International Trade and Economic Dynamics

Koji Shimomura
April 12, 1952 – February 24, 2007

Photograph by Kwan Choi
Midwest International Economics Meeting
Indiana University, Bloomington, USA, October 2003

Takashi Kamihigashi · Laixun Zhao
Editors

International Trade and Economic Dynamics

Essays in Memory of Koji Shimomura

Springer

Editors
Professor Takashi Kamihigashi
Professor Laixun Zhao

RIEB, Kobe University
2-1 Rokkodai, Nada
Kobe 657-8501
Japan
tkamihig@rieb.kobe-u.ac.jp
zhao@rieb.kobe-u.ac.jp

ISBN 978-3-540-78675-7 e-ISBN 978-3-540-78676-4

Library of Congress Control Number: 2008929904

Cover photo by Hidetoshi Yamaji

Cover design: WMXDesign GmbH, Heidelberg, Germany

Printed on acid-free paper

5 4 3 2 1 0

springer.com

Acknowledgements

On 24 February 2007, Koji Shimomura died of complications from liver cancer at the age of 54. His untimely death was mourned by his students, colleagues, coauthors, and friends all over the world. As of December 2007, he published nearly 100 academic papers, with a great majority of them having appeared during the last decade. During this period, he became increasingly productive despite his deteriorating health condition. Many new chapters of his with coauthors are still expected to appear. This volume includes three such chapters.

We express heartfelt thanks to Kazuo Nishimura, Makoto Yano, and Seiichi Katayama for their encouragement and advice during the initial phase of this project. We thank the financial support from the 21 Century COE Program at the Graduate School of Economics and the Research Institute of Economics and Business Administration (RIEB), Kobe University. We thank Shoji Nishijima, Subleader of the COE Program at the RIEB succeeding Koji, Junichi Goto, Director of the RIEB, as well as our staff at the RIEB, including Yachio Yoneda, Kiyoko Sekiguchi, Shiho Magata, Tamaki Murase, and Harumi Watanabe, for their invaluable support and assistance throughout this project.

Many of the contributors also participated in the *Conference on Globalization, International Trade, and Economic Dynamics in Memory of Koji Shimomura*, held in November 2007, and organized by the editors of this volume. Earlier versions of some of the chapters included in this volume were presented at the conference. We express our sincere gratitude to all the contributors for their wholehearted cooperation.

Lastly but not least, we are grateful to Werner A. Mueller and Katharina Wetzel-Vandai of Springer for their editorial support, without which this project would never have materialized.

February 2008

Takashi Kamihigashi
Laixun Zhao

Contents

Introduction 1
Takashi Kamihigashi and Laixun Zhao

Koji Shimomura: Emerging Trade Theorist 5
Murray C. Kemp

Part I Static Theory of International Trade Under Perfect Competition

Rybczynski's Diagram and the Stolper/Samuelson Theorem 9
Ronald W. Jones

On Trade Gains and International Disparities in Factor Proportions 13
Murray C. Kemp and Binh Tran-Nam

A Modified Heckscher–Ohlin Theorem Under Quasilinear Utility Functions 19
Junko Doi, Kenji Fujiwara, Toru Kikuchi, and Koji Shimomura

External Economies of Scale and Comparative Advantage 37
Wilfred J. Ethier and Roy J. Ruffin

Is Free Trade Optimal for a Small Open Economy with Tourism? 49
Chi-Chur Chao, Bharat R. Hazari, Jean-Pierre Laffargue, and Eden S.H. Yu

Factor Mobility and Wage Inequality 63
Masao Oda and Robert Stapp

A Pareto Improvement in Customs Unions Without Intra-Union Transfer 73
Ling Qi and Koji Shimomura

Environment and the Harris and Todaro Paradoxes 87
Makoto Tawada and Azusa Nakamura

Trade Policy and Illegal Immigration 101
Alan Woodland and Chisata Yoshida

Part II Static Theory of International Trade Under Imperfect Competition

Trade in Counterfeit Organic Products 123
E. Kwan Choi

Foreign Economic Aid and Trade Liberalization Under Imperfect Competition 139
Hiroshi Kurata and Masayuki Okawa

Quota as a Competitive Device 151
Sugata Marjit, Tarun Kabiraj, and Arijit Mukherjee

Successive Expansion and Stability of Network Integration in International Trade 161
Noritsugu Nakanishi

Endogenous Leadership with and without Policy Intervention: International Trade When Producer and Seller Differ 187
Zhifang Peng and Sajal Lahiri

Trading Under Strategic Self-Constraint: Conceptual Issues and Factual Evidence 203
Henry Wan, Jr.

Part III Dynamic Theory of International Trade

Dynamic Labor Standards Under International Oligopoly 217
Yunfang Hu and Laixun Zhao

Quotas Under Dynamic Bertrand Competition 239
Kaz Miyagiwa and Yuka Ohno

Imported Inputs: Dynamic Effects on Economic Growth 257
Stefan F. Schubert and Stephen J. Turnovsky

Multiplicity and Stability of Equilibrium in Trade Models with Durable Goods 281
Eric Bond and Robert Driskill

Import Tariffs and Growth in a Model with Habits 299
Been-Lon Chen, Shun-Fa Lee, and Koji Shimomura

Preference Structure and Volatility in a Financially Integrated World ... 323
Kazuo Mino

Part IV Macroeconomic Dynamics

Efficient Fiscal Policy Restrictions in a Monetary Union 345
Costas Azariadis and Raphael W.K. Lam

The Effects of Factor Taxation in Dynamic Economies with Externalities and Endogenous Labor Supply 361
Daisuke Amano, Jun-ichi Itaya, and Kazuo Mino

Status Seeking and Bubbles 383
Takashi Kamihigashi

On the Role of the Rate of Time Preference in Macroeconomics: A Survey 393
Koichi Hamada and Yosuke Takeda

Characterization of Equilibrium Paths in a Two-Sector Economy with CES Production Functions and Sector-Specific Externality 421
Miki Matsuo, Kazuo Nishimura, Tomoya Sakagami, and Alain Venditti

Tobin's "Keynesian Models of Recessions and Depression" Revisited 433
Partha Sen

Inflation Dynamics and the Cross-Sectional Distribution of Prices in the E.U. Periphery 449
Constantina Kottaridi, Diego Méndez-Carbajo, and Dimitrios D. Thomakos

Macro Dynamics and Labor-Saving Innovation: US vs. Japan 477
Ryuzo Sato and Tamaki Morita

Part V Compensation, Entrepreneurship, and Price Leadership

Entrepreneurship, Organization Capital, and the Evolution of the Firm .. 499
Atsushi Oshima, B. Ravikumar, and Raymond Riezman

On Yano's Price Leadership Game 513
Makoto Yano and Takashi Komatsubara

Vilfredo Pareto's Principle of Compensation 525
Murray C. Kemp

Contributors

Daisuke Amano
Graduate School of Economics and Business Administration, Hokkaido University, Sapporo, 060-0809, Japan, e-mail: yogo@pop.econ.hokudai.ac.jp

Costas Azariadis
Department of Economics, Washington University in St. Louis, and Federal Reserve Bank of St. Louis, St. Louis, MO 63130, USA, e-mail: azariadi@artsci.wustl.edu

Eric Bond
Department of Economics, Vanderbilt University, VU Station B #351819, 2301 Vanderbilt Place, Nashville, Tennessee 37235, USA,
e-mail: eric.w.bond@vanderbilt.edu

Chi-Chur Chao
Department of Economics, Chinese University of Hong Kong, Shatin, Hong Kong, China

Been-Lon Chen
Institute of Economics, Academia Sinica, 128 Academia Rd., Section 2, Taipei 11529, Taiwan, e-mail: bchen@econ.sinica.edu.tw and Department of Economics, Washington University, 205 Eliot Hall, St. Louis, MO 63130, USA

E. Kwan Choi
Department of Economics, Iowa State University, Ames, IA 50011, USA,
e-mail: kchoi@iastate.edu

Junko Doi
Faculty of Economics, Kansai University, Suita, Osaka, Japan

Robert Driskill
Department of Economics, Vanderbilt University, VU Station B #351819, 2301 Vanderbilt Place, Nashville, Tennessee 37235, USA,
e-mail: robert.driskill@vanderbilt.edu

Wilfred J. Ethier
Department of Economics, University of Pennsylvania, Philadelphia, PA 19104-6297, USA, e-mail: ethier@econ.sas.upenn.edu

Kenji Fujiwara
School of Economics, Kwansei Gakuin University, Nishinomiya, Hyogo 662-8501, Japan, e-mail: kenjifujiwara@kwansei.ac.jp

Koichi Hamada
Yale University, New Haven, CT 06520-8269, USA

Bharat R. Hazari
Department of Economics and Finance, City University of Hong Kong, Kowloon, Hong Kong, China, e-mail: efedenyu@cityu.edu.hk

Yunfang Hu
Graduate School of International Cultural Studies, Tohoku University, Sendai, Japan, e-mail: yhu@intcul.tohoku.ac.jp

Jun-ichi Itaya
Graduate School of Economics and Business Administration, Hokkaido University, Sapporo 060-0809, Japan, e-mail: itaya@econ.hokudai.ac.jp

Ronald W. Jones
University of Rochester, Rochester, NY 14627, USA, e-mail: rjones@mail.Rochester.edu

Tarun Kabiraj
Indian Statistical Institute, Kolkata, India, e-mail: tarunkabiraj@hotmail.com

Takashi Kamihigashi
RIEB, Kobe University, Rokkodai, Nada, Kobe 657-8501, Japan, e-mail: tkamihig@rieb.kobe-u.ac.jp

Murray C. Kemp
University of New South Wales, Sydney, Australia, e-mail: murraykemp@bigpond.com

Constantina Kottaridi
Department of Economics, University of Peloponnese, 22100 Tripolis, Greece, e-mail: kottarid@uop.gr

Toru Kikuchi
Graduate School of Economics, Kobe University, Kobe, Japan

Takashi Komatsubara
Keio University, Kyoto, Japan

Hiroshi Kurata
Faculty of Economics, Tohoku Gakuin University, Sendai, Japan, e-mail: hkurata@tscc.tohoku-gakuin.ac.jp

Jean-Pierre Laffargue
University of Paris I and CEPREMAP, France

Sajal Lahiri
Department of Economics, Southern Illinois University Carbondale, MC 4515, 1000 Faner Drive, Carbondale, IL 62901, USA, e-mail: lahiri@siu.edu

Raphael W.K. Lam
Department of Economics, Washington University in St. Louis, and Federal Reserve Bank of St. Louis, St. Louis, MO 63130, USA

Shun-Fa Lee
Department of Industrial Economics, Tamkang University, Taiwan

Sugata Marjit
Centre for Studies in Social Sciences, R1 Baishnabghata Patuk Township, Calcutta, 700094, India, e-mail: smarjit@hotmail.com

Miki Matsuo
Institute of Economic Research, Kyoto University, Kyoto, Japan

Diego Méndez-Carbajo
Department of Economics, Illinois Wesleyan University. P.O. Box 2900, Bloomington, IL 61702, USA, e-mail: dmendez@iwu.edu

Kazuo Mino
Graduate School of Economics, Osaka University, 1-7, Machikaneyama, Toyonaka, Osaka 560-0043, Japan, e-mail: mino@econ.osaka-u.ac.jp

Kaz Miyagiwa
Department of Economics, Emory University, Atlanta, GA 30322, USA, e-mail: kmiyagiwa@gmail.com

Tamaki Morita
National Graduate Institute for Policy Studies (GRIPS) 7-22-1, Roppongi, Minato-ku, Tokyo 162 0835, Japan, e-mail: morita@grips.ac.jp

Arijit Mukherjee
University of Nottingham, The Leverhulme Centre for Research in Globalisation and Economic Policy, Nottingham, UK, e-mail: ar25@hotmail.com

Azusa Nakamura
Department of Economics & Information, Gifu Shotoku Gakuen University, 1-38, Nakauzura, Gifu 500-8288, Japan, e-mail: azusa.n@gifu.shotoku.ac.jp

Noritsugu Nakanishi
Graduate School of Economics, Kobe University, Rokkodai-cho 2-1, Nada-ku, Kobe 657-8501, Japan, e-mail: nakanishi@econ.kobe-u.ac.jp

Kazuo Nishimura
Institute of Economic Research, Kyoto University, Kyoto, Japan, e-mail: ishimura@kier.kyoto-u.ac.jp

Masao Oda
Department of Economics, Ritsumeikan University, Kusatsu 525-8577, Japan,
e-mail: odams@mta.biglobe.ne.jp

Yuka Ohno
Deloitte Tax LLP, III Wacker Drive, Chicago, IL 60606-4301, USA,
e-mail: yohno@deloitte.com

Masayuki Okawa
Department of Economics, Ritsumeikan University, Noji-Higashi 1-1-1,
Kusatsu 525 8577, Japan, e-mail: mokawa@ec.ritsumei.ac.jp

Atsushi Oshima
Department of Economics, University of Iowa, Iowa, USA

Zhifang Peng
Department of Economics, Bloomsburg University of Pennsylvania; 312, Bakeless
Center for the Humanities, Bloomsburg, PA 171815, USA

Ling Qi
China Institute for Actuarial Science, Central University of Economics and Finance,
Beijing, China, e-mail: qil@cias.edu.cn

B. Ravikumar
Department of Economics, University of Iowa, Iowa, USA

Raymond Riezman
Department of Economics, University of Iowa, Iowa, USA,
e-mail: raymond-riezman@uiowa.edu

Roy J. Ruffin
Department of Economics, University of Houston, Houston, TX 77204, USA,
e-mail: rruffin@uh.edu

Tomoya Sakagami
Kumamoto Gakuen University, Kumamoto 862-8680, Japan

Ryuzo Sato
New York University and the University of Tokyo, Tokyo, Japan

Stefan F. Schubert
Free University of Bozen-Bolzano, School of Economics and Management,
Via Sernesi 1, 39100 Bolzano, Italy, e-mail: StefanFranz.Schubert@unibz.it

Partha Sen
Delhi School of Economics, Delhi University, Delhi, India

Koji Shimomura
RIEB, Kobe University, Kobe 657-8501, Japan,
e-mail: simomura@rieb.kobe-u.ac.jp

Robert Stapp
Department of Economics, University of Arkansas, Fayetteville 72701, USA,
e-mail: rstapp@walton.uark.edu

Yosuke Takeda
Department of Economics, Sophia University, 7-1 Kioi-cho, Chiyoda-ku Tokyo
102-8554, Japan, e-mail: y-takeda@sophia.ac.jp

Makoto Tawada
Graduate School of Economics, Nagoya University, Furo-cho, Chikusa-ku,
Nagoya 464-8601, Japan, e-mail: mtawada@soec.nagoya-u.ac.jp

Dimitrios D. Thomakos
Department of Economics, University of Peloponnese, 22100 Tripolis, Greece,
e-mail: thomakos@uop.gr

Binh Tran-Nam
Atax, University of New South Wales, Sydney, Australia,
e-mail: b.tran-nam@unsw.edu.au

Stephen J. Turnovsky
Department of Economics, University of Washington, Seattle, WA 98105, USA,
e-mail: sturn@u.washington.edu

Alain Venditti
CNRS-GREQAM, Marseille, France

Henry Wan, Jr.
Department of Economics, Cornell University, 470 Uris Hall, Cornell University,
Ithaca, NY 14853, USA, e-mail: hyw1@cornell.edu

Alan Woodland
Faculty of Economics and Business, University of Sydney, NSW 2006, Australia,
e-mail: A.Woodland@econ.usyd.edu.au

Makoto Yano
Kyoto University, Kyoto, Japan

Chisata Yoshida
Faculty of Economics and Business, University of Sydney, NSW 2006, Australia

Eden S.H. Yu
Department of Economics and Finance, City University of Hong Kong, Kowloon,
Hong Kong, China, e-mail: efedenyu@cityu.edu.hk

Laixun Zhao
RIEB, Kobe University, Research Institute for Economics & Business,
Kobe 657-8501, Japan, e-mail: zhao@rieb.kobe-u.ac.jp

Introduction

Takashi Kamihigashi and Laixun Zhao

This volume is a tribute to Koji Shimomura's memory. After this introduction, Murray C. Kemp, Koji's thesis advisor, offers a portrait of the young Koji as an emerging trade theorist. The rest of the book is divided into five parts in line with Koji's own research.

The chapters in Part I deal with static theory of international trade under perfect competition. Many of the chapters here are based on the Heckscher-Ohlin (HO) model. In Chap. 1, Ronald W. Jones revisits Rybczynski's original diagram and the Stolper-Samuelson Theorem. In Chap. 2, Murray C. Kemp and Binh Tran-Nam consider the HO model and derive necessary and sufficient conditions under which the greater are the international differences in relative factor endowments the larger are the gains from international trade. In Chap. 3, Koji Shimomura teams up with his students-turned-colleagues Junko Doi, Kenji Fujiwara, and Toru Kikuchi to study a HO model with quasi-linear utility functions. In Chap. 4, Wilfred J. Ethier and Roy J. Ruffin investigate the interplay between comparative advantage and external increasing returns to scale. In Chap. 5, Chi-Chur Chao, Bharat R. Hazari, Jean-Pierre Laffargue, and Eden S.H. Yu introduce tourism to a small open economy and explore the welfare effects of tariffs and investment taxes. In Chap. 6, Masao Oda and Robert Stapp analyze the effects of factor mobility on wage inequality and consider a condition under which an inflow of factors into the US could generate wage inequality in favor of skilled labor. In Chap. 7, Ling Qi and Koji Shimomura give an analytical proof of the Kemp-Wan theorem on customs unions. In Chap. 8, Makoto Tawada and Azusa Nakamura introduce environmental elements to the standard Harris and Todaro model and address two well-known paradoxical results. In Chap. 9, Alan Woodland and Chisato Yoshida develop a general equilibrium two-country model in which the home and foreign countries trade two final goods, and legal immigration is restricted.

Part II deals with static theory of international trade under imperfect competition. In Chap. 10, E. Kwan Choi investigates trade in organic and nonorganic products between the North and the South. In Chap. 11, Hiroshi Kurata and Masayuki Okawa examine the possibility of a mutually beneficial policy combination of economic aid by a donor country and tariff reduction in the recipient country

T. Kamihigashi and L. Zhao (eds.) *International Trade and Economic Dynamics – Essays in Memory of Koji Shimomura*.

under imperfect competition. In Chap. 12, Sugata Marjit, Tarun Kabiraj, and Arijit Mukherjee discuss the effects of restricting monopolistic exporters. In Chap. 13, Noritsugu Nakanishi studies an international network formation game in which each country decides whether to join, or exit from, an existing international network integration taking into account subsequent responses by other countries. In Chap. 14, Zhifang Peng and Sajal Lahiri examine the issue of endogenous leadership, using a vertically linked model where producers and sellers are different entities and belong to two different countries. In Chap. 15, using a mechanism-design approach, Henry Wan studies the international division of labor in supplying application-specific integrated circuits.

Part III focuses on dynamic theory of international trade. In Chap. 16, Yunfang Hu and Laixun Zhao model productive labor standards (LS) in a two-stage, two-period model of international oligopoly. In Chap. 17, Kaz Miyagiwa and Yuka Ohno present a model of dynamic Bertrand competition in which a quota is treated as an intertemporal constraint rather than as a capacity constraint. In Chap. 18, Stefan F. Schubert and Stephen J. Turnovsky study the effects of an increase in the price of an intermediate input on economic growth in a small open economy. The last three chapters of this part deal with indeterminacy in two-country models. In Chap. 19, Eric Bond and Robert Driskill examine dynamic stability in Shimomura's durable-goods model of trade when there are multiple steady states. In Chap. 20, Been-Lon Chen, Shun-Fa Lee, and Koji Shimomura study the long-run relationship between tariffs and economic growth in a two-country AK growth model. In Chap. 21, Kazuo Mino investigates a two-country model of capital accumulation with country-specific production externalities.

Part IV deals with macroeconomic dynamics. In Chap. 22, Costas Azariadis and Raphael Lam study the interactions of monetary and fiscal policies in the context of monetary union. In Chap. 23, Daisuke Amano, Jun-Ichi Itaya, and Kazuo Mino examine the long-run effects of factor income and expenditure taxes in an infinitely lived representative agent growth model that allows for production externalities and endogenous labor supply. In Chap. 24, Takashi Kamihigashi examines the possibility of stock market bubbles in a deterministic variant of the Lucas asset pricing model in which utility depends on status in addition to consumption. In Chap. 25, Koichi Hamada and Yosuke Takeda survey the literature on the role of the rate of time preference in macroeconomics. The next two chapters analyze two-sector models. In Chap. 26, Miki Matsuo, Kazuo Nishimura, Tomoya Sakagami, and Alain Venditti study local stability of a two-sector CES economy with sector-specific externalities. In Chap. 27, Partha Sen considers multiplier effects in a two-sector-two-period overlapping generations model. The last two chapters in this part are empirical ones. In Chap. 28, Constantina Kottaridi, Diego Mndez-Carbajo, and Dimitros D. Thomakos explore the connection between inflation and its higher-order moments for three economies in the periphery of the European Union, Greece, Portugal, and Spain. In Chap. 29, Ryuzo Sato and Tamaki Morita conduct the empirical analysis of the economic growth of the United States and Japan from 1970 to 2005.

The three chapters in Part V provide unique perspectives on three fundamental issues in economics. In Chap. 30, Atsushi Oshima, B. Ravikumar, and Raymond

Riezman model the behavior of an entrepreneur who possesses human capital in the form of specific skills or talents. In Chap. 31, Makoto Yano and Takashi Komatsubara extend the price leadership game that Yano constructed in his recent textbook. In Chap. 32, Murray C. Kemp concludes this volume by revisiting Pareto's Principle of Compensation.

Koji Shimomura: Emerging Trade Theorist

Murray C. Kemp

In view of Koji Shimomura's own contribution to the theory of international trade and in view of the focus of Kobe University's 21st Century Center of Excellence, the scope of the present volume is especially appropriate. It is also appropriate that, in these introductory remarks, I turn my thoughts to Koji Shimomura, trade theorist.

Koji's best known and most appreciated contributions to the theory of international trade appeared after 1990. Only a relatively small number of trade theorists know of his earlier work or the path along which he developed into the highly imaginative economist we all came to know and admire. In these introductory remarks, therefore, I will focus narrowly on Koji's early years as an emerging trade theorist.

After receiving his formal training at Kobe University (Bachelor of Economics in 1975, Master of Economics in 1977), Koji was employed as research assistant to Professor Hiromasa Yamamoto, a well-known labor economist in the Research Institute for Economics and Business Administration (RIEB) at the same university. At that time, Professor Yamamoto was especially interested in the determinants and implications of the international migration of labor. However, Koji continued to attend graduate courses, including those offered at Kobe University by Professor Yasuo Uekawa, a highly respected trade theorist who was then a member of the faculty of Kobe University of Commerce.

I met Koji for the first time in 1980, when he arrived in Sydney as a doctoral candidate. The prime mover, both in recommending Koji to the University of New South Wales and in persuading Koji to accept the University's invitation, was Professor Uekawa who not only knew Koji well but had already spent considerable time at the University of New South Wales.

At the time of Koji's arrival, I was engrossed with Ngo Van Long in the economics of exhaustible and renewable resources and suggested to Koji that he work in that field, directing his attention to the optimal order of exploitation of multiple deposits. Koji quickly acquired the necessary mathematics (mainly, control theory) and submitted a highly acceptable dissertation in minimal time.

M.C. Kemp
University of New South Wales

T. Kamihigashi and L. Zhao (eds.) *International Trade and Economic Dynamics – Essays in Memory of Koji Shimomura.*

Parts of the dissertation were published in 1983 and 1984; see References. By then, Koji had returned to the RIEB and resumed his association with Professor Yamamoto; and, after a lengthy absence, I had returned to the theory of international trade. Koji and I might have drifted apart. However, as a result of my shift in interests, I was again in close touch with Yasuo Uekawa, in Kobe. Yasuo and I encouraged Koji to join us on several of our theoretical safaris.

Not surprisingly, some of Koji's early work in trade theory reflects his background in labor economics. Thus in 1985, there appeared an article entitled "Do labor unions drive out capital?" and in 1989 there appeared a further article entitled "A neglected corner: Labor unions and the pattern of international trade." However, even before the second of those chapters, there had appeared (in 1988) a chapter in the Walras-Arrow-Debreu-McKenzie competitive format of modern trade theory. In that chapter it was shown that, in the special $2 \times 2 \times 2$ no-joint-products case, it is impossible in equilibrium for one country to hold an absolute advantage in the production of both commodities if the other country's preferences are homothetic. The result was unexpected; moreover, it is robust in the sense that it can be extended in several directions.[1] It served as a signal of good things to come from Koji's pen.

References

Kemp MC (2001) International trade and national welfare. Routledge, London

Kemp MC, Shimomura K (1985) Do labour unions drive out capital? Econ J 95:1087–1090

Kemp MC, Shimomura K (1988) The impossibility of global absolute advantage in the Heckscher-Ohlin model of trade. Ox Econ P 40:575–576

Kemp MC, Shimomura K (1989) A neglected corner: Labour unions and the theory of international trade. In: Feiwel, G (ed.) Joan Robinson and modern economic theory. Macmillan, Londond and Basingstoke

Shimomura K (1983) On the optimal order of exploitation of deposits of a renewable resource. J Inst and Theo Econ 139:319–322

Shimomura K (1984) The optimal order of exploitation of deposits of a renewable resource. In: Kemp MC and Long NV (eds.) Essays in the economics of exhaustible resources. North-Holland, Amsterdam

[1] These extensions and minor corrections may be found in Kemp (2001, Chap. 12). It is my regret that some confusion of superscripts remains in equation (1) of that chapter.

Part I
Static Theory of International Trade Under Perfect Competition

Rybczynski's Diagram and the Stolper/Samuelson Theorem[1]

Ronald W. Jones

Abstract In his famous 1955 article, Rybczynski used the familiar production box diagram in order to prove, correctly, the theorem that bears his name. However, the construction he used also suggests that the dual theorem, the Stolper–Samuelson theorem, is incorrect. The problem is that the isoquants in the box diagram were not homothetic to such a degree as to yield false Stolper–Samuelson results.

Any graduate course (as well as many undergraduate courses) in international trade theory introduces students to T.M. Rybczynski's famous result contained in his 1955 chapter in *Economica*. This result drew attention to a strong asymmetry facing small growing countries that are competitively involved in international trade: If world prices of a pair of commodities are constant and a country experiences growth in one of a pair of factors of production, national output and income increase, but whereas the output of one commodity expands, that of the other actually *contracts*. (This is a necessary result when production is characterized by constant returns to scale and no joint production.) Rybczynski's own proof of this theorem that bears his name was geometric, based on a box diagram that is faithfully reproduced later. His geometric proof is absolutely correct. Algebraic proofs are easily derived, and the economic intuition is simple: In the standard Heckscher–Ohlin 2×2 model, commodity prices determine factor prices and, thus, factor proportions. If commodity prices remain constant, so do techniques, and if, say, the supply of capital expands, so will the output of the relatively capital-intensive commodity. However, with given techniques the output of the capital-intensive commodity cannot expand without its using more labor, and the only source of labor in a full-employment economy is the other, relatively labor-intensive, sector. Hence, its output must fall.

[1] I am pleased to have this note included in a volume in remembrance of Koji Shimomura. From my memory of him this note is the kind of thing I believe he would have enjoyed.

R.W. Jones
University of Rochester, Rochester, NY 14627, USA, e-mail: rjones@mail. Rochester.edu

T. Kamihigashi and L. Zhao (eds.) *International Trade and Economic Dynamics – Essays in Memory of Koji Shimomura.*

The Rybczynski theorem is often cited as bearing a dual relationship to another famous trade result that appeared 14 years previously, the Stolper–Samuelson theorem (1941).

This latter result, one of the most famous and widely cited propositions in the entire discipline of economics, states that if, in this Heckscher–Ohlin 2×2 context, the price of one commodity increases and the other price remains constant, the *real* return to the factor used relatively intensively in its production must increase, in the sense that the factor's return must rise by a greater relative extent than does the commodity price. The peculiarity in the original Rybczynski box diagram is that whereas the geometric proof of the result named after Rybczynski is correct, the diagram also seems to *disprove* the Stolper–Samuelson result.

The original Rybczynski box diagram also exhibits what would seem to be a rather archaic labeling of factors and commodities by today's common usage: The factors are labeled X and Y, and the commodities are labeled L and K! The first diagram given is a literal copy of the original. Rybczynski's result follows by comparing outputs at points S and P. Point S is a point on the contract curve of the pregrowth box diagram, $ADCB$. Let the endowment of factor X expand (from AB to $A'B$), holding commodity prices, and therefore techniques, constant. This makes point P the production point in the postgrowth situation that corresponds to point S in the original box, with ray $A'S'$ parallel to ray AS. Growth output of the X-intensive commodity (K) clearly expands, but that of the Y-intensive commodity (L) contracts.

The Stolper–Samuelson result can be discussed in terms of the pregrowth box diagram, $ADCB$. Suppose the price of the Y-intensive commodity (L) increases. This must serve to move resources into the L-sector, shown by moving along the contract curve in a northeast direction. But consider what happens to the ratio of factor prices, as indicated by the slopes of the isoquants tangent along the contract curve: the curves become *steeper* with this movement along the contract curve. That implies that the relative (and real) return to the factor (Y) used relatively intensively in the L-sector must actually *fall* as the price of commodity L increases! This is a result that directly contradicts the Stolper–Samuelson theorem!

The problem is not hard to detect. The isoquants as drawn cannot reflect constant-returns-to-scale technology, the assumption about technology that underlies both of these Heckscher–Ohlin results. Indeed, the isoquants are not homothetic. The isoquants that have mutual tangencies along the contract curve as commodity L expands from point A to point C must become progressively *flatter* at the tangency points, as shown in the diagram labeled "*The Corrected Rybczynski Diagram.*" That is, if technology does exhibit constant returns to scale, a lowering of the Y to X factor proportions ratio used to produce commodity L (i.e., a northeasterly movement along the contract curve) must *raise* the relative marginal product of Y to X in its production (which is contradicted by the way isoquants were drawn in the original diagram).

The nonhomothetic feature of the isoquants drawn in the pregrowth box diagram did not interfere with Rybczynski's proof of the necessary output changes with growth, but is enough to reverse the Stolper–Samuelson result. Properly stated,

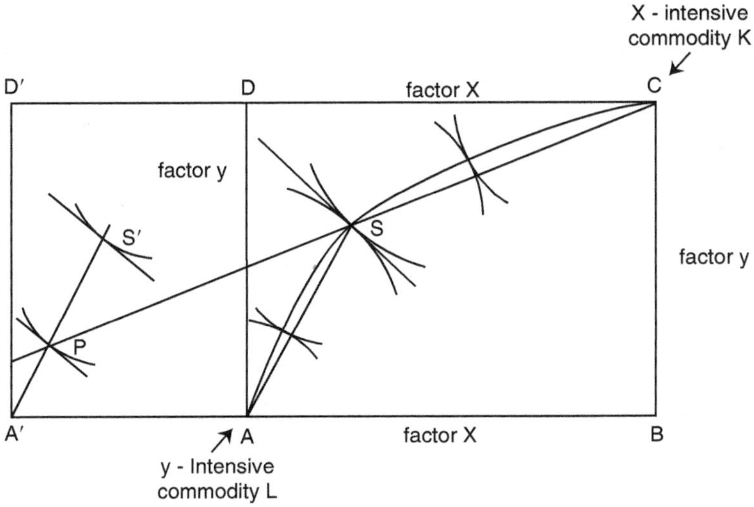

The original Rybczynski box diagram

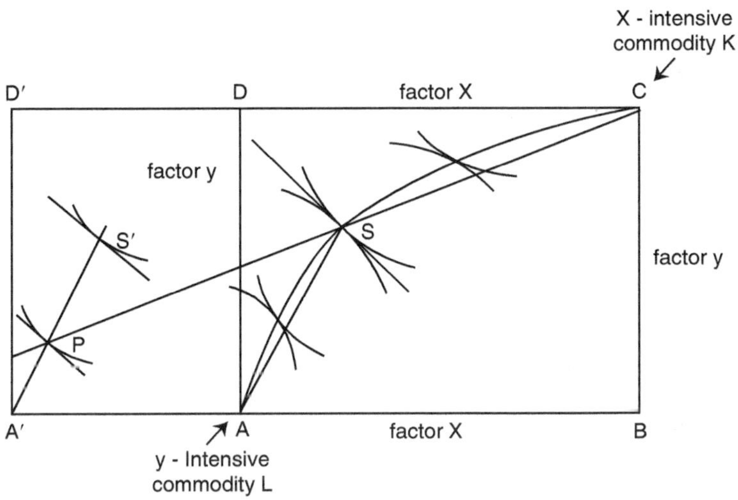

The corrected Rybczynski diagram

these two theorems are both based on constant-returns to scale technology, and bear a dual relationship to each other.[2] In the corrected version of the diagram a movement along the contract curve representing an increase in commodity *L*'s production

[2] Paul Samuelson (1953) established the *Reciprocity Theorem* whereby an increase in the endowment of a factor, with other endowments and all commodity prices constant, affects the output of a particular commodity (say $\partial X_j/\partial V_i$) by an amount equal to the effect of a rise in commodity *j*'s price on the return to factor *i* if endowments and all other commodity prices are constant, $\partial w_i/\partial p_j$.

(encouraged by a relative increase in commodity L's price) must increase factor Y's relative (and real) return, a reflection of the famous Stolper–Samuelson result.

Acknowledgment I am indebted to Hugo Sonnenschein, whose work on the Rybczynski Theorem forced me to check the original article.

References

Rybczynski TM (1955) Factor endowments and relative commodity prices. Economica 22(88):336–341

Samuelson PA (1953) Prices of factors and goods in general equilibrium. Rev Econ Stud 21:1–20

Stolper W, Samuelson PA (1941) Protection and real wages. Rev Econ Stud 9:58–73

On Trade Gains and International Disparities in Factor Proportions[1]

Murray C. Kemp and Binh Tran-Nam(✉)

Abstract It has been suggested that the greater are the international differences in relative factor endowments, the larger are the gains from international trade. The proposition is interesting from a policy-making point of view; for, if it were known to be valid under plausible circumstances, it would provide guidance to any country contemplating reciprocal preferential trading with other countries. However, the proposition has not been accompanied by supporting argument. In the present note, we therefore focus on a conventional Heckscher–Ohlin world economy and derive necessary and sufficient conditions for the validity of a strict version of the proposition.

1 Introduction

It has recently been suggested by Assar Lindbeck (2007: 11) that "...the gains from trade tend to be larger, the more the factor proportions differ among trading partners."[2] The proposition is an interesting one. Indeed it might be viewed as a normative companion to the familiar Heckscher–Ohlin Theorem, focused not on the pattern of international trade but on the pattern of trade gains. If it were shown to be valid in plausible circumstances, it would provide guidance to countries contemplating reciprocal preferential trading with each other; if it were shown to be invalid in

[1] Chapter prepared for the Conference on Globalization, International Trade, and Economic Dynamics – In Memory of Koji Shimomura, held at Kobe University, 22–24 November 2007. We gratefully acknowledge the helpful and spirited comments of conference participants and the very useful written suggestions of Bill Ethier, Koichi Hamada, and an anonymous referee.

[2] We assume that Lindbeck had in mind the gains from trade of *each* trading partner. The concept of *joint* gains from trade is not well defined.

B. Tran-Nam
Atax, University of New South Wales, e-mail: b.tran-nam@unsw.edu.au

T. Kamihigashi and L. Zhao (eds.) *International Trade and Economic Dynamics – Essays in Memory of Koji Shimomura.*

other, equally plausible circumstances, that would help explain why many existing preferential trading associations bring together countries with similar factor proportions. Either way, the proposition would help resolve the chief unanswered questions in the theory of preferential trading associations: What determines the number of associations in existence at any time and what determines the membership of each of them? It is apparent therefore that the proposition deserves more careful study than Lindbeck himself was able to give it.[3]

In the present note we focus on the familiar $2 \times 2 \times 2$ Heckscher–Ohlin world economy and derive necessary and sufficient conditions for the validity of a strict version of Lindbeck's proposition. To appreciate the need to restrict attention to a special version of the proposition, it must be noted that, as stated by Lindbeck, the proposition suffers from an ambiguity: It asserts that the gain from trade for each trading partner increases if the international disparity in factor endowment ratios increases, leaving unclear how one determines whether a country's trade gains are larger or smaller when calculated on the basis of two different factor endowment vectors and, hence, of two different autarkic equilibria. To remove this ambiguity, we confine our attention to increases in the international disparity in factor endowment ratios occasioned by a change in the endowment of just one factor in just one country. The autarkic equilibrium of the other country is unaffected by such a change.

With the aid of the necessary and sufficient conditions obtained in this way, it is a simple matter to construct examples consistent with the proposition as well as counter examples to it. It emerges that, in some circumstances, counter examples may incorporate local inferiority in consumption. This is in sharp contrast to the paradoxical finding of Edgeworth (1894, 1899) that if no commodity is inferior in consumption then factor-neutral technical improvements confined to a country's export industry might impoverish the country.

2 Analysis

The world economy contains two free-trading countries, α and β, and two internationally tradeable commodities, 1 and 2, each producible under constant returns to scale by means of two primary factors of production, labor and physical capital, neither of which is internationally mobile. Each country is inhabited by identical or "representative" households. As is now well understood, this assumption is consistent with the companion assumption of price-taking households only if the households are unaware of their representative status; see Kemp and Long (1992) and Kemp and Shimomura (1995).

[3] Lindbeck did not offer a proof, possibly because the article in which the proposition appeared focused not on abstract trade theory but on China's recent economic reforms, possibly because he had in mind not a precise relationship between factor proportions and the gains from trade but only a tendency, that is, a relationship that holds in some circumstances but not in others.

The following additional notation will be employed; subscripts indicate partial or total derivatives.

p, the price of commodity 1 in terms of commodity 2
u^j, the utility derived from consumption in country j $(j = \alpha, \beta)$
L^j, the constant supply of labor in country j $(j = \alpha, \beta)$
K^j, the parametric stock of capital available in country j $(j = \alpha, \beta)$
$e^j(p, u^j)$, the expenditure function of country j, expenditure in terms of commodity 2 $(j = \alpha, \beta)$
$r^j(p, K^j)$, the revenue function of country j, revenue in terms of commodity 2 $(j = \alpha, \beta)$
$z^{j1}\ (p, u^j, K^j) \equiv e^j_p\ (p, u^j) - r^j_p\ (p, K^j)$ the excess demand by country j for commodity 1 $(j = \alpha, \beta)$

It is assumed (without loss) that $K^\alpha/L^\alpha > K^\beta/L^\beta$ and that, in each country, the first commodity is relatively capital-intensive. It is also assumed that the expenditure and revenue functions are twice differentiable.

The budget constraint of country j is

$$e^j(p, u^j) - r^j(p, K^j) = 0\,(j = \alpha, \beta), \tag{1}$$

and the market-clearing condition for commodity 1 is

$$\sum_{j=\alpha,\beta} z^{j1}(p, u^j, K^j) = 0. \tag{2}$$

Equations (1) and (2) contain the three variables p, u^α, and u^β, and the parameters $K^j(j = \alpha, \beta)$. The system is assumed to possess a unique solution $(p^*, u^{\alpha *}, u^{\beta *})$, with p^* positive and finite. For the time being, it is also assumed that the Jacobian determinant, evaluated at equilibrium values of the variables, is negative.

Consider now any small increase in K^α and any small decrease in K^β, each of which extends the initial inter-country difference in relative factor endowments. Differentiating (1) and (2) with respect to K^α and K^β, choosing units of utility so that $e^j_u \equiv \partial e^j/\partial u^j = 1$ and defining $z^1_p \equiv \sum_{j=\alpha,\beta} z^{j1}_p$, we obtain

$$\begin{bmatrix} z^{\alpha 1} & 1 & 0 \\ z^{\beta 1} & 0 & 1 \\ z^1_p & z^{\alpha 1}_u & z^{\beta 1}_u \end{bmatrix} \begin{bmatrix} \mathrm{d}p \\ \mathrm{d}u^\alpha \\ \mathrm{d}u^\beta \end{bmatrix} = \begin{bmatrix} r^\alpha_K \mathrm{d}K^\alpha \\ r^\beta_K \mathrm{d}K^\beta \\ r^\alpha_{pK} \mathrm{d}K^\alpha + r^\beta_{pK} \mathrm{d}K^\beta \end{bmatrix}. \tag{3}$$

The determinant of coefficients, already assumed to be negative, is denoted by Δ. Evidently, z^{j1}_u is positive or negative as commodity 1 is locally normal or inferior in consumption. With the aid of this information it is now straightforward to produce the promised illustrations of and counter examples to Lindbeck's proposition.

Selectively solving (3), we find that

$$\Delta(\mathrm{d}u^\beta/\mathrm{d}K^\alpha) = z^{\alpha 1}(r^\alpha_{pK} - z^{\alpha 1}_u r^\alpha_K) \tag{4a}$$

and

$$\Delta(\mathrm{d}u^\alpha/\mathrm{d}K^\beta) = -z^{\alpha 1}(r^\beta_{pK} - z^{\beta 1}_u r^\beta_K). \tag{4b}$$

At this point, two cases must be distinguished, depending on whether initially (before any new investment in α or β) α imports or exports the first commodity. Given our assumption of convenience that $K^\alpha/L^\alpha > K^\beta/L^\beta$, and given the Heckscher–Ohlin assumption that the same technology prevails everywhere, α will initially import the first commodity only if α-preferences are suitably biased in favor of the first commodity. However, such a bias is not ruled out by Heckscher or Ohlin, and so both cases must be studied.

Case 1. $z^{\alpha 1} > 0$.

Bearing in mind that $\Delta < 0$ and $r^\alpha_K > 0$, it follows from (4a) that

$$\mathrm{d}u^\beta/\mathrm{d}K^\alpha < (>)\ 0 \text{ if and only if } r^\alpha_{pK}/r^\alpha_K - z^{\alpha 1}_u > (<)\ 0, \tag{5a}$$

that is, β suffers a loss (enjoys a gain) in free-trade utility as a consequence of the increase in the international disparity in endowment ratios associated with an increase in K^α if and only if $r^\alpha_{pK}/r^\alpha_K - z^{\alpha 1}_u > (<)\ 0$. Similarly, from (4b)

$$-(\mathrm{d}u^\alpha/\mathrm{d}K^\beta) < (>)\ 0 \text{ if and only if } r^\beta_{pK}/r^\beta_K - z^{\beta 1}_u > (<)\ 0, \tag{5b}$$

that is, α suffers a loss (enjoys a gain) in free-trade utility as a consequence of the increase in the international disparity in endowment ratios associated with a decrease in K^β if and only if $r^\beta_{pK}/r^\beta_K - z^{\beta 1}_u > (<)\ 0$.

We are now ready to state

Proposition 1. *In response to a small exogenous increase in* K^α *(decrease in* K^β*), the free-trade utility level of country* $\beta(\alpha)$ *will decrease or increase according to whether* $r^\alpha_{pK}/r^\alpha_K - z^{\alpha 1}_u > 0$ $(r^\beta_{pK}/r^\beta_K - z^{\beta 1}_u > 0)$ *or* $r^\alpha_{pK}/r^\alpha_K - z^{\alpha 1}_u < 0$ $(r^\beta_{pK}/r^\beta_K - z^{\beta 1}_u < 0)$, *respectively.*

Recall here that the increase in K^α has no effect on β's autarkic wellbeing and therefore bears on β's gains from trade only indirectly, through its effects on other variables. Similarly, the decrease in K^β has no effect on α's autarkic wellbeing and therefore bears on α's gains from trade only indirectly, through its effects on other variables. Thus, a decrease (an increase) in free-trade utility under these circumstances implies a loss (an increase) in trade gains in both absolute and relative terms. This establishes

Proposition 2. *In response to a small exogenous increase in* K^α *(decrease in* K^β*), country* $\beta(\alpha)$ *will suffer a loss or enjoy an increase in the gains from trade according to whether* $r^\alpha_{pK}/r^\alpha_K - z^{\alpha 1}_u > 0$ $(r^\beta_{pK}/r^\beta_K - z^{\beta 1}_u > 0)$ *or* $r^\alpha_{pK}/r^\alpha_K - z^{\alpha 1}_u < 0$ $(r^\beta_{pK}/r^\beta_K - z^{\beta 1}_u < 0)$, *respectively.*

In particular, from (5a),

$$(\mathrm{d}u^{\beta}/\mathrm{d}K^{\alpha}) < 0 \text{ if commodity 1 is locally inferior in } \alpha \tag{6a}$$

and, from (5b),

$$-(\mathrm{d}u^{\alpha}/\mathrm{d}K^{\beta}) < 0 \text{ if commodity 1 is locally inferior in } \beta. \tag{6b}$$

This can be summarized in

Proposition 3. *In response to a small exogenous increase in K^{α} (decrease in K^{β}), country $\beta(\alpha)$ will suffer a reduction in its free-trade utility and a reduction in its gains from trade if commodity 1 is locally inferior around the initial free-trade equilibrium in country $\beta(\alpha)$.*

That is, a modicum of inferiority in the consumption of each country suffices to rule out Lindbeck's proposition; but, while inferiority suffices, it is not necessary.

Case 2. $z^{\alpha 1} < 0$

The reader may easily discover counterparts to Propositions 1–3 when $z^{\alpha 1} < 0$. It will be found that, under the alternative initial condition, counter examples to Lindbeck's proposition can still be constructed, but only if the first commodity is sufficiently locally normal in the consumption of α and β. The contrast with Edgeworth's finding, noted in Sect. 1, is confined to Case 1.

In summary, under Heckscher–Ohlin assumptions, both illustrative examples and counter examples to Lindbeck's proposition can always be provided. On the other hand, Lindbeck's proposition can be easily established if to the Heckscher–Ohlin assumption of internationally identical technologies are added the familiar textbook assumptions of identical homothetic preferences and international factor price equalization, neither of which was favored by Heckscher or Ohlin and neither of which was mentioned by Lindbeck.

3 The Value Δ

Our calculations in Sect. 2 were based on the assumption that Δ, the determinant of the coefficient matrix, is negative. However, the choice of a negative Δ was for definiteness only, for counter examples to Lindbeck's proposition can be found whether Δ is positive or negative. If Δ is positive, the second inequalities of (5a) and (5b) simply change sign, implying that matched pairs of counter examples can no longer be constructed if either commodity is locally inferior in consumption. In this case, therefore, the sharp contrast with Edgeworth's findings (noted in Sect. 1) must be muted.

Nevertheless, many have been prepared to assume that Δ is negative, justifying this assumption as sufficient for local stability of the dynamic *tâtonnement* process described by Walras. As noted in Kemp et al. (2002) and Kemp and

Shimomura (2003), the Walrasian model is internally inconsistent. It is based on the assumption that markets out of balance adjust costlessly at a finite pace, completely ignoring the profit or utility incentive to increase the rate of adjustment. The Walrasian justification for negative Δ is therefore without value. To derive from stability analysis an acceptable constraint on the sign of Δ, one must develop a model in which market adjustments are costly and chosen optimally over time by producers and consumers. So far, only the small-country models developed by Kemp et al. (2002) and Kemp and Shimomura (2003) are available.

4 Final Remarks

The analysis in Sects. 2 and 3 can be readily extended to accommodate more than two countries. Any attempt to accommodate more than two commodities or factors of production would require conceptual adjustments.

In the analysis of Sects. 2 and 3, only once-over small changes in the stocks of capital are considered. Even under Heckscher–Ohlin assumptions, however, a sequence of small changes in the capital stocks can repeatedly change the signs of (5a) and (5b). Thus small and large changes in the factor endowment ratios of the two countries can have very different effects on the gains from trade.

References

Edgeworth FY (1894) The theory of international values I. Econ J 4:35–50

Edgeworth FY (1899) On a point in the pure theory of international trade. Econ J 9:125–128

Kemp MC, Long NV (1992) Some properties of egalitarian economies. J Publ Econ 49:383–387

Kemp MC, Shimomura K (1995) The apparently innocuous representative agent. Jpn Econ Rev 46:247–256

Kemp MC, Shimomura K (2003) A dynamic Heckscher–Ohlin model: The case of costly factor reallocation. Jpn Econ Rev 54:237–252

Kemp MC, Kimura Y, Shimomura K (2002) A second correspondence principle. In: Woodland AD (ed) Economic theory and international trade, Edward Elgar, Aldershot, Hants

Lindbeck A (2007) China's reformed economy. Cesifo Forum 1:8–14

A Modified Heckscher–Ohlin Theorem Under Quasilinear Utility Functions[1]

Junko Doi, Kenji Fujiwara(✉), Toru Kikuchi, and Koji Shimomura

Abstract Constructing a two-country, two-good, two-factor model of international trade under quasilinear utility functions, we prove a modified Heckscher–Ohlin (MHO) theorem which relates trade patterns to the international distribution of factor endowments in a manner that has parallels with the standard HO theorem. The MHO theorem survives imperfect competition, increasing returns and externalities.

1 Introduction

The determination of trade patterns is a central topic of trade theory. For a long time, the two-country, two-good, two-factor Heckscher–Ohlin (HO) model and its subsequent extensions have been the standard general equilibrium framework that explains the patterns of international trade in terms of intercountry differences in factor endowments.

Most HO models commonly assume homothetic utility functions, which are associated with the unrealistic implication that the income elasticity of the demand for every good is equal to unity.[2] Then, it may be naturally asked whether an alternative trade pattern theorem can be established under nonhomothetic utility functions.

In fact, in the last decade, there has been a growing body of research which is skeptical about the empirical performance of the HO theorem. Among others, Trefler (1995) concludes that the poor empirical performance of the HO theorem

[1] An earlier version of this chapter was presented at Kobe University and Okayama University.

[2] Wong (1995) is a comprehensive survey of perfectly and imperfectly competitive HO models.

K. Fujiwara
School of Economics, Kwansei Gakuin University, Uegahara 1-1-155, Nishinomiya, Hyogo 662-8501, Japan, e-mail: kenjifujiwara@kwansei.ac.jp

T. Kamihigashi and L. Zhao (eds.) *International Trade and Economic Dynamics – Essays in Memory of Koji Shimomura.*

could be attributed to two assumptions in the model.[3] The first is the assumption of identical technologies across countries and its property of factor price equalization and the second is that of homothetic preferences. In view of the developments by Trefler (1995) and his successors, it is of great interest to study the determination of trade patterns by relaxing these assumptions. This chapter examines implications of nonhomotheticity in preferences for trade patterns on the assumption that identical technologies are retained.[4]

Before proceeding further, it might be helpful to outline our argument. We replace a homothetic utility function with a quasilinear one:

$$U = u(Q_1) + Q_2,$$

where $u(\cdot)$ is an increasing and strictly concave function and Q_i, $i = 1,2$, is the consumption of Good i. The quasilinearity implies that the income elasticity of Good 1 is zero, under which we establish a modified Heckscher–Ohlin (MHO) theorem which relates the international distribution of factor endowments to the patterns of international trade in a manner that has parallels with the standard HO theorem.[5]

The standard HO theorem states that each country exports the good the production of which intensively uses the factor of production that is *relatively abundant* in that country. The MHO theorem is based on the same assumption. The difference between the two theorems lies in the meaning of *relative factor abundance*. This can be grasped by referring to Fig. 1, where K and L denote capital and labor endowments of a country, say Home. In the standard HO theorem, the straight line OEM is the border of relative factor abundance whose interpretation is as follows. If the factor endowment point of the other country, say Foreign, (K^*, L^*), is below (resp., above) the borderline, Foreign is defined as a labor-abundant (resp., capital-abundant) country and Home (resp., Foreign) exports the capital-intensive good. On the other hand, in the MHO theorem, the borderline is replaced by either $A'EM'$ or $A''EM''$ whose slope is equal to the equilibrium factor intensity of Good 2 in the above-specified preference under the assumption that the pair of (K^*, L^*) exactly equals (K, L).[6] Then, if Foreign's factor endowment pair is above (resp., below) this redefined locus, it is regarded as a capital-abundant (resp., labor-abundant) country and exports the capital-intensive (resp., labor-intensive) good.

---

[3] Strictly speaking, Trefler's (1995) criticism is concerned with trade volumes rather than trade patterns. However, we are sure that his insight is important in considering trade patterns as well as trade volumes.

[4] Trefler (1995) suggests that the empirical performance can be improved by replacing the homotheticity assumption with the Armington assumption. However, it is often criticized since it has no theoretical foundation.

[5] Markusen (1986) and Chung (2003) also incorporate nonhomothetic preferences into the HO-type trade model. Both chapters aim to examine the volume of trade rather than the determinants of trade patterns.

[6] Whether the borderline becomes $A'EM'$ or $A''EM''$ depends on whether Good 2 is capital-intensive or labor-intensive.

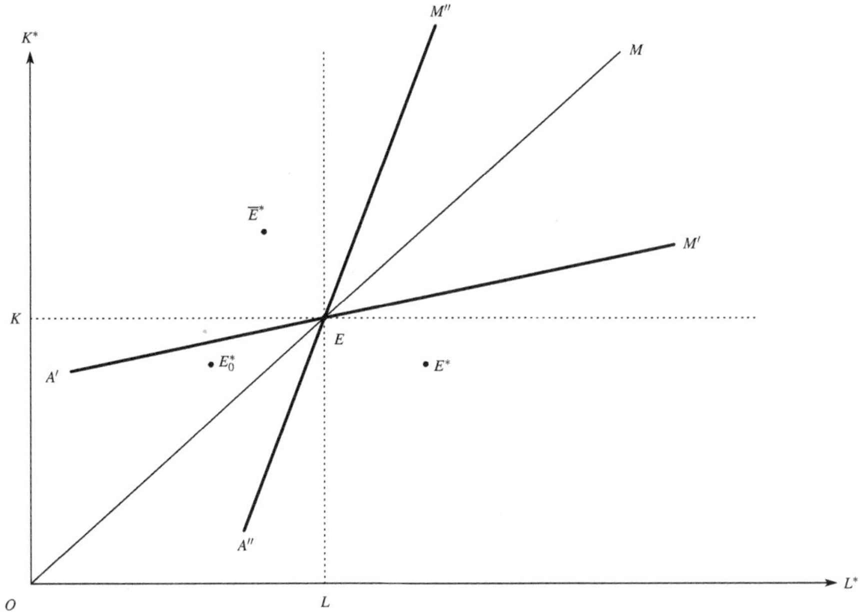

Fig. 1 Borderline of relative factor abundance

The reality lies somewhere between these two polar assumptions.[7] Thus, combining both the standard and modified HO theorems, one could predict that the real borderline is somewhere between OEM and $A'EM'$ or $A''EM''$ and that a more realistic trade pattern is explained more clearly.

Moreover, as will be clear, the scope of the MHO theorem exceeds that of the standard HO theorem since the MHO theorem holds not only under perfect competition but also under monopolistic competition, free entry oligopoly, international duopoly, and national and international external economies of scale. Thus, the MHO theorem could contribute to the literature on general equilibrium trade theory, in the sense that no comparable trade pattern theorem under the homotheticity assumption exists.

This chapter is structured as follows. Section 2 constructs an HO model under quasilinear utility functions. Section 3 proves the MHO theorem in a general environment. Section 4 shows that the generalized model can generate, as its special cases, various types of imperfect competition, increasing returns and externalities and that the MHO theorem is established in each of those market structures. Section 5 presents concluding remarks.

[7] Note also that one cannot say which assumption is more general than the other, since neither logically implies the other.

2 An HO Model with Quasilinear Utility Functions

We consider a world economy consisting of Home and Foreign. There are two goods named Good 1 and Good 2 both of which are produced from two factors of production: capital and labor. Both factors are inelastically supplied and fully employed in each country. An asterisk (*) is attached to each Foreign variable. Assume a representative agent in each country whose preference is specified by

$$U = u(Q_1) + Q_2,$$

which yields the demand function of Good 1 as $D(p) \equiv u'^{-1}(p)$ in both countries, where p is the price of Good 1 in terms of Good 2. Thus, the world market-clearing condition is

$$2D(p) = Y_1 + Y_1^*, \tag{1}$$

where Y_1 and Y_1^* are, respectively, the output of Good 1 in Home and Foreign.

The system of the equilibrium conditions in Home's supply side is described by

$$\Gamma(Y_1, Y_1^*) = c^1(r,w), \tag{2}$$

$$1 = c^2(r,w), \tag{3}$$

$$K = c_r^1(r,w)\Psi(Y_1, Y_1^*) + c_r^2(r,w)Y_2, \tag{4}$$

$$L = c_w^1(r,w)\Psi(Y_1, Y_1^*) + c_w^2(r,w)Y_2, \tag{5}$$

where r and w are the capital rental and wage rates, K and L are Home's endowments of capital and labor, and $c^i(\cdot)$, $i = 1,2$, is a function of factor prices that satisfies all the properties of the standard unit-cost function in a neoclassical model. Following Wong (1995), $\Gamma(\cdot)$ and $\Psi(\cdot)$ are, respectively, called a *virtual* price and output of Good 1. The subscripts indicate the partial derivative. In what follows, we impose:

Assumption 1. $c^i(\cdot)$ is twice continuously differentiable, increasing, quasiconcave, and linearly homogeneous in r and w.

Assumption 2. For any $q > 0$, the system of equations

$$q = c^1(r,w),$$

$$1 = c^2(r,w)$$

has a unique and positive pair of solutions $(r(q), w(q))$.

Assumption 3. The sign of

$$\frac{c_r^1(r(q),w(q))}{c_w^1(r(q),w(q))} - \frac{c_r^2(r(q),w(q))}{c_w^2(r(q),w(q))}$$

does not change for any positive q.

Remark 1. The pair of functions $c^i(r,w)$

$$c^i(r,w) = r^{\alpha_i} w^{1-\alpha_i}, \quad \alpha_i \in (0,1),\ \alpha_1 \neq \alpha_2,$$

is an example that satisfies all the above assumptions.

Noting that both countries share identical production technologies, Foreign's supply side is similarly described by

$$\begin{aligned}
\Gamma(Y_1^*, Y_1) &= c^1(r^*, w^*), && (6)\\
1 &= c^2(r^*, w^*), && (7)\\
K^* &= c_r^1(r^*, w^*)\Psi(Y_1^*, Y_1) + c_r^2(r^*, w^*)Y_2^*, && (8)\\
L^* &= c_w^1(r^*, w^*)\Psi(Y_1^*, Y_1) + c_w^2(r^*, w^*)Y_2^*. && (9)
\end{aligned}$$

The present two-country model consists of (1)–(9) that have nine endogenous variables: $p, r, w, r^*, w^*, Y_1, Y_1^*, Y_2$, and Y_2^*.

To make the subsequent arguments transparent, let us slightly rewrite the model. Using the functions $w(q)$ and $r(q)$, we can derive the following relationship:

$$\begin{aligned}
\Psi(Y_1, Y_1^*) &= r'(\Gamma(Y_1, Y_1^*))\,K + w'(\Gamma(Y_1, Y_1^*))\,L, && (10)\\
\Psi(Y_1^*, Y_1) &= r'(\Gamma(Y_1^*, Y_1))\,K^* + w'(\Gamma(Y_1^*, Y_1))\,L^*, && (11)
\end{aligned}$$

where the prime ($'$) denotes the derivative.

Remark 2. While this completes the description of the basic model, which is fully drawn upon in the subsequent arguments, it is too general and abstract to be easily comprehended. To tackle this difficulty, we explain the structure of the present model in greater detail.

Suppose an HO model with perfect competition and constant returns. Within this simplest case, the supply side is captured by the system of

$$\begin{aligned}
p &= c^1(r,w),\\
1 &= c^2(r,w),\\
K &= c_r^1(r,w)Y_1 + c_r^2(r,w)Y_2,\\
L &= c_w^1(r,w)Y_1 + c_w^2(r,w)Y_2.
\end{aligned}$$

As any elementary textbook declares, the factor prices are determined only in the former two equations, so that they are expressed as $r(p)$ and $w(p)$. Then, substituting them into the latter two equations, these conditions become a linear system of equations whose unknowns are Y_1 and Y_2. It is clear that these equilibrium outputs depend on the factor endowments *linearly*. This fact can be understood in another way by constructing the following function:

$$r(p)K + w(p)L,$$

which is called a factor income or GDP function.[8] Then, the envelope theorem on the factor income function convinces us that

$$Y_1 = r'(p)K + w'(p)L,$$

i.e., the equilibrium output of Good 1 equals the partial derivative of the factor income function with respect to its price.

Some may guess that this convenient property crucially hinges on the assumption of perfect competition and constant returns. This is correct, but we can still make use of a similar property even under imperfect competition and/or increasing returns by specifying the production functions properly. In the cases that deviate from perfect competition and constant returns, the outputs are not generally equal to the partial derivative with respect to the price. However, some other variable which we call a "virtual" output can be assured to be equal to the partial derivative of the factor income function with respect to the "virtual" price. Such a virtual output and price are defined by $\Psi(\cdot)$ and $\Gamma(\cdot)$ in (10) and (11). By using these "virtual" variables, the argument can be drastically simplified and made transparent since many of the useful properties including the above envelope property can be applied.

For example, under perfect competition and constant returns, the two functions simply reduce to

$$\Psi(Y_1, Y_1^*) = Y_1,$$
$$\Gamma(Y_1, Y_1^*) = p\left(\frac{Y_1 + Y_1^*}{2}\right),$$

where the right-hand side in the second equation gives the inverse demand function. How the two functions are specified depends on the market structure under consideration. This section and Sect. 3 discuss the trade pattern within this generalized framework and Sect. 4 applies the trade pattern theorem to a variety of market structures by specifying the two functions.

3 The MHO Theorem

Based on the model developed in Sect. 2, we prove the MHO theorem. Suppose that the system of (10) and (11) has a unique solution for given factor endowments. Then, we can rewrite (1) as

$$D(p) - Y_1(K, L, K^*, L^*) = Y_1^*(K, L, K^*, L^*) - D(p).$$

---

[8] For a detailed definition and properties of the factor income function, see Dixit and Norman (1980), Woodland (1982), and Wong (1995).

Hence, it immediately follows that the trade pattern is determined accordingly as

$$Y_1(K,L,K^*,L^*) > \quad \text{or} \quad < Y_1^*(K,L,K^*,L^*).$$

Like Fig. 1, we fix the Home factor endowments (K,L) and derive the region where Foreign exports Good 1:

$$\Theta \equiv \{(K^*,L^*)|Y_1(K,L,K^*,L^*) < Y_1^*(K,L,K^*,L^*)\},$$

and the other region where it exports Good 2:

$$\overline{\Theta} \equiv \{(K^*,L^*)|Y_1(K,L,K^*,L^*) > Y_1^*(K,L,K^*,L^*)\}.$$

To do this, we focus on the borderline of the two regions which is depicted in Fig. 1.[9] The following lemma characterizes it.

Lemma. *The borderline determining the trade pattern is given by the line which crosses (L,K), the slope of which is equal to the factor intensity of Good 2 evaluated at $(L^*,K^*)=(L,K)$.*

Proof. The borderline is defined as the locus of (L^*,K^*) which guarantees that both countries have no opportunity to trade even after the opening of trade. This is established if and only if $D(p)=Y_1=Y_1^*$, in which we have $\Gamma(Y_1,Y_1^*)=\Gamma(Y_1^*,Y_1)=\Gamma(Y_1,Y_1)$ and $\Psi(Y_1,Y_1^*)=\Psi(Y_1^*,Y_1)=\Psi(Y_1,Y_1)$. Thus, (10) and (11) become

$$\Psi(Y_1,Y_1) = r'(\Gamma(Y_1,Y_1))K + w'(\Gamma(Y_1,Y_1))L, \tag{12}$$
$$\Psi(Y_1,Y_1) = r'(\Gamma(Y_1,Y_1))K^* + w'(\Gamma(Y_1,Y_1))L^*. \tag{13}$$

Note that (12) alone determines Y_1, which is denoted by Y_1^a. Y_1^a clearly depends only on K and L, and (12) becomes

$$\Psi(Y_1^a,Y_1^a) = r'(\Gamma(Y_1^a,Y_1^a))K^* + w'(\Gamma(Y_1^a,Y_1^a))L^*,$$

since $Y_1^a = Y_1 = Y_1^*$ holds along the borderline. Combining (12) and (13), we obtain

$$0 = r'(\Gamma(Y_1^a,Y_1^a))(K^*-K) + w'(\Gamma(Y_1^a,Y_1^a))(L^*-L),$$

which is equivalent to

$$K^* = -\frac{w'(\Gamma(Y_1^a,Y_1^a))}{r'(\Gamma(Y_1^a,Y_1^a))}(L^*-L)+K.$$

[9] Those who know Chung (2003) may notice some similarity between his Fig. 1 and our Fig. 1. However, he assumes that one consumer inelastically supplies one unit of labor and that the population differs between countries. In contrast, we assume that population is fixed to one but that the labor supply of each country is different. This difference in assumption has a significantly different implication when it comes to predicting trade patterns.

Totally differentiating (2) and (3) and invoking the Stolper–Samuelson relationship, we can confirm that the slope of the borderline is equal to the factor intensity of Good 2:

$$-\frac{w'(\Gamma(Y_1^a,Y_1^a))}{r'(\Gamma(Y_1^a,Y_1^a))}=\frac{c_r^2(w(\Gamma(Y_1^a,Y_1^a)),r(\Gamma(Y_1^a,Y_1^a)))}{c_w^2(w(\Gamma(Y_1^a,Y_1^a)),r(\Gamma(Y_1^a,Y_1^a)))},$$

as is to be proved. □

Based on this Lemma, we can establish our main result.

Theorem. *Define Foreign as a labor-abundant (resp., capital-abundant) country if its factor endowment pair* (L^*,K^*) *is below (resp., above)* $A'EM'$ *in the case that Good 2 is labor-intensive and* $A''EM''$ *in the case that Good 2 is capital-intensive, as depicted in Fig. 1. Then, Home exports Good 1 (resp., Good 2) if and only if the functions* $\Gamma(\cdot)$ *and* $\Psi(\cdot)$ *satisfy*

$$\Psi_1-\Psi_2+\Omega(\Gamma_2-\Gamma_1)>0, \tag{14}$$

where

$$\Omega\equiv r''(\Gamma(\cdot))K+w''(\Gamma(\cdot))L>0,\quad \Gamma_1\equiv\frac{\partial\Gamma(\cdot)}{\partial Y_1},\quad \Gamma_2\equiv\frac{\partial\Gamma(\cdot)}{\partial Y_1^*},$$
$$\Psi_1\equiv\frac{\partial\Psi(\cdot)}{\partial Y_1}\quad \text{and}\quad \Psi_2\equiv\frac{\partial\Psi(\cdot)}{\partial Y_1^*},$$

all of which are evaluated at Y_1^a.

Proof. Without loss of generality, we concentrate the argument on the case where Good 2 is labor-intensive, from which $A'EM'$ in Fig. 1 is the borderline. Now, starting from point E, let only Foreign's labor increase by $\mathrm{d}L^*>0$. Then, Foreign becomes a labor-abundant country by our definition. Then, (1) convinces us that Home exports Good 1 when this change induces a larger output change in Home than in Foreign:

$$\frac{\partial Y_1}{\partial L^*}>\frac{\partial Y_1^*}{\partial L^*}.$$

The rest of our task is to derive the condition for this inequality. Totally differentiating (10) and (11) with respect to Y_1, Y_1^*, and L^*, and evaluating at Y_1^a, we obtain

$$\begin{aligned}\Psi_1\mathrm{d}Y_1+\Psi_2\mathrm{d}Y_1^* &= (r''K+w''L)(\Gamma_1\mathrm{d}Y_1+\Gamma_2\mathrm{d}Y_1^*),\\ \Psi_2\mathrm{d}Y_1+\Psi_1\mathrm{d}Y_1^* &= (r''K+w''L)(\Gamma_2\mathrm{d}Y_1+\Gamma_1\mathrm{d}Y_1^*)+w'\mathrm{d}L^*,\end{aligned}$$

whose matrix form is

$$\begin{bmatrix}\Psi_1-\Omega\Gamma_1 & \Psi_2-\Omega\Gamma_2\\ \Psi_2-\Omega\Gamma_2 & \Psi_1-\Omega\Gamma_1\end{bmatrix}\begin{bmatrix}\mathrm{d}Y_1\\ \mathrm{d}Y_1^*\end{bmatrix}=\begin{bmatrix}0\\ w'\end{bmatrix}\mathrm{d}L^*.$$

Hence, simple calculations yield

$$\frac{\partial Y_1^*}{\partial L^*} - \frac{\partial Y_1}{\partial L^*} = \frac{w'}{\Psi_1 - \Psi_2 + \Omega(\Gamma_2 - \Gamma_1)}. \tag{15}$$

Because we have assumed that $w' < 0$, i.e., Good 2 is labor-intensive, it holds that $\partial Y_1^*/\partial L^* - \partial Y_1/\partial L^* < 0$ when the denominator in (17) is positive, which is equivalent to (16). A parallel argument is possible for the case where Good 2 is capital-intensive. □

4 Applications of the MHO Theorem

In this section, we show the validity of the MHO theorem in the following market structures: perfect competition, monopolistic competition, oligopoly with and without free entry, and national and international external economies of scale.[10] For this purpose, we adopt the following strategy. After deriving each of these market structures as a special case of the generalized model developed so far, we demonstrate that all of these models satisfy the condition (16) for the MHO theorem.

4.1 Perfect Competition and Constant Returns to Scale

Let us begin with the canonical model with perfect competition and constant returns. In this case, $\Gamma(\cdot)$ and $\Psi(\cdot)$ are specified as

$$\Gamma(Y_1, Y_1^*) = p\left(\frac{Y_1 + Y_1^*}{2}\right),$$
$$\Psi(Y_1, Y_1^*) = Y_1.$$

Thus, we immediately see $\Gamma_1 = \Gamma_2 < 0$, $\Psi_1 > 0$, and $\Psi_2 = 0$, which leads to (16) and the theorem.

4.2 Monopolistic Competition

Suppose that Good 1 is horizontally differentiated under monopolistic competition, while Good 2 is a perfectly competitive and a constant returns good. For the

[10] The reader interested in the traditional HO theorem used in these models is referred to Dixit and Norman (1980), Ethier (1979), Fujiwara and Shimomura (2005), Helpman and Krugman (1985), Herberg and Kemp (1969), Lahiri and Ono (1995), Markusen (1981), Ohyama (1999), Shimomura (1998), and Wong (1995).

time being, we concentrate on Home's consumer behavior since the same argument applies to Foreign due to the identical preference. Home's preference is given by

$$U = u(Q_1) + Q_2,$$

where Q_1 is the quantity index of the differentiated products:

$$Q_1 \equiv \left(\int_0^n q_i^\theta \mathrm{d}i + \int_0^{n^*} q_j^\theta \mathrm{d}j \right)^{1/\theta}, \quad \theta \in (0,1),$$

where q_i (resp., q_j) denotes the Home consumer's consumption of Home (resp., Foreign) varieties and n (resp., n^*) is their range. The corresponding price index is defined by

$$P \equiv \left(\int_0^n p_i^{\theta/(\theta-1)} \mathrm{d}i + \int_0^{n^*} (p_j^*)^{\theta/(\theta-1)} \mathrm{d}j \right)^{(\theta-1)/\theta},$$

where p_i (resp., p_j^*) is the price of the variety produced by firm i (resp., j) in Home (resp., Foreign).

By solving the utility maximization problem in a two-stage manner as in Helpman and Krugman (1985), we see that both countries' consumer has an identical demand function of variety i:

$$q_i = \left(\frac{p_i}{P} \right)^{1/(\theta-1)} D(P),$$

which yields the following market-clearing condition under free trade:

$$q_i + q_i^* = 2 \left(\frac{p_i}{P} \right)^{1/(\theta-1)} D(P) = x_i.$$

Solving this condition for p_i, the inverse demand function of variety i is derived as

$$p_i = \frac{P}{[2D(P)]^{\theta-1}} x_i^{\theta-1} \equiv A(P) x_i^{\theta-1}.$$

Next, the production technology is introduced. In what follows, we consider only one Home firm's behavior due to no intercountry technological difference and hence the subscript i is dropped. The production function in Sector 1 is assumed to take a homothetic form:

$$x = G(f(k,l)), \tag{16}$$

where k and l are the capital and labor inputs, $G(\cdot)$ is increasing and strictly convex in f with $G(0) = 0$, and $f(\cdot)$ is increasing, quasiconcave, and linearly homogeneous. Then, the corresponding cost function takes a multiplicatively separable form:[11]

$$c^1(r,w)\phi(x),$$

[11] For the derivation, see Wong (1995).

where $\phi(\cdot) \equiv G^{-1}(\cdot)$, which is an increasing and strictly concave function. Making use of the inverse demand function obtained above, a firm i's profit is defined by

$$A(P)x^{\theta} - c^1(r,w)\phi(x).$$

Each monopolistic firm chooses the output to maximize its profit, which yields the following first-order condition:[12]

$$\theta A(P)x^{\theta-1} = c^1(r,w)\phi'(x). \tag{17}$$

Furthermore, free entry and exit drive the long-run profit to zero, implying that the price equals the average cost:

$$A(P)x^{\theta} = c^1(r,w)\phi(x). \tag{18}$$

From (13) and (14), all firms in both countries choose the same output level $\bar{x}$ which is determined by

$$\theta = \frac{\phi'(\bar{x})\bar{x}}{\phi(\bar{x})}.$$

Resorting to the auxiliary results derived, let us relate the generalized model in the previous section to the present context. Due to the quasilinearity of preferences, we immediately have

$$Q_1 + Q_1^* = 2D(P). \tag{19}$$

In addition, the symmetry among all varieties and the market-clearing condition of each variety, $q + q^* = \bar{x}$, enable us to rewrite the left-hand side as

$$\begin{aligned} Q_1 + Q_1^* &= (n+n^*)^{1/\theta}(q+q^*) \\ &= (n+n^*)^{1/\theta}\bar{x}. \end{aligned}$$

In a similar manner, the price index on the right-hand side in (15) is rewritten as

$$\begin{aligned} P &= (n+n^*)^{(\theta-1)/\theta} p \\ &= (n+n^*)^{(\theta-1)/\theta} \frac{c^1(r,w)\phi(\bar{x})}{\bar{x}}, \end{aligned}$$

where the second equality follows from the fact that the price equals the average cost. As a result, (15) is equivalent to

$$(n+n^*)^{1/\theta}\bar{x} = 2D\left((n+n^*)^{(\theta-1)/\theta}\frac{c^1(r,w)\phi(\bar{x})}{\bar{x}}\right).$$

---

[12] Note that P is taken as given by each firm following the standard argument on monopolistic competition.

Solving this equation for $c^1(\cdot)$ yields

$$\frac{D^{-1}\left((n+n^*)^{1/\theta}(\overline{x}/2)\right)}{(n+n^*)^{(\theta-1)/\theta}(\phi(\overline{x})/\overline{x})} = c^1(r,w).$$

Based on these calculations, we can verify that the present model is a special case of the generalized model in Sects. 2 and 3. Since each country's aggregate output of the differentiated good is $Y_1 = n\overline{x}$ and $Y_1^* = n^*\overline{x}$, the functions $\Gamma(\cdot)$ and $\Psi(\cdot)$ take the following forms:

$$\Gamma(Y_1,Y_1^*) = \frac{D^{-1}\left(\frac{1}{2}(Y_1+Y_1^*)^{1/\theta}\overline{x}^{1-(1/\theta)}\right)}{(Y_1+Y_1^*)^{(\theta-1)/\theta}\overline{x}^{(1-2\theta)/\theta}\phi(\overline{x})},$$

$$\Psi(Y_1,Y_1^*) = \frac{Y_1\phi(\overline{x})}{\overline{x}}.$$

Accordingly, it follows that $\Gamma_1 = \Gamma_2$, $\Psi_1 > 0$, and $\Psi_2 = 0$, which ensures (16). Thus, we have proved the MHO theorem under monopolistic competition.

4.3 Free Entry Oligopoly

In the present and next sections, we examine international oligopoly instead of monopolistic competition. Particularly, free entry and exit in the oligopolistic sector are allowed in this section, while they are not in the next section. As will be clear, free entry makes the analysis very close to that of monopolistic competition. The production function of Good 1 is specified by (16).

The market-clearing condition under free trade is

$$2D(p) = nx + n^*x^* \equiv Y_1 + Y_1^*,$$

where n (resp., n^*) and x (resp., x^*), respectively, denote the number of oligopolistic firms and the per-firm output in Home (resp., Foreign). Hence, the inverse demand function is $D'^{-1}\left((Y_1+Y_1^*)/2\right) \equiv p\left((Y_1+Y_1^*)/2\right)$ and the conditions for profit maximization and zero profit are derived as follows:

$$\text{Profit maximization: } p\left(\frac{Y_1+Y_1^*}{2}\right)\left[1 - \frac{x}{(Y_1+Y_1^*)\eta\left(p\left(\frac{Y_1+Y_1^*}{2}\right)\right)}\right] = c^1(r,w)\phi'(x),$$

$$\text{Zero profit: } p\left(\frac{Y_1+Y_1^*}{2}\right)x = c^1(r,w)\phi(x),$$

where $\eta(\cdot)$ is the price elasticity of Good 1:

$$\eta\left(p\left(\frac{Y_1+Y_1^*}{2}\right)\right)^{-1} \equiv -\frac{\mathrm{d}\ln\left[p\left(\frac{Y_1+Y_1^*}{2}\right)\right]}{\mathrm{d}\ln\left[\frac{Y_1+Y_1^*}{2}\right]}.$$

Combining the above two conditions yields

$$1-\frac{x}{(Y_1+Y_1^*)\eta\left(p\left(\frac{Y_1+Y_1^*}{2}\right)\right)}=\frac{\phi'(x)x}{\phi(x)}, \tag{20}$$

for the Home firm and

$$1-\frac{x^*}{(Y_1+Y_1^*)\eta\left(p\left(\frac{Y_1+Y_1^*}{2}\right)\right)}=\frac{\phi'(x^*)x^*}{\phi(x^*)}, \tag{21}$$

for the Foreign firm. Consequently, we can observe from (19) and (20) that $x = x^* = \bar{x}$ if $(1-\phi'x/\phi)/x$ is monotonic in x and that $\bar{x}$ becomes a function of the total output in the world, so that $\bar{x}=\bar{x}(Y_1+Y_1^*)$.[13] Therefore, the functions $\Gamma(\cdot)$ and $\Psi(\cdot)$ are specified by

$$\Gamma(Y_1,Y_1^*) = \frac{p((Y_1+Y_1^*)/2)\bar{x}(Y_1+Y_1^*)}{\phi(\bar{x}(Y_1+Y_1^*))},$$

$$\Psi(Y_1,Y_1^*) = \frac{Y_1\bar{x}(\bar{x}(Y_1+Y_1^*))}{\bar{x}(Y_1+Y_1^*)},$$

and, we have $\Gamma_1=\Gamma_2<0$ and

$$\Psi_1-\Psi_2=\frac{\phi(\bar{x}(Y_1+Y_1^*))}{\bar{x}(Y_1+Y_1^*)}>0.$$

That is, the MHO turns out to be valid under free entry oligopoly.

4.4 International Duopoly

While we have presumed free entry and exit in the previous sections, let us relax them and modify the preceding oligopoly model in such a way to fix the number of oligopolistic firms in each country to one. Then, the zero profit condition is excluded and the profit maximization condition for the Home firm becomes

$$p'\left(\frac{Y_1+Y_1^*}{2}\right)\frac{Y_1}{2}+p\left(\frac{Y_1+Y_1^*}{2}\right)\equiv MR(Y_1,Y_1^*)=c^1(r,w)\phi'(Y_1),$$

13 For a more detailed proof, see Shimomura (1998).

which convinces us that the functions $\Gamma(\cdot)$ and $\Psi(\cdot)$ have the following forms:

$$\Gamma(Y_1, Y_1^*) \equiv \frac{MR(Y_1, Y_1^*)}{\phi'(Y_1)},$$
$$\Psi(Y_1, Y_1^*) \equiv \phi(Y_1),$$

which yields

$$\Gamma_1 = \frac{MR_1\phi' - MR\phi''}{(\phi')^2} = \frac{MR_1 - c^1\phi''}{\phi'},$$
$$\Gamma_2 = \frac{MR_2}{\phi'},$$

where $MR_1 \equiv \partial MR(\cdot)/\partial Y_1$ and $MR_2 \equiv \partial MR(\cdot)/\partial Y_1^*$. The numerator of Γ_1 is negative due to the second-order condition for the Home firm's profit maximization problem. It follows from $\phi' > 0$ that Γ_1 is negative.

Note that (10) and (11) can be regarded as a system of reaction functions in the present context. Therefore, the slope of each firm's reaction curve is derived by totally differentiating it. Carrying this out and subtracting the slope of the Foreign firm's reaction curve from that of the Home firm's reaction curve, we see that

$$\left.\frac{dY_1^*}{dY_1}\right|_{(10)} - \left.\frac{dY_1^*}{dY_1}\right|_{(11)} = \frac{\Psi_1 - \Omega\Gamma_1}{\Omega\Gamma_2} - \frac{\Omega\Gamma_2}{\Psi_1 - \Omega\Gamma_1}$$
$$= \frac{(\Psi_1 - \Omega\Gamma_1 + \Omega\Gamma_2)(\Psi_1 - \Omega\Gamma_1 - \Omega\Gamma_2)}{\Omega\Gamma_2(\Psi_1 - \Omega\Gamma_1)}. \quad (22)$$

Since $\Psi_1 = \phi'(Y_1) > 0$, $\Omega > 0$, and $\Gamma_1 < 0$, we have $\Psi_1 - \Omega\Gamma_1 > 0$. Hence, if Γ_2 is positive (resp., negative), the slopes are both positive (resp., negative). Therefore, if Γ_2 is positive (resp., negative), then the stability condition is equivalent to that when the right-hand side in (22) is positive (resp., negative).

Let us consider the two cases $\Gamma_2 > 0$ and $\Gamma_2 < 0$ separately because both are theoretically possible. First, begin with $\Gamma_2 > 0$. Then, the second-order condition for profit maximization, $\Psi_1 - \Omega\Gamma_1 > 0$, safely guarantees (16). Second, suppose $\Gamma_2 < 0$. Then, the stability of the Cournot–Nash equilibrium requires the right-hand side in (22) to be negative. In view of the fact that $\Psi_1 - \Omega\Gamma_1 - \Omega\Gamma_2 > 0$, we now reach $\Psi_1 - \Omega\Gamma_1 + \Omega\Gamma_2 > 0$. In summary, (16) holds irrespective of the sign of Γ_2, thanks to the second-order condition and the stability condition. This completes the proof of the MHO theorem under international duopoly.

4.5 National Returns to Scale

The final two market structures return to perfect competition while increasing returns work as a Marshallian externality. We deal with two types of externalities, one of which is *national* returnsand the other is *international* returns.

This section sticks to the former type and assumes the following production function:[14]

$$Y_1 = F(Y_1) f^1(K_1, L_1),$$

where K_1 and L_1 are the employment of capital and labor, $F(\cdot)$ is an increasing and strictly concave function, and $f^1(\cdot)$ possesses all the neoclassical properties. From this production function, the total cost function becomes

$$\frac{c^1(r,w)Y_1}{F(Y_1)}.$$

Note that any firm in Sector 1 maximizes profits taking $F(\cdot)$ as given, which makes the profit maximization condition become

$$p = \frac{c^1(r,w)}{F(Y_1)}.$$

Then, $\Gamma(\cdot)$ and $\Psi(\cdot)$ are specified by

$$\Gamma(Y_1, Y_1^*) = p\left(\frac{Y_1 + Y_1^*}{2}\right) F(Y_1),$$
$$\Psi(Y_1, Y_1^*) = \frac{Y_1}{F(Y_1)},$$

from which we immediately see that

$$\Gamma_1 = \frac{p'F}{2} + pF',$$
$$\Gamma_2 = \frac{p'F}{2} < 0,$$
$$\Psi_1 = \frac{F - F'Y_1}{F^2} > 0,$$
$$\Psi_2 = 0.$$

To relate the above results to the condition for the MHO theorem, the stability condition is once again adopted as in the case of international duopoly. Following the existing literature, the following adjustment process of outputs is supposed:

$$\dot{Y}_1 = \Gamma(Y_1, Y_1^*) - c^1, \tag{23}$$
$$\dot{Y}_1^* = \Gamma(Y_1^*, Y_1) - c^{1*}, \tag{24}$$

[14] Herberg and Kemp (1969) and Wong (1995) also employ this specification.

where the dot indicates the time derivative, and c^1 and c^1_* are the "virtual" price which satisfies

$$\Psi(Y_1,Y_1^*) = r'(c^1)K + w'(c^1)L,$$
$$\Psi(Y_1^*,Y_1) = r'(c^{1*})K + w'(c^{1*})L.$$

For deriving the stability condition associated with (21) and (24), the characteristic equation is set up:

$$\begin{aligned} H(\lambda) &\equiv \Omega^{-2}\begin{vmatrix} \Omega\Gamma_1 - \Psi_1 - \Omega\lambda & \Omega\Gamma_2 \\ \Omega\Gamma_2 & \Omega\Gamma_1 - \Psi_1 - \Omega\lambda \end{vmatrix} \\ &= \Omega^{-2}(\Omega\Gamma_1 + \Omega\Gamma_2 - \Psi_1 - \Omega\lambda)(\Omega\Gamma_1 - \Omega\Gamma_2 - \Psi_1 - \Omega\lambda) \\ &= \Omega^{-2}[\Omega\lambda + (\Psi_1 - \Omega\Gamma_1 - \Omega\Gamma_2)][\Omega\lambda + (\Psi_1 - \Omega\Gamma_1 + \Omega\Gamma_2)] \\ &= 0, \end{aligned}$$

where λ is the eigenvalue of the dynamic system. Local stability requires that both $(\Psi_1 - \Omega\Gamma_1 - \Omega\Gamma_2)$ and $(\Psi_1 - \Omega\Gamma_1 + \Omega\Gamma_2)$ be positive. Thus, (16) follows and so does the MHO theorem.

4.6 International Returns to Scale

Following the idea by Ethier (1979), this section examines another type of external economies of scale. When increasing returns prevail internationally, the production function of Good 1 depends on Y_1^* as well as Y_1:

$$Y_1 = F(Y_1 + Y_1^*)f^1(K_1, L_1).$$

Then, the cost function becomes

$$\frac{c^1(r,w)Y_1}{F(Y_1 + Y_1^*)},$$

and the relevant functions in our model are specified as follows:

$$\Gamma(Y_1,Y_1^*) = p\left(\frac{Y_1 + Y_1^*}{2}\right)F(Y_1 + Y_1^*),$$
$$\Psi(Y_1,Y_1^*) = \frac{Y_1}{F(Y_1 + Y_1^*)}.$$

Hence, we obtain $\Gamma_1 = \Gamma_2$ and

$$\Psi_1 = \frac{F - F'Y_1}{F^2} > 0,$$
$$\Psi_2 = -\frac{F'Y_1}{F^2} < 0,$$

which yields

$$\Psi_1 - \Psi_2 = \frac{1}{F} > 0.$$

Thus, we can easily reconfirm the validity of (16) and the MHO theorem.

5 Concluding Remarks

Some recent empirical works represented by Trefler (1995) have suggested that the performance of the HO theorem based on identical technologies and homothetic preferences is hard to accept. However, to our knowledge, there are few theoretical studies that have established a trade pattern theorem by relaxing these assumptions. The present chapter is one such attempt by allowing for nonhomothetic preferences.

We have established a new trade pattern theorem under the assumption that utility functions are quasilinear. While it relates the pattern of trade to the international distribution of factor endowments roughly in the HO manner, we need to emphasize that it covers more market structures than the standard HO theorem based on homothetic preferences.

The difference in the border of *relative factor abundance* between the standard and modified HO theorems has an interesting implication for empirical studies of trade patterns. For instance, let us consider the case that Foreign's factor endowment point is E_0^* in Fig. 1. Since it is above OEM, Foreign is a capital-abundant country in the standard sense. On the other hand, suppose Foreign imports a capital-intensive good. This "paradox" can be resolved by the MHO theorem if empirical evidence shows that the income effect on the demand for the capital-intensive good is small since it suggests that the empirical evidence means that the border of relative factor abundance is not OEM but $A'EM'$. Hence, Foreign is a labor-abundant country in a modified definition and imports the capital-intensive good.

Acknowledgments We are grateful to Been-Lon Chen, Fumio Dei, Elias Dinopoulos, Michihiro Ohyama, Santanu Roy, Henry Y. Wan Jr., Laixun Zhao, and an anonymous referee for their constructive comments. In collaboration with Prof. Koji Shimomura, we derived some of the basic results presented in this chapter while attending his seminar in 2003. Most regrettably, the coauthorship was tragically interrupted when Koji died of cancer on February 24, 2007. Koji was a fine scholar and a very considerate and kind teacher. He is greatly missed (Doi, Fujiwara, and Kikuchi).

References

Chung C (2003) Factor content of trade: nonhomothetic preferences and 'missing trade'. Working Paper, School of Economics, Georgia Institute of Technology

Dixit AK, Norman VD (1980) Theory of international trade. Cambridge University Press, Cambridge

Ethier WJ (1979) Internationally decreasing costs and world trade. J Int Econ 9:1–24
Fujiwara K, Shimomura K (2005) A factor endowment theory of international trade under imperfect competition and increasing returns. Can J Econ 38:273–289
Helpman E, Krugman PR (1985) Market structure and foreign trade. MIT, Cambridge
Herberg H, Kemp MC (1969) Some implications of variable returns to scale. Can J Econ 2:403–415
Lahiri S, Ono Y (1995) The role of free entry in an oligopolistic Heckscher–Ohlin model. Int Econ Rev 36:609–624
Markusen JR (1981) Trade and the gains from trade with imperfect competition. J Int Econ 11:531–551
Markusen JR (1986) Explaining the volume of trade: an eclectic approach. Am Econ Rev 76:1002–1011
Ohyama M (1999) Market, trade and welfare in general equilibrium. Jpn Econ Rev 50:1–24
Shimomura K (1998) Factor income function and an oligopolistic Heckscher–Ohlin model of international trade. Econ Lett 61:91–100
Trefler D (1995) The case of missing trade and other mysteries. Am Econ Rev 85:1029–1046
Woodland AD (1982) International trade and resource allocation. North-Holland, Amsterdam
Wong K (1995) International trade in goods and factor mobility. MIT, Cambridge

External Economies of Scale and Comparative Advantage

Wilfred J. Ethier(✉) **and Roy J. Ruffin**

Abstract We investigate the interplay, in international trade, between comparative advantage and increasing returns to scale that are external to the firm. We focus especially on "advantage reversals," where the country with a comparative-cost disadvantage in producing a good nevertheless is able to export it because of the economies of large-scale production. We examine trade policy in such a situation, looking especially at whether that policy should aim at basic policy-regime change. Koji Shimomura was a delightful person, a warm friend, a dependable follower of sumo, and a thoroughly responsible academic. We miss him. Here we address a subject that he would have appreciated. We return to the implications of increasing returns to scale for the gains from trade and for the role of trade policy. This topic was pioneered by Frank Graham (1923).

1 Introduction

International trade theory identifies three possible reasons for countries to trade: *comparative advantage* (to exploit differences), *economies of scale* (to concentrate more productively on fewer activities), and *imperfect competition* (to expose firms to more competition). This chapter discusses the relation between the first two, with a focus on Graham's concerns about the role of policy.

In recent decades, treatments of international trade featuring economies of scale and imperfect competition have become commonplace. But another, earlier, literature has addressed the former with little or no attention given to the latter.[1] Ethier (1982) addresses *external* economies of scale (without being all that clear

[1] Important contributions include Matthews (1950), Jones (1968), Kemp (1969), Melvin (1969), Panagariya (1981), and Kemp and Shimomura (2000). Helpman (1984) provides a valuable survey.

W.J. Ethier
Department of Economics, University of Pennsylvania, Philadelphia, PA 19104–6297,
e-mail: ethier@econ.sas.upenn.edu

T. Kamihigashi and L. Zhao (eds.) *International Trade and Economic Dynamics – Essays in Memory of Koji Shimomura.*

about it), but, except briefly, ignores comparative-advantage differences and trade policy (beyond the trade vs. autarky choice). Ruffin (2007) addresses *internal* economies of scale (without being all that clear about it) and comparative-cost differences, and looks explicitly at trade policy. The present chapter targets the ground between those two chapters, addressing the interplay between external scale economies and comparative advantage.

A few words about why such an investigation may be of some relevance to reality. We use a two-sector model in which one sector is characterized by external increasing returns to scale. It is natural to think of this sector as manufacturing in general, with individual firms rendered more efficient as a result of the infrastructure, commercial law, industrial labor force, etc. consequent to a large manufacturing sector, that is, to more industrialization. Such a model could supply a natural framework for analyzing the widespread policy choices, in the 1950s and 1960s, by developing countries about whether to open their economies or to rely instead on extensive import-substitution policies. And the framework could also be useful to analyze the choices, in the late 1980s and extending to the current time, by these same countries about the wisdom of basic policy reform (though in this case, ignoring international economies of scale could be questionable).

These constitute two of the four international economic policy events of the past 60 years that are of fundamental significance. Also, in both cases, the policy question was not about marginal changes in trade policy, but about regime change. So, in what follows, we investigate whether or not the role of trade policy implied by the theory is to manage regime change.

2 The Model

Suppose two countries (home and foreign) and two goods: A and B (the good with increasing returns to scale). We employ the familiar Ricardian model of technology, modified by the introduction of scale economies in one sector.

2.1 The Home Economy

The production side of the home economy is as follows.

$$\begin{aligned} L &= L_A + L_B, \\ L_A &= A, \\ k(L_B)^{\alpha} &= B, \end{aligned} \tag{1}$$

where $\alpha > 1$.

One unit of A is defined as the quantity that can be produced by one unit of home labor. We assume that all markets are perfectly competitive. Were B-production characterized by constant returns to scale, the relative price P of B in terms of A would equal $1/k$ in autarky.

The scale economies in the B sector are external to the firm. That is, the representative firm i faces the production function $B_i = [kL_B{}^{\alpha-1}]L_{Bi}$, where L_{Bi} denotes the labor employed by firm i and L_B denotes the sum of all L_{Bi}. The individual firm, unable to influence the overall allocation of resources, takes its labor productivity $[kL_B{}^{\alpha-1}]$ as parametric (Chipman 1970). Summing the production function over all firms gives the aggregate B production function (1).

Assumption 1. The economies of scale in the production of B are external to the firm.

Take home labor as the numeráire, so that $w = 1 = P_A$ if A is being produced. The zero-profit condition for B is $P_B B = L_B$. In view of (1), these zero-profit conditions yield the following supply function for B, if both sectors are active.

$$P_S = k^{-1/\alpha} B^{(1-\alpha)/\alpha}, \tag{2}$$

where P_S denotes the supply price of B in terms of A.

The demand side is described by

$$D_B = (\gamma/2)P^{-\varepsilon},$$

with the demand for A therefore the residual: $D_A = L - (\gamma/2)P^{1-\varepsilon}$. This in turn generates the inverse demand function

$$P_D = ([2/\gamma]D_B)^{-1/\varepsilon}, \tag{3}$$

where P_D denotes the relative demand price.

2.2 Autarky Equilibrium

In autarky equilibrium, $P_S = P_D$ and $B = D_B$, so that (2) and (3) determine that equilibrium. Also, if both goods are produced, the labor allocated to the B sector is

$$L_B = a_0 k^{(\varepsilon-1)/(\alpha+\varepsilon-\alpha\varepsilon)} = L_0, \tag{4}$$

where $a_0 = (\gamma/2)^{1/(\alpha+\varepsilon-\alpha\varepsilon)}$. If $L \geq L_0, L_B = L_0$; otherwise $L_B = L$.

Assume the Marshallian disequilibrium adjustment process:

$$\mathrm{d}B/\mathrm{d}t = P_D - P_S.$$

The local stability condition for this adjustment process (Ethier 1982) is $\alpha/(\alpha-1) > \varepsilon$.

2.3 The Foreign Economy

Analogously for the foreign economy,

$$L^* = L_A^* + L_B^*.$$
$$L_A^* = A^*.$$
$$k^*(L_B^*)^{\alpha} = B^*.$$

A unit of foreign labor is defined as the amount required to produce a unit of good A.

The demand side is

$$D_B^* = (\gamma/2)P^{-\varepsilon}.$$

Assumption 2. $k < k^*$.

In this sense the foreign economy has a comparative-cost advantage in B. Otherwise the two economies are identical, except for size.

Assumption 3. $\alpha/(\alpha - 1) > \varepsilon$.

Proposition 1. *Assumption 3 ensures that each country possesses a Marshallian-stable autarky equilibrium.*

Assumption 3 implies that the elasticity of demand for output is smaller than the numerical elasticity of supply with respect to the price; thus, a smaller output will push the demand price higher than the supply price, which implies firms will want to expand output back to the equilibrium level.

Assumption 3 can also be written as $\alpha + \varepsilon > \alpha\varepsilon$. Thus it places an upper bound on the amount of elasticity (i.e., the magnitudes of α and ε) in the model. If elasticities are high enough to violate the assumption, scale economies are sufficient to allow the home country to have the cost advantage in autarky, despite having the smaller k. We accordingly describe the world as *comparative-cost dominant* if Assumption 3 holds so that stability obtains, and as *scale-dominant* if the assumption fails, implying instability.

If both goods are produced in the autarky equilibrium, the labor allocated to the B sector is given by

$$L_B^* = a_0(k^*)^{(\varepsilon-1)/(\alpha\varepsilon-\alpha-\varepsilon)} \equiv L_0^*. \tag{5}$$

If $L^* \geq L_0^*$, $L_B^* = L_0^*$; otherwise $L_B^* = L^*$.

3 Advantage Reversals

Turn now to free trade between the home and foreign economies. We first consider whether there is an equilibrium in which the home country is the sole supplier of B in the world market despite its cost disadvantage – an *advantage reversal*. If this were so, and if the home country also produces some A,

$$B = \gamma P^{-\varepsilon},$$
$$B = k(L_B)^{\alpha},$$
$$L_B = PB.$$

3.1 An Advantage-Reversal Equilibrium

These are three equations in three variables (P, B, L_B) and so can be solved in terms of the parameters. In particular, we have the solution $L_B = f(\gamma, \alpha, \varepsilon, k)$.

Assumption 4. $L > f(\gamma, \alpha, \varepsilon, k)$.

This assumption ensures that the home economy is large enough so that, in equilibrium, it is able to supply the entire world demand for B. In such an equilibrium, the home economy would produce both goods and export B, while the foreign economy would produce only A.

With the home economy producing both goods, its supply price is still given by (2). As $B^{*} = 0$, the foreign supply price is infinite. Finally, the world demand price is now

$$P_{\mathrm{D}} = ([1/\gamma][D_B + D_B^{*}])^{-1/\varepsilon}. \tag{6}$$

In such an equilibrium, $P_{\mathrm{D}} = P_{\mathrm{S}} < P_{\mathrm{S}}^{*}$ and $B = D_B + D_B^{*}$. Then (2) and (6) determine the equilibrium. The Marshallian stability condition for this equilibrium is easily confirmed to be $\alpha/(\alpha - 1) > \varepsilon$, and thus ensured by Assumption 3.

With the home supply curve unchanged as the negative relation (2), and world demand greater at every P than was the home demand in autarky, the world relative price of B must be lower than it was in the home country in autarky. Since home income in terms of A equals L, home income in terms of B must be higher in the free-trade equilibrium than in autarky. Thus, the home country is better off in the advantage-reversal equilibrium than in autarky, despite exporting the good in which it has a comparative-cost disadvantage – economies of scale dominate comparative advantage. It is possible to construct examples where the foreign economy loses from trade, but they appear to be extreme.[2]

Proposition 2. *If Assumptions 1–4 hold, there exists a Marshallian-stable, advantage-reversal equilibrium in which the home country exports good B and the foreign produces only good A. In this equilibrium the home country is better off than in autarky.*

[2] See Helpman (1984) for a more detailed related argument

3.2 External vs. Internal Economies of Scale

Assumption 1 is critical for the allocation of resources described in the previous subsection actually to describe an equilibrium. With $B^* = 0$ and with foreign firms treating labor productivity as parametric, P_S^* is necessarily infinite, and therefore greater than P_S. But if the scale economies are internal, labor productivity is not parametric, and P_S^* is then determined by what it would cost the foreign economy to supply the quantity $(D_B + D_B^*)$, if it can do so:

$$P_S^* = (k^*)^{-1/\alpha} B^{(1-\alpha)/\alpha}. \tag{7}$$

Then Assumption 2 (that $k^* > k$) implies that $P_S^* < P_S$, so that this allocation of resources, with $B > 0 = B^*$, is not an equilibrium.

Proposition 3. *Assumption 1 is necessary for the existence of the advantage-reversal equilibrium, whenever the foreign economy could instead supply the world demand for good B.*

4 Alternative Equilibria Where the Foreign Economy Supplies the Entire *B* Market

Increasing returns to scale tend to spawn multiple equilibria, and so we consider additional possibilities. As we are interested in the consequences of an advantage-reversal equilibrium, we continue to impose Assumption 4, but we shall vary L^* to consider all alternative relative sizes of the two countries.

4.1 A Large Foreign Economy

If the foreign economy is large enough, it, too, can supply the entire world demand for B.

Assumption 5a. $L^* \geq f(\gamma, \alpha, \varepsilon, k^*)$.

This assumption allows an allocation of resources where the foreign economy produces both goods and exports B. The home economy produces only A.

With the foreign economy producing both goods, its supply price is given by (7). As $B = 0$, the home supply price is infinite, given that the scale economies are external to the firm. Finally, the world demand price is still given by (6). Thus, (6) and (7) determine an equilibrium. In such an equilibrium, $P_D = P_S^* < P_S$ and $B^* = D_B + D_B^*$. The Marshallian stability condition for this equilibrium is again easily confirmed to be $\alpha/(\alpha - 1) > \varepsilon$, and so again ensured by Assumption 3. Trade causes P to fall in both countries, and so both the home and foreign countries are better off in this equilibrium than in autarky.

Proposition 4. *If Assumptions 1–4 and 5a hold, there exist both an advantage-reversal equilibrium and another equilibrium in which the foreign economy exports good B and the home produces only good A. Both equilibria are Marshallian stable, and in each the country exporting B gains from trade.*

This case is treated in Sect. III of Ruffin (2007), except that the advantage-reversal equilibrium is not present, as shown earlier.

Since both equilibria are stable, which obtains is a matter of serendipity. Also the B exporter is better off than in autarky in each of the two equilibria. However, the advantage-reversal case gives only scale-economy gains from trade, whereas the nonreversal equilibrium generates both these and comparative-advantage gains. Thus the latter equilibrium is better in this sense.

4.2 Regime Change

As shown in Ruffin (2007), stability conditions preclude the home country from using conventional tariffs for its own benefit. But there could be a scope for foreign tariff policy. Suppose the world finds itself in the advantage-reversal equilibrium. Let the foreign country implement a prohibitive tariff on B. Suppose that foreign B producers have lower costs than home producers. At this point, the foreign economy begins to export B, its tariff thereby becoming redundant, and the world converges to the nonreversal equilibrium. So consider whether, in autarky, foreign B producers do indeed have the cost advantage. Because the scale economies are external to the B firm, it takes $k\ L^{\alpha-1}$ as parametric (in autarky, this is also the productivity of a unit of A foregone). Then foreign B producers will have an autarkic cost advantage over their counterparts in the home economy if and only if

$$kL_0^{\alpha-1} < kL_0^{*\alpha-1}.$$

Utilizing (4) and (5) this can be written as

$$a_0^{\alpha-1}[(k^*)^{1/(\alpha+\varepsilon-\alpha\varepsilon)} - k^{1/(\alpha+\varepsilon-\alpha\varepsilon)}] > 0,$$

which, in light of Assumption 2 (i.e., $k^* > k$), will hold if and only if the world is comparative-cost dominant. That is, if the stability condition (Assumption 3) is met. This gives the following.

Proposition 5. *With Assumptions 1–4 and 5a, foreign tariff policy can "flip" the world from the advantage-reversal case to the nonreversal case, presumably a social improvement.*

The potential role for trade policy in this case is just to enable regime change. Note that home policy cannot be used to engineer a "flip."

4.3 A Smaller Foreign Economy: Size Reversals

Next, consider an equilibrium in which the foreign economy just supplies the entire world demand for B, producing no A.

$$B = \gamma P^{-\varepsilon}, \tag{8}$$

$$B = k^*(L^*)^{\alpha}, \tag{9}$$

$$w^* L^* = PB, \tag{10}$$

$$w^* \geq 1. \tag{11}$$

Constraint (11) says that in equilibrium positive profit cannot be made in the A sector; it would be satisfied with equality were some A being produced. Equations (8)–(10) can be solved for

$$L^* = F^*(w^*; \gamma, \varepsilon, \alpha, k^*). \tag{12}$$

Let f^* denote $f(\gamma, \varepsilon, \alpha, k^*)$. Then, by definition of f,

$$f^* = F^*(1;\ \gamma, \varepsilon, \alpha, k^*).$$

If L^* exceeds f^*, the extra foreign labor is used to produce A for local consumption. The foreign economy supplies the world market for B, as discussed in the previous subsection, with $w^* = 1$.

Next, consider a reduction in L^* below f^*. Use (8)–(10) to calculate

$$\mathrm{d}w^*/\mathrm{d}L^* = [(\alpha\varepsilon - \alpha - \varepsilon)]a_1\ L^{*(\alpha\varepsilon - \alpha - 2\varepsilon)/\varepsilon}, \tag{13}$$

where $a_1 = (\gamma^{1/\varepsilon}/\varepsilon)k^{*(\varepsilon-1)/\varepsilon}$, a positive constant. A reduction of L^* below f^*, with the foreign economy continuing to supply the world market for B (i.e., (8)–(10)), will be consistent with (11) if and only if $\mathrm{d}w^*/\mathrm{d}L^* < 0$. From (13), this will be true if and only if Assumption 3 holds. The basic intuition is that "too much" elasticity (i.e., high values of α and ε) mean that a fall in L^* causes a rise in PB, so that (10) requires w^* to fall, violating (11). The fact that $\mathrm{d}w^*/\mathrm{d}L^* < 0$ is in itself interesting: It says that the stability condition trumps economies of scale in the impact of the labor supply on wages. One might think that it would be possible with increasing returns to scale for a smaller economy to lower wages, but the stability condition rules this out.

Furthermore, the relation between w^* and L^* in (11) is clearly monotonic, from (13). Thus, if the foreign economy can supply the entire world B market with a L^* slightly below f^*, it can do so with *any* L^* below f^*. Since in such equilibria the smaller country is the supplier of the good with increasing returns to scale, we describe them as *size reversals*. Indeed, if L^* is small enough, $w^*k > k^*$. Assumption 1 would be critical for such an equilibrium, since home B firms would capture the market if they could internalize the scale economies.

Proposition 6. *If Assumptions 1–4 and 5b hold, but 5a does not, there exist both an advantage-reversal equilibrium and a size-reversal equilibrium in which the home economy produces only A and the foreign economy only B. Both equilibria are stable, and in the size-reversal equilibrium the foreign country gains from trade.*

4.4 Regime Change

Size reversals are a characteristic of a comparative-cost dominant world. But this is just the context in which the foreign economy can use a prohibitive tariff on B to engineer regime change from an advantage-reversal equilibrium. The new regime will feature a nonreversal equilibrium if the foreign economy is relatively large, and a size-reversal equilibrium if it is relatively small.

Proposition 7. *If Assumptions 1–4 hold, the foreign economy can use a prohibitive tariff to flip from an advantage-reversal equilibrium to a nonreversal equilibrium, if Assumption 5a holds, or to a size-reversal equilibrium, if 5a fails.*

5 Alternative Equilibria Where the Foreign Economy Supplies Part of the B Market

Now consider the possibility that the foreign economy is not large enough to supply the world demand for B by itself, so that if it does produce only B and export it, it must compete with a home B sector.

5.1 A Knife Edge

An equilibrium in which the foreign economy specializes in the production of B and supplies part of the world market is described as follows:

$$B + B^* = \gamma P^{-\varepsilon},$$
$$B = k(L_B)^{\alpha}, \quad B^* = k^*(L^*)^{\alpha},$$
$$L_B = PB, \; w^* L^* = PB^*,$$
$$w^* \geq 1.$$

Given w^*, these equations determine P, B, B^*, L_B, and L^*. In particular, they can be solved for

$$L^* = G^*(w^*; \gamma, \varepsilon, \alpha, k, k^*). \tag{14}$$

Define $L_1^* = G^*(1; \gamma, \varepsilon, \alpha, k, k^*)$, and let L_B^0 solve $(L_B^0/L^*)^{\alpha-1} = k^*/k$.

Assumption 5b. $L^* = L_1{}^*$

If this holds, we have an equilibrium in which the home country specializes in B and exports it, $w^* = 1$, and $L_B = L_B{}^0$. Costs in the two countries are identical, with the home economy having a B sector just larger enough than the foreign's to offset exactly its comparative disadvantage. But w^* is bounded below by unity, since in a competitive equilibrium the A sector cannot offer positive profit opportunities. Thus, any shock that increases B in the home country will initiate a cumulative movement to the advantage-reversal outcome: The equilibrium will be unstable.

Proposition 8. *If Assumptions 1–4 and 5b hold, there exist both an advantage-reversal equilibrium and a nonreversal equilibrium. The latter is unstable.*

5.2 A Small Foreign Economy

Next consider a foreign economy smaller than the knife-edge size.

Assumption 5c. $L_1^* > L^*$.

This assumption allows an allocation of resources whereby the home economy would produce both goods and import B. The foreign economy would produce only B. In such an allocation, scale economies neutralize exactly the foreign comparative advantage: $w^*(L_B/L_1{}^*)^{\alpha-1} = k^*/k$ and $w^* > 1$. The supply price is now given by (2), where B denotes the home country's supply, and the home demand is

$$B + M = (\gamma/2)P^{-\varepsilon}. \tag{15}$$

where M denotes the home country's import of B from the foreign country. Now, (2) and (15) imply

$$B + M = (\gamma/2)(k^{-1/\alpha}B^{(1-\alpha)/\alpha}]^{-\varepsilon}. \tag{16}$$

Differentiating (16) implicitly,

$$\mathrm{d}B/\mathrm{d}M = -1/[1 + \varepsilon([B+M]/M)([1-\alpha]\alpha) < 0.$$

Thus, the insertion of imports M from the foreign country causes home production B to fall. Thus, P rises at home and the home country loses. The magnitude of the price change also depends on the parameters, and so the foreign country may either gain or lose.

Proposition 9. *If Assumptions 1–4 and 5c hold, there exist both an advantage-reversal equilibrium and a nonreversal equilibrium in which the home economy produces both goods and the foreign economy produces only B. In the nonreversal equilibrium, the home country loses from trade.*

Both equilibria are stable, so it is again a matter of serendipity which obtains. In this case one of the countries (but not both) will be able to gain from a tariff policy.

Section IV of Ruffin (2007) considers this case, and shows that the home economy can gain from a tariff in the nonreversal equilibrium.

5.3 Regime Change

In a comparative-cost dominant world (Assumption 3 holds), the foreign economy can again use a prohibitive tariff to flip from an advantage-reversal equilibrium to the nonreversal situation. In view of the various possible combinations of gains and losses, it is possible that the foreign economy might indeed wish to engineer a regime change. (Of course, if both countries lose from trade, it is in both countries' interest to retreat to autarky – yet another example of regime change).

6 Concluding Remarks

We have investigated the relationship between external economies of scale and comparative advantage regarding the welfare consequences of international trade. The notable feature is the possibility of an advantage-reversal, where the effects of scale economies overwhelm those of comparative-cost differences. The existence of such an equilibrium implies a distinct role for trade policy, namely that such policy could be used to engineer a regime change. But this existence – and thus this role – is crucially sensitive to whether the scale economies are internal or external to the firm.

References

Chipman JS (1970) External economies of scale and competitive equilibrium. Q J Econ 84:347–385

Ethier WJ (1982) Decreasing costs in international trade and Frank Graham's argument for protection. Econometrica 50(5):1243–1268

Graham F (1923) Some aspects of protection further considered. Q J Econ 37:199–227

Helpman E (1984) Increasing returns, imperfect markets, and trade theory. In: Jones RW, Kenen PB (eds) Handbook of international economics, vol 1. North Holland, New York

Jones RW (1968) Variable returns to scale in general equilibrium theory. Int Econ Rev 9:261–272

Kemp MC (1969) The pure theory of international trade and investment. Prentice Hall, Englewood Cliffs

Kemp MC, Shimomura K (2000) Increasing returns and international trade. Rev Int Econ 8:614–618.

Matthews RCO (1950) Reciprocal demand and increasing returns. Rev Econ Stud 17:149–158

Melvin J (1969) Increasing returns to scale as a determinant of trade. Can J Econ 2:389–402

Panagariya A (1981) Variable returns to scale in production and patterns of specialization. Am Econ Rev 71:221–230

Ruffin RJ (2007) Protection with increasing returns and comparative disadvantage. Working paper, Department of Economics, University of Houston

Is Free Trade Optimal for a Small Open Economy with Tourism?[1]

Chi-Chur Chao, Bharat R. Hazari, Jean-Pierre Laffargue, and Eden S.H. Yu(✉)

Abstract We explore the welfare effects of tariffs and investment taxes for a small open economy in the presence of tourism. Inbound tourism converts local non-traded goods into tradeable, generating a tourism terms-of-trade effect. Because of this favourable "expenditure-shifting" effect when goods are substitutes, increases in import tariffs and investment taxes can actually improve welfare of domestic residents. We establish that for a small open economy with tourism, free trade is not the first-best policy. The optimal rates of tariffs and investment taxes are then derived and simulated for the economy with tourism.

1 Introduction

In a small open economy, a tariff necessarily lowers national welfare, so that free trade is the first-best policy. It is also well known that in a large open economy, free trade is not optimal and there is the need for using a non-zero optimal tariff to obtain a first-best solution such that the domestic rate of substitution equals the domestic rate of transformation and that in turn equals the foreign rate of transformation (DRS = DRT = FRT).[2]

These results are also valid in the presence of non-traded goods (markets for these goods clear by equating local supply and demand).[3] Do these universally

[1] We thank the anonymous referee and the participants of the Kobe Conference in memory of Koji Shimomura for useful comments and suggestions. The usual disclaimer applies.

[2] See Jones (1967, 1969, 1987) and Neary (1993).

[3] The studies on non-traded goods in a general equilibrium framework can be found in Komiya (1967) and Batra (1973). Also see a recent study by Yano and Nugent (1999) on the possibility of the transfer paradox in the presence of non-traded goods in the economy. In their model, the prices of non-traded goods are endogenously determined.

E.S.H. Yu
Department of Economics and Finance, City University of Hong Kong, Kowloon, Hong Kong, e-mail: efedenyu@cityu.edu.hk

T. Kamihigashi and L. Zhao (eds.) *International Trade and Economic Dynamics – Essays in Memory of Koji Shimomura.*

Table 1 Tourist spending in the world

(a) Tourism receipts in Hong Kong		
	US billion $	% of GDP
1998	7.28	4.44
2002	9.92	6.09
2005	10.30	7.65
2006	11.60	

(b) Tourism receipts in the world in 2006

Rank	Country	US billion $	Rank	Country	US billion $
1	U.S.	85.4	6	UK	33.5
2	Spain	51.1	7	Germany	32.8
3	France	46.3	8	Australia	17.8
4	Italy	38.1	9	Turkey	16.9
5	China	33.9	10	Austria	16.7

taught and well established propositions survive the introduction of tourism in models of trade? This important policy-oriented question is addressed in this chapter, given that tourism is one of the most important growth industries in the world today (see Table 1). Tourism is defined as the temporary movement of consumers from one country into another to consume non-traded goods and services (Hazari and Sgro 2004). This process transforms non-traded goods and services into tradeable, thereby creating an additional *tourism* terms-of-trade effect in the economy. Thus, there exist two terms of trade: one arising from trade in commodities (traditional terms-of-trade) and another arising from consumption of non-traded goods and services by tourists. The relative price of non-traded goods and services is now determined by equating local and tourists' demand with the local supply of these goods and services.

In this chapter, a three-sector general-equilibrium model is developed to explore this important issue. Following the literature (Hazari and Sgro 2004), foreign tourists are assumed to demand only the domestically produced non-traded goods. This assumption is a reasonable description of tourists' consumption pattern. With flexible prices for these goods we consider for this small open economy the welfare effects of trade restrictive policies: tariffs and investment taxes in this small open economy. An increased tariff results in a consumption substitution effect so that domestic residents switch consumption from the importable to the non-traded good when they are substitutes. This raises the relative price of the non-traded good, thereby creating a favourable tourism terms-of-trade effect. Although this restricts commodity trade, a tariff can actually improve welfare of domestic residents even when a country is a small open economy in commodity trade. This lends support for protection of goods trade via tariffs, and an optimal tariff can be imposed in the presence of tourism in a small open economy. Further, the presence of tariffs leads to tariff-jumping and capital inflows. However, as shown in Brecher and Diaz Alejandro (1977), this type of capital inflows may result in immiserizing growth by aggravating the distortion caused by the tariff. To avoid this distortion, investment taxes on foreign capital are warranted.

In the presence of tourism in a small open economy, adopting protectionist policies to restrict goods trade and factor flows is caused by the favourable movement in the tourism terms-of-trade. This beneficial effect cushions the detrimental shocks, such as changes in tariffs and investment taxes, to the economy. The proposed tourism terms-of-trade mechanism actually matters in the world and this is shown by numerical simulations in Sect. 4. Hence, from the perspective of policy making, the favourable impact of the tourism terms-of-trade effect should be taken into consideration in the modelling of the economy.

It is interesting to mention that as suggested in Brander and Spencer (1985), a tariff has an effect of shifting foreign firm's profits to the domestic firm in an imperfectly competitive framework. Here, the tourism terms-of-trade effect leads to a shift in tourists' expenditures towards domestic non-traded goods. This "expenditure-shifting" effect on foreign tourists is analogous to the "profit-shifting" effect on foreign firms: A tariff can cause tourists to spend more on the locally produced non-traded good, but the expenditure depends on how expensive the good is in the economy. Nonetheless, this expenditure-shifting effect occurs on the demand side of the home economy under a perfectly competitive environment.

The structure of the chapter is as follows. Section 2 presents a general-equilibrium model for the small open economy with inbound tourism. Section 3 examines the welfare effects of tariffs and investment taxes for the economy, and the optimal policies are derived and explained. Section 4 provides numerical simulations for optimal tariffs and investment taxes. The conclusions and remarks are provided in Sect. 5.

2 A Model with Inbound Tourism

It is assumed that the home country produces three goods: an agricultural good, X; a manufacturing good, Y; and a non-traded good, Z, in perfectly competitive markets. The production functions are $X = X(L_X), Y = Y(L_Y, S, K)$ and $Z = Z(L_Z, V)$. Unskilled labour (L_i) is a mobile factor used in all sectors, skilled labour (S) and capital (K) are specific factors to the manufacturing and land (V) is a specific factor to the non-traded goods sector.[4] The production functions display diminishing returns to factors. Letting L be the endowment of unskilled labour, full employment requires that $L_X + L_Y + L_Z = L$. Moreover, there are also inflows of foreign capital but its return is subject to investment taxes. To economize on notations, K denotes foreign capital. Foreign capital flows in until its return equals the world interest rate (r^*) plus the tax (τ) levied by the home country.

It is assumed that the home country exports good X and imports good Y. There are no impediments on exports but imports are subject to a specific tariff, t. Choosing the exportable good X as the numeraire, the domestic price of the importable good

[4] The discussions and applications of specific factors model are, for example, in Jones (1971), Khan (1982), and Beladi and Marjit (1992).

Y is $p(=p^*+t)$, where p^* is the given foreign price. The domestic relative price of the non-traded good Z, denoted by q, is endogenously determined in the home economy. Let w and s denote the wage rates of unskilled and skilled labour, and r and v be the rates of return on capital and land in the economy. Under perfect competition in the goods market, unit price equals its unit cost in equilibrium:

$$1 = c^X(w), \tag{1}$$

$$p = c^Y(w,s,r), \tag{2}$$

$$q = c^Z(w,v), \tag{3}$$

where $c^X(\cdot), c^Y(\cdot)$ and $c^Z(\cdot)$ denote, respectively, the unit cost functions of goods X, Y and Z. By the envelope property, $c^X_w(=\partial c^X/\partial w)$ represents unit demand for unskilled labour in sector X, and so on. Under full employment, the employment conditions for unskilled labour, skilled labour, capital and land are given in (4)–(7):

$$c^X_w(w)X + c^Y_w(w,s,r)Y + c^Z_w(w,v)Z = L, \tag{4}$$

$$c^Y_s(w,s,r)Y = S, \tag{5}$$

$$c^Y_r(w,s,r)Y = K, \tag{6}$$

$$c^Z_v(w,v)Z = V. \tag{7}$$

Equations (1)–(7) present the supply side of the economy, which consists of seven endogenous variables, w, s, r, v, X, Y and Z, for given prices p and q and capital inflow of K. Note that at this stage the other exogenous variables are ignored. As the above system is block recursive, the endogenous variables can be solved in a stepwise manner: w is fixed by (1), and then s, r and Y are solved from (2), (5) and (6) as functions of p and K. From (3) and (7), v and Z are determined as functions of q alone. Finally, X is obtained from (4) as a function of p, q and K.

The above supply side information can be compactly represented by the revenue function: $R(p,q,K) = \max\{X(L_X) + pY(L_Y,S,K) + qZ(L_Z,V)\colon L_X + L_Y + L_Z = L\}$ with respect to $L_i, i = X,Y,Z$. Using subscripts in $R(\cdot)$ to denote partial derivatives, by the envelope property we have $R_p = Y, R_q = Z$ and $R_K = r$. Further, we have $R_{qq} > 0$, showing that the positive supply of good Z is increasing in q, and $R_{qp} = R_{qK} = 0$ because Z depends only on its own price q. Note that because of the specific factor model in (1)–(3), we have $R_{pK} > 0$ and $R_{KK} < 0$. That is, a rise in capital raises the output of good Y but reduces the rate of return on capital.

Consider next the demand side of the economy, which consists of domestic residents and foreign tourists. Domestic residents demand all the three goods and their expenditure function is $E(p,q,u) = \min\{C_X + pC_Y + qC_Z\colon U(C_X,C_Y,C_Z) = u\}$, where C_i is demand for good $i, U(\cdot)$ is the utility function and u is the utility level of domestic residents. Using the envelope property, we have $E_q = C_Z$ for the compensated demand for good Z by domestic residents, with $E_{qq} < 0$ for the downward-sloped compensated demand function. Note that $E_{qp} > (<)\ 0$ when goods Y and Z are substitutes (complements) in consumption.[5] As far as tourists' demand is concerned, we follow the literature of assuming that they demand the non-traded good Z only and their demand function is $D_Z(q,T)$, with $\partial D_Z/\partial q < 0$ and $\partial D_Z/\partial T > 0$, where T is a shift parameter that captures tourists' expenditure and other things, for example, taste.

Using the above demand and supply information, the equilibrium conditions of the economy are characterized by[6]

$$E(p,q,u) = R(p,q,K) - r^*K + tM, \tag{8}$$

$$M = E_p(p,q,u) - R_p(p,q,K), \tag{9}$$

$$R_K(p,q,K) - \tau = r^*, \tag{10}$$

$$E_q(p,q,u) + D_Z(q,T) = R_q(p,q,K), \tag{11}$$

where M denotes the imports of good Y. Assuming that tariff revenue is returned to domestic residents, (8) expresses the budget constraint of the economy, in which domestic residents' expenditure equals net income from production plus revenue from tariff. Equation (9) is the import demand function for good Y, while (10) describes the equilibrium condition that after-tax returns on capital between countries. Equation (11) gives the market-clearing condition for the non-traded good Z, in which total demand by domestic residents and foreign tourists equals supply from domestic production.

The tourist-receiving home economy described in (8)–(11) consists of four unknowns, u, M, K and q, with an exogenous tariff t and investment tax τ. We now examine the welfare effects of these two policies for a small open economy with inbound tourism.

3 Optimal Tariff and Investment Tax

The general expression of the change in welfare of domestic residents can be obtained by totally differentiating (8):

$$E_u\,\mathrm{d}u = t\,\mathrm{d}M + \tau\,\mathrm{d}K + D_Z\,\mathrm{d}q, \tag{12}$$

where E_u is the inverse of the marginal utility of income. The first two terms on the right hand side of (12) show the traditional welfare effects arising from changes in the volume of trade and capital inflows. An increase in them raises domestic welfare, since tariffs and investment taxes restrict imports of good Y and inflows of capital K. The last term in (12) captures the *tourism* terms-of-trade effect via the change in the relative price of the non-traded good Z. This is because tourism

[5] We thank the referee for pointing out the case that $E_{qp} < 0$.

[6] The duality approach for the general-equilibrium model can be found, for example, in Hatzipanayotou and Michael (1993, 2001) and Neary (1995).

converts the formally non-traded good to exports. A higher relative price of the non-tradable yields a gain from exporting tourism, which contributes positively to domestic welfare.

The change in imports of good Y can be derived from (9) as follows:

$$\mathrm{d}M = E_{pu}\,\mathrm{d}u + (E_{pp} - R_{pp})\,\mathrm{d}t + E_{pq}\,\mathrm{d}q - R_{pK}\,\mathrm{d}K, \tag{13}$$

where $R_{pK} > 0$. The demand factors, such as real income (utility) and the prices of good Y and Z, all affect the change of imports in (13). In particular, when goods Y and Z are substitutes (complements) in consumption [i.e., $E_{pq} > (<)\ 0$], a rise in the relative price of non-tradable q raises (lowers) demand for good Y according to the third term on the right hand side of (13). As far as the supply factors are concerned, the change of capital affects production of good Y and hence the imports in the last term of (13). Note that the change in capital can be obtained by differentiating (10):

$$R_{KK}\,\mathrm{d}K = -R_{pK}\,\mathrm{d}t + \mathrm{d}\tau, \tag{14}$$

where $R_{KK} < 0$. Equation (14) indicates that the changes in tariffs and investment taxes affect inflows of foreign capital. It is important to note that increases in tariffs may lead to the tariff-jumping inflow of foreign capital.[7]

By differentiating (11), we obtain the change in the relative price of the non-traded good:

$$(E_{qq} + \partial D_Z/\partial q - R_{qq})\,\mathrm{d}q = -E_{qu}\,\mathrm{d}u - E_{qp}\,\mathrm{d}t, \tag{15}$$

where $E_{qu}(=\partial C_Z/\partial u)$ expresses the income effect of demand for good Z by domestic residents. We assume that all goods are normal in consumption (i.e., $E_{pu} > 0$). Hence, both the income and substitution/complement effects as indicated in the first and the second term on the right hand side of (15) affect the relative price of the domestic non-traded good Z.

3.1 Tariffs

We examine first the welfare effect of tariffs for a given and also for a zero investment tax. Solving (12)–(15), we obtain

$$\begin{aligned}\mathrm{d}u/\mathrm{d}t = &-\{t[(E_{qq} + \partial D_Z/\partial q - R_{qq}) + R_{pK}^2 + R_{KK}H]\\ &- \tau(E_{qq} + \partial D_Z/\partial q - R_{qq})R_{pK}\}/\Delta + D_Z E_{pq} R_{KK}/\Delta,\end{aligned} \tag{16}$$

[7] See Brecher and Diaz Alejandro (1977) for a related study on the welfare effect of capital inflows under tariffs. Also see Beladi and Parai (1993) for a related study.

where $H = (E_{pp} - R_{pp})(E_{qq} + \partial D_Z/\partial q - R_{qq}) - E_{pq}^2 > 0$.[8] By the stability condition, we have $\Delta = -R_{KK}[(E_u - tE_{pu})(E_{qq} + \partial D_Z/\partial q - R_{qq}) + E_{qu}(D_Z + tE_{pq})] < 0$.[9] In the absence of tourism (i.e., $D_Z = 0$) in (16), the conventional welfare result on tariffs for a small open economy is obtained. A rise in tariffs unambiguously reduces domestic welfare and hence free trade in goods is optimal when the investment tax is absent (i.e., $\tau = 0$). More importantly, the presence of tourism ($D_Z > 0$) in the economy alters this free-trade result. When the non-traded and importable goods are substitutes ($E_{pq} > 0$) (in the last term of (16)),[10] tariffs can actually improve domestic welfare of a small open economy. Because of the substitution effect, the higher importable price of good Y by tariffs leads domestic residents to switch consumption to the non-traded good Z. This raises the relative price of the non-tradable, yielding a favourable tourism terms-of-trade or expenditure-shifting effect on foreign tourists. In this case, raising the price of the imports by tariffs can improve domestic welfare. Setting $\mathrm{d}u/\mathrm{d}t = 0$ in (16), we can derive the optimum tariff, t^o, as

$$t^o = [D_Z E_{pq} R_{KK} + \tau(E_{qq} + \partial D_Z/\partial q - R_{qq})R_{pK}]/[(E_{qq} + \partial D_Z/\partial q - R_{qq})R_{pK}^2 + R_{KK}H], \tag{17}$$

which is positive for $D_Z > 0$ even in the absence of investment taxes (i.e., $\tau = 0$). This proves an important result that *free trade in goods is not optimal for the economy with inbound tourism.*

Figure 1 provides a graphical illustration for the t^o schedule in the space of policy instruments (t, τ), in which the t^o schedule is positively sloped and $t^o > 0$ when $\tau = 0$. Notice that domestic welfare is maximized at t^o for a given τ. This can be seen by checking the curvature of the domestic welfare function. Following the technique used by Neary (1993), we substitute the expressions from (17) into (16) to obtain[11]

$$\mathrm{d}u/\mathrm{d}t = -[(E_{qq} + \partial D_Z/\partial q - R_{qq})R_{pK}^2 + R_{KK}H](t - t^o)/\Delta. \tag{18}$$

Since $\Delta < 0$, we have $\mathrm{d}u/\mathrm{d}t > (<)\ 0$ when $t < (>)\ t^o$. This implies that u is a concave function of t. When t increases horizontally in Fig. 1, domestic welfare increases initially, reaches a maximum at t^o, and then starts to decline. The horizontal arrows indicate these changes in domestic welfare. In view of this result, the conventional trade theory needs to be modified. In the presence of tourism with

---

[8] Because the expenditure function is concave in prices, we have: $E_{pp}E_{qq} - E_{pq}^2 > 0$. This gives $H > 0$.

[9] Following Dei (1985), the adjustment for the price q of the non-traded good is $\dot{q} = \rho A(q)$, where the dot over q is the time derivative, ρ is the speed of adjustments and A denotes excess demand for good Z, that is $A = E_q(p,q,u) + D_Z(q,T) - R_q(p,q,K)$ in (5). A necessary and sufficient condition for stability of the economy is $\mathrm{d}A/\mathrm{d}q < 0$. From (6) and (7), we obtain $\mathrm{d}q/\mathrm{d}A = -E_u R_{KK}(1 - m_Y t/p)/\Delta$, where $m_Y (= pE_{pu}/E_u)$ is the marginal propensity to consume good Y and is less than 1. Hence, stability requires $\Delta < 0$.

[10] The results below are reversed when the two goods are complements ($E_{pq} < 0$).

[11] Because of the third-order partial derivatives involved in the functions of $E(\cdot)$ and $R(\cdot)$, it is impossible to check the second-order condition of welfare maximization for t^o in (17) (i.e. $\mathrm{d}^2u/\mathrm{d}t^2 < 0$). Therefore, a direct proof in (18) is used to look at the curvature of the welfare function around point t^o.

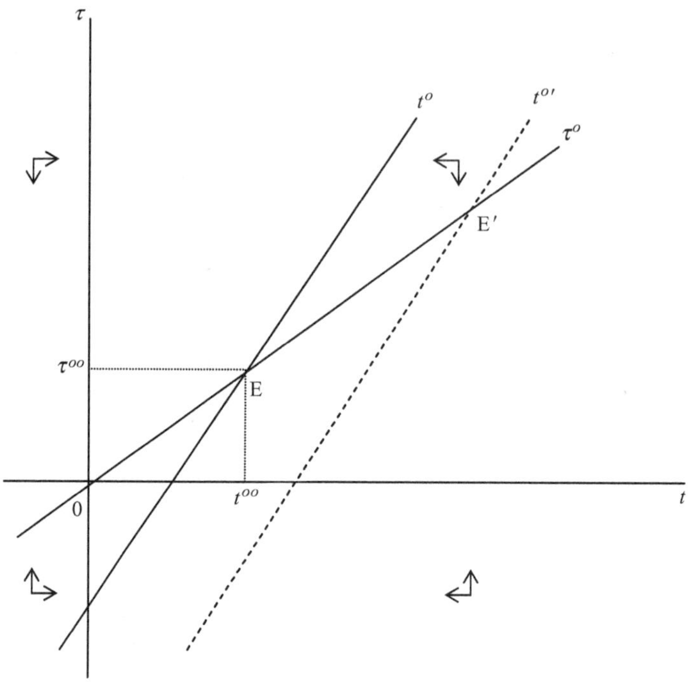

Fig. 1 Optimal tariffs and investment taxes

flexible prices for the non-traded good, there exists an optimal tariff on traded goods that maximizes resident welfare.

3.2 Investment Taxes

We now examine the welfare effect of investment taxes for a given tariff. From (12)–(15), we obtain

$$\mathrm{d}u/\mathrm{d}\tau = -(E_{qq} + \partial D_Z/\partial q - R_{qq})(\tau - tR_{pK})/\Delta. \tag{19}$$

A rise in investment taxes immediately reduces inflows of foreign capital by (14) and hence less domestic production of good Y. This leads to two forces that can conflict with each other on domestic welfare as shown in the first and the second term on the right hand side of (19): The former reduces welfare via less tax revenue, whereas the latter raises welfare by more tariff revenue. By setting $\mathrm{d}u/\mathrm{d}\tau = 0$, we can obtain the optimal investment taxes, τ^{o}, as follows:

$$\tau^{o} = tR_{pK}. \tag{20}$$

Since $R_{pK} > 0$, the positive-sloped τ^{o} schedule is depicted in Fig. 1, in which $\tau^{o} = 0$ when $t = 0$. Notice that for a given t, domestic welfare is maximized at τ^{o}. This can be shown by substituting τ^{o} in (20) into (19) to rewrite the change in domestic welfare as

$$\mathrm{d}u/\mathrm{d}\tau = -(E_{qq} + \partial D_Z/\partial q - R_{qq})(\tau - \tau^{o})/\Delta. \tag{21}$$

Because of $\Delta < 0$, we have $\mathrm{d}u/\mathrm{d}\tau > (<)\ 0$ when $\tau < (>)\tau^{o}$ in (21). That is, any vertical movements of the investment tax τ towards its optimal rate τ^{o} are necessarily welfare-improving.

3.3 Jointly Optimal Tariffs and Investment Taxes

We are now in a position to consider the jointly optimal tariffs and investment taxes, denoted by t^{oo} and τ^{oo}, for the domestic economy in the presence of tourism. Solving (17) and (20), we obtain

$$t^{oo} = D_Z E_{qp}/H, \tag{22}$$

$$\tau^{oo} = D_Z E_{qp} R_{pK}/H. \tag{23}$$

Hence, contrary to conventional wisdom, the presence of tourism in the economy supports positive rates of tariffs and investment taxes. This is again due to the favourable tourism terms-of-trade effect induced by the consumption substitution effect between the importable good Y and the non-traded good Z, as measured by $E_{qp} > 0$ in (22) and (23).

The jointly optimal tariff and investment tax, t^{oo} and τ^{oo}, are depicted at point E in Fig. 1.[12] From (17) and (20), an increase in the tourism activity via a larger D_Z shifts the t^{o} schedule to the right, while leaving the τ^{o} schedule unchanged. This gives a new equilibrium at E′, which yields higher optimal rates for tariffs and investment taxes. Hence, contrary to the common belief, it should be more protection of goods trade and factor flows as tourism expands. This result will be verified by numerical simulation in the next section.[13]

[12] In Fig. 1, the slope of the t^{o} schedule is $\mathrm{d}\tau/\mathrm{d}t|_t = R_{pK} + R_{KK}H/R_{pK}(E_{qq} + \partial D_Z/\partial q - R_{qq}) > 0$ and the slope of the τ^{o} schedule is $\mathrm{d}\tau/\mathrm{d}t|_\tau = R_{pK} > 0$. These give that the slope of the t^{o} schedule is larger than the slope of the τ^{o} schedule.

[13] It should be more interesting to examine the change in tourists' expenditure T on t^{oo} and τ^{oo} in (22) and (23). However, it is analytically infeasible because the change in T affects not only D_Z but also H. Therefore, we rely on simulations, provided in Table 1 below to obtain the effects of changes in T on t^{oo} and τ^{oo}.

4 Simulations for Optimal Tariffs and Investment Taxes

In this section, we calibrate the impact of tourism on optimal tariffs and capital taxes by specifying the functional forms for the utility and production functions.

4.1 Specifications

The production functions of the traded and non-traded goods are assumed to possess the Cobb–Douglas (CD) forms:

$$X = AL_X^{\delta}, \tag{24}$$

$$Y = BL_Y^{\alpha}K^{\beta}S^{1-\alpha-\beta}, \tag{25}$$

$$Z = GL_Z^{\gamma}V^{1-\gamma}, \tag{26}$$

where A, B and G are the technology factors, and δ, α, β and γ are the respective factor shares in the production of goods X, Y and Z. Since the factors S and V are exogenously fixed, we set $S = V = 1$. Total employment for sectors X, Y and Z in the economy is given by $L = L_X + L_Y + L_Z$. Given the relative prices, wage rate and capital rental, profit maximization yields the equilibrium allocation of labour and demand for capital:

$$\delta X/L_X = p\alpha Y/L_Y = q\gamma Z/L_Z = w, \tag{27}$$

$$p\beta Y/K = r. \tag{28}$$

On the demand side of the economy, we assume a CD-CES utility function in which the non-traded and importable goods are substitutes:

$$U = C_X^a\left[b^{1/(1+\sigma)}C_Y^{\sigma/(1+\sigma)} + \bar{b}^{1/(1+\sigma)}C_Z^{\sigma/(1+\sigma)}\right]^{\bar{a}(1+\sigma)/\sigma}/[b^1/(1+\sigma)+\bar{b}^{1/(1+\sigma)}]^{\bar{a}(1+\sigma)/\sigma}, \tag{29}$$

where $a, b, \bar{a}, \bar{b} > 0$ and $a + \bar{a} = b + \bar{b} = 1$. The elasticity of substitution between the consumption of the non-traded and manufacturing goods is captured by $1+\sigma$, where $\sigma > -1$. Utility maximization yields the following demand functions for goods X and Y:

$$C_X = (a/\bar{a})[1 + (b/\bar{b})(q/p)^{\sigma}]qC_Z, \tag{30}$$

$$C_Y = (b/\bar{b})(q/p)^{1+\sigma}qC_Z. \tag{31}$$

Substituting (30) and (31) into the utility function in (29) yields

$$U = \bar{b}^{\bar{a}/\sigma}(aq/\bar{a})^a[1 + (b/\bar{b})(q/p)^c]^{1+\bar{a}/\sigma}C_Z/[b^{1/(1+\sigma)} + \bar{b}^{1/(1+\sigma)}]^{\bar{a}(1+\sigma)/\sigma}. \tag{32}$$

The model is closed by considering the market-clearing condition for the non-traded good Z:

$$C_Z + D_Z = Z, \tag{33}$$

where the demand for the non-traded good by tourists is specified as

$$D_Z = T/q^{\eta}. \tag{34}$$

Note that η, the price elasticity of demand for good Z by tourists, provides a measure for tourists how to substitute to other destinations as the price of the non-traded good rises in the country.

Finally, the budget constraint of the economy is

$$C_X + p^*C_Y + qC_Z = X + p^*Y + qZ - r^*K. \tag{35}$$

This can give the balance-of-trade condition: $(X - C_X) + qD_Z = p^*(C_Y - Y) + r^*K$, which states that the value of the exports from good X and tourism equals the value of the imports from good Y and capital.

We proceed to solve the system in (24)–(35). Given $p(=p^* + t)$ and $r(=r^* + \tau)$, we can obtain $X = A^{1/(1-\delta)}(\delta/w)^{\delta/(1-\delta)}$ and $L_x = \delta X/w$ from (24) and (27), $Y = [B(\alpha/w)^{\alpha}(\beta/r)^{\beta}p^{\alpha+\beta}]^{1/(1-\alpha-\beta)}$, $K = \beta pY/r$ and $L_Y = \alpha pY/w$ from (25), (27) and (28), and $Z = G^{1/(1-\gamma)}(\gamma q/w)^{\gamma/(1-\gamma)}$ and $L_Z = \gamma qZ/w$ from (26) and (27). By setting $I = X + p^*Y + qZ - r^*K$ and using (30), (31) and (35), we obtain $C_Z = \bar{a}\bar{b}I/q\{1 - b[1 - (q/p)^{\sigma}(p^* + at)/p]\}$ and hence C_X and C_Y in (30) and (31). Therefore, we can compute welfare U in (32). Finally, w and q are the solutions of the system of two equations: $L = L_X + L_Y + L_Z$ and $C_Z + D_Z = Z$.

4.2 Calibrations

We start by setting the values of the main endogenous variables of the reference equilibrium of the model: $X = 2, Y = 2, Z = 6, L_X = 2, C_Y = 3, C_Z = 5, r^* = 0.1$, $p^* = 1, q = 1, t = 0$ and $\tau = 0$, and the values of the elasticity parameters: $\alpha = 0.6, \beta = 0.2, \gamma = 0.6, \delta = 0.6$ and $\sigma = 3$. When tourism is absent in the economy $(T = 0)$, the optimal policy is free trade in goods and no taxes on capital ($t^{oo} = 0$ and $\tau^{oo} = 0$) and the utility is $U^{oo} = 3.4416$, indicated in Table 2.

We consider next a case with tourism, say $T = 1$; that is, tourism revenue is 10% of GDP.[14] For an inelastic tourists' demand function ($\eta = 0.5$) in (34), we have the values of the variables $p = 1, D_Z = 1, w = 0.6, L_Y = 2, L_Z = 6, K = 4, L = 10, C_X = 1.6$ and $r = 0.1$. The values of the scale parameters are $A = 1.3195, B = 1$ and $G = 2.0477$, and the values of the parameters are $b = 0.375$ and $a = 0.1667$.

---

[14] This ratio of tourism revenue to GDP can be illustrated by the Hong Kong economy. In 2005, total tourism expenditure associated to inbound tourism was HK\$10.30 billion, or 7.65% of Hong Kong's GDP, while GDP was HK\$1,290.81 billion. The service sectors related to tourism and non-traded goods, including restaurants and hotels, wholesale and retail trades, transport and communications, financing, real estate and business services, and community, social and personal services, account for roughly 54.17% of GDP. See the Hong Kong Tourism Board's website: www.tourism.gov.hk, and *Hong Kong Monthly Digest of Statistics*, January 2006 (p. 223), Census and Statistics Department, Hong Kong Special Administrative Region.

Table 2 Sensitivity analysis for tourism

T	η	$t^{oo}(\%)$	$\tau^{oo}(\%)$	U^{oo}	$U(0,0)$	Change in U
0	3	0.00	0.00	3.4416	3.4416	0.00
1	3	14.14	1.64	3.4718	3.4566	0.44
1.5	3	17.40	1.99	3.4942	3.4701	0.69
0	1	0.00	0.00	3.4416	3.4416	0.00
1	1	25.14	2.85	3.4863	3.4566	0.86
1.5	1	38.13	4.19	3.5353	3.4737	1.77
0	0.5	0.00	0.00	3.4416	3.4416	0.00
1	0.5	34.03	3.79	3.4962	3.4566	1.15
1.5	0.5	66.33	6.95	3.5750	3.4749	2.88
0	0.2	0.00	0.00	3.4416	3.4416	0.00
1	0.2	47.37	5.15	3.5077	3.4566	1.48
1.5	0.2	244.6	22.35	3.6812	3.4758	5.91

In addition, we have the households' utility $U(0,0) = 3.4566$ at free trade in goods and no taxes on capital.

Nevertheless, in the presence of tourism, welfare of domestic households can be further increased by imposing tariffs and investment taxes. In calibration, we increase them from their free-trade levels. The consequent welfare profile under $T = 1$ and $\eta = 0.5$ is plotted in Fig. 2, in which the utility function is concave in the space of tariffs and investment taxes. The optimal tariff and tax rates are $t^{oo} = 34.03\%$ and $\tau^{oo} = 3.79\%$, and the corresponding utility is $U^{oo} = 3.4962$. These optimal policies raise welfare by 1.15%, which confirms that free trade is not optimal for a small open economy with tourism.

We next increase the tourism activity T from 1 to 1.5 (i.e., tourism revenue is 15% of GDP) under $\eta = 0.5$. In this case, the optimal tariff and investment tax are $t^{oo} = 66.33\%$ and $\tau^{oo} = 6.95\%$. Hence, an increase in the tourism activity gives higher optimal tariff and investment tax. This raises welfare of domestic households by 2.88% from the free-trade level.

It is noted that the price elasticity of tourists' demand for the non-traded good (η) can be used as a measure for the intensity of the competition from other destinations. Table 2 gives a sensitivity analysis for the optimal policies to the different price elasticities of tourists' demand. When the demand by tourists becomes less elastic (smaller η) and hence less competitive from other destinations, the optimal tariffs and investment taxes become larger and the levels of utility rise. When this price elasticity approaches to zero (say, $\eta = 0.2$), utility can be raised by 5.91% when tourism revenue is 15% of GDP ($T = 1.5$).

5 Conclusions

Incorporating the demand of the non-traded good by tourists into a general-equilibrium model, we have examined the welfare effects of tariffs and investment

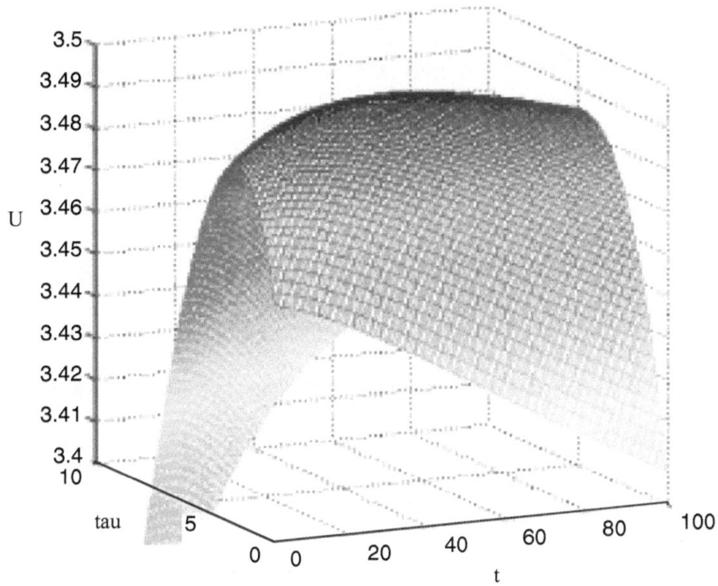

Fig. 2 Welfare profile of tariffs and investment taxes

taxes for the economy with inbound tourism. Inbound tourism converts local non-traded goods into tradable and hence generates a tourism terms-of-trade effect to the economy. Because of this favourable expenditure-shifting effect on foreign tourists, we have found that increases in import tariffs and investment taxes can actually improve welfare of domestic households when the non-traded and importable goods are substitutes in consumption. This suggests that for a small open economy with tourism, free trade is not the first-best policy. Hence, the impact of the tourism terms-of-trade should be considered in making the tariff and investment tax policies for the economy with tourism. In tourism dependent economies, all this suggests is import tariffs are useful in raising welfare of domestic residents as they correct a foreign distortion arising from the movements in the tourism terms of trade.

This proposed mechanism for using tariffs and investment taxes to improve welfare has been numerically verified. This calibrated model has also shown that the optimal tariffs and investment taxes become larger when the economy faces less competition from other tourist destinations.

References

Batra R (1973) Nontraded goods, factor market distortions, and the gains from trade. Am Econ Rev 63:706–713

Beladi H, Marjit S (1992) Foreign capital and protectionism. Can J Econ 25:233–238

Beladi H, Parai AK (1993) Sluggish intersectoral factor movements and alternative trade policies. South Econ J 59:760–767

Brander JA, Spencer BJ (1985) Export subsidies and international market share rivalry. J Int Econ 18:83–100

Brecher RA, Alejandro CFD (1977) Tariffs, foreign capital and immiserizing growth. J Int Econ 7:317–322

Dei F (1985) Voluntary export restraints and foreign investment. J Int Econ 19:305–312

Hatzipanayotou P, Michael MS (1993) Import restrictions, capital taxes and welfare. Can J Econ 26:727–738

Hatzipanayotou P, Michael MS (2001) Public goods, tax policies, and unemployment in LDCs. South Econ J 68:107–119

Hazari BR, Sgro PM (2004) Tourism, trade and national Welfare. Elsevier, Amsterdam

Jones RW (1967) International capital movements and the theory of tariffs and trade. Q J Econ 81:1–38

Jones RW (1969) Tariffs and trade in general equilibrium: comment. Am Econ Rev 59:418–424

Jones RW (1971) A three-factor model in theory, trade and history. In: Bhagwati JN et al. (eds) Trade, balance of payments and growth: essays in honor of C. P. Kindleberger. North-Holland, Amsterdam

Jones RW (1987) Tax wedges and mobile capital. Scand J Econ 89:335–346

Khan MA (1982) Social opportunity costs and immiserizing growth: some observations on the long run versus the short. Q J Econ 97:353–362

Komiya R (1967) Non-traded goods and the pure theory of international trade. Intl Econ Rev 8:132–152

Neary JP (1993) Welfare effects of tariffs and investment taxes. In: Ethier WJ (ed) Theory, policy and dynamics in international trade. Cambridge University Press, Cambridge

Neary JP (1995) Factor mobility and international trade. Can J Econ 28:S4–S23

Yano M, Nugent JB (1999) Aid, nontraded goods, and the transfer paradox in small countries. Am Econ Rev 89:431–449

Factor Mobility and Wage Inequality[1]

Masao Oda(✉) and Robert Stapp

Abstract This chapter provides a model to analyze the effects of factor mobility on wage inequality and considers a condition under which an inflow of factors into the US could generate wage inequality in favor of skilled labor. It is shown that the factor intensity and the degree of factor mobility play crucial roles in generating wage inequality. Furthermore, we demonstrate that the conventional wisdom concerning the wage gap no longer holds when capital is mobile.

1 Introduction

The drastic increase in wage inequality in the US since the 1980s has become a subject of controversy among trade and labor theorists. Seminal chapters such as Autor et al. (1998), Bhagwati and Kosters (1994), Bound and Johnson (1992), Davis (1998), Deardorff (2000), Dasgupta and Osang (2007), Krugman (2000), Tokarick (2005), Xu (2001) and Zhu (2004) have speculated on the causes and their effects. Research by various authors in Choi and Greenaway (2001) and Feenstra (2000) have focused on the effects of growing integration of the world economy on wage inequality.[2] These chapters have identified two suspects as the determinants of wage inequality, namely bias in technological progress and trade expansion.

[1] This chapter is dedicated as a memorial to Koji's sincere friendship which will dearly be missed.

[2] In addition, two trade journals, JIE and RIE, have edited special issues on wage inequality. Surprisingly, however, little attention has been paid to the analyses on the effects of factor mobility on wage inequality.

M. Oda
Department of Economics, Ritsumeikan University, Kusatsu 525-8577 Japan

T. Kamihigashi and L. Zhao (eds.) *International Trade and Economic Dynamics – Essays in Memory of Koji Shimomura.*

The most significant feature in the world economy today has been the tremendous increase in international factor movements. Despite this fact, only Kar and Beladi (2004), Marjit and Kar (2005), and Yabuuchi and Chaudhuri (2007) have examined this aspect while the central body of the literature has paid scant attention to the impact that factor mobility has on wage inequality leaving it as an unexplained black box.[3] Our chapter is motivated by this fact. By deriving the elasticity of wage inequality with respect to factor mobility, we consider how international factor mobility affects wage inequality in a developed country. We show that given some reasonable assumptions, wage inequality in favor of skilled labor is an inevitable outcome in the US.

The rest of this chapter is organized as follows. In Sect. 2, we set up a simple specific factor model with factor mobility. Section 3 considers the effects of factor mobility on wage inequality and shows that factor intensity and the degree of factor mobility play key roles in generating wage inequality in favor of skilled labor. In Sect. 4, we show that the conventional wisdom of labor movements on the wage gap no longer holds with capital mobility. Section 5 concludes the chapter. To focus on the effects that factor mobility has on wage inequality and the wage gap, we will neglect its welfare and repatriation effects.

2 The Model

This section sets up a simple model that relates factor mobility to wage inequality. We envision a developed economy (e.g., the USA) that produces two commodities with three factors with the usual properties, including perfect competition, full employment, constant returns to scale, and decreasing marginal productivity. The model of this (home) economy is

$$c_j(w_j, r) = p_j, \tag{1}$$

$$c_{jw}(w_j, r)X_j = \bar{L}_j + L_j, \tag{2a}$$

$$c_{1r}(w_1, r)X_1 + c_{2r}(w_2, r)X_2 = \bar{K} + K, \tag{2b}$$

$$\dot{L}_j = f_j(w_j - w_j^*),\ f_j(0) = 0,\ f_j'(\cdot) > 0, \tag{3a}$$

$$\dot{K} = g(r - r^*),\ g(0) = 0,\ g'(\cdot) > 0, \tag{3b}$$

$$w_j = w_j^*,\ r = r^*. \tag{4}$$

[3] Feenstra and Hanson (1996) show that foreign investment and trade are important parts of the explanation for the pattern of wage and employment changes while Markusen and Venables (1997) focus on the role of multinational firms in explaining wage inequality.

This model is comprised of two parts. The first consists of (1), (2a), and (2b). The zero profit condition is expressed in (1) while (2a) and (2b) are the full employment conditions. The second part consists of (3a), (3b), and (4) with (3a) and (3b) revealing the mechanisms of how the inflow of foreign factors occur that are dependent on the differences in factor rewards between two countries. The equilibrium conditions in factor markets are shown in (4).

Here, $c_j(\cdot)$ is the unit cost function, p_j is the price of the jth $(j = 1, 2)$ commodity, w_1 and w_2 are the wage rates of unskilled and skilled labor, respectively, with $w_2 - w_1$ serving as the expression of wage inequality. The return to capital is r. Output of the jth commodity is X_j, $\bar{L}_j$, and $\bar{K}$ are the fixed domestic endowments of labor and capital, while L_j and K are the inflows of these factors from a foreign country. Dots denote time derivatives and asterisks signify foreign variables. The subscripts of w and r in (2a) and (2b) are partial derivatives. Given p_j, $\bar{L}_j$, $\bar{K}$, L_j, and K, the first part of the model determines the five variables of w_1, w_2, r, X_1, and X_2.

The use of a specific factor model with outsourcing factors of production can be justified for the following reasons. First, labor is differentiated into skilled and unskilled and it takes time and expense for an unskilled labor to transition into skilled labor. They are specific in the short run. Second, as a result of globalization, the acquisition of factors from foreign countries has become much easier while increasing to a significant degree.

3 Wage Inequality with Factor Mobility

In this section, we consider a condition in which the simultaneous inflow of all factors into the US could generate wage inequality in favor of skilled labor. In the first three subsections, the conventional approach of factor mobility is used in which each factor migrates depending on the differences in factor rewards between the two countries. It will be shown that while the inflow of both types of labor can change wage inequality against skilled labor, importing capital alters this inequality in favor of skilled labor. Gathering these results in the three subsection, we provide a condition in which the simultaneous inflow of all three factors could generate the wage inequality in favor of skilled labor. Throughout this section, we assume the following:

(i) The inflow of foreign factors is motivated by the differences in factor rewards, which are produced by technological superiority in the home country.
(ii) The second sector is capital intensive relative to the first sector and commodity prices are fixed.[4]

[4] The assumption of fixed commodity prices has the following merits. First, the changes in nominal wages imply that of real wages. Second, the effects of international factor mobility on factor prices become strong and clear.

(iii) If $\hat{w}_2 > \hat{w}_1$ ($\hat{w}_2 < \hat{w}_1$), then wage inequality changes in favor of (against) skilled labor, where the hat denotes the relative change of the variables.

3.1 The Inflow of Unskilled Labor

To begin this analysis, we assume that each country starts with the same level of technology. Now, suppose technological progress occurs in the home country generating $w_1 > w_1^*$; thereby causing foreign unskilled labor to move into this country. Assuming $\dot{L}_2 = \dot{K} = 0$, from (1), (2a), and (2b), we obtain

$$\hat{w}_2 - \hat{w}_1 = \left(\left(\frac{\theta_{K1}}{\theta_{L1}} - \frac{\theta_{K2}}{\theta_{L2}} \right) \frac{\lambda_{K1}}{\Phi} \right) \hat{L}_1, \tag{5}$$

where $\theta_{ij} > 0$ is the distributive share of the ith ($i = K, L$) factor in the jth ($j = 1, 2$) sector; ($\theta_{Kj} + \theta_{Lj} = 1$), $\lambda_{Kj} > 0$ is the fraction of capital used in the jth sector ($\lambda_{K1} + \lambda_{K2} = 1$); $\Phi = (\lambda_{K1}\sigma_1/\theta_{L1} + \lambda_{K2}\sigma_2/\theta_{L2}) > 0$; $\sigma_j = (\hat{a}_{Kj} - \hat{a}_{Lj})/(\hat{w}_j - \hat{r}) > 0$ is the elasticity of factor substitution in the jth sector; and $(\theta_{Kj}/\theta_{Lj})$ is the capital intensity in the value sense in jth sector.

The coefficient of $\hat{L}_1$ in (5) is the elasticity of wage inequality with respect to the inflow of unskilled labor. This is the product of the difference in the capital intensity and some weights. Assuming $\hat{L}_1 > 0$, from (5) we have

Result 1. *If the second sector is capital intensive, then an inflow of unskilled labor changes wage inequality against skilled labor.*

Result 1 has the following implications. An inflow of unskilled labor reduces the scarcity of unskilled labor and its wage rate. This is the negative direct effect of unskilled labor inflow. However, it also generates an indirect effect on both unskilled and skilled labor. An increase in the productivity of capital in the first sector initiated by the inflow of unskilled labor induces capital to move from the second sector to the first sector. This increases the productivity of unskilled labor and reduces that in the second sector. This is the indirect effect of an inflow of unskilled labor. While two opposite effects work on the wage rate of unskilled labor, only the negative effect impacts skilled labor. Result 1 shows that by considering these effects an inflow of unskilled labor changes the wage inequality against skilled labor.

3.2 The Inflow of Skilled Labor

As in the previous section, we initially assume that each country begins with the same level of technology. Now suppose the home country experiences technological progress producing $w_2 > w_2^*$, providing an incentive for foreign skilled labor to move into this country. Assuming $\dot{L}_1 = \dot{K} = 0$, from (1), (2a), and (2b), we obtain

$$\hat{w}_2 - \hat{w}_1 = \left(\left(\frac{\theta_{K1}}{\theta_{L1}} - \frac{\theta_{K2}}{\theta_{L2}} \right) \frac{\lambda_{K2}}{\Phi} \right) \hat{L}_2. \tag{6}$$

By assuming $\hat{L}_2 > 0$, from (6) we obtain

Result 2. *If the second sector is capital intensive, then the inflow of skilled labor changes wage inequality against skilled labor.*

The implications of the Result 2 are as follows. An inflow of skilled labor reduces the scarcity of skilled labor and its wage rate. This is the negative direct effect of skilled labor inflow. However, it increases the rental of capital in the second sector and domestic capital moves into this sector. This in turn increases the productivity of skilled labor while reducing that of unskilled labor. Two opposite effects are at work on skilled labor but only the negative indirect effect impacts unskilled labor. Result 2 shows that by considering these effects an inflow of skilled labor changes the wage rate against skilled labor.

As can be seen, (5) and (6) have $(\theta_{K1}/\theta_{L1} - \theta_{K2}/\theta_{L2})$ as a common element. However, they differ in λ_{Kj}/Φ. From the two cases above, we see that an inflow of both types of labor could change wage inequality against skilled labor.

3.3 The Inflow of Capital

As in the previous two sections, we start by assuming that the level of technology is initially the same in both countries. Now suppose technological progress occurs in the home country that generates $r > r^*$. Thus, foreign capital will move into this country. Assuming $\dot{L}_j = 0$, from (1), (2a), and (2b), we obtain

$$\hat{w}_2 - \hat{w}_1 = \left(\left(\frac{\theta_{K2}}{\theta_{L2}} - \frac{\theta_{K1}}{\theta_{L1}} \right) \frac{1}{\Phi} \right) \hat{K}. \tag{7}$$

Assuming $\hat{K} > 0$, from (7) we obtain

Result 3. *If the second sector is capital intensive, then an inflow of capital changes wage inequality in favor of skilled labor.*

Result 3 provides the following implications. Since capital is mobile between the two sectors, the inflow of foreign capital increases the marginal product of both types of labor and therefore both types of labor gain from this capital inflow. However, since the second sector is capital intensive, the marginal product of labor in the second sector increases more than that of the first sector, tilting wage inequality in favor of skilled labor. It is interesting to note that while the importation of the two types of labor changes wage inequality against skilled labor, the inflow of capital alters it in favor of skilled labor. From Results 1, 2, and 3, we obtain

Result 4. *If the factor intensity is the same between the two sectors, international factor mobility does not affect wage inequality. Thus, the difference in factor intensity is a necessary and sufficient condition in generating wage inequality.*

3.4 The Inflow of All Three Factors

As a result of technological superiority in the home country, suppose the rewards of all three factors in the home country are higher than those of the foreign country and all three factors move into this country. Gathering the results in the previous subsections, this section provides a condition under which the simultaneous inflow of all three factors generates wage inequality in favor of skilled labor. It will be shown that factor intensity and the degree of factor inflow play key roles in producing wage inequality in favor of skilled labor

Davis and Weinstein (2002) points out that all factors of production in the world are moving into the US due to its level of technology being the highest in the world. However, they did not consider how this type of factor mobility is related to wage inequality in the US.[5] In this section, we provide a condition in which the Davis–Weinstein type factor inflow generates wage inequality in favor of skilled labor. From (5), (6), and (7) and assuming $\dot{L}_j > 0$ and $\dot{K} > 0$, we obtain:

$$(\hat{w}_2 - \hat{w}_1) = \frac{1}{3}\left(\left(\frac{\theta_{K2}}{\theta_{L2}} - \frac{\theta_{K1}}{\theta_{L1}}\right)\frac{1}{\Phi}\right)\left(\hat{K} - (\lambda_{K1}\hat{L}_1 + \lambda_{K2}\hat{L}_2)\right). \tag{8}$$

From (8), we obtain:

Result 5. *A necessary and sufficient condition for an inflow of all three factors to cause wage inequality in favor of skilled labor is that the second sector is capital intensive and the degree of capital mobility is greater than that of the weighted sum of the two types of labor.*

Result 5 provides a condition in which an inflow of all three factors could generate wage inequality in favor of skilled labor. At first glance, it may be difficult to see why skilled labor in the US gains from the simultaneous inflow of all three factors. Intuitively, however, it is evident that if the degree of capital inflow is high and the second sector is capital intensive, the marginal product of skilled labor increases more than that of unskilled labor.

What remains to consider is the plausibility of our assumptions. First is the factor intensity ranking. As the skilled labor using sector is usually more capital intensive than the unskilled labor using sector, it is reasonable to assume that the second sector is capital intensive. Second to consider is the degree of factor inflow. While labor mobility is restricted by many institutional and political barriers, capital mobility is very high. Thus, it is plausible that the degree of capital inflow is higher than that of the weighted sum of both types of labor.[6] Third, we assumed the level of technology of the home country is high enough to attract foreign factors. Considering this aspect, as the US is the most innovative country in the world, the level of technology

[5] Their interest is on the effects of immigration of factors on welfare. By the use of a Ricardian framework, they show that a country that experiences immigration of factors motivated by technological differences will suffer from the migration.

[6] For the evidence about the surge of capital mobility, see Wong (1995), Chap. 1.

in the US is therefore the highest in the world. Thus, we can conclude that the wage inequality in favor of skilled labor is an inevitable outcome with factor mobility. The following remarks on our results are necessary.

Remark 1. Our results depend on the model and assumptions. It is neither correct nor trivial that our results carry over to a higher dimension.

Remark 2. It is interesting to see that if both terms of the parentheses in (8) are negative, we still obtain $\hat{w}_2 - \hat{w}_1 > 0$. In other words, wage inequality in favor of skilled labor is established if the second sector is labor intensive and the degree of capital inflow is less than that of the weighted sum of labor inflows. As the degree of capital inflow is less than that of the weighted average of labor, the output of the capital intensive first good declines and that of the labor intensive second good expands, which increases w_2 and reduces w_1, making wage inequality in favor of skilled labor. Furthermore, if both terms of the parentheses have opposite signs the inflow of all three factors could generate wage inequality in favor of unskilled labor.

4 The Wage Gap with Capital Mobility

In the analyses of labor mobility, conventional wisdom tells us that labor movement between two countries reduces the initial wage gap and consequently hampering the incentives for further labor migration.[7] However, this conventional wisdom is derived with the assumption that capital is not mobile. This section considers the effects of labor movement on the wage gap when capital is mobile. It is shown that this traditional thought will no longer hold with capital mobility. In this section, we assume that due to the differences in factor endowments between two countries, the home country readily accepts unskilled labor while skilled labor exits the home country.

4.1 The Inflow of Unskilled Labor

Consider the case of unskilled labor movement with capital mobility. Suppose that this home (developed) country accepts unskilled labor from a foreign (developing) country due to $w_1 > w_1^*$, with $w_2 = w_2^*$ and $r = r^*$ initially. This unskilled labor inflow will decrease w_1 while increasing w_1^*, which reduces the initial wage gap in unskilled labor retarding the incentive for further migration. This is the direct effect of unskilled labor movement. However this exodus of unskilled labor from the foreign country reduces r^* and increases r, which then induces capital to move from the foreign country to the home country. This movement of capital will increase w_1

[7] We give different meanings to wage inequality and the wage gap. Wage inequality is the wage differential between skilled and unskilled labor within a country, while the wage gap is the wage differential of same type of labor between the two countries.

and reduce w_1^*, which is the indirect effect of capital movement on the wage gap. Thus the inflow of unskilled labor accompanies the inflow of capital. This capital movement will continue until $r = r^*$ is attained. At the final situation, we are not sure whether the initial wage gap ($w_1 > w_1^*$) diminishes and as a result will reduce the incentive for further unskilled labor migration. The net results depend on the magnitude of these two effects.

4.2 *The Outflow of Skilled Labor*

Next, consider the case of skilled labor movement when capital is mobile. Suppose that skilled labor moves out from the home country to the foreign country due to $w_2 < w_2^*$, while $w_1 = w_1^*$ and $r = r^*$ initially. This exit of skilled labor from the home country will increase w_2 and decrease w_2^*, reducing the initial wage gap in skilled labor. This is the direct effect of skilled labor movement. However, the departure of skilled labor reduces r and increases r^*, which induces capital to move out from the home country to the foreign country. This capital movement will reduce w_2 and increase w_2^* and is the indirect effect of capital movement on the wage gap. Consequently, such an exodus of skilled labor is accompanied by the exit of capital. This capital movement will continue until $r = r^*$ is attained. Without qualification, we cannot be sure whether the initial wage gap in skilled labor between the two countries is reduced or not. The net result depends on the magnitude of these two effects. Should the indirect effect of capital mobility dominate the direct effect of labor mobility, then the initial wage gap in skilled labor between the two countries may increase. Thus we have

Result 6. *The conventional wisdom of the wage gap no longer holds with capital mobility.*

The implications of Result 6 are explained by the following facts. The inflow of unskilled labor accompanies the inflow of capital while the outflow of skilled labor accompanies the outflow of capital. In other words, labor movement is accompanied by capital movement and both factors move in the same direction. We see that capital mobility negates the validity of the conventional wisdom that labor movement has on the wage gap. Result 6 provides a reason why international labor mobility does not reduce the incentive for labor to move in the presence of capital mobility. Since capital mobility is high in the real world, labor movement will not reduce the incentive of labor mobility.

5 Conclusions

By the use of a specific factor model with factor mobility, this chapter provided the following novel results on wage inequality and the wage gap in a developed economy. First, by deriving the elasticity of wage inequality with respect to factor mobility, we showed that an inflow of foreign capital could change wage inequality in favor of skilled labor. Second, we provided a condition under which the Davis–Weinstein type factor inflow generates wage inequality in favor of skilled labor and demonstrated how this could occur in the US. Third, we showed that the conventional wisdom on the wage gap no longer holds when capital is mobile.

The following aspects seem to be fertile ground for further research. First, the welfare analysis of factor inflows would be necessary in order to obtain policy implications in the presence of wage inequality. Second, factor inflows accompany the repatriations of proceeds, which may in turn affect wage inequality. Third, the effects of trade on wage inequality should be included. Deardorff (2000) along with Feenstra and Hanson (2003) have provided a backdrop for this particular feature. In spite of these facts, we added new results to the analysis of wage inequality from the aspect of factor mobility.

Acknowledgment This chapter benefited from presentations at the SEA in 2006 and APEA in 2007. We are very grateful to Daniel Millimet, John Laitner, Kenji Fujiwara, Masayuki Hayashibara, Makoto Tanaka, Shigemi Yabuuchi as well as the referee and editors of this book for their comments.

References

Autor D, Katz L, Krueger A (1998) Computing inequality: Have computers changed the labor market? Q J Econ 114:1169–1213

Bhagwati J, Kosters M (eds) (1994) Trade and wages: Leveling wages down. AEI Press, Washington DC

Bound J, Johnson G (1992) Changes in the structure of wages in the 1980's: An evaluation of alternative explanations. Am Econ Rev 82:371–392

Choi K, Greenaway D (eds) (2001) Globalization and labor market. Blackwell, Oxford

Dasgupta I, Osang T (2007) Trade, wages, and specific factors. Rev Intl Econ 15:45–61

Davis D (1998) Does european unemployment prop up American wage? National labor market and global trade. Am Econ Rev 88:478–494

Davis D, Weinstein D (2002) Technological superiority and the losses from migration. NBER Working Paper 8971

Deardorff A (2000) Policy implications of the trade and wage debate. Rev Intl Econ 8:478–496

Feenstra R (ed) (2000) The impact of international trade on wages. University of Chicago Press, California

Feenstra R, Hanson G (1996) Foreign investment, outsourcing, and relative wages. The political economy of trade policy. MIT Press, Cambridge, MA, pp 89–127

Feenstra R, Hanson G (2003) Global production sharing and rising inequality: A survey of trade and wages. Handbook of international trade. Blackwell, Malden, MA, pp 146–185

Hijzen A (2007) International outsourcing, technology change, and wage inequality. Rev Intl Econ 15:188–205

Kar S, Beladi H (2004) Skill formation and international migration: Welfare perspective of developing countries. Jpn World Econ 16:35–54

Krugman P (2000) And now for something completely different: An alternative model of trade, education, and inequality. The impact of international trade on wages. National Bureau of Economic Research, Cambridge, MA, pp 15–28

Marjit S, Kar S (2005) Emigration and wage inequality. Econ Lett 88:141–145

Markusen J, Venables A (1997) The role of multinational firms in the wage-gap debate. Rev Intl Econ 5:435–451

Ruffin R (2001) Quasi-specific factors: Worker comparative advantage in the two-sector production model. J Intl Econ 53:445–461

Tokarick S (2005) Quantifying the impact of trade on wages: The role of nontraded goods. Rev Intl Econ 13:841–860

Wong K-Y (1995) International trade in goods and factor mobility. MIT Press, Cambridge, MA

Xu B (2001) Factor bias, sector bias, and the effects of technical progress on relative factor prices. J Intl Econ 54:5–25

Yabuuchi S, Chaudhuri S (2007) International migration of labor and skilled-unskilled wage inequality in a developing economy. Econ Model 24:128–137

Zhu S (2004) Trade, product cycles, and inequality within and between countries. Can J Econ 37:1042–1060

A Pareto Improvement in Customs Unions Without Intra-Union Transfer

Ling Qi(✉) and Koji Shimomura

Abstract Kemp and Wan (1976) proved a theorem on the formation of customs unions: a common tariff vector can be found in the union such that there exists a Pareto improvement in the union without changing the international prices and the purchases from the rest of the world in the associated tariff-ridden competitive equilibrium. However, this Pareto-optimum may imply a tariff-ridden competitive equilibrium with an intra-union income transfer that does not seem to be very realistic.

We give a strictly analytical proof to show that under some conditions on the tariff vector, the equilibrium can be established without intra-union income transfer and the utility of every country in the customs union can be improved when the customs union consists of three countries.

1 Introduction

Kemp and Wan, (1976) considered the problem of customs unions in the international trade model, in which there exists a competitive world trade equilibrium with different tariffs on tradable goods across countries. A customs union is formed by several countries, and within the union, goods are traded with the same tariff vectors from one country to another. They show that there exists a compensation scheme within the union such that members in the union are better off or at least no worse off, leaving international prices and purchases from the rest of the world unchanged. This theorem provides the basis for the possibility of free trade: forming customs unions and enlarging them till free trade is reached. However, the Pareto-optimum may imply a tariff-ridden competitive equilibrium with an intra-union

L. Qi
Research Institute for Economics and Business Administration, Kobe University,
2–1, Rokkodai-cho, Nada-ku, Kobe 657–8501, Japan, e-mail: qiling@rieb.kobe-u.ac.jp

T. Kamihigashi and L. Zhao (eds.) *International Trade and Economic Dynamics – Essays in Memory of Koji Shimomura.*

income transfer that does not seem to be very realistic. For instance, Grinols (1981) gives an example that shows the difficulty of establishing a compensation scheme in practice. Thus, it remains an open question as to whether or not there exists a Pareto improvement in a customs union without intra-union income transfer.

A lot of literature has attempted to extend the Kemp–Wan theorem in various directions. Ohyama (1972) obtained the same result as the Kemp–Wan theorem. Grinols (1981) extended the Kemp–Wan theorem to provide a particular compensation scheme that shows how the intra-union income transfer can be constructed to compensate members of the union so that no member will be worse off. Panagariya and Krishna (2002) studied preferential trade areas where members can use member-specific tariff vectors, and the domestic-price vectors differ across member countries. They showed that the Kemp–Wan theorem can be extended to cover free-trade areas. Kemp and Shimomura (2001) showed that the Kemp–Wan Theorem remains valid, even though nonmember countries adjust their tariffs in response to the common tariff vector in the union. However, there is a scarcity of literature on the Kemp–Wan theorem, showing that the Pareto improvement can be established without intra-union income transfer. Iwasa, Riezman and Shimomura (2008) studied the same problem addressed in our chapter, with a more general formulation that contains production in the model. However, the proof still needs to be completed.

The purpose of this chapter is to give a strictly analytical proof of the existence of the tariff-ridden competitive equilibrium in the Kemp–Wan theorem without intra-union income transfer. Although the result can be extended to the m-country case, where $m > 3$, because we want to emphasize the essence of the proof, we only consider the case where a union contains three countries. We show that when the international tariff vector is not so large, there exists a Pareto-optimal allocation due to the formation of the union without intra-union income transfer, so as to leave international prices and the utilities of the rest of the world unchanged. In this Pareto-optimum, the utilities of all countries in this union are improved. This chapter may be considered as an extension of the Kemp–Wan theorem in the sense of giving a condition for the existence of the equilibrium without intra-union income transfer.

2 The Model

We consider the world economy in which there exists more than three countries, countries 1,2,3, and the rest of the countries, $n+1$ goods are traded and indexed as $0, 1, \ldots, j, \ldots, n$, where good 0 serves as the numeraire. Here, assume $n > 3$, for if not, there may exist no solution to the problem.

Suppose that the government of each country imposes a specific tariff on the non-numeraire goods; we denote the tariff rate imposed by country i on good j by τ^i_j, $j = 1, \ldots, n$. The tariff rate τ^i_j can be of either sign; a negative τ^i_j means that the government of country i subsidizes the international trade of good j. Let $\tau^i \equiv (\tau^i_1, \ldots, \tau^i_n)$ be the tariff vector of country i and

$$\Upsilon \equiv \begin{bmatrix} \tau^1 \\ \vdots \\ \tau^m \end{bmatrix}$$

the international tariff vector.

Assume that there exists a general equilibrium international price vector denoted as $p(\Upsilon)$, and the countries attain their maximum utilities $\tilde{u}_i$, $i = 1,2,3$, under their own tariffs τ^i, at the international price vector $p(\Upsilon)$, where the tariffs are different from each other. Now, consider that the group of three countries forms a union in which the goods can be traded in the same tariff vector from one country to another.

Let an $n+1$-dimensional vector s be the vector of the amount of goods imported by the group of three countries from the rest of the world. At the world trade equilibrium, $ps = 0$. Let $\bar{c}^i$ and $\tilde{c}^i$ be, respectively, the endowment vector and the consumption vector of country i preunion. Namely, $u_i(\tilde{c}^i) = \tilde{u}_i$, $i = 1,2,3$.

First, we formulate the problem and give some preliminaries of the proof. Consider the following optimization problem:

$$\begin{aligned} &\max_{(c^2,c^3)} u_1\left(s - \sum_{i=2}^{3}(c^i - \bar{c}^i) + \bar{c}^1\right), \\ &\text{s.t.}\, u_i(c^i) \geq u_i,\, i = 2,3, \\ &s - \sum_{i=2}^{3}(c^i - \bar{c}^i) + \bar{c}^1 \geq 0, \\ &c^i \geq 0,\, i = 2,3, \end{aligned} \tag{1}$$

and define the maximum of this problem by $U_1(u_2,u_3)$. For brevity, we define the set of constraints as follows:

$$\Gamma(u_2,u_3,s) \equiv \left\{(c^2,c^3) \geq 0 : s - \sum_{i=2}^{3}(c^i - \bar{c}^i) + \bar{c}^1 \geq 0,\, u_i \leq u_i(c^i),\, i = 2,3\right\}.$$

Similarly, consider problem (2) as follows:

$$\max_{(c^2,c^3)\in\Gamma'(u_2,u_3,s,p)} u_1\left(s - \sum_{i=2}^{3}(c^i - \bar{c}^i) + \bar{c}^1\right), \tag{2}$$

where

$$\begin{aligned} \Gamma'(u_2,u_3,s,p) \equiv \Bigg\{ &(c^2,c^3) \geq 0 : s - \sum_{i=2}^{3}(c^i - \bar{c}^i) + \bar{c}^1 \geq 0; \\ &u_i \leq u_i(c^i);\, p(c^i - \bar{c}^i) = 0,\, i = 2,3\Bigg\}. \end{aligned}$$

For the use of the proof, consider

$$\max_{(c^1,c^3)\in\Gamma^2(u_2,u_3,s)} u_2\left(s-\sum_{i\neq 2}^{3}(c^i-\bar{c}^i)+\bar{c}^2\right), \tag{3}$$

and

$$\max_{(c^1,c^2)\in\Gamma^3(u_2,u_3,s)} u_3\left(s-\sum_{i=1}^{2}(c^i-\bar{c}^i)+\bar{c}^3\right), \tag{4}$$

and define $U_2(u_1,u_3)$ and $U_3(u_1,u_2)$ as the maximums of problem (3) and (4), respectively, where

$$\Gamma^2(u_1,u_3,s) \equiv \left\{(c^1,c^3)\geq 0: s-\sum_{i\neq 2}^{3}(c^i-\bar{c}^i)+\bar{c}^2\geq 0,\, u_i\leq u_i(c^i),\, i=1,3\right\} \text{ and}$$

$$\Gamma^3(u_1,u_2,s) \equiv \left\{(c^1,c^2)\geq 0: s-\sum_{i=1}^{2}(c^i-\bar{c}^i)+\bar{c}^3\geq 0,\, u_i\leq u_i(c^i),\, i=1,2\right\}.$$

We want to show (a) there exists a Pareto improvement brought about by formation of the union. (b) This improvement can be established without intra-union income transfer. (a) implies that problem (1) has a solution (c^2,c^3), where $u_i(c^i)>\tilde{u}_i$, $i=2$, 3, such that $U_1(u_2,u_3)\geq\tilde{u}_1$. (b) implies that the solution must satisfy $p(c^i-\bar{c}^i)=0, i=2,3$, that is, it must be a solution to problem (2) also. Now, our task is to show that there exists $(u_2,u_3)>(\tilde{u}_2,\tilde{u}_3)$, such that the two problems have the same solution and $U_1(u_2,u_3)\geq\tilde{u}_1$.

In the preunion case, $\tilde{u}_i=u_i(\tilde{c}^i)$, $i=1,2,3$, and $p(\tilde{c}^i-\bar{c}^i)=0$ hold, we know that $\Gamma'(\tilde{u}_2,\tilde{u}_3,s,p)\neq\emptyset$. Since $\Gamma(\tilde{u}_2,\tilde{u}_3,s)\supseteq\Gamma'(\tilde{u}_2,\tilde{u}_3,s,p)$, we also have $\Gamma(\tilde{u}_2,\tilde{u}_3,s)\neq\emptyset$. However, when (u_2,u_3) is sufficiently large, it is possible that $\Gamma(u_2,u_3,s)=\emptyset$, so we have to define a set to exclude such (u_2,u_3). Thus, second, we determine a set consisting of such points (u_2,u_3), so that the constraint set is nonempty. We give the result in Lemma 1. Before stating the lemma, we assume that the initial state $(\tilde{u}_1,\tilde{u}_2,\tilde{u}_3)$ is not Pareto optimal.

Lemma 1. *There exists a domain D^* of $\Gamma(u_2,u_3,s)$ in problem (1), such that for any $(u_2,u_3)\in D^*,\Gamma(u_2,u_3,s)\neq\emptyset$. Moreover, $(\tilde{u}_2,\tilde{u}_3)$ lies in the interior of D^*.*

Proof. See Appendix 1. □

The last result in this lemma allows us to assume that all the countries in the union can be better off than in the preunion state. This ensures that Assumption 1(2) in Sect. 3 is reasonable.

Third, we show that there exists a maximum in problem (1) by Lemma 2.

Lemma 2. *Suppose that every utility function $u_i(c^i)$ is twice continuously differentiable, and strictly quasi-concave for $i=1,2,3$. For any $(u_2,u_3)\in D^*$, there exists a maximum in problem (1). Let the solution to problem (1) be $(\varphi^2(u_2,u_3),\varphi^3(u_2,u_3))$.*

Let $\varphi^1 \equiv s - \sum_{i=2}^{3} \varphi^i(u_2,u_3) + \sum_{i=1}^{3} \bar{c}^i$ *and* $\psi^i(u_2,u_3) \equiv p[\varphi^i(u_2,u_3) - \bar{c}^i]$, i = *1,2,3. Then,* $\varphi^i(u_2,u_3)$ *and* $\psi^i(u_2,u_3)$ *are continuously differentiable with respect to* (u_2,u_3)*,* i *=1,2,3.*

Proof. See Appendix 2. □

In the proof of this lemma, we first show the uniqueness of the solution to problem (1), next we show the continuous differentiability of the solution function by the implicit function theorem.

3 The Result

In this section, we show the main result: if $(\tilde{u}_1,\tilde{u}_2,\tilde{u}_3)$ is close to the Pareto frontier, then there exists a Pareto improvement in which the utilities of all countries in the union are improved, without intra-union income transfer.

In Lemma 3, we examine the signs of $\psi^2(u_2,u_3)$ and $\psi^3(u_2,u_3)$ on the frontier of D^* and in the initial state. With this, we examine the effect on the expenditure of country i according to the changes in its utility and the utilities of other countries. Before stating the lemma, we assume that there exists a free trade equilibrium in the union for given s.

Assumption 1. (1) There exists a fictitious competitive free trade equilibrium (p^*, c^{*1},c^{*2},c^{*3}) in the union, such that $p^*c^{*i} = p^*\bar{c}^i$, i = 1,2,3; ${u^*}_i \equiv u_i(c^{*i}) > \tilde{u}_i$, i=1,2,3, and $\sum_{i=1}^{3} c^{*i} = s + \sum_{i=1}^{3} \bar{c}^i$.
(2) The initial state $(\tilde{u}_1,\tilde{u}_2,\tilde{u}_3)$ lies in the neighborhood of (u_1^*,u_2^*,u_3^*).

From the first welfare theorem, we see that (u_1^*,u_2^*,u_3^*) lies on the Pareto frontier. Since we have shown that $(\tilde{u}_1,\tilde{u}_2,\tilde{u}_3)$ lies in the interior of the utility possibility set, it seems plausible to assume that ${u^*}_i = u_i(c^{*i}) > \tilde{u}_i$, $i = 1,2,3$. If the international tariff vector Υ is close to zero, the international price vector of the tariff-ridden equilibrium $p(\Upsilon)$ is close to p^*, then $(\tilde{u}_1,\tilde{u}_2,\tilde{u}_3)$ can be close to (u_1^*,u_2^*,u_3^*). In fact, we only use the assumption that p is close to $p*$ in the proof. Conversely, Assumption 1 (2) implies that p is close to p^*. This is shown by Lemma 3.

Lemma 3. *Suppose that every utility function* $u_i(c^i)$ *is strictly quasi-concave for* $i = 1,2,3$. *Let* $G(u_2)$ *be defined as in the last section. Under Assumption 1,*

1. $\psi^2(u_2,G(u_2)) + \psi^3(u_2,G(u_2)) > 0,$ *for any* $G^{-1}(\tilde{u}_3) \geq u_2 \geq \tilde{u}_2$,
2. $\psi^2(\tilde{u}_2,u_3) < 0$ for $\tilde{u}_3 \leq u_3 \leq G(\tilde{u}_2)$; and $\psi^3(u_2,\tilde{u}_3) < 0$, for $\tilde{u}_2 \leq u_2 \leq G^{-1}(\tilde{u}_3)$,
3. $\psi^3(\tilde{u}_2,G(\tilde{u}_2)) > 0$, $\psi^2(G^{-1}(\tilde{u}_3),\tilde{u}_3) > 0$.

Proof. See Appendix 3. □

The first result follows from the fact that on the frontier of D^*, $\psi^1(u_2, G(u_2)) < 0$ for any $\tilde{u}_2 \le u_2 \le G^{-1}(\tilde{u}_3)$. The second result can be shown with a similar argument.

In Lemma 4, we show that there exists $(u_2^0, u_3^0) > (\tilde{u}_2, \tilde{u}_3)$ such that problem (1) associated with (u_2^0, u_3^0) has the same solution as problem (2). That is, if countries 2 and 3 obtain utilities u_2^0 and u_3^0, respectively, then the income is equal to the expenditure in every country of the union under the international prices, and countries 2 and 3 in the union are better off.

Lemma 4. *By Lemmas 2–3, (1) there exists a continuous function* $\vartheta : [\tilde{u}_2, u_2^f] \to [\tilde{u}_3, G(\tilde{u}_2)]$ *such that* $\psi^3(u_2, \vartheta(u_2)) = 0$. *(2) There exists* $u_2^0 \in (\tilde{u}_2, u_2^f)$ *such that* $\psi^2(u_2^0, \vartheta(u_2^0)) = 0$. *Moreover,* $\tilde{u}_3 < \vartheta(u_2^0) < G(u_2^0)$.

Proof. See Appendix 4. □

From the proof of this lemma, we see that the last two countries are better off in the postunion equilibrium. Now, we show by the following theorem that country 1 is better off postunion.

Theorem. *Suppose that the utility function* $u_i(c^i)$ *is strictly quasi-concave for* $i = 1, 2, 3$. *Under Assumption 1, there exists* $(u_2^0, u_3^0) > (\tilde{u}_2, \tilde{u}_3)$ *such that problems (1) and (2) with respect to* (u_2^0, u_3^0) *have the same solution. Moreover, the maximum of problem (2) is larger than* $\tilde{u}_1$.

Proof. In the proof of Lemma 4, we have shown that there exist u_2^0 and continuous function ϑ with $\tilde{u}_2 < u_2^0 < u_2^f$ and $\tilde{u}_3 < \vartheta(u_2^0) < G(u_2^0)$ such that $\psi^2(u_2^0, \vartheta(u_2^0)) = 0$ and $\psi^3(u_2^0, \vartheta(u_2^0)) = 0$. Let $u_3^0 \equiv \vartheta(u_2^0)$. Now, it remains to be shown that the maximum $U_1(u_2^0, u_3^0)$ of problem (1) is larger than $\tilde{u}_1$. Recall the definition of the frontier of D^*; we know that $U_1(u_2^0, G(u_2^0)) = \tilde{u}_1$. Consider the Lagrange function (10) defined in the proof of Lemma 2,

$$L(c^2, c^3, \lambda, \mu) \equiv u_1\left(s - \sum_{i=2}^{3}(c^i - \bar{c}^i) + \bar{c}^1\right) + \lambda[u_2(c^2) - u_2] + \mu[u_3(c^3) - u_3].$$

By the envelope theorem, we obtain that

$$\frac{\partial U_1(u_2, u_3)}{\partial u_3} = -\mu < 0. \tag{5}$$

That is, $U_1(u_2, u_3)$ is decreasing in u_3.

Since $u_3^0 = \vartheta(u_2^0) < G(u_2^0)$, we must have

$$U_1\left(u_2^0, u_3^0\right) > U_1\left(u_2^0, G(u_2^0)\right) = \tilde{u}_1.$$

Thus, we have completed the proof of the theorem. □

Now, it still remains to point out the common tariff vector of the union and to show that the intra-union transfer is zero. By the second welfare theorem, the solution (c^{02}, c^{03}) to problem (1) associated with (u_2^0, u_3^0) satisfies $\frac{1}{\partial u_1/\partial c_0^1} \frac{\partial u_1}{\partial c^{01}}(c^{0i} - \bar{c}^i) = 0$, $i = 1, 2, 3$, where $\tilde{c}^i$ is the consumption vector of country i in the preunion. By the theorem, $p(c^{0i} - \bar{c}^i) = 0$, $i = 1, 2, 3$. Recalling that at the preunion equilibrium, $p(\tilde{c}^i - \bar{c}^i) = 0$, we have $p(c^{0i} - \tilde{c}^i) = 0$. Summing up the two equations, for $i = 1, 2, 3$, respectively, we have

$$\left(\alpha_1 \frac{\partial u_1}{\partial c^1} - p\right)[c^{0i} - \bar{c}^i - (\tilde{c}^i - \bar{c}^i)] = \left(\alpha_1 \frac{\partial u_1}{\partial c^1} - p\right)(c^{0i} - \tilde{c}^i) = 0, \quad i = 1,2,3, \tag{6}$$

where $\alpha_1 \equiv \frac{1}{\partial u_1/\partial c_0^1}$. The left hand side of (6) is the intra-union transfer, and $\alpha_1 \frac{\partial u_1}{\partial c^1} - p$ is the common tariff vector in the union.

4 Concluding Remarks

In this chapter, we have analytically shown that there exists a Pareto-improvement due to the formation of a customs union in a group of three countries. The tariff vector of the union can be computed as the difference between the shadow price vector in the optimization problem and the international price vector p. With the same tariff vector there exists an equilibrium in the sense of $pc^{*i} = p\bar{c}^i$, $i = 1, 2, 3$, while $u_i(c^{*i}) > \tilde{u}_i$, $i = 1,2,3$, under the assumption that the initial state is close to the Pareto frontier. This implies that if the original equilibrium is efficient enough, then there exists a Pareto improvement without intra-union income transfer, because the international price vector has performed its role to allocate consumption goods in the world efficiently.

By mathematical induction, this result can also be extended to the m-country case where $m > 3$. To shorten the chapter, we omitted the proof in this case.

Appendix 1

Proof of Lemma 1

(1) Defining a set D such that for any $(u_2, u_3) \in D, \Gamma(u_2, u_3, s) \neq \emptyset$.
Consider the set of $\Pi^{\varepsilon}(s) \equiv \left\{(c^2, c^3) \geq 0 : s - \sum_{i=2}^{3}(c^i - \bar{c}^i) + \bar{c}^1 \geq \varepsilon e\right\}$ for some $\varepsilon > 0$ small enough and $e \equiv (1, \ldots, 1)$. Let $c_2^M \equiv \frac{s + \bar{c}^1 - \varepsilon e}{2} + \bar{c}^2$, $c_3^M \equiv \frac{s + \bar{c}^1 - \varepsilon e}{2} + \bar{c}^3$, $u_2^M \equiv u_2\left(c_2^M\right)$, and $u_3^M \equiv u_3\left(c_3^M\right)$. Let $D \equiv \left[0, u_2^M\right] \times \left[0, u_3^M\right]$. To show that $\Gamma(u_2, u_3, s) \neq \emptyset$, we only need to show that $\Gamma\left(u_2^M, u_3^M, s\right) \neq \emptyset$ because $\left(u_2^M, u_3^M\right)$ is the largest utilities combination among $(u_2, u_3) \in D$. It can be shown straightforwardly by examination that $s - \sum_{i=2}^{3}\left(c_i^M - \bar{c}^i\right) + \bar{c}^1 = \varepsilon e > 0$.

(2) Setting a Pareto frontier in (u_2, u_3) as a boundary of D^*.
To guarantee that $U_1(u_2, u_3) \geq \tilde{u}_1$, we further restrict the domain to D^*. We do this by setting a Pareto frontier in (u_2, u_3) as a boundary of D^*, on which the utility of country 1 is fixed as $\tilde{u}_1$. First, let $u_2^1 = \min\left\{u_2\left(s + \sum_{i=1}^{3} \bar{c}^i - c^1\right) : s + \sum_{i=1}^{3} \bar{c}^i - c^1 \geq 0, u_1(c^1) = \tilde{u}_1\right\}$. Second, let $u_2^m \equiv \min\{u_2^1, u_2^M\}$. Third, consider problem (4) in the context, and let $G(u_2) = U_3(\tilde{u}_1, u_2) = \max\left\{u_3(c^3) : c^3 = s - \sum_{i=1}^{2} c^i + \sum_{i=1}^{3} \bar{c}^i,\ u_2(c^2) = u_2,\ u_1(c^1) = \tilde{u}_1\right\}$, for $u_2 \leq u_2^m$. By the maximum theorem, $G(u_2)$is continuous. Consider the following Lagrange function:

$$L(c^1, c^2, \lambda, \mu) \equiv u_3\left(s - \sum_{i=1}^{2}(c^i - \bar{c}^i) + \bar{c}^3\right) + \lambda[u_2(c^2) - u_2] + \mu[u_1(c^1) - \tilde{u}_1]. \tag{7}$$

By the envelope theorem, we obtain that

$$\frac{\mathrm{d}G(u_2)}{\mathrm{d}u_2} = -\lambda < 0. \tag{8}$$

That is, $G(u_2)$ is decreasing in u_2, and then the inverse function $G^{-1}(u_3)$ exists. In what follows we simply say G as the frontier of D^*.
Let

$$D^* \equiv \{(u_2, u_3) : 0 \leq u_2 \leq u_2^m, 0 \leq u_3 \leq G(u_2)\}.$$

(3) Finally, we show that $(\tilde{u}_2, \tilde{u}_3)$ lies in the interior of D^*.

This can be shown by considering $U_1(\tilde{u}_2, \tilde{u}_3)$ defined in the context.

From the assumption that there exist $\tilde{c}^i$, $i = 1, 2, 3$, such that $\sum_{i=1}^{3} \tilde{c}^i = s + \sum_{i=1}^{3} \bar{c}^i$, $u_2(\tilde{c}^2) = \tilde{u}_2$, and $u_3(\tilde{c}^3) = \tilde{u}_3$ hold preunion, it follows that $(\tilde{c}^2, \tilde{c}^3) \in \Gamma(\tilde{u}_2, \tilde{u}_3, s)$. That is, $(\tilde{c}^2, \tilde{c}^3)$ is feasible for problem (1) for $(\tilde{u}_2, \tilde{u}_3)$. Since we have assumed that the initial state $(\tilde{u}_1, \tilde{u}_2, \tilde{u}_3)$ is not Pareto optimal, we see that $\tilde{u}_1 = u_1(\tilde{c}^1)$ is not the maximum of problem (1) and $U_1(\tilde{u}_2, \tilde{u}_3) > \tilde{u}_1$. Suppose that $c^1 = (c_0^1, \ldots, c_n^1)$ is the solution to problem (1). Because $u_1(c^1) > u_1(\tilde{c}^1)$, we can choose $\varepsilon > 0$, such that $c_j^1 - \varepsilon \geq 0$ and $u_1(c^1 - \varepsilon e_j) \geq \tilde{u}_1$, where $e_j = (0, \ldots, 0, 1, 0, \ldots, 0)$ for some j, with $c_j^1 > 0$. Providing good j with the amount ε to country 2 and country 3, we have $u_2\left(c^2 + \frac{\varepsilon}{2} e_j\right) > \tilde{u}_2$ and $u_3\left(c^3 + \frac{\varepsilon}{2} e_j\right) > \tilde{u}_3$. Thus, $\left(u_2\left(c^2 + \frac{\varepsilon}{2} e_j\right), u_3\left(c^3 + \frac{\varepsilon}{2} e_j\right)\right) \in D^*$, and we have that $(\tilde{u}_2, \tilde{u}_3)$ lies in the interior of D^* □

Appendix 2

Proof of Lemma 2

(1) For the fixed $s \in R^n$, showing that $\Gamma(u_2,u_3,s)$ is a compact set.
Let $\Pi(s) \equiv \left\{(c^2,c^3) \geq 0 : s - \sum_{i=2}^{3}(c^i - \bar{c}^i) + \bar{c}^1 \geq 0\right\}$ and $\mathrm{M}(u_2,u_3) \equiv \{(c^2,c^3) : u_i \leq u_i(c^i), i = 2,3\}$. We see that $\Gamma(u_2,u_3,s) = \mathrm{M}(u_2,u_3) \cap \Pi(s)$. To show that $\Gamma(u_2,u_3,s)$is compact, first we show that $\Pi(s)$ is nonempty and compact. Since $(\bar{c}^2,\bar{c}^3) \in \Pi(s)$, $\Pi(s) \neq \emptyset$. It is obvious that $\Pi(s)$ is bounded. Next, we show that $\Pi(s)$ is closed. For any $(c^2_\upsilon,c^3_\upsilon) \in \Pi(s)$, and $(c^2_n,c^3_n) \to (c^2_0,c^3_0)$, since $(c^2_\upsilon,c^3_\upsilon) \in \Pi(s)$, we have $s - \sum_{i=2}^{3}(c^i_\upsilon - \bar{c}^i) + \bar{c}^1 \geq 0$. By taking the limit on both sides, we have $s - \sum_{i=2}^{3}(c^i_0 - \bar{c}^i) + \bar{c}^1 \geq 0$. Then $(c^2_0,c^3_0) \in \Pi(s)$. Thus, $\Pi(s)$ is compact. Second, obviously, $M(u_2,u_3)$ is closed. Since $\Gamma(u_2,u_3,s) = M(u_2,u_3) \cap \Pi(s)$, we see that $\Gamma(u_2,u_3,s)$ is compact. Since $u_1\left[s - \sum_{i=2}^{3}(c^i - \bar{c}^i) + \bar{c}^1\right]$ is continuous in (c^2,c^3), there exists a maximum of problem (1).

(2) The uniqueness of the solution
It can be shown in two steps.

(a) $\Gamma(u_2,u_3,s)$ is a convex set.
For any (c'^2,c'^3) and $(c''^2,c''^3) \in \Gamma(u_2,u_3,s)$, $\lambda \in (0,1)$, let $(c^2_\lambda,c^3_\lambda) = \lambda(c'^2,c'^3) + (1-\lambda)(c''^2,c''^3)$. Since the function $u_i(c^i)$, $i = 2,3$, is strictly quasi-concave, we have $u_i(c^i_\lambda) > \min\{u_i(c'^i),u_i(c''^i)\} \geq u_i$, $i = 2,3$.
Furthermore,

$$s - \sum_{i=2}^{3}(c^i_\lambda - \bar{c}^i) + \bar{c}^1 = \lambda\left[s - \sum_{i=2}^{3}(c'^i - \bar{c}^i) + \bar{c}^1\right] + (1-\lambda)$$

$$\left[s - \sum_{i=2}^{3}(c''^i - \bar{c}^i) + \bar{c}^1\right] \quad \geq \lambda\varepsilon + (1-\lambda)\varepsilon = \varepsilon.$$

Therefore, $(c^2_\lambda,c^3_\lambda) \in \Gamma(u_2,u_3,s)$, and then $\Gamma(u_2,u_3,s)$ is a convex set.

(b) The uniqueness of the solution to problem (1).

Suppose that more than one solution to problem (1) exists. Suppose that (c'^2,c^3) and (c'^2,c''^3) are solutions to problem (1), and $(c'^2,c'^3) \neq (c''_2,c''_3)$. Let $c'^1 = s - \sum_{i=2}^{3}(c'^i - \bar{c}^i) + \bar{c}^1$, and $c''^1 = s - \sum_{i=2}^{3}(c''^i - \bar{c}^i) + \bar{c}^1$, $(c^2_\lambda,c^3_\lambda) \equiv \lambda(c'^2,c'^3) + (1-\lambda)(c''^2,c''^3)$, and $c^1_\lambda = s - \sum_{i=2}^{3}(c^i_\lambda - \bar{c}^i) + \bar{c}^1 = \lambda c'^1 + (1-\lambda)c''^1$. From (a), on the one hand, we have $(c^2_\lambda,c^3_\lambda) \in \Gamma(u_2,u_3,s)$. On the other hand, by the strict quasi-concavity of u_1, we have

$$u_1\left(c_\lambda^1\right) = u_1(\lambda c'^1 + (1-\lambda)c''^1) > \min\{u_1(c'^1), u_1(c''^1)\} = u_1(c'^1). \qquad (9)$$

The last equality holds because $u_1(c'^1) = u_1(c''^1)$, by the assumption. This contradicts that $u_1(c'^1)$ is a maximum. Thus, the solution to problem (1) is unique.

Consider the Lagrange function

$$L(c^2, c^3, \lambda, \mu) \equiv u_1\left(s - \sum_{i=2}^{3}(c^i - \bar{c}^i) + \bar{c}^1\right) + \lambda[u_2(c^2) - u_2] + \mu[u_3(c^3) - u_3]. \qquad (10)$$

We obtain the following first order conditions:

$$-\frac{\partial u_1}{\partial c_j^1} + \lambda\frac{\partial u_2}{\partial c_j^2} = 0,\ j = 1, \ldots, n \qquad (11)$$

$$-\frac{\partial u_1}{\partial c_j^1} + \mu\frac{\partial u_3}{\partial c_j^3} = 0,\ j = 1, \ldots, n,\ j = 1, \ldots, n, \qquad (12)$$

$$u_2(c^2) - u_2 = 0, \qquad (13)$$

and

$$u_3(c^3) - u_3 = 0. \qquad (14)$$

Let

$$\Delta \equiv \begin{bmatrix} 0 & 0 & \frac{\partial u_2}{\partial c_1^2} & \frac{\partial u_2}{\partial c_2^2} & \cdots & \frac{\partial u_2}{\partial c_n^2} & 0 & \cdots & 0 \\ 0 & 0 & 0 & \cdots & 0 & \frac{\partial u_3}{\partial c_1^3} & \frac{\partial u_3}{\partial c_2^3} & \cdots & \frac{\partial u_3}{\partial c_n^3} \\ \frac{\partial u_2}{\partial c_1^2} & 0 & u_{11}^1 + \lambda u_{11}^2 & u_{21}^1 + \lambda u_{21}^2 & \cdots & u_{n1}^1 + \lambda u_{n1}^2 & u_{11}^1 & u_{21}^1 & \cdots & u_{n1}^1 \\ \vdots & \vdots & \vdots & & & & & & & \\ \frac{\partial u_2}{\partial c_n^2} & 0 & u_{1n}^1 + \lambda u_{1n}^2 & u_{2n}^1 + \lambda u_{2n}^2 & \cdots & u_{nn}^1 + \lambda u_{nn}^2 & u_{1n}^1 & u_{2n}^1 & \cdots & u_{nn}^1 \\ 0 & \frac{\partial u_3}{\partial c_1^3} & u_{11}^1 & u_{21}^1 & \cdots & u_{n1}^1 & u_{11}^1 + \mu u_{11}^3 & u_{21}^1 + \mu u_{21}^3 & \cdots & u_{n1}^1 + \mu u_{n1}^3 \\ \vdots & \vdots & \vdots & & & & & & & \\ 0 & \frac{\partial u_3}{\partial c_n^3} & u_{1n}^1 & u_{2n}^1 & \cdots & u_{nn}^1 & u_{1n}^1 + \mu u_{1n}^3 & u_{2n}^1 + \mu u_{2n}^3 & \cdots & u_{nn}^1 + \mu u_{nn}^3 \end{bmatrix}$$

Because of the uniqueness of the solution to the problem, $\Delta \neq 0$. By the implicit function theorem, there exists a neighborhood of (u_2, u_3) such that $c^i = \varphi^i(u_2, u_3)$ is continuously differentiable in the neighborhood, $i = 1, 2$. From the definition of ψ^i, it follows that ψ^i is continuously differentiable in this neighborhood also. □

Appendix 3

Proof of Lemma 3

(A) By Assumption 1, there exists $p^* > 0$ such that $p^*[\varphi^1(u_2^*, u_3^*) - \bar{c}^1] = 0$, $p^*[\varphi^2(u_2^*, u_3^*) - \bar{c}^2] = 0$, and $p^*[\varphi^3(u_2^*, u_3^*) - \bar{c}^3] = 0$, for (u_1^*, u_2^*, u_3^*) on the Pareto frontier, with $u_1^* > \tilde{u}_1$, $u_2^* > \tilde{u}_2$, and $u_3^* > \tilde{u}_3$. Since $u_1^* > \tilde{u}_1$, $u_2^* > \tilde{u}_2$, and $u_3^* > \tilde{u}_3$, there exists $\tilde{c}'^1, \tilde{c}'^2, \tilde{c}'^3$, such that $\tilde{u}_i = u_i(\tilde{c}'^i)$ and $p^*[\tilde{c}'^i - \bar{c}^i] < 0$. The consumption bundle $\tilde{c}'^i$ can be obtained by reducing some components of $\varphi^i(u_2^*, u_3^*)$ till the utility of the new consumption bundle reaches $\tilde{u}_i$, for $i = 1, 2, 3$.

(B) Let $G^{-1}(u_3) \equiv U_2(\tilde{u}_1, u_3)$. Noting that $(U_2(\tilde{u}_1, u_3), u_3)$ lies on the boundary of D^*, we can denote $U_2(\tilde{u}_1, u_3)$ as $G^{-1}(u_3)$. Now, we show that on the Pareto frontier, $(U_1(\tilde{u}_2, \tilde{u}_3), \tilde{u}_2, \tilde{u}_3)$, $(\tilde{u}_1, \tilde{u}_2, G(\tilde{u}_2))$, and $(\tilde{u}_1, G^{-1}(\tilde{u}_3), \tilde{u}_3)$ are close to (u_1^*, u_2^*, u_3^*).
This can be shown as follows (we only show the last case):

From Assumption 1 (1), $u_2^* = \max\limits_{(c^1,c^3)\in\Gamma(u_1^*,u_3^*)} u_2\left(s - c^1 - c^3 + \sum\limits_{i=1}^{3} \bar{c}^i\right) = U_2(u_1^*, u_3^*)$. By the maximum theorem, $U_2(u_1, u_3)$ is continuous with respect to (u_1, u_3). Since $(\tilde{u}_1, \tilde{u}_3)$ is close to (u_1^*, u_3^*), $U_2(\tilde{u}_1, \tilde{u}_3) = G^{-1}(\tilde{u}_3)$ is close to $U_2(u_1^*, u_3^*) = u_2^*$. That is, $(\tilde{u}_1, G^{-1}(\tilde{u}_3), \tilde{u}_3)$ is close to (u_1^*, u_2^*, u_3^*).

(C) Next, we show that $(\tilde{u}_1, u_2, G(u_2))$ and $(\tilde{u}_1, G^{-1}(u_3), u_3)$ are close to (u_1^*, u_2^*, u_3^*) for every $\tilde{u}_2 \le u_2 \le G^{-1}(\tilde{u}_3)$ and $\tilde{u}_3 \le u_3 \le G^{-1}(\tilde{u}_2)$, respectively.

For $\tilde{u}_2 \le u_2 \le G^{-1}(\tilde{u}_3)$, since both $\tilde{u}_2$ and $G^{-1}(\tilde{u}_3)$ are close to u_2^*, u_2 is close to u_2^* also. Since G is continuous and decreasing for $\tilde{u}_2 \le u_2 \le G^{-1}(\tilde{u}_3)$, we have $\tilde{u}_3 \le G(u_2) \le G(\tilde{u}_2)$. From the fact that $G(\tilde{u}_2)$ and $\tilde{u}_3$ are close to u_3^*, it follows that $G(u_2)$ is close to u_3^*. Thus, $(\tilde{u}_1, u_2, G(u_2))$ is close to (u_1^*, u_2^*, u_3^*) for every $\tilde{u}_2 \le u_2 \le G^{-1}(\tilde{u}_3)$. Similarly, we can show the latter case.

(D) The shadow prices defined as

$$p'^*(u_2, u_3) = \alpha_1\left(\frac{\partial u_1}{\partial c_0^1}, \ldots, \frac{\partial u_1}{\partial c_n^1}\right) = \alpha_2\left(\frac{\partial u_2}{\partial c_0^2}, \ldots, \frac{\partial u_2}{\partial c_n^2}\right) = \alpha_3\left(\frac{\partial u_3}{\partial c_0^3}, \ldots, \frac{\partial u_3}{\partial c_n^3}\right),$$

$\alpha_i > 0, i = 1, 2, 3$, where $\alpha_1 = \frac{1}{\partial u_1/\partial c_0^1}$, $\alpha_2 = \alpha_1\lambda$, and $\alpha_3 = \alpha_1\mu$ in problem (1) are close to p^*, whenever (u_2, u_3) is close to (u_2^*, u_3^*). This is because$p'^*(u_2, u_3)$ is continuous with the solution (c^2, c^3), and the solution is continuous with respect to (u_2, u_3).

Now, we proceed to show (1) of this lemma.

(1) Let (c'^{*1}, c'^{*2}) be a solution so that $G(u_2)$ is the maximum of problem (4). From (D), we have $\alpha_3(p'_{0^*}, \ldots, p'_{n^*}) \equiv \left(\frac{\partial u_3}{\partial c_0'^{*3}}, \ldots, \frac{\partial u_3}{\partial c_n'^{*3}}\right)$, with $\alpha_3 > 0$, where $c'^{*3} = s - \sum\limits_{i=1}^{2} c'^{*i} + \bar{c}^3$. To show that $\psi^1(u_2, G(u_2)) < 0$ on the frontier of D^*, first we

show that $p(c'^{*1} - \bar{c}^1) < 0$. Consider a new function

$$f(\lambda) \equiv u_3 \left[s - (1-\lambda)c'^{*1} - \lambda \tilde{c}'^1 - c'^{*2} + \sum_{i=1}^{3} \bar{c}^i \right].$$

Since (c'^{*1}, c'^{*2}) is the unique solution to problem (4), we have $f(\lambda) < f(0)$ for any $\lambda > 0$. It follows that $\frac{f(\lambda)-f(0)}{\lambda} < 0$. Taking the limit on both sides of the inequality, we have $\lim_{\lambda \to 0} \frac{f(\lambda)-f(0)}{\lambda} = f'(0) \leq 0$. On the other hand, by differentiating f with respect to λ, we have $f'(0) = \sum_{j=0}^{n} \frac{\partial u_3}{\partial c_j^3}\Big|_{(c'^{*1}, c'^{*2})} \left[c_j'^{*1} - \tilde{c}_j'^1 \right] = \alpha_3 \sum_{j=0}^{n} p_j'^* \left[c_j'^{*1} - \tilde{c}_j'^1 \right] \leq 0$. Suppose $f'(0) < 0$. We have $\sum_{j=0}^{n} p'^*[c'^{*1} - \tilde{c}_j'^1] < 0$. That is, $p'^* c'^{*1} < p'^* \tilde{c}'^1$. Since p'^* is close to p^*, we also have $p^* c'^{*1} < p^* \tilde{c}'^1$, and then $p^*[c'^{*1} - \bar{c}^1] < p^*(\tilde{c}'^1 - \bar{c}^1) < 0$. Since p is close to p^*, we have $p[c'^{*1} - \bar{c}^1] < p(\tilde{c}'^1 - \bar{c}^1) < 0$.

If $f'(0) = 0$, then $p'^* c'^{*1} = p'^* \tilde{c}'^1$. We also have $p'^* c'^{*1} - p'^* \bar{c}^1 = p'^* \tilde{c}'^1 - p'^* \bar{c}^1$, that is, $p'^*(c'^{*1} - \bar{c}^1) = p'^*(\tilde{c}'^1 - \bar{c}^1)$. Since $p^*(\tilde{c}'^1 - \bar{c}^1) < 0$, and p'^* is close to p^*, we also have $p'^*(\tilde{c}'^1 - \bar{c}^1) < 0$. Thus, we have $p'^*(c'^{*1} - \bar{c}^1) = p'^*(\tilde{c}'^1 - \bar{c}^1) < 0$. Since p is close to p'^*, we have $p(c'^{*1} - \bar{c}^1) < 0$. Now, we have shown that in either case $p(c'^{*1} - \bar{c}^1) < 0$ holds.

Next, we calculate $\psi^1(u_2, G(u_2))$according to the above result. Substituting $G(u_2) = u_3(c'^{*3})$for u_3 in problem (1), we obtain that $U_1(u_2, G(u_2)) = \tilde{u}_1$, and $c'^{*1} = \varphi^1(u_2, G(u_2))$, because problem (1) for $(u_2, G(u_2))$ and problem (4) for $(\tilde{u}_1, u_2)$ are the same problems. Then, by the definition of ψ^1, we have $p(c'^{*1} - \bar{c}^1) = \psi^1(u_2, G(u_2)) < 0$ for any $\tilde{u}_2 \leq u_2 \leq G^{-1}(\tilde{u}_3)$. From $0 = ps = \sum_{i=1}^{3} \psi^i(u_2, u_3)$, we have $\psi^2(u_2, G(u_2)) + \psi^3(u_2, G(u_2)) > 0$ on the frontier for $\tilde{u}_2 \leq u_2 \leq G^{-1}(\tilde{u}_3)$.

(2) Substituting $\tilde{u}_2$ and u_3 in problem (1), by an argument similar to (1), we can show that $\psi^2(\tilde{u}_2, u_3) < 0$ for $\tilde{u}_3 \leq u_3 \leq G(\tilde{u}_2)$. Similarly, we can show that $\psi^3(u_2, \tilde{u}_3) < 0$ for $\tilde{u}_2 \leq u_2 \leq G^{-1}(\tilde{u}_3)$.

(3) Especially, from (1) and (2), $\psi^2(\tilde{u}_2, G(\tilde{u}_2)) + \psi^3(\tilde{u}_2, G(\tilde{u}_2)) > 0$ and $\psi^2(\tilde{u}_2, G(\tilde{u}_2)) < 0$, we have $\psi^3(\tilde{u}_2, G(\tilde{u}_2)) > 0$. Similarly, we have $\psi^2(G^{-1}(\tilde{u}_3), \tilde{u}_3) > 0$.

Appendix 4

Proof of Lemma 4

We show this lemma in the following steps:

(1) There exists $\tilde{u}_3 < u_3^l < G(\tilde{u}_2)$, such that $\psi^3(\tilde{u}_2, u_3^l) = 0$ and $\psi^2(\tilde{u}_2, u_3^l) < 0$.

By Lemma 3 (2) and (3), $\psi^3(\tilde{u}_2,\tilde{u}_3)<0$ and $\psi^3(\tilde{u}_2,G(\tilde{u}_2))>0$. By the mean value theorem, there exists $\tilde{u}_3<u_3^l<G(\tilde{u}_2)$ such that $\psi^3(\tilde{u}_2,u_3^l)=0$. By Lemma 3 (2), we have $\psi^2(\tilde{u}_2,u_3^l)<0$.

(2) There exists $(u_2^f,G(u_2^f))$ on the frontier of D^*, such that $\psi^3(u_2^f,G(u_2^f))=0$.
From Lemma 3 (2) and (3), $\psi^3(G^{-1}(\tilde{u}_3),\tilde{u}_3)<0$ and $\psi^3(\tilde{u}_2,G(\tilde{u}_2))>0$, by the mean value theorem, there exists $\tilde{u}_2<u_2^{<}G^{-1}(\tilde{u}_3)$ such that $\psi^3(u_2,G(u_2))=0$. If there exists more than one such point, let u_2^f be the smallest one. From Lemma 3 (1), $\psi^2(u_2^f,G(u_2^f))+\psi^3(u_2^f,G(u_2^f))>0$ and $\psi^3(u_2^f,G(u_2^f))=0$, it follows that $\psi^2(u_2^f,G(u_2^f))>0$.

(3) For any $u_2\in[\tilde{u}_2,u_2^f]$, there exists a correspondence $\vartheta(u_2)$, such that $\psi^3(u_2,\vartheta(u_2))=0$.
In Lemma 3 (3), we have shown that $\psi^3(\tilde{u}_2,G(\tilde{u}_2))>0$. Now, we want to show that $\psi^3(u_2,G(u_2))>0$ for $u_2\in(\tilde{u}_2,u_2^f)$. Conversely, suppose there exists $u_2'\in(\tilde{u}_2,u_2^f)$ such that $\psi^3(u_2',G(u_2'))\le 0$. Since u_2^f is the smallest number such that $\psi^3(u_2^f,G(u_2^f))=0$, we see that $\psi^3(u_2',G(u_2'))\neq 0$. Then $\psi^3(u_2',G(u_2'))<0$. Since $\psi^3(\tilde{u}_2,G(\tilde{u}_2))>0$, by the mean value theorem, $\tilde{u}_2<u_2''<u_2'<u_2^f$ would exist such that $\psi^3(u_2'',G(u_2''))=0$. This contradicts the definition of u_2^f. Thus, $\psi^3(u_2,G(u_2))>0$, for $u_2\in(\tilde{u}_2,u_2^f)$.
For any $u_2\in(\tilde{u}_2,u_2^f)$, from Lemma 3 (2), $\psi^3(u_2,\tilde{u}_3)<0$. By the above, $\psi^3(u_2,G(u_2))>0$. By the mean value theorem, there exists $\tilde{u}_3<u_3^{u_2}<G(u_2)$ such that $\psi^3(u_2,u_3^{u_2})=0$ for any $u_2\in(\tilde{u}_2,u_2^f)$. On the two points $\tilde{u}_2$ and u_2^f, from (1) and (2) in this proof, we have $\psi^3(\tilde{u}_2,u_3^l)=0$ and $\psi^3(u_2^f,G(u_2^f))=0$. Thus, for any $u_2\in[\tilde{u}_2,u_2^f]$, there exists a correspondence $\vartheta(u_2)\neq\emptyset$, such that $\psi^3(u_2,u_3^{u_2})=0$ for $u_3^{u_2}\in\vartheta(u_2)$.

(4) $\vartheta(u_2)$ is upper-hemi continuous.
Let $\{u_2^n\}\subset[\tilde{u}_2,u_2^f]$, $u_2^n\to u_2^0$, and $u_3^n\in\vartheta(u_2^n)$, $n=1,\ldots$. We want to show that there exists a subsequence $\{u_3^{n_k}\}$ of $\{u_3^n\}$, such that $u_3^{n_k}\to u_3^0$ and $u_3^0\in\vartheta(u_2^0)$. Since D^* is bounded, we see that $\{u_3^n\}$ is bounded. Thus, there exists a subsequence $\{u_3^{n_k}\}\subset\vartheta(u_2^{n_k})$, such that $u_3^{n_k}\to u_3^0$. Now, we show that $u_3^0\in\tau(u_2^0)$. From the definition of $\vartheta(u_2^{n_k})$, $\psi^3(u_2^{n_k},u_3^{n_k})=0$. By taking the limit on both sides, since ψ^3 is continuous, we have $\psi^3(u_2^0,u_3^0)=0$ and $u_3^0\in\vartheta(u_2^0)$. Thus, $\vartheta(u_2)$ is an upper-hemi continuous correspondence.

(5) $\vartheta(u_2)$ is a singleton and then $\vartheta(u_2)$ is a continuous function.
Differentiating (14) with respect to u_3, we have

$$1=\frac{\partial u_3}{\partial c_1^3}\frac{\partial c_1^3}{\partial u_3}+\cdots+\frac{\partial u_3}{\partial c_n^3}\frac{\partial c_n^3}{\partial u_3}. \tag{15}$$

Since $\left(\frac{\partial u_3}{\partial c_1^3},\ldots,\frac{\partial u_3}{\partial c_n^3}\right)=\alpha_3(p_1'^*,\ldots,p_n'^*)$, $\alpha_3>0$ (15) implies that $\frac{1}{\alpha_3}=p_1'^*\frac{\partial c_1^3}{\partial u_3}+\cdots+p_n'^*\frac{\partial c_n^3}{\partial u_3}$. That is, $p_1'^*\frac{\partial c_1^3}{\partial u_3}+\cdots+p_n'^*\frac{\partial c_n^3}{\partial u_3}>0$ for $\alpha_3>0$. By our assumption, p'^* is close to p. It follows that $p_1\frac{\partial c_1^3}{\partial u_3}+\ldots+p_n\frac{\partial c_n^3}{\partial u_3}>0$. Namely,

$\frac{\partial \psi^3}{\partial u_3}(u_2,u_3) > 0$. That is, $\psi^3(u_2,u_3)$ is strictly increasing in u_3. Thus, there exists only one u_3' such that $\psi^3(u_2,u_3') = 0$, for each $u_2 \in [\tilde{u}_2, u_2^f]$. Namely, $\vartheta(u_2)$ is a function. From the fact that $\vartheta(u_2)$ is upper-hemi continuous, it follows that $\vartheta(u_2)$ is a continuous function.

(6) There exists $u_2^0 \in (\tilde{u}_2, u_2^f)$, such that both $\psi^2(u_2^0, \vartheta(u_2^0)) = 0$ and $\psi^3(u_2^0, \vartheta(u_2^0)) = 0$ hold.

Let $\xi(u_2) \equiv \psi^2(u_2, \vartheta(u_2))$. Then $\xi(u_2)$ is a continuous function of u_2, since ψ^2 and ϑ are continuous. From (1) and (2) in this proof, we have $\xi(\tilde{u}_2) = \psi^2(\tilde{u}_2, \vartheta(\tilde{u}_2)) = \psi^2(\tilde{u}_2, u_3^l) < 0$ and $\xi(u_2^f) = \psi^2(u_2^f, \vartheta(u_2^f)) = \psi^2(u_2^f, G(u_2^f)) > 0$. Then by the mean value theorem, there exists $u_2^0 \in (\tilde{u}_2, u_2^f)$ such that $\xi(u_2^0) = 0$. That is, $\xi(u_2^0) = \psi^2(u_2^0, \vartheta(u_2^0)) = 0$. At the same time, from the definition of ϑ, we also have $\psi^3(u_2^0, \vartheta(u_2^0)) = 0$. □

Acknowledgment Qi Ling thanks Professor Kazuo Nishimura and Professor Makoto Tawada for their constant encouragement. Thanks are also due to Professor Murray Kemp for his helpful comments on this chapter.

References

Debreu G (1959) Theory of value. Wiley, New York

Kemp MC, Shimomura K (2001) A second elementary proposition concerning the formation of customs unions. Jpn Econ Rev 52:64–69

Kemp MC, Wan HY Jr (1976) An elementary proposition concerning the formation of customs unions. J Int Econ 6:95–97

Iwasa, Riezman and Shimomura (2008) Pareto-improving trading clubs without income transfers are generally possible, mimeographed

Ohyama M (1972) Trade and welfare in general equilibrium. Keio Econ Stud 9:37–73

Panagariya A, Krishna P (2002) On necessarily welfare-enhancing free trade areas. J Int Econ 57:353–367

Environment and the Harris and Todaro Paradoxes

Makoto Tawada(✉) and Azusa Nakamura

Abstract There are two well-known paradoxical results in the Harris and Todaro model. One is that subsidization policies for the manufacturing sector are not effective, but those for the agricultural sector are effective for reducing urban unemployment. The other is that unemployment expands as a result of an increase in the capital endowment, but contracts as a result of an increase in the labor endowment. In the present analysis, environmental elements are introduced into the model, and we show that a decrease in the discharge rate of pollution may enhance urban unemployment, while the paradoxical results that occur with a change in the factor endowment disappear.

1 Introduction

Many studies have appeared in which policies aimed at the economic development of developing countries are analyzed. In the theoretical approach, there are two main well-known models. One is the model constructed by Lewis (1954), who focused on the agricultural sector in a rural area where a large amount of surplus labor existed. The other model, considered by Harris and Todaro (1970), focused on the manufacturing sector in an urban area where unemployed workers remained in the hope of obtaining a job opportunity in the manufacturing sector. To rationalize this aspect, Harris and Todaro assumed that the government introduces minimum wage legislation in the urban area. In the recent economic experience of developing countries, the existence of unemployment in urban areas has become a serious obstacle to smooth economic development. So the latter model, namely the Harris and Todaro model, has attracted the interest of many development economists in recent decades.

M. Tawada
Graduate School of Economics, Nagoya University, Furo-cho, Chikusa-ku, Nagoya 464-8601, Japan, e-mail: mtawada@soec.nagoya-u.ac.jp

T. Kamihigashi and L. Zhao (eds.) *International Trade and Economic Dynamics – Essays in Memory of Koji Shimomura.*

In their model, Harris and Todaro considered a developing country where two sectors exist: a manufacturing sector in an urban area and an agricultural sector in a rural area. There are two productive factors, capital and labor. The government adopts minimum wage legislation in the urban manufacturing sector, so that the wage in the manufacturing sector is fixed at a certain wage level, which is above the agricultural wage. Consequently, this legislation generates unemployment in the urban area. The workers in the rural area, however, tend to move to the urban area as long as the expected wage in the urban area is higher than the agricultural wage. In an economy having this characteristic, Harris and Todaro (1970), Corden and Findley (1975), Neary (1981), and many others investigated desirable policies for the promotion of economic development and the reduction of urban unemployment.[1]

One of their main results, particularly in the case of mobile capital, is that subsidization policies for the manufacturing sector are not effective for reducing urban unemployment, but those policies are suitable for the agricultural sector. The result seems intuitively paradoxical, and it is thus regarded as one of the Harris and Todaro paradoxes. Another paradoxical result arises in the case of mobile capital. If the endowment of capital increases, urban unemployment increases. In contrast, if the endowment of labor increases, then urban unemployment decreases.

One of the contemporary and serious issues facing developing countries is an environmental pollution problem arising from the strong promotion of economic growth. Thus, we focus on this aspect of the Harris and Todaro framework by assuming that the production activity in the manufacturing sector generates pollution, which affects the productivity of the agricultural sector. We then investigate the economic effects of environmental pollution and of factor endowment by a simple comparative static analysis and examine whether or not those paradoxical results still hold. Before going into the main analysis, we examine the stability of equilibrium. The stability condition obtained in our analysis is rather opposite to the one obtained by Neary (1981). In our comparative static analysis, it is shown that there emerges a paradoxical result for the generation rate of pollution, but that the paradox caused by a change in the factor endowment disappears.

The chapter is organized as follows. The Sect. 2 introduces the model, Sect. 3 presents the stability analysis. Then we proceed with the comparative static analysis in Sect. 4. The final section offers some summary remarks.

2 Model

Consider a small open economy where there are two production sectors and two productive factors. The two sectors include a manufacturing sector located in an urban area and an agricultural sector located in a rural area. The two factors are capital and

[1] In their analyses, Harris and Todaro (1970) considered a model where capital is sector-specific and goods are non-tradable, while Corden and Findley (1975), Neary (1981), and others assumed in the model that capital is mobile and goods are tradable.

labor, both of which are domestically mobile between sectors but internationally immobile. The goods produced in the two sectors are assumed to be tradable.

In the urban area, the government adopts minimum wage legislation, so that the workers in the manufacturing sector are paid the minimum wage that is fixed by the government. We assume that the minimum wage is higher than the wage prevailing in the agricultural sector initially. This induces labor movement from the rural to the urban areas. In the urban area, workers are uncertain about whether they can be employed or not. Even if a worker could not get a job in the urban area, he/she would stay there to seek a manufacturing job opportunity. Therefore, when workers make a decision about whether to move between the two areas, they compare the agricultural wage with the expected wage of the urban area. This implies that the arbitrage condition in the labor movement is to equate the agricultural wage with the expected wage of the urban area.

We consider that pollution is generated by the production activity in the manufacturing sector. And the pollution damages the quality of the natural environment, which in turn affects the productivity of the agricultural sector.[2]

The production functions of both sectors are described as

$$M = F^M(L_M, K_M) \tag{1}$$

and

$$A = G(E)F^A(L_A, K_A), \tag{2}$$

where M and A are the outputs of the manufacturing and agricultural sectors, respectively; L_i and K_i are the labor and capital employed in each sector, respectively ($i = A, M$); E stands for the quality of the natural environment, and $G(E)$, with the properties $G > 0$, $G' \equiv \mathrm{d}G/\mathrm{d}E > 0$, and $G'' \equiv \mathrm{d}^2G/\mathrm{d}E^2 < 0$, represents the effect of the natural environment on agricultural productivity. We assume that F^i is strictly quasi-concave and linearly homogeneous. Therefore, the better is the quality of the natural environment, the higher is the productivity of the agricultural sector.

Pollution is generated in the following fashion:

$$Z = \lambda M, \tag{3}$$

where Z is the amount of pollution and λ is a positive parameter expressing the generation rate of pollution. Thus one unit of manufacturing output generates λ units of pollution.

The quality of the natural environment changes from time to time according to the difference between the self-recovering rate and the temporal amount of pollution. Thus, the dynamic process of the natural environment is expressed as

$$\dot{E} = g(\bar{E} - E) - Z, \tag{4}$$

where $\bar{E}$ is a positive and constant parameter showing the best quality of the natural environment and g is a positive and constant parameter expressing the self-recovering rate of the natural environment. At the steady state of (4), it holds

[2] This formulation of environmental externalities relies on Copeland and Taylor (1999)

from (1) and (3) that

$$E = \bar{E} - (\lambda/g)F^M(L_M, K_M), \tag{5}$$

where we assume E to be always positive in our analysis.

The labor endowment of this country, say L, is supposed to be given and is a constant. The full employment condition of labor is assumed, so that we have

$$L_M + L_A + L_U = L, \tag{6}$$

where L_U is the amount of urban unemployment.

Let the minimum wage of the urban manufacturing sector be $\bar{w}$, which is institutionally fixed. Then, the arbitrage condition for the workers is

$$w_A = \frac{\bar{w}L_M}{L_M + L_U}, \tag{7}$$

where w_A is the wage of the rural agricultural sector and the RHS of (7) is the expected wage in the urban area.

We assume that perfect competition is prevailing in both sectors. This implies

$$pF_L^M(L_M, K_M) = \bar{w} \tag{8}$$

and

$$G(E)F_L^A(L_A, K_A) = w_A, \tag{9}$$

by profit maximization in each sector, where p is the price of the manufacturing sector relative to that of the agricultural sector and $F_L^i \equiv \partial F^i/\partial L_i$, for $i = M, A$.

We assume that the capital endowment, say K, is given and is constant. The full employment condition of capital is also assumed, so that

$$K_M + K_A = K. \tag{10}$$

In the equilibrium of the capital market, the following condition must be satisfied by profit maximization in each sector:

$$pF_K^M(L_M, K_M) = G(E)F_K^A(L_A, K_A) = r, \tag{11}$$

where r is the rental price of capital and $F_K^i \equiv \partial F^i/\partial K_i$, $i = M, A$.

To sum up, ten endogenous equations, (1), (2), (5), (6), (7), (8), (9), (10), and (11), determine ten endogenous variables, M, A, E, L_M, L_A, L_U, K_M, K_A, w_A, and r.

3 The Stability Analysis

The general equilibrium model presented in the previous section differs from the traditional neoclassical model in two aspects. One is the introduction of the institutionally fixed urban minimum wage, which yields urban unemployment. The other is that the agricultural productivity is influenced by the quality of the natural environment characterized as an externality in the economy. These features may disturb the stability assured in the traditional neoclassical economy. Thus, prior to our main analysis, we have to examine the stability in the present model.[3]

The adjustment process of the natural environment presented in the previous section can be rewritten as

$$\dot{E} = g(\bar{E} - E) - \lambda F^M(L_M, K_M) \equiv \phi(E). \tag{12}$$

The global stability condition of this adjustment process is

$$\begin{aligned} \frac{\mathrm{d}\phi}{\mathrm{d}E} &= -g - \lambda F_L^M \frac{\mathrm{d}L_M}{\mathrm{d}E} - \lambda F_K^M \frac{\mathrm{d}K_M}{\mathrm{d}E} \\ &= -g - \lambda \left[F_L^M \frac{\mathrm{d}L_M}{\mathrm{d}E} + F_K^M \frac{\mathrm{d}K_M}{\mathrm{d}E} \right] < 0. \end{aligned} \tag{13}$$

To examine whether condition (13) is satisfied, we first study $F_L^M(\mathrm{d}L_M / \mathrm{d}E) + F_K^M(\mathrm{d}K_M / \mathrm{d}E)$ in (13). Total differentiation of (6)–(11) yields the following equation system:

$$\begin{bmatrix} 1 & 1 & 1 & 0 & 0 & 0 \\ \bar{w}L_U/(L_M+L_U)^2 & 0 & -\bar{w}L_M/(L_M+L_U)^2 & 0 & 0 & -1 \\ pF_{LL}^M & 0 & 0 & pF_{LK}^M & 0 & 0 \\ 0 & GF_{LL}^A & 0 & 0 & GF_{LK}^A & -1 \\ 0 & 0 & 0 & 1 & 1 & 0 \\ pF_{KL}^M & -GF_{KL}^A & 0 & pF_{KK}^M & -GF_{KK}^A & 0 \end{bmatrix} \begin{bmatrix} \mathrm{d}L_M \\ \mathrm{d}L_A \\ \mathrm{d}L_U \\ \mathrm{d}K_M \\ \mathrm{d}K_A \\ \mathrm{d}w_A \end{bmatrix} = \begin{bmatrix} 0 \\ 0 \\ 0 \\ -G'F_L^A \\ 0 \\ G'F_K^A \end{bmatrix} \mathrm{d}E, \tag{14}$$

where $F_{KL}^i \equiv \partial^2 F^i / \partial K_i \partial L_i = \partial^2 F^i / \partial L_i \partial K_i \equiv F_{LK}^i > 0, F_{KK}^i = \partial^2 F^i / \partial K^2 < 0$, and $F_{LL}^i = \partial^2 F^i / \partial L_i^2$, for $i = M, A$.

We define the determinant of the square matrix of LHS in (14) as J. Then, after tedious calculation, we obtain the determinant J as

$$J = pG \frac{\bar{w}}{(L_M + L_U)} \frac{F_{LK}^M F_{KL}^A L_A}{K_A} \left(\frac{K_A}{L_A} - \frac{K_M}{L_M + L_U} \right).$$

Thus the following relation holds:

$$K_A/L_A > (<) K_M/(L_M + L_U) \Leftrightarrow J > (<)\ 0. \tag{15}$$

[3] Here we introduce a dynamic adjustment of E, while other variables like K and L are assumed to adjust instantaneously. This is because we consider the environment to take quite a long time to adjust in comparison with other variables. See Tawada (2007) for the stability discussion, including the dynamic adjustment of other variables.

Let $\boldsymbol{a}$ be the coefficient vector of dE in the RHS of (14) and $\boldsymbol{i}$ be the ith column vector of the square matrix of the LHS in (14), for $\mathbf{i} = \mathbf{1}, \ldots, \mathbf{6}$. Then, applying Cramer's rule to (14), we have

$$\begin{aligned}
&\left(F_L^M \frac{\mathrm{d}L_M}{\mathrm{d}E} + F_K^M \frac{\mathrm{d}K_M}{\mathrm{d}E}\right) J \\
&= F_L^M \left| \boldsymbol{a},\mathbf{2},\mathbf{3},\mathbf{4},\mathbf{5},\mathbf{6} \right| + F_K^M \left| \mathbf{1},\mathbf{2},\mathbf{3},\boldsymbol{a},\mathbf{5},\mathbf{6} \right| \\
&= \left| \boldsymbol{a},\mathbf{2},\mathbf{3},F_L^M \mathbf{4},\mathbf{5},\mathbf{6} \right| + \left| F_K^M \mathbf{1},\mathbf{2},\mathbf{3},\boldsymbol{a},\mathbf{5},\mathbf{6} \right| \\
&= \left| \boldsymbol{a},\mathbf{2},\mathbf{3},F_L^M \mathbf{4},\mathbf{5},\mathbf{6} \right| - \left| \boldsymbol{a},\mathbf{2},\mathbf{3},F_K^M \mathbf{1},\mathbf{5},\mathbf{6} \right| \\
&= \left| \boldsymbol{a},\mathbf{2},\mathbf{3},F_L^M \mathbf{4} - F_K^M \mathbf{1},\mathbf{5},\mathbf{6} \right| \equiv J^*.
\end{aligned}$$ [4]

Again, after tedious calculation, we obtain

$$J^* = \begin{vmatrix}
0 & 1 & 1 & -F_K^M & 0 & 0 \\
0 & 0 & \frac{-\bar{w}L_M}{(L_m+L_U)^2} & \frac{-F_K^M \bar{w}L_U}{(L_M+L_U)^2} & 0 & -1 \\
0 & 0 & 0 & pF_L^M F_{LK}^M - pF_K^M F_{LL}^M & 0 & 0 \\
-G'F_L^A & GF_{LL}^A & 0 & 0 & GF_{LK}^A & -1 \\
0 & 0 & 0 & F_L^M & 1 & 0 \\
G'F_K^A & -GF_{KL}^A & 0 & pF_L^M F_{kk}^M - pF_K^M F_{KL}^M & -GF_{kk}^A & 0
\end{vmatrix}$$

$$= p\left(F_L^M F_{LK}^M - F_K^M F_{LL}^M\right) G' \left(G\left(F_L^A F_{KL}^A - F_K^A F_{LL}^A\right) + \frac{F_K^A \bar{w} L_M}{(L_M+L_U)^2} \right) > 0.$$

Subsequently, it is shown from (15) that

$$F_L^M \frac{\mathrm{d}L_M}{\mathrm{d}E} + F_K^M \frac{\mathrm{d}K_M}{\mathrm{d}E} = \frac{J^*}{J} > (<) 0 \Leftrightarrow \frac{K_A}{L_A} > (<) \frac{K_M}{L_M + L_U}.$$

Hence, if $K_A/L_A > K_M/(L_M + L_U)$, implying that the urban area is more labor-abundant than the rural area, the equilibrium is globally stable under (12).

Theorem 1. *If the urban area is more labor-abundant than the rural area, the equilibrium is globally stable under the dynamic process given in (12).*

Therefore, we make the following assumption.

Assumption 1. The urban area is more labor-abundant than the rural area, that is, $K_A/L_A > K_M/(L_M + L_U)$.

Neary (1981) examined the stability condition of the Harris and Todaro model without environmental pollution. He employed the dynamic adjustment of factors according to the difference in factor reward between sectors. Under this process, he showed that a sufficient condition for the stability is that $K_A/L_A < K_M/(L_M + L_U)$,

[4] In the formulation, $|\mathbf{a}, \mathbf{2}, \mathbf{3}, \mathbf{4}, \mathbf{5}, \mathbf{6}|$ is defined as a determinant of the matrix associated with vectors **a**, **2**, **3**, **4**, **5**, and **6**, for example.

that is, the urban area is more capital-abundant. Thus, the sufficient condition of our case is rather opposite to that of their case.

4 Comparative Static Analysis

We are now in a position to tackle the comparative static analysis in our model. In the present H-T model with environmental elements, our main concern is how the generation rate of pollution affects the economy. In most developing countries, one of the contemporary issues is how economic development can be achieved without the environmental damage caused by pollution. Thus, these countries are eager to introduce better production technologies so that less pollution will be generated by production activities. One of the direct ways to obtain better technologies is to rely on technology transfer from advanced countries through ODA without any cost. In fact, the Japanese government has been carrying out such technology transfer to south-east Asian countries. The economic impact of this type of technology transfer to developing countries would be reflected by a decrease in λ in the present model. Thus, first we investigate the economic impact of a change in λ.

To this end we differentiate (5) and (6)–(11) totally and obtain

$$\begin{bmatrix} (\lambda/g)F_L^M & 0 & 0 & (\lambda/g)F_K^M & 0 & 1 & 0 \\ 1 & 1 & 1 & 0 & 0 & 0 & 0 \\ \bar{w}L_U/(L_M+L_U)^2 & 0 & -\bar{w}L_M/(L_M+L_U)^2 & 0 & 0 & 0 & -1 \\ pF_{LL}^M & 0 & 0 & pF_{LK}^M & 0 & 0 & 0 \\ 0 & GF_{LL}^A & 0 & 0 & GF_{LK}^A & G'F_L^A & -1 \\ 0 & 0 & 0 & 1 & 1 & 0 & 0 \\ pF_{LK}^M & -GF_{LK}^A & 0 & pF_{KK}^M & -GF_{KK}^A & -G'F_K^A & 0 \end{bmatrix}$$
$$\cdot \begin{bmatrix} \mathrm{d}L_M \\ \mathrm{d}L_A \\ \mathrm{d}L_U \\ \mathrm{d}K_M \\ \mathrm{d}K_A \\ \mathrm{d}E \\ \mathrm{d}w_A \end{bmatrix} = \begin{bmatrix} -(1/g)F^M \\ 0 \\ 0 \\ 0 \\ 0 \\ 0 \\ 0 \end{bmatrix} \mathrm{d}\lambda + \begin{bmatrix} 0 \\ 1 \\ 0 \\ 0 \\ 0 \\ 0 \\ 0 \end{bmatrix} \mathrm{d}L + \begin{bmatrix} 0 \\ 0 \\ 0 \\ 0 \\ 0 \\ 1 \\ 0 \end{bmatrix} \mathrm{d}K. \tag{16}$$

Now, denoting Ω as the determinant of the square matrix of LHS in (16), we have

$$\begin{aligned} \Omega &= (\lambda/g)F_L^M\,|\mathbf{2,3,4,5,-a,6}| - (\lambda/g)F_K^M\,|\mathbf{1,2,3,5,-a,6}| - J \\ &= -(\lambda/g)\left[|\mathbf{2,3},F_L^M\,\mathbf{4,5,a,6}| - |F_K^M\,\mathbf{1,2,3,5,a,6}|\right] - J \\ &= -(\lambda/g)\,|\mathbf{2,3},\,F_L^M\,\mathbf{4} - F_K^M\,\mathbf{1,5,a,6}| - J \\ &= -(\lambda/g)\,|\mathbf{a,2,3},\,F_L^M\,\mathbf{4} - F_K^M\,\mathbf{1,5,6}| - J = -(\lambda/g)J^* - J. \end{aligned}$$

Subsequently, Ω is negative in sign under Assumption 1. This is because $J^* > 0$ is always true and $J > 0$ under the assumption. Hence it is assured that $\Omega < 0$.

Now we examine the effect of a change in λ. Solving (16), we obtain the following:

$$\frac{\mathrm{d}L_M}{\mathrm{d}\lambda} = \frac{(1/g)F^M pF^M_{LK}G'}{\Omega}\left[\frac{\bar{w}L_M F^A_K}{(L_M+L_U)^2} - G\left(F^A_{LL}F^A_K - F^A_{LK}F^A_L\right)\right] < 0, \tag{17}$$

$$\frac{\mathrm{d}L_A}{\mathrm{d}\lambda} = \frac{(1/g)F^M pG'}{\Omega}\left[-F^M_{LK}F^A_K\frac{\bar{w}}{L_M+L_U} + F^M_{LL}G\left(F^A_{LK}F^A_K - F^A_{KK}F^A_L\right)\right] > 0, \tag{18}$$

$$\frac{\mathrm{d}L_U}{\mathrm{d}\lambda} = \frac{(1/g)F^M pG'}{\Omega}\left[\frac{\bar{w}L_U F^M_{LK}F^A_K}{(L_M+L_U)^2} + GF^M_{LL}\left(1-\frac{K_A L_M}{L_A K_M}\right)\left(F^A_{KK}F^A_L - F^A_{LK}F^A_K\right)\right], \tag{19}$$

$$\frac{\mathrm{d}K_M}{\mathrm{d}\lambda} = -\frac{(1/g)F^M pF^M_{LL}G'}{\Omega}\left[\frac{\bar{w}L_M F^A_K}{(L_M+L_U)^2} + G\left(F^A_{LK}F^A_L - F^A_{LL}F^A_K\right)\right] < 0, \tag{20}$$

$$\frac{\mathrm{d}K_A}{\mathrm{d}\lambda} = -\frac{\mathrm{d}K_M}{\mathrm{d}\lambda} > 0, \tag{21}$$

$$\frac{\mathrm{d}E}{\mathrm{d}\lambda} = -\frac{(1/g)F^M p\bar{w}G}{\Omega(L_M+L_U)^2}\left[F^M_{LL}F^A_{KK}L_M - F^M_{LK}F^A_{LK}(L_U+L_M)\right], \tag{22}$$

$$\frac{\mathrm{d}w_A}{\mathrm{d}\lambda} = -\frac{F^M p\bar{w}GG'}{g\Omega(L_M+L_U)^2}\left[(F^M_{LL}F^A_{KK}L_M - F^M_{LK}F^A_{LK}(L_U+L_M)\right]\left(F^A_L + F^A_K\frac{K_A}{L_A}\right). \tag{23}$$

In view of (17) and (18), it is clear that a decrease in the discharge rate of pollution induces labor movement from rural to urban areas and an increase in the labor employment in the manufacturing sector. Whether the urban unemployment increases or not is, however, ambiguous. If the manufacturing sector is more capital-intensive than the agricultural sector, that is, $1-(K_A/L_A)(L_M/K_M) > 0$, then we obtain $\mathrm{d}L_U/\mathrm{d}\lambda < 0$ from (19). Thus, a decrease in the discharge rate of pollution enhances urban unemployment.

We must note the following to investigate the effect of a decrease in the discharge rate of pollution on the natural environment:

$$F^M_{LL}F^A_{KK}L_M - F^M_{LK}F^A_{LK}(L_U+L_M) = \frac{F^M_{LK}F^A_{LK}L_A(L_U+L_M)}{K_A}\left(\frac{K_M}{L_M+L_U} - \frac{K_A}{L_A}\right).$$

This together with (22) and (23) gives

$$\frac{K_M}{L_M+L_U} < \frac{K_A}{L_A} \Rightarrow \frac{\mathrm{d}E}{\mathrm{d}\lambda} < 0 \Leftrightarrow \frac{\mathrm{d}w_A}{\mathrm{d}\lambda} < 0.$$

Therefore, under Assumption 1 that the urban area is labor-abundant, a decrease in the discharge rate of pollution produces a favorable effect on the natural environment as well as on the agricultural wage, namely on the average income of workers.

Our analysis of a change in λ can be summarized as follows:

Theorem 2. *Under Assumption 1, a decrease in the discharge rate of pollution in the manufacturing sector generates the following outcomes:*

1. *Capital and labor inputs expand in the manufacturing sector, but contract in the agricultural sector. Thus the output of the manufacturing sector undoubtedly increases.*
2. *If the manufacturing sector is more capital-intensive than the agricultural sector, urban unemployment increases.*
3. *The quality of the natural environment and the agricultural wage, that is, the workers' average income, rises.*

The assertion of Theorem 2(2) seems to be paradoxical, for it shows that the lower generation rate of pollution is not necessarily favorable to a reduction in urban unemployment. In fact, the assumption that $K_M/L_M > K_A/L_A > K_M/(L_M+L_U)$ assures that the urban unemployment is swollen by the reduction of the pollution discharge.

Our interest is then directed to the effect of the generation rate of pollution on the national welfare. Note that, the higher the national income, the better the national welfare. This is because we assume the country to be a small country. Hence, to investigate the national welfare, we simply focus on the national income, which is denoted as $Y = pM + A$. In view of (11) and (21), we have

$$\frac{dY}{d\lambda} = p\frac{dM}{d\lambda} + \frac{dA}{d\lambda} = \bar{w}\frac{dL_M}{d\lambda} + w_A\frac{dL_A}{d\lambda} + G'F^A\frac{dE}{d\lambda},$$

where $dE/d\lambda < 0$ provided that $K_M/(L_M+L_U) < K_A/L_A$. Moreover, it holds that

$$\begin{aligned}
&\bar{w}\frac{dL_M}{d\lambda} + w_A\frac{dL_A}{d\lambda},\\
&= \frac{F^M pGG'}{g\Omega}\left[-\bar{w}\left(F^A_{LL}F^A_K - F^A_{LK}F^A_L\right)F^M_{LK} + w_A\left(F^A_{LK}F^A_K - F^A_{KK}F^A_L\right)F^M_{LL}\right]\\
&= \frac{F^M pGG'}{g\Omega}\frac{\bar{w}}{L_M+L_U}\\
&\times\left[\left(F^M_{LK}F^A_{LK}(L_U+L_M) - F^M_{LL}F^A_{KK}L_M\right)F^A_L + \left(L_M F^M_{LL}F^A_{KL} - (L_M+L_U)F^M_{LK}F^A_{LL}\right)F^A_K\right]\\
&= \frac{F^M pGG'}{g\Omega}\bar{w}F^M_{LK}F^A_{LK}\left(\frac{K_A}{L_A} - \frac{K_M}{L_M+L_U}\right)\left(\frac{F^A_L L_A}{K_A} + F^A_K\right) < 0,
\end{aligned}$$

under the assumption that $K_M/(L_M+L_U) < K_A/L_A$. Hence, we have

$$\frac{dY}{d\lambda} < 0 \Leftarrow \frac{K_M}{L_M+L_U} < \frac{K_A}{L_A},$$

which establishes the following theorem.

Theorem 3. *Under Assumption 1, the country welfare is improved by a decrease in the discharge rate of pollution.*

Theorem 3 is obvious, even if there is a case in which the urban unemployment expands due to a decrease in the discharge rate of pollution. This is because, according to Theorem 2, the average income of the workers goes up while capital income is unchanging.[5]

It is known from Neary's analysis that, if capital is mobile between sectors, two impacts produce a paradoxical result: the impact of factor endowment and that of production or wage subsidies. Thus, we proceed in our analysis to an examination of the impact of a change in factor endowment.

We return to our equation system (16) and solve it with respect to a change in labor endowment. Then we obtain the following results:

$$\frac{dL_M}{dL} = -\frac{1}{\Omega}\frac{\bar{w}L_M}{(L_M+L_U)^2}pGF^M_{LK}F^A_{LK} > 0,$$

$$\frac{dL_A}{dL} = \frac{1}{\Omega}\frac{\bar{w}L_M}{(L_M+L_U)^2}p\left[GF^M_{LL}F^A_{KK} + G'(\lambda/g)F^A_K\left(F^M_{LL}F^M_K - F^M_{LK}F^M_L\right)\right],$$

$$\frac{dL_U}{dL} = -\frac{1}{\Omega}\left[\frac{\bar{w}L_U}{(L_M+L_U)^2}pF^M_{LK}GF^A_{LK} + \frac{\lambda}{g}pGG'\left(F^A_{LL}F^A_K - F^A_{LK}F^A_L\right)\left(F^M_{LL}F^M_K - F^M_{LK}F^M_L\right)\right] > 0,$$

$$\frac{dK_M}{dL} = \frac{1}{\Omega}\frac{\bar{w}L_M}{(L_M+L_U)^2}pGF^M_{LL}F^A_{LK} > 0,$$

$$\frac{dK_A}{dL} = -\frac{dK_M}{dL} < 0,$$

$$\frac{dE}{dL} = \frac{1}{\Omega}\frac{\bar{w}L_M}{(L_M+L_U)^2}\frac{\lambda}{g}pGF^A_{LK}\left(F^M_{LK}F^M_L - F^M_{LL}F^M_K\right) < 0,$$

$$\frac{dw_A}{dL} = \frac{1}{\Omega}\frac{\bar{w}L_M}{(L_M+L_U)^2}GG'P\frac{\lambda}{g}\left(F^M_{LL}F^M_K - F^M_{LK}F^M_L\right)\left(F^A_{LL}F^A_K - F^A_{LK}F^A_L\right) < 0.$$

Therefore, an expansion in labor endowment necessarily brings forth an increase in both labor employment in the manufacturing sector and unemployment in the urban area. Capital shifts from the rural area to the urban area, so that the production of the manufacturing sector expands and the natural environment is further damaged. This additional damage lowers the agricultural productivity. The direction of the change in agricultural labor employment depends on the substitution effect between labor and capital in that sector and the impact of the environmental damage on the agricultural productivity. If the former is stronger than the latter, the agricultural labor employment increases.

[5] The reason that capital income is unchanging is that K_M/L_M is not influenced by a shift in λ because of (8), and thus r does not change in view of (11).

Our main results are summarized in the following theorem:

Theorem 4. *Under Assumption 1, an expansion in labor endowment will cause both the labor employment in the manufacturing sector and the urban unemployment to increase, the natural environment to deteriorate, and the agricultural wage, which is the worker's average income, to fall.*

We now turn our attention to a change in capital endowment. A similar analysis can be applied to this case. Solving (15) we obtain

$$\frac{dL_M}{dK} = -\frac{1}{\Omega}\frac{\bar{w}L_M}{(L_M+L_U)^2}pGF^A_{KK}F^M_{LK} < 0,$$

$$\frac{dL_A}{dK} = \frac{1}{\Omega}pG\left[\frac{\bar{w}}{(L_M+L_U)}F^M_{LK}F^A_{KK} + \frac{\lambda}{g}G'\left(F^M_{LL}F^M_K - F^M_{LK}F^M_L\right)\left(F^A_{KL}F^A_K - F^A_{KK}F^A_L\right)\right]$$
$$> 0,$$

$$\frac{dL_U}{dK} = \frac{-1}{\Omega}pG\left[\frac{\bar{w}L_U}{(L_M+L_U)^2}F^A_{KK}F^M_{LK} + \frac{\lambda}{g}G'\left(F^M_{LL}F^M_K - F^M_{LK}F^M_L\right)\left(F^A_{KL}F^A_K - F^A_{KK}F^A_L\right)\right]$$
$$< 0,$$

$$\frac{dK_M}{dK} = \frac{1}{\Omega}\frac{\bar{w}L_M}{(L_M+L_U)^2}pGF^M_{LL}F^A_{KK} < 0,$$

$$\frac{dK_A}{dK} = 1 - \frac{dK_M}{dK} > 0,$$

$$\frac{dE}{dK} = \frac{1}{\Omega}\frac{\bar{w}L_M}{(L_M+L_U)^2}\frac{\lambda}{g}GF^A_{KK}p\left(F^M_{KL}F^M_L - F^M_{LL}F^M_K\right) > 0,$$

$$\frac{dw_A}{dK} = \frac{1}{\Omega}\frac{\bar{w}L_M}{(L_M+L_U)^2}\frac{\lambda}{g}GG'p\left(F^A_{LK}F^A_K - F^A_{KK}F^A_L\right)\left(F^M_{LL}F^M_K - F^M_{LK}F^M_L\right) > 0.$$

Thus, in the case where capital endowment expands, the labor employment of the manufacturing sector and the urban unemployment decline, which implies a rise in the labor employment of the agricultural sector. Moreover, some capital shifts from the manufacturing to the agricultural sector. Thus, the manufacturing output contracts while the agricultural output expands. A fall in the manufacturing output leads to the improvement of the environmental quality and hence a rise in the agricultural wage.

Theorem 5. *Under Assumption 1, an expansion of capital endowment will cause urban unemployment to decrease, the production level of the manufacturing sector to fall, and that of the agricultural sector to rise. Therefore, the natural environment improves and the agricultural wage, that is, the workers' average income, goes up.*

In the traditional Harris and Todaro economy where there exists no pollution and the urban area is capital-abundant, Corden and Findley (1975) and Neary (1978) showed the paradoxical result that the expansion of labor endowment reduces urban unemployment but the expansion of capital endowment increases it. In our setting, the result is the opposite, and thus the paradox disappears. This difference in the result is heavily dependent on the difference in the assumption of factor abundance. Recall the Rybczynski effect that an increase in a factor endowment expands the production sector where that factor is intensively used but causes the other production sector to contract. This, together with the assumption that the urban area is labor-abundant, tends to support the validity of Theorems 4 and 5.

5 Conclusion

In this chapter, we carried out a simple comparative analysis of a Harris and Todaro model that incorporated the natural environment. Prior to the main analysis, we investigated the dynamic adjustment process of the natural environment in order to make full use of the stability condition for the comparative static analysis. The sufficient condition for the stability was shown to be the factor-intensity condition that the urban area is more labor-abundant than the rural area.

Under this stability condition, we obtained the result that, if the manufacturing sector is more capital-intensive than the agricultural sector, a fall in the generation rate of pollution in the manufacturing sector leads to an increase in urban unemployment. The result implies that technological progress in protecting the environment, which may be possible via technology transfer from an advanced country, is not favorable for labor employment under certain conditions. The result seems to be paradoxical, but is not paradoxical in the sense that this technological improvement eventually raises the level of the national welfare.

We also derived the result that urban unemployment expands due to an increase in the labor endowment, but contracts due to an increase in the capital endowment. In the original Harris and Todaro framework that does not include the natural environmental element, the result is opposite to ours, and is known as the one of the Harris and Todaro paradoxes. Hence, this paradox concerning changes in factor endowment disappears in our setting that incorporates the natural environment.

These results are heavily dependent on the assumption of factor abundance between regions. Our factor abundance condition, given as Assumption 1, is only sufficient but not necessary for the stability of our model. Thus, even if the urban area is capital-abundant, the economy may still be stable. In this case, our results would seriously change. Consider Theorem 3, for example. If the urban area is capital-abundant under the condition that $\Omega < 0$, it is true that a decrease in the discharge rate of pollution is harmful to the natural environment and lowers the level of the national welfare.

In our present analysis, we concentrated on the type of natural environment that influences production activities. In a developing economy, however, much attention is paid to the fact that pollution generated by production activities affects people living in the region where the pollution is generated. The labor movement between regions should then be determined by the difference in migrant's utility received from a region. Treating this type of environmental pollution is another topic of interest generated by our present analysis.

Acknowledgment We are very grateful to an anonymous referee for constructive comments and suggestions.

References

Copeland BR, Taylor MS (1999) Trade, spatial separation and the environment. J Int Econ 47:137–168

Corden WM, Findley R (1975) Urban unemployment, intersectoral capital mobility and development policy. Economica 42:59–78

Harris JR, Todaro M (1970) Migration, unemployment and development: a two-sector analysis. Am Econ Rev 60(1):126–142

Lewis WA (1954) Economic development with unlimited supplies of labor. Manchester School of Economics and Social Studies 22(2):139–191

Neary P (1981) On the Harris–Todaro model with intersectoral capital mobility. Economica 48:219–234

Tawada M (2007) On the stability conditions of the Harris–Todaro model with natural environment. Mimeographed, Nagoya University

Trade Policy and Illegal Immigration[1]

Alan Woodland(✉) and Chisata Yoshida

Abstract We develop a general equilibrium two-country model in which the home and foreign countries trade two final goods and legal immigration is restricted. International trade is distorted via tariffs imposed by both countries. Foreign migrants attempt illegally entry to the home country but face a probability of detection and arrest by border patrol of the home country. The primary concern is with the interaction between tariff policy and illegal immigration. Tariff settings affect the real wages that illegal immigrants can attract and so have an influence on the amount of illegal immigration. Conversely, the existence of illegal immigrants can influence the effectiveness of changes in tariffs. Our analysis attempts to draw out the important interactions between tariff policy and illegal immigration. We establish conditions under which unilateral and bilateral tariff reforms reduce successful illegal immigration, and determine the welfare implications of these policy changes. We conclude that the mutual liberalization of trade does not necessarily reduce successful illegal immigration.

1 Introduction

During the post-World War II period, the world has witnessed a significant reduction in tariffs and other barriers to international trade in goods and services. This has been achieved primarily through multilateral reductions carried out through the World Trade Organization (and its predecessor, the General Agreement on Tariffs and Trade) and through the more recent proliferations of customs unions and preferential trading arrangements between groups of countries. This increased freedom in

[1] Chapter written in memory and honor of Koji Shimomura.

A. Woodland
Faculty of Economics and Business, University of Sydney, NSW 2006, Australia,
e-mail: A.Woodland@econ.usyd.edu.au

T. Kamihigashi and L. Zhao (eds.) *International Trade and Economic Dynamics – Essays in Memory of Koji Shimomura.*

international trade of goods and services has not been matched by the international movement of labor, for which substantial impediments continue to exist.

The European Union (EU), which became effective in 1994, had already established the free movement of goods and persons within the European Economic Community by the Schengen Agreement enacted in 1985. Since the agreement came into force in March 1995, member nations implement a common policy of the temporary entry of persons with the Schengen Visa, the unification of external border patrols, and crossborder police cooperation. Of the 30 nations comprising the European Union, all except the United Kingdom, Ireland, and three non-EU members (Iceland, Norway, and Switzerland) have signed the agreement, and it is currently implemented by 15 nation members. Border checks have been removed among countries in Schengen area. Thus, the EU provides for the free intraunion movement of labor.

However, there are impediments to the movement of labor between nonmember and member nations. Hence, migrants from outside the Schengen area become illegal migrants if they enter the EU with no checks at the frontier. Also, migrants who stay in the EU with expired temporary visas become illegal aliens.[2] It has been estimated that there are approximately 4.5–8 million illegal migrants in the EU (Nihon Keizai Shimbun 2007). Recently, illegal immigration from the so-called Mediterranean countries (such as Turkey, the Middle Eastern and North African countries) has increased. This trend is attributed to a large income gap between EU and the countries along the Mediterranean Sea: per capita gross domestic product in this region is roughly 10% of that in the EU. Hence, there is a strong incentive to illegally immigrate to the EU to earn higher income. Recently, French President Sarközy has proposed plan for a Mediterranean Union (including France, Spain, Portugal, Italy, Malta, Cyprus, Greece, Turkey, Syria, Lebanon, Palestine, Israel, Egypt, Libya, Algeria, Tunisia, and Morocco) to curb illegal immigration toward EU from the Mediterranean countries by promoting free trade within member countries to reduce the regional income disparity.

In other regional agreements, internal movement of labor is restricted. For example, the 1992 North American Free Trade Agreement (NAFTA) between the United States (US), Canada, and Mexico provided for the gradual elimination of tariffs and stimulation to trade and investment, but not for labor mobility. The disparity between incomes in the US and Mexico has resulted in a large body of illegal immigrants in the US.

Within this backdrop, the current chapter is concerned with the interaction between tariff policy and illegal immigration. Tariff settings affect the real wages that illegal immigrants can attract and so have an influence on the amount of illegal immigration. Conversely, the existence of illegal immigrants can influence the effectiveness of changes in tariffs. Below, we propose a model of trade between two countries that have tariffs on trade and that experience illegal immigration and use this model to draw out the important interactions between tariff policy and illegal immigration.

[2] An illegal immigrant may be defined as a person dwelling in a country with no official residence permit (Staring 2000).

Research on illegal immigration was pioneered by contributions of Ethier (1986a,b). Ethier introduced decision making based upon expected income differentials by a potential risk-neutral illegal immigrant facing border patrol in the event of illegally entering a host country, and risk-neutral behavior against the internal scrutiny by a home firm that illegally hires illegal migrants, making use of the Harris–Todaro model. Subsequent contributions, including Bond and Chen (1987), Bandyopadhyay and Bandyopadhyay (1998), Djajic (1987, 1999), Gaytan-Fregoso and Lahiri (2000), and Levine (1999), also suppose no risk or assume risk-neutral behavior by the prospective illegal immigrant and home firm. However, Woodland and Yoshida (2006) generalized behavior of a potential illegal migrant to allow for non-neutral risk preferences when being confronted with border interdiction, extending Ethier's one-country model to a two-country context.

None of these models explicitly analyzed commodity trade, and hence do not consider tariff reforms by groups of countries. However, some recent literature has considered illegal immigration in the context of models involving commodity trade and tariff distortions. Gaytan-Fregoso and Lahiri (2000) developed a two-country model of commodity trade and illegal immigration, in which the host country provides foreign aid to the source country of illegal immigration. They conclude that (1) additional aid to the source country raises (lessens) the level of illegal immigration when the level of aid is initially small (large) and that (2) a transfer of resources from border patrol to foreign aid will increase illegal immigration if aid is sufficiently small in the initial equilibrium.

Gaytan-Fregoso and Lahiri (2002) introduced a general equilibrium trade model comprising two small open economies and in which legal labor movement is disallowed. The volume of illegal immigration and the level of remittances are set such that family welfare is maximized. Accordingly, they implicitly assume away the existence of aggregate uncertainty for the family, although the immigrants face the risk of getting caught at the border between the two countries. They show that, under certain conditions, uniform percentage reductions in all tariffs in both countries (1) reduce the number of illegal immigration and (2) raise the welfare of nationals in the host country. Kahana and Lecker (2005) presented a multicountry trade model consisting of one rich country A and several source countries S_i, where legal migration from S_i to A is not allowed. They follow Gaytan-Fregoso and Lahiri (2002) in assuming that decisions to migrate are made at the family level. The receiving (rich) country has basically two policy tools: funds allocated for strengthening its border patrol and foreign aid given to the source countries. They suggest that the rich country would use financial aid to the source countries as an instrument to prevent illegal immigration. They state that the rich country, by choosing an appropriate mix of these two policies, can minimize the expected number of uncaught illegal immigrants.

We develop a general equilibrium two-country model of international trade in commodities in which immigration is restricted, thus providing the incentive for illegal immigration. Unlike the previous researches on illegal immigration, we explicitly consider decision making of potential illegal migrants based upon expected utility maximization. Thus, we allow for non-neutral risk preferences.

To focus on the relations between international trade and illegal immigration, we examine how border controls act on commodity trade and illegal immigration, and how unilateral and bilateral tariff reductions by the two countries affect trade and illegal immigration.

2 The Model

2.1 Introduction

We introduce a model of illegal immigration in which there are two small countries (North and South) and many traded commodities. Assuming good 1 to be the numeraire, the world price vector is $(1,\pi)$. We assume that legal immigration is disallowed but that there is illegal immigration from South to North due to higher wage rates in North, perhaps due to a superior technology or factor endowments. We further assume that the two countries impose import tariffs and that tariff revenues in each country are transferred to its legal residents in a lump-sum manner. The domestic prices for non-numeraire goods are denoted $P=\pi+T$ and $p=\pi+t$, where T and t are the specific tariff rates.

The representative legal resident of the host country, North, has expenditure function $E(P,G,U)$, where P is the domestic price vector (for non-numeraire goods), G is the government public good supply, and U is the level of utility. Illegal residents have expenditure function $\tilde{e}(P,G,\tilde{u})$.[3] The expenditure function for the residents of South is given by $e(p,u)$. The expenditure functions have the properties that they are increasing, concave, and linearly homogeneous in prices and increasing in utility levels. As is well known, the partial derivatives denoted by $E_P(\cdot)$, $-E_G(\cdot)$, and $E_U(\cdot)$ are, respectively, the compensated demand functions for non-numeraire goods, the marginal willingness to pay for the government good, and the marginal cost of utility (inverse of the marginal utility of income). Similar interpretations apply to the partial derivatives $\tilde{e}_P(\cdot)$, $-\tilde{e}_G(\cdot)$, and $\tilde{e}_u(\cdot)$ of the expenditure function for illegal immigrants, and to the partial derivatives $e_p(\cdot)$ and $e_u(\cdot)$ of the expenditure function for South residents.

The technology in North is specified through the revenue function $R(P,L,I)$, where L is the amount of home labor used and I is the number of illegal residents (and their labor supply). In South, the revenue function is $r(p,l)$, where l is the amount of home labor used. The revenue functions have the properties that they are increasing, convex, and linearly homogeneous in prices and they are increasing, concave, and linearly homogeneous in factor inputs.[4] As is well known, the partial derivatives of the revenue function denoted by $R_P(\cdot)$, $R_L(\cdot)$, and $R_I(\cdot)$ are, respectively, the (net) supply functions for non-numeraire goods, the wage rate

[3] For properties of expenditure and revenue functions, see Woodland (1982).

[4] It is assumed that the factor inputs include capital but, since capital is not changed in the analysis, reference to capital inputs is subsumed.

for domestic labor, and the wage rate for the labor of illegal immigrants in North. Similar interpretations apply to the partial derivatives $r_p(\cdot)$ and $r_l(\cdot)$ of the revenue function in South.

The North government employs labor to produce the public good and to patrol borders to detect illegal immigrants. These employments are denoted by L^{G} and L^{B} with total government employment being $L^{\theta} = L^{\mathrm{G}} + L^{\mathrm{B}}$. The output of the public good is $G(L^{\mathrm{G}})$, while the probability of detection of an illegal immigrant at the border is $g(L^{\mathrm{B}})$. The detection probability function obeys the restrictions $g' > 0$, $g'' < 0$. This means that the employment of more labor resources in border patrol raises the probability of detection, but with decreasing marginal returns.

The number of citizens (legal residents) in North is $\overline{L}$, while employment of citizens in the private sector is $L = \overline{L} - (L^{\mathrm{G}} + L^{\mathrm{B}}) = \overline{L} - L^{\theta}$. In South, employment is $l = \overline{l} - I$, where $\overline{l}$ is the number of citizens.

Because it is assumed that residents of South have a lower standard of living than residents of North and legal immigration is not permitted, there is an incentive for residents of South to contemplate illegal immigration to North. If they remain in South, their income, and hence their level of utility u, will be known with certainty. However, an attempt at illegal immigration entails the possibility that they will be detected at the border and deported. Accordingly, their expected utility depends upon the utility, $\tilde{u}$, received upon successful migration, obtained with probability $1 - g$, and the utility, $u - k$, they receive upon detection and deportation, which occurs with probability g. If this expected utility exceeds the utility obtained from staying in South, residents of South will attempt to migrate illegally. This attempt will reduce the expected gain. Equilibrium will be established when the expected gain in utility from illegal immigration is zero; at the margin, South residents will be indifferent as to whether to attempt migration or not. Accordingly, in equilibrium, the indifference condition $(1 - g(L^{\mathrm{B}}))\tilde{u} + g(L^{\mathrm{B}})(u - k) = u$ will be satisfied.

2.2 Model Specification

The model comprises the budget constraints for the legal residents of North and South, the budget constraint of illegal immigrants from South residing in North, and the equilibrium condition for the illegal immigration decision. The endogenous variables are the utility levels for the three types of individuals and the level of successful illegal immigration. The model may be expressed as

$$R(P,\overline{L} - L^{\theta},I) - IR_I(P,\overline{L} - L^{\theta},I) + T'M - E(P,G(L^{\mathrm{G}}),U)\overline{L} = 0, \quad (1)$$

$$(1-\alpha)R_I(P,\overline{L} - L^{\theta},I) - e(P,G(L^{\mathrm{G}}),\tilde{u}) = 0, \quad (2)$$

$$r(p,\overline{l} - I) + \alpha IR_I(P,\overline{L} - L^{\theta},I) + t'm - e(p,u)(\overline{l} - I) = 0, \quad (3)$$

$$(1 - g(L^{\mathrm{B}}))\tilde{u} + g(L^{\mathrm{B}})(u - k) = u, \quad (4)$$

where $P = \pi + T$, $p = \pi + t$, $R_L = R_L(P, \overline{L} - L^{\theta}, I)$ and import vectors M and m are given by

$$M = \overline{L}E_P + I\tilde{e}_P - R_P, \tag{5}$$

$$m = (\overline{l} - I)e_p - r_p. \tag{6}$$

These four equations (substituting for imports) determine the four endogenous variables $U, u, \tilde{u}$, and I. The exogenously given policy parameters of interest are $L^{\mathrm{B}}, \alpha, T$, and t.

The first equation describes the budget constraint of the citizens of North. The sum of the first two terms is the income of the citizens of North, comprising revenue from the production sector minus the payments to illegal immigrants. The third term is the tariff revenue, which is distributed to citizens as a lump-sum payment. The final term is total expenditure. Thus, the first equation states that total expenditure by the citizens of North equals income plus net tariff revenue distributed in a lump-sum form to citizens.[5] The second equation equates expenditure by a representative illegal immigrant to the wage earned from employment minus remittances sent back to South. The third equation states that total expenditure by the residents of South comprises revenue from the production sector plus remittances received from illegal immigrants in North plus the net tariff revenue accruing to the government and distributed in a lump-sum form to residents. The final equation requires that the expected utility for a prospective illegal immigrant is equal to the certain utility attained by remaining in South and so is the equilibrium condition for illegal immigration as explained by Woodland and Yoshida (2006).

It is instructive and useful to note that the last equilibrium condition may be rewritten as

$$\tilde{u} = u + hk, \tag{7}$$

where $h \equiv g/(1-g)$ is the odds of being caught at the border in the attempt at illegally immigrating. This states that the utility level obtained upon successful immigration $\tilde{u}$ is to be greater than the utility attained by not attempting illegal immigration u by the amount hk. An increase in the odds of being caught and/or the penalty k will make this required utility wedge larger.

---

[5] The equilibrium condition for the North citizens may, alternatively, be expressed as

$$R(P, \overline{L} - L^{\theta}, I) - IR_I(P, \overline{L} - L^{\theta}, I) + R_L L^{\theta} + \mathrm{BS} - E(P, G(L^{\mathrm{G}}), U)\overline{L} = 0,$$

where BS is the government's budget surplus. The sum of the first three terms is the income of the citizens of North, comprising revenue from the production sector minus the payments to illegal immigrants plus earnings of public servants. The fourth term is the government net budget surplus assumed to be distributed to citizens as a lump-sum payment. The budget surplus is, in turn, determined as $\mathrm{BS} = T'M - R_L L^{\theta}$, equal to the net tariff revenue minus the cost of paying government employees. Using this equality, we can simplify the first equilibrium condition and so rewrite the system of equilibrium conditions as in the text.

2.3 Equilibrium Conditions

The equilibrium conditions (suppressing mention of G in the first two, since it remains fixed) may be rewritten as

$$
\begin{aligned}
E(P,U) &= Y \equiv \left[R(P,L,I) - IR_I(P,L,I) + T'M\right]/\overline{L}, && (8)\\
\tilde{e}(P,\tilde{u}) &= \tilde{y} \equiv (1-\alpha)R_I(P,L,I), && (9)\\
e(p,u) &= y \equiv \left[r(p,l) + \alpha IR_I(P,L,I) + t'm\right]/l, && (10)\\
\tilde{u} &= u + hk, && (11)
\end{aligned}
$$

where it is recalled that $P = \pi + T$, $p = \pi + t$, $L = \overline{L} - L^{\theta}$, and $l = \overline{l} - I$, that M and m are given by (5) and (6), and that $h \equiv g/(1-g)$.

The first three equations determine the utility levels of the three agents and therefore may be used to obtain the three indirect utility functions expressed in terms of the prices they face and their incomes $Y, \tilde{y}$, and y. These three indirect utility functions are denoted as $V(P,Y)$, $\tilde{v}(P,\tilde{y})$, and $v(p,y)$.

2.4 Comparative Statics Equations

Now, consider the model expressed in (8)–(11) in which each country imposes tariffs on its trade. The complications of having tariffs in the model are threefold. First, domestic prices are affected by tariffs. Second, income depends upon the tariff revenue generated and returned to legal residents in a lump-sum form. Third, the policy instruments available to governments include the tariff vectors. A particular complication is that imports depend on utilities and, especially, the imports of North depend upon the utilities of legal and illegal residents. Each of these complications has to be taken into account in computing the comparative statics solutions.

The comparative statics equations may be obtained as follows. Differentiating (8)–(11), we get that

$$
\begin{aligned}
\overline{L}E_U\mathrm{d}U + \overline{L}E_P'\mathrm{d}T &= -IR_{II}\mathrm{d}I - (R_L - IR_{IL})\mathrm{d}L^{\mathrm{B}} + (R_P' - IR_{IP})\mathrm{d}T\\
&\quad + M'\mathrm{d}T + T'\mathrm{d}M, && (12)\\
\tilde{e}_u\mathrm{d}\tilde{u} + \tilde{e}_P'\mathrm{d}T &= (1-\alpha)R_{II}\mathrm{d}I - (1-\alpha)R_{IL}\mathrm{d}L^{\mathrm{B}} - R_I\mathrm{d}\alpha\\
&\quad + (1-\alpha)R_{IP}\mathrm{d}T, && (13)\\
le_u\mathrm{d}u + le_p'\mathrm{d}t - e\,\mathrm{d}I &= \left[-r_l + \alpha(R_I + IR_{II})\right]\mathrm{d}I - \alpha IR_{IL}\mathrm{d}L^{\mathrm{B}} + IR_I\mathrm{d}\alpha\\
&\quad + r_p'\mathrm{d}t + \alpha IR_{IP}\mathrm{d}T + m'\mathrm{d}t + t'\mathrm{d}m, && (14)\\
\mathrm{d}\tilde{u} &= \mathrm{d}u + \lambda\,\mathrm{d}L^{\mathrm{B}}, && (15)
\end{aligned}
$$

where the changes in imports are

$$
\begin{aligned}
\mathrm{d}M &= (\overline{L}E_{PP} + I\tilde{e}_{PP} - R_{PP})\mathrm{d}T + \overline{L}E_{PU}\mathrm{d}U + I\tilde{e}_{Pu}\mathrm{d}\tilde{u} + (\tilde{e}_P - R_{PI})\,\mathrm{d}I + R_{PL}\mathrm{d}L^{\mathrm{B}}\\
&= S_{PP}\mathrm{d}T + \overline{L}E_{PU}\mathrm{d}U + I\tilde{e}_{Pu}\mathrm{d}\tilde{u} + (\tilde{e}_P - R_{PI})\,\mathrm{d}I + R_{PL}\mathrm{d}L^{\mathrm{B}}, && (16)
\end{aligned}
$$

$$\begin{aligned} \mathrm{d}m &= (le_{pp} - r_{pp})\mathrm{d}t + le_{pu}\mathrm{d}u + (r_{pl} - e_p)\mathrm{d}I \\ &= s_{pp}\mathrm{d}t + le_{pu}\mathrm{d}u + (r_{pl} - e_p)\mathrm{d}I, \end{aligned} \tag{17}$$

where

$$S_{PP} = \overline{L}E_{PP} + I\tilde{e}_{PP} - R_{PP} \tag{18}$$

and

$$s_{pp} = le_{pp} - r_{pp} \tag{19}$$

are the net substitution matrices in North and South, and where $\lambda = kg'/(1-g)^2 > 0$.

Using all these equations, the comparative statics equations may be re-expressed as

$$\begin{aligned} \overline{L}(E_U - T'E_{PU})\mathrm{d}U &= -\left[IR_{II} + T'(R_{PI} - \tilde{e}_P)\right]\mathrm{d}I - (R_L - T'R_{PL})\mathrm{d}L^{\mathrm{B}} \\ &\quad + [T'S_{PP} + I\tilde{e}'_P]\mathrm{d}T + IT'\tilde{e}'_{Pu}\mathrm{d}\tilde{u}, &(20)\\ \tilde{e}_u\mathrm{d}\tilde{u} &= (1-\alpha)R_{II}\mathrm{d}I - (1-\alpha)R_{IL}\mathrm{d}L^{\mathrm{B}} - R_I\mathrm{d}\alpha \\ &\quad + [(1-\alpha)R_{IP} - \tilde{e}'_P]\mathrm{d}T, &(21)\\ l(e_u - t'e_{pu})\mathrm{d}u &= \left[e - r_l + \alpha(R_I + IR_{II}) + t'(r_{pl} - e_p)\right]\mathrm{d}I - \alpha IR_{IL}\mathrm{d}L^{\mathrm{B}} \\ &\quad + IR_I\mathrm{d}\alpha + t's_{pp}\mathrm{d}t + \alpha IR_{IP}\mathrm{d}T, &(22)\\ \mathrm{d}\tilde{u} &= \mathrm{d}u + \lambda\,\mathrm{d}L^{\mathrm{B}}. &(23) \end{aligned}$$

Combining the first two rows of the comparative statics equations, we can obtain the "reduced form" for the utility change for North's legal residents, and further re-express the equilibrium conditions as

$$\begin{aligned} \overline{L}\widehat{E}_U\mathrm{d}U &= \left[IT'\tilde{c}_y(1-\alpha)R_{II} + T'(\tilde{e}_P - R_{PI}) - IR_{II}\right]\mathrm{d}I \\ &\quad + \left[T'R_{PL} - (R_L - IR_{IL}) - IT'\tilde{c}_y(1-\alpha)R_{IL}\right]\mathrm{d}L^{\mathrm{B}} \\ &\quad + [T'S_{PP} + IT'\tilde{c}_y(1-\alpha)R_{IP} + I(1 - T'\tilde{c}_y)\tilde{e}'_P]\mathrm{d}T - IT'\tilde{c}_yR_I\mathrm{d}\alpha, &(24)\\ \tilde{e}_u\mathrm{d}\tilde{u} &= (1-\alpha)R_{II}\mathrm{d}I - (1-\alpha)R_{IL}\mathrm{d}L^{\mathrm{B}} - R_I\mathrm{d}\alpha + [(1-\alpha)R_{IP} - \tilde{e}'_P]\mathrm{d}T, &(25)\\ l\widehat{e}_u\mathrm{d}u &= \left[e - r_l + \alpha(R_I + IR_{II}) + t'(r_{pl} - e_p)\right]\mathrm{d}I - \alpha IR_{IL}\mathrm{d}L^{\mathrm{B}} + IR_I\mathrm{d}\alpha \\ &\quad + t's_{pp}\mathrm{d}t + \alpha IR_{IP}\mathrm{d}T, &(26)\\ \mathrm{d}\tilde{u} &= \mathrm{d}u + \lambda\,\mathrm{d}L^{\mathrm{B}}, &(27) \end{aligned}$$

where $\tilde{c}_y = (\tilde{e}'_{Pu}/\tilde{e}_u)$ is the income effect on consumption for an illegal immigrant and where $\widehat{e}_u \equiv e_u - t'e_{pu} > 0$ and $\widehat{E}_U \equiv E_U - T'E_{PU} > 0$ under Hatta normality. Alternative expressions for these Hatta normality terms are provided by $\widehat{e}_u \equiv e_u(1 - t'e_{pu}/e_u) = e_u(1 - t'c_y)$ and $\widehat{E}_U \equiv E_U(1 - T'E_{PU}/E_U) = E_U(1 - T'C_Y)$, where $c_y = e_{pu}/e_u$ and $C_Y = E_{PU}/E_U$ are the income effects on consumption for foreign and home residents, respectively.

The comparative statics equations (24)–(27) may be combined to first solve for the change in the level of immigration as a result of policy changes. The final comparative statics equation, using the others, becomes

$$
\begin{aligned}
0 = &\ \mathrm{d}\tilde{u} - \mathrm{d}u - \lambda\,\mathrm{d}L^{\mathrm{B}} \\
= &\ \left\{\tilde{e}_u^{-1}(1-\alpha)R_{II} - l^{-1}\widehat{e}_u^{-1}\left[e - r_l + \alpha(R_I + IR_{II}) + t'(r_{pl} - e_p)\right]\right\}\mathrm{d}I \\
&- \left\{\lambda + \tilde{e}_u^{-1}(1-\alpha)R_{IL} - l^{-1}\widehat{e}_u^{-1}\alpha IR_{IL}\right\}\mathrm{d}L^{\mathrm{B}} - \left\{\tilde{e}_u^{-1}R_I + l^{-1}\widehat{e}_u^{-1}IR_I\right\}\mathrm{d}\alpha \\
&+ \left\{\tilde{e}_u^{-1}[(1-\alpha)R_{IP} - \tilde{e}'_P] - l^{-1}\widehat{e}_u^{-1}\alpha IR_{IP}\right\}\mathrm{d}T - l^{-1}\widehat{e}_u^{-1}t's_{pp}\mathrm{d}t \\
= &\ C_I\mathrm{d}I + C_B\mathrm{d}L^{\mathrm{B}} + C_A\mathrm{d}\alpha + C_T\mathrm{d}T + C_t\mathrm{d}t, \qquad (28)
\end{aligned}
$$

where

$$
\begin{aligned}
C_I &= \tilde{e}_u^{-1}(1-\alpha)R_{II} - l^{-1}\widehat{e}_u^{-1}H, & (29)\\
C_B &= -\left\{\lambda + \left(\tilde{e}_u^{-1}(1-\alpha) - l^{-1}\widehat{e}_u^{-1}\alpha I\right)R_{IL}\right\}, & (30)\\
C_A &= -\left\{\tilde{e}_u^{-1} + \widehat{e}_u^{-1}l^{-1}I\right\}R_I < 0, & (31)\\
C_T &= \tilde{e}_u^{-1}[(1-\alpha)R_{IP} - \tilde{e}'_P] - l^{-1}\widehat{e}_u^{-1}\alpha IR_{IP}, & (32)\\
C_t &= -l^{-1}\widehat{e}_u^{-1}t's_{pp}, & (33)
\end{aligned}
$$

and $H \equiv e - r_l + \alpha(R_I + IR_{II}) + t'(r_{pl} - e_p)$. The solution for the change in illegal immigration, obtained from (28), is

$$
\mathrm{d}I = -C_I^{-1}\left[C_B\mathrm{d}L^{\mathrm{B}} + C_A\mathrm{d}\alpha + C_T\mathrm{d}T + C_t\mathrm{d}t\right]. \qquad (34)
$$

Once this solution is obtained, the solution for the remaining endogenous variables (changes in utility levels) can be obtained by substituting this solution into the other comparative statics equations and evaluating the right-hand sides.

The sign of C_A in (31) is unconditional. However, the signs of the other coefficients appear ambiguous in general. To help resolve some of the coefficient signs, we make some further assumptions. First, in Appendix, it is shown that a sufficient condition for Hicksian stability of the model is that $C_I < 0$ provided that Hatta normality is a maintained hypothesis. Second, it is also shown in Appendix that a sufficient condition for $C_I < 0$ is that $H > 0$. Thus, the condition $H > 0$ is, under Hatta normality, sufficient to guarantee Hicksian stability. Accordingly, we will henceforth assume that

$$
H \equiv e - r_l + \alpha(R_I + IR_{II}) + t'(r_{pl} - e_p) > 0. \qquad (35)
$$

This sign restriction will be referred to as Condition *A*.

Having set up the model equations and assumptions, we now proceed to utilize the comparative statics properties of the model to determine the effects of various tariff reforms upon illegal immigration and welfare.[6]

[6] It is also possible to use the model to determine the effects of changes in the level of remittances (α) and the level of resources devoted to border patrols (L^{B}) upon illegal immigration and welfare. The model may also be readily extended to include employer surveillance by government patrols. However, these extensions are not included in the present research to concentrate attention upon tariff reform.

3 Effects of Tariff Reforms

Consider now the effects of changing the level of tariff protection. First, we consider unilateral tariff reforms by each country and then move to a consideration of a bilateral tariff reform. In each case, our attention is focused on the effect of the reforms upon the level of illegal immigration and upon the welfare effects of the reforms.

3.1 Tariff Reform by South

The effect of a unilateral tariff change by South is given by $\mathrm{d}I = -C_I^{-1}C_t\mathrm{d}t$, where $C_t = -l^{-1}\widehat{e_u}^{-1}t's_{pp}$ and $C_I < 0$, i.e.,

$$\mathrm{d}I = C_I^{-1}l^{-1}\widehat{e_u}^{-1}t's_{pp}\mathrm{d}t. \tag{36}$$

If South chooses a proportional tariff reduction of the form $\mathrm{d}t = -t\,\mathrm{d}\kappa$, where $\mathrm{d}\kappa > 0$, then $\mathrm{d}I/\mathrm{d}\kappa = -C_I^{-1}l^{-1}\widehat{e_u}^{-1}t's_{pp}t < 0$ due to the negative definiteness property of the substitution matrix s_{pp}. Accordingly, this tariff reform by South brings about a reduction in the level of illegal immigration to North. This is achieved by South reducing its tariff distortions and thereby raising welfare for its residents, thus reducing the incentive for South citizens to migrate. Accordingly, unilateral tariff reform by South is a very effective policy choice for reducing illegal immigration.

The welfare effects of the reform $\mathrm{d}t = -t\,\mathrm{d}\kappa$, where $\mathrm{d}\kappa > 0$, are as follows:

$$\overline{L}\widehat{E}_U\mathrm{d}U/\mathrm{d}\kappa = \left[T'(\tilde{e}_P - R_{PI}) - IR_{II}\left\{1-(1-\alpha)T'\tilde{c}_y\right\}\right]\mathrm{d}I/\mathrm{d}\kappa, \tag{37}$$

$$\tilde{e}_u\mathrm{d}\tilde{u}/\mathrm{d}\kappa = (1-\alpha)R_{II}\mathrm{d}I/\mathrm{d}\kappa, \tag{38}$$

$$l\widehat{e}_u\mathrm{d}u/\mathrm{d}\kappa = H\,\mathrm{d}I/\mathrm{d}\kappa - t's_{pp}t, \tag{39}$$

$$\mathrm{d}\tilde{u}/\mathrm{d}\kappa = \mathrm{d}u/\mathrm{d}\kappa. \tag{40}$$

These equations show the welfare effects arising from the tariff reform by South, taking into account the indirect effects of the tariff reform upon the level of illegal immigration. If there were no indirect effects, then it is clear from (37)–(39) that the proportional tariff reform by South would raise the welfare of South residents (since $-t's_{pp}t > 0$) through the usual efficiency gains, while the residents of North (both legal and illegal) would be unaffected (since $\mathrm{d}I/\mathrm{d}\kappa = 0$). We now proceed to take account of welfare changes, taking into account the indirect effects contributed by $\mathrm{d}I/\mathrm{d}\kappa$ being nonzero.

From (40), it follows that South residents and illegal immigrants gain equally. The successful illegal immigrants clearly gain since $R_{II} < 0$ and $\mathrm{d}I/\mathrm{d}\kappa < 0$ in (38) and this means higher wages for successful illegal immigrants and hence higher welfare. At first glance, (39) for the utility change for South residents appears ambiguous in sign since $-t's_{pp}t > 0$ while $H\,\mathrm{d}I/\mathrm{d}\kappa < 0$. The tariff reform itself raises utility by reducing the tariff distortions (as explained above). However, an indirect effect is to reduce the number of illegal immigrants and this reduces utility. The greater the efficiency gain, the greater the chance that welfare of South residents will increase. Yet, we see that South residents and illegal immigrants gain equally, and the latter definitely gain. Accordingly, the direct efficiency gain outweighs the indirect welfare loss and there is no ambiguity after all.

For the citizens of North, there are competing forces in general. If North is a free trader, the expression on the right-hand side of (37) simplifies to $-IR_{II}\mathrm{d}I/\mathrm{d}\kappa < 0$. The indirect effect of a reduction in the number of illegal immigrants is for an increase in the marginal productivity (wages) of illegal immigrants and this reduces the net revenue accruing to locals from the production sector. North's residents therefore suffer a loss in welfare.

If North is not a free trader, there are additional effects upon tariff revenue in (37). The second term is now given by $-IR_{II}\left\{1-(1-\alpha)T'\tilde{c}_y\right\}\mathrm{d}I/\mathrm{d}\kappa$. In this expression, the effect of fewer illegal immigrant upon the net revenue accruing to local resident is now tempered by the term $(1-\alpha)T'\tilde{c}_y$, which takes into account the illegal immigrants' income effect on tariff revenue. Under the assumption that $1-(1-\alpha)T'\tilde{c}_y > 0$, the second term will continue to be negative and to contribute to a decrease in the welfare of North residents.

On the other hand, the sign of the first term in (37) could go either way depending upon the technology and immigrant's preferences. This term, given by $T'(\tilde{e}_P - R_{PI})$, may be interpreted as the additional tariff revenue arising from an additional illegal immigrant. This interpretation follows since the vector $\tilde{e}_P - R_{PI}$ is the change in the net import vector if there were to be a unit increase in the number of illegal immigrants and, therefore, $T'(\tilde{e}_P - R_{PI})$ is the resulting additional tariff revenue. Accordingly, the sign of this term is positive if immigrants contribute positively to tariff revenue at the margin and negatively if they do not.

In the present context, there is a reduction in the number of illegal immigrants as a result of South's tariff reform. Accordingly, $T'(\tilde{e}_P - R_{PI})\mathrm{d}I/\mathrm{d}\kappa$ will be negative if $T'(\tilde{e}_P - R_{PI}) > 0$, in which case this term also contributes to a loss of welfare for North's legal residents; fewer illegal immigrants mean lower tariff revenue earned and distributed to citizens. Both terms in (37) therefore work together to ensure that North's citizens suffer a loss in welfare. On the other hand, if $T'(\tilde{e}_P - R_{PI}) < 0$, then the two terms in (37) are of opposite sign and so the welfare effect is ambiguous. In this case, fewer illegal immigrants mean lower net production revenue but greater tariff revenue. In sum, if North is not a free trader, the welfare effect seems ambiguous in sign in general.

The results obtained thus far may be summarized in the following proposition.

Proposition 1. *Assume that Condition A ($H > 0$) holds. Then, a unilateral proportional tariff reduction of the form* $\mathrm{d}t = -t\,\mathrm{d}\kappa$, *where* $\mathrm{d}\kappa > 0$, *by South reduces successful illegal immigration. The welfare level of illegal immigrants and residents of South increase equally. If North is a free trader, Northern citizens suffer a loss in welfare. If North is not a free trader, North will suffer a loss of welfare if* $T'(\tilde{e}_P - R_{PI}) > 0$ *and* $1-(1-\alpha)T'\tilde{c}_y > 0$.

3.2 Tariff Reform by North

Attention is now turned to a unilateral tariff reform by North. Our concern is with the effect of this tariff reform on the level of illegal immigration and upon the welfare of the various individuals. The analysis of North's tariff reform is a little more complicated than the analysis of South's tariff reform. This is primarily because the imports, and hence tariff revenue, of North depend upon the role illegal immigrants play in determining the consumption and production of goods. In addition, the remittances of income to South by illegal immigrants provide an avenue whereby the tariff change in North is transmitted directly to South.

The effect of a unilateral tariff change by North is given by $\mathrm{d}I = -C_I^{-1}C_T\mathrm{d}T$, where $C_I < 0$, i.e.,

$$\mathrm{d}I = -C_I^{-1}\left\{\tilde{e}_u^{-1}[(1-\alpha)R_{IP} - \tilde{e}_P'] - \widehat{e}_u^{-1}\alpha I l^{-1}R_{IP}\right\}\mathrm{d}T. \tag{41}$$

The expression $\{\cdot\}$ contains two terms. The first represents the effect of the tariff change $\mathrm{d}T$ upon the real income of illegal immigrants, while the second is the real income effect for South residents. If illegal immigrants gain more than South residents ($C_T\mathrm{d}T > 0$), there will be an incentive for increased illegal migration as a result of $\mathrm{d}T$. Illegal immigration will rise since $C_I < 0$. Alternatively, if $C_T\mathrm{d}T < 0$, then the impact effect is to lower the real incomes of immigrants relative to South residents and so the tariff reform will reduce illegal immigration.

If North chooses a proportional tariff reduction of the form $\mathrm{d}T = -T\,\mathrm{d}\kappa$, where $\mathrm{d}\kappa > 0$, then the effect upon illegal immigration is given by

$$\mathrm{d}I/\mathrm{d}\kappa = -C_I^{-1}\left\{\tilde{e}_u^{-1}T'[\tilde{e}_P - (1-\alpha)R_{PI}] + \widehat{e}_u^{-1}\alpha I l^{-1}T'R_{IP}\right\}. \tag{42}$$

The term $\{\cdot\}$ in this equation is the change in the real income differential for immigrants and South residents for the special case of a proportional tariff reform. What is the sign of $\mathrm{d}I/\mathrm{d}\kappa$?

To simplify the analysis, let us first assume that there are no remittances from illegal immigrants to the residents of South. The effect on illegal immigration then simply depends on whether illegal immigrants gain real income from the reform, since real incomes in the South are unaffected at the margin. If $\alpha = 0$, then $\mathrm{d}I/\mathrm{d}\kappa = -C_I^{-1}\tilde{e}_u^{-1}T'[\tilde{e}_P - R_{PI}]$, which will be negative provided $T'[\tilde{e}_P - R_{PI}] < 0$. This condition means, as noted above, that the change in the real income of illegal immigrants (at the margin) is negative. Accordingly, in this case, the tariff reform by North brings about a reduction in the level of illegal immigration. This is achieved by North reducing its tariff distortions and thereby reducing the real income of illegal immigrants, thus reducing the incentive for South's citizens to migrate.

Proposition 2. *Assume that Condition A ($H > 0$) holds. Then, a unilateral proportional tariff reduction of the form $\mathrm{d}T = -T\,\mathrm{d}\kappa$, where $\mathrm{d}\kappa > 0$, by North reduces successful illegal immigration if (i) there are no remittances ($\alpha = 0$) and (ii) $T'[\tilde{e}_P - R_{PI}] < 0$.*

If there are remittances ($\alpha \neq 0$), then the analysis becomes more complicated. The term given by $T'(\tilde{e}_P - (1-\alpha)R_{PI})$ in (42) may be interpreted as the direct effect of the tariff reform upon the real income of illegal immigrants, taking into account the effect on income (after remittances) and expenditure. That is, the direct welfare effect of the reform by North on the real income of an illegal immigrant is given by $\tilde{e}_u \partial\tilde{u}/\partial\kappa = T'(\tilde{e}_P - (1-\alpha)R_{PI})$. Thus, an illegal immigrant's welfare directly increases or decreases as a result of a proportional tariff reduction by North according to whether $T'(\tilde{e}_P - (1-\alpha)R_{PI}) > 0$ or $T'(\tilde{e}_P - (1-\alpha)R_{PI}) < 0$. The first part given by $T'\tilde{e}_P$ is the effect on the cost of living, while the second part, $(1-\alpha)T'R_{PI}$, is the effect on the after-remittances income of the immigrant. If the illegal immigrant suffers a loss in real income, then $T'(\tilde{e}_P - (1-\alpha)R_{PI}) > 0$. The second term in (42) given by $\alpha Il^{-1}T'R_{IP}$ is the effect of the resulting change in the illegal immigrant's income upon average remittances for residents of South. They gain or lose depending on whether remittances rise or fall. If $T'R_{PI} > 0$, which means that the tariff reform $\mathrm{d}T = -T\,\mathrm{d}\kappa$ lowers the wage rate for illegal immigrants, then the term $\widehat{e}_u^{-1}\alpha Il^{-1}T'R_{PI} > 0$ works against $\mathrm{d}I/\mathrm{d}\kappa$ being negative. However, if $T'R_{PI} < 0$, then both effects work together.[7] The overall effect upon illegal immigration of the tariff reform depends on whether the illegal immigrants gain in real income relative to those in South.

It is possible to rewrite the right-hand side of (42) in a different ways that provides a compact expression similar to, but generalizing, that arising in the $\alpha = 0$ case. Specifically, the change in illegal immigration may be expressed in alternative ways as

$$\begin{aligned}\mathrm{d}I/\mathrm{d}\kappa &= -C_I^{-1}\left\{\tilde{e}_u^{-1}T'[\tilde{e}_P - (1-\alpha)R_{PI}] + \widehat{e}_u^{-1}\alpha Il^{-1}T'R_{PI}\right\}\\ &= -C_I^{-1}\tilde{e}_u^{-1}T'\left[\tilde{e}_P - \tilde{e}_u\left\{\tilde{e}_u^{-1}(1-\alpha) - \widehat{e}_u^{-1}\alpha Il^{-1}\right\}R_{PI}\right]\\ &= -C_I^{-1}\tilde{e}_u^{-1}T'\left[\tilde{e}_P - \delta R_{PI}\right], \end{aligned} \tag{43}$$

where $\delta = \tilde{e}_u\left\{\partial\tilde{v}/\partial\tilde{y}(1-\alpha) - \partial v/\partial y\, \alpha Il^{-1}\right\}$. Under our normality assumptions, $\delta > 0$ if and only if $\frac{\partial\tilde{v}/\partial\tilde{y}}{\partial v/\partial y} > \beta \equiv \alpha I/(1-\alpha)l$. This means that the marginal utility of income for illegal immigrants ($\partial\tilde{v}/\partial\tilde{y} = \tilde{e}_u^{-1}$) relative to that for the residents of South ($\partial v/\partial y = \widehat{e}_u^{-1}$) (adjusting for tariffs) is greater than a critical number β that depends on the remittance proportion α and the ratio I/l of immigrants to those who stay in South. The term $\beta = (\alpha I/l)/(1-\alpha)$ is interpreted as the ratio of remittances received per South resident to the income retained per immigrant.

In the case of no remittances, the condition for obtaining a reduction in illegal immigrants following the tariff reform by North was that $T'[\tilde{e}_P - R_{PI}] < 0$. The complication created by the existence of remittances is that this condition now becomes $T'[\tilde{e}_P - \delta R_{PI}] < 0$. This term is complex and combines the effects of the tariff change upon the welfare of illegal immigrants and the residents of South.

Summarizing the discussion above, we have the following proposition relating the tariff reform by North to the level of illegal immigration.

---

[7] This may be a stringent condition since then $T'[\tilde{e}_P - (1-\alpha)R_{PI}] < 0$ implies that $T'\tilde{e}_P < 0$.

Proposition 3. *Assume that Condition A ($H > 0$) holds. Then, a unilateral proportional tariff reduction of the form* $\mathrm{d}T = -T\,\mathrm{d}\kappa$, *where* $\mathrm{d}\kappa > 0$, *by North reduces successful illegal immigration if* $T'[\tilde{e}_P - (1-\alpha)R_{PI}] + \widehat{e}_u^{-1}\alpha I l^{-1} T' R_{PI} = T'[\tilde{e}_P - \delta R_{PI}] < 0$, *where* $\delta = \tilde{e}_u\left\{\partial\tilde{v}/\partial\tilde{y}(1-\alpha) - \partial v/\partial y\,\alpha I l^{-1}\right\}$.

The welfare effects of the reform $\mathrm{d}T = -T\,\mathrm{d}\kappa$, where $\mathrm{d}\kappa > 0$, are as follows:

$$\begin{aligned}\overline{L}\widehat{E}_U \mathrm{d}U/\mathrm{d}\kappa &= \left[T'(\tilde{e}_P - R_{PI}) - IR_{II}\left\{1-(1-\alpha)T'\tilde{c}_y\right\}\right]\mathrm{d}I/\mathrm{d}\kappa \\ &\quad - T'S_{PP}T - I[T'\tilde{c}_y(1-\alpha)T'R_{PI} + (1-T'\tilde{c}_y)T'\tilde{e}_P], \qquad (44)\\ \tilde{e}_u \mathrm{d}\tilde{u}/\mathrm{d}\kappa &= (1-\alpha)R_{II}\mathrm{d}I/\mathrm{d}\kappa + T'[\tilde{e}_P - (1-\alpha)R_{PI}], \qquad (45)\\ l\widehat{e}_u \mathrm{d}u/\mathrm{d}\kappa &= H\,\mathrm{d}I/\mathrm{d}\kappa - \alpha I T' R_{PI}, \qquad (46)\\ \mathrm{d}\tilde{u}/\mathrm{d}\kappa &= \mathrm{d}u/\mathrm{d}\kappa. \qquad (47)\end{aligned}$$

Before proceeding to the full determination of the welfare effects, it will help the exposition to first consider the direct welfare effects of the tariff reform by ignoring the indirect effects due to the change in the number of illegal immigrants. From (45), we observe that $\tilde{e}_u\mathrm{d}\tilde{u}/\mathrm{d}\kappa = T'[\tilde{e}_P - (1-\alpha)R_{PI}]$ when $\mathrm{d}I/\mathrm{d}\kappa = 0$. As previously noted, the right-hand side of this expression may be interpreted as the direct effect of the tariff reform upon the real income of illegal immigrants, taking into account the effect on income (after remittances) and expenditure. Thus, illegal immigrants (obviously) gain welfare if their real income increases as a result of the reform. Similarly, from (46), we observe that $l\widehat{e}_u\mathrm{d}u/\mathrm{d}\kappa = -\alpha I T' R_{PI}$ when $\mathrm{d}I/\mathrm{d}\kappa = 0$. If $-T'R_{PI} > 0$, then the wage rate of, and hence remittance payments from, illegal immigrants rises as a result of the tariff reform and so South residents experience a gain in welfare.

For citizens of North, the direct welfare effects given by $\overline{L}\widehat{E}_U\mathrm{d}U/\mathrm{d}\kappa = -T'S_{PP}T - I[T'\tilde{c}_y(1-\alpha)T'R_{PI} + (1-T'\tilde{c}_y)T'\tilde{e}_P]$ are complex. The first term is the usual efficiency gain from a proportional tariff reform in a small open economy and is clearly positive due to the net substitution matrix being negative definite. The second term arises because of illegal immigrants. It weights by $T'\tilde{c}_y$ and $1 - T'\tilde{c}_y > 0$ (the Hatta normality assumption) the income ($(1-\alpha)T'R_{PI}$) and expenditure ($T'\tilde{e}_P$) effects for illegal immigrants arising from the tariff reform. The weighting translates this into tariff revenue effects. The sign of this expression appears ambiguous in general. In any case, this term reflects the fact that the tariff revenue distributed to North citizens is affected by the consumption behavior of illegal immigrants and their role in production. Accordingly, the evaluation of the welfare effects of the tariff reform has to take account of illegal immigrants as well as the usual efficiency gains.

Having considered the direct effects, attention is now turned to the full effects of the tariff reform. First, consider the simpler case where there are no remittances ($\alpha = 0$) as assumed in Proposition 2. In this case, it is readily observed from (46) that $l\widehat{e}_u\mathrm{d}u/\mathrm{d}\kappa = H\,\mathrm{d}I/\mathrm{d}\kappa < 0$ if $\mathrm{d}I/\mathrm{d}\kappa < 0$, so that the residents of South suffer a loss in welfare. Since illegal residents have the same welfare effect, it must be the case from (45) that the positive effect of $R_{II}\mathrm{d}I/\mathrm{d}\kappa > 0$ on their welfare is overcompensated by the negative effect given by $T'[\tilde{e}_P - R_{PI}] < 0$ under condition (ii) of Proposition 2. Thus, both South residents and illegal immigrants suffer utility losses as a result of North's tariff reform. The effect of the tariff reform on the welfare of the citizens of North appears ambiguous. The usual efficiency gain for a small open economy from a proportional tariff reform given by $-T'S_{PP}T$ is positive due to the substitution matrix being negative definite. However, the indirect effect comprises terms of each sign, as does the direct effect (as previously discussed). These results may be summarized in the following proposition.

Proposition 4. *Assume that Condition A ($H > 0$) holds, and that (i) there are no remittances ($\alpha = 0$) and (ii) $T'[\tilde{e}_P - R_{PI}] < 0$. Then, a unilateral proportional tariff reduction of the form $\mathrm{d}T = -T\,\mathrm{d}\kappa$, where $\mathrm{d}\kappa > 0$, by North reduces the welfare level of illegal immigrants and residents of South equally. The effect upon the welfare of North citizens is ambiguous.*

Second, consider the more complicated case where there are remittances ($\alpha \neq 0$). If the assumptions of Proposition 3 are satisfied, then $\mathrm{d}I/\mathrm{d}\kappa < 0$. In this case, it is readily observed from (46) that $\mathrm{d}u/\mathrm{d}\kappa < 0$, so that the residents of South suffer a loss in welfare, provided that we also observe $T'R_{PI} > 0$. Since illegal residents have the same welfare effect as South residents due to (47), it must be the case that the positive effect of $(1-\alpha)R_{II}\mathrm{d}I/\mathrm{d}\kappa > 0$ on their welfare is overcompensated by the negative effect in (45) given by $T'[\tilde{e}_P - (1-\alpha)R_{PI}] < 0$.[8] As with the case of no remittances, the effect of the tariff reform on the welfare of the citizens of North appears ambiguous. The indirect effect comprises terms of each sign, as does the direct effect. These results yield the following proposition.

Proposition 5. *Assume that Condition A ($H > 0$) holds, and that (i) $T'[\tilde{e}_P - \delta R_{PI}] < 0$ and (ii) $T'R_{PI} > 0$. Then, a unilateral proportional tariff reduction of the form $\mathrm{d}T = -T\,\mathrm{d}\kappa$, where $\mathrm{d}\kappa > 0$, by North reduces the welfare level of illegal immigrants and residents of South equally. The effect upon the welfare of North citizens is ambiguous.*

3.3 Bilateral Tariff Reform

Having dealt with unilateral tariff reforms by South and North, attention is now turned to a coordinated bilateral reform of the tariffs of both countries.

The effect of a bilateral tariff change is given by $\mathrm{d}I = -C_I^{-1}(C_t\mathrm{d}t + C_T\mathrm{d}T)$, where $C_I < 0$, i.e.,

$$\mathrm{d}I = -C_I^{-1}\left[-l^{-1}\widehat{\tilde{e}_u}^{-1}t's_{pp}\mathrm{d}t + \left\{\tilde{e}_u^{-1}[(1-\alpha)R_{IP} - \tilde{e}'_P] - l^{-1}\widehat{\tilde{e}_u}^{-1}\alpha IR_{IP}\right\}\mathrm{d}T\right]. \quad (48)$$

Clearly, this is complicated without some specification of the nature of the tariff reforms. Therefore, we consider a bilateral reform of tariffs whereby both countries

[8] This term is negative under the assumption of Proposition 3 that $T'[\tilde{e}_P - (1-\alpha)R_{PI}] + \widehat{\tilde{e}_u}^{-1}\alpha Il^{-1}T'R_{PI} < 0$ and the postulated condition that $T'R_{PI} > 0$.

reduce all tariffs in the same proportion, given by $\mathrm{d}T = -T\,\mathrm{d}\kappa$ and $\mathrm{d}t = -t\,\mathrm{d}\kappa$, where $\mathrm{d}\kappa > 0$.

The effect of this bilateral tariff reform upon illegal immigration then becomes

$$\begin{aligned}\mathrm{d}I/\mathrm{d}\kappa &= -C_I^{-1}\left[l^{-1}\widehat{e_u}^{-1}t's_{pp}t + \left\{l^{-1}\widehat{e_u}^{-1}\alpha IT'R_{PI} + \tilde{e}_u^{-1}T'[\tilde{e}_P - (1-\alpha)R_{PI}]\right\}\right] \\ &= -C_I^{-1}\left[l^{-1}\widehat{e_u}^{-1}t's_{pp}t + \tilde{e}_u^{-1}T'\left[\tilde{e}_P - \delta R_{PI}\right]\right]. \qquad (49)\end{aligned}$$

The first term in parenthesis is due to the reform by South and is clearly negative, while the second term is due to the reform by North. It is apparent that a sufficient condition (in addition to Hicksian stability) for the outcome $\mathrm{d}I/\mathrm{d}\kappa < 0$ is that $T'\left[\tilde{e}_P - \delta R_{PI}\right] < 0$, which was the corresponding condition when North had a unilateral tariff reform. It is also apparent from the first line that sufficient conditions for $T'\left[\tilde{e}_P - \delta R_{PI}\right] < 0$ are (1) $T'[\tilde{e}_P - (1-\alpha)R_{PI}] < 0$ and (2) $R_{IP}T > 0$. Thus, we have the following proposition.

Proposition 6. *Assume that Condition A ($H > 0$) holds and that $T'\left[\tilde{e}_P - \delta R_{PI}\right] < 0$. Then, a bilateral proportional tariff reduction of the form $\mathrm{d}T = -T\,\mathrm{d}\kappa$ and $\mathrm{d}t = -t\,\mathrm{d}\kappa$, where $\mathrm{d}\kappa > 0$, by South and North reduces successful illegal immigration.*

The welfare effects of the bilateral reform $\mathrm{d}T = -T\,\mathrm{d}\kappa$ and $\mathrm{d}t = -t\,\mathrm{d}\kappa$, where $\mathrm{d}\kappa > 0$, are as follows:

$$\begin{aligned}\overline{L}\widehat{E}_U\mathrm{d}U/\mathrm{d}\kappa &= \left[T'(\tilde{e}_P - R_{PI}) - IR_{II}\left\{1-(1-\alpha)T'\tilde{c}_y\right\}\right]\mathrm{d}I/\mathrm{d}\kappa \\ &\quad - T'S_{PP}T - I[T'\tilde{c}_y(1-\alpha)T'R_{PI} + (1-T'\tilde{c}_y)T'\tilde{e}_P], \qquad (50)\\ \tilde{e}_u\mathrm{d}\tilde{u}/\mathrm{d}\kappa &= (1-\alpha)R_{II}\mathrm{d}I/\mathrm{d}\kappa + T'[\tilde{e}_P - (1-\alpha)R_{PI}], \qquad (51)\\ l\widehat{e}_u\mathrm{d}u/\mathrm{d}\kappa &= H\,\mathrm{d}I/\mathrm{d}\kappa - t's_{pp}t - \alpha IT'R_{PI}, \qquad (52)\\ \mathrm{d}\tilde{u}/\mathrm{d}\kappa &= \mathrm{d}u/\mathrm{d}\kappa. \qquad (53)\end{aligned}$$

It is clear from the last condition that, as previously, South citizens all have the same utility change as a result of the bilateral tariff reform. Equation (51) leads to an ambiguously signed welfare gain for illegal immigrants. Specifically, the first term is positive since $R_{II} < 0$ and $\mathrm{d}I/\mathrm{d}\kappa < 0$ (by Proposition 6), while the second term is negative because of condition (i). The effect of the bilateral reform upon the welfare level of South residents therefore appears to be ambiguous in sign. Looking at (52), the positive second term ($-t's_{pp}t > 0$) must outweigh the other negative terms (due to $\mathrm{d}I/\mathrm{d}\kappa < 0$ and condition (ii) in Proposition 6) to ensure that South residents get a welfare gain, but this cannot be guaranteed in general. As with the welfare effects in (50) for North citizens under the unilateral reforms, the effects here are also ambiguous. In short, the bilateral tariff reform does not readily yield clear answers regarding the welfare effects, as recorded in the following proposition.

Proposition 7. *Assume that Condition A ($H > 0$) holds and that $T'\left[\tilde{e}_P - \delta R_{PI}\right] < 0$. Then, a bilateral proportional tariff reduction of the form $\mathrm{d}T = -T\,\mathrm{d}\kappa$ and $\mathrm{d}t = -t\,\mathrm{d}\kappa$, where $\mathrm{d}\kappa > 0$, by South and North raises or reduces the welfare level of illegal immigrants and residents of South equally. The effect upon the welfare of North citizens is also ambiguous.*

Before leaving this section, it is useful to contrast our results with those of Gaytan-Fregoso and Lahiri (2002), who also considered the effects of an equiproportional, bilateral tariff reform. Their model has a similar structure to ours, but their specification of the illegal immigration decision is based upon a family approach rather than our individual approach based on expected utility maximization. Gaytan-Fregoso and Lahiri obtain the results that (1) $\mathrm{d}I/\mathrm{d}\kappa < 0$ if $T'[\tilde{e}_P - R_{PI}] < 0$ and a particular matrix is positive definite and (2) North gains under the same conditions supplemented by some additional conditions. By contrast, we only get the result that $\mathrm{d}I/\mathrm{d}\kappa < 0$ if $T'[\tilde{e}_P - R_{PI}] < 0$ in the special case where there are no remittances. Moreover, as is clear from Proposition 7, we are unable to establish an unambiguous welfare effect. A lesson to be drawn from this comparison is that results depend crucially upon the model specification.

4 Conclusions

The issue of illegal immigration and the appropriate policy response by source and destination countries is of vital interest. In this chapter, we have investigated the role of various government policies in the determination of the level of illegal immigration and have also examined the welfare implications of these policies. Rather than deal with the direct policy of the host country devoting more resources to border patrols, we have considered the use of tariff reform as an indirect policy measure. More specifically, we have been concerned with the interaction between tariff distortions, illegal immigration, and welfare. This investigation has been undertaken in a general equilibrium model in which prospective illegal immigrants choose whether to attempt the broach of a border on the basis of expected utility maximization in the face of a probability of detection and deportation.

Our results concerning the effects of tariff reforms are much clearer when there are no remittances. The relaxation of this assumption to allow remittances creates complications by adding dependencies between the budget constraints of the agents. Remittances clearly connect the budget constraints of the citizens of South, since the illegal immigrants reduce their disposable income and remit this reduction to residents of South; one thereby suffers a loss in welfare while the other benefits. The budget constraints of North citizens and the illegal immigrants are interconnected, since the latter not only contribute to production but also extract income. Tariffs imposed by North further complicate this interdependency. The illegal immigrants contribute to tariff revenue through consumption and production. For example, their consumption of goods attracts import duties through import, while their contribution to production of dutiable goods reduces tariff revenue. As a result, the role of illegal immigrants in production and consumption affects tariff revenue, which is distributed to North citizens. This complicates the illegal immigration and welfare effects of tariff reforms, especially upon welfare of North citizens. Our research reported in this chapter highlights these effects.

Appendix: Stability

In this appendix, we specify a dynamic adjustment model and derive the Hicksian stability conditions that are used in the body of the chapter.

We consider the adjustment procedure

$$\dot{U} = \beta_1 \left[R(P, \overline{L} - L^{\theta}, I) - IR_I(P, \overline{L} - L^{\theta}, I) + T'M - E(P, G(L^G), U)\overline{L} \right], \quad (54)$$

$$\dot{\tilde{u}} = \beta_2 \left[(1-\alpha) R_I(P, \overline{L} - L^{\theta}, I) - e(P, G(L^G), \tilde{u}) \right], \quad (55)$$

$$\dot{u} = \beta_3 \left[r(p, \bar{l} - I) + \alpha I R_I(P, \overline{L} - L^{\theta}, I) + t'm - e(p,u)(\bar{l} - I) \right], \quad (56)$$

$$\dot{I} = \beta_4 \left[\tilde{u} - hk - u \right], \quad (57)$$

where a dot over variables denotes the time derivative and the positive constants $\beta_i\,(i = 1, \ldots, 4)$ are the speeds of adjustment. The assumed adjustment mechanism implies that utilities will rise if income exceeds expenditure and that the level of illegal immigration will rise if the expected utility from attempted immigration exceeds the utility level obtained from not making the attempt.

Linearization of these differential equations around the equilibrium gives

$$\begin{bmatrix} \dot{U} \\ \dot{\tilde{u}} \\ \dot{u} \\ \dot{I} \end{bmatrix} = \begin{bmatrix} -\beta_1 \overline{L}(E_U - T'E_{PU}) & \beta_1 I T' \tilde{e}'_{Pu} & 0 & -\beta_1 \left[IR_{II} + T'(R_{PI} - \tilde{e}_P) \right] \\ 0 & -\beta_2 \tilde{e}_u & 0 & \beta_2 (1-\alpha) R_{II} \\ 0 & 0 & -\beta_3 l(e_u - t'e_{pu}) & \beta_3 H \\ 0 & \beta_4 & -\beta_4 & 0 \end{bmatrix} \begin{bmatrix} dU \\ d\tilde{u} \\ du \\ dI \end{bmatrix},$$

where

$$H = e - r_l + \alpha(R_I + IR_{II}) + t'(r_{pl} - e_p).$$

Let the coefficient matrix be denoted by J and the ith principal minor by J_i. If J is a totally stable matrix, then J is a Hicksian matrix. This implies that (1) every principal minor of J of even order is positive and (2) every principal minor of J of odd order is negative. Thus, the Hicksian sufficient stability conditions are that

$$\begin{aligned} J_1 &= -\beta_1 \overline{L}(E_U - T'E_{PU}) < 0, \\ J_2 &= \beta_1 \beta_2 \overline{L}(E_U - T'E_{PU}) \tilde{e}_u = -\beta_2 J_1 \tilde{e}_u > 0, \\ J_3 &= -\beta_1 \beta_2 \beta_3 \overline{L}(E_U - T'E_{PU}) \tilde{e}_u l(e_u - t'e_{pu}) = -\beta_3 J_2 \tilde{e}_u l(e_u - t'e_{pu}) < 0, \\ J_4 &= \beta_1 \beta_2 \beta_3 \beta_4 \overline{L}(E_U - T'E_{PU}) K = -\beta_2 \beta_3 \beta_4 J_1 K > 0, \end{aligned}$$

where

$$K = \tilde{e}_u H - l(e_u - t'e_{pu})(1-\alpha) R_{II}.$$

We find that $E_U - T'E_{PU} = E_U(1 - T'E_{PU}/E_U) = E_U(1 - T'C_Y) > 0$ and $e_u - t'e_{pu} = e_u(1 - t'e_{pu}/e_u) = e_u(1 - t'c_y) > 0$, where $C_Y = E_{PU}/E_U$ and $c_y = e_{pu}/e_u$ are vectors of the income derivatives of the Marshallian demand functions for non-numeraire goods and the positive signs are the Hatta (1977) normality (or stability) conditions. Thus, the sign conditions on J_1, J_2, and J_3 for stability are automatically satisfied if Hatta normality is assumed. Stability condition $J_4 > 0$ will hold (under Hatta normality) if

$$K = \tilde{e}_u H - l e_u (1 - t' c_y)(1 - \alpha) R_{II} > 0.$$

It is readily shown that $C_I = \tilde{e}_u^{-1}(1-\alpha)R_{II} - l^{-1}\widehat{e}_u^{-1}H$ appearing in the body of the chapter is related to K by the equation $C_I \tilde{e}_u e_u (1 - t'c_y) + K = 0$. Thus, the sufficiency condition $K > 0$ may be equivalently expressed as $C_I < 0$. Finally, it is noted that a sufficient, but not necessary, condition for $K > 0$ ($C_I < 0$) is that $H > 0$.

Alternative approach to stability Assume that the utility budget constraints adjust instantaneously, but that the response of illegal immigration to differences in expected utilities is not instantaneous. Then, the adjustment model is $\dot{I} = \beta_4[\tilde{u} - hk - u]$, where the utility levels are determined by the three budget constraints. The differential approximation is given by $I = \beta_4 C_I \mathrm{d}I$ and the stability condition is that $\beta_4 C_I < 0$ or, equivalently, that $C_I < 0$.

Acknowledgment We wish to thank the participants at the Conference on Globalization, International Trade and Economic Dynamics in Memory of Koji Shimomura at Kobe University and the referee for very helpful comments. This research was initiated while Woodland was visiting Ritsumeikan University, whose kind and generous hospitality is gratefully acknowledged. Woodland also thanks the Australian Research Council for financial support for this research.

References

Bandyopadhyay S, Bandyopadhyay SC (1998) Illegal immigration: a supply side analysis. J Dev Econ 57:343–360

Bond EW, Chen T-J (1987) The welfare effects of illegal migration. J Int Econ 23:315–328

Djajic S (1987) Illegal aliens, unemployment, and immigration policy. J Dev Econ 25:235–249

Djajic S (1999) Dynamics of immigration control. J Popul Econ 12:45–61

Ethier WJ (1986a) Illegal immigration: the host country problem. Am Econ Rev 76:56–71

Ethier WJ (1986b) Illegal immigration. Am Econ Rev 76:258–262

Gaytan-Fregoso H, Lahiri S (2000) Foreign aid and illegal immigration. J Dev Econ 63:515–527

Gaytan-Fregoso H, Lahiri S (2002) Regionalism and illegal immigration in North America. In: Lahiri S (ed) Regionalism and globalization. Routledge, London, pp 92–109

Hatta T (1977) A recommendation for a better tariff structure. Econometrica 45:1859–1869

Kahana N, Lecker T (2005) Competition as a track for preventing illegal immigration. Econ Gov 6:33–39

Levine P (1999) The welfare economics of immigration control. J Popul Econ 12:23–43

Nihon Keizai Shimbun (2007) EU, Chichukai shokoku to jiyuboueki-ken koso (in Japanese), 15 November

Staring R (2000) International migration, undocumented immigrants and immigrant entrepreneurship. In: Rath J (ed) Immigrant business – the economic, political and social environment. Macmillan, London

Woodland AD (1982) International trade and resource allocation. North-Holland/Elsevier Science, Amsterdam/New York

Woodland AD, Yoshida C (2006) Risk preference, illegal immigration and immigration policy. J Dev Econ 81:500–513

Part II
Static Theory of International Trade Under Imperfect Competition

Trade in Counterfeit Organic Products

E. Kwan Choi

Abstract This chapter investigates trade in organic and nonorganic products between the North and the South. The labor-abundant South exports the labor-intensive organic product to the North, but imports from the South contain some counterfeits. In the absence of labels, consumers cannot differentiate between the two products using naked eye. When properly labeled, organic and nonorganic products are close substitutes, but the former commands a higher market price. Accordingly, traders have an incentive to pass off the nonorganic product as an organic product. There is no need for the government to regulate the production of organic or nonorganic products. If law enforcement is costly, controlling counterfeit imports is socially optimal, but total elimination of counterfeits or an import ban is not socially optimal.

1 Introduction

Organic products have come into vogue in developing as well as developed economies.[1] Conventional or processed goods are produced by capital-intensive methods, whereas organic products are labor-intensive and are produced by small firms. Organic products entering the world markets generally are produced by small firms in developing countries and sold in high-income countries of North America, Europe, and Asia. Also, consumers have become sensitive to organic production and animal welfare in Europe and America. Demand for organic products has risen so steadily that supply is not keeping up with demand in high-income countries.

[1] Organic farming was practiced throughout history until the use of herbicides and pesticides became widespread during the last century. Chemically intensive farming was gradually adopted because nonorganic fruit and vegetables cost less but command almost the same prices as their organic counterparts.

E.K. Choi
Department of Economics, Iowa State University, Ames, IA 50011, USA,
e-mail: kchoi@iastate.edu

T. Kamihigashi and L. Zhao (eds.) *International Trade and Economic Dynamics – Essays in Memory of Koji Shimomura.*

Gradually, a two-tier price system has developed: consumers pay a higher price for organic products and a lower price for the conventional products.

In the absence of product labels, it is difficult for consumers to distinguish between the two products by visual inspection. Producers of processed foods have an incentive to pass off conventional products as organic products. Nonorganic goods produced in developing countries may be exported as organic products to developed economies. After several recalls of hazardous imports in recent years, consumers in developed economies are calling for better guarantees of the safety of imports. Some regions of Europe also ban imports of genetically modified (GM) products. Differing standards for organic products also can be a trade barrier.[2]

Grossman and Shapiro (1988) noted that counterfeits usually are of inferior quality to genuine products and undermine the functioning of property rights.[3] Moreover, they may pose health risks to consumers. Governments of various countries are issuing product safety alerts and importers are recalling their products imported from developing countries.[4]

Counterfeit manufactured goods are a relatively recent phenomenon, but counterfeiting of agricultural products is not new. Pliny the Elder, the first century Roman historian, noted that even their royal families rarely enjoy wines that are genuine. Counterfeit organic foods are widespread in developed as well as developing countries. The organic industry is plagued by widespread fraud. China Daily (2007) noted that "in a random selection of 268 goods labeled organic, including rice, oil, eggs, vegetables, and drinks, 25 samples were counterfeit." Similarly, according to the Times Online (2007), 1.5 million items of counterfeit food and drink were confiscated in the European Union in 2003.

This chapter considers international trade of organic and nonorganic products.[5] Wage–rent ratio is lower in the South. Since organic production is less chemical-intensive and more labor-intensive, developing countries are better suited for producing and exporting organic products. Higgins and Rubin (1986) suggest that in some cases consumers may be deceived and think that they are buying genuine goods when they are not. Consumers may have difficulty differentiating the two products by visual inspection or through consumption, but organic products generally command higher market prices. Accordingly, Southern exporters have an incentive to pass off nonorganic products as organic products. Counterfeit products

[2] There are three major arbiters of organic standards: the U.S. government's National Organic Program (NOP), the EU standard, and Japan's Japanese Agricultural Standard (JAS). Organic standards differ among countries, and thus constitute a trade barrier. American firms are targeting Asian countries because of their lack of organic standards. Consumers do not exactly know what "organic" means, and lack of common standards causes "a sea of counterfeit organic foods" (Ellsworth 2001).

[3] Grossman and Shapiro (1988) first considered trade in counterfeit products. In their model, counterfeit products of inferior quality are produced in developing countries.

[4] For instance, Food Standards Agency (2007) regularly issues consumer alerts warning of dangerous products.

[5] This is a partial equilibrium model of two traded goods that are close substitutes, not a full-fledged general equilibrium model.

may be produced in developed economies as well,[6] but in practice, the majority of counterfeit goods are produced in developing countries.

The plan of this chapter is as follows: Sect. 2 lays out an autarky Nash equilibrium of two markets producing close substitutes. When imports are banned, Nash-type producers choose outputs, ignoring their impacts on the other market. Section 3 considers an optimal autarky equilibrium that maximizes joint profits. Section 4 investigates optimal regulation when imports contain counterfeit nonorganic products. Section 5 discusses long-run equilibrium with counterfeit imports, while Sect. 6 examines socially optimal regulation of counterfeit trade. Concluding remarks are found in Sect. 7.

2 Autarky Equilibrium of Organic and Nonorganic Industries

There are two countries or regions. The North is capital-abundant and the South is labor-abundant. Each country produces two goods. The conventional processed product is capital-intensive while the organic product is labor-intensive. We first consider autarky equilibrium of two industries, which sell close substitutes. Each market may be characterized by perfect competition (PC), monopoly (M), oligopoly (O), or monopolistic competition (MP). With or without product differentiation, there can be several pairings of two markets. In this chapter, we consider only the PC–PC mode. In the first market, many firms sell nonorganic products, and in the second many competitive firms sell the organic product, which competes with its close substitute in the first market.

Organic products are considered to be of higher quality, and generally command higher prices than their conventional counterparts in the same product category. Organic products and conventional products are difficult to distinguish by naked eye or through consumption, and consumers generally rely on product labels to differentiate between the two. Thus, they are perfect substitutes in the absence of labels, but are "close substitutes" when labels correctly identify them.

Consider the autarky equilibrium in the North without counterfeit imports. When imports include some counterfeits, an import ban can ensure total elimination of counterfeits. For instance, some European countries ban imports of GM products. Let X and Y denote outputs of the organic and nonorganic product. The inverse demand for the conventional food in the North is given by

$$p = a - bY - gX. \quad (1)$$

All parameters, a, b, and g, are positive. Since the two products are close but not perfect substitutes ($g < b$), the presence of the organic product decreases the demand for the conventional product ($g > 0$).

Assume that there is a large number of organic producers, and let X denote the industry output. The inverse demand function for the organic product in the North

[6] For instance, Coca-Cola promoted its bottled water Dasani in 2004 as "pure, still water," but later withdrew the claim after it was revealed to be purified tap water.

is given by

$$P = A - BX - GY, \tag{2}$$

where P is the price of the organic product and A is a positive constant. Since the nonorganic and organic products are close substitutes, the price of a product is inversely related, not only to its own quantity, but also to the quantity of the other product ($G > 0$). Since they are not perfect substitutes, the slopes of cross demand curves are less than those of own demand curves, that is, $g < b$ and $G < B$.

2.1 Autarky Equilibrium

Consider the autarky equilibrium of the North. Although the supply of the nonorganic product decreases the demand for the organic product, each competitive firm is a *price taker* and assumes that the output of the other industry is given. The aggregate profit of the nonorganic industry is given by

$$\pi = (a - bY - gX)Y - c(Y), \tag{3}$$

where $c(Y)$ is the industry's production cost. Since the nonorganic producers act as price takers,

$$\frac{\partial \pi}{\partial Y} \equiv p - c' = 0, \tag{4}$$

which defines the nonorganic industry's best response $Y = r(X)$ to the organic industry output X. Differentiating (4), we obtain the slope of the nonorganic industry's best response function,

$$r'(X) \equiv \left.\frac{\mathrm{d}Y}{\mathrm{d}X}\right|_r = -\frac{\pi_{YX}}{\pi_{YY}} = -\frac{g}{b} < 0,$$

that is, the nonorganic industry decreases its output as the organic industry expands.

Next, consider the production decision of the organic producers in the North. The industry profit is

$$\Pi = (A - BX - GY)X - C(X), \tag{5}$$

where $C(X)$ is the industry's production cost. The first order condition is

$$\frac{\partial \Pi}{\partial X} \equiv P - C' = 0. \tag{6}$$

Organic producers also are price takers. Market demand for their product depends on the output of the other industry that produces a close substitute. Equation (6) defines the organic industry's best response $X = R(Y)$ to the nonorganic industry's aggregate output. Differentiating (6), we obtain the slope of the organic industry's best response function,

$$R'(Y) \equiv \left.\frac{\mathrm{d}X}{\mathrm{d}Y}\right|_R = -\frac{\Pi_{XY}}{\Pi_{XX}} = -\frac{G}{B} < 0.$$

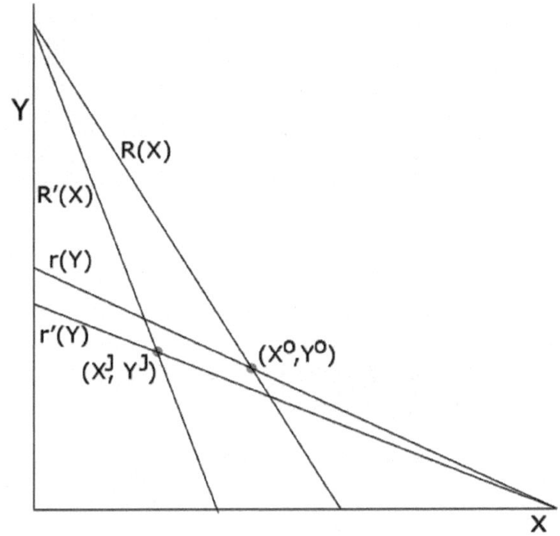

Fig. 1 Nash equilibrium and joint profit maximizing outputs

Thus, the organic industry's output decreases as the nonorganic industry expands. Let $(X^{\mathrm{o}}, Y^{\mathrm{o}})$ denote the pair of outputs of the organic and the nonorganic firms at a Nash equilibrium, where producers assume that the output of the other market is given. Combining the behavioral equations (6) and (4), we obtain a Nash autarky equilibrium in Fig. 1:

$$X^{\mathrm{o}} = \frac{b(A-C') - G(a-c')}{bB - gG}, \tag{7}$$

$$Y^{\mathrm{o}} = \frac{B(a-c') - g(A-C')}{bB - gG}, \tag{8}$$

where $\Delta \equiv bB - gG > 0$ by assumption. Note that $g > 0$ and $G > 0$ imply that cross demand curves are positively sloped, that is, an increase in the price of one good increases the demand for the other product. It can be shown that the best response curve of the organic industry is steeper than that of the nonorganic industry, as shown in Fig. 1.

3 Optimal Autarky Equilibrium

When the probability of hazardous imports is zero, free trade is optimal, and the North imports organic products from the South. If the probability of hazardous imports is one, then banning all imports from the South may be an optimal policy.[7]

[7] In some cases, the counterfeits are not hazardous, but simply nonfunctional. For example, EPA (2007) urged retailers and distributors to watch for counterfeit pet products marketed to control flees and ticks.

In the present model, we assume that both goods are safe. While the North intends to import the organic product, counterfeits are mingled with the genuine organic products. Consequently, some imports from the South are nonorganic products.

We first consider the optimal autarky equilibrium when all imports are banned. For instance, some countries of Europe declare themselves as genetically modified organism (GMO)-free areas. The import ban may eliminate counterfeit imports, but the country sacrifices gains from trade. Thus, an import ban may not be an optimal policy.

It is important to note that the intermarket Nash equilibrium in the previous section is a noncooperative equilibrium, and hence joint profit of the two industries is not maximized. How is the socially optimal output mix of organic and nonorganic products determined? Consider optimal autarky equilibrium that maximizes joint profit or the total profits of the two industries:

$$J = \pi + \Pi = (a - bY - gX)Y - c(Y) + (A - BX - GY)X - C(X). \tag{9}$$

The first order conditions are

$$\frac{\partial J}{\partial X} \equiv P - gY - C'(X) = 0, \tag{10}$$

$$\frac{\partial J}{\partial Y} \equiv p - GX - c'(Y) = 0. \tag{11}$$

The solution is

$$X^J = \frac{A^*b - a^*(g+G)}{bB - (g+G)^2}, \quad Y^J = \frac{A^*(g+G) - a^*B}{bB - (g+G)^2}, \tag{12}$$

where $a^* = a - c'$ and $A^* = A - C'$. Note that $gG < (g+G)^2$. Thus, $bB - gG > bB - (g+G)^2$. Thus, $X > X' = \frac{A^*b - a^*(g+G)}{bB} < X^{\text{o}} = \frac{A^*b - a^*G}{bB}$.

Let (X^J, Y^J) denote the optimal outputs for joint profit maximum. Then the left hand side of (11) is negative when evaluated at $(X^{\text{o}}, Y^{\text{o}})$. This implies that for any given output of Y, joint profit would be higher if the organic producers were to produce less than their noncooperative output level. Likewise, the left hand side of (10) is negative when evaluated at $(X^{\text{o}}, Y^{\text{o}})$.

In Fig. 1, $R'(Y)$ is the locus of (X,Y) satisfying $\partial J/\partial X = 0$, and lies below $R(Y)$. Similarly, $r'(X)$ is the locus of (X,Y) along which $\partial J/\partial Y = 0$ lies below $r(X)$. Accordingly, the relationship between the socially optimal output (X^J, Y^J) and the Nash equilibrium output $(X^{\text{o}}, Y^{\text{o}})$ cannot be determined a priori.

From the first order conditions in (10) and (11), we obtain

$$\frac{P - gY}{p - GX} = \frac{C'(X)}{c'(Y)}, \tag{13}$$

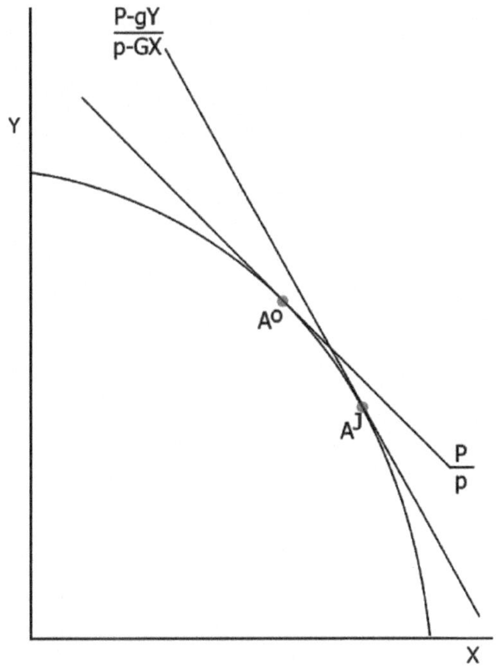

Fig. 2 Intermarket dependence and joint profit maximizing output

where $MRT \equiv C'(X)/c'(Y)$ is the marginal rate of transformation. Note that for given factor supplies, the total costs of the two industries are fixed, $C(X)+c(Y) = wL+rK$. Thus, for joint profit maximization, MRT must be equal to the ratio of marginal revenues, $(P-gY)/(p-GX)$, which is not equal to the price ratio, P/p. If $(P-gY)/(p-GX) > P/p$, and MRT must be greater than at competitive equilibrium. In this case, $A^J = (X^J, Y^J)$ is to the right of $A^o = (X^o, Y^o)$, as shown in Fig. 2. We summarize these results:

Proposition 1. *When imports are banned, either the nonorganic industry or the organic industry produces more than is socially optimal, that is, either* $X^J < X^o$ *or* $Y^J < Y^o$. *Moreover,*

(i) if $\frac{P-gY}{p-GX} > \frac{P}{p}$, *then* $X^J > X^o$ *and* $Y^J < Y^o$,
(ii) if $\frac{P-gY}{p-GX} < \frac{P}{p}$, *then* $X^J < X^o$ *and* $Y^J > Y^o$, *and*
(iii) if $\frac{P-gY}{p-GX} = \frac{P}{p}$, *then* $X^J = X^o$ *and* $Y^J = Y^o$.

Nash equilibrium does not necessarily maximize national income because of the interdependence of the two markets, that is, an increase in one industry's output affects the price of the other product. In the special case where the two market demands are independent of each other, Nash equilibrium maximizes joint profit.

4 Counterfeit Imports and Regulation

When the North opens up to trade, it begins to import allegedly organic products from the South. Unlike ordinary consumer goods, the organic and nonorganic products are not distinguishable by naked eye or through consumption. Despite the apparent resemblance, production of the organic product is less costly than that for the nonorganic product, that is, $C(X) < c(Y)$ for $X = Y$.

When there is a significant price difference, firms have an incentive to pass off nonorganic product as organic product. *Counterfeiting* is said to occur when a trader passes off a low-quality product as a high-quality product. Thus, exporting a nonorganic product as an organic product constitutes counterfeit trade. When a nonorganic product is correctly labeled and sold, it is a legitimate product. However, when a safe but chemical-intensive product is labeled and sold as an organic product, it is a counterfeit. Since the quality of the processed product is considered inferior to the organic product, it is assumed that $P > p$.

There are at least three possible ways for counterfeit trade to occur between the South and the North. First, an organic producer may purchase some nonorganic products and export them as organic products. This method hurts the reputation of the firm as an organic exporter, and is less likely to be adopted by the going concerns.[8]

Second, an independent exporter in a developing country or an importer in the developed country can engage in counterfeiting. It is assumed that the counterfeit trader does not engage in production activities. Third, if law enforcement is lax, a producer of conventional products may pass off some or all his output as an organic product. In this case, his profit is simply the sum of profits from production and profits from counterfeiting. His counterfeiting profit is the same as that when counterfeiting is practiced by an independent firm. Thus, we consider the second scenario.

4.1 Counterfeit Trade Distorts Market Demands

Counterfeit imports by an independent importer materially affect and distort market demands for the organic and nonorganic products in the North.[9] The price of the organic product will be affected in the same manner, whether the product supplied is a genuine organic product or a counterfeit.

Assume that there are no tariff barriers, and the North imports a supposedly organic product from the South. However, inspection at the border is not perfect,

[8] Alternatively, an importer may knowingly import nonorganic product from the South and pass it as organic product. But this scenario is not likely because nonorganic products are also available in the North. The stigma cost for counterfeiting producers is so high that no Northern producers engage in counterfeiting.

[9] This approach is similar to that in Choi (2007), which considers counterfeiters that pass off GM product as GMO-free product. Because of the high cost of GM technology, GM product is produced by a monopolist, but organic products are produced at many competitive firms in the present model.

and some counterfeits are concealed among the imports. There are two types of importers, genuine organic importers and counterfeit importers. Let Q denote the quantity of the genuine organic product the North imports from the South, and let Z denote the quantity of the nonorganic product in the imports. Thus, the total quantity of supposedly organic imports is $(Q+Z)$. Since the two products are difficult to differentiate, the government hires L workers to detect counterfeits among imports.

Possession or sale of the nonorganic product is not illegal, but it is illegal to pass it off as an organic product. Because of the law enforcement activity, only F units of counterfeits are caught and resold to consumers in the nonorganic market. We assume that the catch rate $F(L,Z)$ increases with the number of policing agents and the quantity of counterfeits imported, that is, $F_L > 0$ and $F_Z > 0$. However, $(Z-F)$ units of the nonorganic product are sold as organic product. In the absence of counterfeiting, $(X+Q)$ units of organic product are available and sold as such in the organic food market. When counterfeiting occurs, only $(X+Q+Z-F)$ units of supposedly organic products are made available in the organic product market, but among these, only $(X+Q)$ units are genuine organic products, and the remainders, $Z-F$ units, are counterfeits. When caught, the counterfeits are resold in the nonorganic market. Accordingly, the supply of the nonorganic product increases by F. Thus, the inverse demand for the organic product is written as

$$P = A - B(X+Z+Q-F) - G(Y+F). \tag{14}$$

Note that $\partial P/\partial Z = -B(1-F_Z) - GF_Z < 0$. Thus, imports of counterfeit Z lower the price of the organic product. Since counterfeiting increases the quantity supplied, the price of the organic product declines. The inverse demand for the conventional product is written as

$$p = a - b(Y+F) - g(X+Q+Z-F). \tag{15}$$

Differentiating (15) with respect to Z, we get $\partial p/\partial Z = (b-g)(1-F_Z) > 0$. Thus, *counterfeiting raises the price of the nonorganic product but depresses the price of the organic product.* Accordingly, counterfeiting reduces the price gap between the two goods,

$$\partial(P-p)/\partial Z < 0. \tag{16}$$

The moment the two prices are equalized, there is no need to engage in counterfeiting. Thus, we assume that the price of the organic product is always higher, $P > p$.

4.2 Counterfeit Importers

Note that importers of the genuine organic product buy and sell Q units at the same price P, and hence make zero profits. Thus, their profits or activities will not be investigated. Consider the counterfeiting profit of an independent firm that purchases the nonorganic product in the South and sells it as organic product in the North.[10] These counterfeiter traders may exist in the South or the North, but their geographic location is economically irrelevant. Their nationality or ownership also is meaningless, as long as their profits are made in the North. We assume that their profits are made in the North and they will be treated as counterfeit importers.

The catch or failure rate $F(L,Z)$ is positively related to the volume of counterfeit imports, Z, and the number of policing agents, L. In the absence of policing effort, no counterfeits are caught, $F(0,Z) = 0$. Recall that $F_L > 0$ and $F_Z > 0$. Marginal catch rate increases with counterfeiting ($F_{LZ} > 0$), that is, the catch rate of an extra policing agent is greater when more counterfeits flood the market.

Because of diminishing returns ($F_{LL} < 0$), not all counterfeits are caught, $F(L,Z) < Z$. $(Z - F)$ units of counterfeits are sold at $P$and the revenue from undetected counterfeits is $P(Z-F)$. The importer makes no profit from the nonorganic product when caught, but pays penalty TF. The firm buys the nonorganic product at price p but sells it at P, if not caught. Revenue from uncaught counterfeits is $(P-p)(Z-F)$. Thus, profit from counterfeit imports is

$$\Phi = (P-p)(Z-F(L,Z)) - TF. \tag{17}$$

Cheating is profitable if $\Phi > 0$, or

$$\frac{Z-F}{F} > \frac{T}{P-p}. \tag{18}$$

Note that T is the penalty per unit of counterfeit when caught, and $(P-p)$ is the gain per unit when not caught. When counterfeiting is regulated ($L > 0$), F is the failure rate and $(Z-F)$ is the number of counterfeits that survive the policing effort. Let $\sigma \equiv (Z-F)/F$ denote the survival rate or the relative fraction of counterfeits not caught. For example, if three out of four counterfeits attempted succeeds and one is caught, the relative survival rate is 3 to 1, or $\sigma = 3$.

In the absence of any policing effort, $T = 0$ and $F(0,Z) = 0$, and counterfeiting is profitable and hence needs to be regulated. If counterfeiting is regulated ($L > 0$) and the pain-to-gain ratio, $\theta \equiv T/(P-p)$ exceeds the survival rate$(Z-F)/F$, no cheating is optimal. On the other hand, if the pain-to-gain ratio is less than the survival rate, then counterfeiting is profitable despite the policing effort.

Recall that competitive producers of the nonorganic and organic products are price takers. Since there are a large number of counterfeiters, we assume they are price takers. Differentiating (17) with respect to Z gives

$$\Phi_Z \equiv (P-p)(1-F_Z) - TF_Z = 0. \tag{19}$$

---

[10] The counterfeiting firm also may purchase nonorganic products from domestic producers, and pass them off as organic products. But this scenario with both domestic and foreign counterfeiters is not considered here.

Since only a fraction of additional counterfeits are caught, the marginal detection rate is positive but less than unity ($0 < F_Z < 1$). Note that $(P-p)(1-F_Z)$ is marginal revenue and TF_Z is the marginal penalty cost of counterfeiting. Note that $T=0$ in the absence of policing agents. In this case, the left hand side of (19) reduces to $(P-p)(1-F_Z) > 0$, and hence counterfeiting occurs when there are no police agents. On the other hand, if there are enough policing agents that each additional counterfeit is caught ($F_Z = 1$), then the left hand side of (19) reduces to $-T < 0$ and counterfeiting disappears. If not all counterfeits are caught and condition (18) holds, then some counterfeiting is profitable.

How does increased policing effort affect cheating by the counterfeiters? Differentiating (19) with respect to L gives

$$\frac{\partial Z}{\partial L} = -\frac{\pi_{ZL}}{\pi_{ZZ}} < 0, \tag{20}$$

where $\pi_{ZZ} < 0$ and $\pi_{ZL} = -(P-p+T)F_{ZL} < 0$. We now summarize the results on counterfeiting:

Proposition 2. *(1) In the absence of regulation ($L=0$ and $T=0$), counterfeiting is profitable, (2) if the pain-to-gain ratio is greater than the survival rate ($\theta \geq \sigma$), then no counterfeiting is optimal, (3) if $\theta < \sigma$, then counterfeiting is profitable, and (4) if $F_{LZ} > 0$, then increased policing effort deters counterfeiting, $\partial Z/\partial L < 0$.*

5 Long-Run Equilibrium with Counterfeit Trade

Long-run equilibrium is a situation in which producers of the nonorganic and organic products coexist with counterfeit importers. Also, except for the penalty, there are no entry barriers to counterfeiting. Thus, long-run equilibrium is characterized by zero profit of counterfeit importers.

If the representative counterfeit importer receives a positive profit ($\phi \equiv \Phi/n > 0$), more counterfeiters will enter the market. The number of counterfeiters n continues to increase until the representative counterfeit importer's profit is zero ($\phi = 0$) or when the aggregate profit of counterfeit importers is zero ($\Phi = 0$).

Profits of the counterfeiting importers are positive if and only if the representative counterfeit importer obtains profits. Let $z = Z/n$ denote the number of nonorganic products that the representative counterfeiter imports and passes off as organic products, and let $f(L,z) = F(L,Z)/n$ be the number of counterfeits caught by policing agents. The total profit of counterfeit importers in (17) is written as

$$\Phi = (P-p)(Z - F(L,Z)) - TF(L,Z), \tag{21}$$

where

$$P - p = (A-a) - (G-b)Y - (g-B)(X+Q+Z-F). \tag{22}$$

From (17), in long-run equilibrium,

$$\frac{T}{p-P} = \frac{Z-F}{F},$$

that is, the pain-to-gain ratio must be equal to the survival rate.

We show that the ensuing entry reduces the profit of the representative counterfeit importer, and ensures the stability of long-run equilibrium. Assume that initially aggregate counterfeiting profits are positive. Differentiating (21) with respect to n and holding z constant, we get

$$\frac{\partial \Phi}{\partial n} \equiv (P_Z - p_Z)z(Z-F) + n((P-p)(1-F_Z) - TF_Z) < 0. \tag{23}$$

From (16), the first term on the left hand side of (23) is negative. That is, an increase in the number of counterfeiting importers decreases the price gap, $\delta \equiv (P-p)$. The second term is zero for short-run profit maximization, as shown in (19). Thus, as the number of counterfeiters increases, industry profit declines. Let $\phi = \Phi/n$ denote the profits of the representative counterfeit importer. Then $\phi_n = (\Phi_n n - \Phi)/n^2 < 0$ if the industry is earning nonnegative profits. Thus, the representative counterfeit importer's profit declines as more counterfeiters enter the market, $\partial\phi/\partial n < 0$. Long-run equilibrium is characterized by zero industry profit.

6 Optimal Regulation of Counterfeit Trade

The ultimate question is whether counterfeit imports are harmful to the importing country. Should counterfeit imports be eliminated at all cost, or should some counterfeit trade be tolerated? The importing country needs to eliminate counterfeit products that are intrinsically harmful and jeopardize public health or safety. Recalls of dangerous toys and other unsafe products are a good indication of the importing country's resolve to eliminate hazardous imports.

In this chapter, we consider only a nonorganic product, in itself a legitimate product, which is passed off as organic product. Counterfeit products generally originate in the nonorganic markets in the South and are mingled and sold in the organic market in the North. We now investigate whether it is necessary to regulate the outputs of the North's nonorganic and organic industries.

6.1 Total Profit Maximization

Consider the problem of a regulator that maximizes joint profit,

$$\begin{aligned} J \equiv \pi + \Pi + \Phi + G &\equiv (a - b(Y+F) - g(X+Q+Z-F))Y - c(Y) \\ &+ (A - B(X+Q+Z-F) - G(Y+F))X - C(X) + (P-p)(Z-F(L,Z)) - wL \\ &= pY - c(Y) + PX - C(X) + (P-p)(Z-F(L,Z)) - wL, \end{aligned} \tag{24}$$

where $p = a - b(Y+F) - g(X+Q+Z-F), P = A - B(X+Q+Z-F) - G(Y+F)$, and $\Phi + G = (P-p)(Z-F) - wL$.

Recall that counterfeit importers are price takers and treat prices, p and P, as given. Differentiating (24) with respect to Y and X yields

$$\frac{\partial J}{\partial Y} \equiv p - c'(Y) = 0, \tag{25}$$

$$\frac{\partial J}{\partial X} \equiv P - C'(X) = 0. \tag{26}$$

Equations (25) and (26) are the same as those for the Nash intermarket equilibrium of competitive firms in (4) and (6). Thus, there is no need for the regulator to directly control the outputs in these markets. Moreover, this is true even if Z were counterfeits originated in the domestic market.

Proposition 3. *There is no need to regulate directly the prices or outputs of the nonorganic and organic products in the North.*

Next, we consider whether it is necessary to regulate counterfeit imports. Differentiating (24) with respect to L gives

$$\frac{\partial J}{\partial L} \equiv -(P-p)F_L - w \leq 0 \tag{27}$$

for $L > 0$. The left hand side of (27) is negative for all $L > 0$, and hence $L = 0$. In other words, if the regulator maximizes joint profit of the North, including the illegal profits of the counterfeit importers, then no law enforcement is optimal ($L = 0$).

Proposition 4. *If the government maximizes joint profit, inclusive of profits of counterfeit importers, no policing is optimal* ($L = 0$).

6.2 Legal Profit Maximization

Proposition 2 shows that in the absence of regulation, counterfeiting proliferates, and hence needs to be regulated. However, will it be socially optimal to eliminate counterfeit imports completely? We now assume that the regulator maximizes only legal profits. Excluding profits from counterfeit imports, the sum of legal profits is

$$\begin{aligned} J^o \equiv \pi + \Pi + G &\equiv (a - b(Y+F) - g(X+Q+Z-F))Y - c(Y) \\ &+ (A - B(X+Q+Z-F) - G(Y+F))X - C(X) + TF - wL \\ &= pY - c(Y) + PX - C(X) + TF(L,Z) - wL. \end{aligned} \tag{28}$$

Differentiating (28) with respect to X and Y, again we get (26) and (25). Since the first order conditions for optimal choice of (X,Y) by the regulator are the same as those made by the competitive firms in the two markets, there is no need for the government to directly regulate the two markets. In other words, there is no need to be mindful of the profits of the two industries. Thus, Proposition 3 holds, whether the government is interested in maximizing legal or total profits.

We now assume that the regulator is mindful only of its own revenue and law enforcement costs. The government receives penalty revenue $TF(L,Z)$ from counterfeit traffickers, but incurs enforcement cost. The policing cost is wL, where w is wage. Net government revenue is

$$G = TF(L,Z) - wL. \tag{29}$$

First, consider the policing decision of a naïve government, which assumes counterfeiting attempt Z is given. Differentiating (29) with respect to L gives

$$\frac{\partial G}{\partial L} \equiv TF_L - w = 0. \tag{30}$$

Recall that the marginal catch rate is positive but less than unity, $0 < F_L < 1$. It follows that penalty is $T > w$. Let L^* denote the number of policing agents needed to eliminate counterfeits, that is, $F_L(L^*, Z) = 0$ and $F(L^*, Z) = Z$. If policing agents are volunteers and work for free, the left hand side of (30), $F_L T$, is positive for all $L < L^*$ and counterfeiting is eliminated. However, if policing agents are paid the market wage, then the government hires some workers, $L < L^*$ and some counterfeit imports remain.

How high should the penalty be? If the policing cost exceeds penalty revenue, the policing branch of the government needs to be subsidized by taxes. We assume that the government's goal is to regulate counterfeit trafficking at zero cost. Then optimal penalty is then

$$T = \frac{wL}{F}.$$

6.3 Government as Stackelberg Leader

Next, assume that the government behaves as a Stackelberg leader in law enforcement. A Stackelberg-type government recognizes the counterfeit importers' response to the policing effort. In this case, the government's objective function is

$$G = TF\,(L, Z(L)) - wL. \tag{31}$$

The first order condition is

$$\frac{\partial G}{\partial L} \equiv T\left(F_L + F_Z \frac{\partial Z}{\partial L}\right) - w = 0. \tag{32}$$

Recall that counterfeit importers' response to the policing effort is given in (20), that is, $\partial Z/\partial L < 0$. When comparing (30) and (32), the latter has an extra term,

$F_L(\partial Z/\partial L)$, on the left hand side. Let L_N and L_S denote the numbers of policing agents hired for the naïve and the Stackelberg-type governments, respectively. When evaluated at L_N, the left hand side of (32) is negative, which implies that $L_S < L_N$. That is, a Stackelberg-type government hires fewer policing agents when the counterfeiters' reaction is taken into account.

Proposition 5. *If the government maximizes only legal joint profits and law enforcement is costly* $(w > 0)$, *then some policing of counterfeit imports is optimal, but total elimination of counterfeit trade is not optimal* $(L < L^*)$. *A Stackelberg-type government hires fewer policing agents than a naïve government,* $L_S < L_N$.

7 Concluding Remarks

This chapter considered trade in counterfeit organic products between the North and the South. Because of the price differences, traders have an incentive to pass off the nonorganic product as organic product, which constitutes counterfeiting. The majority of counterfeit products are produced in the South and some are exported to the high-income, developed countries of the North.

In a sense, counterfeit products are like goods that generate pollution and impose spillover costs on other producers. The Southern government has little incentive to regulate the counterfeit exporters, while the Northern government has no jurisdiction to regulate Southern industries. Accordingly, the Northern government can regulate only counterfeit imports.

Regulations designed to control counterfeit trade are socially optimal but total elimination of counterfeit trade may be too costly.

References

China Daily (2007) Consumers swallow organic food claims. http://www.chinadaily.com.cn/english/doc/2005–03/15/content_424824.htm. Accessed 15 September 2007

Choi EK (2001) Genetically modified products and counterfeiting, Iowa State University, IA

Choi EK (2005) Mixed markets with counterfeit producers. In: Choi EK, Hartigan J (eds) Handbook of international trade – economic and legal analysis of trade policy and institutions, vol. 2. Blackwell Publishing, Oxford, pp 427–458

Ellsworth J (2001) A history of organic food regulation. http://leda.law.harvard.edu/leda/data/383/Ellsworth.html. Accessed 5 October 2007

Environmental Protection Agency (2007) Couterfeit pet products for dogs and cats. http://www.epa.gov/pesticides/factsheets/petproduct.htm. Accessed on 25 February 2007

Food Standards Agency, UK (2007) food standards agency alerts. http://rbkc.gov.uk/EnvironmentalServices/FoodHygieneandStandards/fsa_warnings.asp. Accessed 15 September 2007

Grossman G, Shapiro C (1988) Counterfeit-product trade, Am Econ Rev 78:59–75

Higgins R, Rubin P (1986) Counterfeit goods, J Law Econ 29:211–30

Times Online (2004) Coca Cola faces probe over bottled tap water, http://www.timesonline.co.uk/tol/news/article1035332.ece. Accessed 12 September 2007

Times Online (2007) Is it really organic?, http://women.timesonline.co.uk/tol/life_and_style/women/body_and_soul/article1394983.ece. Accessed 15 September 2007

U.S. International Trade Commission (1984) The effects of foreign production counterfeiting on US industry. USITC Publication No. 1479

Foreign Economic Aid and Trade Liberalization Under Imperfect Competition

Hiroshi Kurata and Masayuki Okawa(✉)

Abstract This chapter examines the possibility of a mutually beneficial policy combination of economic aid by a donor country and tariff reducing trade liberalization in the recipient country under imperfect competition. We set up a simple two country Ricardian trading model in which the donor's export good is supplied by a monopoly firm and the recipient country imposes tariff on imports from the donor country. We derive the condition that mutually beneficial policy coordination can be agreed by the two countries.

1 Introduction

In 2008, the number of member countries in the WTO was reported to have increased to 153. About 80% of these member countries are regarded as developing countries, some of which receive economic assistance from developed countries. As members of the WTO, these countries are now liberalizing their goods and/or capital markets to trading partners. For example, according to OECD (2007), Mexico received 128.6 million dollars and 5.8 million dollars as Official Development Assistance (ODA) from the United States and Canada, respectively, in 2005. It is also well known that Mexico formed NAFTA with the United States and Canada in 1994 and liberalized its markets to these countries. Indonesia received 1,223.1 million dollars as ODA from Japan in 2005. On the other hand, Indonesia and Japan agreed to form a FTA in 2006. We often observe that economic aid from a donor country and trade liberalization by the recipient country are parallelly conducted.

M. Okawa
Department of Economics, Ritsumeikan University, Noji-Higashi 1-1-1, Kusatsu 525 8577, Japan, e-mail: mokawa@ec.ritsumei.ac.jp

T. Kamihigashi and L. Zhao (eds.) *International Trade and Economic Dynamics – Essays in Memory of Koji Shimomura.*

International income transfer and/or foreign aid have been extensively studied in the literature of international trade for a long time.[1] Main attention has been focused on the "transfer problem": does a transfer make the donor less well off and the recipient better off? It was shown that the paradoxical welfare outcomes of income transfers are possible even in stable international trade frameworks (Gale 1974; Yano 1983; Bhagwati et al. 1983; Kemp and Shimomura 2002, 2003). Also, tied aid has attracted much attention in the literature. Foreign aid can be tied in various forms. For example, it is tied to the purchase of the exports of the donor country. This case is analyzed, among others, by Ohyama (1974), Kemp and Kojima (1985), and Schweinberger (1990). The case where the economic aids are tied to the tariffs or quotas is studied, for example, by Lahiri and Raimondos-Møller (1995, 1997) and Lahiri et al. (2001). All analyses have derived fruitful results in the general equilibrium frameworks of trade.

One common assumption in the above studies is that all markets are assumed to be perfectly competitive. It is, however, common wisdom that the majority of exports of developed countries to developing countries, such as automobiles, machines, electricities, etc, are characterized by imperfectly competitive markets. How does tied aid affect the donor's and the recipient's welfare under imperfect competition? It is worthwhile to answer this question in order to provide a more realistic description about international policy coordination. Brakman and Marrewijk (1995) study the effects of tied and untied aid under monopolistic competition. In their analysis, aid is tied to the consumption of exports from the donor country. Okawa (2007), on the other hand, introduces a pure monopoly firm in the exporting industry of the donor country and examines the welfare effects of an income transfer. He assumes that there exist two distinct agents in the donor country, a monopolist and factor owners, and that the income for the transfer is collected from the agents with different lump-sum tax rates. It is shown that the government of the donor country can raise social welfare of both donor and recipient countries. The chapter assumes that free trade prevails throughout and does not study the effects of an economic aid tied to the trade policy reform by the recipient country.

The purpose of this chapter is to study the effects of economic aid, which is tied to the trade liberalization policy by the recipient country, on the welfare of both donor and recipient countries under imperfect competition. We assume that economic aid is provided by the donor country under condition of the adoption of a tariff reduction policy by the recipient country. The export good of the donor country is supplied by a monopoly firm. This assumption reflects the fact that major exports from the developed countries to the developing countries are produced in imperfectly competitive markets. Brander and Spencer (1984) examine the optimal tariff policy of a country importing from a monopoly or oligopoly firms and show that the country can extract a monopoly rent by imposing a tariff (or a subsidy), even when there is no domestic producer to protect. Our model is an extension of

[1] The terms *international income transfer* and *foreign aid* are interchangeable throughout this chapter. For a review of the literature, see among others, Brakman and Marrewijk (1998).

Brander and Spencer's setting in introducing foreign economic aid by the exporting country.[2]

We set up a simple two country Ricardian trading model and study the circumstances under which policy coordination between economic aid and tariff reduction can be beneficial for both countries. Then under such circumstances, both countries will have an endogenous incentive for the policy coordination.

The structure of the chapter is as follows: Sect. 2 sets up the model, Sect. 3 analyses the effects of economic aid tied to a tariff reduction policy by the recipient country. Concluding remarks are made in Sect. 4.

2 The Model

Consider a two-country, two-good, one-factor trading model. In each country, good 1 is produced by employing labor in a perfectly competitive market under constant returns to scale. Good 1 is taken as the numeraire and the price is normalized to one. We assume that one unit of good 1 is produced by one unit of labor. Thus, wage rate is also equal to one. Good 2 is produced by a monopoly firm under increasing returns to scale in country α. The production technology of good 2 is of a type with fixed input and constant marginal input of labor. Thus, country α produces two goods while country β is specialized in the production of good 1. Labor is fully employed in both countries. We assume that country α is a donor country and provides an economic aid (an income transfer) in terms of good 1 to the recipient, country β. Country α exports good 2 and country β exports good 1.

There are two types of agents: households and a monopolist. Households in each country provide labor to firms, earn labor income, and consume two goods. All households in each country are identical in all respects. Thus, without loss of generality the number of households in each country is normalized to one. On the other hand, the source of monopolist's income is monopoly profit, and he or she consumes good 1 only.

We focus on the market for good 2 and assume that the income transferred to the recipient β is directed to consumption of good 1 and is not directed the demand for good 2.[3] To reflect the above setting on the consumption and to make our analysis tractable and meaningful, we restrict the preference of the household to a type expressed by a quasi-linear utility function:

$$U^i(D_1^i, D_2^i) = u^i(D_2^i) + D_1^i, \quad i = \alpha, \beta, \tag{1}$$

[2] We set up an integrated world market model where the monopoly firm supplies both exporting and importing countries, while Brander and Spencer (1984) set up a segmented market model where a monopoly firm or oligopoly firms export only to the importing country.

[3] Our setting would fit the cases where the income provided by economic aid is used for acquiring foods, clothes, and/or the other necessities of life, not for importing goods such as high-tech machines, electricities, etc.

where U^i is the utility level of consumer in country i, D^i_j $(i=\alpha,\beta;\ j=1,2)$ is the consumption of good j in country i, and $u^i(\cdot)$ is consumer's subutility function for consumption of D^i_2 in country i. The first-order condition for utility maximization is

$$u^i(D^i_2)' = p^i, \quad i=\alpha,\beta, \tag{2}$$

where $u^i(.)' \equiv \mathrm{d}u^i/\mathrm{d}D^i_2 > 0$ and p^i is the price of good 2 in country i.

Good 2 is produced by the monopoly firm in country α and is sold in countries α and β. The profit of the monopolist α, π^α, is written as

$$\pi^\alpha(x^\alpha) = (p^\alpha - c)x^\alpha - F - T_{\mathrm{m}}, \tag{3}$$

where c is a constant marginal cost and is equal to the units of labor to produce one unit of good 2, x^α is the output of the monopolist, F is a fixed cost, and T_{m} is the lump-sum tax imposed on the monopolist to finance the income for economic aid. We assume that the level of T_{m} is set at a level such that it guarantees $\pi^\alpha > 0$: the operation of the monopoly firm is profitable.[4]

We assume that country β imposes a specific tariff, t, on the imports of good 2, that is, $p^\beta = p^\alpha + t$. The world market equilibrium condition for good 2 can be written as

$$\textstyle\sum_{i=\alpha,\beta} D^i_2(p^i) = x^\alpha. \tag{4}$$

The first order condition for the profit maximization by monopolist α can be written as

$$x^\alpha \left(\sum D^{i'}_2\right)^{-1} + p^\alpha = c, \tag{5}$$

where $D^{i'}_2 \equiv \mathrm{d}D^i_2/\mathrm{d}p^i < 0$.

3 The Effects of the Policy Coordination of the Economic Aid and Trade Liberalization

We now examine the effects of a change in the specific tariff t on the output of monopolist α, x^α, and the price of good 2, p^α. To that end, totally differentiating (4) and (5), we find that

$$\begin{bmatrix} \left(\sum D^{i'}_2\right) & -1 \\ a & \left(\sum D^{i'}_2\right)^{-1} \end{bmatrix} \begin{bmatrix} \mathrm{d}p^\alpha \\ \mathrm{d}x^\alpha \end{bmatrix} = \begin{bmatrix} -D^{\beta'}_2 \\ b \end{bmatrix} \mathrm{d}t, \tag{6}$$

where $a \equiv -x^\alpha\left[\left(\sum D^{i'}_2\right)^{-2} \sum D^{i''}_2\right] + 1$, $b \equiv x^\alpha \left(\sum D^{i'}_2\right)^{-2} D^{\beta''}_2$, and $D^{i''}_2 \equiv \mathrm{d}^2 D^i_2/(\mathrm{d}p^i)^2$. Let Δ be the determinant of the coefficient matrix of LHS, we find that $\Delta = 1 + a$.

[4] As T_{m} can be regarded as a fixed cost for the monopoly firm, large T_{m} can work as entry deterrence.

We assume that the second order condition for profit maximization is satisfied and that $\Delta > 0$. Solving (6), we obtain that

$$\frac{\mathrm{d}p^{\alpha}}{\mathrm{d}t} = \frac{g}{\Delta}, \tag{7}$$

$$\frac{\mathrm{d}x^{\alpha}}{\mathrm{d}t} = \frac{h}{\Delta}, \tag{8}$$

where $\quad g \equiv -(\sum D_2^{i\prime})^{-1} D_2^{\beta\prime} + x^{\alpha}(\sum D_2^{i\prime})^{-2} D_2^{\beta\prime\prime}$ and

$$h \equiv x^{\alpha}(\sum D_2^{i\prime})^{-1} D_2^{\beta\prime\prime} + D_2^{\beta\prime}[-x^{\alpha}((\sum D_2^{i\prime})^{-2} \sum D_2^{i\prime\prime}) + 1].$$

In addition, the effect of a change in t on the price in country β is derived as $\mathrm{d}p^{\beta}/\mathrm{d}t = \mathrm{d}p^{\alpha}/\mathrm{d}t + 1 = (g/\Delta) + 1$.

Let us now turn to the welfare of countries α and β. The social surplus of the recipient country β consists of consumer surplus, tariff revenue, economic assistance in the form of income transferred from country α and wage income. It can be written as

$$w^{\beta} = u^{\beta}(D_2^{\beta}) - p^{\beta} D_2^{\beta} + t D_2^{\beta} + T + L^{\beta}, \tag{9}$$

where $T > 0$ is total income transferred from country α as an economic aid and L^i $(i = \alpha, \beta)$ is the labor endowment in country i. The first two terms of the RHS denote the consumer's surplus and the third term stands for tariff revenue.

On the other hand, the social surplus of the donor country α consists of the consumer surplus, the profit of monopolist α, income payments for economic aid to country β, and wage income. Thus the social surplus of country α can be written as

$$w^{\alpha} = u^{\alpha}(D_2^{\alpha}) - p^{\alpha} D_2^{\alpha} + (p^{\alpha} - c)x^{\alpha} - F - T + L^{\alpha}. \tag{10}$$

We see that an income transfer from country α to country β, if it is not tied to any policy change by country β, simply reduces the social surplus of country α and raises the social surplus of country β by the same amount. Therefore, the government α will not have any endogenous incentive to provide a transfer to country β. However, if the income transfer by government α is tied to a trade liberalization policy by government β and if both donor and recipient countries can be better off after a combination of the two policies, then both governments will have an endogenous incentive to work on such mutually beneficial policy coordination.

We now first examine the welfare effects of changes in t and T. To that end, differentiating (9) and (10) with respect to t and T, we find that

$$\mathrm{d}w^{\beta} = (\partial w^{\beta}/\partial t)\,\mathrm{d}t + \mathrm{d}T, \tag{11}$$

$$\frac{\partial w^{\beta}}{\partial t} = -D_2^{\beta}\left[\frac{g}{\Delta} + \left(\frac{\eta^{\beta}}{p^{\beta}}\right)\left(\frac{g}{\Delta} + 1\right)t\right], \tag{12}$$

$$\mathrm{d}w^{\alpha} = (\partial w^{\alpha}/\partial t)\,\mathrm{d}t - \mathrm{d}T, \tag{13}$$

and

$$\frac{\partial w^\alpha}{\partial t} = -x^\alpha \left[\theta^\alpha \left(\frac{g}{\Delta} \right) + \frac{\theta^\beta \eta^\beta}{p^\beta} \left(\sum \frac{\theta^i \eta^i}{p^i} \right)^{-1} \right], \tag{14}$$

where $\eta^i \equiv -\frac{p^i}{D_2^i} \frac{\mathrm{d}D_2^i}{\mathrm{d}p^i} > 0$ is the price elasticity of demand for good 2 in country i, and $\theta^i \equiv \frac{D_2^i}{x^\alpha} \in [0,1]$ is the consumption share of country i $(i = \alpha, \beta)$. We define $H(t) \equiv \frac{g}{\Delta} + \left(\frac{\eta^\beta}{p^\beta} \right) \left(\frac{g}{\Delta} + 1 \right) t$. The sign of $\frac{\partial w^\beta}{\partial t}$ negatively corresponds to that of $H(t)$.

We now restrict our attention to circumstances in which the imposition of a tariff on good 2 by government β raises the welfare of country β. This implies from (7) and (12) that

$$\left. \frac{\partial w^\beta}{\partial t} \right|_{t=0} = D_2^\beta \left\{ -\left(\frac{g}{\Delta} + 1 \right) + 1 \right\} = -D_2^\beta \left(\frac{g}{\Delta} \right) > 0 \Leftrightarrow \frac{\partial p^\alpha}{\partial t} = \frac{g}{\Delta} < 0 \Leftrightarrow g < 0. \tag{15}$$

We hereafter assume, therefore, that $g < 0$; that is, an imposition of a tariff by government β reduces p^α.[5] This assumption implies that the demand curves for good 2 in both countries are not too convex to the origin. If $D_2^{i''} \leq 0$ $(i = \alpha, \beta)$, we obtain $g < 0$. Even if $D_2^{i''} > 0$, however, as long as the value is sufficiently small, we still have the same sign condition. Thus, hereafter, we assume that the demand function is not too convex to the origin, such that the second order condition for profit maximization and $g < 0$ are satisfied. In addition, notice that this assumption determines the sign of $(\mathrm{d}p^\beta/\mathrm{d}t)$ as well as the signs of (7) and (8). Under this assumption, we have $h < 0$ and $(g/\Delta) + 1 > 0$. We thus obtain $\mathrm{d}p^\alpha/\mathrm{d}t$, $\mathrm{d}p^\beta/\mathrm{d}t > 0$, and $\mathrm{d}x^\alpha/\mathrm{d}t < 0$. We also see that there exists a unique optimal tariff rate, t^{op}:

$$t^{\mathrm{op}} = \theta^\beta \left\{ \Delta \frac{\theta^\alpha \eta^\alpha}{p^\alpha} + (\Delta + 1) \frac{\theta^\beta \eta^\beta}{p^\beta} \right\}^{-1} > 0.$$

On the other hand, the first term in the parenthesis in (14) represents a change in consumer surplus in country α and the second term is the change in monopolist α's profit. It is seen from (14) that consumer in country α benefits from an increase in the tariff, because it reduces p^α (see (7)), while monopolist α unambiguously loses. We can speculate that if consumption share of country α is relatively small, then country α loses as the tariff on good 2 is imposed and raised.

We now turn to the welfare effects of the economic aid from country α, which is tied to a trade policy reform by government β to liberalize the good 2 market. To that end, we first obtain changes in the tariff rate, which keeps the social surplus of

[5] Brander and Spencer (1984) focus on *rent-extracting tariffs* and show that either a tariff or a subsidy may be the optimal response of government, depending on the relative curvature of demand. Concretely speaking, if the relative curvature of demand, $p''X/p'$ (where X is aggregate output in the corresponding market), falls short of minus one, then the import subsidy is the optimal policy. However, since import subsidies are not common in the real world, we assume that the demand curve is not too convex such that $g < 0$. If we assume $D_2^{\alpha} = 0$, then our condition reduces to that in Brander and Spencer (1984).

the donor country α constant when a further income transfer is provided to country β. Letting $\mathrm{d}w^{\alpha} = 0$ and assuming $\partial w^{\alpha}/\partial t \neq 0$ in (13), we find that

$$\left.\frac{\mathrm{d}T}{\mathrm{d}t}\right|_{w^{\alpha}=\text{const.}} = \frac{\partial w^{\alpha}}{\partial t} = -x^{\alpha}\left[\frac{\eta^{\beta}}{p^{\beta}}\left(\sum\frac{\theta^{i}\eta^{i}}{p^{i}}\right)^{-1} - \frac{g}{\Delta}\right]\left[\tilde{\theta}^{\alpha} - \theta^{\alpha}\right], \tag{16}$$

where $\tilde{\theta}^{\alpha} \equiv \left[\frac{\eta^{\beta}}{p^{\beta}}\left(\sum\frac{\theta^{i}\eta^{i}}{p^{i}}\right)^{-1}\right]\left[\frac{\eta^{\beta}}{p^{\beta}}\left(\sum\frac{\theta^{i}\eta^{i}}{p^{i}}\right)^{-1} - \frac{g}{\Delta}\right]^{-1}$ and $\tilde{\theta}^{\alpha} \in (0,1)$. Then we see that if $\theta^{\alpha} \in (0, \tilde{\theta}^{\alpha})$ (respectively, $\theta^{\alpha} \in (\tilde{\theta}^{\alpha}, 1)$), then $\mathrm{d}T/\mathrm{d}t|_{w^{\alpha}=\text{const.}} < 0$ (respectively, $\mathrm{d}T/\mathrm{d}t|_{w^{\alpha}=\text{const.}} > 0$). The economic intuition is straightforward; since a reduction of a tariff raises $p^{\alpha}$and also raises the profit of monopolist α, if the consumption share of country α is smaller than $\tilde{\theta}^{\alpha}$, then the increase in the profit of monopolist α can be kept equal to the sum of the loss of consumer surplus plus income reduction caused by a further income transfer. Thus, the social surplus is kept constant at the level before the further income transfer is provided and the tariff reduction is conducted.

We next look at the relationship between a change in both the tariff rate and the income transfer which keeps the social surplus of the recipient β constant at the same level as that before such policies are made by both countries α and β. Letting $\mathrm{d}w^{\beta} = 0$ in (11), we obtain that

$$\left.\frac{\mathrm{d}T}{\mathrm{d}t}\right|_{w^{\beta}=\text{const.}} = -\frac{\partial w^{\beta}}{\partial t} = D_{2}^{\beta}\left(\frac{\theta^{\alpha}\eta^{\alpha}}{p^{\alpha}} + \left(\frac{\Delta-1}{\Delta}\right)\frac{\theta^{\beta}\eta^{\beta}}{p^{\beta}}\right)\left(\sum\frac{\theta^{i}\eta^{i}}{p^{i}}\right)^{-1}(t - t^{\text{op}}). \tag{17}$$

Therefore, if $t < t^{\text{op}}$ (respectively, $t^{\text{op}} < t$) initially, then $\mathrm{d}T/\mathrm{d}t|_{w^{\beta}=\text{const.}} < 0$ (respectively, $\mathrm{d}T/\mathrm{d}t|_{w^{\beta}=\text{const.}} > 0$).

We now proceed to examine whether it is possible for both countries α and β to agree with the mutually beneficial policy coordination that consists of a further economic assistance by the donor country α and a trade liberalization policy by the recipient country β. We study this point by using diagrams shown in Figs. 1 and 2. In the figures, the specific tariff rate is measured along the horizontal axis, while the amount of income transferred to the recipient β is measured along the vertical axis. In the figures, $w^{\alpha}w^{\alpha'}$ and $w^{\beta}w^{\beta'}$ are the iso-welfare lines of countries α and β, respectively. The iso-welfare line of each country indicates the combination of $T$and t, which keeps the welfare of each country constant at the initial level. Point E_0 represents the initial configuration of the transfer and the specific tariff level, (T_0, t_0). The $(+)$ and $(-)$ signs of each iso-welfare line indicate how the social welfare of each country will change when the iso-welfare line shifts to those directions. We denote $w^{i}(+)$ (respectively, $w^{i}(-)$) to express the combination of T and t or areas in which country i is better off (respectively, worse off) than in the initial situation characterized by the configuration (T_0, t_0). Fig. 1 shows that, for example, if a new equilibrium combination moves vertically up from the initial point (T_0, t_0), the social

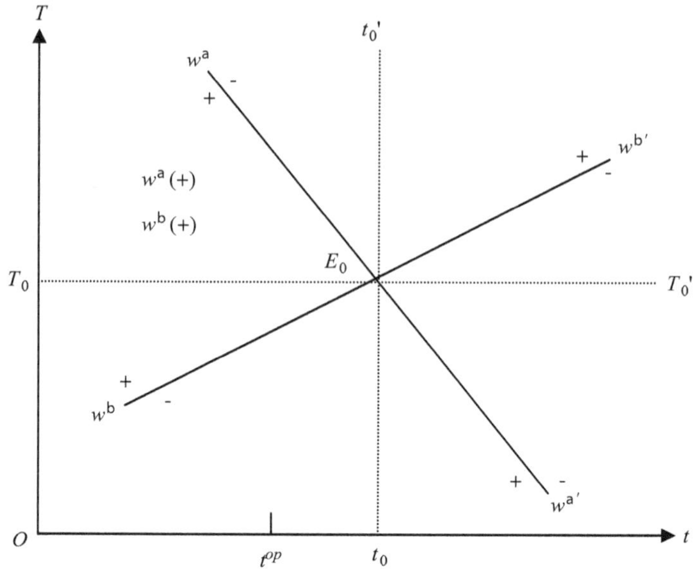

Fig. 1 $t^{op} < t$ and $\theta^\alpha < \tilde{\theta}^\alpha$

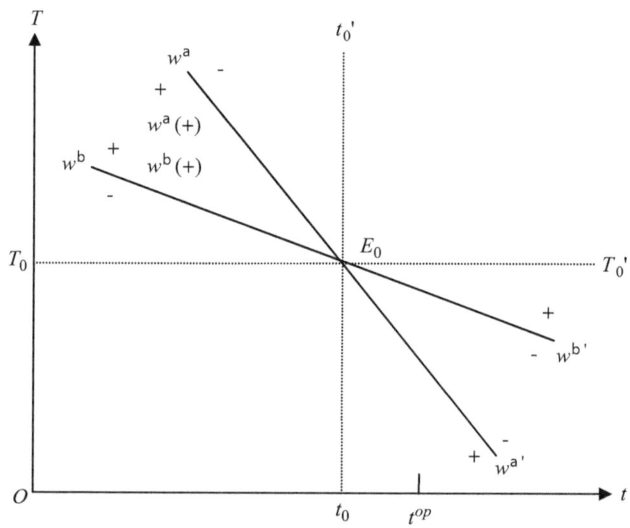

Fig. 2 $t < t^{op}$, $\theta^\alpha < \tilde{\theta}^\alpha$, and slope of $w^\alpha w^{\alpha'}$ < slope of $w^\beta w^{\beta'}$

surplus of country α decreases while that of country β increases, respectively. In the west area from Point E_0, both countries are better off.

Since we are interested in a policy combination of the economic aid from the donor α and the tariff reduction by the recipient β, we restrict our attention to the case where $\mathrm{d}T > 0$ and $\mathrm{d}t < 0$; that is, we focus on the area above the T_0T_0' line and on the left side of the t_0t_0' line.[6]

The slopes of the iso-welfare lines of countries α and β are determined by (16) and (17), respectively. We see that the slope of the iso-welfare line of country α is positive (respectively, negative) if $\tilde{\theta}^\alpha < \theta^\alpha$ (respectively, $\theta^\alpha < \tilde{\theta}^\alpha$). Also the slope of the iso-welfare line of country β is positive (respectively, negative) if $t^{\mathrm{op}} < t$ (respectively, $t < t^{\mathrm{op}}$). We have six possible cases, and two cases of them include a common intersection area of $w^\alpha(+)$ and $w^\beta(+)$, which implies that mutually beneficial policy coordination is possible above the T_0T_0' line and on the left side of the t_0t_0' line.

Fig. 1 illustrates the case where $t^{\mathrm{op}} < t$ and $\theta^\alpha < \tilde{\theta}^\alpha$. Since the initial tariff rate is higher than the optimal rate, a reduction of the tariff rate raises the welfare of country β. The income transfer provided by country α causes a further increase in the surplus of country β. The reduction of tariff rate, at the same time, raises the price of good 2 in country α. This increase in the price of good 2 increases the profit of the monopolist α while reducing the consumer surplus in country α. However, since $\theta^\alpha < \tilde{\theta}^\alpha$, the increase in the monopoly profit outweighs the sum of the loss of consumer surplus and the income reduction transferred to country β.

We also see in Fig. 2, the case where $t < t^{\mathrm{op}}$ and $\theta^\alpha < \tilde{\theta}^\alpha$, and the slope of iso-welfare line $w^\alpha w^{\alpha'}$ is steeper than that of iso-welfare line $w^\beta w^{\beta'}$. The reduction in the tariff lowers the social surplus of the recipient β, but this is compensated for and dominated by the income transfer by the donor α. The process on the donor α follows the same line as the case in Fig. 1. The condition that the slope of line $w^\alpha w^{\alpha'}$ is steeper than that of line $w^\beta w^{\beta'}$ means that the positive impact of tariff reduction on the donor country α is greater than the negative impact on country β. Otherwise, the donor α's economic aid cannot compensate the loss of the recipient β's welfare. Thus we assume the following:

Assumption 1. When $t < t^{\mathrm{op}}$, the slope of line $w^\alpha w^{\alpha'}$ is smaller than that of line $w^\beta w^{\beta'}$.

We now summarize our result in Proposition 1.

Proposition 1. *Suppose that the consumption share of the donor country α is smaller than the critical value (i.e., $\theta^\alpha < \tilde{\theta}^\alpha$) and Assumption 1 is satisfied, then both countries are better off after a policy coordination that the donor provides a further economic assistance and the recipient liberalizes its import market by a reduction of the tariff.*

It would be of some help to see a specific example in order to make the results more transparent. We here assume that the utility function is of a quadratic type and the demand is linear: $D_2^{i''} = 0$ $(i = \alpha, \beta)$. Then we have that $a = 1$, $b = 0$, $\Delta = 2$,

---

[6] Though our focus is on the combination of economic aid and the reduction of import tariff (i.e., $\mathrm{d}t < 0$), if the cases where $\mathrm{d}t > 0$ are allowed, it may be possible that both countries are better off after the donor provides a further transfer and the recipient raises the import tariff.

$g = -\left(\Sigma D_2^{i'}\right)^{-1} D_2^{\beta'} < 0$, $h = D_2^{\beta'} < 0$, $\mathrm{d}p^\alpha/\mathrm{d}t = g/\Delta < 0$, $\mathrm{d}x^\alpha/\mathrm{d}t = h/\Delta < 0$, and $\mathrm{d}p^\beta/\mathrm{d}t = (g/\Delta) + 1 = \left\{-\left(\Sigma D_2^{i'}\right)^{-1} D_2^{\beta'} + 2\right\}/2 > 0$. In this case, (16) can be written as

$$\left.\frac{\mathrm{d}T}{\mathrm{d}t}\right|_{w^\alpha=\text{const.}} = \frac{\partial w^\alpha}{\partial t} = -\frac{x^\alpha}{2}\left(\frac{\theta^\beta \eta^\beta}{p^\beta}\right)\left(\Sigma \frac{\theta^i \eta^i}{p^i}\right)^{-1}(2-\theta^\alpha) < 0. \qquad (16')$$

Thus, the slope of the donor's iso-welfare curve is unambiguously negative. On the other hand, (17′) can be written as

$$\left.\frac{\mathrm{d}T}{\mathrm{d}t}\right|_{w^\beta=\text{const.}} = -\frac{\partial w^\beta}{\partial t} = D_2^\beta\left(\frac{\theta^\alpha \eta^\alpha}{p^\alpha} + \left(\frac{1}{2}\right)\frac{\theta^\beta \eta^\beta}{p^\beta}\right)\left(\Sigma \frac{\theta^i \eta^i}{p^i}\right)^{-1}(t - t^{\text{op}}). \qquad (17')$$

Thus, if $t < t^{\text{op}}$ (respectively, $t^{\text{op}} < t$) initially, then $\mathrm{d}T/\mathrm{d}t|_{w^\beta=\text{const.}} < 0$ (respectively $\mathrm{d}T/\mathrm{d}t|_{w^\beta=\text{const.}} > 0$). We also see, from (16′) and (17′), that, under a quadratic utility, assumption 1 is satisfied. Thus, whatever the market share of the donor country is, a mutually beneficial policy coordination with the donor's further aid and the recipient's tariff reduction is possible.

We have set up an integrated world market model in which monopoly firm α sells in both countries α and β. Thus we see that this case includes a special segmented world market setting in which two markets α and β are segmented and monopolist α independently decides the optimal outputs in the two markets. In the segmented market case, we can regard the market in country β as an export market of monopolist α. This case corresponds to the case where $\theta^\alpha = 0$ in our setting. We see, therefore, that a policy combination that the donor α provides further economic assistance and the recipient β liberalizes its import market by a reduction of the tariff will always be beneficial for the two countries. In this case, both countries always have an endogenous incentive for the policy coordination.

4 Concluding Remarks

We have examined the possibility of mutually beneficial policy coordination with economic assistance by a donor country and trade liberalization policy by a recipient country under imperfect competition where a monopoly firm in the donor country sells its products in both countries. It was shown that, under assumption 1, if the donor's consumption share of the export good is smaller than a critical value, then the donor's further income transfer and the recipient's tariff reduction policy can raise both countries' wellbeing. In this case, both countries have an endogenous incentive to form a free trade agreement.

This chapter has assumed that the recipient country is merely an importer of the monopolist's products. It would be interesting to extend this setting to an international duopoly framework in which a duopoly firm in the recipient country competes with another duopoly firm in the donor country on the world market. Also, in this chapter, the level of economic aid and the tariff rate are treated as exogenous. As Lahiri et al. (2001) have examined in a perfectly competitive setting, it would be interesting to endogenize two policy measures to analyze how a change in the level of economic aid affects the optimal tariff, or to pursue a policy game between the donor and recipient countries. These works are, however, left for our future research.

Acknowledgment We appreciate Colin Davis, Murray C. Kemp, Alan D. Woodland, and an anonymous referee for their helpful comments and suggestions. The usual disclaimer applies. Authors gratefully acknowledge financial support from MEXT. OPEN RESEARCH (2004–2008) and Grants-in-Aid for Scientific Research (No. 17530150).

References

Brander JA, Spencer BJ (1984) Trade welfare: tariffs and cartels. J Int Econ 16:227–242

Brakman S, Marrewijk C (1995) Transfers, returns to scale, tied aid and monopolistic competition. J Dev Econ 47:333–354

Brakman S, Marrewijk C (1998) The economics of international transfer. Cambridge, Cambridge University Press

Bhagwati JN, Brecher RA, Hatta T (1983) The generalized theory of transfers and welfare: bilateral transfers in a multilateral world. Am Econ Rev 73:606–618

Gale D (1974) Exchange equilibrium and coalitions: an example. J Math Econ 1:63–66

Kemp M, Kojima S (1985) Tied aid and paradoxes of donor-enrichment and recipient-improvement. Int Econ Rev 26:721–729

Kemp M, Shimomura K (2002) A theory of voluntary unrequited international transfers. Jpn Econ Rev 53:290–300

Kemp M, Shimomura K (2003) A theory of involuntary unrequited international transfers. J Polit Econ 111:682–692

Lahiri S, Raimondos-Møller P (1995) Welfare effects of aid under quantitative trade restrictions. J Int Econ 39:297–315

Lahiri S, Raimondos-Møller P (1997) On the tying of aid to tariff reform. J Dev Econ 54:479–491

Lahiri S, Raimondos-Møller P, Wong K, Woodland AD (2001) Optimal foreign aid and tariffs. J Dev Econ 67:79–99

Ohyama M (1974) Tariffs and the transfer problem. Keio Econ Stud 11:29–45

Okawa M (2007) International income transfer under imperfect competition. Rev Dev Econ 11:242–257

Organization for Economic Co-Operation and Development (2007) Geographical distribution of financial flows to aid recipients, 2001–2005. OECD Publications, Paris

Schweinberger AG (1990) On the welfare effects of tied aid. Int Econ Rev 31:457–462

Yano M (1983) The welfare aspects of the transfer problem. J Int Econ 15:277–289

Quota as a Competitive Device

Sugata Marjit(✉), Tarun Kabiraj, and Arijit Mukherjee

Abstract When entry of the relatively inefficient firms is deterred due to fixed costs, leading to a monopoly of the relatively efficient firm, guaranteed production quota for the less efficient ones can increase consumers' surplus. In other words, restricting the output of more efficient firm helps to reduce the price compared to the monopoly level. If the emergence of monopoly is independent of the level of fixed costs of the inefficient competitors, monopoly is the more efficient outcome. This has relevance for the recent entry of China in WTO and the abolition of export quotas in textiles. This also qualifies the conventional wisdom in the trade policy literature that quantitative restrictions are necessarily anticompetitive. The optimal policy can be to keep in place a quota but allow it to be licensed to the more efficient exporter.

1 Introduction

China's entry into WTO has brought mixed reactions from the textile exporters in the developing world, particularly when the Multi-Fiber-Arrangement (MFA) is also being phased out. Countries such as Bangladesh and Vietnam are worried that China will significantly affect their market shares, both because it will henceforth enjoy the Most-Favored-Nation (MFN) status, and the quota protection provided by the MFA will no longer be there. Such country-specific concerns are quite reasonable. But these should not perturb the consumers of textiles in the importing countries. If we ignore the import-competing production in rest of the world, and look at the interest of the consumers, the entry or exit in the market does not matter as long as the price comes down. If China is more efficient than other countries and the other countries fail to live up to the standard, Chinese monopoly should also be welcome to the

S. Marjit
Centre for Studies in Social Sciences, R 1 Baishnabghata Patuli Township, Calcutta 700094, India, e-mail: smarjit@hotmail.com

T. Kamihigashi and L. Zhao (eds.) *International Trade and Economic Dynamics – Essays in Memory of Koji Shimomura.*

consumers. Typically, the monopoly price charged by China should be lower than the marginal cost of production in other countries. We start off from this benign argument and pose an interesting theoretical problem.

We show that if there is sufficiently large fixed cost of production that prevents relatively inefficient exporters from entering the market in the absence of any export quota, the consumers in the importing country can be worse-off without such a quota. So, protecting relatively inefficient exporters may actually make the consumers of the importing country better-off. However, if the entry barrier is due to a difference in the marginal cost, the consumers in the importing country are better-off in absence of a quota. Whether the consumers in the importing country are better-off under a quota may depend on the type of industry, which can be characterized by the cost of fixed investment. For example, one is likely to observe higher fixed cost for the manufacturing industry, whereas it is less likely to be the case for the service sectors.

Hence, our findings have important implications for the abolition of MFA. It suggests that arrangements such as the MFA may not be bad for the consumers of textiles in the developed countries if the exporting countries face a significant fixed cost, but do not differ that much in terms of their marginal costs of production.

Even if quota allows the technologically inefficient firm to enter the product market, the technologically inefficient firm will prefer to sub-contract the production of its quota to the efficient firm. Sub-contracting with the technologically efficient firm will help to save the cost of production, and thus it makes the firms better-off. Therefore, even if the technologically efficient firm produces all the output, the presence of quota helps to eliminate monopoly of the technologically efficient firm, making the consumers of the importing country better-off.[1] As an alternative to sub-contracting, technology licensing by the technologically efficient firm to the technologically inefficient firm may also help to achieve the same outcome, provided the licensing contract specifies the amount of output that could be produced through the licensed technology. Thus, our chapter can also be related to the literature on international technology transfer.

Hence, our chapter contributes to the general literature on strategic trade policy (Brander and Spencer 1983, 1985; Helpman and Krugman 1989; Jones and Takemori 1989; Krishna 1987, 1989; Krugman 1994), and more specifically to Kabiraj and Marjit (2003) and Mukherjee and Pennings (2006). Kabiraj and Marjit (2003) show that the government of an importing country may use the tariff policy to induce technology licensing from a technologically efficient foreign firm to a technologically inefficient domestic firm, thus making the consumers of the importing country better-off. Mukherjee and Pennings (2006) extend this line of research and show that a monopolist has the incentive to license its technology to another firm in the presence of the strategic trade policy of the importing country. However, whether the technology will be licensed to a domestic firm or to a foreign firm will depend

[1] In a recent chapter, Choi and Marjit (2005) show that quota can be less restrictive than a tariff even in a competitive model.

on the cost of international technology transfer and whether the importing country commits to its tariff policy or not.[2]

The remainder of the chapter is organized as follows: Section 2 describes the basic model and derives the results. Section 3 provides the conclusion.

2 Model

Consider an industry with two exporters, 1 and 2, of a homogeneous product and there is an importing country for this product. Let the demand function of the importing country be given by $p(q_1+q_2)$, where q_1 and q_2 are the output levels of firm 1 and 2, respectively, with $p'<0$. To show the effects of quota on entry and market competition, we assume away any domestic competition in the importing country.

Assume that firm 1 is technologically superior to that of firm 2 and the firms have constant marginal costs of production. For simplicity, we assume that the marginal cost of firm 1 is zero, and the constant marginal cost of firm 2 is $c>0$. However, each firm needs to incur a fixed cost of production, $F>0$.

Let us first consider a scenario where initially the institutional arrangement prevents firm 1 from exporting its product, and therefore firm 2 has monopoly to export the good to the importing country. The monopoly price it will charge is given by $p_2^m=\phi(c)$. We assume that the operating profit (i.e., total revenue minus total variable cost) of firm 2 covers the fixed cost of production, that is,

$$\pi_2^m(c)>F. \tag{1}$$

Now, assume that the institutional barrier on firm 1's export has been removed completely. This creates the threat of competition in the product market. Since firm 1 has low cost of production, either it will emerge as monopoly or the market structure will be duopoly. We consider the following game under competition. At stage 1, the firms decide simultaneously whether to produce (or enter) or not. If both firms decide to produce, at stage 2 they choose their output levels like Cournot duopolists. If, at stage 1, only one firm decides to produce, then at stage 2, this firm produces like a monopolist. A firm will produce a positive output level if it derives a nonnegative (net) payoff. We solve the game through backward induction.

We denote by $\pi_i(c_1,c_2)$ the operating profit of firm i under Cournot duopoly, where c_j is the marginal cost of firm j; $i,j=1,2$, and we restrict to the standard assumption of falling industry marginal revenue curve. This will yield downward sloping reaction functions with absolute slope less than one. Clearly, the existence of a positive fixed cost implies that each reaction function will be discontinuous with a part degenerating to the axis.

When firm 1 emerges as the monopolist, it charges a monopoly price $p_1^m=\phi(0)$. Since monopoly price decreases with lower marginal cost of production, we must

[2] One may refer to Saggi (2002) for a survey on international technology transfer.

have $p_1^m < p_2^m$. It is also clear, on the one hand, that under assumption (1) firm 1's net payoff is positive since

$$\pi_1^m(0) > F.$$

On the other hand, under duopoly market structure, firm 1's operating payoff will be $\pi_1(0,c)$. Therefore, if assumption (1) is replaced by

$$\pi_1(0,c) > F \tag{2}$$

so that $\pi_1^m(0) > \pi_1(0,c) > F$, then we must have a unique pure strategy equilibrium at stage 1 under free trade,[3] where firm 1 will always produce.

Let us now define $\widetilde{c}$ as the level of marginal cost that equals the monopoly price charged by firm 1, that is,

$$\tilde{c} = p_1^m. \tag{3}$$

Then if $c \geq \tilde{c}$, firm 2 will necessarily cease to operate even if the fixed cost were zero, and so firm 1 will emerge as monopoly. Firm 2's operating profit (i.e., total revenue minus total variable cost) is positive if and only if $c < \widetilde{c}$. However, $c < \widetilde{c}$ does not necessarily mean that firm 2 will operate at a positive output level. Firm 2 will decide to produce provided that its net profit is nonnegative, that is, $\pi_2(0,c) \geq F$.

Let us now assume[4]

$$\pi_2(0,0) > F. \tag{4}$$

With the standard curvature restrictions on the demand function, we shall have $\frac{\partial \pi_1(0,c)}{\partial c} > 0$ for all $c < \tilde{c}$. Then clearly (2) holds under this assumption. Again since $\frac{\partial \pi_2(0,c)}{\partial c} < 0$ for $c \in (0,\tilde{c})$, for any F satisfying (4) we can define the following:

$$\exists \hat{c} \in (0,\tilde{c}) | \pi_2(0,c) \geq F \quad \text{iff } \mathrm{c} \leq \hat{\mathrm{c}}. \tag{5}$$

Therefore, given assumption (4), when $F > 0$, on the one hand, the market structure will be duopoly and firm 2 will operate at a positive output level if and only if $\mathrm{c} \leq \hat{\mathrm{c}}$. On the other hand, if $\mathrm{c} \in (\hat{\mathrm{c}}, \tilde{\mathrm{c}})$, while firm 2's operating profit is positive, but it cannot cover its fixed cost, therefore it will not enter the market and the market structure will be monopoly of firm 1. Finally, if $c \geq \tilde{c}$, firm 1 becomes monopoly under free trade even if $F = 0$.

We can now write the following proposition.

Proposition 1. *(a) If $c \geq \tilde{c}$, the equilibrium price will be $p_1^m < p_2^m$ for any $F \geq 0$.*

(b) Let p_d denote the duopoly price when both firms produce positive output. Then the equilibrium price will be $p_d < p_1^m$ for $c \in (0,\hat{c})$, and p_1^m for $c \in (\hat{c},\tilde{c})$.

---

[3] If $\pi_1(0,c) < F$, there will be two pure strategy equilibria where either only firm 1 or only firm 2 will decide to produce, and one mixed strategy equilibrium. However, we avoid this situation, since it will not add anything to the main purpose of this chapter.

[4] If $\pi_2(0,0) < F$, there will be two Nash equilibria for some values of c, where either only firm 1 or only firm 2 enters the market. Our assumption of $\pi_2(0,0) > F$ helps us to avoid this unnecessary complication by ensuring a unique pure strategy Nash equilibrium for the market entry decision, and without loosing any insight for our analysis.

Proof. (a) Even if $F = 0$, the definition of $\tilde{c}$ implies that firm 2 does not find it profitable to produce even if firm 1 charges its monopoly price, given its marginal cost $c \geq \tilde{c}$. Hence, firm 1 will charge p_1^m, which is less than p_2^m.

(b) If firm 1 produces as a monopolist, the first order condition for profit maximization implies

$$p(q_1^m) + q_1^m p' = 0, \tag{6}$$

where q_1^m is the monopoly output of firm 1.

When both firms produce positive outputs, the optimal output levels of firm 1 and 2 will satisfy

$$p(q_\mathrm{d}) + q_1 p' = 0 \tag{7}$$

and

$$p(q_\mathrm{d}) + q_2 p' - c = 0, \tag{8}$$

where $q_\mathrm{d} = q_1 + q_2$ is the total output produced under duopoly.

Then adding (7) and (8) we get

$$2p(q_\mathrm{d}) + q_\mathrm{d} p' - c = 0. \tag{9}$$

Since $p(q_\mathrm{d}) > c$, subtraction of (6) from (9) implies

$$p(q_\mathrm{d}) + q_\mathrm{d} p'(q_\mathrm{d}) < p(q_1^m) + q_1^m p'(q_1^m). \tag{10}$$

Given that the marginal revenue for the industry, $p(q_1 + q_2) + (q_1 + q_2)p'$, is negatively sloped, (10) implies $q_\mathrm{d} > q_1^m$, and therefore $p_\mathrm{d} < p_1^m$ when both firms operate in the market.

However, given the positive fixed cost of production, both firms produce positive output if and only if $c \in (0, \hat{c})$. So, we have $p_\mathrm{d} < p_1^m$ for $c \in (0, \hat{c})$.

But, the positive fixed cost of production deters entry of firm 2 for $c \in (\hat{c}, \tilde{c})$, and this generates the equilibrium price p_1^m. □

Given the initial monopoly of firm 2, Proposition 1(a) tells that firm 1 is so much better than firm 2, that it will deter entry of firm 2 even if there is no fixed cost of production. The entry of firm 1 certainly benefits the consumers in this situation. Proposition 1(b) shows that if firm 1's cost efficiency is not large, both firms will produce in the market if the fixed cost of production does not prevent firm 2 from entering. Since, in this situation, the duopoly price is lower than firm 1's monopoly price, consumers will be better off if the market structure is duopoly than monopoly of firm 1. However, if $c \in (\hat{c}, \tilde{c})$, free trade will not be able to ensure duopoly market structure, and firm 1 will be monopolist in this situation.

Let us now consider the policy option of the importing country. In particular, consider an export-quota assigned to firm 2 (the inefficient firm). Let $\overline{q_2}$ be the export-quota assigned to firm 2 such that the following condition holds:

$$[p(q_1(\overline{q_2}) + \overline{q_2}) - c]\overline{q_2} = F. \tag{11}$$

With the standard tie-breaking assumption one can argue that if such $\overline{q_2}$ exists, the inefficient firm will enter the market. It should be noted that to make entry of firm 2 profitable, $\overline{q_2}$ must be greater than firm 2's Cournot output when both firms produce in the market.

Note that setting such a policy is exactly similar to allow firm 2 to act as a Stackelberg leader. However, even with this quota, firm 2 will enter provided the net profit of firm 2 behaving as the Stackelberg leader (which is the maximal payoff firm 2 can earn, given that firm 1 produces in the market) covers the fixed cost of production. So let us now assume that firm 2 makes a nonnegative payoff when it acts as Stackelberg leader, that is,

$$\pi_2^S(0,c) \geq F. \tag{12}$$

If (12) holds, it is easy to check that there exists $\overline{q_2}$ satisfying (11), the corresponding industry output will be $\overline{q_2} + q_1(\overline{q_2}) = \overline{q_S}$. It may be noted that $\pi_2^S(0,c) > \pi_2(0,c)\, \forall c < \tilde{c}$, that is, firm 2 as leader makes a larger profit compared to its Cournot profit.

In Fig. 1 the shaded portion gives combinations of c and F satisfying $\pi_2(0,c) < F < \pi_2^S(0,c)$ and $\pi_2(0,0) > F$. Therefore, for such a parameter situation the market structure under free trade will be monopoly of firm 1, whereas an intervention by the importing country in the form of imposing a quota on firm 2's exports will result in a duopoly structure with firm 2 acting as Stackelberg leader. To illustrate further, consider any $F = \hat{F} < \pi_i(0,0)$; then $\exists\{\hat{c}(\hat{F}), \hat{c}'(\hat{F})\}$ such that $\forall c \in (\hat{c}, \hat{c}')$, $\pi_2(0,c) < F < \pi_2^S(0,c)$. Thus, our result shows that there are situations when an export quota levied on the inefficient firm can create competition in the product market.

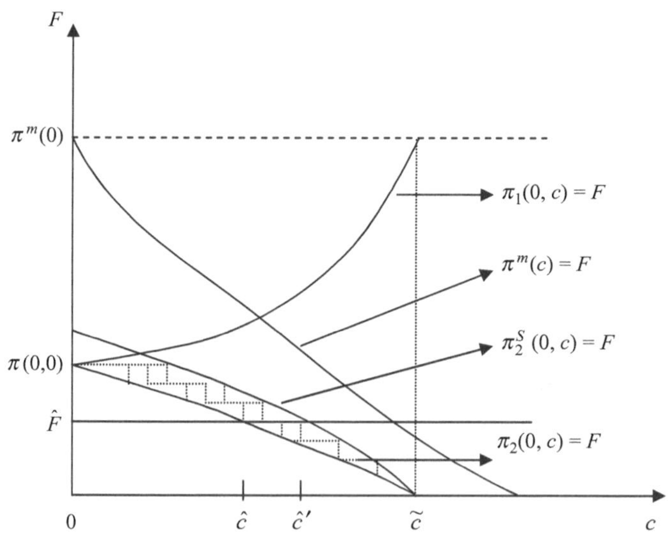

Fig. 1 Parameter situations where quota leads to more competition

Since we are talking about policy option, the importing country would impose a quota restriction provided that it makes the consumers better off. The following proposition will show that it is indeed the case.

Proposition 2. *Let q_S denote the optimal industry output when firms 2 and 1 behave like Stackelberg leader and follower, respectively. Then, $p(q_S) < p_1^m$.*

Proof. Firm 1 maximizes the following objective function:

$$p(q_1^S + q_2^S)q_1^S. \tag{13}$$

The FOC for profit maximization for firm 1 implies

$$p + q_1^S p' = 0. \tag{14}$$

As a Stackelberg leader firm 2 maximizes

$$p(q_1^S(q_2^S) + q_2^S)q_2^S - cq_2^S. \tag{15}$$

FOC for profit maximization implies

$$p + q_2^S p' \left(1 + \frac{\mathrm{d}q_1^S}{\mathrm{d}q_2^S}\right) - c = 0, \tag{16}$$

where $\frac{\mathrm{d}q_1^S}{\mathrm{d}q_2^S}$ is the slope of firm 1's reaction function. It is easy to derive

$$\frac{\mathrm{d}q_1^S}{\mathrm{d}q_2^S} = -\frac{(p' + q_1^S p'')}{(2p' + q_1^S p'')} < 0 \quad \text{and} \quad \left|\frac{\mathrm{d}q_1^S}{\mathrm{d}q_2^S}\right| < 1.$$

Adding (14) and (16), we get the total output under Stackelberg competition that will satisfy

$$2p + q_S p' + q_S p' \frac{\mathrm{d}q_1^S}{\mathrm{d}q_2^S} - c = 0. \tag{17}$$

Since $p(q_S) > c$, subtraction of (6) from (17) implies

$$p(q_S) + q_S p'(q_S)\left(1 + \frac{\mathrm{d}q_1^S}{\mathrm{d}q_2^S}\right) < p(q_1^m) + q_1^m p'(q_1^m). \tag{18}$$

Since the marginal revenue for the industry is negatively sloped, it follows from (18) that $q_S > q_1^m$, and therefore, $p_S < p_1^m$. □

The above proposition shows that the industry output under Stackelberg competition is greater than that under monopoly. This happens because a shift of equilibrium from monopoly of firm 1 to the Stackelberg equilibrium with firm 2 as leader is a movement along the reaction function of firm 1, which is negatively sloped with absolute slope less than one. Then the importing country to maximize its benefit will chose a quota level at which the industry output is maximum and hence it will set the quota at firm 2's Stackelberg leadership output level. This is stated in the following proposition.

Proposition 3. *When (12) holds, the importing country will set the quota equal to firm 2's Stackelberg leader output.*

The above discussion shows that if free entry prevents relatively inferior firm from entering the market, an importing country might be better off by imposing quota on the exporting firms. However, the above argument has assumed away any contracting between the firms. In fact, if contracting between the exporting firms is not costly, the firms will prefer to produce all the output under Stackelberg competition in firm 1, since it will help to save cq_2^S amount of cost of production, though the outputs will be sold by both firms. In other words, given the imposition of quota, we may observe outsourcing by firm 2 to firm 1. Further, outsourcing by firm 2 will also relax condition (12). However, it should be remembered that though firm 1 would produce all the outputs, the imposition of quota would be necessary to create competition in the product market.

3 Conclusion

This chapter shows that if entry of a relatively cost inefficient firm is deterred due to fixed cost of production, the imposition of quota on the exporting firms can make the consumers of the importing country better-off. However, though the technologically inefficient firm may outsource its production to the technologically efficient firm, the imposition of quota is important to keep the competition between the exporting firms. Our chapter suggests that the abolition of MFA and the entry of China in WTO may make the importing countries of textiles worse-off by eliminating technologically inefficient textile exporters.

As a final remark, though we have assumed away import competing sector in our analysis to show the results in the simplest way, quota on the exporting firms may reduce output of the import competing firm by inducing entry of some exporters. Hence, quota on the exporters is likely to be a preferable option if the importance of import competing sector can be neglected for the welfare of the importing country.

Acknowledgement We thank an anonymous referee for helpful comments. However, we are responsible for any remaining errors.

References

Brander JA, Spencer BJ (1985) Export subsidies and international market share rivalry. J Int Econ 18:83–100

Brander JA, Spencer BJ (1983) International R&D rivalry and industrial strategy. Rev Econ Stud 50:707–722

Choi EK, Marjit S (2005) On the non-equivalence of tariff and quota in a competitive general equilibrium framework. Mimeo, City University of Hong Kong
Helpman E, Krugman P (1989) Trade policy and market structure. MIT Press, Massachusetts
Jones R, Takemori S (1989) Foreign monopoly and optimal tariffs for the small open economy. Eur Econ Rev 33:1691–1707
Kabiraj T, Marjit S (2003) Protecting consumers through protection: the role of tariff induced technology transfer. Eur Econ Rev 47:113–124
Krishna K (1987) Tariffs versus quotas with endogenous quality. J Int Econ 23:97–112
Krishna K (1989) Trade restrictions as facilitating practices. J Int Econ 26:251–270
Krugman P (1994) Rethinking international trade. MIT Press, Massachusetts
Mukherjee A, Pennings E (2006) Tariffs, licensing and market structure. Eur Econ Rev 50:1699–1707
Saggi K (2002) Trade, foreign direct Investment, and international technology transfer: a survey. World Bank Res Observ 17:191–235

Successive Expansion and Stability of Network Integration in International Trade[1]

Noritsugu Nakanishi

Abstract We construct a model of an international network integration formation game in which each country decides whether to join or exit from the existing international network integration and is assumed to be sufficiently farsighted to understand not only the immediate outcome of its own entry–exit but also the ultimate outcome resulting from the successive entry–exit by other countries. We demonstrate that there exists a unique farsighted stable set for this game that supports a Pareto-efficient network integration. In most cases, the worldwide network integration can be supported by the farsighted stable set.

1 Introduction

The globalization of economic activities assumes various forms: e.g., the liberalization of trade in physical goods and services, the promotion of temporal and/or permanent migration, foreign direct investment by multinational firms, and the standardization of various rules. The advancement of communication technologies and networks provides people with faster and larger means of the transportation of goods, easier ways of providing services, and quicker and clearer transmission of information, thereby facilitating globalization. By making use of communication networks (e.g., the Internet), producers are enabled to reduce communication costs and, therefore, distribute their products and services (in particular, intermediate business services such as informational services, business consulting, and system engineering) more efficiently than before. Then, if communication networks come

[1] I cordially dedicate this chapter to Prof. Koji Shimomura.

N. Nakanishi
Graduate School of Economics, Kobe University, Rokkodai-cho 2-1, Nada-ku, Kobe 657-8501, Japan, e-mail: nakanishi@econ.kobe-u.ac.jp

T. Kamihigashi and L. Zhao (eds.) *International Trade and Economic Dynamics – Essays in Memory of Koji Shimomura.*

to cover a wider range of the world, the efficiency of the worldwide production structure might be enhanced and the welfare of the world might be improved.

The expansion of communication networks has similar effects to that of economic integrations. If some countries interconnect their domestic networks and form a larger international network, each of the countries is enabled to use the resources (factors of production) in the other countries *indirectly* through the network. In effect, the expanded network can be considered as an economic integration in which not only goods but also factors of production are traded freely. Alternatively, the expansion of communication networks can be regarded as the standardization (among countries) of some industrial articles, facilities, and rules. Examples of this include chapter sizes (US letter, A4, etc.), the shape and size of transportation containers, the formats of business/legal documents, and rules for consumers safety and hygiene. If a country adopts its own industrial standard that is different from those in other countries, then it may become highly costly for the domestic producers who have adjusted themselves to their home country's standard to use other countries' products that conform other countries' standards. On the other hand, if some countries adopt a common industrial standard, then the producers in these countries are enabled to utilize products in other common-standard countries easily and at a lower cost.

Considering these features of communication networks, Nakanishi and Kikuchi (2005) have examined the effects of expanding communication networks on the trade patterns and welfare of countries.[2] They have considered two different scenarios: one is the "successive expansion of a single network integration" and the other is the "parallel expansion of plural network integrations." In the former scenario, each country joins the only existing network integration at a point in time and expands the size of the existing network integration by 1 until all the countries join the worldwide network integration. On the other hand, in the latter scenario, pairs of countries form new network integrations of size 2, and subsequently, pairs of size-2 network integrations form new network integrations of size 4; in each stage, pairs of small network integrations of the same size form network integrations twice as large as the original networks until all the countries join the worldwide network integration.

Based on a comparative statics analysis, Nakanishi and Kikuchi (2005) have shown that the parallel expansion of plural network integrations can be Pareto-improving in each stage of the expansion, while the successive expansion of a single network integration can have harmful effects on the welfare of outside countries. In their model, however, the expansion of the network integration(s) along each scenario has been treated *exogenously*; each country's decision whether or not to interconnect its domestic network with other countries' networks has not been analyzed. In addition, they have assumed away the interconnection cost, i.e., the cost that accrues to each country from establishing and maintaining the connection of its domestic network with other countries' networks.

In this chapter, taking into account some strategic interactions between countries and incorporating the interconnection costs into the model, we construct a model

[2] Examples of other studies incorporating the features of the communication networks include Harris (1998), MacKie-Mason and Varian (1995), and Kikuchi (2002, 2003).

of the network integration formation game and examine how the countries behave along with the successive expansion scenario and whether the worldwide network integration (or, at least, some efficient network integrations) can be established.[3] Along the scenario of the successive expansion of a single network integration, if one country decides to join the existing network integration and actually does so, an expanded network integration will be established. However, this is not the only possibility. Another country may decide to enter the expanded network integration, and consequently, the size of the expanded network integration increases further. In this manner, one country's entry to the existing network integration may be followed by subsequent entries by other countries. Of course, it may be the case that some countries successively exit from the existing network integration after one country's entry. When we analyze the successive expansion, it is appropriate to assume that each country (player) is sufficiently *farsighted* to understand not only an immediate outcome attained by its own action but also the "ultimate" outcome resulting from the subsequent actions (reactions) of other countries.

Technically, the structure of our network integration formation game is similar (but not identical) to the cartel formation game developed by D'Aspremont et al. (1983) and also to the n-person prisoner's dilemma game. Farsightedness on the part of players has been taken into account by Diamantoudi (2005), Kamijo and Muto (2007), and Kamijo and Nakanishi (2007) in the context of the cartel formation game and by Suzuki and Muto (2005) and Nakanishi (2007) in the context of prisoner's dilemma games. Following these studies, we adopt the farsighted stable set as the solution concept in this chapter. We demonstrate that, in each of the cases classified by the magnitude of the interconnection cost, there exists a unique farsighted stable set and it supports at least one Pareto-efficient network integration. In most of the cases, the worldwide network integration can be supported by the farsighted stable set.

To facilitate the discussion, we relegate all the proofs of lemmas and theorems to the appendices.

2 The Basic Trade Model

Before constructing a game-theoretical model, we describe the background trade model. Most of the materials in the background model are borrowed from Nakanishi and Kikuchi (2005).

[3] We will not consider the scenario of the parallel expansion of plural network integrations. We believe that an appropriate model for the parallel expansion scenario can be constructed and examined by using the same solution concept (i.e., the farsighted stable set), as in the current chapter. The resulting model, however, may become much more complicated than that in this chapter, because we have to incorporate into the model not only *whether* each country participates in one of existing network integrations but also *which* network integration each country wants to join. In other words, we have to consider the externalities among the existing network integrations; this situation can be represented by a game in *partition function form*.

2.1 Production

We consider a world economy comprising n-identical countries ($n \geqq 2$). Let $N \equiv \{1,2,\ldots,n\}$ be the set of all countries. Each country is endowed with L units of labor and can produce two consumption goods: X and Y. Both markets for goods X and Y are assumed to be competitive. Good Y is produced under constant-returns-to-scale (CRS) technology using only labor as input. We assume that the input coefficient of labor for good Y equals unity; this implies that the equilibrium wage rate of a country also equals unity provided a positive amount of good Y is produced in equilibrium.

Good X is produced using only differentiated business services as inputs. The range of the available differentiated business services is represented by a closed interval $M \equiv [0,m]$ on the real line. The production technology of good X exhibits CRS and constant-elasticity-of-substitution (CES), and it is represented by the following production function:

$$x = \left[\int_0^m z(\tau)^{(\sigma-1)/\sigma} \mathrm{d}\tau\right]^{\sigma/(\sigma-1)}, \quad \sigma > 1, \tag{1}$$

where x is the quantity of good X, $z(\tau)$ is the amount of the τth variety of business services, and σ is the elasticity of substitution between each pair of services. The dual of the production function is the following unit cost function:

$$c = \left[\int_0^m q(\tau)^{1-\sigma} \mathrm{d}\tau\right]^{1/(1-\sigma)}, \quad \sigma > 1, \tag{2}$$

where $q(\tau)$ is the price of the τth variety of business services. By applying Shepard's lemma to (2), we obtain the derived demand function for the ith variety of business services:

$$z(i) = \frac{q(i)^{-\sigma}}{\int_0^m q(\tau)^{1-\sigma} \mathrm{d}\tau} x. \tag{3}$$

As is well known, the price elasticity of the demand for the ith variety of business services is approximated by σ if m is sufficiently large.

Each differentiated business service is produced by a monopolistically competitive *service firm*. The production and distribution of each differentiated business service entail communications through a country-specific network that is provided by a natural monopolist in each country. We assume that the total cost (in terms of labor) of producing $z(i)$ units of service is represented by $\alpha + \beta z(i)$, where $\alpha > 0$ is a fixed fee that a service firm has to pay to the network monopolist to enter the network and $\beta > 0$ is a constant marginal cost. We assume that α and β are identical across service firms.

Let w be the wage rate in a country. Then, the first-order condition for the profit maximization of the ith service firm is given as follows:

$$q(i)\left[1-\frac{1}{\sigma}\right]=w\beta, \quad i\in M. \tag{4}$$

By this, we obtain a symmetric equilibrium in which the service prices are identical across service firms, i.e., $q=q(i)$ for all $i\in M$. Further, by choosing units of services appropriately, we can set $\beta=(\sigma-1)/\sigma$, and therefore, we have $q=w$. Then, the unit cost function c of good X is simplified to

$$c=m^{1/(1-\sigma)}q=m^{1/(1-\sigma)}w. \tag{5}$$

The above equation implies that the unit cost of good X decreases as the degree of input differentiation measured by m increases.

We assume that free entry–exit is allowed in the market for differentiated business services. By substituting $q=w$ into the zero-profit condition for a (representative) service firm, we obtain the long-run output of the business service per firm:

$$z(i)=\alpha\sigma, \quad \forall i\in M. \tag{6}$$

We simply write the common value of $z(i)$ as z. With this, the production function of good X is reduced to

$$x=m^{\sigma/(\sigma-1)}z. \tag{7}$$

As good X is supplied in a perfectly competitive market, the unit cost of X must be equal to a given price of X in terms of good Y, denoted by p, provided incomplete specialization prevails:

$$p=c=m^{1/(1-\sigma)}w=z^{1/\sigma}x^{-1/\sigma}. \tag{8}$$

Note that we have $w=1$ under incomplete specialization and that the last equality follows from (7). By solving the above equation for x and taking account of the resource constraint, we obtain the supply function S_1 for X of a single country:[4]

$$S_1(p)\equiv\begin{cases} zp^{-\sigma}, & \text{if} \quad p\geqq\bar{c}(1),\\ \bar{x}, & \text{otherwise},\end{cases} \tag{9}$$

where $\bar{x}\equiv L^{\sigma/(\sigma-1)}z^{1/(1-\sigma)}$ is the maximum amount of X that can be supplied by a country and $\bar{c}(1)\equiv z^{1/\sigma}(\bar{x})^{-1/\sigma}=z^{1/(\sigma-1)}L^{1/(1-\sigma)}$ is the height of the supply curve corresponding to $\bar{x}$. Note that $\bar{x}$ depends on the labor endowment L of a country; as L increases, $\bar{x}$ increases and, accordingly, $\bar{c}(1)$ decreases. This fact, as we will discuss later, plays an important role in determining the supply function of the network integration. Further, note that the supply function S_1 is "decreasing" in p and the price elasticity of supply is equal to σ provided incomplete specialization prevails.

[4] At the moment, we concentrate our attention on the production structure of a single country that does not connect its own communication network to other countries' networks.

2.2 Consumption

Let us consider the consumption side. We assume that each country's preference over the consumption of X and Y is represented by an identical Cobb–Douglas utility function with share coefficients δ on X and $1-\delta$ on Y:

$$u = x^{\delta} y^{1-\delta}, \quad 0 < \delta < 1, \tag{10}$$

where x and y denote the consumption levels of goods X and Y, respectively, and u is the utility level of a country. Let I be the income level of a country. Then, through the usual procedure, we obtain the demand functions for consumption goods:

$$x = \delta I/p, \quad y = (1-\delta)I. \tag{11}$$

By substituting the above results into (10), we obtain the indirect utility function of a country:

$$u = AIp^{-\delta}, \tag{12}$$

where $A \equiv \delta^{\delta}(1-\delta)^{1-\delta} > 0$.

2.3 Supply Function of a Network Integration

As mentioned in Sect. 1, we consider the scenario of the successive expansion of a single network integration examined by Nakanishi and Kikuchi (2005). This scenario is as follows. Initially, the world economy is in a situation where the consumption goods X and Y are freely traded among the countries, while the business services are not traded internationally at all, because country-specific networks are not interconnected. From this situation, two (and only two) countries interconnect their country-specific networks and form a network integration of size 2. Then, given the network integration of size 2, another country joins the network integration and expands the size of the integration by 1; at this point, the network integration of size 3 is established. Thus, the network integration expands its size successively.[5]

One important assumption in this chapter is that interconnecting each country's network to the existing network integration is costly. For simplicity, we assume that the interconnecting cost takes the form of a fixed cost in terms of labor.[6] That is,

---

[5] If a country exits from the network integration, the network integration reduces in size by 1.

[6] Similar to the cost-sharing externality for the firms supplying business services over the communication network, as assumed in Kikuchi (2002), the interconnecting cost may depend on the size of the existing network integration. Even if we assume the interconnection cost externality and incorporate it into the model, we can qualitatively obtain the same results concerning the stability/efficiency properties of the network integration to the extent that each country's welfare can be represented by a function of both the status of the country (i.e., whether or not the country is a member of the existing network integration) and the size of the existing network integration, as in (18) and (19).

when a country participates in the existing network integration, it needs to devote a certain amount of labor, say $\ell > 0$, to the establishment and maintenance of the connection. Consequently, if a country interconnects its network to the network integration, the labor force that can be used for the production of consumption goods decreases from L to $L - \ell$. To simplify the calculation, let us define a coefficient $\lambda \equiv (L - \ell)/L$. We have $0 < \lambda < 1$. Then, instead of ℓ, the interconnecting cost can be represented by the coefficient λ; a higher λ corresponds to a lower interconnecting cost.

Let us consider how the supply function for good X of a single network integration changes according to its size.[7] Suppose that h countries have formed a network integration. Then, through the integrated networks, each member country can employ the business services produced not only in the country itself but also in other member countries. In effect, this is equivalent to each member country being enabled to employ the labor forces located in the other member countries. In this sense, a network integration can be regarded as though it were a single country whose labor endowment equals h times λL. Hence, the supply function of a network integration with h members is equivalent to that of a single country with $h\lambda L$ labor endowment. By replacing L in (9) with $h\lambda L$, we obtain the supply function S_h of a network integration with h members, as follows: For $h = 2, 3, \ldots, n$,

$$S_h(p) \equiv \begin{cases} zp^{-\sigma}, & \text{if } \; p \geqq \bar{c}(h), \\ (\lambda h)^{\sigma/(\sigma-1)}\bar{x}, & \text{otherwise,} \end{cases} \tag{13}$$

where $\bar{c}(h) \equiv z^{1/\sigma}\left[(\lambda h)^{\sigma/(\sigma-1)}\bar{x}\right]^{-1/\sigma} = (\lambda h)^{1/(1-\sigma)}\bar{c}(1)$. Clearly, $\bar{c}(h)$ is decreasing in h. It should be noted that the supply function of a network integration is obtained *not* by summing the individual supply functions of the member countries, but by extending an individual supply function downward.

2.4 Equilibrium Prices

The aggregate world supply function S of good X when a network integration with h members exists can be written as a function of p and h: For $h = 1, 2, \ldots, n$,

$$S(p,h) \equiv S_h(p) + (n-h)S_1(p). \tag{14}$$

For completeness, we assume that $S(p,0) = nS_1(p)$.

Let us consider the demand side. The income level I of a country depends on both the price of X and the status of the country (i.e., whether the country is *in* or *out* of the network integration). Let I^{in} and I^{out} be the income levels in terms of Y of an inside country and that of an outside country, respectively. As shown by Nakanishi and Kikuchi (2005), the network integration as a whole always diversifies in the

---

[7] The size of a network integration is measured in terms of the number of member countries.

course of the successive expansion of the network integration. This implies that the wage rate in the network integration is always equal to unity (i.e., $w = 1$). Then, we have $I^{\text{in}} = \lambda L$ for an appropriate (sufficiently wide) domain of p. On the other hand, I^{out} varies according to p and, therefore, to the production structure of the country. If p is higher than $\bar{c}(1)$, then an outside country diversifies, and similar to the case of I^{in}, we have $w = 1$ in this country; if p is lower than $\bar{c}(1)$, then an outside country specializes in X and produces $\bar{x}$, and hence, its income becomes $p\bar{x}$. That is,

$$I^{\text{out}} = \begin{cases} L, & \text{if} \quad p \geqq \bar{c}(1), \\ p\bar{x}, & \text{otherwise.} \end{cases} \tag{15}$$

Summarizing these facts, we can express the aggregate world demand for good X as a function of p and h: For $h = 2, 3, \ldots, n$,

$$\begin{aligned} D(p,h) &= h\delta I^{\text{in}}/p + (n-h)\delta I^{\text{out}}/p \\ &= \begin{cases} h\delta\lambda L/p + (n-h)\delta L/p, & \text{if} \quad p \geqq \bar{c}(1), \\ h\delta\lambda L/p + (n-h)\delta\bar{x}, & \text{otherwise.} \end{cases} \end{aligned} \tag{16}$$

When there is no network integration (i.e., $h = 0$), we have $D(p,0) = n\delta I^{\text{out}}/p$. A network integration with only one member is analytically meaningless; we identify a one-member network integration with no network integration. Therefore, we assume that $D(p,1) = D(p,0)$.

With (14) and (16), the market equilibrium condition can be written as follows: For $h = 0, 1, \ldots, n$,

$$S(p,h) = D(p,h). \tag{17}$$

The above equation implicitly determines the equilibrium price of good X as a function of h, which is denoted by $p(h)$. By the definitions of the world supply and demand functions, we have $p(0) = p(1)$. Except for this case, as Nakanishi and Kikuchi (2005) have shown, $p(h)$ is monotonically decreasing in h.

Let $\bar{n}$ be the maximum integer that satisfies $p(\bar{n}) \geqq \bar{c}(1)$. Under certain conditions, we can show that $1 < \bar{n} < n$.[8] If the size of the network integration does not exceed $\bar{n}$, then the equilibrium price becomes higher than $\bar{c}(1)$ and all the countries diversify; if, on the other hand, the size of the network integration exceeds $\bar{n}$, then the equilibrium price becomes lower than $\bar{c}(1)$ and all the outside countries begin to specialize in good X.

2.5 Welfare of a Country

Given a network integration of size h, a unique equilibrium price $p(h)$ is determined. A country's welfare depends on the equilibrium price $p(h)$ and the status of the country (i.e., whether or not the country is a member of the existing

[8] See the Appendices 1 and 2.

network integration). Let $\{C,D\}$ be the set of possible statuses of a country, where C represents "Connected" (to the existing integration) and D represents "Disconnected." By substituting $p(h)$ into (12) and taking into account the definitions of I^{in}, I^{out}, and $\bar{n}$, we can express the welfare level of a country as a function of the status (C or D) and the size of existing network integration:

$$f(C,h) \equiv A\lambda L[p(h)]^{-\delta}, \quad h = 2,3,\ldots,\bar{n},\ldots,n, \tag{18}$$

$$f(D,h) \equiv \begin{cases} AL[p(h)]^{-\delta}, & \text{if} \quad h = 0,1,\ldots,\bar{n}, \\ A\bar{x}[p(h)]^{1-\delta}, & \text{if} \quad h = \bar{n}+1,\bar{n}+2,\ldots,n. \end{cases} \tag{19}$$

For the reason we mentioned before, we assume that $f(C,1) = f(D,0)$.[9] Further, because $p(0) = p(1)$, we have $f(D,0) = f(D,1)$. Because $p(h)$ is decreasing in h (except for $p(0) = p(1)$) and $0 < \lambda < 1$, it is easy to verify the following lemma.

Lemma 1. *The function f satisfies the following properties:*

(i) $f(C,h) < f(C,h+1)$, $h = 2,3,\ldots,\bar{n}-1,\bar{n},\ldots,n-1$.
(ii) $f(D,h) < f(D,h+1)$, $h = 1,2,\ldots,\bar{n}-1$.
(iii) $f(D,h) > f(D,h+1)$, $h = \bar{n}+1,\bar{n}+2,\ldots,n-2$.
(iv) $f(D,h) > f(C,h)$, $h = 2,3,\ldots,\bar{n}$.

The proofs to these are straightforward; therefore, we omit them.

Lemma 1(i) implies that a country's entry into the existing network integration (i.e., the expansion of the network integration) is beneficial to each inside country. Lemma 1(ii) means that if the size of a network integration is small enough (i.e., smaller than $\bar{n}$), the expansion of the network integration will produce *positive* external effects on the welfare of the outside countries. On the other hand, Lemma 1(iii) indicates that if the size of a network integration has already become large enough (i.e., larger than $\bar{n}$), the further enlargement of the network integration will produce *negative* external effects on the outside countries. Lemma 1(iv) means that because of the interconnecting cost, it is better for a country to stay outside of the network integration than to be inside provided the size of the network integration is not too large.

Lemma 1(ii) and (iii) together imply that $f(D,h)$ attains its maximum at $h = \bar{n}$ or at $h = \bar{n}+1$. For simplicity, we assume the former.

Assumption 1. $f(D,\bar{n}) \geqq f(D,h)$ for all $h = 0,1,\ldots,n$.

In addition, to avoid unnecessary complexities, we assume the following.

Assumption 2. Except for the case $f(D,0) = f(D,1) = f(C,1)$, we have $f(C,h) \neq f(D,k)$ and $f(D,h) \neq f(D,k)$ for any distinct integers h and k.

[9] It should be noted that neither $f(C,0)$ nor $f(D,n)$ can be defined.

It is logically possible to have $f(C,h) = f(D,k)$ or $f(D,h) = f(D,k)$ for some pair of h and k. These equalities, however, can be violated easily by a slight perturbation of the fundamental parameters of the model. By Assumption 2, we ignore these degenerate cases in this chapter.

If an outside country joins the existing network integration of size h, then the size of the network integration increases from h to $h+1$ and the joining country now becomes a member of the expanded network integration; in this case, the welfare of the joining country changes from $f(D,h)$ to $f(C,h+1)$. The difference between $f(D,h)$ and $f(C,h+1)$ depends on the interconnection cost.

Lemma 2. *For $h = 1,2,\ldots,\bar{n}$, we have $f(D,h) < f(C,h+1)$ if the interconnection cost is sufficiently low and $f(D,h) > f(C,h+1)$ if the interconnection cost is sufficiently high.*

The maximum welfare that a country can obtain by staying outside the network integration is $f(D,\bar{n})$. On the other hand, the maximum welfare that a country can obtain by joining the network integration is $f(C,n)$. Again, the difference between $f(D,\bar{n})$ and $f(C,n)$ depends on the interconnecting cost.

Lemma 3. *Suppose $\delta n > 1$. Then, $f(D,\bar{n}) < f(C,n)$ if the interconnection cost is sufficiently low and $f(D,\bar{n}) > f(C,n)$ if the interconnecting cost is sufficiently high.*

The condition $\delta n > 1$ can be satisfied if the number of countries in the world is sufficiently large or if the expenditure share δ on good X is sufficiently high; in fact, as we assumed that $n \geqq 2$, then $\delta > 1/2$ is a sufficient condition for $\delta n > 1$.

Because $f(C,h)$ is increasing in h, $f(D,\bar{n}) > f(C,n)$ implies that $f(D,\bar{n}) > f(C,\bar{n}+1)$. Conversely, even if the interconnection cost is sufficiently high to satisfy $f(D,h) > f(C,h+1)$ for all $h = 1,2,\ldots,\bar{n}$, it is still possible to have $f(D,\bar{n}) < f(C,n)$. Based on this observation, we distinguish between the following three cases:

1. *The high-cost case*, where $f(D,h) > f(C,h+1)$ for $h = 1,2,\ldots,\bar{n}$ and $f(D,\bar{n}) > f(C,n)$
2. *The intermediate-cost case*, where $f(D,h) > f(C,h+1)$ for $h = 1,2,\ldots,\bar{n}$ and $f(D,\bar{n}) < f(C,n)$
3. *The low-cost case*, where $f(D,h) < f(C,h+1)$ for $h = 1,2,\ldots,\bar{n}$ and $f(D,\bar{n}) < f(C,n)$

If the interconnection cost is prohibitively high, it is possible to have $f(D,0) > f(C,h)$ for all $h = 1,\ldots,n$. In this case, regardless of the size of the network integration, all the countries who form the integration become worse off than when there is no network integration. Then, in this case, we can conclude that no network integration will be formed. To avoid such a degenerate case, we assume the following.

Assumption 3. In each of the high-, intermediate-, and low-cost cases, there exists an integer $\tilde{n}$ such that $f(D,0) < f(C,\tilde{n})$ and $2 \leqq \tilde{n} \leqq n$.

3 Formation and Stability of the Network Integration

Having described the background trade model, we now construct a game-theoretical model of the network integration formation. $N \equiv \{1,2,\dots,n\}$ is the set of all countries (players) and $\{C,D\}$ is the set of possible statuses, where C represents "Connected" and D represents "Disconnected." Because each country chooses whether or not to join the network integration, we can regard $\{C,D\}$ as the set of strategies of a country. Let $\Gamma \equiv \prod_{j\in N}\{C,D\}$ be the set of all the possible combinations of strategies. An n-vector $\xi \in \Gamma$ is called an "outcome." For $\xi = (\xi_1, \xi_2, \dots, \xi_n) \in \Gamma$, $\xi_j = C$ means that country j is a member of the current network integration and $\xi_j = D$ implies that country j remains outside the network integration. We denote the all-C outcome as $\xi^C \equiv (C,C,\dots,C)$, which corresponds to the worldwide network integration. With a slight abuse of notation, let $C(\xi)$ be the set of members of the network integration that corresponds to ξ, i.e., $C(\xi) \equiv \{j \in N | \xi_j = C\}$. Further, let $s(\xi) \equiv |C(\xi)|$ be the size of the current network integration. Furthermore, let $V(h)$ be a subset of all outcomes in which the number of countries who play C is equal to h:

$$V(h) \equiv \{\xi \in \Gamma | s(\xi) = h\}, \quad h = 0,1,2,\dots,n. \tag{20}$$

Of course, $V(0)$ is a singleton set comprising the all-D outcome and $V(n)$ is also a singleton set consisting of ξ^C, i.e., $V(0) = \{(D,D,\dots,D)\}$ and $V(n) = \{(C,C,\dots,C)\} = \{\xi^C\}$.

Given $\xi \in \Gamma$, the following economic variables are determined: a network integration with $s(\xi)$ members, a trade equilibrium, the corresponding equilibrium price $p(s(\xi))$, and the welfare level of each country, which depends on the status of a country. In this sense, an outcome ξ describes the current state of an economy, and therefore, Γ can be considered as the set of all the possible states of an economy.

The payoff function $U_j : \Gamma \to \mathbb{R}$ of country j is a function that assigns the welfare level of country j to ξ: For $j \in N$,

$$U_j(\xi) \equiv \begin{cases} f(C,s(\xi)), & \text{if} \quad j \in C(\xi), \\ f(D,s(\xi)), & \text{if} \quad j \notin C(\xi). \end{cases} \tag{21}$$

For two outcomes $\xi, \zeta \in \Gamma$, we say that "ζ Pareto-dominates ξ" or "ζ is Pareto-superior to ξ" if $U_j(\xi) \leqq U_j(\zeta)$ for all $j \in N$ with strict inequality for some $j \in N$. An outcome $\xi \in \Gamma$ is said to be *Pareto-efficient* if and only if there is no other outcome $\zeta \in \Gamma$ that Pareto-dominates ξ. Let $\Gamma^{\mathrm{P}} \subset \Gamma$ be the set of all the Pareto-efficient outcomes. The following lemma characterizes the Pareto-efficient outcomes.

Lemma 4. *Under Assumptions 2 and 3, an outcome ξ is Pareto-efficient if and only if it satisfies either one of the following two conditions* (i) $f(D,s(\xi)) \geqq f(C,n)$ *or* (ii) $\xi = \xi^C$.

Suppose that the current state of the economy is $\xi \in \Gamma$. By joining the current network integration or by exiting from it, country j can change the state of the economy from ξ to another $\zeta \in \Gamma$ such that $\zeta_j \neq \xi_j$ and $\zeta_k = \xi_k$ for all $k \in N \backslash \{j\}$. When country j changes a given outcome ξ to another outcome ζ, we say that "country j induces ζ from ξ" or "ζ is induced from ξ through country j." We write this inducement relation as $\xi \xrightarrow{j} \zeta$.

If $\xi \xrightarrow{j} \xi'$ and $U_j(\xi) < U_j(\xi')$ for some $j \in N$, we can say that country j has the power to change the current state of the economy ξ to a new state ξ' and can benefit from doing so. If country j believes that ξ' will be maintained after its own deviation from ξ (in other words, if country j is so *myopic* that it only takes account of the immediate outcome after its deviation from the initial outcome), then country j actually deviates from ξ. On the contrary, suppose that country j is *farsighted* enough to understand not only the direct outcome ξ' of its own deviation from the current outcome ξ but also the ultimate outcome that results from subsequent deviations by other countries. In this case, even if both $\xi \xrightarrow{j} \xi'$ and $U_j(\xi) < U_j(\xi')$ hold, country j may not deviate from ξ, anticipating that it will become worse off under the ultimate outcome realized by the deviations by other countries subsequent to its own deviation than under ξ. Conversely, even if $\xi \xrightarrow{j} \xi'$ but $U_j(\xi) > U_j(\xi')$, a farsighted country j may deviate from ξ to ξ', anticipating that successive deviations by other countries after its own deviation may lead to an ultimate outcome under which country j would be better off than under ξ. The farsightedness of the countries is captured by the notion of the indirect domination, which is a binary relation $\ll$ defined on Γ.

Definition 1 (Indirect domination). For $\xi, \zeta \in \Gamma$, we have $\xi \ll \zeta$ if and only if there exist a sequence of outcomes $\xi^0, \xi^1, \ldots, \xi^R$ and countries $j_1, j_2, \ldots, j_R$,

$$\xi = \xi^0 \xrightarrow{j_1} \xi^1 \xrightarrow{j_2} \xi^2 \xrightarrow{j_3} \cdots \xrightarrow{j_R} \xi^R = \zeta,$$

such that for all $r = 1, 2, \ldots, R$, (a) $\xi^{r-1} \xrightarrow{j_r} \xi^r$ and (b) $U_{j_r}(\xi^{r-1}) < U_{j_r}(\zeta)$.

Condition (a) in the above definition implies that country j_r has the power to change a given outcome ξ^{r-1} to another ξ^r. However, this does not necessarily imply that country j_r will be better off in ξ^r than in ξ^{r-1}. Condition (b) implies that each country in the sequence can be better off in the last outcome (i.e., ζ) than in the outcome from which the country deviates. When $\xi \ll \zeta$, we simply say that "ζ indirectly dominates ξ" or "ξ is indirectly dominated by ζ." The pair $(\Gamma, \ll)$ is an abstract system that describes the network integration formation game in which all countries are farsighted.

Now, let us define the solution concept in this chapter.[10]

Definition 2 (Farsighted stable set). A subset K of Γ is said to be a "farsighted stable set" for $(\Gamma, \ll)$ if and only if it satisfies the following two conditions:

---

[10] The (von Neumann–Morgenstern) stable set was originally defined as a solution concept for games in characteristic function form (von Neumann and Morgenstern 1953). Greenberg's (1990) *Theory of Social Situations* (TOSS) has revitalized the notion of the stable set and paved the way to apply it to games in various forms.

(i) For any $\xi \in K$, there does not exist $\zeta \in K$ such that $\xi \ll \zeta$.
(ii) For any $\xi \in \Gamma \backslash K$, there exists $\zeta \in K$ such that $\xi \ll \zeta$.

Conditions (i) and (ii) are known as "internal stability" and "external stability," respectively. The intuition behind internal/external stability requirements can be explained as follows. Suppose that every country considers (or believes) that a subset K of Γ comprises all the "ultimate" outcomes and does not include any outcome that is not ultimate. Consider an outcome ξ in K. If, contrary to the internal stability, there exists another "ultimate" outcome ζ in K such that $\xi \ll \zeta$, then ξ cannot be an "ultimate" outcome. Indeed, ξ will be replaced by ζ through a sequence $\xi = \xi^0 \xrightarrow{j_1} \xi^1 \xrightarrow{j_2} \dots \xrightarrow{j_R} \xi^R = \zeta$ such that $U_{j_r}(\xi^{r-1}) < U_{j_r}(\zeta)$ for all $r = 1, 2, \dots, R$. In this case, every country's belief that ξ is one of the ultimate outcomes is disproved. In turn, consider an outcome ξ not in K. Suppose that the external stability is violated. Then, no country has the incentive to deviate from ξ; consequently, once ξ has reached, it will be maintained. Again, every country's belief that ξ is *not* one of the ultimate outcomes is disproved. In sum, a subset K that satisfies both internal and external stabilities is a set of outcomes that are consistent with every countries' belief concerning whether or not some outcomes are "ultimate."

The first theorem establishes the existence of a unique farsighted stable set in the low-cost and intermediate-cost cases.

Theorem 1. *In both the low-cost and intermediate-cost cases, there exists a unique farsighted stable set K^*, which is given by $K^* = V(n)$.*

Before stating our next theorem, we need to introduce one more definition, which will play an important role in establishing the existence of the farsighted stable set in the high-cost case. Let us define positive integers h_t $(t = 1, 2, \dots)$ recursively, as follows:

$$h_0 \equiv 0, \quad h_1 \equiv 1, \tag{22}$$

$$h_t = \min\{h \mid f(D,h) > f(C,h) > f(D,h_{t-1})\}, \quad t = 2, 3, \dots. \tag{23}$$

Clearly, there exists an integer T at which the recursive process stops. Let $H = \{h_0, h_1, \dots, h_T\}$ be the set of the integers defined above. Because $f(C,h)$ is increasing in h and because $f(D,h) > f(C,h)$ for $h = 2, 3, \dots, \bar{n}$, we have $h_t < h_{t+1}$ for $t = 1, 2, \dots, T-1$.

Theorem 2. *In the high-cost case, there exists a unique farsighted stable set K^*, which is given by:*

(i) $K^* = \bigcup_{t=0}^{T} V(h_t)$ *if* $f(D,h_T) > f(C,n)$.
(ii) $K^* = \left[\bigcup_{t=0}^{T} V(h_t)\right] \cup V(n)$ *if* $f(D,h_T) < f(C,n)$ *and* $h_T < \bar{n}$.
(iii) $K^* = \left[\bigcup_{t=0}^{T-1} V(h_t)\right] \cup V(n)$ *if* $f(D,h_T) < f(C,n)$ *and* $h_T > \bar{n}$.

From Theorems 1 and 2, we obtain the following proposition.

Proposition 1. *In the international network integration formation game, at least one Pareto-efficient outcome is supported by the unique farsighted stable set K^*.*

4 Remarks

By Theorem 1, we can say that in both the low-cost and intermediate-cost cases, the worldwide network integration *will* be established. In the low-cost case, this result may seem almost trivial. Because $f(D,h) < f(C,h+1)$ in this case, even if each country is *myopic* in the sense that it only takes into account the immediate outcome resulting from its own deviation, each country has an incentive to join the existing network integration. Then, one may consider it as a matter of course that the worldwide network integration will be formed eventually.

In the intermediate-cost case, on the other hand, the result in Theorem 1 is somewhat surprising. Because $f(D,h) > f(C,h+1)$ for $h = 1,\ldots,\bar{n}$ in this case, if the existing network integration is not sufficiently large, each myopic outside country has no incentive to join the existing integration and each myopic inside country has an incentive to disconnect itself from the existing integration. Accordingly, if countries are myopic in the intermediate-cost case, it seems natural to have no network integration. Because $f(D,\bar{n}) < f(C,n)$ in the intermediate-cost case (which implies that $f(D,h) < f(C,n)$ for all h), then each *farsighted* country, who can foresee the ultimate outcome (i.e., the worldwide network integration), decides to join the existing network integration despite the fact that its own participation in the existing network integration gives rise to a lower welfare in the immediate outcome.

The situation in the high-cost case is more complicated. By Proposition 1, we can show that the worldwide network integration (or, at least, some Pareto-efficient network integrations) can be supported by the farsighted stable set. However, unfortunately, in the high-cost case, we cannot conclude that the worldwide (or, efficient) network integration *will* indeed be established. Remember that $V(0) \subset K^*$ in the high-cost case; i.e., the worldwide (or, efficient) network integration is a possibility on the one hand, but *no network integration* is another possibility on the other hand. Which network integration will be actually established depends on the initial situation. If the world economy is in a situation with no network integration and the interconnection cost is very high, then the status quo will remain. If the interconnection cost gradually decreases and it reaches the intermediate-cost case, then before the interconnection cost reaches the low-cost case, the network begins to grow into the worldwide network integration.

Appendix 1: Some Properties of the Basic Model

Characterization of $\bar{n}$

Define $\bar{p} \equiv \bar{c}(1)$. Because $\bar{c}(1) = z^{1/\sigma}\bar{x}^{-1/\sigma}$ and $\bar{x} = L^{\sigma/(\sigma-1)}z^{1/(1-\sigma)}$, then we have $\bar{p} = (z/L)^{1/(\sigma-1)}$. Using $\bar{p}$, we can characterize $\bar{n}$ as the integer that simultaneously satisfies the following two inequalities:

$$S(\bar{p},\bar{n}) \geqq D(\bar{p},\bar{n}), \tag{24}$$
$$S(\bar{p},\bar{n}+1) < D(\bar{p},\bar{n}+1). \tag{25}$$

Using the definitions of S and D, the first inequality is expanded as follows:

$$\begin{aligned} & (n+1-\bar{n})z(\bar{p})^{-\sigma} \geqq (n+[\lambda-1]\bar{n})\delta L(\bar{p})^{-1} \\ \Leftrightarrow \quad & n+1-\bar{n} \geqq (n+[\lambda-1]\bar{n})\delta L(\bar{p})^{\sigma-1}/z \\ \Leftrightarrow \quad & n+1-\bar{n} \geqq (n+[\lambda-1]\bar{n})\delta. \end{aligned} \tag{26}$$

Similarly, (25) is expanded as follows:

$$\begin{aligned} & (n+1-[\bar{n}+1])z(\bar{p})^{-\sigma} < (n+[\lambda-1][\bar{n}+1])\delta L(\bar{p})^{-1} \\ \Leftrightarrow \quad & n+1-[\bar{n}+1] < (n+[\lambda-1][\bar{n}+1])\delta L(\bar{p})^{\sigma-1} \\ \Leftrightarrow \quad & n-\bar{n} < (n+[\lambda-1]\bar{n})\delta + (\lambda-1)\delta. \end{aligned} \tag{27}$$

Combining the above results, we obtain the following relation:

$$\begin{aligned} & n+1-\bar{n} \geqq (n+[\lambda-1]\bar{n})\delta > n-\bar{n}-[\lambda-1]\delta \\ \Leftrightarrow \quad & \frac{(1-\delta)n+1}{1-(1-\lambda)\delta} \geqq \bar{n} > \frac{(1-\delta)n+(1-\lambda)\delta}{1-(1-\lambda)\delta}. \end{aligned} \tag{28}$$

The above inequalities provide a complete characterization of $\bar{n}$.

Dividing both the sides of (28) by n and letting n tend to infinity, we have the following result:

$$\lim_{n\to+\infty}\left(\frac{\bar{n}}{n}\right) = \frac{1-\delta}{1-(1-\lambda)\delta}. \tag{29}$$

The right-hand side of (29) is strictly positive and less than unity. The above result implies that if n is sufficiently large, $\bar{n}$ can be approximated by the product of the right-hand side of (29) and n:

$$\bar{n} \doteqdot \frac{(1-\delta)n}{1-(1-\lambda)\delta} \quad \text{(for sufficiently large } n\text{)}. \tag{30}$$

Hence, if the number of the countries is sufficiently large, we have

$$1 < \bar{n} < n. \tag{31}$$

Calculation of the Equilibrium Price

For h with $1 \leqq h \leqq \bar{n}$, the market equilibrium condition is as follows:

$$zp^{-\sigma} + (n-h)zp^{-\sigma} = h\delta\lambda Lp^{-1} + (n-h)\delta Lp^{-1}. \tag{32}$$

By solving the above equation for p, we can write the equilibrium price as a function of h:

$$p(h) \equiv \left[\frac{(n+1-h)z}{(n+[\lambda-1]h)\delta L}\right]^{1/(\sigma-1)}, \quad 1 \leqq h \leqq \bar{n}. \tag{33}$$

On the other hand, for h with $\bar{n}+1 \leqq h \leqq n$, the market equilibrium condition is as follows:

$$zp^{-\sigma} + (n-h)\bar{x} = h\delta\lambda Lp^{-1} + (n-h)\delta\bar{x}. \tag{34}$$

Rearranging the above equation, we have

$$\psi(p,h) \equiv (1-\delta)(n-h)\bar{x}p^{\sigma} - h\delta\lambda Lp^{\sigma-1} + z = 0. \tag{35}$$

In general, (34) (or (35)) cannot be solved explicitly for p. Moreover, because (34) is a nonlinear equation, there may be multiple solutions for p. In any case, if there exist solutions of (34) for p, one of them is the equilibrium price $p(h)$.

Let us examine the number of the solutions of (34) for p and determine which of them is the equilibrium price. The number of the solutions of (34) depends on the shape of ψ. To find the extreme points of ψ, let us differentiate ψ with respect to p and set the result equal to zero:

$$\frac{\partial \psi(p,h)}{\partial p} \equiv p^{\sigma-2}\{\sigma(n-h)(1-\delta)\bar{x}p - (\sigma-1)h\delta\lambda L\} = 0. \tag{36}$$

The above equation has *at most* two solutions for p:

$$p = \frac{(\sigma-1)h\delta\lambda L}{\sigma(n-h)(1-\delta)\bar{x}} \tag{37}$$

is always a solution; further, if $\sigma > 2$, $p = 0$ can also be another solution. As is easily verified, (37) yields a unique, local minimum point of ψ. This, together with the fact that $\psi(0,h) = z > 0$ and $\lim_{p\to+\infty}\psi(p,h) = +\infty$, implies that (34) (or (35)) has *at most* two positive solutions for p: p_{L} and p_{H} with $p_{\mathrm{L}} < p_{\mathrm{H}}$.

As Nakanishi and Kikuchi (2005) have shown by using a diagrammatical technique, the equilibrium price $p(h)$ is decreasing in h; therefore, either p_{L} or p_{H} that satisfy this condition is the equilibrium price. To show which is the one that satisfies this condition, it suffices to examine the sign of the partial derivative of ψ with respect to h. By simply calculating, we have

$$\frac{\partial \psi(p,h)}{\partial h} = -(1-\delta)\bar{x}p^{\sigma} - \delta\lambda Lp^{\sigma-1} < 0. \tag{38}$$

This implies that p_{H} is increasing in h, while p_{L} is decreasing in h. Hence, we can conclude that p_{L} (if it exists) is the equilibrium price $p(h)$.

Appendix 2: Proofs

Proof of Lemma 2

Taking into account the definitions of $f(D,h)$, $f(C,h)$, and $p(h)$, the condition $f(D,h) > f(C,h+1)$ will be expanded as follows:

$$\begin{aligned}
\frac{f(D,h)}{f(C,h+1)} > 1 \quad &\Leftrightarrow \quad \frac{AL[p(h)]^{-\delta}}{A\lambda L[p(h+1)]^{-\delta}} > 1 \\
&\Leftrightarrow \quad \left[\frac{p(h)}{p(h+1)}\right]^{-\delta} > \lambda \\
&\Leftrightarrow \quad \left[\frac{\left\{\frac{(n+1-h)z}{(n+[\lambda-1]h)\delta L}\right\}^{1/(\sigma-1)}}{\left\{\frac{(n-h)z}{(n+[\lambda-1][h+1])\delta L}\right\}^{1/(\sigma-1)}}\right]^{-\delta} > \lambda \\
&\Leftrightarrow \quad \left[\frac{(n+1-h)(n+[\lambda-1][h+1])}{(n+[\lambda-1]h)(n-h)}\right]^{-\delta/(\sigma-1)} > \lambda \\
&\Leftrightarrow \quad \left[\frac{(n+[\lambda-1]h)(n-h)}{(n+1-h)(n+[\lambda-1][h+1])}\right] > \lambda^{(\sigma-1)/\delta}. \qquad (39)
\end{aligned}$$

Then, to prove the lemma, it suffices to show that the above inequality holds for λ sufficiently close to zero.

Let us consider the left-hand side of (39) as a function g_{L} of λ and h. Then, we can demonstrate the following results:

$$\lim_{\lambda\downarrow 0} g_{\mathrm{L}}(\lambda,h) = \frac{(n-h)^2}{(n-h)^2-1} > 1, \qquad (40)$$

$$\lim_{\lambda\uparrow 1} g_{\mathrm{L}}(\lambda,h) = \frac{n-h}{n-h+1} < 1, \qquad (41)$$

$$\frac{\partial g_{\mathrm{L}}(\lambda,h)}{\partial\lambda} = \frac{-n(n-h)}{(n-h+1)\{n-h-1+(h+1)\lambda\}^2} < 0. \qquad (42)$$

Similarly, if we take the right-hand side of (39) as a function g_{R} of λ and h, we have the following results:

$$\lim_{\lambda\downarrow 0} g_{\mathrm{R}}(\lambda,h) = 0, \quad \lim_{\lambda\uparrow 1} g_{\mathrm{R}}(\lambda,h) = 1. \qquad (43)$$

It is apparent that g_{R} is increasing in λ.

Because both g_{L} and g_{R} are continuous in (λ,h), the above results imply that, for each h, there exists a unique critical value $\tilde{\lambda}(h)$ such that $g_{\mathrm{L}}(\tilde{\lambda}(h),h) \equiv g_{\mathrm{R}}(\tilde{\lambda}(h),h)$ and $0 < \tilde{\lambda}(h) < 1$. Of course, we have $g_{\mathrm{L}}(\lambda,h) > g_{\mathrm{R}}(\lambda,h)$ if $\lambda < \tilde{\lambda}(h)$ and $g_{\mathrm{L}}(\lambda,h) < g_{\mathrm{R}}(\lambda,h)$ if $\lambda > \tilde{\lambda}(h)$. Define $\tilde{\lambda}_{\min} \equiv \min_h \tilde{\lambda}(h)$ and $\tilde{\lambda}_{\max} \equiv \max_h \tilde{\lambda}(h)$.

Because h runs over a finite set, $\tilde{\lambda}_{\min}$ and $\tilde{\lambda}_{\max}$ are well defined and $0 < \tilde{\lambda}_{\min} < \tilde{\lambda}_{\max} < 1$. Then, if $\lambda < \tilde{\lambda}_{\min}$, we have $g_{\mathrm{L}}(\lambda,h) > g_{\mathrm{R}}(\lambda,h)$ for all $h = 1,2,\ldots,n$. On the other hand, if $\lambda > \tilde{\lambda}_{\max}$, we have $g_{\mathrm{L}}(\lambda,h) < g_{\mathrm{R}}(\lambda,h)$ for all $h = 1,2,\ldots,n$. □

Proof of Lemma 3

Ignoring the fact that h in (33) is an integer and, instead, regarding it as a real number, $p(h)$ can be considered as a continuous function of the real h. By (28), we can use the upper limit of $\bar{n}$ as an approximation of $\bar{n}$:

$$\bar{n} \doteqdot \frac{(1-\delta)n+1}{1-(1-\lambda)\delta}. \tag{44}$$

Substituting the above into the definition of the equilibrium price yields the following:

$$\begin{aligned}
p(\bar{n}) &\doteqdot \left(\frac{z}{\delta L}\right)^{1/(\sigma-1)} \left[\frac{n+1-\frac{(1-\delta)n+1}{1-(1-\lambda)\delta}}{n-(1-\lambda)\frac{(1-\delta)n+1}{1-(1-\lambda)\delta}}\right]^{1/(\sigma-1)} \\
&= \left(\frac{z}{\delta L}\right)^{1/(\sigma-1)} \left[\frac{(n+1)(1-[1-\lambda]\delta)-(1-\delta)n-1}{n(1-[1-\lambda]\delta)-(1-\lambda)[(1-\delta)n+1]}\right]^{1/(\sigma-1)} \\
&= \left(\frac{z}{\delta L}\right)^{1/(\sigma-1)} \left[\frac{\delta(\lambda n-1+\lambda)}{\lambda n-1+\lambda}\right]^{1/(\sigma-1)} \\
&= \left(\frac{z}{\delta L}\right)^{1/(\sigma-1)} \delta^{1/(\sigma-1)} \\
&= \left(\frac{z}{L}\right)^{1/(\sigma-1)} = \bar{p}.
\end{aligned} \tag{45}$$

Thus, $p(\bar{n})$ can be approximated by $\bar{p}$. Then, we have

$$f(D,\bar{n}) \doteqdot AL[\bar{p}]^{-\delta}. \tag{46}$$

Substituting $h = n$ into the definition of the equilibrium price yields

$$p(n) = \left(\frac{z}{\delta L}\right)^{1/(\sigma-1)} \left[\frac{n+1-n}{n-(1-\lambda)n}\right]^{1/(\sigma-1)} = (\lambda\delta n)^{1/(1-\sigma)}\,\bar{p}. \tag{47}$$

Then, we have

$$f(C,n) = \lambda AL\left[(\lambda\delta n)^{1/(1-\sigma)}\,\bar{p}\right]^{-\delta}. \tag{48}$$

Combining these results, we obtain the following:

$$\frac{f(C,n)}{f(D,\bar{n})} = \frac{\lambda AL\left[(\lambda\delta n)^{1/(1-\sigma)}\bar{p}\right]^{-\delta}}{AL[\bar{p}]^{-\delta}} = \lambda^{(\delta+\sigma-1)/\delta}\delta n. \tag{49}$$

Consequently, the following relation (approximately) holds:

$$f(C,n) \gtreqqless f(D,\bar{n}) \quad \Leftrightarrow \quad \lambda^{(\delta+\sigma-1)/\delta} \gtreqqless \frac{1}{\delta n}. \tag{50}$$

By the condition given in the lemma, $0 < 1/(\delta n) < 1$. If λ is sufficiently close to zero (i.e., if the interconnection cost is sufficiently high), then $f(C,n) < f(D,\bar{n})$; if λ is sufficiently close to unity (i.e., if the interconnection cost is sufficiently high), then $f(C,n) > f(D,\bar{n})$. □

Proof of Lemma 4

Sufficiency

First, let us consider ξ^C, which is the only outcome that satisfies $s(\xi) = n$. Take an arbitrary outcome ζ other than ξ^C; $s(\zeta) < n$. If $s(\zeta) \geqq 2$, by the monotonicity of $f(C,h)$ with respect to h and by Assumption 3, we obtain $U_j(\zeta) = f(C,s(\zeta)) < f(C,n) = U_j(\xi^C)$ for all $j \in C(\zeta)$. If $s(\zeta) = 0$ or 1, $U_j(\zeta) = f(D,0) = f(C,1) < f(C,n)$ for all $j \in N$. That is, no other outcome Pareto-dominates ξ^C.

Next, take an arbitrary outcome ξ such that $f(D,s(\xi)) \geqq f(C,n)$; by Assumption 2, this inequality can be made strict. Suppose, in negation, that there exists another outcome ζ that Pareto-dominates ξ. If there exists a country $j \in C(\zeta) \cap [N\backslash C(\xi)]$, we must have $U_j(\xi) = f(D,s(\xi)) \geqq f(C,n) > f(C,s(\zeta)) = U_j(\zeta)$. This contradicts the fact that ζ Pareto-dominates ξ. Therefore, $C(\zeta) \cap [N\backslash C(\xi)] = \emptyset$. Put differently, $C(\zeta) \subset C(\xi)$. In turn, this implies $s(\zeta) < s(\xi)$.

If $s(\zeta) \geqq 2$, then by the result obtained in the last paragraph and by Lemma 1, $U_j(\xi) = f(C,s(\xi)) > f(C,s(\zeta)) = U_j(\zeta)$ for all $j \in C(\zeta)$. This contradicts the Pareto-superiority of ζ over ξ. Therefore, we must have $s(\zeta) = 0$ or 1. By Assumption 3, we have $U_j(\xi) = f(D,s(\xi)) > f(C,n) > f(D,0) = f(C,1) = U_j(\zeta)$ for all $j \in N\backslash C(\xi)$. This again is a contradiction. Hence, there is no ζ that Pareto-dominates ξ.

Necessity

Take an arbitrary outcome ξ such that $s(\xi) < n$ *and* $f(D,s(\xi)) < f(C,n)$. We show that ξ^C Pareto-dominates ξ. For any $j \in C(\xi)$, we have $U_j(\xi) = f(C,s(\xi)) < f(C,n) = U_j(\xi^C)$ by Lemma 1. On the other hand, for any $j \in N\backslash C(\xi)$, we have $U_j(\xi) = f(D,s(\xi)) < f(C,n) = U_j(\xi^C)$ by the definition of ξ. Hence, ξ cannot be Pareto-efficient. □

Proof of Theorem 1

Stability

Since $V(n)$ is a singleton, the internal stability is obvious. Let us turn to the external stability. Take an arbitrary $\xi \in \Gamma \backslash V(n)$. Consider $N \backslash C(\xi) = \{j_1, j_2, \ldots, j_R\}$ and a corresponding sequence of outcomes such that $\xi = \xi^0 \xrightarrow{j_1} \xi^1 \xrightarrow{j_2} \ldots \xrightarrow{j_R} \xi^R = \xi^C$. Note that each country j_r in the sequence switches its strategy from D to C and, therefore, $U_{j_r}(\xi^{r-1}) = f(D, s(\xi^{r-1}))$ for all $r = 1, \ldots, R$. In the low-cost and intermediate-cost cases, $f(D, \bar{n}) < f(C, n)$ by definition. Then, by Lemma 1, we have $f(D, h) < f(C, n)$ for all $h \neq n$. Because $s(\xi) \neq n$, we have $U_{j_r}(\xi^{r-1}) = f(D, s(\xi^{r-1})) < f(C, n) = U_{j_r}(\xi^C)$ for all $r = 1, \ldots, R$. That is, ξ^C indirectly dominates any other $\xi \in \Gamma$. Hence, $V(n)$ is a farsighted stable set for $(\Gamma, \ll)$.

Uniqueness

Suppose, in negation, that there is a farsighted stable set $K \neq V(n)$. Of course, we must have $K \backslash V(n) \neq \emptyset$. Further, because ξ^C indirectly dominates any other outcome as shown in the above paragraph, ξ^C cannot be included in K; otherwise, the internal stability of K will be violated. Then, by the external stability, there must be an outcome $\xi \in K$ that indirectly dominates ξ^C. However, for any $j \in N$, we have $U_j(\xi) = [f(C, s(\xi)) \text{ or } f(D, s(\zeta))] < f(C, n) = U_j(\xi^C)$. ξ cannot indirectly dominate ξ^C; this would be a contradiction. □

Proof of Theorem 2(i)

To prove Theorem 2(i), we need an additional lemma:

Lemma 5. *No outcome in* $V(0) \cup V(1)$ *can be indirectly dominated by other outcomes.*

Proof. Take an arbitrary $\xi \in V(0) \cup V(1)$ and suppose, in negation, that there exists another $\zeta \in \Gamma$ that indirectly dominates ξ. Let $\xi = \xi^0 \xrightarrow{j_1} \xi^1 \xrightarrow{j_2} \ldots \xrightarrow{j_R} \xi^R = \zeta$ be the sequence that realizes $\xi \ll \zeta$. We distinguish between two cases (a) $s(\zeta) \leqq \bar{n}$ and (b) $s(\zeta) > \bar{n}$.

Case (a). Suppose that there exists a step (say, the kth step) $\xi^{k-1} \xrightarrow{j_k} \xi^k$ in the sequence such that $s(\xi^{k-1}) = s(\zeta)$ and $s(\xi^k) = s(\zeta) + 1$. Note that country j_k switches its strategy from D to C. If $j_k \in C(\zeta)$, we have $U_{j_k}(\xi^{k-1}) = f(D, s(\xi^{k-1})) = f(D, s(\zeta)) > f(C, s(\zeta)) = U_{j_k}(\zeta)$ by Lemma 1; on the other hand, if $j_k \in N \backslash C(\zeta)$, then $U_{j_k}(\xi^{k-1}) = f(D, s(\xi^{k-1})) = f(D, s(\zeta)) = U_{j_k}(\zeta)$. In sum, we have $U_{j_k}(\xi^{k-1}) \geqq U_{j_k}(\zeta)$, contradicting $\xi \ll \zeta$. Then, there is no such step. It follows that the last country in the sequence (i.e., country j_R) must be the one who switches its strategy from D to C. Therefore, by the definition of the high-cost case, we have $U_{j_R}(\xi^{R-1}) = f(D, s(\zeta) - 1) > f(C, s(\zeta)) = U_{j_R}(\zeta)$. This again is a contradiction.

Case (b). Then, there must exist at least one step $\xi^{k-1} \xrightarrow{j_k} \xi^k$ in the sequence such that $s(\xi^{k-1}) = \bar{n}$ and $s(\xi^k) = \bar{n} + 1$; i.e., country j_k switches its strategy from D to C. By Lemma 1 and by the definition of the high-cost case, we have $f(D,\bar{n}) > f(C,n) \geqq f(C,h)$ for all h. Therefore, if $j_k \in C(\zeta)$, then $U_{j_k}(\xi^{k-1}) = f(D, s(\xi^{k-1})) = f(D,\bar{n}) > f(C, s(\zeta)) = U_{j_k}(\zeta)$; on the other hand, if $j_k \in N \backslash C(\zeta)$, then $U_{j_k}(\xi^{k-1}) = f(D, s(\xi^{k-1})) = f(D,\bar{n}) > f(D, s(\zeta)) = U_{j_k}(\zeta)$. This contradicts $\xi \ll \zeta$. Hence, ξ cannot be indirectly dominated. □

Now, let us prove the theorem.

Internal Stability

Take an arbitrary $\xi \in K^*$. Then, we have $s(\xi) = h_{t'}$ for some integer t'. Contrary to the internal stability, suppose there is another outcome $\zeta \in K^*$ that indirectly dominates ξ; again, we must have $s(\zeta) = h_{t''}$ for some t''. Let $\xi = \xi^0 \xrightarrow{j_1} \xi^1 \xrightarrow{j_2} \dots \xrightarrow{j_R} \xi^R = \zeta$ be the sequence that realizes $\xi \ll \zeta$. As shown in Lemma 5, no outcome in $V(0) \cup V(1)$ can be dominated. Therefore, $t' > 1$ or, equivalently, $s(\xi) > h_1 = 1$. We distinguish between two cases (a) $t' \leqq t''$ and (b) $t' > t''$.

Case (a). Suppose that there exists a step (say, the kth step) $\xi^{k-1} \xrightarrow{j_k} \xi^k$ in the sequence such that $s(\xi^{k-1}) = h_{t''}$ and $s(\xi^k) = h_{t''} + 1$. For country j_k, we have $U_{j_k}(\xi^{k-1}) = f(D, h_{t''}) = U_{j_k}(\zeta)$ if $j_k \in N \backslash C(\zeta)$ or $U_{j_k}(\xi^{k-1}) = f(D, h_{t''}) > f(C, h_{t''}) = U_{j_k}(\zeta)$ if $j_k \in C(\zeta)$, implying that $U_{j_k}(\xi) \geqq U_{j_k}(\zeta)$. This contradicts $\xi \ll \zeta$. Then, such a step in the sequence does not exist. It follows that the last country in the sequence (i.e., country j_R) must be the last one of those who switch their actions from D to C. By the definition of the high-cost case, we have $U_{j_R}(\xi^{R-1}) - f(D, s(\xi^{R-1})) > f(C, s(\xi^{R-1}) + 1) = f(C, s(\xi^R)) = f(C, s(\zeta)) = U_{j_R}(\zeta)$. Again, this contradicts $\xi \ll \zeta$. Case (a) is not possible.

Case (b). By the definition of h_t, we have

$$
\begin{aligned}
&f(D,h_{t'}) > f(C,h_{t'}) > f(D,h_{t'-1}) > f(C,h_{t'-1}) > \cdots \\
&\quad \cdots > f(D,h_{t''+1}) > f(C,h_{t''+1}) > f(D,h_{t''}) > f(C,h_{t''}).
\end{aligned}
\tag{51}
$$

Since, for any $j \in N$, $U_j(\xi)$ is equal to either $f(D,h_{t'})$ or $f(C,h_{t'})$ and $U_j(\zeta)$ is equal to either $f(D,h_{t''})$ or $f(C,h_{t''})$, then $U_j(\xi) > U_j(\zeta)$. This contradicts $\xi \ll \zeta$. Case (b) is not possible either. Hence, $\xi \in K^*$ cannot be dominated by any other outcome in K^*. The internal stability of K^* is obtained.

External Stability

Take an arbitrary $\xi \in \Gamma\backslash K^*$; we have $s(\xi) \neq h_t$ for all $t = 0, 1, \ldots, T$. Let t' be the maximum integer that satisfies $h_{t'} < s(\xi)$. We show that ξ is dominated by an outcome in $V(h_{t'})$.

Let $\{j_1, j_2, \ldots, j_R\}$ be a subset of $C(\xi)$ with $R \equiv s(\xi) - h_{t'}$ countries and consider a sequence $\xi = \xi^0 \xrightarrow{j_1} \xi^1 \xrightarrow{j_2} \ldots \xrightarrow{j_R} \xi^R$ in which each country in the sequence switches its strategy from C to D. Clearly, $\xi^R \in V(h_{t'}) \subset K^*$. By the definition of h_t and by Lemma 1, we have $U_{j_r}(\xi^{r-1}) = f(C, s(\xi^{r-1})) < f(D, s(\xi^R)) = U_{j_r}(\xi^R)$ for all $r = 1, 2, \ldots, R$. Hence, ξ^R indirectly dominates ξ. The external stability of K^* is obtained.

Uniqueness

Let K be a farsighted stable set for $(\Gamma, \ll)$. Since, by Lemma 5, no outcome in $V(h_0) \cup V(h_1)$ (i.e., $V(0) \cup V(1)$) can be indirectly dominated by other outcomes, we must have $[V(h_0) \cup V(h_1)] \subset K$. Similar to the proof of the external stability, we can show that any $\xi \in \Gamma$ with $h_1 < s(\xi) < h_2$ is indirectly dominated by an outcome in $V(h_1)$. Therefore, such an outcome cannot be included in K.

Next, consider an arbitrary outcome $\xi \in V(h_2)$. If $\xi \notin K$, then by the external stability of K, there must exist an outcome $\zeta \in K$ that indirectly dominates ξ. We distinguish between two cases (a) $s(\zeta) < h_2$ and (b) $s(\zeta) \geqq h_2$.

In case (a), we have $\zeta \in V(h_0) \cup V(h_1)$. Without loss of generality, we can assume $\zeta \in V(h_1)$. By the definition of h_t, we have $f(D, h_2) > f(C, h_2) > f(D, h_1) > f(C, h_1)$. Since, for any $j \in N$, $U_j(\xi)$ is equal to either $f(D, h_2)$ or $f(C, h_2)$ and $U_j(\zeta)$ is equal to either $f(D, h_1)$ or $f(C, h_1)$, then $U_j(\xi) > U_j(\zeta)$. ζ cannot indirectly dominate ξ. Hence, case (a) is not possible.

In case (b), let us consider a sequence $\xi = \xi^0 \xrightarrow{j_1} \xi^1 \xrightarrow{j_2} \ldots \xrightarrow{j_R} \xi^R = \zeta$ that realizes $\xi \ll \zeta$. Similar to case (a) in the proof of the internal stability, the last country in the sequence (i.e., country j_R) must be the last one of those who switch their strategy from D to C. However, by the definition of the high-cost case, we have $U_{j_R}(\xi^{R-1}) = f(D, s(\zeta) - 1) > f(C, s(\zeta)) = U_{j_R}(\zeta)$. Again, ζ cannot indirectly dominate ξ. Case (b) is not possible either. Hence, $\xi \in K$. Consequently, we obtain $V(h_2) \subset K$.

By repeatedly applying the same argument, we can show that any outcome ξ with $h_t < s(\xi) < h_{t+1}$ $(t = 1, 2, \ldots, T-1)$ or $h_T < s(\xi)$ is excluded from K and that $V(h_t) \subset K$ for all $t = 1, 2, \ldots, T$. Hence, $K = K^*$. □

Proof of Theorem 2(ii)

Remember that $f(D, h_T) < f(C, n)$ and $h_T < \bar{n}$ in this case. Most of the proof of Theorem 2(ii) can be demonstrated in the same manner as that of Theorem 2(i).

It remains to show that (a) $\xi^C \in V(n)$ cannot be indirectly dominated by some outcome in K^* nor can it dominate some outcome in K^* and (b) any outcome ξ with $h_T < s(\xi) < n$ is indirectly dominated by some outcome in K^*.

First, let us consider case (a). Take any $\zeta \in K^*$ other than ξ^C. We have $s(\zeta) = h_{t'}$ for some t'. By the definition of h_t, the following inequalities hold:

$$\begin{aligned} f(C,n) > f(D,h_T) > f(C,h_T) > \cdots \\ \cdots > f(D,h_{t'}) > f(C,h_{t'}) > \cdots \\ \cdots > f(C,h_2) > f(D,h_1). \end{aligned} \tag{52}$$

For any $j \in N$, either $U_j(\zeta) = f(D,h_{t'})$ or $U_j(\zeta) = f(C,h_{t'})$ holds. Then, $U_j(\xi) = f(C,n) > U_j(\zeta)$ for all $j \in N$. Hence, ξ^C cannot be indirectly dominated by ζ.

Conversely, we show that any outcome $\zeta \in K^*$ cannot be indirectly dominated by ξ^C. We assume that $s(\zeta) = h_{t'}$. Suppose, in negation, that $\zeta \ll \xi^C$ and let $\zeta = \xi^0 \xrightarrow{j_1} \xi^1 \xrightarrow{j_2} \ldots \xrightarrow{j_R} \xi^R = \xi^C$ be the sequence that realizes $\zeta \ll \xi^C$. Because $h_{t'} \leqq h_T < \bar{n} < n$, there exists a step (say, the kth step) $\xi^{k-1} \xrightarrow{j_k} \xi^k$ in the sequence such that $s(\xi^{k-1}) = \bar{n}$ and $s(\xi^k) = \bar{n}+1$. Country j_k switches its strategy from D to C. By the definition of the high-cost case, $U_{j_k}(\xi^{k-1}) = f(D,\bar{n}) > f(C,n) = U_{j_k}(\xi^C)$. This contradicts $\zeta \ll \xi^C$. Therefore, ζ cannot be indirectly dominated by ξ^C. Hence, case (a) holds.

In turn, let us consider case (b). Let $\hat{n}$ be the minimum integer that satisfies $f(D,h_T) < f(C,\hat{n})$. Because $f(C,h)$ is increasing in h and because $f(D,h_T) > f(C,h_T)$ and $f(C,n) > f(D,h_T)$, the existence of $\hat{n}$ is guaranteed and we have $h_T < \hat{n}$. Note that, by the definition of h_T, $f(D,\hat{n}) > f(C,\hat{n})$ cannot hold. Then, by Assumption 2 and Lemma 1, we have $f(D,\hat{n}) < f(C,\hat{n})$; this implies $\bar{n} \leqq \hat{n}$.

Take an arbitrary ξ with $h_T < s(\xi) < \hat{n}$. Similar to the proof of the external stability of K^* in Theorem 2(i), we can show that there exists an outcome in $V(h_T)$ that indirectly dominates ξ.

Take an arbitrary ξ with $s(\xi) \geqq \hat{n}$. If $\hat{n} = n$, then $\xi = \xi^C$ and the proof ends. Suppose $\hat{n} < n$. We now show that ξ is indirectly dominated by ξ^C. Let $\{j_1, j_2, \ldots, j_R\}$ be a subset of $N \backslash C(\xi)$ with $R \equiv n - s(\xi)$ countries, and consider a sequence $\xi = \xi^0 \xrightarrow{j_1} \xi^1 \xrightarrow{j_2} \ldots \xrightarrow{j_R} \xi^R = \xi^C$ in which each country switches its strategy from D to C. By Lemma 1, $f(D,h)$ is decreasing in h for $h \geqq \hat{n}$ since $\bar{n} < \hat{n}$. Then, the following relation holds:

$$\begin{aligned} f(D,s(\xi^0)) = U_{j_1}(\xi^0) > f(D,s(\xi^1)) = U_{j_2}(\xi^1) > \cdots \\ \cdots > f(D,s(\xi^{R-1})) = U_{j_R}(\xi^{R-1}). \end{aligned} \tag{53}$$

Note that $s(\xi^{r-1}) + 1 = s(\xi^r)$ for all $r = 1,2,\ldots,R$. Further, because $f(D,\hat{n}) < f(C,\hat{n})$ and because $f(C,h)$ is increasing in h, we have

$$\begin{aligned} f(D,s(\xi^0)) < f(D,s(\xi^0)-1) < f(D,s(\xi^0)-2) < \cdots \\ \cdots < f(D,\hat{n}) < f(C,\hat{n}) < f(C,\hat{n}+1) < \cdots < f(C,n). \end{aligned} \tag{54}$$

Combining the above inequalities, we obtain $U_{j_r}(\xi^{r-1}) < f(C,n) = U_{j_r}(\xi^C)$ for all $r = 1, 2, \ldots, R$. Hence, case (b) holds. □

Proof of Theorem 2(iii)

By replacing the role of $\hat{n}$ in the proof of case (ii) with that of h_T in this case, we can apply the same proof as that for Theorem 2(ii) to Theorem 2(iii). □

Proof of Proposition 1

By Lemma 4, ξ^C is Pareto-efficient. In the low-cost and intermediate-cost cases, we have $\Gamma^{\mathrm{P}} = \{\xi^C\} = V(n)$. In (ii) and (iii) of the high-cost case, we have $V(n) \subset K^*$. In (i) of the high-cost case, we have $\xi \in \Gamma^{\mathrm{P}}$ for all $\xi \in V(h_T) \subset K^*$ since $f(D, h_T) > f(C,n)$ by the definition of the high-cost case. Then, in all cases, $\Gamma^{\mathrm{P}} \cap K^* \neq \emptyset$. □

Acknowledgments This chapter is an outgrowth of researches conducted by a working group, led by (the late) Prof. Koji Shimomura, of the 21st Century COE Program in Kobe University ("Research and Education Center of New Japanese Economic Paradigm"). I am very grateful to Prof. Toru Kikuchi for his insightful comments on an earlier version of this chapter.

References

D'Aspremont C, Jacquemin A, Gabszewicz JJ, Weymark JA (1983) On the stability of collusive price leadership. Can J Econ 16(1):17–25

Diamantoudi E (2005) Stable cartels revisited. Econ Theory 26:907–921

Greenberg J (1990) The theory of social situations – an alternative game-theoretic approach. Cambridge University Press, Cambridge

Harris RG (1998) Internet as the GTP. In: Helpman E (ed) General purpose technologies and economic growth. MIT, Cambridge

Kamijo Y, Muto S (2007) Farsighted stability of collusive price leadership. Discussion Papers 07–09, Tokyo Institute of Technology. http://www.soc.titech.ac.jp/%7Elibrary/discuss/index_e.html

Kamijo Y, Nakanishi N (2007) Stability of price leadership cartel with endogenous pricing. Discussion Paper 706, Kobe University. http://www.econ.kobe-u.ac.jp/katudou/publication/paper/discussion/0706.pdf

Kikuchi T (2002) Country-specific communications networks and international trade in a model of monopolistic competition. Jpn Econ Rev 53:167–176

Kikuchi T (2003) Interconnectivity of communications networks and international trade. Can J Econ 36:155–167

MacKie-Mason JK, Varian H (1995) Pricing congestible network resources. IEEE J Sel Area Commun 13:1141–1149

Nakanishi N (2007) Purely noncooperative farsighted stable set in an n-player prisoners' dilemma. Discussion Paper 707, Kobe University. http://www.econ.kobe-u.ac.jp/katudou/publication/paper/discussion/0707.pdf

Nakanishi N, Kikuchi T (2005) Expansion of network integrations: two scenarios, trade patterns, and welfare. J Econ Integr 20(4):631–643

von Neumann J, Morgenstern O (1953) Theory of games and economic behavior, 3rd edn. Princeton University Press, Princeton

Suzuki A, Muto S (2005) Farsighted stability in an n-person prisoner's dilemma. Int J Game Theory 33:431–445

Endogenous Leadership with and without Policy Intervention: International Trade When Producer and Seller Differ

Zhifang Peng and Sajal Lahiri(✉)

Abstract Using a vertically linked model of international trade where producers and sellers are different entities and belong to two different countries, we examine the issue of endogenous leadership. In the absence of policy intervention, there are two cases depending on whether the producer or the seller is the leader. In the presence of policy intervention, the nationality of the leader and that of the follower also becomes important. We find necessary and sufficient conditions for endogenous leadership to arise, and find that in the presence of policy intervention and lump-sum transfers, leadership by the domestic firm – whether it is a producer or a seller – will emerge as the equilibrium.

1 Introduction

International interfirm collaboration has been growing hand in hand with the overall process of integration of the international economy. Such collaborations have been attracting the attention of scholars from many fields including economics (see, e.g., Backman 1965; Berg and Friedman 1977; Duncan 1982; McConnell and Nantell 1985). However, bulk of this literature in the field of international business organization concerns themselves primarily with the situation where both domestic and foreign firms have complementary specific inputs and join together to produces a product, sell the product, and share in the resulting profits and losses. However, sellers are commonly distinct from producers in real life. For example, in China, Shanghai General Motors Co., Ltd produce automobiles, sells them to General Motors Warehousing and Trading (Shanghai), a wholly owned GM enterprise which in turn sells automobiles at home and at abroad.

S. Lahiri
Department of Economics, Southern Illinois University Carbondale, MC 4515, 1000 Faner Drive, Carbondale, IL 62901, USA, e-mail: lahiri@siu.edu

T. Kamihigashi and L. Zhao (eds.) *International Trade and Economic Dynamics – Essays in Memory of Koji Shimomura.*

In spite of its prevalence in real life, the study of vertical interfirm collaboration is relatively uncommon in the literature of international trade. Nearly 80 years ago, Bowley (1928) studied the implications of vertical relationships and presented the first formal statement of the price leadership problem. Subsequently, others considered a joint-profit-maximization model to solve the problem of indeterminacy of the quantity of intermediate inputs traded (see, e.g., Fellner 1947; Machlup and Taber 1960; Truett and Truett 1993). Henderson and Quandt (1980) analyzed four possibilities that arise in the determination of equilibrium in a bilateral monopoly model, viz., (1) seller is the leader, the producer takes the price as given, (2) producer is the leader, the seller takes the price as given, (3) collusion by the seller and the buyer, and (4) noncooperation by the seller and buyer in which both of them may go out of business. Other studies that provide game-theoretic solution to the problem include Devadoss and Cooper (2000) where the two entities have equal bargaining power, and Dasgupta and Devadoss (2002) where the two parties have unequal bargaining power. Lahiri and Ono (1999) put the bilateral monopoly structure in the international context and examined the question of optimal tariffs under different market structures.

In the studies discussed above, the issue of leadership, whenever applied, is exogenous in nature; i.e., who is the leader and who is the follower is not determined endogenously inside the model. There is, however, a separate literature in which the issue of leadership is determined endogenously under different contexts. Ono (1978, 1982), Hamilton and Slutsky (1990), and Matsumura (1995, 2003) examine the issue in a domestic context under different market structures. Das and Lahiri (2006) develop a model of terrorist activity and examine the issue of endogenous leadership between a terrorist organization and a government trying to deal with potential terrorist attacks. Jafarey and Lahiri (2008) consider interactions between a borrowing country and a monopolist lender, and analyze if one and the two parties can emerge as the leader.

In the present chapter, we integrate the two different literatures discussed above. To be more specific, we shall consider a model in which there are a producer and a seller who are engaged in a vertical relationship. We shall examine if the leadership by one of the parties can be agreed upon by both parties, considering their own self-interests. We provide an international dimension to the problem by assuming that the two parties are nationals of two different countries, called the home and the foreign country. The good is consumed in the home country. We also consider two situations depending on whether the domestic government is passive or it is active in the sense of optimally setting tax/subsidy instruments. In the latter situation, the ownership of the two different parties becomes particularly relevant. In this situation, it also matters as to which of the two is a producer and which one is the seller.

Section 2 considers the case where the domestic government is passive and does not intervene at all. In Sect. 3, we consider the optimal tax/subsidy policy of the domestic government. This section is divided into a number of subsections depending on who is the producer and who is the seller, and in each case who is the leader and who is the follower. Some concluding remarks are made in Sect. 4.

2 The Model with No Government Intervention

We consider a single homogeneous-commodity partial-equilibrium model with two entities: a producer and a seller. The government is passive in this section, so that the nationalities of the two parties are not relevant for our analysis here. We model a simple vertical relationship between these two entities.

The inverse demand function for the commodity is given by:

$$p = a - bx, \tag{1}$$

where p and x are, respectively, the price and demand/output of the commodity and a and b are positive parameters. Since we do not consider government behavior, it does not matter, for the purpose of this section, where this good is consumed.

The cost function for the producer and that for the seller are, respectively,

$$c^{\mathrm{p}} = \beta^{\mathrm{p}}x + \theta^{\mathrm{p}}x^2, \tag{2}$$
$$c^{\mathrm{s}} = \beta^{\mathrm{s}}x + \theta^{\mathrm{s}}x^2, \tag{3}$$

where β and θ are positive parameters. Whereas, c^{p} represents purely production costs and c^{s} includes costs associated with retailing, marketing, etc.

The profit of the producer and that of the seller, respectively, are

$$\pi^{\mathrm{p}} = \rho x - \beta^{\mathrm{p}}x - \theta^{\mathrm{p}}x^2, \tag{4}$$
$$\pi^{\mathrm{s}} = (a - bx - \rho - \beta^{\mathrm{s}} - \theta^{\mathrm{s}}x)x, \tag{5}$$

where ρ is the inside price of the commodity, i.e., the price which the producer receives from the seller.

Before proceeding any further, i.e., before specifying profit-maximizing conditions, we need to consider two scenarios depending on who the leader is, and these are taken up in Sects. 2.1 and 2.2.

2.1 The Case of Leadership by the Seller

Using the model developed so far, we now derive the profit-maximization conditions when the seller is the leader. We consider the following two-stage game, working with backward induction. When the seller acts as a leader, the producer, in the second stage, takes the inside price ρ as given, and maximizes its profit given by (4) yielding the first-order condition:

$$\frac{\partial \pi^{\mathrm{p}}}{\partial x} = \rho - \beta^{\mathrm{p}} - 2\theta^{\mathrm{p}}x = 0,$$

which gives the reaction function of the producer:

$$\rho(x) = \beta^{\mathrm{p}} + 2\theta^{\mathrm{p}}x. \tag{6}$$

Since the seller is the leader and moves first, it maximizes its profits π^{s} given in (5), taking into account the producer's reaction function given by (6). The first-order profit-maximizing condition is given by

$$\begin{aligned}\frac{\partial \pi^{\mathrm{s}}}{\partial x} &= \frac{\partial[((a-\beta^{\mathrm{s}})-(b+\theta^{\mathrm{s}})x-\beta^{\mathrm{p}}-2\theta^{\mathrm{p}}x)x]}{\partial x} \\ &= (a-\beta^{\mathrm{s}})-(b+\theta^{\mathrm{s}})x-\beta^{\mathrm{p}}-2\theta^{\mathrm{p}}x-(b+\theta^{\mathrm{s}})x-2\theta^{\mathrm{p}}x=0. \end{aligned} \tag{7}$$

From (6) and (7), output x and inside price ρ are calculated, respectively, as

$$x_{\mathrm{s}1} = \frac{a-\beta^{\mathrm{s}}-\beta^{\mathrm{p}}}{2(b+\theta^{\mathrm{s}}+2\theta^{\mathrm{p}})}, \tag{8}$$

$$\rho_{\mathrm{s}1} = \frac{(a-\beta^{\mathrm{s}}+\beta^{\mathrm{p}})\theta^{\mathrm{p}}+(b+\theta^{\mathrm{s}})\beta^{\mathrm{p}}}{b+\theta^{\mathrm{s}}+2\theta^{\mathrm{p}}}, \tag{9}$$

and then profits of the producer and that of the seller are calculated, respectively, as

$$\pi_2^{\mathrm{p}} = \frac{(a-\beta^{\mathrm{s}}-\beta^{\mathrm{p}})^2\theta^{\mathrm{p}}}{4(b+\theta^{\mathrm{s}}+2\theta^{\mathrm{p}})^2}, \tag{10}$$

$$\pi_1^{\mathrm{s}} = \frac{(a-\beta^{\mathrm{s}}-\beta^{\mathrm{p}})^2}{4(b+\theta^{\mathrm{s}}+2\theta^{\mathrm{p}})}. \tag{11}$$

This completes the analysis when the seller is the leader, and we now turn to the case where the producer is the leader.

2.2 The Case of Leadership by the Producer

When the producer is the leader, the seller takes the inside price ρ as given, and hence its first-order profit-maximizing condition is

$$\frac{\partial \pi^{\mathrm{s}}}{\partial x} = a-bx-\rho-\beta^{\mathrm{s}}-\theta^{\mathrm{s}}x-bx-\theta^{\mathrm{s}}x=0,$$

which gives the reaction function of the seller as

$$\rho(x) = a-\beta^{\mathrm{s}}-2(b+\theta^{\mathrm{s}})x. \tag{12}$$

Since the producer is the leader, it maximizes π^{p} given by (4), taking into account the seller's reaction function given by (12). The profit-maximizing condition is given by

$$\begin{aligned}\frac{\partial \pi^{\mathrm{p}}}{\partial x} &= \frac{\partial[((a-\beta^{\mathrm{s}})-2(b+\theta^{\mathrm{s}})x-\beta^{\mathrm{p}}-\theta^{\mathrm{p}}x)x]}{\partial x} \\ &= (a-\beta^{\mathrm{s}})-2(b+\theta^{\mathrm{s}})x-\beta^{\mathrm{p}}-\theta^{\mathrm{p}}x-2(b+\theta^{\mathrm{s}})x-\theta^{\mathrm{p}}x=0. \end{aligned} \tag{13}$$

The output x and the inside price ρ are calculated, respectively, as

$$x_{s2} = \frac{a-\beta^s-\beta^p}{2(2b+2\theta^s+\theta^p)}, \tag{14}$$

$$\rho_{s2} = \frac{(a-\beta^s+\beta^p)(b+\theta^s)+a\theta^p}{2b+2\theta^s+\theta^p}. \tag{15}$$

The profit of the producer and that of the seller are

$$\pi_1^p = \frac{(a-\beta^s-\beta^p)^2}{4(2b+2\theta^s+\theta^p)}, \tag{16}$$

$$\pi_2^s = \frac{(a-\beta^s-\beta^p)^2(b+\theta^s)}{4(2b+2\theta^s+\theta^p)^2}. \tag{17}$$

2.3 Leadership Preferences

Having derived the levels of profits for the two firms under different leadership scenario, we can now examine if one of the scenarios will be accepted by both parties. Comparing the profit of each firm under the two scenarios, we find

$$\pi_1^p - \pi_2^p = \frac{(a-\beta^s-\beta^p)^2((b+\theta^s)^2-2(b+\theta^s)\theta^p+3(\theta^p)^2)}{4} > 0,$$

$$\pi_1^s - \pi_2^s = \frac{(a-\beta^s-\beta^p)^2(3(b+\theta^s)^2+2(b+\theta^s)\theta^p+(\theta^p)^2)}{4(b+\theta^s+2\theta^p)(2b+2\theta^s+\theta^p)^2} > 0.$$

That is, each firm prefers its own leadership. In other words, in the absence of any side payments, there will be no unanimity about who should be the leader. Formally,

Proposition 1. *In the absence of side payment, both entities will prefer their own leadership and unanimity cannot be reached.*

Thus, in the absence of side payments, the relationship between the two firms may break down. However, if side payments are possible, then we only need to look at the differences in the aggregate profits of the two firms. If the aggregate profit is higher under one scenario, that scenario can be acceptable to both parties and should be the equilibrium outcome.

The levels of, and the difference between, aggregate profits when the seller is the leader and that when the producer is the leader are calculated as

$$\pi_{s1} = \pi_2^p + \pi_1^s = \frac{(a-\beta^s-\beta^p)^2(b+\theta^s+3\theta^p)}{4(b+\theta^s+2\theta^p)^2},$$

$$\pi_{p1} = \pi_1^p + \pi_2^s = \frac{(a-\beta^s-\beta^p)^2(3b+3\theta^s+\theta^p)}{4(2b+2\theta^s+\theta^p)^2},$$

$$\pi_{s1} - \pi_{p1} = \frac{[(a-\beta^s-\beta^p)^2(b+\theta^s)^2+(b+\theta^s)\theta^p+(\theta^p)^2+3(b+\theta^s)\theta^p](b+\theta^s-\theta^p)}{4(b+\theta^s+2\theta^p)^2(2b+2\theta^s+\theta^p)^2}.$$

From the last of the above three equations, it follows that

$$\pi_{s1} - \pi_{p1} > 0 \iff b+\theta^s > \theta^p.$$

Proposition 2. *In the presence of side payments, both firms will prefer seller's (producer's) leadership if and only if* $b+\theta^s > \theta^p$ $(b+\theta^s < \theta^p)$.

The intuition for the above result is as follows. Note that when $\theta^p \simeq 0$, the leadership by the seller is preferred by both. In this case, the marginal cost of production is effectively constant and the equilibrium inside price is nearly equal to the lowest possible value for the marginal cost of production. That is, production is almost at the most efficient level and the total unit cost for the seller is almost at the highest possible level. Not surprisingly therefore, under the leadership of the seller, efficiency level of operation and thus total surplus is very high. As the marginal cost of production increases with output level, we move more and more away from the efficiency of the leadership by the seller as θ^p gets bigger and bigger, and after some stage total surplus becomes higher when the producer is the leader.

3 The Model with Government Intervention

In Sect. 2, we did not consider government policy intervention, and therefore the nationalities of the two firms were of no concern to us. In this section, we add the government of the home country as the third player who commits on a specific sales tax t at the first stage of the game, the subsequent two stages of the game are the same as before. When the domestic firm is the seller and the foreign firm is the producer (Sect. 3.1), the tax t is the consumption tax, and when the foreign firm is the seller and the domestic is the producer (Sect. 3.2), the tax t is an exports tax.

The profit of the producer and that of the seller, respectively, are

$$\pi^p = \rho x - \beta^p x - \theta^p x^2,$$
$$\pi^s = (a - bx - \rho - \beta^s - \theta^s x - t)x.$$

In Sects. 3.1 and 3.2, we shall consider two scenarios depending on what the domestic firm does (a) domestic firm is the seller and (b) domestic firm is the producer. Each section will then be subdivided according to the types of producer–seller relationships (1) leadership by seller and (2) leadership by producer.

3.1 Domestic Firm Is the Seller

First, we consider the case when the domestic firm is the seller and also the leader.

3.1.1 Domestic Seller Is the Leader

In stage 3 of the game, foreign producer who is the follower takes the inside price ρ as given. Its profit-maximizing condition, as before, is

$$\frac{\partial \pi^{\mathrm{f}}}{\partial x} = \rho - \beta^{\mathrm{p}} - 2\theta^{\mathrm{p}}x = 0,$$

giving rise to its reaction function:

$$\rho(x) = \beta^{\mathrm{p}} + 2\theta^{\mathrm{p}}x. \tag{18}$$

In stage 2, the domestic seller who is the leader maximizes its profits, given by $\pi^{\mathrm{d}} = (a - bx - \beta^{\mathrm{p}} - 2\theta^{\mathrm{p}}x - \beta^{\mathrm{s}} - \theta^{\mathrm{s}}x - t)x$, taking into account the producer's reaction function (18). The first-order profit-maximizing condition is

$$\frac{\partial \pi^{\mathrm{d}}}{\partial x} = a - 2bx - \beta^{\mathrm{p}} - 4\theta^{\mathrm{p}}x - \beta^{\mathrm{s}} - 2\theta^{\mathrm{s}}x - t = 0. \tag{19}$$

From (19), the solution of output/sales x_{ds1} and then from (18) the inside price ρ_{ds1} are given by

$$x_{\mathrm{ds1}} = \frac{a - \beta^{\mathrm{s}} - \beta^{\mathrm{p}} - t}{2(b + \theta^{\mathrm{s}} + 2\theta^{\mathrm{p}})}, \tag{20}$$

$$\rho_{\mathrm{ds1}} = \frac{(a - \beta^{\mathrm{s}} + \beta^{\mathrm{p}} - t)\theta^{\mathrm{p}} + (b + \theta^{\mathrm{s}})\beta^{\mathrm{p}}}{b + \theta^{\mathrm{s}} + 2\theta^{\mathrm{p}}}.$$

For a given tax rate t, profits of the domestic firm and that of the foreign firm can be calculated as

$$\pi^{\mathrm{f}}_{\mathrm{p2}} = \frac{(a - \beta^{\mathrm{s}} - \beta^{\mathrm{p}} - t)^2\theta^{\mathrm{p}}}{4(b + \theta^{\mathrm{s}} + 2\theta^{\mathrm{p}})^2}, \tag{21}$$

$$\pi^{\mathrm{d}}_{\mathrm{s1}} = \frac{(a - \beta^{\mathrm{s}} - \beta^{\mathrm{p}} - t)^2}{4(b + \theta^{\mathrm{s}} + 2\theta^{\mathrm{p}})}. \tag{22}$$

In stage 1 of the game, the domestic government chooses the tax rate t to maximize the welfare of the home country W, which is the sum of consumers' surplus CS, domestic seller's profits π^{d}, and the government's tax revenue tx, i.e.,

$$W = \mathrm{CS} + \pi^{\mathrm{d}} + \mathrm{tx}, \tag{23}$$

where it is well known that $\mathrm{dCS} = -x\mathrm{d}p$.

Substituting π^{d} from (22) and x from (20) into (23) and then setting $\partial W/\partial t = 0$, we can solve the optimal tax rate t as

$$t = -\frac{(a-\beta^{\mathrm{s}}-\beta^{\mathrm{p}})b}{b+2\theta^{\mathrm{s}}+4\theta^{\mathrm{p}}} < 0. \tag{24}$$

Now, substituting (24) into (21) and (22), we get

$$\pi^{\mathrm{f}}_{\mathrm{p2}} = \frac{(a-\beta^{\mathrm{s}}-\beta^{\mathrm{p}})^2\theta^{\mathrm{p}}}{(b+2\theta^{\mathrm{s}}+4\theta^{\mathrm{p}})^2},$$

$$\pi^{\mathrm{d}}_{\mathrm{s1}} = \frac{(a-\beta^{\mathrm{s}}-\beta^{\mathrm{p}})^2(b+\theta^{\mathrm{s}}+2\theta^{\mathrm{p}})}{(b+2\theta^{\mathrm{s}}+4\theta^{\mathrm{p}})^2}.$$

3.1.2 Domestic Seller Is the Follower

When the foreign producer is the leader and the domestic seller is the follower, in stage 3, the domestic firm's profit-maximizing behavior gives rise to its reaction function as

$$\rho(x) = a-\beta^{\mathrm{s}}-2(b+\theta^{\mathrm{s}})x-t. \tag{25}$$

Since the producer who is the leader maximizes π^{f} $(= ((a-\beta^{\mathrm{s}})-2(b+\theta^{\mathrm{s}})x-\beta^{\mathrm{p}}-\theta^{\mathrm{p}}x-t)x)$, taking into account the seller's reaction function (25), its profit-maximization behavior gives rise to the solutions of output x and then the inside price ρ in this case as

$$x_{\mathrm{ds2}} = \frac{a-\beta^{\mathrm{s}}-\beta^{\mathrm{p}}-t}{2(2b+2\theta^{\mathrm{s}}+\theta^{\mathrm{p}})},$$

$$\rho_{\mathrm{ds2}} = \frac{(a-\beta^{\mathrm{s}}+\beta^{\mathrm{p}}-t)(b+\theta^{\mathrm{s}})+(a-t)\theta^{\mathrm{p}}}{2b+2\theta^{\mathrm{s}}+\theta^{\mathrm{p}}}.$$

The profits of the producer and that of the seller in this case are

$$\pi^{\mathrm{f}}_{\mathrm{p1}} = \frac{(a-\beta^{\mathrm{s}}-\beta^{\mathrm{p}}-t)^2}{4(2b+2\theta^{\mathrm{s}}+\theta^{\mathrm{p}})}, \tag{26}$$

$$\pi^{\mathrm{d}}_{\mathrm{s2}} = \frac{(a-\beta^{\mathrm{s}}-\beta^{\mathrm{p}}-t)^2(b+\theta^{\mathrm{s}})}{4(2b+2\theta^{\mathrm{s}}+\theta^{\mathrm{p}})^2}. \tag{27}$$

The first stage of the game is similar to the previous case here, and the optimal tax rate is given by

$$t = \frac{(a-\beta^{\mathrm{s}}-\beta^{\mathrm{p}})(b+2\theta^{\mathrm{s}}+2\theta^{\mathrm{p}})}{5b+6\theta^{\mathrm{s}}+4\theta^{\mathrm{p}}} > 0. \tag{28}$$

Substituting (28) into (26) and (27), profits of the two firms in this case are given by

$$\pi_{s2}^{d} = \frac{(a-\beta^{s}-\beta^{p})^2(b+\theta^{s})}{(5b+6\theta^{s}+4\theta^{p})^2}, \tag{29}$$

$$\pi_{p1}^{f} = \frac{(a-\beta^{s}-\beta^{p})^2(2b+2\theta^{s}+\theta^{p})}{(5b+6\theta^{s}+4\theta^{p})^2}. \tag{30}$$

Note that while the optimal tax rate is positive in the case when the domestic seller is the follower, it is negative when the domestic seller is the leader.[1] The reason for the change in the sign of the optimal tax is that the domestic firms' profits are higher when it is the leader, and therefore in the determination of the optimal tax rate, the interest of the domestic firm plays a bigger role when the domestic firm is the leader than when it is the follower. This results in a lower optimal tax (in fact a subsidy) when the domestic firm is a leader rather than a follower.

3.1.3 Leadership Preference

In this section, we check if there is a certain producer–seller relationship that both firms prefer. Comparing profits of each firm under the two scenarios, we get

$$\pi_{p1}^{f} - \pi_{p2}^{f} = \frac{(a-\beta^{s}-\beta^{p})^2\Delta^{f}}{(5b+6\theta^{s}+4\theta^{p})^2(b+2\theta^{s}+4\theta^{p})^2},$$

$$\pi_{s1}^{d} - \pi_{ds2}^{d} = \frac{(a-\beta^{s}-\beta^{p})^2\Delta^{d}}{(5b+6\theta^{s}+4\theta^{p})^2(b+2\theta^{s}+4\theta^{p})^2} > 0,$$

where

$$\Delta^{f} = (2b+2\theta^{s}+\theta^{p})(b+2\theta^{s}+4\theta^{p})^2 - \theta^{p}(5b+6\theta^{s}+4\theta^{p})^2,$$

$$\Delta^{d} = [(b+\theta^{s})((5b+6\theta^{s}+4\theta^{p})^2-(b+2\theta^{s}+4\theta^{p})^2)] + 2\theta^{p}(5b+6\theta^{s}+4\theta^{p})^2 > 0.$$

That is, the domestic firm would prefer to be the leader. Moreover, in this case, the foreign firm may also prefer the domestic seller's leadership to its own if $\theta^{s} < (4/5)\theta^{p}$ since $\Delta^{f} < 0$ under this condition. This result is stated formally in Proposition 3.

Proposition 3. *In the absence of side payments, leadership by the domestic seller is an equilibrium if* $\theta^{s} < (4/5)\theta^{p}$.

The intuition is as follows. Since the domestic seller receives a higher subsidy when it is the leader, the vertically related foreign firm also benefits from this higher

[1] It is to be noted that Lahiri and Ono (1999) also found that the sign of optimal tariffs can crucially depend on who is the leader.

subsidy. This competes with the natural tendency for the foreign firm to prefer its own leadership. The net effect goes in favor of the foreign firm preferring the domestic firm's leadership when the foreign firm's marginal cost function is sufficiently steep, i.e., θ^{p} is sufficiently high.

The levels of, and the differences between, aggregate profits when the domestic seller is the leader and that when the foreign producer is the leader are

$$\begin{aligned}
\pi_{\mathrm{ds1}} &= \pi^{\mathrm{d}}_{\mathrm{s1}} + \pi^{\mathrm{f}}_{\mathrm{p2}} = \frac{(a-\beta^{\mathrm{s}}-\beta^{\mathrm{p}})^2(b+\theta^{\mathrm{s}}+3\theta^{\mathrm{p}})}{(b+2\theta^{\mathrm{s}}+4\theta^{\mathrm{p}})^2},\\
\pi_{\mathrm{ds2}} &= \pi^{\mathrm{d}}_{\mathrm{s2}} + \pi^{\mathrm{f}}_{\mathrm{p1}} = \frac{(a-\beta^{\mathrm{s}}-\beta^{\mathrm{p}})^2(3b+3\theta^{\mathrm{s}}+\theta^{\mathrm{p}})}{(5b+6\theta^{\mathrm{s}}+4\theta^{\mathrm{p}})^2},\\
\pi_{\mathrm{ds1}} - \pi_{\mathrm{ds2}} &= \frac{(a-\beta^{\mathrm{s}}-\beta^{\mathrm{p}})^2\Delta}{(5b+6\theta^{\mathrm{s}}+4\theta^{\mathrm{p}})^2(b+2\theta^{\mathrm{s}}+4\theta^{\mathrm{p}})^2} > 0,
\end{aligned}$$

where

$$\Delta = (b+\theta^{\mathrm{s}}+3\theta^{\mathrm{p}})(5b+6\theta^{\mathrm{s}}+4\theta^{\mathrm{p}})^2 - (3b+3\theta^{\mathrm{s}}+\theta^{\mathrm{p}})(b+2\theta^{\mathrm{s}}+4\theta^{\mathrm{p}})^2 > 0.$$

That is, when side payments are allowed, the foreign firm will unambiguously prefer leadership by the domestic firm, which will be the equilibrium outcome. Formally,

Proposition 4. *In the presence of side payments, when government optimally employs sales tax and when the domestic firm is the seller, both firms will prefer the domestic firms' leadership.*

A higher subsidy when the domestic firm is the leader makes the scenario so much efficient in the sense of higher income that the aggregate profits become unambiguously higher in this case than in the case where the domestic firm is the follower.

3.2 Domestic Firm Is the Producer

In this section, we consider the case when domestic firm is the producer and the foreign firm is the seller. In this situation, it more reasonable to assume that the good is consumed outside the country and the sales tax t needs to be reinterpreted as an exports tax. Once, we shall consider two scenarios here, depending on who is the leader, and these are taken up in the two subsections below.

3.2.1 Domestic Producer Is the Leader

When the domestic producer acts as a leader, the foreign seller takes inside price ρ as given, and hence its profit-maximization condition gives the following reaction function of the foreign seller:

$$\rho(x) = a - \beta^{\mathrm{s}} - 2(b + \theta^{\mathrm{s}})x - t. \tag{31}$$

The producer who is the leader maximizes π^{d} $(= ((a - \beta^{\mathrm{s}}) - 2(b + \theta^{\mathrm{s}})x - \beta^{\mathrm{p}} - \theta^{\mathrm{p}}x - t)x)$ by taking into account the seller's reaction function as given in (31). The first-order profit-maximizing condition gives the solution of x and thus ρ from (31) as

$$\begin{aligned} x_{\mathrm{dp1}} &= \frac{a - \beta^{\mathrm{s}} - \beta^{\mathrm{p}} - t}{2(2b + 2\theta^{\mathrm{s}} + \theta^{\mathrm{p}})}, \\ \rho_{\mathrm{dp1}} &= \frac{(a - \beta^{\mathrm{s}} + \beta^{\mathrm{p}} - t)(b + \theta^{\mathrm{s}}) + (a - t)\theta^{\mathrm{p}}}{2b + 2\theta^{\mathrm{s}} + \theta^{\mathrm{p}}}. \end{aligned}$$

Profits of the domestic producer and that of the foreign seller are calculated, respectively, as

$$\pi^{\mathrm{d}}_{\mathrm{p1}} = \frac{(a - \beta^{\mathrm{s}} - \beta^{\mathrm{p}} - t)^2}{4(2b + 2\theta^{\mathrm{s}} + \theta^{\mathrm{p}})}, \tag{32}$$

$$\pi^{\mathrm{f}}_{\mathrm{s2}} = \frac{(a - \beta^{\mathrm{s}} - \beta^{\mathrm{p}} - t)^2(b + \theta^{\mathrm{s}})}{4(2b + 2\theta^{\mathrm{s}} + \theta^{\mathrm{p}})^2}. \tag{33}$$

As before, in stage 1, the domestic government chooses tax t to maximize the welfare of the home country $\tilde{W}$, which is the sum of the domestic producer's profit π^{d} and the government's tax revenue tx, i.e.,

$$\tilde{W} = \pi^{\mathrm{d}} + \mathrm{tx}. \tag{34}$$

Note that since the good is assumed to be sold by the foreign firm abroad, consumers' surplus is not a part of welfare of the home country.

Substituting the expressions of π^{d} and x from above and then setting $\mathrm{d}\tilde{W}/\mathrm{d}t = 0$, we solve the optimal level of t as

$$t = 0.$$

The negative effect of increasing t on profits cancels with the positive effect of increasing t on tax revenue (for a given level of x), leaving only the deadweight loss, and thus the optimal exports tax is zero.

By substituting the optimal values of t in the expression for profits in (32) and (33), we get

$$\begin{aligned} \pi^{\mathrm{d}}_{\mathrm{p1}} &= \frac{(a - \beta^{\mathrm{s}} - \beta^{\mathrm{p}})^2}{4(2b + 2\theta^{\mathrm{s}} + \theta^{\mathrm{p}})}, \\ \pi^{\mathrm{f}}_{\mathrm{s2}} &= \frac{(a - \beta^{\mathrm{s}} - \beta^{\mathrm{p}})^2(b + \theta^{\mathrm{s}})}{4(2b + 2\theta^{\mathrm{s}} + \theta^{\mathrm{p}})^2}. \end{aligned}$$

3.2.2 Domestic Producer Is the Follower

We now consider the second scenario where the domestic producer is the follower. Here, in stage 3, the follower, i.e., the domestic firm, takes inside price ρ as given. Its profit-maximizing condition gives the following reaction function of the domestic firm:

$$\rho(x) = \beta^{\mathrm{p}} + 2\theta^{\mathrm{p}} x. \tag{35}$$

In stage 2, the foreign firm who is the leader maximizes profits π^{f} $(= (a - bx - \beta^{\mathrm{p}} - 2\theta^{\mathrm{p}}x - \beta^{\mathrm{s}} - \theta^{\mathrm{s}}x - t)x)$, taking into account the reaction function given in (35). The first-order profit-maximizing condition solves the output level and then inside price from (35) as

$$x_{\mathrm{dp2}} = \frac{a - \beta^{\mathrm{s}} - \beta^{\mathrm{p}} - t}{2(b + \theta^{\mathrm{s}} + 2\theta^{\mathrm{p}})},$$

$$\rho_{\mathrm{dp2}} = \frac{(a - \beta^{\mathrm{s}} + \beta^{\mathrm{p}} - t)\theta^{\mathrm{p}} + (b + \theta^{\mathrm{s}})\beta^{\mathrm{p}}}{b + \theta^{\mathrm{s}} + 2\theta^{\mathrm{p}}}.$$

The profit of the domestic firm and that of the foreign firm are calculated, respectively, as

$$\pi^{\mathrm{d}}_{\mathrm{p2}} = \frac{(a - \beta^{\mathrm{s}} - \beta^{\mathrm{p}} - t)^2 \theta^{\mathrm{p}}}{4(b + \theta^{\mathrm{s}} + 2\theta^{\mathrm{p}})^2}, \tag{36}$$

$$\pi^{\mathrm{f}}_{\mathrm{s1}} = \frac{(a - \beta^{\mathrm{s}} - \beta^{\mathrm{p}} - t)^2}{4(b + \theta^{\mathrm{s}} + 2\theta^{\mathrm{p}})}. \tag{37}$$

As in Sect. 3.2.1, in stage 1, the domestic government chooses tax t to maximize the welfare of the home country as given in (34). In this case, the optimum tax is solved as

$$t = \frac{(a - \beta^{\mathrm{s}} - \beta^{\mathrm{p}})(b + \theta^{\mathrm{s}} + \theta^{\mathrm{p}})}{(2b + 2\theta^{\mathrm{s}} + 3\theta^{\mathrm{p}})} > 0. \tag{38}$$

As in the case when the domestic firm was a seller and for similar reasons, the optimal tax is higher when the domestic firm is the follower than when it is the leader.

By substituting (38) in (36) and (37), we get the levels of profits of the two parties as

$$\pi^{\mathrm{d}}_{\mathrm{p2}} = \frac{(a - \beta^{\mathrm{s}} - \beta^{\mathrm{p}})^2 \theta^{\mathrm{p}}}{4(2b + 2\theta^{\mathrm{s}} + 3\theta^{\mathrm{p}})^2},$$

$$\pi^{\mathrm{f}}_{\mathrm{s1}} = \frac{(a - \beta^{\mathrm{s}} - \beta^{\mathrm{p}})^2 (b + \theta^{\mathrm{s}} + 2\theta^{\mathrm{p}})}{4(2b + 2\theta^{\mathrm{s}} + 3\theta^{\mathrm{p}})^2}.$$

3.2.3 Leadership Preference

In this section, we check if there is a certain producer–seller relationship that both entities prefer, when the domestic firm is the producer. Comparing profits under the two scenarios, we find

$$\pi^{\mathrm{f}}_{\mathrm{s1}} - \pi^{\mathrm{f}}_{\mathrm{s2}} = \frac{2(a-\beta^{\mathrm{s}}-\beta^{\mathrm{p}})^2(\theta^{\mathrm{p}})^3}{4(2b+2\theta^{\mathrm{s}}+3\theta^{\mathrm{p}})^2(2b+2\theta^{\mathrm{s}}+\theta^{\mathrm{p}})^2} > 0,$$

$$\pi^{\mathrm{d}}_{\mathrm{p1}} - \pi^{\mathrm{d}}_{\mathrm{p2}} = \frac{(a-\beta^{\mathrm{s}}-\beta^{\mathrm{p}})^2\Delta^{\mathrm{d}}}{4(2b+2\theta^{\mathrm{s}}+3\theta^{\mathrm{p}})^2(2b+2\theta^{\mathrm{s}}+\theta^{\mathrm{p}})} > 0,$$

where

$$\Delta^{\mathrm{d}} = (2b+2\theta^{\mathrm{s}}+3\theta^{\mathrm{p}})^2 - (2b+2\theta^{\mathrm{s}}+\theta^{\mathrm{p}})\theta^{\mathrm{p}} > 0.$$

That is, in the absence of any side payments, both firms would prefer their own leadership. Although the optimal tax rate is lower when the domestic producer is the leader than when it is the follower, the difference in the optimal tax rates is bigger when the domestic firm is a seller. That is why, in this case, the foreign firm would never accept leadership by the domestic firm, but it would do under certain conditions (see Proposition 3) when the domestic firm is the seller and the foreign firm is the producer.

Proposition 5. *In the absence of side payment, both firms would prefer their own leadership.*

In the presence of side payments, we consider again aggregate profits. The levels of, and the differences in, aggregate profits are

$$\pi_{\mathrm{dp1}} = \pi^{\mathrm{d}}_{\mathrm{s2}} + \pi^{\mathrm{f}}_{\mathrm{p1}} = \frac{(a-\beta^{\mathrm{s}}-\beta^{\mathrm{p}})^2(3b+3\theta^{\mathrm{s}}+\theta^{\mathrm{p}})}{4(2b+2\theta^{\mathrm{s}}+\theta^{\mathrm{p}})^2},$$

$$\pi_{\mathrm{dp2}} = \pi^{\mathrm{d}}_{\mathrm{p2}} + \pi^{\mathrm{f}}_{\mathrm{s1}} = \frac{(a-\beta^{\mathrm{s}}-\beta^{\mathrm{p}})^2(b+\theta^{\mathrm{s}}+3\theta^{\mathrm{p}})}{4(2b+2\theta^{\mathrm{s}}+3\theta^{\mathrm{p}})^2},$$

$$\pi_{\mathrm{dp1}} - \pi_{\mathrm{dp2}} = \frac{(a-\beta^{\mathrm{s}}-\beta^{\mathrm{p}})^2\tilde{\Delta}}{4(2b+2\theta^{\mathrm{s}}+\theta^{\mathrm{p}})^2(2b+2\theta^{\mathrm{s}}+3\theta^{\mathrm{p}})^2} > 0,$$

where

$$\tilde{\Delta} = (3b+3\theta^{\mathrm{s}}+\theta^{\mathrm{p}})(2b+2\theta^{\mathrm{s}}+3\theta^{\mathrm{p}})^2 - (2b+2\theta^{\mathrm{s}}+\theta^{\mathrm{p}})^2(b+\theta^{\mathrm{s}}+3\theta^{\mathrm{p}}) > 0.$$

That is, in the presence of side payments, the foreign seller can be made to prefer the leadership by the domestic producer. Formally,

Proposition 6. *In the presence of side payments, when domestic firm is the producer and the government imposes exports tax optimally, both firms would prefer domestic firms' leadership.*

Since the optimal tax is higher when the foreign firm is the leader, the foreign firm benefits sufficiently when it is not the leader and this overcompensates for the loss the foreign seller incurs being a follower.

4 Conclusion

In economic analysis, it is normally assumed that there is no difference between a producer and a seller, i.e., the producer directly sells to the consumers. But, in reality, more often than not, a producer sells its product to a seller and who then in turn sells the product to consumers. This vertical relationship between a producer and a consumer has been considered in the literature and it opens up new issues and problems. This chapter is about one such problem: who should be the leader in such a vertical relationship. We consider several cases depending on the nationality of the two parties, on whether side payments between the two firms are allowed, and on whether the domestic government is passive or active in setting optimal sales tax.

In the case where the government is passive, we find that in the absence of any side payment, both firms will prefer their own leadership. However, when side payments are allowed, it is possible that both parties agree on the leadership of one of the two firms. We also find that when the government sets sales tax optimally, they can agree on the leadership issue even in the absence of side payments. This is true when the domestic firm is the seller. When side payments are allowed and the government is active, the leadership by the domestic firm emerges as the equilibrium.

References

Backman J (1965) Joint ventures in the light of recent antitrust developments: joint ventures in the chemical industry. Antitrust Bull 10:7–24

Berg S, Friedman P (1977) Joint ventures, competition, and technological complementarities. Southern Econ J 43:1330–1337

Bowley AL (1928) Bilateral monopoly. Econ J 38:651–659

Das SP, Lahiri S (2006) A strategic analysis of terrorist activity and counter-terrorism policies. Top Theor Econ 6(1):Article 6. http://www.bepress.com/bejte/topics/vol6/issl/art6

Dasgupta S, Devadoss S (2002) Equilibrium contracts in a bilateral monopoly with unequal bargaining powers. Int Econ J 16:43–71

Devadoss S, Cooper K (2000) Simultaneous price and quantity determination in a joint profit maximizing bilateral monopoly under dynamic optimization. Int Econ J 14:71–84

Duncan L (1982) Impact of new entry and horizontal joint ventures on industrials rates of return. Rev Econ Stat 64:339–342

Fellner W (1947) Price and wages under bilateral monopoly. Q J Econ 61:503–532

Hamilton JH, Slutsky SM (1990) Endogenous timing in duopoly games: Stackelberg or Cournot equilibria. Games Econ Behav 2:29–46

Henderson JM, Quandt RE (1980) Microeconomic theory: a mathematical approach. McGraw-Hill, New York, NY

Jafarey S, Lahiri S (2008) Developing-country borrowing from a monopolistic lender: strategic interactions and endogenous leadership. Jpn Econ Rev (in press)

Lahiri S, Ono Y (1999) Optimal tariffs in the presence of middlemen. Can J Econ 32:55–70

Machlup F, Taber M (1960) Bilateral monopoly, successive monopoly, and vertical integration. Economica 28:101–119

Matsumura T (1995) Endogenous timing in multi-stage duopoly games. Jpn Econ Rev 46:257–265

Matsumura T (2003) Stackelberg mixed duopoly with a foreign competitor. Bull Econ Res 55:275–287

McConnell J, Nantell J (1985) Common stock returns and corporate combination: the case of joint venture. J Finance 40:519–536

Ono Y (1978) The equilibrium of duopoly in a market of homogeneous goods. Economica 45:287–295

Ono Y (1982) Price leadership: a theoretical analysis. Economica 49:11–20

Truett DD, Truett LJ (1993) Joint profit maximization, negotiation, and the determinacy of price in bilateral monopoly. J Econ Educ 24:260–270

Trading Under Strategic Self-Constraint: Conceptual Issues and Factual Evidence

Henry Wan, Jr.

Abstract One of the most important aspects in the current world economy is the rise of microelectronics, which is regarded as a general purpose technology (GPT). In particular, a significant instrument is the application-specific integrated circuits (ASICs).

This instrument is supplied by international division of labor, under a novel production relationship, between a few capital-intensive "chip-foundries" and the large pool of "chip-designers". To exclude itself from chip design, the foundry can avoid conflict of interest with potential chip designers. This behavior is modeled as a problem of mechanism design. It is shown that the commitment of the foundry enhances social welfare.

1 Introduction

Every era, the world economy functions under the prevailing technological environment. As technology improves with innovation, trade theory evolves to rise up to the emerging issues, and economists must sally forth onto uncharted waters. In serving the purpose of the profession, novel topics of pragmatic significance must be analyzed, even though the resultant new theory – at least in its initial stage – may not yet match the elegance or generality one customarily finds in the traditional canon. In his exceptionally fruitful but unfortunately short career, Professor Koji Shimomura set an example for such valuable endeavor of the profession, like the study of trade-dependent preferences in Kemp et al. (2001), which I was fortunate to join. It is appropriate here to carry on in the spirit of his good deeds.

H. Wan, Jr.
Department of Economics, Cornell University, 470 Uris Hall, Ithaca, NY 14853, USA,
e-mail: hyw1@cornell.edu

T. Kamihigashi and L. Zhao (eds.) *International Trade and Economic Dynamics – Essays in Memory of Koji Shimomura.*

This chapter focuses on the international division of labor in supplying the application-specific integrated circuits (ASICs). These customized assemblages of semiconductors have made the microelectronics into such a versatile technology and radically transform modern life, from photography, telecommunication, machine tooling, pharmaceutical research, to financial trading, and so forth. As a result, microelectronics is rated as a general-purpose technology (GPT) defined by Helpman (1998) and Lipsey et al. (2005) and ranked with the printing press. It brings about a broad range of innovations with profound impact in a rapid and continuous pace. It is the hallmark of our era.

The production of ASICs mirrors much of the modern inventive process. To supply such devices, the worldwide division of labor marks the implementation of the Smithian ideal, through the close cooperation across the world of a few very capital-intensive chip foundries and the large pool of experienced chip designers.

As one might expect, in the interplay of information, control, and incentive, the new technological environment has given rise to new economic challenges. The fabrication of the product provides the chip foundry not only the experience for production, but also potent insight for chip design. This may allow the chip foundry to become an irresistible rival to the original chip designers, before the latter can earn enough profit to cover their sunk cost on design work. In turn, this prospect would inhibit many would-be designers from entering the market. The inhibition of would-be designers both causes loss to the social welfare and reduces the clientele to the chip foundry. Yet, difficulties in contract enforcement make it ineffective for a chip foundry to offer any no-compete promise to individual designers. Such consideration induces the rise of the "dedicated chip foundry," which refrains from doing any design work. This possibility is examined here.

Traditionally, the variety of goods and the production technology are taken as given. The simplicity of the timeless structure has allowed for the exploration of basic issues like efficiency, comparative advantage, and market power. This study now focuses on not only the effects of, but also the causes for the rise of new goods with new technology.

In what follows a conceptual digression is provided into the question of self–constraint, which underlies the institution of the dedicated chip foundry. We then set up a model under some simple assumptions. Some concluding remarks then follow.

2 Self-Constraint, General Considerations

In decision theory, it is the implication of the Axiom of Independence from Irrelevant Alternatives that there can be no incentive to impose restrictions on one's own constrained set. If A is the global optimum over the set $\{A, B, X\}$, excluding option X that is not chosen (equivalently to limit one's choice to the subset $\{A, B\}$) should not improve one's payoff. If self-restraining makes a difference, the global optimality of A is suspect.

But in the "inter-agent" context, self-constraint is justified in at least three cases.

(a) For restricting the circumstance-dependent action of *the agent-tomorrow*, the *agent-today* may behave as described in the Ulysses–Strotz paradox (Strotz 1955), such as placing savings in a piggy bank. In a sense, this topic bears some resemblance to Kemp et al., op. cit.
(b) In negotiating a "golden parachute," the departing corporate executive is offered the opportunity to qualify for a severance package, by signing a *non-compete agreement*, that forbids the employment with rival firms over some period.
(c) To appeal to chip designers in the market, a chip foundry may proclaim that it is solely *dedicated* to the foundry business (thus, becoming a "*dedicated foundry*"), *to the exclusion of any chip designing by itself.*

In the last case, three characteristics can he identified forthwith:

First, there is *information externality*. In producing the chip for the designer, the foundry acquires specific knowledge that enhances its own productive capacity.

Second, unless constrained from doing so, the chip foundry has the motive to use this specific knowledge under its *control* to enter the market and compete against the chip designer. Here, the information externality short-circuits the market, benefits one agent (the foundry) at the expense of the other (the designer), and hence reduces the *incentive* of the latter to undertake inventive action, in the first place.

Third, since each transaction alone may be quite insignificant for the foundry, its promise for self-constraint is likely to be *self-enforcing*. Any breach of promise would harm its own over-all interest.

To obtain deeper insight, a more formal analysis is given in Sect. 3 under simplifying assumptions.

3 A Simple Example

There is a set of S designers of ASICs facing a particular foundry. Each designer $s = 1, \ldots, S$ can complete the design at cost $c(s) \geq 0$, which is strictly increasing in s.

For all s, the demand for a produced chip is h^{t-1} units in period $t \geq 1$, after the production. The *unit market revenue* is 1 for any produced chip, in any period.

For any chip, the chip foundry charges a *unit foundry fee* of $f \in (0,1)$ for production. The unit production cost of any chip for the foundry is $k \in (0,1)$.

The time preference factor is $b \in (0,1)$.

The payoff streams of both the designer and the foundry depend upon whether the foundry is dedicated or not. For simplicity, the following specification is adopted.

Assumptions. 1. Whether the foundry is *dedicated* or not, the ratio of the revenue shares between the chip-designer and the chip-foundry is $1-f : f-k$ for the first period.

Table 1 Payoffs from the chip s (where designer's payoff depends on s)

	For the chip – designer	For the chip – foundry	
The foundry is dedicated	$\pi_0^d(s) = -c(s) + (1-f)/(1-bh)$		(1)
		$\pi_0^f = (f-k)/(1-bh)$	(2)
The foundry is not	$\pi_1^d(s) = -c(s) + (1-f)$		(3)
		$\pi_1^f = f + (bh-k)/(1-bh)$	(4)

2. If the foundry is "dedicated," this ratio remains the same for all future periods.
3. Otherwise, from the second period on, the ratio becomes 0:1, as the foundry enters the market and out-competes the chip-designer.

Regarding chip s, the present values of the net payoff streams are tabulated in Table 1.

By the condition of incentive compatibility, no chip designer would enter into business for a negative present value of income stream. Thus, the chip foundry faces the optimization problem:

Problem F

$$Max\{\Pi_0^*, \Pi_1^*\} \tag{5}$$

subject to

$$\Pi_0^* = \underset{f_0, s_0}{\text{Max}}\,[(f_0 - k)\,/\,(1-bh)]\,s_0 \quad \text{(Operating as a dedicated foundary)} \tag{6}$$

For all $s = 1, 2, \ldots, s_0$,

$$s_0 \leq S, \tag{7}$$

$$c(s) \leq (1-f_0)\,/\,(1-bh), \quad \text{(Incentive compatibility condition)} \tag{8}$$

$$\Pi_1^* = \underset{f_1, s_0}{Max}\,[f_1 + (bh-k)\,/\,(1-bh)]\,s_1 \quad \text{(Not operating as a dedicated foundary)} \tag{9}$$

For all $s = 1, 2, \ldots, s_1$,

$$s_1 \leq S, \tag{10}$$

$$c(s) \leq 1 - f_1 \quad \text{(incentive compatibility condition).} \tag{11}$$

This yields immediately:

Proposition 1. *(Existence of an optimal solution). The maximization problem facing the chip foundry has a solution.*

Proof. Straightforward. □

Table 1 implies:

Lemma 1. *(a) For a particular fee f and a particular chip designer s, if the incentive compatibility condition holds when the chip foundry does not operates as a dedicated foundry, then the condition continues to hold when it does.*

(b) *If the same chip designer is a client of the chip foundry, whether or not the chip foundry operates as a dedicated foundry, the chip foundry enjoys a higher present value of the net revenue stream by not operating on a dedicated basis.*

Proof. Part (a) follows the fact that

$$1 - f < (1 - f)/(1 - bh). \tag{12}$$

Part (b) follows the fact that

$$\begin{aligned}(f-k)/(1-bh) &= f - k + (f-k)bh/(1-bh),\\ &< f - k + (1-k)bh/(1-bh),\\ &= f + (bh-k)/(1-bh).\end{aligned} \tag{13}$$

It then follows, □

Proposition 2. *(Characterization of the optimal basis and volume)*

(a) *If under f_1^*, the optimal fee for a nondedicated chip foundry, the incentive compatibility condition is satisfied for all the S chip designers, then the foundry has no incentive to operate on the dedicated basis.*
(b) *Conversely, if it is optimal for the chip foundry to operate on a dedicated basis, then the justification must be to attract chip designers who would be excluded otherwise.*

Proof. Straightforward. □

To gain further insight into Problem F for the present value maximization of the chip foundry in (5), one may additionally adopt the following:

Assumptions. 4. There is a continuum of chip designers, $s \in [0, S]$.
5. The start-up cost function $c(s)$ is differentiable in s.
Now in the sub-problems of solving for Π_0^* and Π_1^*, one has the following result.

Proposition 3. *(Characterization of the optimal fee level).*

(a) *The solution for Π_0^* satisfies either*

$$s_0 = S \quad and \quad f_0 = 1 - (1 - bh)c(S), \quad \textit{(a corner optimum)} \tag{14}$$

or

$$s_0 < S \quad and \quad c(s_0) = (1 - f_0)/(1 - bh); \quad c'(s_0) = (f_0 - k)/(1 - bh)s_0 = \pi_0^f/s_0 \quad \textit{(an interior optimum)} \tag{15}$$

The solution for Π_0^* satisfies either

$$s_1 = S \quad and \quad f_1 = 1 - c(S), \quad \textit{(a corner optimum)} \tag{16}$$

or

$$s_1 < S \quad and \quad c(s_1) = (1 - f_1); \quad c'(s_1) = [f_1 + (bh-k)/(1-bh)]s_1 = \pi_1^f s_1$$

$$\text{(an interior optimum)} \qquad (17)$$

Proof. For corner solutions, the fee equals what maximum level designer S will bear.

For interior solutions,

$$\Pi_0^* = \pi_0^f s_0 \quad \text{and} \quad \Pi_1^* = \pi_1^f s_1. \qquad (18)$$

The first order necessary condition for their maximum is that their logarithmic derivatives with respect to f_0 and f_1 be zero:

$$\begin{aligned} \frac{1}{(1-bh)f_0} &= \frac{-\mathrm{d}s_0/\mathrm{d}f_0}{s_0}, \quad (\text{from}\,(2)) \\ \frac{1}{f+(bh-k)/(1-bh)} &= \frac{-\mathrm{d}s_1/\mathrm{d}f_1}{s_1}. \quad (\text{from}\,(4)) \end{aligned} \qquad (19)$$

By the rule of derivative of inverse functions,

$$\begin{aligned} \frac{\mathrm{d}s_0}{\mathrm{d}f_0} &= \left(\frac{\mathrm{d}s_0}{\mathrm{d}c}\right)\left(\frac{\mathrm{d}c}{\mathrm{d}f_0}\right) = \frac{-1}{c'(s_0)(1-bh)}, \quad \text{where} \quad c(s_0) = \frac{1-f_0}{(1-bh)}, \quad (\text{from}(1)) \\ \frac{\mathrm{d}s_1}{\mathrm{d}f_1} &= \left(\frac{\mathrm{d}s_1}{\mathrm{d}c}\right)\left(\frac{\mathrm{d}c}{\mathrm{d}f_1}\right) = \frac{-1}{c'(s_1)}, \quad \text{where} \quad c(s_1) = 1 - f_1. \quad (\text{from}(3)) \end{aligned} \qquad (20)$$

By rearrangement, one obtains (15) and (17). □

Next, following part (b), Proposition 3.2, one has,

Proposition 4. *(Welfare implications). A dedicated chip foundry implies a more efficient resource allocation than if it has operated otherwise.*

Proof. In bringing to the market chip designers in $(s_0, s_1]$, the dedicated foundry has increased producers' surplus by the area,

$$\int_{s_1}^{s_0} [(1-k)/(1-bh) - c(s)]\,\mathrm{d}s = (s_0 - s_1)\pi_0^f + \int_{s_1}^{s_0} \pi_0^d(s)\,\mathrm{d}s. \qquad (21)$$

□

Remark 1. Problem F is completely determined by the parameter values of b, h, k, and S, as well as the differentiable function c(.).

Proposition 5. *(Characterization of the cost schedule c(s)). If the chip foundry chooses to operate on the dedicated basis, then the increasing, continuously differentiable function, $c(s)$, is not weakly convex.*

Proof. For a foundry to operate optimally on a dedicated basis,

$$\begin{aligned} \pi_0^f s_0 &= \Pi_0^* \\ &> \Pi_1^* = \pi_1^f s_1. \end{aligned} \qquad (22)$$

But,

$$\forall s \le s_0,\ \pi_0^f + \pi_0^s(s) + c(s) = (1-k)/(1-bh);$$
$$\forall s \le s_1,\ \pi_1^f + \pi_1^s(s) + c(s) = (1-k)/(1-bh) \tag{23}$$

Also, for the "marginal chip designer,"

$$\pi_0^s(s_0) = 0 = \pi_1^s(s_1). \tag{24}$$

The fact that $c(s)$ is increasing means

$$\begin{aligned} \pi_0^f &= (1-k)/(1-bh) - c(s_0) \\ &< (1-k)/(1-bh) - c(s_1) = \pi_1^f. \end{aligned} \tag{25}$$

Hence, by the last equalities in (15) and (17),

$$\begin{aligned} c'(s_0) &= \pi_0^f/s_0 \\ &< \pi_1^f/s_1 = c'(s_1). \end{aligned} \tag{26}$$

Thus, $c(.)$ is not even weakly convex. □

3.1 A Graphic Recapitulation

Figure 1a shows two specimens of the cost schedule, $c(s)$ and $c^0(s)$. Fig. 1b is constructed on the basis of $c(s)$. An inverted $c(s)$ locus divides the present value rectangle into two separate areas. Above the locus represents costs paid by the foundry and the designers to "third parties." Below the locus represents what the foundry and the designers share between the two. By using the properties of the hyperbola, we can identify the two solutions at (s_0, f_0) and (s_1, f_1).

For expository convenience, the conditions characterize the equilibrium are contained in Table 2.

3.2 Sensitivity Analysis

(a) The curve aspect (The *arc-elasticity* criterion)

A nonconvex $c(s)$ curve is necessary for a dedicated foundry, but this is not sufficient. Taking b, h, and k as given, interested reader can verify graphically that a cost schedule like $c(s)$ would cause a foundry to become dedicated, but not one like $c^0(s)$. In either case, the potential clientele breaks down into two subsets: a low cost

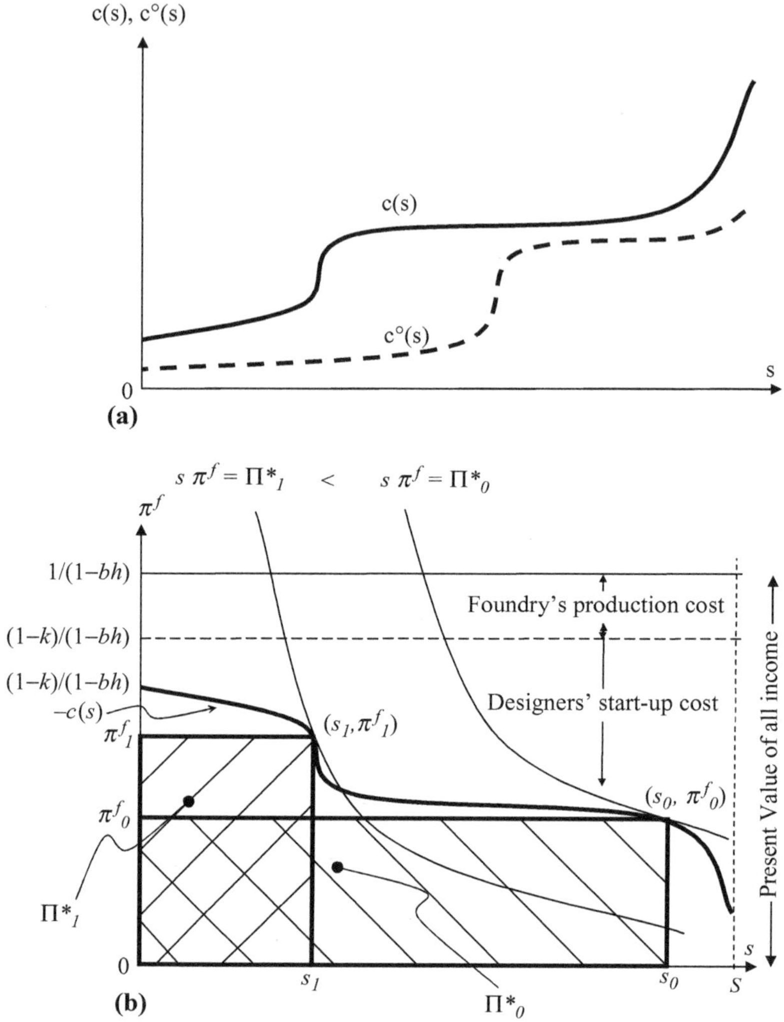

Fig. 1 Graphic interpretation

Table 2 Equilibrium conditions

Equilibrium conditions	At (s_1, π_1) (15)	At (s_0, π_0) (17)	Remark
For the marginal designer	$-c(s_1) + (1 - f_1) = 0$		Zero π^d
		$-c(s_0) + (1 - f_0)/(1 - bh) = 0$	
For the foundry	$c'(s_1) - \pi_1^f / s_1 = 0$		Tangency
		$c'(s_0) - \pi_0^f / s_0 = 0$	

section $[0,s_1)$ and a high cost section $(s_1,s_0]$. The promise of *non-compete* lowers the payoff of the chip foundry per designer, but in return, gains more than enough of a proportion of new clientele as compensation for $c(s)$, but not for $c^0(s)$. Formally, these can be stated as

$$\frac{\log(\pi_1^f)-\log(\pi_0^f)}{\log(s_0)-\log(s_1)}>1 \quad \text{for the case of } c(s),$$
$$\frac{\log(\pi_1^f)-\log(\pi_0^f)}{\log(s_0)-\log(s_1)}<1 \quad \text{for the case of } c^0(s). \tag{27}$$

(b) The scalar aspect (The critical magnitude criterion)

The dedicated foundry trades the net payoff in the future for the clientele of the present. Given the same cost schedule $c(s)$, the scalar value making the litmus test is

$$r=\frac{1-k}{1-bh}, \tag{28}$$

where in Fig. 2, there is the knife-edge case, under which the locus, $r-c(s)$, is tangential to a hyperbola at two distinct points, and the ratio of total present value of net payoff to the present is $r:1$.

Formally, define the gain from dedicated operation as

$$\Delta\Pi=\Pi_0^*-\Pi_1^*, \tag{29}$$

one has the comparative static results

$$\frac{\partial(\Delta\Pi)}{\partial b}>0,\ \frac{\partial(\Delta\Pi)}{\partial h}>0,\ \frac{\partial(\Delta\Pi)}{\partial k}<0. \tag{30}$$

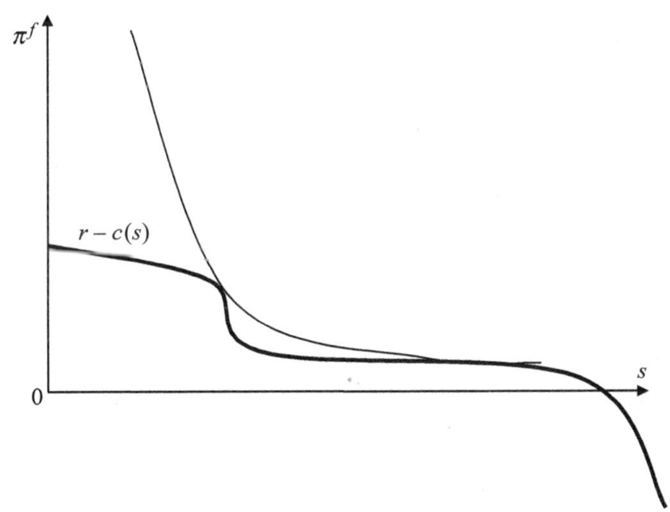

Fig. 2 The knife-edge case

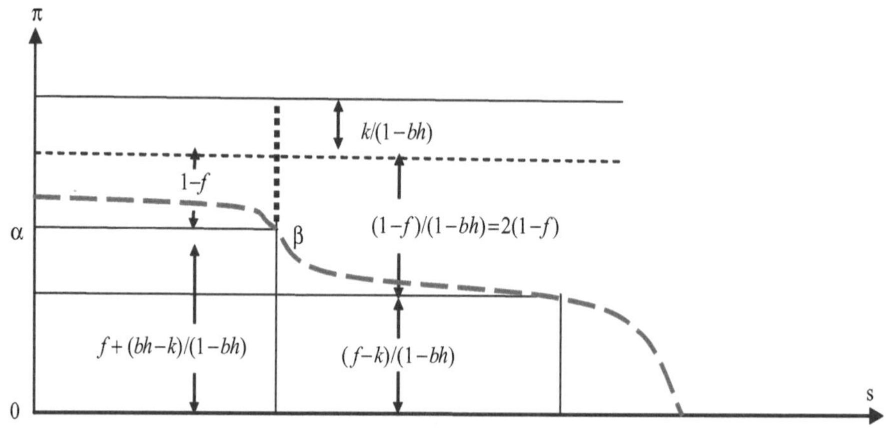

Fig. 3 The dedicated foundry may or may not adjust the fee level

3.3 Comparison of Fee Levels

Would a dedicated foundry charge a lower (or higher) level of fee than if it operates not on a dedicated basis? By a constructive proof, one can conclude that nothing can be definitely excluded. Now, reproduce Fig. 1b in Fig. 3, and assume that $bh = \frac{1}{2}$ for simplicity. Assume first the neutral case

$$0 = \Delta f = f_0 - f_1, \quad \text{or} \quad f_1 = f = f_0. \tag{31}$$

So there need be no difference in the fee level at all. Next, one can keep $f_0 = f$ as before, but move the line $\alpha\beta$ up or down a bit, changing the value of f_1 accordingly, and shift the cost curve to fit. Thus, Δf can take either positive or negative sign. Hence, one has established the desired result:

In becoming a dedicated foundry, the fee level may stay the same, raised, or lowered.

4 Concluding Remarks

It is time to address the following issues:

First, from the international trade perspective, the industry of *dedicated foundry* is interesting in its own right. The product of this industry relates to the change of technology. By the existence of this industry, many chip designers manage to translate their talents into novel, practical devices to serve diverse purposes. Although chip designers come from all over the world, the top four dedicated foundries[1] happen to be in economies like Taiwan, Mainland China, and Singapore, rather than

[1] The value of a single plant can reach 4.5 billion US dollars.

the technologically leading lands. Initially, the source of their comparative advantage was first the *market insight*, and then the *institution* to establish the dedicated operation. Next, the effect of *learning-by-doing* provides these firms with the specialized expertise, so that they remain to be leaders of the trade, because market evolution is path-dependent. All these are related to the development of the Hsinchu Science Park in Taiwan, as part of the fruit of the *industrial policy* in that economy (Tung 2001; Thorbecke et al. 2002).

Second, for the clarity of analysis, this study focuses on what is novel in the problem, leaving out certain aspects that are more familiar to economists. For instance, from the view of public interest, it is a second-best solution – just like the granting of patent right – to restrict the future entry by foundries in the market of chip design. This encourages the current entry of would-be chip-designers. Likewise, for each foundry, the *present* scale of operation influences the *future* cost of fabrication for each foundry, due to the effect of learning. Furthermore, both the level of fee charged and the size of the clientele pool served by individual foundries are mutually dependent among the oligopolies, under the Cournot model.

Finally, with the recent development of "system on a chip" (SoC), the fabrication technology becomes increasingly complex, so that the foundry–designer relationship may evolve from the mode "at arm's length" as represented here, toward the mode of *incomplete contract* (Ernst 2006), in which partners in enduring associations invest in relationship-specific human capital. That would call for another campaign in trade-theoretic research.

Acknowledgment In taking responsibility for all the remaining imperfections of this study, the author gratefully acknowledges the valuable discussions that have contributed to the analysis, with Professor David Easley, Cornell University and Dr. C. C. Yang, Institute of Economics, Academia Sinica.

References

Ernst D (2006) Upgrading through innovation in a small network economy: insights from Taiwan's IT industry. Paper for the conference High Tech Regions 2.0 – Sustainability and Reinvention

Helpman E (1998) General purpose technologies and economic growth. MIT Press, Cambridge, MA

Kemp MC, Shimomura K, Wan HY Jr (2001) Trade gains when the opportunity to trade changes the state of information. Rev Int Econ 9(1):24–28

Lipsey RG, Carlaw KI, Bekar CT (2005) Economic transformations: general purpose technologies and long-term economic growth. Oxford University Press, New York

Strotz RH (1955) Myopia, inconsistency in dynamic utility maximization. Rev Econ Stud 23(3):165–180

Thorbecke E, Tung A-C, Wan H Jr (2002) Industrial targeting: lessons from past errors and successes of Hong Kong and Taiwan. World Dev 25(8):1047–1061

Tung A-C (2001) Taiwan's semiconductor industry: what the state did and did not. Rev Dev Econ 5(2):266–288

Part III
Dynamic Theory of International Trade

Dynamic Labor Standards Under International Oligopoly

Yunfang Hu and Laixun Zhao(✉)

Abstract This chapter models productive labor standards (LS) in a two-stage, two-period model of international oligopoly, where a home government chooses subsidies on LS and output first, and oligopolistic firms determine productions of LS and output later. We show that the optimal LS maintained is higher in a dynamic setup (i.e., across periods) than in a static setup (or when firms behave myopically). Thus, even in poor countries, it benefits to maintain a certain level of LS. A minimum international LS directly affecting only the less efficient firm may lower the profits of the rival firm also. With inter-temporal LS carryovers, first-period optimal subsidies are more efficient on LS than on output. If the home government cares about LS (or human rights) in the foreign country, then it is better not to provide home subsidies, because such subsidies reduce foreign LS.

1 Introduction

There have been heated debates concerning international labor standards (LS) recently,[1] especially in forums of the ILO (International Labor Organization), the former GATT, and now the WTO. Labor unions, human rights groups, and other

[1] A simple search on the net will turn out many websites maintained by labor organizations, which organize campaigns to improve working conditions and the treatment of workers. Some of the examples are Clean Clothes Campaign, Toy Campaign, Solidarity Campaign, and Work Safety Campaign. They are against multinational firms such as Adidas, Disney, GAP, Levi's, Mattel, New Balance, Nike, Reebok, Timberland, Wal Mart, etc. These campaigns call for monitoring by independent human rights organizations, and for multinationals to abide by international LS and local labor law. It is believed that there are more violations of LS in low skilled industries, which developing countries have a comparative advantage in. Specific violations include child labor, minimum wage violations, illegal overtime, hazardous chemicals and machinery, poor ventilation and lighting, and so on.

L. Zhao
Research Institute for Economics & Business, Kobe University, Kobe 657-8501, Japan,
e-mail: zhao@rieb.kobe-u.ac.jp

T. Kamihigashi and L. Zhao (eds.) *International Trade and Economic Dynamics – Essays in Memory of Koji Shimomura.*

NGOs in a few industrialized countries have campaigned for LS to be included in WTO clauses. They argue that weak LS is a means for generating artificially low wages and thus firms able to adopt a lower LS gain a competitive edge. Some even advocate for trade sanctions against countries that do not enforce a set of agreed LS.

Many economists counter this point of view. Bhagwati (1995) and Basu (1999) believe that the recent surge in the demands for LS stems overwhelmingly from lobbies whose true agenda is protectionism. Srinivasan (1995) and Brown et al. (1996, 1998) demonstrate that the diversity of LS between nations reflect differences in factor endowments and levels of income. Martin and Maskus (2001) show that a failure to establish and enforce LS may reduce an economy's efficiency and interferes with its comparative advantage. Bagwell and Staiger (2001) argue that efficiency can be achieved without negotiating over LS. In contrast, some other economists such as Rodrik (1996) and Elliot (2000) embrace linking LS to trade and FDI.[2]

The basic guidelines of LS provided by the ILO includes broad contents such as freedom of association, freedom to unionize, no child labor, no forced labor, no forced overtime work, no hazardous work environment, no discrimination based on age, gender or religion, etc. It is hard to squeeze all these into a single model. However, there are common elements in them that can be extracted and modeled, which we attempt to do in this chapter.

The existing theoretical literature and most of the ongoing debates are based on the assumption that LS improvements mainly increase production costs and also consumer utility or national welfare directly. In contrast, *workers or firms* do not benefit from LS investments. If goods are exported, as in the widely cited Brander and Spencer (1985) model in which consumption is in a third-country, then the countries that manufacture the goods do not gain anything from LS improvements. It is then no surprise that such countries have no incentives to improve LS.

In our view, while it is costly to maintain a certain level of LS, a higher LS also improves labor productivity. Our justification is as follows. If LS is interpreted as work safety or work environment, then an increase in LS reduces accidents and presumably raises work spirits. One can provide many other examples. If one agrees that LS contributes to productivity, then it is not hard to see that even in poor countries, maintaining a certain level of LS is beneficial to the firms and national welfare there. Furthermore, this effect becomes even stronger in a dynamic setting where LS upgraded at present contributes to production in the future. To induce countries with poor LS to make improvements, these points must be emphasized.

The present chapter models the ideas above in a two-firm, two-country framework of Spencer and Brander (1983) and Brander and Spencer (1985), with consumption in a third market. Firms produce an identical product and compete à la

[2] "Increasing domestic pressures on labor matters will lead to a new set of grey-area-protectionist measures because there are no internationally agreed rules to channel these pressures into less harmful directions. If that happens, the consequences will be more damaging to developing-country interests than those of a social-safeguards clause negotiated multilaterally." Rodrik (1996, p 68) and Elliot (2000) examine the US Generalized System of Preferences and finds that external pressure can be helpful in improving treatment of workers and that linkage of trade and worker rights need not develop into protectionism.

Cournot. To incorporate the effects of LS carryovers, we consider a dynamic model in its simplest form – two periods. A fraction of LS produced in the first period can be reused in the second period. A home government decides simultaneously whether to subsidize LS or output production, and whether to subsidize in the first period or the second period. Given government policies, firms choose how much to invest in LS, and how much output to produce for each period. Note that the way LS contributes to production is similar to human capital or R&D investments, but in the present model, the home government's utility can increase if foreign LS (or human rights) rises. These features of LS distinguish themselves from human capital or R&D.

In this dynamic setup, we first show that *the average total* and *per-worker* LS maintained inter-temporally is higher than in a static setup, due to the existence of inter-temporal LS carryovers, which induces the firm to produce a higher LS than in a static setup. It is often argued that the enforcement of LS incurs transitory costs, whereas the benefits are more likely to accrue in the longer run. Our results can shed some light on this. If a firm behaves myopically and sees only one period, then it does not consider the benefits that manifest only in the following periods, which in turn leads it to under-produce LS.

Next we investigate the effects of a minimum international LS imposed on both countries. Consider a simplest case in which it affects directly only the less efficient country, such that it is below the LS level chosen in the more efficient country. We demonstrate that the minimum LS raises the cost and also output of the less efficient firm, but reduces its profit. However, the surprising result is that the profit of the more efficient, rival firm also falls, because its market share is reduced by the output expansion of the other firm.

Regarding government policies, we have the following findings. Compared with static policies, in the present dynamic setup, the government over-subsidizes LS in the first period, but under-subsidizes it in the second period, because first-period LS can be carried over to the second period. In contrast, the government over-subsidizes output in the first period (which also increases second-period LS), but does *not* under-subsidize and instead maintains the static level of output subsidy in the second period, because output is not carried over to the second period. Thus, first-period subsidy is more efficient on LS than on output, because the former saves the cost of subsidy in the second period.

Following popular claims that governments in developed countries also care about LS (or human rights) in developing countries, we suppose that government utility in the developed country increases if LS in the other developing country rises. Then we find that the optimal home subsidies are lowered, because a lower subsidy raises the LS in the other country. This result implies that contrary to conventional wisdom, using home subsidies to force the foreign country to raise LS may not work.

To the best of our knowledge, there is no formal dynamic analysis of LS in the literature.[3] Some recent studies on child labor are related to the present chapter. For

[3] For dynamic analysis related to Spencer and Brander (1983), see for instance Tanaka (1994), Ohkawa and Shimomura (1995), and Benchekroun (2003). Notice at least three major differences

instance, Basu and Van (1998) demonstrate that child labor may arise out of the parents' concern for the household's survival, and it may be difficult to ban child labor. Ranjan (2001) and Jafarey and Lahiri (2002) examine the interaction between credit markets and child labor. The latter also shows that trade sanctions can increase child labor, especially among poor households. Hussain and Maskus (2003) model and test econometrically the interaction between child labor and human capital accumulation through schooling. However, all these studies take an approach that is based on household decisions on whether to invest in child schooling or to make them work, which is quite different from ours in an international duopoly setup, with firms maximizing profits and governments maximizing welfare.

The rest of the chapter is organized as follows: Sect. 2 sets up the basic model. Section 3 solves the firm's inter-temporal problem. Section 4 compares optimal government policies. Section 5 examines the effects of a minimum international LS imposed on both countries. Section 6 looks into the issue of human rights. And finally Sect. 7 concludes.

2 Basic Model Setup

Consider two firms located respectively in two countries Home and Foreign. They produce an identical product which is sold in a third country. For notational convenience, we use a superscript * to denote foreign variables, wherever necessary.

2.1 Production

We consider LS to be costly to obtain on the one hand, and that it contributes to final production on the other hand. Specifically, it can exhibit in three forms. One is work safety, ventilation, clean and comfortable work environment, etc., which is not embodied in the worker physically; the second is health improvement, which is embodied in the worker; the third is a reduction of child labor or an increase in the minimum wage, which can increase productivity indirectly. In addition, the home government's utility can increase if foreign LS (or human rights) rises. These features of LS distinguish themselves from human capital or R&D.

Denote θ the LS in each country. There is no market for θ. Firms must produce it internally by using labor input. Let the production function of LS be

$$\theta = \alpha L_{\theta}, \tag{1}$$

between the basic structure of the present model and Spencer and Brander (1983). While they consider a two-stage game of R&D investment and output competition, with R&D affecting only the marginal cost of production, in a one-period setup, we assume a *simultaneous game* of LS investment and output competition, in *two periods* with *LS affecting inter-temporal production and costs*, which is the focus of our model.

where L_θ is labor used for the production of LS and $\alpha > 0$ is an exogenous technology parameter.

To produce the final output, both labor and LS are needed such that

$$y = \theta L_y, \tag{2}$$

where y is the final output and L_y is labor used for final production. This setup implies that lowering LS reduces the cost, which is why firms prefer a lower LS. However, lowering LS also reduces productivity. These two effects work against each other.

We consider a two-period model, and assume that LS in the two periods is related in the following manner:

$$\tilde{\theta}_2 = (1-\delta)\theta_1 + \theta_2, \tag{3}$$

where θ_1 and θ_2 are the LS actually produced in periods 1 and 2, respectively, such that $\theta_1 = \alpha L_{\theta 1}$ and $\theta_2 = \alpha L_{\theta 2}$ for each firm. A portion of LS in period 1, $(1-\delta)\theta_1$, can be reused in period 2. Thus, the total LS that can be used in period 2 is $\tilde{\theta}_2$. As such, δ is the depreciation rate of LS. It is not hard to think of some examples. For instance, most classroom facilities including the floor, chairs, desks, and blackboards are cleaned early morning before classes begin. That is, once cleaned, the room is used for a day, during which many classes are held. However, cleanness deteriorates after each class.

2.2 Static Profits

Let the static profit function for each firm be

$$\begin{aligned} \pi(L_\theta, L_y) &= (p+s)y - w(L_\theta + L_y) + w\sigma\theta, \\ &= (p+s)y - wL_y - (1-\alpha\sigma)wL_\theta, \end{aligned} \tag{4}$$

where $p = p(y+y^*)$ is the inverse demand, with $p' < 0$; s is an output subsidy to the domestic firm; w is the given wage rate, and $w\sigma$ is a unit subsidy to LS production of the domestic firm, with $(1-\alpha\sigma) > 0$. For simplicity, we assume $p = a - (y+y^*)$.

2.3 Timing

We consider a two-stage game. In the first stage, at the very beginning of the first period, both governments choose a subsidy on outputs in the first period and another one in the second period, respectively, and simultaneously a separate subsidy on the production of LS in the first period and another one in the second period, respectively. In the second stage, firms compete à la Cournot by choosing labor inputs in the two kinds of productions, simultaneously and respectively for each period. That is, firms are forward looking and can see two periods when making decisions. Subsidies in the two periods are independent in the sense that each subsidy is given for just one period. However, as we shall show that subsidies have cross-period inter-temporal strategic effects. To ensure consistency, the firms' problems are solved first. Then we substitute the outcomes to solve for the government's optimal subsidies, in which our equilibrium concept is Markov sub-game perfect.

3 Firm Behavior

In this section, we examine the forward-looking firms, who maximize inter-temporal profits, by choosing LS and outputs for each period, given government policies. We start by assuming identical firms, so that it suffices to focus on the home firm, whose inter-temporal profits can be written as

$$\Pi(L_{y1}, L_{\theta 1}, L_{y2}, L_{\theta 2}) \equiv \pi_1(L_{y1}, L_{\theta 1}; y_1^*) + \gamma \pi_2(L_{\theta 1}, L_{y2}, L_{\theta 2}; y_2^*), \tag{5}$$

where $\pi_1(L_{y1}, L_{\theta 1}; y_1^*) = \{(a + s_1 - y_1^*) - \theta_1 L_{y1}\}\theta_1 L_{y1} - (1 - \alpha\sigma_1)wL_{\theta 1} - wL_{y1}$,
$\pi_2(L_{\theta 1}, L_{y2}, L_{\theta 2}; y_2^*) = \{(a + s_2 - y_2^*) - \tilde{\theta}_2 L_{y2}\}\tilde{\theta}_2 L_{y2} - (1 - \alpha\sigma_2)wL_{\theta 2} - wL_{y2}$,

and $\gamma \in (0, 1]$ is an exogenous discount rate. Since second-period firm choices do not affect first-period profits, time inconsistency does not arise. The home firm chooses $L_{\theta 1}, L_{y1}, L_{\theta 2}, L_{y2}$ simultaneously to maximize (5). The first order conditions can be obtained, respectively, as

$$\frac{\partial \Pi}{\partial L_{\theta 1}} = \frac{\partial \pi_1}{\partial L_{\theta 1}} + \gamma \frac{\partial \pi_2}{\partial L_{\theta 1}} = 0, \tag{6a}$$

$$\frac{\partial \Pi}{\partial L_{y1}} = \frac{\partial \pi_1}{\partial L_{y1}} + \gamma \frac{\partial \pi_2}{\partial L_{y1}} = 0, \tag{6b}$$

$$\frac{\partial \Pi}{\partial L_{\theta 2}} = \frac{\partial \pi_1}{\partial L_{\theta 2}} + \gamma \frac{\partial \pi_2}{\partial L_{\theta 2}} = 0, \tag{6c}$$

$$\frac{\partial \Pi}{\partial L_{y2}} = \frac{\partial \pi_1}{\partial L_{y2}} + \gamma \frac{\partial \pi_2}{\partial L_{y2}} = 0. \tag{6d}$$

To gain basic insights into our problem, especially on the inter-temporal effects, let us investigate the firm's choices for the two periods separately. We first examine the second-period choices $L_{\theta 2}, L_{y2}$, and then move on to the first-period ones $L_{\theta 1}, L_{y1}$. The reason is that in the second period, the problem is identical to a static one, which enables us to do interesting comparisons.

3.1 Second Period Analysis

From (5), since second-period choice variables $L_{\theta 2}$, L_{y2} do not enter first-period functions, (6c) and (6d) become, respectively,

$$\frac{\partial \Pi}{\partial L_{\theta 2}} = \frac{\partial \pi_2}{\partial L_{\theta 2}} = 0, \tag{6c'}$$

$$\frac{\partial \Pi}{\partial L_{y2}} = \frac{\partial \pi_2}{\partial L_{y2}} = 0. \tag{6d'}$$

Thus, if the firm is myopic and sees only one period, it also maximizes profits according to (6c′) and (6d′). Using (5), we can rewrite them as

$$\{(a+s_2-y_2^*)-2\tilde{\theta}_2 L_{y2}\}\alpha L_{y2}-(1-\alpha\sigma_2)w=0,$$
$$\{(a+s_2-y_2^*)-2\tilde{\theta}_2 L_{y2}\}\tilde{\theta}_2-w=0,$$

which can be combined to give

$$L_{y2} = \frac{(1-\alpha\sigma_2)\tilde{\theta}_2}{\alpha}, \tag{6c''}$$

$$-\frac{2(1-\alpha\sigma_2)\tilde{\theta}_2^3}{\alpha} + (a+s_2-y_2^*)\tilde{\theta}_2 - w = 0, \tag{6d''}$$

where $\tilde{\theta}_2$ is the total LS used in period 2, which is the sum of that carried over from period 1 and that produced in period 2, according to (3).

Condition (6c″) provides the relationship between output produced and LS used in the second period, in the equilibrium to maximize inter-temporal profits. Condition (6d″) gives the optimal solution to LS used in the second period, from which one sees that $\tilde{\theta}_2$ is independent of the depreciation parameter δ. Appendix 1 proves the existence and uniqueness of $\tilde{\theta}_2$. In Fig. 1, the optimal $\tilde{\theta}_2$ is shown at the right intersection of the concave function $g(\tilde{\theta}_2)$ (defined in (25) in Appendix 1) and the wage cost line w. Condition (6d″) implies

Lemma 1. *Second-period LS, $\tilde{\theta}_2$, is identical to the level chosen optimally in a static model.*

Lemma 1 says that the realized LS in the second period is fixed at the optimal level to maximize inter-temporal profits. In other words, the LS carried over from the first period does not affect $\tilde{\theta}_2$. Of course, it affects the LS actually produced in the second period θ_2. If the LS carryover is small, then the firm produces more LS in the second period to maintain $\tilde{\theta}_2$ at the optimal level. If the carryover is large, then it produces less in the second period.

It is straightforward to calculate the LS per worker in the second period:

$$\hat{\theta}_2 = \frac{\tilde{\theta}_2}{L_{y2}+L_{\theta 2}}. \tag{7a}$$

And using (3) we obtain

$$\frac{\partial \hat{\theta}_2}{\partial L_{\theta 1}} > 0. \tag{7b}$$

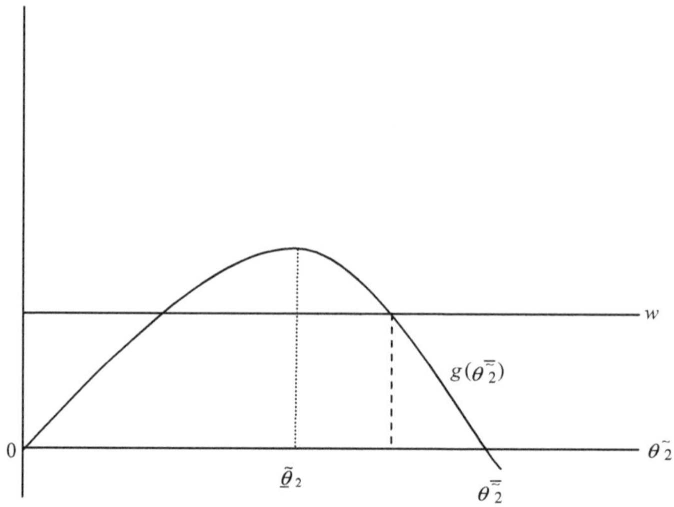

Fig. 1 Optimal $\tilde{\theta}_2$

Thus, we can state

Proposition 1. *LS maintained per worker in the second period is higher than that in a static setup.*

Proposition 1 contrasts with Lemma 1. While total LS in the second period, $\tilde{\theta}_2$, is identical to that in a static setup, as the depreciation rate decreases from $\delta = 1$ (i.e., LS carryover increases), $L_{\theta 2}$ can be reduced to maximize inter-temporal profits. Thus, LS per worker rises.

Combined with (6c$''$), Lemma 1 implies that first-period LS does not affect second-period output,

$$\frac{\partial y_2}{\partial L_{\theta 1}} = \frac{\partial y_2^*}{\partial L_{\theta 1}} = 0. \tag{8a}$$

Also, given the inter-temporal (3), Lemma 1 in turn implies that $L_{\theta 2}$ is lower than that chosen in a static model. That is, an increase in θ_1 reduces the labor input used to upgrade LS in period 2, $L_{\theta 2}$,

$$\frac{\partial L_{\theta 2}}{\partial L_{\theta 1}} < 0. \tag{8b}$$

3.2 First-Period Analysis

Now we come to the first period. First order conditions (6a) and (6b) can be expanded as

$$L_{y1} = \{[1 - \gamma(1-\delta)] - [\sigma_1 - \gamma(1-\delta)\sigma_2]\alpha\}\frac{\theta_1}{\alpha}, \tag{9a}$$

$$-\frac{2\theta_1^3}{\alpha}\{[1-\gamma(1-\delta)] - [\sigma_1 - \gamma(1-\delta)\sigma_2]\alpha\} + (a + s_1 - y_1^*)\theta_1 - w = 0. \tag{9b}$$

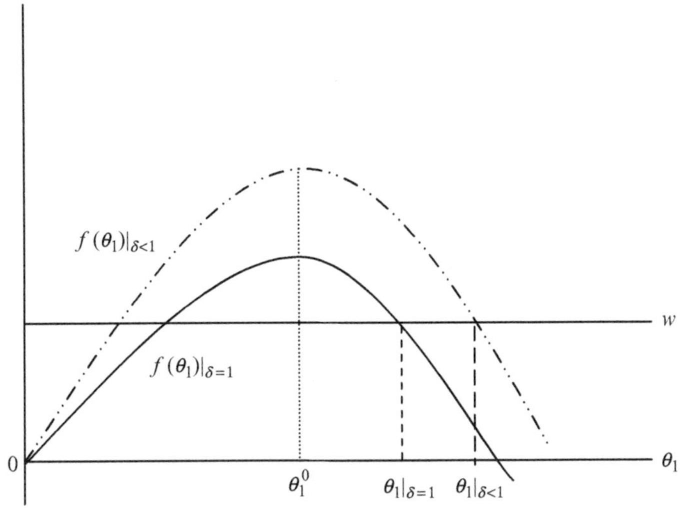

Fig. 2 Dynamic LS is higher

In a one-period model, $\delta = 1$, and condition (9a′) collapses to (6c″). However, because of the carryover effect in a two-period model, $\delta < 1$, and condition (9a′) says that the firm over produces LS in the first period, from the point of maximizing single-period profits.

Just as in (6d″), there exists one unique solution satisfying condition (9b′). Let us define the first two terms on the LHS of (9b′) to be

$$f(\theta_1) = -\frac{2\theta_1^3}{\alpha}\{[1-\gamma(1-\delta)] - [\sigma_1 - \gamma(1-\delta)\sigma_2]\alpha\} + (a + s_1 - y_1^*)\theta_1. \quad (10)$$

Figure 2 illustrates the situation. The static case corresponds to $\delta = 1$. When the carryover rate $1-\delta$ increases (i.e., δ decreases from $\delta = 1$), curve $f(\theta_1)$ shifts up, resulting in a higher θ_1. Further, LS per worker in the first period can be calculated as

$$\frac{\theta_1}{L_{y1} + L_{\theta 1}} = \frac{\alpha}{1 + L_{y1}/L_{\theta 1}}. \quad (11a)$$

Using (9a′) and (9b′), and differentiation yields,

$$\frac{\partial (L_{y1}/L_{\theta 1})}{\partial \delta} = (1 - \alpha\sigma_2)\gamma > 0. \quad (11b)$$

That is, as δ decreases from $\delta = 1$, the expression in (11a) increases.

Summing up, we can establish

Proposition 2. *The total LS and LS per worker in the first period are both higher than in a static setup.*

Combining Lemma 1, Propositions 1 and 2, it is clear that both the average total LS and the LS per worker maintained across periods are higher in a dynamic setup than in a static one. It is worthy of noting that if a firm behaves myopically and sees only one period, then it maximizes single-period profits. As a result, it under-produces LS compared to when it is forward looking.

3.3 Nash Equilibrium

We have so far considered only the home firm's activities, assuming given those of the foreign firm. The foreign firm's response can be analyzed analogously for given outputs of the home firm. Take the second period as an example, from (6c″), (6d″), and (2), we obtain the best response curve of the home firm in $y_2 \sim y_2^*$ plane as

$$y_2(y_2^*)|_{\text{home}} : -2A^{-\frac{1}{2}}(y_2)^{\frac{3}{2}} + (a + s_2 - y_2^*)A^{-\frac{1}{2}}(y_2)^{\frac{1}{2}} - w = 0. \quad (12a)$$

We prove in Appendix 1 that it is downward sloped and concave to the origin. Symmetrically, we have the foreign firm's best response curve as

$$y_2^*(y_2)|_{\text{foreign}} : -2A^{-\frac{1}{2}}(y_2^*)^{\frac{3}{2}} + (a + s_2^* - y_2)A^{-\frac{1}{2}}(y_2^*)^{\frac{1}{2}} - w = 0, \quad (12b)$$

in $y_2 \sim y_2^*$ plane, which has the same shape as the home firm's. These two best response curves are depicted in Fig. 3, where the Nash equilibrium is determined at the intersection of the two curves.

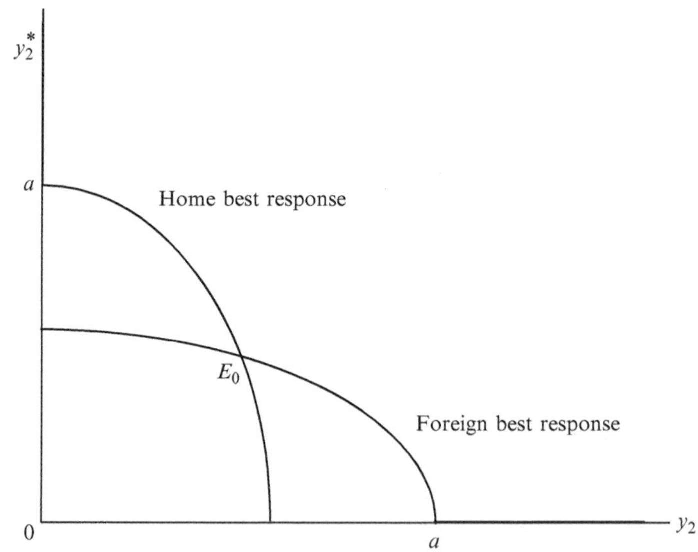

Fig. 3 $\delta = 1, w = 0$

In Appendix 2, we prove the existence, uniqueness, and stability of the Nash Equilibrium in the second period.[4] Similar analysis also applies to the first-period game.

3.4 Comparative Statics

Total differentiation of (6d″) yields, respectively,

$$\frac{\partial \tilde{\theta}_2}{\partial s_2} > 0, \tag{13a}$$

$$\frac{\partial \tilde{\theta}_2}{\partial \sigma_2} > 0. \tag{13b}$$

Conditions (13a) and (13b) say that an increase in either home output subsidy or LS subsidy in the second period raises home LS in the same period. Alternatively, for given $\alpha$and w, an increase in s_2 or σ_2 increases the value of function $g(\tilde{\theta}_2)$ in Appendix 1, which leads to a higher $\tilde{\theta}_2$. Combined with (6c″), it implies that both subsidies raise the home production of the final output. These are illustrated by an upward shift of the home firm's best response curve in Fig. 4, moving the equilibrium from point E_0 to E_s.

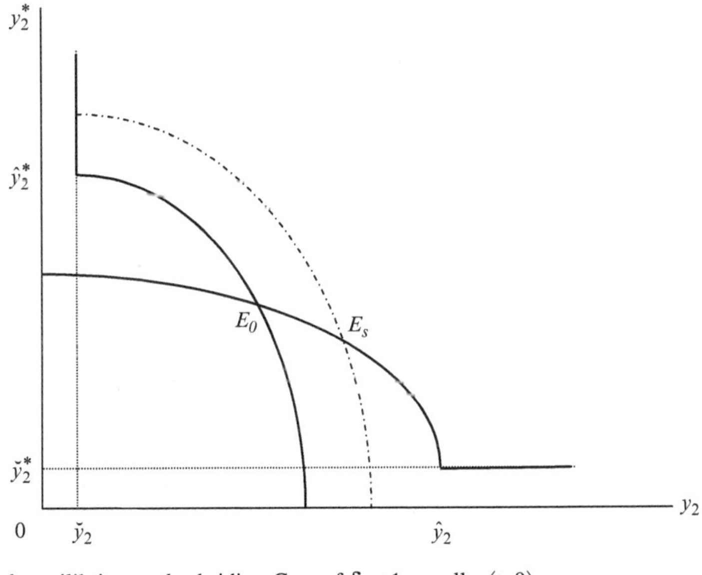

Fig. 4 Nash equilibrium and subsidies. Case of $\delta < 1$, small $w(>0)$

[4] The existence, uniqueness, and stability of the Nash equilibrium in $\tilde{\theta}_2 \sim \tilde{\theta}_2^*$ plane can be proved analogously.

Total differentiation of (9b′) yields, respectively,

$$\frac{\partial \theta_1}{\partial s_1} > 0, \tag{14a}$$

$$\frac{\partial \theta_1}{\partial \sigma_1} > 0, \tag{14b}$$

$$\frac{\partial \theta_1}{\partial \sigma_2} < 0, \tag{14c}$$

$$\frac{\partial \theta_2}{\partial \sigma_1} < 0, \tag{14d}$$

$$\frac{\partial \theta_2}{\partial s_1} < 0. \tag{14e}$$

In deriving the above, we have used the second order condition,

$$\frac{\partial^2 \pi_1}{(\partial L_{\theta 1})^2} \frac{\partial^2 \pi_1}{(\partial L_{y1})^2} - \left(\frac{\partial^2 \pi_1}{\partial L_{\theta 1} \partial L_{y1}} \right)^2 > 0,$$

which is equivalent to $\frac{\partial f(\theta_1)}{\partial \theta_1} > 0$.

The interpretations of conditions (14a) and (14b) are similar to (13a) and (13b). Basically, an increase in either home output subsidy or LS subsidy raises home LS in the same period, leading to a higher home final output. Foreign subsidies would have opposite effects on home variables in the same period. In Fig. 2, an increase in either s_1 or σ_1 causes curve $f(\theta_1)$ to shift up, resulting in a higher θ_1, whereas an increase in σ_2 does the opposite.

Condition (14c) states that an increase in home LS subsidy in the second period reduces home LS in the first period, because the firm expects to receive subsidy in the second period, and thus it under-produces LS in the first period. This in turn reduces home output but raises foreign output in the first period.

Next, we are interested in how first-period subsidies affect second-period variables. Condition (14d) says that first-period subsidy on LS reduces second-period production of LS. Even though an increase in first-period subsidy does not affect the total LS used in the second period $\tilde{\theta}_2$ according to Lemma 1, LS produced in the second period θ_2 must fall, because an increase in σ_1 raises θ_1 in (14b). And the same applies to condition (14e).

It then follows that by Lemma 1, (14d), and (14e), the home firm gains in the second period by saving on $L_{\theta 2}$. That is, the home firm's profit increases, even though its output remains unaffected by first-period subsidies.

How do first-period home subsidies affect second-period foreign variables? We already know that foreign LS and output fall as a consequence of home subsidies in either form in the first period. This in turn leads to a lower foreign LS that is carried over in the second period. Even though foreign output is not changed, the foreign firm must input more $L^*_{\theta 2}$ to maintain an optimal LS. Thus, cost increases and profit falls in the second period.

In summary, the comparative static results above lead to

Proposition 3. *First-period home subsidy on either output or LS increases (decreases) second-period home (foreign) profits.*

4 Optimal Subsidies

The previous sections have completed solving the firm's inter-temporal problem. In this section, we investigate optimal subsidies. To preserve the simplicity and clarity of the model, we assume that the foreign government does not change its policies, and only the home government chooses optimal subsidies on LS and outputs, for both periods, respectively. We are interested in whether it is better to subsidize output or LS production; whether to subsidize in the first period or in the second period; and comparing dynamic subsidies with static ones.

Before deriving the home government's objective function, note that from conditions (9a′) and (9b′), we can obtain, respectively

$$y_1 = y_1(s_1, \sigma_1, \sigma_2; y_1^*), \tag{9a$'$}$$

$$L_{\theta 1} = L_{\theta 1}(s_1, \sigma_1, \sigma_2; y_1^*); \quad \theta_1 = \theta_1(s_1, \sigma_1, \sigma_2; y_1^*). \tag{9b$'$}$$

Thus, government subsidy on LS for the second period affects the firm's choices in the first period. This leads to the possibility of time inconsistency across periods. To be more specific, the home government may not commit to the promised second-period policy at the end of the first period. To avoid this problem, we adopt Markov sub-game perfect equilibrium as our equilibrium concept. That is, we use backward induction.

Since final sales of the good are in a third-country market, the home country's welfare is the sum of profits in the two periods, subtracted by the sum of subsidy costs. However, Markov sub-game perfect equilibrium requires that we first look at the welfare in the second period only, which is the home firm's profit minus subsidy costs in the second period; that is,

$$\begin{aligned}\Phi_2(s_2(s_1,\sigma_1);\sigma_2(s_1,\sigma_1);s_1,\sigma_1) \equiv\ & \pi_2(s_2,\sigma_2;L_{\theta 2}(s_2,\sigma_2);L_{y2}(s_2,\sigma_2)) \\ & -(s_2 y_2 + \sigma_2 w \theta_2).\end{aligned} \tag{15}$$

In the subgame in the second period, the home government maximizes (15) with respect to s_2 and σ_2, given s_1 and σ_1. Differentiation yields

$$\frac{\partial \Phi_2}{\partial s_2} = \frac{\partial \pi_2}{\partial s_2} + \frac{\partial \pi_2}{\partial y_2^*}\frac{\partial y_2^*}{\partial s_2} - \left(y_2 + s_2\frac{\partial y_2}{\partial s_2} + \sigma_2 w\,\frac{\partial \theta_2}{\partial s_2}\right), \tag{16a}$$

$$\frac{\partial \Phi_2}{\partial \sigma_2} = \frac{\partial \pi_2}{\partial \sigma_2} + \frac{\partial \pi_2}{\partial L_{\theta 1}}\frac{\partial L_{\theta 1}}{\partial \sigma_2} + \frac{\partial \pi_2}{\partial y_2^*}\frac{\partial y_2^*}{\partial \sigma_2} - \left(w\theta_2 + s_2\,\frac{\partial y_2}{\partial \sigma_2} + \sigma_2 w\,\frac{\partial \theta_2}{\partial \sigma_2}\right). \tag{16b}$$

In deriving the above, we have used (3), conditions (6c″), (6d″), and (9a′) and (9b′). Equating (16a) and (16b) to zero results in the following first order conditions:

$$-\left\{\sigma_2 w\,\frac{\partial\theta_2}{\partial s_2}+s_2\,\frac{\partial y_2}{\partial s_2}+y_2\,\frac{\partial y_2^*}{\partial y_2}\frac{\partial y_2}{\partial s_2}\right\}=0, \tag{16a$'$}$$

$$\frac{\partial\pi_2}{\partial L_{\theta 1}}\frac{\partial L_{\theta 1}}{\partial\sigma_2}-\left\{\sigma_2 w\,\frac{\partial\theta_2}{\partial\sigma_2}+s_2\,\frac{\partial y_2}{\partial\sigma_2}+y_2\,\frac{\partial y_2^*}{\partial\sigma_2}\frac{\partial y_2}{\partial\sigma_2}\right\}=0. \tag{16b$'$}$$

Conditions (16a′) and (16b′) give the equilibrium levels of (s_2,σ_2) as implicit functions of (s_1,σ_1), such that the following holds: $s_2\equiv s_2(s_1,\sigma_1)$, $\sigma_2\equiv\sigma_2(s_1,\sigma_1)$.

Some explanations are in order. Condition (16a′) is identical to the case of static subsidies, implying that the optimal subsidy on output in the second period is equal to the static one.

To analyze (16b′), let us first obtain

$$\frac{\partial\pi_1}{\partial L_{\theta 1}}<0, \tag{17a}$$

$$\frac{\partial\pi_2}{\partial L_{\theta 1}}>0. \tag{17b}$$

Conditions (17a) and (17b) are distortion effects of marginal profits of LS investments. They arise because the firm over-invests in θ_1, which can be reused in period two.

Now we go back to condition (16b′). The term in the curled brackets is identical to the condition determining the optimal static subsidy on LS. The term before that is negative, using condition (17b) and (14d). It captures a cross-period tradeoff effect: raising second-period LS subsidy decreases first period LS, which in turn reduces second-period profit by lowering the carryover of LS in the first period. The home government takes these into consideration and chooses a lower LS subsidy in period 2.

From the above discussions, conditions (16a′) and (16b′) give rise to

Proposition 4. *In a dynamic setup, the second-period subsidy on output (LS) is identical to (lower than) the static subsidy.*

Next we move on to the first period. Using $s_2\equiv s_2(s_1,\sigma_1),\sigma_2\equiv\sigma_2(s_1,\sigma_1)$, the government's objective function in the first period can be written as

$$\Phi=\pi_1(s_1,\sigma_1;L_{\theta 1},L_{y1},y_1^*)-(s_1y_1+\sigma_1 w\theta_1)+\gamma\Phi_2(s_2(s_1,\sigma_1),\sigma_2(s_1,\sigma_1);s_1,\sigma_1). \tag{18}$$

Differentiation with respect to s_1 yields

$$\frac{\partial\Phi}{\partial s_1}=\frac{\partial\pi_1}{\partial s_1}+\frac{\partial\pi_1}{\partial L_{\theta 1}}\frac{\partial L_{\theta 1}}{\partial s_1}+\frac{\partial\pi_1}{\partial y_1^*}\frac{\partial y_1^*}{\partial s_1}-y_1-s_1\,\frac{\partial y_1}{\partial s_1}-\sigma_1 w\,\frac{\partial\theta_1}{\partial s_1}+\gamma\,\frac{\partial\Phi_2}{\partial s_1}, \tag{19a}$$

in deriving which we have used the envelope theorem, $\frac{\partial \pi_1}{\partial L_{y1}} = \frac{\partial \Phi_2}{\partial s_2} = \frac{\partial \Phi_2}{\partial \sigma_2} = 0$, and Lemma 1, which implies $\frac{\partial y_2^*}{\partial s_1} = \frac{\partial y_2}{\partial s_1} = 0$. Similarly, differentiating (18) with respect to σ_1 yields

$$\frac{\partial \Phi}{\partial \sigma_1} = \frac{\partial \pi_1}{\partial \sigma_1} + \frac{\partial \pi_1}{\partial L_{\theta 1}} \frac{\partial L_{\theta 1}}{\partial \sigma_1} + \frac{\partial \pi_1}{\partial y_1^*} \frac{\partial y_1^*}{\partial \sigma_1} - s_1 \frac{\partial y_1}{\partial \sigma_1} - w\theta_1 - \sigma_1 w \frac{\partial \theta_1}{\partial \sigma_1} + \gamma \frac{\partial \Phi_2}{\partial \sigma_1}. \tag{19b}$$

Letting (19a) and (19b) equal to zero, and invoking the comparative static results in (13a) to (14f), substitution gives rise to, respectively,

$$-\left\{\sigma_1 w \frac{\partial \theta_1}{\partial s_1} + s_1 \frac{\partial y_1}{\partial s_1} + y_1 \frac{\partial y_1^*}{\partial s_1}\right\} - \gamma \sigma_2 w \frac{\partial \theta_2}{\partial s_1} = 0, \tag{19a$'$}$$

$$-\left\{\sigma_1 w \frac{\partial \theta_1}{\partial \sigma_1} + s_1 \frac{\partial y_1}{\partial \sigma_1} + y_1 \frac{\partial y_1^*}{\partial \sigma_1}\right\} - \gamma \sigma_2 w \frac{\partial \theta_2}{\partial \sigma_1} = 0. \tag{19b$'$}$$

Condition (19a′) and (19b′) have one more term each than (16a′) does, that is, the term after the curled braces on the LHS of (19a′) and (19b′). They are positive, including the negative sign before them. They capture the following cross-period inter-temporal effect: an increase in first-period output or LS subsidy reduces government expenditure on second-period subsidy, which arises due to LS carryover to the second period. This effect tends to raise first-period subsidy on both output and LS. Therefore, we can state the following:

Proposition 5. *In a dynamic setup, the first-period subsidy is higher than the static subsidy either on output or LS.*

Propositions 4 and 5 imply that compared with static policies, in the present dynamic setup, the government over-subsidizes LS in the first period, but under-subsidizes it in the second period, because first-period LS can be carried over to the second period. In contrast, the government over-subsidizes output in the first period (which also increases second-period LS), but does *not* under-subsidize, instead maintain the static level of output subsidy in the second period, because output is not carried over to the second period. Thus, first-period subsidy is more efficient on LS than on output, because the former saves the cost of subsidy in the second period.

5 Minimum International Labor Standards

As proposed by labor unions, human rights groups, and other NGOs, suppose there is a minimum international labor standard that must be observed by both countries, that is, $\underline{\theta}_i > \theta$, $\underline{\theta}_i^* > \underline{\theta}$, for $i = 1,2$. For the minimum LS to be binding, it must be above the original one prevailing in the country with a lower technology of producing LS, α. Without loss of generality, suppose that it is the foreign country. Since $\alpha > \alpha^*$, then $L_\theta < L_\theta^*$. That is, the foreign country must devote more resources to improve LS than the home country.

We consider the simplest case, namely that the minimum international LS is binding only in the foreign country. Also, since Propositions 1 and 2 imply that $\theta_1^* > \tilde{\theta}_2^*$ in equilibrium, we assume that the minimum LS $\underline{\theta}$ is slightly above $\tilde{\theta}_2^*$, such that

$$\theta_1^* > \underline{\theta} > \tilde{\theta}_2^* \quad \text{and} \quad \theta_1 > \tilde{\theta}_2 > \underline{\theta}. \tag{20}$$

Thus, given that the firm's optimal choices in the first period are made according to (9a′) and (9b′), $\underline{\theta}$ does not affect LS and other variables in the first period in the foreign country, and we can focus only on the second period. Using (6c″) and (6d″), it is immediate that

$$y_2^*(\underline{\theta}) > y_2^*(\tilde{\theta}_2^*) \quad \text{and} \quad y_2(\underline{\theta}) < y_2(\tilde{\theta}_2^*). \tag{21}$$

In other words, the final output of the foreign firm is increased while that of the home firm is reduced. Since the minimum LS is above the optimal level in the second period for the foreign firm, optimization results in

$$\pi_2^*(\underline{\theta}) < \pi_2^*(\tilde{\theta}_2^*). \tag{22a}$$

That is, the minimum LS lowers the foreign firm's profits in the second period, because it produces too much final output induced by the minimum LS. Analogously, the following holds for the home firm

$$\pi_2(\underline{\theta}) < \pi_2(\tilde{\theta}_2^*), \tag{22b}$$

because it now is forced to produce too little final output, by the output expansion of the foreign firm. Thus, we can state the following:

Proposition 6. *In a static setup, under the minimum LS given in (20), the foreign firm's final output and cost increase but profit falls. The home firm's profit also falls, because its final output is reduced to below the optimal level.*

6 Human Rights Concerns

Labor unions, human rights groups, other NGOs, and even governments in developed countries are also concerned about human rights and social justice in developing countries. Some even advocate for trade sanctions against countries that do not enforce a set of agreed LS. Following such popular claims, in this section, we suppose that government utility in the developed country increases if LS in the other country rises. To make the discussions relevant, we assume again Home is the developed country, whose objective function can now be modified as

$$\Psi = \Phi(s_1, \sigma_1; s_2(s_1, \sigma_1), \sigma_2(s_1, \sigma_1)) + \{h(\theta_1^*) + \gamma h(\tilde{\theta}_2^*)\}, \tag{23}$$

where Φ is given in (18), and $h(\theta)$ represents how foreign LS affects home government objectives, with $h' > 0,\ h'' < 0$. Note that Home LS does not enter (23) directly because LS in developed countries has reached a certain threshold level, enabling the government not to worry about it.

Again, invoking the concept of Markov sub-game perfect equilibrium, and using (16a′), (16b′), (19a′), and (19b′), the first order conditions to maximize (23) in the second period are obtained, respectively, as

$$\frac{\partial \Psi_2}{\partial s_2} = \frac{\partial \Phi_2}{\partial s_2} + \left(\gamma \frac{\partial \tilde{\theta}_2^*}{\partial s_2} + \frac{\partial \theta_1^*}{\partial s_2}\right) h' = 0, \tag{24a}$$

$$\frac{\partial \Psi_2}{\partial \sigma_2} = \frac{\partial \Phi_2}{\partial \sigma_2} + \left(\frac{\partial \theta_1^*}{\partial \sigma_2} + \gamma \frac{\partial \tilde{\theta}_2^*}{\partial \sigma_2}\right) h' = 0. \tag{24b}$$

And those in the first period are, respectively,

$$\frac{\partial \Psi}{\partial s_1} = \frac{\partial \Phi}{\partial s_1} + \left(\frac{\partial \theta_1^*}{\partial s_1} + \gamma \frac{\partial \tilde{\theta}_2^*}{\partial s_1}\right) h' = 0, \tag{24c}$$

$$\frac{\partial \Psi}{\partial \sigma_1} = \frac{\partial \Phi}{\partial \sigma_1} + \left(\frac{\partial \theta_1^*}{\partial \sigma_1} + \gamma \frac{\partial \tilde{\theta}_2^*}{\partial \sigma_1}\right) h' = 0, \tag{24d}$$

where

$$\frac{\partial \theta_1^*}{\partial s_1} = \frac{\partial \theta_1^*}{\partial y_1}\left\{\frac{\partial y_1}{\partial s_1} + \frac{\partial y_1}{\partial \sigma_2}\frac{\partial \sigma_2}{\partial s_1}\right\} < 0$$

and

$$\frac{\partial \theta_1^*}{\partial \sigma_1} = \frac{\partial \theta_1^*}{\partial y_1}\left\{\frac{\partial y_1}{\partial \sigma_1} + \frac{\partial y_1}{\partial \sigma_2}\frac{\partial \sigma_2}{\partial \sigma_1}\right\} < 0.$$

These first order conditions give rise to the following:

Proposition 7. *When the home government considers foreign LS (human rights) in its objective, (i) the optimal subsidies on outputs in both periods and the optimal subsidy on LS in the first period become lower; (ii) the optimal subsidy on LS in the second period also becomes lower if $\gamma \approx 1$ and the cross-period effect of the subsidy is lower than the within-period effect.*

Proof. We only need to examine the terms in the parentheses in (24a)–(24d).

(i) In conditions (24a), (24c), and (24d), the second terms in parentheses are all equal to zero by Lemma 1 and condition (9b″), that is, $\frac{\partial \theta_1^*}{\partial s_2} = 0$, $\frac{\partial \tilde{\theta}_2^*}{\partial s_1} = 0$, and $\frac{\partial \tilde{\theta}_2^*}{\partial \sigma_1} = 0$. Now we examine the first terms. In (24a), $\frac{\partial \theta_2^*}{\partial s_2} < 0$ because of $\frac{\partial \tilde{\theta}_2}{\partial s_2} > 0$, $\frac{\partial \tilde{\theta}_2^*}{\partial \tilde{\theta}_2} < 0$, and $\frac{\partial \theta_1^*}{\partial s_2} = 0$; In (24c) and (24d), as explained under them, $\frac{\partial \theta_1^*}{\partial s_1} < 0$ and $\frac{\partial \theta_1^*}{\partial \sigma_1} < 0$.

(ii) In (24b), the cross-period effect is $\frac{\partial \theta_1^*}{\partial \sigma_2} > 0$, because $\frac{\partial \theta_1}{\partial \sigma_2} < 0$ and $\frac{\partial \theta_1^*}{\partial \theta_1} < 0$ hold. However, the within-period effect is $\frac{\partial \tilde{\theta}_2^*}{\partial \sigma_2} < 0$. These two effects work against each other. Under the conditions that $\gamma \approx 1$ and that the cross-period effect of the subsidy is lower than the within-period effect, then the sum of the terms in parentheses becomes negative.

In summary, incorporating foreign LS adds only negative terms to the first order conditions of the government's maximization problem, lowering the optimal subsidies.

Proposition 7 implies that if the home government cares about LS in a developing country, then home subsidies on either output or LS, in either period, would reduce foreign LS, eventually leading to a lower welfare in the home country.

7 Concluding Remarks

This chapter has modeled productive labor standards in a two-stage, two-period model of international oligopoly, where the home government chooses subsidies on LS and output first, and oligopolistic firms determine productions of LS and outputs later. Under-productive LS, "a race to the bottom" of LS does not arise. We showed that even in poor countries, maintaining a certain level of LS is beneficial to the workers, the firm, and national welfare there. The effect becomes even stronger in a dynamic setting where LS upgraded today contributes to production tomorrow. This result also implies that firms might behave myopically and under-produce LS if they see only one period instead of being forward looking, which partially explains why LS in developing countries might be lower.

We further demonstrated that a minimum international LS directly affecting the less efficient firm may lower the profits of the rival firm also, because the minimum LS forces the less efficient firm to expand output, which squeezes the market share of the rival firm. With inter-temporal LS carryovers, first-period optimal subsidies are more efficient on LS than on output. If the home government cares about LS (or human rights) in the foreign country, then it is better not to provide home subsidies on either LS or output, because such subsidies reduce foreign LS. We hope these findings can help to shed light on the current debate on international LS.

We have assumed that firms compete in quantity in the goods market. They could also compete in prices. It is well known that under-price competition, prices are lower and outputs higher under-price competition than under-quantity competition (see for instance, Cheng 1985), and that export taxes rather than subsidies may be called for (Eaton and Grossman 1986).

A very interesting extension of the model would be to allow labor turnover and migration between firms. Then LS upgraded in one firm benefits other firms. In this case, we conjecture that the equilibrium LS chosen by firms falls. In addition, we have adopted a simple, two-period model to gain intuitive insights. A more general setup would be a multi-period model of differential games, which could yield new insights. These represent fruitful avenues for future research.

Appendix 1

Existence and Uniqueness of $\tilde{\theta}_2$

In this Appendix, we prove that given any y_2^*, there exists only one optimal $\tilde{\theta}_2 > 0$. From (6d″), we can define

$$g(\tilde{\theta}_2) \equiv -2A\tilde{\theta}_2^3 + (a+s_2-y_2^*)\tilde{\theta}_2, \quad \text{for} \quad \tilde{\theta}_2 > 0,\, A = \alpha^{-1}(1-\alpha\sigma_2). \qquad (24)$$

This is a concave function with its positive zero-point at $\bar{\tilde{\theta}}_2 = \sqrt{(a+s_2-y_2^*)/2A}$ (see Fig. 1). The function reaches maximum at $\underline{\tilde{\theta}}_2 = \sqrt{(a+s_2-y_2^*)/6A}$. Thus, for any wage satisfying $0 \le w \le -2A\underline{\tilde{\theta}}_2^3 + (a+s_2-y_2^*)\underline{\tilde{\theta}}_2$, there are two solutions of (6d″) positioned in $[0, \underline{\tilde{\theta}}_2]$ and $[\underline{\tilde{\theta}}_2, \bar{\tilde{\theta}}_2]$, respectively. However, the first one is ruled out by the second order conditions. Specifically, $\partial^2\pi_2/(\partial L_{\theta 2})^2 < 0$ and $\partial^2\pi_2/(\partial L_{y2})^2 < 0$ always hold, but

$$\frac{\partial^2\pi_2}{(\partial L_{\theta 2})^2}\frac{\partial^2\pi_2}{(\partial L_{y2})^2} - \left(\frac{\partial^2\pi_2}{\partial L_{\theta 2}\partial L_{y2}}\right)^2 = (2\alpha\tilde{\theta}_2 L_{y2})^2 - \alpha^2\left[(a+s_2-y_2^*) - 4\alpha\tilde{\theta}_2 L_{y2}\right]^2 > 0$$

holds only for $\tilde{\theta}_2$ in $[\underline{\tilde{\theta}}_2, \bar{\tilde{\theta}}_2]$. That is, there is only one optimal $\tilde{\theta}_2$ satisfying (6d″), which is when curve $g(\tilde{\theta}_2)$ crosses the horizontal wage line on the right.

The existence and uniqueness of θ_1 can be proven in a similar fashion.

Appendix 2

Best Response and Nash Equilibrium

The home firm's best response is given in (12a). And y_2 is bounded by

$$y_2 \subset \left[\frac{a+s_2-y_2^*}{6}, \frac{a+s_2-y_2^*}{2}\right],$$

which is identical to

$$\tilde{\theta}_2 \in \left[\underline{\tilde{\theta}}_2, \bar{\tilde{\theta}}_2\right].$$

Differentiation yields

$$\frac{\mathrm{d}y_2}{\mathrm{d}y_2^*} = \frac{2y_2}{\Delta} < 0 \text{ and } \frac{\mathrm{d}^2 y_2}{(\mathrm{d}y_2^*)^2} = \frac{6y_2[(a+s_2-y_2^*) - 2y_2]}{\Delta^3} < 0,$$

where

$$\Delta = a + s_2 - y_2^* - 6y_2 < 0.$$

Therefore, we obtain a downward sloping, concave-to-origin best response curve within its bounds.

Next, we examine the Nash equilibrium. There are basically two cases to be considered.

(i) $\delta = 1$, $w = 0$. In this case, the home firm's best response curve is concave-to-origin for $y_2^* \leq a + s_2$. The concaved portion and straight portion are connected at $(0, a + s_2)$, which is depicted in Fig. 3.[5] Analogously, similar first order conditions to (6c″) and (6d″) exist for the foreign firm, from which we can draw the best rsesponse curves of both firms in output space. The intersection of these curves determines the Nash equilibrium.

(ii) $\delta < 1, w > 0$. In this case, LS produced in the first period is carried over to the second period. For a sufficiently small w, continuous best response curves are still available (Fig. 4). The difference from case (i) is that with LS carryovers, the home best response curve reaches a vertical line $\breve{y}_2 = A[(1-\delta)\theta_1]^2$ rather than the vertical axis. To see this, given $p \geq 0$ by the demand function, we must have $y_2^* \leq a$, leading to $y_2 > 0$ for any y_2^* within its bounds.

Continuity, concavity, and the relative position of the two best response curves in Fig. 3 reveal that a unique, stable Nash equilibrium exists in the present model. When the LS carryover is small, the relative position of the two best response curves in Fig. 4 is similar to that in Fig. 3. That is, a unique, stable Nash equilibrium still exists.

Finally, the existence, uniqueness, and stability of the Nash equilibrium in period 1 can be investigated analogously.

Acknowledgment We are grateful to E. Dinopoulos, T. Haruyama, Y. Ichino, P. Segerstrom, K. Shimomura, and Y. Takarada for detailed comments, and to participants of seminars at Kobe University, the Japanese International Economics Association's Kansai Seminar (July 2004) and the Hitotsubashi International Economics Workshop (August 2004) for helpful comments. The usual disclaimer applies.

References

Bagwell K, Staiger RW (2001) The WTO as a mechanism for securing market access property rights: implications for global labor and environmental issues. J Econ Perspect 15(3):69–88

Basu K (1999) International labor standards and child labor. Challenge 42(5):80–93

Basu K, Van PH (1998) The economics of child labor. Am Econ Rev 88(3):412–427

[5] For any y_2^* satisfying $w > g(\sqrt{(a+s_2-y_2^*)/6A})$, the best response of the home firm jumps to $y_2 = 0$ when $w = g(\sqrt{(a+s_2-y_2^*)/6A})$, and stays there thereafter. Similarly, for $\delta < 1$ and relatively large w > 0, such jumps are possible. Even if jumping occurs, the existence of Nash equilibrium is still ensured if w is not too large.

Benchekroun H (2003) Unilateral production restrictions in a dynamic duopoly. J Econ Theory 111(2):214–239

Bhagwati J (1995) Trade liberalization and 'fair trade' demands: addressing environmental and labor standards issues. World Econ 18:745–759

Brander JA, Spencer BJ (1985) Export subsidies and international market share rivalry. J Int Econ 18(1–2):83–100

Brown DK (2001) Labor standards, where do they belong on the international trade agenda? J Econ Perspect 15(3):89–112

Brown DK, Deardorff AV, Stern RM (1996) International labor standards and trade: a theoretical analysis. In: Bhagwati J, Hudec R (eds) Fair trade and harmonization: prerequisites for free trade? Economic analysis, vol 1. MIT Press, Cambridge, pp 227–280

Cheng L (1985) Comparing Bertrand and Cournot equilibria: a geometric approach. Rand J Econ 16:146–152

Eaton J, Grossman G (1986) Optimal trade and industrial policy under oligopoly. Q J Econ 101:383–406

Elliot KA (2000) Preferences for workers? Worker Rights and the US Generalized System of Preference. Peterson Institute, Washington DC

Hussain M, Maskus K (2003) Child labor use and economic growth: an econometric analysis. World Econ 26(7):993–1017

Itaya J-I (1995) Dynamic tax incidence in a finite horizon model. Publ Fin 50(2):246–266

Jafarey S, Lahiri S (2002) Will trade sanctions reduce child labor? The role of credit markets. J Dev Econ 68(1):137–156

Martin WJ, Maskus K (2001) The economics of core labor standards: implications for global trade policy. Rev Int Econ 9(2):317–328

Mino K (1986) Optimality, credibility, and time consistency: alternative solutions in a dynamic policy game. Hiroshima Econ Rev 10(2):59–77

Ohkawa T, Shimomura K (1995) Dynamic effects of subsidies on outputs and r&d in an international export rivalry model. In: Chang W, Katayama S (eds) Imperfect competition in international trade. Kluwer, Dordrecht, pp 175–184

Ranjan P (2001) Credit constraints and the phenomenon of child labor. J Dev Econ 64:81–102

Robert S (1999) Labor standards and international trade in INTAL. Integr Trade 3(7–8):15–38

Rodrik D (1996) Labor standards in international trade: Do they matter and what do we do about them? In: Lawrence R et al (eds) Emerging agenda for global trade: high stakes for developing countries. Overseas Development Council, Washington DC

Spencer BJ, Brander JA (1983) International R & D rivalry and industrial strategy. Rev Econ Stud 50(4):707–722

Srinivasan TN (1995) International trade and labor standards. In: Van Dyck P, Faher G (eds) Challenges to the new world trade organization. Martin's Nijhoff, Amsterdam

Tanaka Y (1994) Export subsidies under dynamic duopoly. Eur Econ Rev 38(5):1139–1151

Quotas Under Dynamic Bertrand Competition

Kaz Miyagiwa(✉) and Yuka Ohno

Abstract We present a new model of dynamic Bertrand competition, where a quota is treated as an intertemporal constraint, rather than as a capacity constraint. The firm under a quota then can still vary the rates of exports over time, provided that its annual sales do not exceed the quota. We show that a quota results in higher prices than a tariff of equal imports. We also find that firms never play mixed strategies in equilibrium, which contrasts from the result of a one-shot game, in which the only equilibrium under a quota is in mixed strategies (Krishna 1989).

1 Introduction

This chapter presents a new model of dynamic Bertrand competition under a quota. The model reflects the idea that an exporter facing a quota behaves quite differently from a firm facing a capacity constraint. A quota specifies how much a firm is allowed to export in, say, 1 year. Thus, a firm can still vary the rates of exports within the year as long as total sales do not exceed the quota. In contrast, a capacity-constrained firm is subject to the production limit per unit of time, say, due to the plant size, and therefore does not face a dynamic constraint like a firm under a quota. This distinction between a quota and a capacity constraint is lost in the literature, however. Practically every dynamic model of oligopoly examining the effect of quotas, no doubt influenced by the capacity constraint literature (Kreps and Sheinkman 1983), treats a quota as a capacity constraint.

The objective of this chapter is therefore to explore the nature of a quota as a dynamic quantity constraint. To that end, we consider duopolistic competition between a foreign firm and a domestic firm in the domestic market during a given period. Firms produce differentiated goods, and choose prices continuously during

K. Miyagiwa
The Institute of Social and Economic Research, Osaka University, 6–1 Mihogaoka, Ibaraki, Osaka 567–0047, Japan, e-mail: kmiyagiwa@gmail.com

T. Kamihigashi and L. Zhao (eds.) *International Trade and Economic Dynamics – Essays in Memory of Koji Shimomura.*

this period to maximize total profits. In addition, the foreign firm is subject to a quota during that period. We solve this model for a subgame-perfect equilibrium.

Our analysis makes two main contributions to the literature. A first is to the literature on the relative effect of tariffs and quotas. It is well know that tariffs and quotas are equivalent under perfect competition in the sense that replacement of a tariff with an equal-import quota leaves the domestic price intact. Over the last quarter-century the validity of this proposition, however, has been examined under various forms of market structure.[1] In particular, Itoh and Ono (1982, 1984), Harris (1985), and Krishna (1989) showed for Bertrand duopoly that the quota results in a higher domestic price than the tariff. In contrast, Hwang and Mai (1988) reaffirmed the equivalence for Cuournot duopoly.

The relative effect of tariffs and quotas has also been examined in dynamic contexts. Rotemberg and Saloner (1989) analyzed a collusive equilibrium in a repeated-game setting and found that a quota results in a lower domestic price than a tariff of equal imports. The reason for this surprising result is that the quota prevents the foreign firm from punishing the home firm as harshly as the tariff when the latter cheats. Hence, the equilibrium price must be set lower to curb the home firm's temptation to cheat. Dockner and Haug (1990), considering a dynamic Cournot model with slow price adjustment, showed that a quota results in higher prices than the quota. However, why the market remains out of equilibrium in the first place is not explained. Miyagiwa and Ohno (1995,1999) re-examined the infant-industry argument for protection, showing that a quota generally delays adoption or innovation of new technology relative to a tariff. All these authors assumed the quota binding at each point in time, thereby ignoring the possibility of intra-period variations in prices, which is the focus of this chapter. The exception is the work of Miyagiwa and Ohno (2001). Treating quotas as dynamic constraints and examining the intra-period variations in prices and output for Cournot duopoly, they found that the equilibrium price is higher under the quota, thereby showing the static result of Hwang and Mai (1988) does not extend to a dynamic setting.

A second contribution this chapter makes to the literature concerns the fact that models of oligopoly under a quota may not possess equilibria in pure strategies. A basic reference is Krishna (1989), who showed that for differentiated Bertrand competition, the only Nash equilibrium under the quota is in mixed strategies, with the domestic firm randomizing between two prices and the foreign firm playing a pure strategy. In repeated-game setting, Rotemberg and Saloner (1989) also showed that the stage game has homogeneous-goods Bertrand firms playing mixed strategies in equilibrium. Furthermore, the absence of pure-strategy equilibrium under quotas is not unique to Bertrand competition, however. Reitzes and Grawe (1994) showed that Cournot duopoly has the equilibrium only in mixed strategies under market-share quotas, that is, when the foreign firm is constrained not to exceed the prescribed fraction of sales in the domestic market.

The logic underling these results cannot be faulted. Some researchers have nonetheless expressed skepticism about mixed-strategy equilibriums. The following

[1] See, for example, Helpman and Krugman (1989) and Brander (1995) for surveys of early work.

statement by Brander (1995, p. 1,436) summarizes this sentiment: "The value of Krishna is not so much that it is likely to be a literal description of an actual outcome. The chapter's contribution is that it focuses attention on the idea that a VER (and, by extension, any trade policy instrument) can have important effects through the effects on imperfectly competitive rivalries between firms." Our model throws light on this issue. The above-mentioned models possess no pure-strategy Nash equilibrium under the quota because the game is static (Krishna 1989; Reitzes and Grawe 1994) or equivalently a quota is binding at every instant (Rotemberg and Saloner 1989). Using Krishna's (1989) model as a benchmark, we show that, when a quota serves as a dynamic constraint, firms never play mixed strategies.

Section 2 reviews the Krishna model, which serves as a benchmark. Section 3 sets out the dynamic Bertrand model, showing the absence of mixed strategy equilibrium under a quota. Section 4 presents additional properties of the equilibrium, and shows that normally a quota leads to higher price trajectories than the equal-import tariff. Section 5 reconsiders the facilitating nature of quotas. Concluding remarks are in Sect. 6.

2 The One-Shot Price-Setting Game Under the Quota

This section provides a quick review of the Krishna (1989) model, pointing out its essential features that will be useful in Sect. 3. The Krishna model is an application of the standard differentiated-goods Bertrand duopoly model, where a domestic and a foreign firm play a one-shot price-setting game in the domestic market. Let P and p denote the prices of the domestic and the foreign good, respectively. Write the demand function for the domestic and the foreign good as $X(P,p)$ and $x(P,p)$, respectively. Assume that demands are downward sloping ($X_P < 0$ and $x_p < 0$), and goods are substitutes ($X_p > 0$ and $x_P > 0$), where the subscripts denote partial derivatives.

Suppose that free trade prevails. The foreign firm takes P as given and chooses p to maximize the profit:

$$v(P,p) \equiv px(P,p) - c[x(P,p)],$$

where $c(\cdot)$ is the foreign firm's cost function, with $c' > 0$ and $c'' \geq 0$ (primes denote derivatives). Similarly, the domestic firm takes p as given and chooses P to maximize the profit:

$$V(P,p) \equiv PX(P,p) - C[X(P,p)],$$

where $C(\cdot)$ is the domestic firm's cost function, with $C' > 0$ and $C'' \geq 0$. The first-order condition

$$v_p(P,p) = x(P,p) + px_p(P,p) - c'[x(P,p)]x_p(P,p) = 0 \tag{1}$$

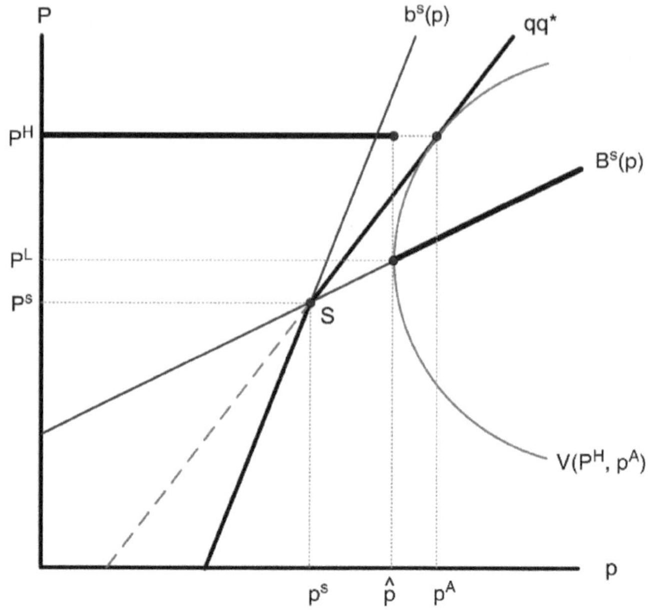

Fig. 1

implicitly defines the foreign firm's best-response function, $p = b^s(P)$. The domestic firm's best-response function, $P = B^s(p)$, obtains analogously from the first-order condition:

$$V_P(P, p) = X(P, p) + PX_P(P, p) - C'[X(P, p)]X_P(P, p) = 0. \tag{2}$$

Assume that $v(P, p)$ is strictly concave in p and $V(P, p)$ is strictly concave in P so that the best-response functions are indeed "functions."

Solving the two best-response functions simultaneously yields the one-shot Nash equilibrium denoted by (P^s, p^s). (We call this the "static" Nash equilibrium later and use the superscript s to denote it). The best-response functions and the Nash equilibrium (P^s, p^s) under free trade are shown in Fig. 1. The best-response functions slope upward since prices are strategic complements as assumed by Krishna (1989). The intersection point S of the two best-response functions corresponds to the Nash equilibrium. The usual conditions are invoked to ensure the uniqueness of the equilibrium.[2] The equilibrium outputs and profits are readily obtained by substituting P^s and p^s into each firm's demand and objective functions. Let $X^s \equiv X(P^s, p^s)$ and $x^s \equiv x(P^s, p^s)$ denote, respectively, the domestic and the foreign firm's static equilibrium output.

[2] $|v_{pp}| > |v_{pP}|$ and $|V_{PP}| > |V_{Pp}|$ guarantee the equilibrium to be unique and stable.

Suppose the quota is set at $\tilde{q} = x^{\mathrm{s}}$, the equilibrium quantity of imports under free trade. The effect is seen in Fig. 1.[3] The curve qq^* represents the locus of P and p such that the demand for the foreign product just satisfies the quota; that is, $\tilde{q} = x(P, p)$. It necessarily goes though S. Given P, if the foreign firm charges a price less than the price that satisfies this equation, the demand for the foreign product exceeds the quota. But the foreign firm is not allowed to set a price below the price implied by the locus qq^*. Therefore, its best-response function consists of the part of qq^* to the right of the b^{s} schedule and the part of b^{s} below the locus qq^*, as indicated by the thick line with a distinct kink at the point S. The domestic firm's best-response function under the quota (also shown in bold) is not even continuous, consisting of the part of its original best-response curve B^{s} to the right of $\hat{p}$ and the horizontal line at P^{H} up to $\hat{p}$.

Since the two best-response functions do not intersect each other, there is no Nash equilibrium in pure strategies. However, there is a unique Nash equilibrium in which the domestic firm randomizes between P^{H} and P^{L} and the foreign firm charges $\hat{p}$. Since both P^{H} and P^{L} are higher than P^{s}, and $\hat{p}$ is higher than p^{s}, we conclude that the quota raises prices of both firms. This conclusion holds even when there is a tariff initially, and when the quota is set equal to the volume of imports under the tariff. That is, the quota raises prices of both the foreign and the domestic firm relative to the tariff.

Notice that, when the domestic firm chooses P^{H}, the demand for imports exceeds the quota, thereby creating a shortage of imported goods. This shortage is assumed to vanish through costless arbitrage among consumers. That is, consumers lucky enough to get the imports at $\hat{p}$ make profits by selling them at p^{A}, the market-clearing price. The effect on the domestic firm's demand therefore is exactly what it would be if the foreign firm charged p^{A} instead of $\hat{p}$, that is, the demand for the domestic good is given by $X(P^{\mathrm{H}}, p^{\mathrm{A}})$.

Notice also that, since the domestic firm randomizes between P^{H} and P^{L}, its profit from each action must be identical, as indicated by the iso-profit curve. Thus, the domestic firm earns a greater profit under the quota. The foreign firm's profit is also increased as the domestic firm raises its price.

3 The Quota as a Dynamic Constraint

3.1 Setup

We now consider the model of differentiated-goods Bertrand duopoly in an infinite-time setting, where time t flows continuously from zero to infinity. Divide the time set $[0, \infty)$ into infinitely many nonoverlapping unit intervals, called years, that is,

$$(0, \infty) = [0, 1) \cup [1, 2) \cup [2, 3) \cup \ldots$$

[3] Figure 1 duplicates Krishna's Fig. 3, where the quota is set at the free-trade level of imports.

$X[P(t),p(t)]$ and $x[P(t),p(t)]$ now denote instantaneous demand functions at time t. The demand functions are stationary over time. Finite reservation prices exist and quantities demanded are finite for all (p,P). The Markov-perfect equilibrium is used as the solution concept, and so the properties of the one-shot game are preserved.

Under free trade, firms choose prices simultaneously at each time to maximize profits over an infinite time horizon. Since there are no "state variables," the model is stationary in the sense that subgames starting at any $t \in [0,\infty)$ are identical. Therefore, the equilibrium outcome at any t is exactly the same as that in the one-shot Bertrand game. That is, in the Markov-perfect equilibrium the foreign firm produces x^{s} units and charges p^{s}, while the domestic firm produces X^{s} units and sells them at p^{s} at each $t \in [0,\infty)$.

3.2 Quotas

Suppose that the foreign firm is subject to an annual quota $\bar{q}$. Since a year is a unit interval, we can write the constraint facing the foreign firm as

$$\int_{\tau}^{\tau+1} x[P(t),p(t)]\,\mathrm{d}t \leq \bar{q}, \tag{3}$$

for all $\tau = 0,1,2,\ldots$. To make the analysis interesting, we assume that the quota is binding, that is, $\bar{q}$ is less than the total volume of exports under free trade:

$$\bar{q} \leq \int_{\tau}^{\tau+1} x^{\mathrm{S}}\,\mathrm{d}t.$$

The constraint (3) implies that how much more output the foreign firm can sell during the remainder of a given year depends on the total output it has sold to date in that year. Thus, the past sales become a "state variable" in the dynamic optimization problem facing the foreign firm. However, the foreign firm cannot usually carry the unused portion of the quota over to the following year. Then, by the property of Markov-perfect equilibrium, whatever happens during the year has no effect on the subgames beginning in the following or later years. This fact lets us focus on the first year, that is, $t \in [0,1)$.

Since we are interested in the subgame perfect equilibrium, we solve the model backward, using dynamic programming techniques. Suppose we are at a given time $z \in [0,1)$. Let $\mu(z)$ denote the foreign firm's total output up to a time $z < 1$, that is,

$$\mu(z) \equiv \int_{0}^{z} x(P(t),p(t))\,\mathrm{d}t.$$

Then, the maximum quantity the foreign firm is allowed to sell in the interval $[z, 1)$ is equal to $\bar{q} - \mu(z)$. Thus, the foreign firm's quantitative constraint at time z is written as

$$\int_z^1 x[P(t), p(t)]\,\mathrm{d}t \leq \bar{q} - \mu(z). \tag{4}$$

Subject to this constraint, the foreign firm takes $\mu(z)$ and $P(z)$ as given and chooses $p(t)$ for $t \in [z, 1)$ to maximize the sum of profits over the interval $[z, 1)$

$$\int_z^1 \mathrm{e}^{-rt}\left\{(p(t)x[P(t), p(t)] - c(x[P(t), p(t)])\right\}\mathrm{d}t.$$

where r is the instantaneous rate of interest. The domestic firm faces no quantitative restriction, so it takes $p(z)$ as given and chooses $P(t)$ to maximize the following intertemporal profit over $t \in [z, 1)$:

$$\int_z^1 \mathrm{e}^{-rt}\left\{P(t)X[P(t), p(t)] - C(X[P(t), p(t)])\right\}\mathrm{d}t.$$

3.3 Characterization of the Equilibrium under the Quota

We first prove the following proposition, which is useful in solving the model.

Proposition 1. *Both the firms play pure strategies at each $t \in [0, 1)$.*

Proof is by contradiction. Suppose that a mixed strategy is played at any time $t^0 \in [0, 1)$. When the quantitative restriction does not bind, strict concavity of the flow profit functions $V(P, p)$ and $v(P, p)$ implies that firms play pure strategies. Therefore, for firms to play mixed strategies at t^0, at least one firm must have a nonconcave flow profit function. Then the discussion developed in Sect. 2 leads to the following result.

Result. *When the quota binds at t^0, at a time $t \in [t^0, t^0 + \varepsilon]$, where $\varepsilon(>0)$ is arbitrarily small, the domestic firm randomizes between $\bar{P} \equiv P^{\mathrm{H}}(t^0)$ and $\underline{P} \equiv P_{\mathrm{L}}(t^0)$ while the foreign firm charges $\hat{p} \equiv \hat{p}(t^0)$. (Strict concavity of the profit function rules out other types of mixed-strategy equilibria).*

Let $\Omega(P, \hat{p}, t^0)$ denote the domestic firm's future profit when it charges the price P during $[t^0, t^0 + \varepsilon]$. When it randomizes between $\bar{P}$ and P, the domestic firm's future profits must be identical; that is, $\Omega(\bar{P}, \hat{p}, t^0) = \Omega(\underline{\mathrm{P}}, \hat{p}, t^0)$. We show that this is a contradiction.

Begin with the case in which the domestic firm charges $\bar{P}$ during $[t^0, t^0 + \varepsilon]$. Since the restriction is binding and consumer arbitrage takes place, the effect on the domestic firm's demand is exactly what it would be if the foreign firm charged some arbitrage price $p^{\mathrm{A}}(\geq \hat{p})$.[4] Thus, during the interval $[t^0, t^0+\varepsilon]$, the domestic firm makes the profit:

$$\int_{t^0}^{t^0+\varepsilon} \mathrm{e}^{-r(t-t^0)}\{\bar{P}X(\bar{P},p^{\mathrm{A}}) - C[X(\bar{P},p^{\mathrm{A}})]\}\,\mathrm{d}t = \varepsilon\{\bar{P}X(\bar{P},p^{\mathrm{A}}) - C[X(\bar{P},p^{\mathrm{A}})]\},$$

where we used the fact that for small ε

$$\int_{t}^{t+\varepsilon} f(z)\,\mathrm{d}z = f(t)\varepsilon.$$

Then, the foreign firm reaches the quantitative limit $\bar{q}$ by the time $t^0+\varepsilon$, and will make no more sales after that. This will allow the domestic firm to charge the monopoly price P^{m} for the rest of the year. The domestic firm therefore earns the monopoly profit for the rest of the year. Let $\Phi^{\mathrm{m}}(t^0+\varepsilon)$ denote the discounted sum of the monopoly profits earned in the interval $[t^0+\varepsilon, 1)$. Now, we can write the profit from charging $\bar{P}$ as

$$\Omega(\bar{P},\hat{p},t^0) = \varepsilon\{\bar{P}X(\bar{P},p^{\mathrm{A}}) - C[X(\bar{P},p^{\mathrm{A}})\} + \Phi^m(t^0+\varepsilon).$$

Consider next the case in which the domestic firm charges the low price $\underline{P}$ in $[t^0, t^0+\varepsilon]$. The domestic firm's profit during this short interval is given by

$$\varepsilon\{\underline{P}X(\underline{P},\hat{p}) - C[X(\underline{P},\hat{p}]\}.$$

In this case the foreign firm will not use up its quota by time $t^0+\varepsilon$, so will continue to engage in duopolistic competition for some time after $(t^0+\varepsilon)$. Let $\Phi(t^0+\varepsilon)$ denote the discounted sum of the profits to the domestic firm in the interval $[t^0+\varepsilon, 1)$. Then, the domestic firm's future profit is given by

$$\Omega(\underline{P},\hat{p},t^0) = \varepsilon(\underline{P}X(\underline{P},\hat{p}) - C[X(\underline{P},\hat{p})]\} + \Phi(t^0+\varepsilon).$$

Comparing the profits after $t^0+\varepsilon$, we have that

$$\Phi(t^0+\varepsilon) < \Phi^m(t^0+\varepsilon),$$

since $\Phi^{\mathrm{m}}(t^0+\varepsilon)$ sums up all the monopoly profits between $t^0+\varepsilon$ and 1.[5] Therefore, for ε arbitrarily small, we have

$$\Omega(\bar{P},\hat{p},t^0) > \Omega(\underline{P},\hat{p},t^0),$$

[4] The actual value of p^{A} is different from that in Sect. 2.

[5] The difference between $\Phi^{\mathrm{m}}(t^0+\varepsilon)$ and $\Phi(t^0+\varepsilon)$ may be small if the quota is used up shortly after $t^0+\varepsilon$ or if the rates of exports are low. However small, the difference, $\Phi^{\mathrm{m}}(t^0+\varepsilon) - \Phi(t^0+\varepsilon)$, does not vanish when ε goes to zero, which is sufficient to produce a desired contradiction.

implying that the domestic firm strictly prefers charging $\bar{P}$ to charging $\underline{P}$. But this contradicts the initial hypothesis that the domestic firm randomizes between $\bar{P}$ and $\underline{P}$ in the interval $[t^0, t^0 + \varepsilon]$. Since t^0 is arbitrary, this contradiction proves that the domestic firm does not randomize at $t \in [0, 1)$.[6]

To complete the proof, we must show that the quota is not used up at $t < 1$ in a pure-strategy equilibrium, either. To see this, suppose the contrary; that is, suppose that the foreign firm makes the final sale of x units at $t < 1$. Should it postpone the sale of one unit of output to $t + \varepsilon$ instead, the foreign firm would lose $p'(x)x + p(x) - c'(x)$ in profit at time t but would gain $p(0) - c'(0)$ at time $t + \varepsilon$. For an arbitrarily small ε, therefore, such postponement would always increase the foreign firm's intertemporal profit. The proof of Proposition 1 is now complete.

As we already noted, a mixed-strategy equilibrium outcome emerges only at the moment when the quota is all used up. But Proposition 1 says that a mixed-strategy outcome is never observed at $t < 1$. These two results lead to the next proposition.

Proposition 2. *In the equilibrium the foreign firm does not use up its quota before the end of the year. That is*

$$\mu(t) < \bar{q} \quad \textit{for all } t < 1$$

and

$$\lim_{[t \to 1]} \mu(t) = \bar{q}.$$

4 Equilibrium Paths under the Quota

Now we solve the model. Propositions 1 and 2 let us focus on a pure-strategy equilibrium. We use dynamic programming techniques to obtain a subgame-perfect equilibrium.[7]

Let $\tilde{P}[t; j, \mu(j)]$ and $\tilde{P}[t; j, \mu(j)]$ denote the equilibrium paths for the subgame starting at time j (<1) with the initial condition that the foreign firm has sold $\mu(j)(< \bar{q})$ between $[0, j)$. Then the intertemporal equilibrium profits for this subgame are given by

$$\Pi[j, \mu(j)] \equiv \int_j^1 e^{-rz}(\tilde{P}X(\tilde{P}, \tilde{p}) - C[X(\tilde{P}, \tilde{p})]\} \, dz,$$

for the domestic firm and,

$$\pi[j, \mu(j)] \equiv \int_j^1 e^{-rz}\{\tilde{p}x(\tilde{P}, \tilde{p}) - c[x(\tilde{P}, \tilde{p})]\} \, dz,$$

---

[6] This result is not affected by the size of r ($< \infty$).

[7] See Kamien and Schwartz (1981, Chap. 20) for an exposition of dynamic programming techniques.

for the foreign firm. Now divide the interval $[t,\ 1)$ into two disjoint subintervals $[t, t+\Delta t)$ and $[t+\Delta t, 1)$, where Δt is small. Assume that the optimization problem is solved for the second subinterval, with the maximum profit from that subinterval denoted by $\Pi[t+\Delta t, \mu(t+\Delta t)]$. Then, by the principle of optimality we can express the domestic firm's optimization problem for the interval $[t,\ 1)$ as

$$\max_{P}\left\{\int_{t}^{t+\Delta t} \mathrm{e}^{-rz}\{P(z)X[P(z),p(z)] - C(X[P(z),p(z)])\,\mathrm{d}z + \Pi[t+\Delta t, \mu(t+\Delta t)]\}\right\}. \tag{5}$$

Note that $\mu(t+\Delta t) = \mu(t) + \Delta\mu$. Since Δt is small, $P(z)$ can be treated as a constant in (5). Also, for small Δt we have:

$$\int_{t}^{t+\Delta t} f(z)\,\mathrm{d}z = f(t)\Delta t. \tag{6}$$

Using (6) on the first term of (5) and expanding the second term by a Taylor-series expansion, we can rewrite (5) as

$$\begin{aligned}\max_{P}\{&\Delta t\{PX(P,p) - C[X(P,p)]\}\mathrm{e}^{-rt}\\ &+\Pi[t,\mu(t)] + \Pi_t[t,\mu(t)]\Delta t + \Pi_\mu[t,\mu(t)]\Delta\mu + \text{h.o.t}\},\end{aligned} \tag{7}$$

where the h.o.t. represents all the higher-order terms in the Taylor-series expansion.

Since the second and the third term in (7) do not depend on P, they can be ignored in the optimization problem. Then, dividing through the remaining terms by Δt and taking the limit $\Delta t \to 0$, we can rewrite the domestic firm's objective function as

$$\max\{\mathrm{e}^{-rt}(PX(P,p) - C[X(P,p)\} + \Pi_\mu[t,\mu(t)]x(P,p)\}, \tag{8}$$

where $x(P,p)$ is used to replace $\mu'(t)$.[8] The first-order condition to (8) is given by

$$\Psi \equiv \mathrm{e}^{-rt}\{X(P,p) + PX_P(P,p) - C'[X(P,p)X_P(P,p)\} + \Pi_\mu[t,\mu(t)]x_P(P,p) = 0, \tag{9}$$

which defines the domestic firm's best-response function $B(p,t)$ at time t.

The first-order condition (9) has the following interpretation. The first term measures the change in the domestic firm's profit at time t due to a small increase in P. Raising P also induces an instantaneous increase in imports ($x_P > 0$), which reduces the remaining quota through the increase in $\mu(t)$, which in turn raises the domestic firm's profits from sales made during the remainder of the year ($\Pi_\mu > 0$). This dynamic effect of a price change is captured in the second term on the right-hand side of (9). For an optimum the domestic firm chooses P to equate these two marginal effects on profits.

[8] By definition, $\mu'(t) = x(P,p)$. Note also that the h.o.t. vanishes when the limit is taken.

The properties of the best-response function $B(p,t)$ can now be examined. We first compare $B(p,t)$ with the best-response function $B^{s}(p)$ from the static game of Sect. 2. Notice that the expression in braces in (9) is the same as the first-order condition of the static game [see (2)]. The second term in (9) is positive by the preceding argument. Therefore, for a given p the domestic price P must be higher in the dynamic game than in the static game, that is, $P(t) = B(p,t) > B^{s}(p)$. Graphically, $B(p,t)$ lies "outside" $B^{s}(p)$.

We next examine how the domestic firm's best-response function shifts over time. Differentiating (9), while holding p constant, we obtain

$$\mathrm{d}P/\mathrm{d}t = -\frac{(\Pi_{\mu t} + \Pi_{\mu\mu}x)x_P + r\Pi_{\mu}x_P}{\mathrm{e}^{-rt}(2X_P + PX_{PP} - C''X_P^2 - C'X_{PP}) + \Pi_{\mu}x_{PP}}. \tag{10}$$

The denominator is negative by the second-order condition. Lemma 1 in the Appendix shows that $(\Pi_{\mu t} + \Pi_{\mu\mu}x)x_P$ is positive. Since Π_{μ} and x_P are also positive, we have $\mathrm{d}P/\mathrm{d}t > 0$, meaning that the domestic firm's best-response function shifts out over time. To sum the result so far, the domestic firm's dynamic best-response function under the quota is located outside its static-game (and hence free-trade) best-response function, and shifts out over time.

Turning to the foreign firm, we write its optimization problem as

$$\max_{p} \left\{ \int_{t}^{t+\Delta t} \mathrm{e}^{-rz}\{p(z)x[P(z),p(z),p(z) - c\{x[P(z),p(z)]\}\,\mathrm{d}z + \pi[t+\Delta t, \mu(t+\Delta t)] \right\}.^{9} \tag{11}$$

The procedure used in the case of the domestic firm can be applied to simplify (11) to the following problem:

$$\max_{p} \mathrm{e}^{-rt}\{px(P,p) - c[x(P,p)]\} + \pi_{\mu}[t, \mu(t)x(P,p).$$

The first order condition is

$$\psi \equiv \mathrm{e}^{-rt}\{x(P,p) + px_p(P,p) - c'[x(P,p)]x_p(P,p)\} + \pi_{\mu}[t,\mu(t)]x_p(P,p) = 0, \tag{12}$$

which yields the foreign firm's best-response function, $p = b(P,t)$, at time $t < 1$.

How does $b(P,t)$ compare with the best-response function $b^{s}(P)$ from the one-shot game in Sect. 2? The expression in braces in (12) is the same as that in the first-order condition in the static game [see (1)], so the position of $b(P,t)$ relative to $b^{s}(P)$ depends on the second term in (12), which captures the following dynamic effect. A small increase in p decreases the demand for exports ($x_p < 0$), thereby relaxing the quota constraint for the remainder of the year and affecting the foreign firm's future profit by π_{μ}. Thus the term $(-\pi_{\mu})$ may be interpreted as the dynamic shadow price of the quota.[10]

---

[9] By definition π is the equilibrium profit under the quota, so it subsumes the quota constraint (4).

[10] See Kamien and Schwartz (1981, p. 240) for this interpretation.

This shadow price is positive (i.e., $\pi_\mu < 0$) when the quota is binding. The intuition is that when μ increases the foreign firm has less to export for the rest of year and hence earns a smaller profit. Formally, suppose contrarily that $\pi_\mu \geq 0$, implying that the foreign firm's equilibrium profit is increased by a decrease in the (remaining) quota. Then, the foreign firm would voluntarily give up a portion of the quota until π_μ becomes negative. In the absence of such an option, the foreign firm would export in an instant whatever quantity is needed to make π_μ negative. While such an action may yield a negative profit instantaneously, its effect on total profit is of measure zero and is overwhelmed by an increase in profits due to a smaller quota that it now faces.

Given that $\pi_\mu < 0$, the second term on the right-hand side of (12) is positive, implying that $p = b(P,t) > b^{\mathrm{s}}(P)$, that is, for a given P, the domestic firm charges a higher price than it does in a static game.

We next examine the transition of the foreign firm's best-response function over time. Differentiating (12), while holding P constant, yields

$$\mathrm{d}p/\mathrm{d}t = -\frac{(\pi_{\mu t} + \pi_{\mu\mu}x)x_p + r\pi_\mu x_p}{\mathrm{e}^{-rt}(2x_p + px_{pp} - c''x_p^2 - c'x_{pp}) + \pi_\mu x_{pp}}.$$

The denominator is negative by the second-order condition. Lemma 2 in the appendix shows that the first term of the numerator is positive. Thus, the direction of shift again depends on the sign of π_μ. π_μ is strictly negative, so $\mathrm{d}p/\mathrm{d}t > 0$ so that the foreign firm's best-response function shifts out over time.

Solving the best-response functions (9) and (12) simultaneously, we can find the equilibrium prices at each t. Let $P^*(t)$ and $p^*(t)$ denote the equilibrium outcome for the whole game, that is, $P^*(t) \equiv \tilde{P}[t;0,\mu(0)]$ and $p^*(t) \equiv \tilde{P}[t;0,\mu(0)]$for $t \in [0,1)$

We now present some properties of the equilibrium price paths. We already established that under the quota the domestic firm's best-response function is located outside its static-game counterpart, $B^{\mathrm{s}}(p)$, and shifts out over time. We then proved that the foreign firm's best-response function also is placed on or outside the best-response function $b^{\mathrm{s}}(P)$ and shifts out after some $t \geq 04$. These facts lead to the following general result.

Proposition 3. *The prices under the quota are higher than what they are under free trade and increasing over time:*

$$P^*(t) > P^{\mathrm{s}}(t), p^*(t) > p^{\mathrm{s}}(t), P^{*\prime}(t) > 0, \quad \textit{and } p^{*\prime}(t) > 0 \quad \textit{for } t \in [0,1).$$

We now ask what happens when the home government imposes a more restrictive quota. A tighter quota raises the shadow price of the quota at each point in time, thereby inducing the foreign firm to raise its price at $t \in (0,1]$ Further, since prices are strategic complements, the domestic price also rises throughout the period. We state this in the next proposition, while relegating the proof to the appendix (see lemma 3).

Proposition 4. *Decreasing the quota raises both firms' price trajectories.*

5 Quotas as Facilitating Practices

Krishna (1989) showed for a one-shot differentiated-good Bertrand game that both the foreign and the home firm earn greater profits under a quota than under free trade. This result holds when there is a tariff, that is, a quota results in a more collusive equilibrium than the equal-import tariff. In this section we examine whether this property extends to the dynamic setting we consider.

As before, focus on the interval [0,1), and set the quota equal to the quantity of imports under free trade:

$$\bar{q}^{\mathrm{f}} = \int_0^1 x(P^{\mathrm{s}}, p^{\mathrm{s}})\,\mathrm{d}t. \tag{13}$$

The free-trade prices P^{s} and p^{s} obviously meet the constraint (13). They fail to satisfy the first-order conditions (9) and (12), however, and hence no longer constitute a subgame-perfect equilibrium.[11] Thus, the imposition of the quota at the free-trade level of imports affects the equilibrium behavior in our model.

Our analysis of Sect. 4 is fully applicable here. Thus, under the quota, the domestic firm's best-response function is located outside its free-trade position and shifts out over time. The foreign firm's best-response function also behaves similarly although it may be identical to its static counterpart momentarily. With both the best-response functions being displaced outward from their respective free-trade positions, the equilibrium prices are higher under the quota than under free trade. Thus, $P^{*\mathrm{f}}(t) > P^{\mathrm{s}}$ and $p^{*\mathrm{f}}(t) > p^{\mathrm{s}}$ for all $t \in [0,1)$. Then, both firms' profits are greater under the quota $\bar{q}^{\mathrm{f}}$ than under free trade. By an extension, the foreign firm earns a greater profit under a quota than under the equal-import tariff even if the tariff revenue were returned to the foreign firm. In other words, a quota facilitates collusion relative to the equal-import tariff.

Proposition 5. *Both the foreign firm and the domestic firm earn greater profits under a quota than they do under the equal-import tariff.*

6 Concluding Remarks

This chapter explores the fundamental difference between the capacity-constrained firm and the quota-constrained firm. Quotas limit the total quantity the foreign firm is allowed to export within a given period, say, a year. As a consequence the firm under the quota can strategically vary rates of export at every instant as long as the sum of exports does not exceed the quota. In contrast, capacity constraints are more physical, limiting the firm's production ability per unit of time, say, due to the

[11] To see this, suppose that firms charge $P^{\mathrm{s}}, p^{\mathrm{s}}$ at time zero (the moment the quota is imposed). Then the first expression on the right-hand side of (9) vanishes. Since $\Pi_\mu[0,\mu(0)]x_P > 0$ the first-order condition (9) is not satisfied.

plant size. As a result, the capacity-constrained firm does not face the isoperimetric problem as the firm does under the quota. This difference is obscured in the literature examining the relative effect of quota, which analyzes firms under a quota as capacity-constrained ones.

One benefit from treating the quota as an isoperimetric problem is that firms play pure strategies at all times. This fact is helpful in solving the dynamic profit-maximization problems under the quota. We develop techniques to solve this type of differential games, and fully characterize the equilibrium path for the quota-constrained Bertrand duopoly model, the one-shot version of which was considered in Krishna (1989).

We show that the quota results in higher and increasing prices than the tariff of equal imports. Our result also shows that price variations are greater under the quota as prices increase over time. Further, if the annual quota is renewed every year, the saw-toothed price trajectories appear every year: the quota produces price and output cycles while they are stationary under the tariff.

The techniques we developed are useful in analyzing other models of one-shot games under the quota that have mixed-strategy equilibriums, for example, Reitzes and Grawe (1994). We leave such applications of the present analysis to future work.

Appendix

Proofs of the three lemmas mentioned in the text are presented.

Lemma 1

$$(\Pi_{\mu t} + \Pi_{\mu\mu} x) x_p > 0$$

Proof. First, since goods are substitutes, we have $x_P > 0$. Therefore, the proof is complete if we show $\Pi_{\mu t} + \Pi_{\mu\mu} x > 0$. The definition of the maximum profit function and the principle of optimality imply

$$\begin{aligned}\Pi[t,\mu(t)] &\equiv \Delta t \left\{\tilde{P}X(\tilde{P},\tilde{p}) - C\left[X(\tilde{P},\tilde{p})\right]\right\} \mathrm{e}^{-rt} + \Pi[t+\Delta t, \mu(t)+\Delta\mu] \\ &= \Delta t \left\{\tilde{P}X(\tilde{P},\tilde{p}) - C\left[X(\tilde{P},\tilde{p})\right]\right\} \mathrm{e}^{-rt} \\ &\quad + \Pi[t,\mu(t)] + \Pi_t[t,\mu(t)]\Delta t + \Pi_\mu[t,\mu(t)]\Delta\mu + \text{h.o.t},\end{aligned}$$

where the equality follows from a Taylor series expansion. Dividing throughout by Δt and taking the limit $\Delta t \to 0$ yields the Bellman equation:

$$-\Pi_t[t,\mu(t)] = \mathrm{e}^{-rt}\left\{\tilde{P}X(\tilde{P},\tilde{p}) - C\left[X(\tilde{P},\tilde{p})\right]\right\} + \Pi_\mu[t,\mu(t)]x\left(\tilde{P},\tilde{p}\right) \tag{14}$$

Since this holds for all μ, we can differentiate (14) with respect to μ to obtain

$$-\Pi_{t\mu}\left[t,\mu(t)\right] = \mathrm{e}^{-rt}\left\{\tilde{P}X_p(\tilde{P},\tilde{p}) - C'\left[X(\tilde{P},\tilde{p})\right]X_p\right\}\tilde{p}_\mu + \Pi_{\mu\mu}\left[t,\mu(t)\right]x(\tilde{P},\tilde{p})$$
$$+\Pi_\mu\left[t,\mu(t)\right]x_p(\tilde{P},\tilde{p})\tilde{p}_\mu,$$

which simplifies to

$$\begin{aligned}&\Pi_{\mu\mu}\left[t,\mu(t)\right]x(\tilde{P},\tilde{p}) + \Pi_{t\mu}\left[t,\mu(t)\right]\\ &\quad = -\left\{\mathrm{e}^{-rt}\left\{\tilde{P}X_p(\tilde{P},\tilde{p}) - C'\left[X(\tilde{P},\tilde{p})\right]X_p\right\} + \Pi_\mu\left[t,\mu(t)\right]x_p(\tilde{P},\tilde{p})\right\}\tilde{p}_\mu.\end{aligned} \tag{15}$$

Rearranging the first-order condition (9) yields

$$\begin{aligned}&\mathrm{e}^{-rt}\left\{\tilde{P}X_p(\tilde{P},\tilde{p}) - C'\left[X(\tilde{P},\tilde{p})\right]X_p(\tilde{P},\tilde{p})\right\}\\ &\quad = -\Pi_\mu\left[t,\mu(t)\right]x_p(\tilde{P},\tilde{p}) - \mathrm{e}^{-rt}X(\tilde{P},\tilde{p}).\end{aligned}$$

Substituting this expression to the right-hand side of (15), we obtain

$$\begin{aligned}&\Pi_{\mu\mu}\left[t,\mu(t)\right]x(\tilde{P},\tilde{p}) + \Pi_{t\mu}\left[t,\mu(t)\right]\\ &\quad = -\left\{\mathrm{e}^{-rt}\left\{\tilde{P}X_p(\tilde{P},\tilde{p}) - C'\left[X(\tilde{P},\tilde{p})\right]X_p\right\} + \Pi_\mu\left[t,\mu(t)\right]x_p(\tilde{P},\tilde{p})\right\}\tilde{p}_\mu\\ &\quad = -\left\{-\mathrm{e}^{-rt}X(P,p) + \Pi_\mu\left[t,\mu(t)\right]\left[x_p(\tilde{P},\tilde{p}) - x_P(\tilde{P},\tilde{p})\right]\right\}\tilde{p}_\mu.\end{aligned}$$

Since we have $\Pi_\mu > 0$, the terms in the braces are negative. Also, in Lemma 3 below, we show $\tilde{p}_\mu > 0$. Therefore, we have $\Pi_{\mu\mu}x + \Pi_{t\mu} > 0$. □

Lemma 2

$$(\pi_{\mu t} + \pi_{\mu\mu}x)x_p > 0$$

Proof. Following a procedure similar to the one leading to (14) in the proof of Lemma 1, we can obtain the Bellman equation for the foreign firm:

$$-\pi_t\left[t,\mu(t)\right] = \mathrm{e}^{-rt}\left\{\tilde{p}x(\tilde{P},\tilde{p}) - c\left[x(\tilde{P},\tilde{p})\right]\right\} + \pi_\mu\left[t,\mu(t)\right]x(\tilde{P},\tilde{p}). \tag{16}$$

Differentiating (16) with respect to μ yields

$$\begin{aligned}-\pi_{t\mu}\left[t,\mu(t)\right] &= \mathrm{e}^{-rt}\left\{\tilde{p} - c'\left[x(\tilde{P},\tilde{p})\right]\right\}x_P(P,p)P_\mu\\ &\quad + \pi_{\mu\mu}\left[t,\mu(t)\right]x(\tilde{P},\tilde{p}) + \pi_\mu\left[t,\mu(t)\right]x_p(\tilde{P},\tilde{p})\tilde{P}_\mu\end{aligned}$$

or

$$\begin{aligned}&\pi_{t\mu}\left[t,\mu(t)\right] + \pi_{\mu\mu}\left[t,\mu(t)\right]x(\tilde{P},\tilde{p})\\ &\quad = -\left\{\mathrm{e}^{-rt}\left\{\tilde{p} - c'\left[x(\tilde{P},\tilde{p})\right]\right\} + \pi_\mu\left[t,\mu(t)\right]\right\}x_p(\tilde{P},\tilde{p})\tilde{P}_\mu.\end{aligned} \tag{17}$$

The expression in braces on the right-hand side of (17) is positive since rewriting the first-order condition (12) from the text yields

$$\mathrm{e}^{-rt}\left\{\tilde{p}-c'\left[x(\tilde{P},\tilde{p})\right]\right\}+\pi_{\mu}\left[t,\mu(t)\right]=-\mathrm{e}^{-rt}x(\tilde{P},\tilde{p})/x_{p}(\tilde{P},\tilde{p})>0.$$

Furthermore, $x_P > 0$ because products are substitutes, and $\tilde{p}_{\mu} > 0$ as we prove later in Lemma 3. We have shown that the right-hand side of (17) is negative. Lemma 2 then follows immediately from the fact that $x_p < 0$. □

Lemma 3

$$\tilde{p}_{\mu} > 0 \quad \text{and} \quad \tilde{P}_{\mu} > 0.$$

Proof. Differentiating the first-order conditions (9) and (12) simultaneously yields

$$\begin{aligned}|D|\,\mathrm{d}P/\mathrm{d}\mu &= -\Pi_{\mu\mu}x_{P}\Psi_{p}+\pi_{\mu\mu}x_{p}\Psi_{p},\\ |D|\,\mathrm{d}p/\mathrm{d}\mu &= \Pi_{\mu\mu}x_{P}\Psi_{P}-\pi_{\mu\mu}x_{p}\Psi_{p},\end{aligned} \tag{18}$$

where $|D| \equiv \psi_p\Psi_P - \psi_P\Psi_p > 0$ by the standard stability and uniqueness conditions. We also know that $\Psi_P < 0, \psi_p < 0$ by the second-order conditions, and $\Psi_p > 0, \psi_P > 0$ due to strategic complementarity of prices.

We first show that $\pi_{\mu\mu} < 0$. To do so, note that

$$\begin{aligned}&\pi(t,\mu_0) > \pi(t,\mu_1)+(\mu_1-\mu_0)\mathrm{e}^{-rt}(x+px_p-c'x_p)/x_p\\ &=\pi(t,\mu_1)-(\mu_1-\mu_0)\pi_{\mu}(t,\mu_0)\end{aligned} \tag{19}$$

for given t, μ_1, and $\mu_0 (\mu_1 > \mu_0)$. The inequality holds for the following reason. Both sides of the inequality measure profits the foreign firm makes by exporting the quantity $\bar{q}-\mu_0$ between time t and 1. The left-hand side, $\pi(t,\mu_0)$, is by definition the foreign firm's maximum profit attainable. The first term, $\pi(t,\mu_1)$, on the right-hand side of the inequality is the maximum profit attainable by exporting the smaller quantity $\bar{q}-\mu_1$ during this period. The next term represents the profit resulting from exporting the quantity, $\mu_1-\mu_0$, at $\mathrm{e}^{-rt}(x+px_p-c'x_p)$. However, since this term is not the maximum profit to the foreign firm from exporting $\mu_1-\mu_0$ units, the inequality is established. The equality in (19) follows from the first-order condition (12). But (19) means that $\pi(t,\mu)$ is concave in μ, that is, $\pi_{\mu\mu} < 0$.

We next show that $\Pi_{\mu\mu} > 0$. Let μ_1 and μ_0 be given, with $\mu_1 > \mu_0$.$\Pi(t,\mu_1)$ represents the maximum profit the domestic firm can make when $\bar{q}-\mu_1$ units of the foreign good are imported between t and 1. If $\bar{q}-\mu_0$ units were allowed to be imported instead during the same period, the domestic firm would suffer the loss $\Pi(t,\mu_1)-\Pi(t,\mu_0) > 0$. Now suppose that the domestic firm receives a compensation for this loss in the amount of

$$-\mathrm{e}^{-rt}(X+PX_p-C'X_p)(\mu_1-\mu_0)/x_p.$$

This has the following interpretation. Since x_P measures the increase in imports induced by a unit increase in the domestic price, $(\mu_1 - \mu_0)/x_P$ represents the price increase necessary to induce the increase in imports by $\mu_1 - \mu_0$. But according to the first-order condition (9), the marginal cost of a price increase (a deviation from optimality) is

$$-e^{-rt}(X + PX_p - C'X_p).$$

However, since the profit function is concave, this compensation evaluated at the margin underestimates the true cost of the discrete price change necessary to induce the increase in imports, $\mu_1 - \mu_0$. Therefore,

$$\Pi(t,\mu_1) - \Pi(t,\mu_0) > -(\mu_1 - \mu_0)e^{-rt}(X + PX_p - C'X_p)/x_p = (\mu_1 - \mu_0)\Pi_\mu(t,\mu_0),$$

where the equality follows from (9). However, this means that $\Pi(t,\mu)$ is convex in μ, and hence $\Pi_{\mu\mu} > 0$. Using these results in (18), we have $\tilde{p}_\mu > 0$ and $\tilde{P}_\mu > 0$. □

Acknowledgment We thank an anonymous referee and participants at the Hitotsubashi COE/RES Conference on International Trade and FDI and Economics Department seminars at the University of Texas-Arlington and Osaka University for comments and suggestions. We alone are responsible for any errors.

References

Brander JA (1995) Strategic trade policy. In: Grossman GM, Rogoff K (eds) Handbook of international economics, vol 3. North-Holland, Amsterdam

Dockner EJ, Haug AA (1990) Tariffs and quotas under dynamic duopolistic competition. J Int Econ 29:147–160

Itoh M, Ono Y (1982) Tariffs, quotas, and market structure. Q J Econ 97:295–305

Itoh M, Ono Y (1984) Tariffs vs. quotas under duopoly of heterogeneous goods. J Int Econ 17:359–374

Harris R (1985) Why voluntary export restraints are 'voluntary'. Can J Econ 18:799–809

Helpman E, Krugman PR (1989) Trade policy and market structure. MIT Press, Cambridge

Hwang H, Mai C (1988) On the equivalence of tariffs and quotas under duopoly: a conjectural variation approach. J Int Econ 24:373–380

Kamien MI, Schwartz NL (1981) Dynamic optimization: the calculus of variations and optimal control in economics and management. North-Holland, Amsterdam

Kreps DM, Sheinkman JA (1983) Quantity precommitment and Bertrand competition yield Cournot outcomes. Bell J Econ 14:326–337

Krishna K (1989) Trade restrictions as facilitating practices. J Int Econ 26:251–270

Miyagiwa K, Ohno Y (1995) Closing the technology gap under protection. Am Econ Rev 85:755–770

Miyagiwa K, Ohno Y (1999) Credibility of protection and incentives to innovate. Int Econ Rev 40:143–164

Miyagiwa K, Ohno Y (2001) Quota-induced cycles. Int Econ Rev 42:451–472

Reitzes JD, Grawe OR (1994) Market-share quotas. J Int Econ 36:431–447

Rotemberg J, Saloner G (1989) Tariffs vs. quotas with implicit collusion. Can J Econ 22:237–244

Imported Inputs: Dynamic Effects on Economic Growth[1]

Stefan F. Schubert and Stephen J. Turnovsky(✉)

Abstract This chapter studies the effects of an increase in the price of an intermediate input on economic growth of a small open economy. Most of the analysis employs a nonscale growth model, although for comparative purposes we also briefly consider a simple endogenous growth model. The economy has access to a perfect world capital market, a consequence of which is that the equilibrium growth rates of consumption and output can diverge indefinitely. Both models imply that following an oil shock consumption level, although its subsequent growth rate remains unaffected. But the two models yield sharply contrasting implications for the growth rate of capital and ouput. The nonscale growth model implies that the effects on the growth rate are only temporary. Eventually, the growth rate of capital and output recovers back to its initial balanced growth rate, although output, capital, and consumption are all permanently lower. In the case of the endogenous growth model, there are no transitional dynamics; a permanent increase in the price of the imported input leads to a permanent constant reduction in the growth rate of capital and output.

1 Introduction

The price of imported raw materials has been of concern to economists since the 1970s, with the occurrence of supply shocks associated with the "oil-crisis" of that period. This experience spawned substantial research, much of it motivated by the

[1] This chapter is dedicated to the memory of Koji Shimomura, a fine scholar and good friend, who made significant contributions to many areas of international economics.

S.J. Turnovsky
Department of Economics, University of Washington, Seattle, WA 98105, USA,
e-mail: sturn@u.washington.edu

T. Kamihigashi and L. Zhao (eds.) *International Trade and Economic Dynamics – Essays in Memory of Koji Shimomura.*

concern for "stagflation," that is, for the economy to experience inflation in conjunction with a decline in output; see, for example, Corden (1975), Findlay and Rodriguez (1977), Obstfeld (1980), Sachs et al. (1981), Bruno and Sachs (1982a, 1982b), Sachs (1983), Golub (1983), Krugman (1983), Marion (1984), Marion and Svensson (1984), Svensson (1984), and Bhandari and Turnovsky (1984). This literature was almost entirely short-run in nature, focusing particular attention on the short-run consequences of the oil shocks and the appropriate macroeconomic policies to deal with them. No doubt this was in part a consequence of the conventional international macrodynamic models of the time – the fact that virtually all ignored the role of physical capital accumulation – but it also reflected the contemporary concern with the issue of short-run macroeconomic stability. One of the conclusions to emerge from this literature is that the macroeconomic impacts of oil price shocks depend crucially upon their specific nature, that is, whether they are permanent or temporary, on the one hand, and anticipated or untanticipated, on the other.

With the continuing instability in the Middle East and the associated periodic dramatic movements in world oil prices, the question of its macroeconomic consequences continues to engage the attention of economists; see Barsky and Kilian (2004) for a recent review. Indeed, the recent increases in oil price causing it to approach $100 a barrel confirms the ongoing importance of this issue.

In this chapter we address the effects of oil price shocks on the long-run economic growth performance of a small open economy. Recent empirical evidence for New Zealand, for example, suggests that while small economies are potentially vulnerable to fluctuations in oil prices, their effects on the long-run growth performance is unclear; see, for example, Grounder and Bartleet (2007). Somewhat surprisingly, we find that the analytical literature on this topic is surprisingly sparse.[2]

The model we employ is an extension of the class of model developed by Eicher and Turnovsky (1999), augmented to include an imported intermediate input, we identify as oil. We consider two alternative parameterizations of that model. The first, and more general, yields the kind of "nonscale growth equilibrium" emphasized in their work. However, for a specific "knife-edge" parameterization, an endogenous growth equilibrium of the type pioneered by Romer (1986) emerges. Using this framework we analyze the effects of a permanent increase in the price of the intermediate input. Responses differ markedly between the two alternative parameteriztions. For the more general case, our analysis predicts that a permanent increase in the imported input price pushes the economy from its balanced growth path, causes an economic slump, and lowers growth during transition. Eventually, the economy recovers and returns back to its initial balanced growth rate, although at a permanently lower level of output. In the endogenous growth equilibrium, the higher input price leads to a permanently lower growth rate of output and capital.

[2] Two early exceptions to analyze imported input shocks in a growing economy should be noted. Bardhan and Lewis (1970) address the issue in the context of a standard neoclassical growth model of trade and growth, while Sen (1991) studied the effects of an oil-price increase in a small open economy populated with intertemporally optimizing agents. Neither chapter allows for international capital mobility.

Fluctuations in the price of the imported input are an important source of fluctuations in the country's terms of trade (the relative price of its exports in terms of its inputs). Our analysis is therefore related to the broader literature dealing with the effects of changes and fluctuations in the terms of trade on the country's economic performance. The importance of this literature stems from the fact that adverse shocks to a country's terms of trade not only disrupt output growth, but also represent fundamental sources of risk and instability, especially for developing economies, and also for developed countries.[3] For example, Mendoza (1995) and Kose (2002) found that they account for at least half of the output volatility in developing countries, while Barro (1997, 2003) provides evidence that sustained terms of trade deteriorations have a negative and significant impact on economic growth. Kandil (2006) shows that a currency depreciation (i.e., a terms of trade deterioration) results in a decrease in output growth in many developing countries. Becker and Mauro (2006) estimate that in developing countries the expected cost of a terms of trade shock counts about 40% of pre-event per capita GDP. Turnovsky and Chattopadhyay (2003) provide evidence showing that volatility in the terms of trade has adverse effects on the growth rate.[4]

The theoretical literature analyzing terms of trade shocks dates back to the seminal contributions of Laursen and Metzler (1950) and Harberger (1950), who predicted that a deterioration in the terms of trade would reduce real income, thereby lowering savings and investment to cause a deterioration in the current account balance. The original Laursen–Metzler–Harberger effect was purely static and gave rise to an extensive literature that reexamined the effects of terms of trade shocks within an intertemporal framework.[5] Without exception, these models abstract from the presence of imported inputs. The terms of trade shocks are due to fluctuations in the relative price of consumption goods, and therefore represent pure demand effects. From this standpoint, the present chapter can be viewed as extending this literature to the important situation where the terms of trade fluctuations, being due to import prices, originate on the supply side.

The remainder of the chapter is structured as follows: Sect. 2 sets out the model. The macroeconomic equilibrium is derived and discussed in Sect. 3. The consequences of a permanent increase in price of the imported input are analyzed in

[3] The importance of terms of trade shocks and their economic effects can also be inferred from the fact that the International Monetary Fund (IMF) recently established an Exogenous Shocks Facility within the Poverty Reduction and Growth Facility. According to the IMF, the aim is to assist low income countries meet balance of payment needs arising from sudden and exogenous shocks in the terms of trade.

[4] Mendoza (1995) first analyzed the quantitative importance of terms of trade shocks in a dynamic stochastic small open economy model. He finds that terms of trade disturbances explain 56% of aggregate output fluctuations in developing countries. Kose (2002) studies a broader set of world price shocks (including intermediate and primary goods) to find that they explain roughly 88% of aggregate output fluctuations.

[5] This reappraisal was initiated by Obstfeld (1982) and further pursued in a number of different directions by Svensson and Razin (1983), Persson and Svensson (1985), Bean (1986), Matsuyama (1988), and Sen (1989), and more recently by Serven (1999), Ikeda (2001), Otto (2003), Huang and Meng (2007), and Eicher et al. (2008).

Sect. 4, while the effects of a temporary increase are briefly discussed in Sect. 5. Section 6 compares the implications of the oil price shock in the polar case of the endogenous growth model, while Sect. 7 concludes the chapter. A brief appendix includes some of the technical material.

2 Analytical Framework

We extend the one-sector "nonscale" open economy growth model developed by Eicher and Turnovsky (1999) to include a foreign import, used as an intermediate input in domestic production.[6] The economy is small and produces a traded good, Y, that can be consumed, invested, or exported. The imported intermediate good is used solely as an input in production, the relative price of which, expressed in terms of the traded final good, is p. The economy is small in the sense that the relative price of the imported input (oil) is determined in the world market. We assume that p remains constant over time and analyze the dynamic effects of a one-time unanticipated permanent increase in p. We assume that the economy is populated with identical agents, subscripted by i, and that each individual's labor supply, L_i, is fixed at unity. Full employment prevails, implying that total labor supply equals the population size, N, the growth rate of which is $\dot{N}/N = n$. Each individual produces the traded output, Y_i, using private capital, K_i, labor, L_i, and the imported intermediate good, Z_i, according to the production function

$$Y_i = \alpha' L_i^{1-\sigma-\xi} K_i^{\sigma} Z_i^{\xi} K^{\eta} \equiv \alpha K_i^{\sigma} Z_i^{\xi} K^{\eta}, \tag{1a}$$

where $\alpha \equiv \alpha' L_i^{1-\sigma-\xi}$, $0 < \sigma < 1$, $0 < \xi < 1$, $0 < \sigma + \xi < 1$, and $\eta \gtreqless 0$. Spillovers from the economy-wide capital stock, $K \equiv NK_i$, are captured by η, see Romer (1986). In addition, we assume constant returns to scale in private factors, L_i, K_i, and Z_i, but total returns to scale of $1+\eta$ in all factors. Aggregate returns to scale are thus increasing or decreasing, depending on the qualitative nature of the spillover.[7]

Each agent's utility is represented by the intertemporal iso-elastic utility function

$$\Omega \equiv \int_0^{\infty} \frac{1}{\gamma} C_i^{\gamma} \mathrm{e}^{-\beta t}\, \mathrm{d}t, \quad -\infty < \gamma < 1, \tag{1b}$$

[6] The "non-scale" growth model is a generalization of the neoclassical growth model to allow for nonconstant returns to scale. It was developed by Jones (1995a, b) under the label "semi-endogenous" growth model as an attempt to respond to some of the counterfactual implications of first generation endogenous growth models.

[7] An alternative specification of the aggregate spillover is to express it in terms of the average economy-wide capital stock, replacing (1a) by $Y_i = \alpha K_i^{\sigma} Z_i^{\xi} (K/N)^{\eta}$. This has virtually identical implications to the specification we have adopted. The only difference is that the scale effect is eliminated and the long-run growth rate (4) reduces to the population growth rate, n, as in the standard neoclassical model. All of the transitional dynamics remain unchanged.

where $1/(1-\gamma)$ measures the intertemporal elasticity of substitution, and β denotes the agent's constant time preference rate.

The representative agent accumulates physical capital, K_i. Investment is associated with installation costs. We therefore assume a Hayashi (1982) type investment adjustment cost function, resulting in a total investment cost function

$$\Phi(I_i, K_i) = I_i + h\frac{I_i^2}{2K_i} = I_i\left(1 + \frac{h}{2}\frac{I_i}{K_i}\right), \tag{1c}$$

where adjustment costs are proportional to the rate of investment per unit of installed capital, I_i/K_i. The linear homogeneity of this function is necessary if a steady-state equilibrium showing ongoing growth is to be sustained. For simplicity, we further assume that the capital stock does not depreciate, so that the net rate of capital accumulation per agent, taking population growth into account, is given by

$$\dot{K}_i = I_i - nK_i. \tag{1d}$$

In addition, domestic agents have access to a perfect world capital market, allowing them to accumulate world bonds, denominated in terms of the traded good and paying a fixed given world interest rate, r, yielding a net return to individual agents of $(r-n)$. The agent's short-run budget constraint, expressed in terms of the traded good as numeraire is

$$\dot{B}_i = Y_i - C_i - pZ_i - \Phi(I_i, K_i) + (r-n)B_i, \tag{1e}$$

where $B_i > 0$ denotes its holdings of foreign (traded) bonds.[8] According to (1e) to the extent that the agent's income from production plus net interest income exceeds his consumption, investment costs, and raw material costs, he accumulates traded bonds. For simplicity we abstract from taxes.

The representative agent chooses his rates of consumption, C_i, investment, I_i, and use of imported input, Z_i, together with the rates of accumulation of capital, K_i, and traded bonds, B_i, so as to maximize his intertemporal utility function (1b), subject to the accumulation equations, (1d) and (1e), the production function, (1a), and the given initial stocks of capital and bonds, $K_i(0) = K_{i0}$, $B_i(0) = B_{i0}$, respectively. The optimality conditions with respect to C_i, Z_i, I_i are, respectively,

$$C_i^{\gamma-1} = \lambda_i, \tag{2a}$$

$$Z_i = \xi\frac{Y_i}{p}, \tag{2b}$$

$$1 + h\frac{I_i}{K_i} = q_i, \tag{2c}$$

[8] Note that it is possible for $B_i < 0$, in which case the agent is a debtor.

where λ_i is the shadow value (marginal utility) of wealth in form of internationally traded bonds, and q denotes the value of capital in terms of the (unitary) price of foreign bonds.[9]

Equation (2a) is the usual static optimality condition, requiring that along an optimal path, the marginal utility of consumption has to equal the shadow value of wealth. Equation (2b′) determines the optimal choice of the imported input, Z_i, equating the marginal product of the imported input to its relative price in terms of the domestic good, p. For the Cobb–Douglas production function this implies that the demand is directly proportional to output and inversely proportional to its relative price. Equation (2c) asserts that the marginal cost of investment must be equated to the marginal value of installed capital, q_i, and gives rise to a Tobin-q theory of investment.

Optimizing with respect to B_i and K_i yields the dynamic efficiency conditions

$$\beta - \frac{\dot{\lambda}_i}{\lambda_i} = r - n, \tag{2d}$$

$$\frac{\sigma Y_i}{q_i K_i} + \frac{\dot{q}_i}{q_i} + \frac{h}{2q_i}\left(\frac{q_i - 1}{h}\right)^2 = r. \tag{2e}$$

Equation (2d) requires that the rate of return on consumption, denoted in terms of the traded good, $\beta - \dot{\lambda}_i/\lambda_i$, must equal the net of growth interest rate, $r - n$. With r, n, β all being constants, it implies a constant growth rate of the agent's marginal utility. Equation (2e′) equates the rate of return on domestic capital to the rate of return on the traded bond. The former comprises three components. The first is the marginal output per unit of installed capital, valued at the price q, the second is the capital gain, and the third reflects the benefits arising from the fact that higher capital stock reduces the installation costs. Solving (2b′) for Z_i, we may write

$$Z_i = \left(p^{-1}\alpha\xi\right)^{1/(1-\xi)} K_i^{\sigma/(1-\xi)} K^{\eta/(1-\xi)}, \tag{2b$'$}$$

and substituting together with (1a) into (2e′) permits us to rewrite the no-arbitrage condition for capital and traded bonds in the form

$$\frac{\alpha\sigma\left(p^{-1}\alpha\xi\right)^{\xi/(1-\xi)} K_i^{\sigma-1+\xi\sigma/(1-\xi)} K^{\eta+\xi\eta/(1-\xi)}}{q_i} + \frac{\dot{q}_i}{q_i} + \frac{h}{2q_i}\left(\frac{q_i - 1}{h}\right)^2 = r. \tag{2e$'$}$$

Finally, to ensure that the agent's intertemporal budget constraint is met, the following transversality conditions must be imposed:

$$\lim_{t\to\infty} \lambda_i B_i \mathrm{e}^{-\beta t} = \lim_{t\to\infty} q_i \lambda_i K_i \mathrm{e}^{-\beta t} = 0. \tag{2f}$$

[9] If we let q_i' be the shadow value of capital, then $q_i = q_i'/\lambda_i$ is unit-free.

3 Macroeconomic Equilibrium

We now use the optimality conditions for individual agents to derive the aggregate macroeconomic equilibrium. First, we note that since all agents are assumed to be identical and face the same market conditions, $\lambda_i = \lambda$ and $q_i = q$. Second, since our objective is to analyze the dynamics of the economy in response to an oil shock about a stationary growth path, we must determine the economy's long-run growth rate along a balanced growth path. To do so, we note that in steady-state $\dot{q} = 0$. Hence (2e′) implies that along a balanced growth path Y_i/K_i remains constant, while the optimality condition for imported input (2b′) requires Y_i/Z_i to remain constant at all points of time. Thus, along the balanced growth path Y_i, K_i, and Z_i, all grow at a common constant rate. Moreover, with all agents being identical, the aggregate quantities are defined by $Y \equiv NY_i, K \equiv NK_i, Z \equiv NZ_i$, from which it follows that Y, K, Z also grow at a common rate, that is, $\hat{Y} = \hat{K} = \hat{Z}$.[10]

Summing the production function (1a) over the N agents, the aggregate production function is

$$Y = N\alpha(K/N)^{\sigma}(Z/N)^{\xi}K^{\eta} = \alpha K^{\sigma_K}N^{\sigma_N}Z^{\sigma_Z}, \tag{3}$$

where $\sigma_K \equiv \sigma + \eta$, $\sigma_N \equiv 1 - \sigma - \xi > 0$, and $\sigma_Z \equiv \xi$ are the shares of capital, labor, and imported input in aggregate output, respectively. Thus $\sigma_K + \sigma_N + \sigma_Z = 1 + \eta$ measures total returns to scale of the aggregate production function. Taking percentage changes of (3′) and imposing the long-run equilibrium relationship $\hat{Y} = \hat{K} = \hat{Z}$ implies the steady-state growth rate

$$\hat{Y} \equiv g = \frac{\sigma_N}{1 - \sigma_K - \sigma_Z}n = \frac{1 - \sigma - \xi}{1 - \sigma - \xi - \eta}n. \tag{4}$$

The equilibrium growth rate depends thus on the production technology as summarized in the shares σ_j and the exogenous rate of population growth, n. Balanced growth is positive if and only if $\sigma_K + \sigma_Z < 1$, an assumption that we shall maintain until Sect. 5. Under constant aggregate returns to scale, the economy's long-run growth rate equals the population growth rate, $g = n$. In the presence of spillovers, g exceeds or is less than n, depending on the qualitative form of the spillover, that is, on $\eta \gtrless 0$, that is, whether aggregate returns to scale are increasing or decreasing. Note, in particular, that whether the introduction of an imported raw material aids or impedes the long-run growth rate depends upon $\eta \gtrless 0$.[11]

Because of the existence of the perfect world capital market, the equilibrium dynamics of this economy has a simple sequential structure. First, consumption dynamics proceeds independently of output dynamics; second, output dynamics, which depends upon the productive characteristics of the economy, proceeds

---

[10] The ^ denotes a growth rate, that is, $\hat{X} \equiv \dot{X}/X$. Because $Y_i \equiv Y/N$ and $K_i \equiv K/N$, $\dot{Y}_i/Y_i = \dot{K}_i/K_i$ implies $\dot{Y}/Y = \dot{K}/K$.

[11] If the externality is expressed as in footnote 6, the introduction of the imported raw material has no effect on the long-run growth rate.

independently of consumption dynamics; third, output and consumption dynamics taken together then influence the country's external dynamics in such a way so as to ensure that it remains intertemporally solvent.

3.1 Consumption Dynamics

To determine the growth rate of consumption, we take the time derivative of (2a) and combine with (2d), implying that individual's consumption grows at the rate

$$\frac{\dot{C}_i}{C_i} = \frac{r-n-\beta}{1-\gamma} \equiv \psi_i, \tag{5}$$

so that the growth rate of aggregate consumption $C \equiv C_i N$ is

$$\frac{\dot{C}}{C} = \frac{r-n\gamma-\beta}{1-\gamma} \equiv \psi = \psi_i + n. \tag{5'}$$

As in Eicher and Turnovsky (1999), the growth rate of consumption proceeds at a constant rate and is independent of the production conditions characterizing the economy, including the role of the imported input. These aspects of consumption dynamics remain unchanged from the basic AK growth model discussed by Turnovsky (1996).

3.2 Capital and Output Dynamics

In contrast to the consumption growth rate, which is always on its balanced growth path, the dynamics of capital and output converge to a long-run steady growth rate along a transitional growth path. To analyze this path, it is convenient to express these dynamics in terms of the relative price of installed capital, q, and the stationary "scale-adjusted" capital stock.[12]

$$k \equiv K/N^{\sigma_N/(1-\sigma_K-\sigma_Z)}.$$

To obtain the rate of capital accumulation, we first substitute (2c) in (1d) to obtain

$$\frac{\dot{K}_i}{K_i} = \frac{q_i-1}{h} - n.$$

Recalling the definition of $K \equiv NK_i$, in equilibrium, the growth rate of the aggregate capital stock is given by

$$\frac{\dot{K}}{K} = \frac{q-1}{h} \equiv \varphi \tag{6}$$

[12] This is further discussed by Eicher and Turnovsky (1999). If the production function has constant returns to scale so that $\sigma_K + \sigma_N + \sigma_Z = 1$, then k is simply the standard per capita stock of capital.

and hence

$$\frac{\dot{k}}{k} = \frac{q-1}{h} - \frac{\sigma_N}{1-\sigma_K-\sigma_Z}n = \varphi - g. \tag{7a}$$

To determine the evolution of the market price of installed capital, q, we first recall (2e′), which we then combine with the definitions of $K \equiv NK_i$ and $k \equiv K/N^{\sigma_N/(1-\sigma_K-\sigma_Z)}$. The result can be expressed as

$$\frac{\dot{q}}{q} = r - \frac{(q-1)^2}{2hq} - \frac{1}{q}\sigma\alpha^{1/(1-\sigma_Z)}\left(p^{-1}\sigma_Z\right)^{\sigma_Z/(1-\sigma_Z)}k^{(\sigma_K+\sigma_Z-1)/(1-\sigma_Z)}. \tag{7b}$$

Equations (7a) and (7b) thus comprise a pair of autonomous equations in q and k that evolve independently of consumption. As capital is accumulated along the equilibrium transitional path, the aggregate intermediate imported input ($Z \equiv NZ_i$) and aggregate output ($Y \equiv NY_i$) follow directly from (2b′) and (1a) and are given by

$$Z = (p^{-1}\alpha\sigma_Z)^{1/(1-\sigma_Z)}K^{\sigma_K/(1-\sigma_Z)}N^{\sigma_N/(1-\sigma_Z)},$$

$$Y = \alpha^{1/(1-\sigma_Z)}(p^{-1}\sigma_Z)^{\sigma_Z/(1-\sigma_Z)}K^{\sigma_K/(1-\sigma_Z)}N^{\sigma_N/(1-\sigma_Z)}.$$

From these equations it follows that, given the economy's capital stock and population, an increase in p reduces the use of the imported input and therefore output. Moreover, the dynamics of the capital stock and of population determine the dynamic evolution of Z and Y.[13] Expressed in terms of their corresponding "scale-adjusted" per capita quantities $z \equiv Z/N^{\sigma_N/(1-\sigma_K-\sigma_Z)}$ and $y \equiv Y/N^{\sigma_N/(1-\sigma_K-\sigma_Z)}$, we obtain the direct relationship between the time path of capital and the imported input and output

$$z = \left(p^{-1}\alpha\sigma_Z\right)^{1/(1-\sigma_Z)}k^{\sigma_K/(1-\sigma_Z)}, \tag{8a}$$

$$y = \alpha^{1/(1-\sigma_Z)}\left(p^{-1}\sigma_Z\right)^{\sigma_Z/(1-\sigma_Z)}k^{\sigma_K/(1-\sigma_Z)}. \tag{8b}$$

For the domestic stock and output ultimately to converge to a balanced growth path with a constant rate of growth, the stationary solution to (7a) and (7b), attained when $\dot{k} = \dot{q} = 0$, must have least one real solution. Setting $\dot{k} = \dot{q} = 0$, we see that the steady-state values of $\tilde{k}$ and $\tilde{q}$ are in fact unique and are determined as follows. First, (7a) implies

$$\tilde{q} = 1 + gh, \tag{9a}$$

so that $\tilde{q}$ is determined by the growth rate (4). Having determined $\tilde{q}$, the steady-state scale-adjusted capital–labor ratio, $\tilde{k}$, is then determined from the steady-state arbitrage relationship, (7b), being given by

$$\tilde{k} = \left[\frac{r(1+gh) - g^2h/2}{\sigma\alpha^{1/(1-\sigma_Z)}(p^{-1}\sigma_Z)^{\sigma_Z/(1-\sigma_Z)}}\right]^{\frac{1-\sigma_Z}{\sigma_K+\sigma_Z-1}}. \tag{9b}$$

[13] Specifically, $\dot{Z}/Z = \dot{Y}/Y = (\sigma_K/(1-\sigma_Z))(\dot{K}/K) + (\sigma_N/(1-\sigma_Z))n$.

To be viable, the long-run equilibrium must satisfy the transversality conditions. Substituting (2d) and (6) in (2f) and evaluating this requires $r > g$, so that the right hand side of (9b) is clearly positive and $\tilde{k} > 0$.[14]

Linearizing (7a) and (7b) around their respective steady states, the local transitional dynamics of capital and its shadow value are described by

$$\begin{pmatrix} \dot{k} \\ \dot{q} \end{pmatrix} = \begin{pmatrix} 0 & \tilde{k}/h \\ a_{21} & r-g \end{pmatrix} \begin{pmatrix} k-\tilde{k} \\ q-\tilde{q} \end{pmatrix}, \tag{10}$$

where

$$a_{21} \equiv \frac{1-\sigma_K-\sigma_Z}{1-\sigma_Z}\sigma\alpha^{1/(1-\sigma_Z)}(p^{-1}\sigma_Z)^{\sigma_Z/(1-\sigma_Z)}\tilde{k}^{\frac{\sigma_K}{1-\sigma_Z}-2}.$$

The two eigenvalues, μ_1 and μ_2, are

$$\mu_i = \frac{1}{2}\left[(r-g) \pm \sqrt{(r-g)^2 + 4a_{21}\tilde{k}/h}\right] \tag{11}$$

and the system is saddle-point stable if and only if $a_{21} > 0$, that is, if and only if $1-\sigma_K-\sigma_Z > 0$. In terms of the basic parameters, this imposes an upper bound on the magnitude of the externality, namely $\eta < 1-\sigma-\xi$. Imposing this condition, it follows that $g > 0$.[15]

Hence, the equilibrium balanced growth rate of capital (output) g, consistent with the transversality condition, and with a staddle-point equilibrium, is given by

$$0 < g \equiv \frac{\sigma_N}{1-\sigma_K-\sigma_Z}n < r. \tag{12}$$

Assuming that (12) is met, and denoting the negative eigenvalue by $\mu_1 < 0$, the stable solution to (10) is

$$\begin{pmatrix} k(t)-\tilde{k} \\ q(t)-\tilde{q} \end{pmatrix} = (k_0-\tilde{k}) \begin{pmatrix} 1 \\ \mu_1 h/\tilde{k} \end{pmatrix} e^{\mu_1 t}. \tag{13}$$

As usual, we assume that the capital stock accumulates gradually from its given initial stock, k_0, whereas the market price of installed capital, q, may adjust instantaneously to new information.

Figure 1 illustrates the phase diagram for the linearized dynamic subsystem (10). The value q corresponds to the $\dot{k} = 0$ locus. The value $q^* = 1+hr$ denotes the value of q at which the slope of the $\dot{q} = 0$ locus becomes vertical. Steady-state equilibrium is at the intersection of the $\dot{k} = 0$ and the $\dot{q} = 0$ loci, with XX being the negatively sloped saddlepath through that point, having the slope $\mu_1 h/\tilde{k}$.

14 To see this, note first that in steady-state, $\dot{K}_i/K_i = (\tilde{q}_i - 1)/h - n = g - n$. Hence $K_i(t) = K_i(0)\,e^{(g-n)t}$. Second, the solution of (2d) is $\lambda(t) = \lambda(0)\,e^{(\beta+n-r)t}$. Third, at steady-state $q(t) = \tilde{q}$. Inserting these expressions into the transversality condition yields $p\tilde{q}\lambda(0)K_i(0)\lim_{t\to\infty} e^{(g-r)t} = 0$, which is satisfied if and only if $r > g$.

15 Note that the condition $1-\sigma_Z-\sigma_K > 0$ is imposed directly on the production function.

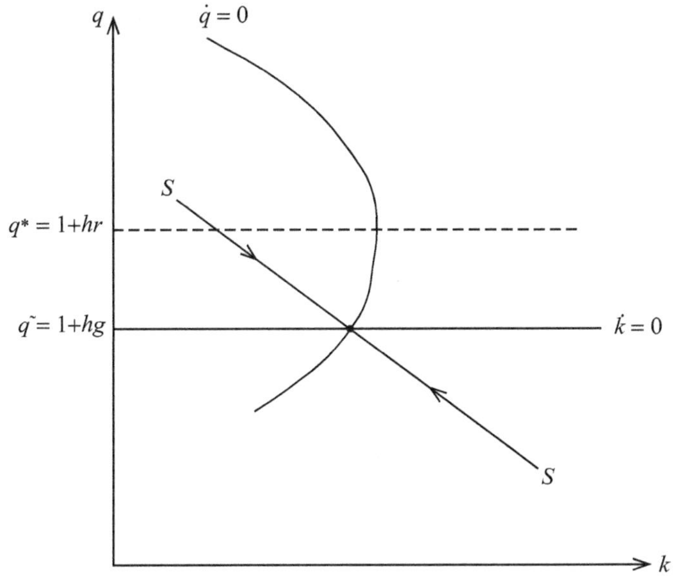

Fig. 1 Phase diagram

3.3 Accumulation of Foreign Assets

An important aspect of this equilibrium is that differential growth rates of consumption and domestic output can be sustained. This is a consequence of the economy being small in the world financial market and we now consider the implications of this for its net asset position.[16]

Aggregating the individual consumer's flow budget constraint, (1e), implies that the aggregate net rate of accumulation of traded bonds by the private sector, the nation's current account balance, is described by

$$\dot{B} = rB + Y - C - pZ - I\left(1 + \frac{h}{2}\frac{I}{K}\right), \tag{14}$$

which, when converted to scale-adjusted form and with substitution, becomes

$$\dot{b} = (r-g)b + (1-\sigma_Z)\alpha^{1/(1-\sigma_Z)}\left(p^{-1}\sigma_Z\right)^{\sigma_Z/(1-\sigma_Z)}k^{\sigma_K/(1-\sigma_Z)} - \frac{q^2-1}{2h}k - c. \tag{15}$$

[16] We shall assume that the country is sufficiently small so that it can maintain a growth rate that is unrelated to that in the rest of the world. Ultimately, this requirement imposes a constraint on the growth rate of the economy. If it grows faster than the rest of the world, at some point it will cease to be small. While we do not pursue the issue here, we should note that the issue of convergence in international growth rates is an important one.

In the Appendix we show that provided the transversality conditions (2f) hold, the linearized solution to the scale-adjusted per capita stock of bonds, starting from the initial stock of bonds, b_0, is given by

$$b(t) = -\frac{M}{r-g} - \frac{L}{r-g-\mu_1} e^{\mu_1 t} + \frac{c(0)}{r-\psi} e^{(\psi-g)t}, \tag{16a}$$

where M and L are constants defined in the Appendix and

$$c(0) = (r-\psi)\left[b_0 + \frac{M}{r-g} + \frac{L}{r-g-\mu_1}\right]. \tag{16b}$$

As we note in the Appendix, (16b) is effectively the economy's intertemporal budget constraint and reflects the present value of the resources available for initial consumption after the investment needs along the transition path have been met. The term $M/(r-g)$ reflects the resources for consumption if the economy were to reach the new steady state instantaneously, while $L/(r-g-\mu_1)$ reflects an adjustment due to the fact that the new steady state is reached only gradually.

We observe from (16a) that traded bonds are subject to transitional dynamics, in the sense that their growth rate $\dot{b}/b$ varies through time. There are two cases. First, if $\psi < g$, $b \to -M/(r-g)$ so that asymptotically bonds grow at the same rate as capital, g. If $\psi > g$, the scale adjusted stock of traded bonds grows at the rate $\psi - g$, with the aggregate stock of traded bonds growing at the rate ψ. Which case is relevant depends critically upon the size of the consumer rate of time preference relative to the rate of return on investment opportunities, among other parameters.[17]

4 Increase of the Price of the Intermediate Input *p*

4.1 Steady-State Changes

We now consider the effects of an unanticipated permanent increase in the price of the imported input ($dp > 0$), occuring at time $t = 0$. Assuming perfect foresight, the dynamic evolution of the economy is determined in part by agents' expectations of the ultimate steady-state response. It is therefore convenient to start our analysis with the investigation of the long-run steady-state effects of an increase in p. Starting from an initial steady-state, (9a) implies that the long-run market price of installed capital, $\tilde{q}$, does not change, since the economy's steady-state growth rate, g, is independent of the price of the intermediate input. From (9b), together with (8a′) and (8b), we see that the price of the imported input has the following long-run effects on the scale-adjusted capital stock, output, and the demand for the imported

[17] This issue is discussed in more detail in Turnovsky (1996) in the context of an endogenous growth model. But the same issue is relevant here.

input:

$$\frac{d\tilde{k}}{\tilde{k}} = -\frac{\sigma_Z}{1-\sigma_K-\sigma_Z}\frac{dp}{p} = -\frac{\xi}{1-\sigma-\eta-\xi}\frac{dp}{p} < 0, \tag{17a}$$

$$\frac{d\tilde{z}}{\tilde{z}} = -\frac{1}{1-\sigma_Z}\frac{dp}{p} + \frac{\sigma_K}{1-\sigma_Z}\frac{d\tilde{k}}{\tilde{k}} = -\frac{1-\sigma_K}{1-\sigma_K-\sigma_Z}\frac{dp}{p} = -\frac{1-\sigma-\eta}{1-\sigma-\eta-\xi}\frac{dp}{p} < 0, \tag{17b}$$

$$\frac{d\tilde{y}}{\tilde{y}} = -\frac{\sigma_Z}{1-\sigma_Z}\frac{dp}{p} + \frac{\sigma_K}{1-\sigma_Z}\frac{d\tilde{k}}{\tilde{k}} = -\frac{\sigma_Z}{1-\sigma_K-\sigma_Z}\frac{dp}{p} = -\frac{\xi}{1-\sigma-\eta-\xi}\frac{dp}{p} < 0. \tag{17c}$$

Thus, an increase in the price of the imported input leads to a more than proportionate reduction in the use of the input. It reduces the economy's scale-adjusted capital stock and output levels by the same proportionate amounts, though in both cases by a lesser amount than the usage of the input itself. Hence, although the long-run growth rate of output does not change, the new balanced growth path following a higher oil price is associated with lower capital, lower output, and reduced usage of the imported input.

4.2 *Impact Effects*

Equations (8) reveal that an increase in the price of the imported input leads to an immediate reduction in its usage, and because the capital stock is given in the short run, production falls as well, that is,

$$\frac{dz(0)}{\tilde{z}} = -\frac{1}{1-\sigma_Z}\frac{dp}{p} = -\frac{1}{1-\xi}\frac{dp}{p} < 0, \tag{18a}$$

$$\frac{dy(0)}{\tilde{y}} = -\frac{\sigma_Z}{1-\sigma_Z}\frac{dp}{p} = -\frac{\xi}{1-\xi}\frac{dp}{p} < 0. \tag{18b}$$

Comparing (18a) and (18b) with (17b) and (17c), we see that the short-run decline in both the usage of the input and output is less than the long-run decline, implying that following the initial drop, both $z(t), y(t)$ will continue to fall steadily as the economy evolves over time.

From (13) considered at the initial time, $t = 0$, we obtain the relationship

$$q(0) - \tilde{q} = \frac{\mu_1 h}{\tilde{k}}\left(k_0 - \tilde{k}\right),$$

from which the impact effect on the market price of installed capital can be found by differentiating with respect to p and noting that k_0 is historically given, and $\tilde{q}$ does not change, yielding

$$\frac{dq(0)}{dp} = -\frac{\mu_1 h}{\tilde{k}}\frac{d\tilde{k}}{dp} < 0. \tag{18c}$$

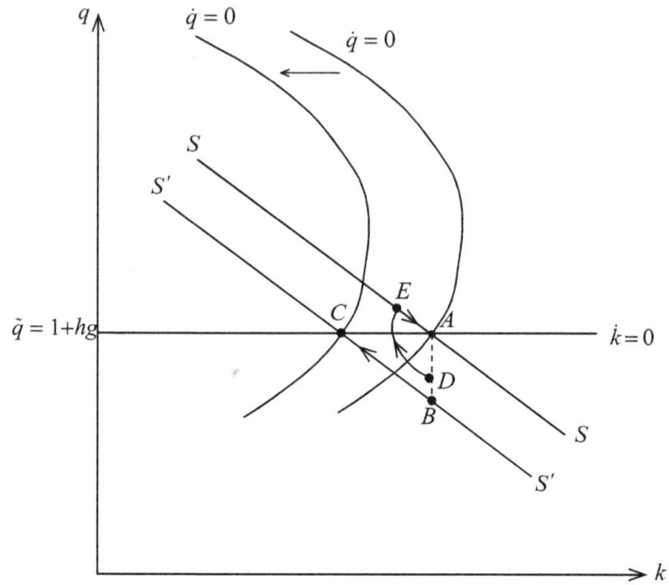

Fig. 2 Increase in price of input

Thus an increase in the imported input price causes $q(0)$ to drop on impact. In Fig. 2, the economy jumps down from point A to point B, lying on the stable saddle-path $S'S'$ associated with the new steady-state, located at C. Intuitively, the reduction of the imported input and the resulting decline in its usage lowers the marginal product of capital, now and in the future; thus reducing the current market price of capital.

The initial response of scale-adjusted consumption, resulting from an increase in the price of the imported input can be derived from (16b), and is given by

$$\frac{\mathrm{d}c(0)}{\mathrm{d}p} = (r-\psi)\left[\frac{1}{r-g}\frac{\mathrm{d}M}{\mathrm{d}p} + \frac{1}{r-g-\mu_1}\frac{\mathrm{d}L}{\mathrm{d}p}\right], \tag{18d}$$

where it turns out that the eigenvalue, μ_1, can be shown to be independent of p.[18] The effect of an increase in the price of the imported input on initial consumption depends upon the net effect of the overall resources after investment needs have been met. To evaluate $\mathrm{d}c(0)/\mathrm{d}p$ from (18d) is tedious and instead, we can argue directly that $\mathrm{d}c(0)/\mathrm{d}p < 0$. Suppose instead that $\mathrm{d}c(0)/\mathrm{d}p > 0$. It then follows that $\mathrm{d}C(0)/\mathrm{d}p > 0$ and with the consumption growth rate being independent of p that the level of consumption, and therefore utility, increases at all points of time. If that is the case, agents in the small economy are unambiguously better off with the higher import price, which clearly makes no economic sense. Thus, we can conclude that at least in any plausible context, initial consumption and thus consumption at all points of time decline with the increase in the price of the imported input.

[18] This implies that the asymptotic speed of convergence is independent of p.

Finally, the impact on the country's current account follows from differentiating (15) with respect to p, yielding

$$\frac{\mathrm{d}\dot{b}(0)}{\mathrm{d}p} = -(\sigma_Z p^{-1}\alpha)^{1/(1-\sigma_Z)} k^{\sigma_K/(1-\sigma_Z)} - \frac{qk}{h}\frac{\mathrm{d}q(0)}{\mathrm{d}p} - \frac{\mathrm{d}c(0)}{\mathrm{d}p}. \tag{18e}$$

The formal expression (16e) summarizes the two offsetting effects in operation. First, the direct effect of the increase in the price of the imported input is to reduce its usage, thereby reducing productivity and domestic output; thus adversely affecting the trade balance. At the same time, the reduction in $q(0)$ and the reduction in $c(0)$ reduce domestic demand and thus improve the current account, with the net effect depending upon which influence dominates.

4.3 Dynamic Transition

The subsequent transitional adjustment in capital and its price is also illustrated in Fig. 2. Immediately following the initial drop in the price of capital,$q(0)$, the economy is located at the point B on the new stable saddlepath, $S'S'$. At that point $q < 1 + gh$ and the economy begins gradually to reduce its stock of capital. As this occurs, its market price starts to increase, as a consequence of the increased scarcity of capital. Thus, the capital stock and its price gradually evolve toward point C, the new steady-state. Along this path, the market price of capital is expected to rise, yielding a capital gain ($\dot{q}/q > 0$), which offsets the lower marginal product of capital, thereby maintaining financial market equilibrium.

After the initial drops in scale-adjusted input z and output y, (8) imply that the gradual reduction of the scale-adjusted capital stock reduces z and y further over time, a fact that we have already observed. Therefore, investment, imported inputs, and output show transitional dynamics. However, after its impact reaction, consumption continues to grow at the constant rate $\psi - g$. The dynamics of traded bonds are governed by (16a). From this equation we see that if $\psi < g$, the economy's foreign position approaches asymptotically $-M/(g-r)$, where M measures the difference between steady-state investment expenditure and input imports, and steady-state production. If, on the other hand, $\psi > g$, in the long-run b will grow asymptotically at rate $\psi - g > 0$, see also Eicher and Turnovsky (1999).

Noting that the growth rates of the economy's aggregate key variables are linked to their scale adjusted growth rates by $\hat{X} = \hat{x} + g$, it follows that the higher imported input price has severe economic effects. As both the scale-adjusted capital stock and scale-adjusted output fall, during transition the economy's aggregate capital stock, K, and production, Y, grow at slower rates than g, there is a slump in per capita production. Only in the long-run does growth revert to its balanced path. This is precisely what one had observed during the 1970s, as the sharp increase in oil prices caused sharp reductions in western countries' economic performance.

5 Temporary Increase in Price of Imported Input

As we noted at the outset, one of the concerns of the early literature dealing with oil price shocks was with the contrasting effects of different qualitative shocks (temporary vs. permanent, etc). Here we briefly compare the effects of the permanent increase with those of a temporary increase on the growth rates. Just as a permanent increase in the price of the imported input has no effect on the growth rate of consumption, neither does a temporary increase, although it will affect the level of consumption, temporarily.

In contrast, there is a temporary effect on the growth rate of capital, which can be informally illustrated in Fig. 2.[19] Suppose that the economy starts out at the initial equilibrium A and at $t = 0$ learns that the price of the imported input is to be increased temporarily until time T, when it will revert to its original level. At the initial time the stable path SS will drop to $S'S'$, which would take the economy to a new steady state at C, if the increase were to be permanent. However, since the increase is only temporary, the economy discounts it somewhat, so that $q(0)$ drops only partially to the point D. With $q(0) < 1 + gh$, the rate of investment declines, but at a slower rate, and the output side of the economy begins to follow the unstable path DE. Along this path, the tendency for capital accumulation is subject to two offsetting forces. First, $q < 1 + gh$ is a signal to reduce the capital stock. But at the same time, the knowledge that the higher input price is only temporary and that the productivity of capital will be increased when the original input price and input usage are restored to their original levels is an incentive to increase the capital stock. As time T and the end of the higher price approaches, the latter effect strengthens and after the economy crosses the $\dot{k} = 0$ axis it actually dominates, so that k increases. At time T, when the input price returns to its original level, the economy reaches the point E, and the stable locus reverts to SS, which it then follows back to the original steady state A.

6 Endogenous Growth

Thus far we have made the critical assumption that $\sigma_K + \sigma_Z < 1$, or in terms of the underlying parameters, $\sigma + \xi + \eta < 1$. This emerged as a stability condition insofar as the capital adjustment of the economy is concerned. We now address the polar, but important, case where $\sigma + \xi + \eta = 1$, so that the production function has constant returns to scale in the factors that are being endogenously accumulated. In this case, if in addition there is positive population growth ($n > 0$), there can be no balanced growth path for output or capital. We will therefore require the additional assumption that the population is constant, and without loss of generality normalize it at unity. This of course is the assumption underlying the conventional endogenous growth model of the Romer (1986) type.

[19] A formal analysis can be carried out following the procedure set out in Schubert and Turnovsky (2002).

Under these conditions, the consumption dynamics remains unchanged. With $n = 0$, (5′) and (5′) coincide, yielding the equilibrium consumption growth rate

$$\frac{\dot{C}}{C} = \frac{r-\beta}{1-\gamma} \equiv \psi. \tag{19}$$

In contrast to the previous model, the capital and output dynamics now degenerate. In particular, under the present knife-edge condition, the aggregate production function (3′) reduces to

$$Y = \alpha K^{\sigma_K} Z^{1-\sigma_K}, \tag{3'}$$

while the equilibrium demand for the imported input is now

$$Z = (p^{-1}\alpha\sigma_Z)^{1/\sigma_K} K. \tag{8a'}$$

Substituting this expression in (3′), the equilibrium production function is of the AK form

$$Y = \alpha^{1/(1-\sigma_Z)}(p^{-1}\sigma_Z)^{\sigma_Z/\sigma_K} K, \tag{20}$$

where it will be observed from (20) that the productivity of capital varies inversely with the price of the imported input, as firms economize on its usage.

Under these conditions, the the arbitrage condition (7b) reduces to

$$\frac{1}{q}\sigma\alpha^{1/\sigma_K}\left(p^{-1}\sigma_Z\right)^{\sigma_Z/\sigma_K} + \frac{\dot{q}}{q} + \frac{(q-1)^2}{2hq} = r \tag{21}$$

and is independent of k. This equation is of the same form as (5b) in Turnovsky (1996) and represents a simple quadratic differential equation in q alone. For the capital stock and output of this small economy ultimately to follow a path of steady growth, the stationary solution to this equation, attained when $\dot{q} = 0$, must have (at least) one real solution. Setting $\dot{q} = 0$ in (20) implies that the steady-state value of q, $\tilde{q}$ say, must be a solution to the quadratic equation:

$$\sigma\alpha^{1/\sigma_K}\left(p^{-1}\sigma_Z\right)^{\sigma_Z/\sigma_K} + \frac{(q-1)^2}{2h} = rq. \tag{22}$$

A necessary and sufficient condition for the capital stock ultimately to converge to a steady growth path is that this equation have real roots, and this will be so if and only if

$$\sigma\alpha^{1/\sigma_K}\left(p^{-1}\sigma_Z\right)^{\sigma_Z/\sigma_K} \leq r\left[1+\frac{hr}{2}\right]. \tag{23}$$

Thus, the existence of an equilibrium balanced growth path involves a comprehensive tradeoff between the parameters appearing in (23).

Assuming that (23) holds, so that a steady asymptotic growth path for capital does indeed exist, there are two real solutions to the quadratic equation (22), indicating the potential existence of two steady equilibrium growth rates for capital. As shown in Turnovsky (1996) for the model with no intermediate input, the equilibrium corresponding to the smaller value, q_1 say, is an unstable equilibrium, while the equilibrium that corresponds to the larger value, q_2 say, is locally stable. However, any time path for q that converges to the locally stable equilibrium can be shown to violate the transversality condition. Consequently, the only solution for q that is consistent with the transversality condition is that q will always be at the (unstable) steady-state solution q_1, given by the smaller root to (22).

Consequently, there are *no* transitional dynamics in the market price of capital q. In response to any shock, q immediately jumps to its new equilibrium value and as a result, domestically domiciled capital is always on its steady growth path, growing at the rate $\varphi = (q_1 - 1)/h$. In particular, an increase in the price of the imported input leads to an instantaneous one-time permanent reduction in q_1, leading to corresponding permanent reductions in the growth rates of capital and output.

Substituting the expressions I,$K(t)$, and Z from (6) and (8a′), and $C(t)$ from (5′) in (14), this accumulation equation can be written in the form

$$\dot{B} = rB + \vartheta K_0 \mathrm{e}^{\varphi t} - C(0)\mathrm{e}^{\psi t}, \tag{24}$$

where $\varphi = (q_1 - 1)/h$, $\psi = (r - \beta)/(1 - \gamma)$, and

$$\vartheta \equiv \sigma_K \alpha^{1/\sigma_K} \left(p^{-1}\sigma_Z\right)^{\sigma_Z/\sigma_K} - \frac{(q_1^2 - 1)}{2h}. \tag{25}$$

The final step is to solve (24), which describes the accumulation of traded bonds. Starting from a given initial stock B_0, the stock of traded bonds at time t is given by

$$B(t) = \left(B_0 + \frac{\vartheta K_0}{r - \varphi} - \frac{C(0)}{r - \psi}\right)\mathrm{e}^{rt} - \frac{\vartheta K_0}{r - \varphi}\mathrm{e}^{\varphi t} + \frac{C(0)}{r - \psi}\mathrm{e}^{\psi t}. \tag{26}$$

To ensure national intertemporal solvency, the transversality conditions now require

$$C(0) = (r - \psi)\left(B_0 + \frac{\vartheta K_0}{r - \varphi}\right) \tag{27}$$

so that

$$B(t) + \frac{\vartheta}{r - \varphi}K(t) = \left(B_0 + \frac{\vartheta K_0}{r - \varphi}\right)\mathrm{e}^{\psi t}. \tag{28}$$

Using (22), we see that

$$\frac{\vartheta}{r - \varphi} = q_1 + \frac{\eta \alpha^{1/\sigma_K}\left(p^{-1}\sigma_Z\right)^{\sigma_Z/\sigma_K}}{r - \varphi}, \tag{25′}$$

which can be interpreted as being the price of capital, adjusted for the externality, η. Thus the "externality-adjusted" wealth grows at the same rate as does consumption. It immediately follows from (27) and (28) that the reduction in q_1 stemming from the higher oil price leads to an immediate reduction in initial consumption and wealth, which then both continue to grow at their previous rates, although on a permanently reduced base. Moreover, this effect is compounded to the extent that the externality from aggregate capital $\eta > 0$.

7 Conclusions

In this chapter we studied the effects of an increase in the price of an intermediate input (say oil) on the dynamic time path of a small open economy. Most of our analysis has employed an extension of the nonscale growth model, developed by Eicher and Turnovsky (1999), although for comparative purposes we have also briefly considered a simple endogenous growth model as well. Both models assume that the economy has access to a perfect world capital market, a consequence of which is that the equilibrium growth rates of consumption and output can diverge indefinitely. Both models yield similar implications for consumption following an oil shock; the initial consumption level drops, although its subsequent growth rate remains unaffected.

However, the two models yield sharply contrasting implications for the growth rate of capital and its price. In the case of the nonscale growth model, the effects on the growth rate are only temporary. That is, an increase in the price of the input pushes the economy off its balanced growth path, causes an economic slump, and lowers growth during transition. However, eventually, the growth rate of capital and output recovers back to its initial balanced growth rate, although output, capital, and consumption are all permanently lower. In the case of endogenous growth model, the behavior of the production side is fundamentally different. There are no transitional dynamics; instead there is instantaneous adjustment in the growth rate of capital and output. Thus, a permanent increase in the price of the imported input leads to a permanent reduction in the growth rate of capital and output.

There are other differences as well. For example, the flexibility of the capital–labor ratio in the nonscale model always ensures the existence of an equilibrium balanced growth rate of output. In the case of the endogenous growth model, this need be so and depends upon tradeoffs among the productive parameters. To the extent that the recent evidence suggests that recent oil shocks have had only temporary effects on growth rates, this is an argument favoring the more flexible nonscale model over the more rigid Romer-type endogenous growth model.

As one final point, we recall the observation that developing countries are particularly vulnerable to fluctuations in oil prices and imported inputs in general. It is therefore important that this type of analysis be adapted to the context of a developing economy. To do this, the most important modification is to drop the assumption of unlimited access to a perfect world capital market, assumed in this analysis, to the more relevant situation of limited access. One way to formulate this is to assume that the economy is a debtor nation facing an upward sloping supply curve of debt. The effect of this is to tie the growth rates of consumption and output so that the decoupling of the two steady-state growth rates, characteristic of the present analysis, no longer holds. Eicher et al. (2008) have carried out such an analysis to examine the consequences for the conventional Laursen–Metzler–Harberger terms of trade effects. A natural extension of the present analysis would be to consider the impact of oil price shocks in this framework.

Appendix

Solution for b(t)

For notational simplicity we write (15) in the form

$$\dot{b}(t) = (r-g)b(t) + x(t) - c(t), \tag{29}$$

where

$$Q \equiv (1-\sigma_Z)\alpha^{1/(1-\sigma_Z)}\left(p^{-1}\sigma_Z\right)^{\sigma_Z/(1-\sigma_Z)}, \tag{30a}$$

$$x(t) \equiv Qk(t)^{\sigma_K/(1-\sigma_Z)} - \frac{q(t)^2-1}{2h}k(t), \tag{30b}$$

so that (30b) denotes output net of total resource costs of investment at time t. Starting from an initial stock of bonds, $b_0(0)$, the solution to (29) is

$$b(t) = \mathrm{e}^{(r-g)t}\left(b_0 + \int_0^t x(\tau)\mathrm{e}^{-(r-g)\tau}\mathrm{d}\tau - \int_0^t c(\tau)\mathrm{e}^{-(r-g)\tau}\mathrm{d}\tau\right). \tag{31}$$

To ensure national intertemporal solvency, the transversality condition $\lim_{t\to\infty} \lambda B \mathrm{e}^{-\beta t} = \lim_{t\to\infty} \lambda(0)b(t)N_0\mathrm{e}^{-(r-g)t} = 0$ must hold, and this will hold if and only if

$$\int_0^\infty c(\tau)\mathrm{e}^{-(r-g)\tau}\mathrm{d}\tau = b_0 + \int_0^\infty x(\tau)\mathrm{e}^{-(r-g)\tau}\mathrm{d}\tau. \tag{32}$$

This intertemporal constraint asserts that the present value of consumption equals the present value of resources available for consumption after investment needs have been met.

Recalling the aggregate consumption growth rate, (5′), we see that $c(t) \equiv C/N^{\sigma_N/(1-\sigma_K-\sigma_Z)}$ is

$$c(t) = c(0)\mathrm{e}^{(\psi-g)t}. \tag{33}$$

Substituting this expression in (32), we obtain

$$c(0) = (r-\psi)\left(b_0 + \int_0^\infty x(\tau)\mathrm{e}^{-(r-g)\tau}\mathrm{d}\tau\right), \tag{34}$$

where $r > \psi$ in order for consumption to be nonnegative, thus imposing an upper bound on the rate of growth of consumption. This condition reduces to $\gamma < \rho/(r-n)$, imposing an upper limit on the intertemporal elasticity of substitution.

This is certainly met for the logarithmic utility function and given the empirical evidence indicating small elasticities of substitution $\gamma < \rho/(r-n)$ will hold under less restrictive conditions as well. Equation (33) thus determines the initial consumption level, such that given its growth, the economy's intertemporal budget constraint will be met.

To determine the corresponding feasible time path for bonds, we substitute the solution for $c(t)$ in (31) and evaluate

$$b(t) = \mathrm{e}^{(r-g)t}\left(b_0 + \int_0^t x(\tau)\,\mathrm{e}^{-(r-g)\tau}\,\mathrm{d}\tau - \frac{c(0)}{r-\psi}\left[1-\mathrm{e}^{-(r-\psi)t}\right]\right).$$

We then substitute (34) enabling us to write the solution in the form

$$b(t) = \mathrm{e}^{(\psi-g)t}\left(b_0 + \int_0^\infty x(\tau)\mathrm{e}^{-(r-g)\tau}\,\mathrm{d}\tau\right) - \int_t^\infty x(\tau)\,\mathrm{e}^{-(r-g)(\tau-t)}\,\mathrm{d}\tau. \tag{35}$$

To obtain operational approximations to (34) and (35), we linearize $x(t)$ around its steady state

$$\tilde{x} \equiv Q\tilde{k}^{\sigma_K/(1-\sigma_Z)} - \frac{\tilde{q}^2-1}{2h}\tilde{k},$$

and substitute the transitional dynamic adjustment paths for $k(t), q(t)$. The resulting expressions are

$$c(0) = (r-\psi)\left[b_0 + \frac{M}{r-g} + \frac{L}{r-g-\mu}\right] \tag{36a}$$

and

$$b(t) = -\frac{M}{r-g} - \frac{L}{r-g-\mu_1}\,\mathrm{e}^{\mu_1 t} + \left(b_0 + \frac{M}{r-g} + \frac{L}{r-g-\mu_1}\right)\mathrm{e}^{(\psi-g)t}, \tag{36b}$$

where

$$M \equiv Q\tilde{k}^{\sigma_K/(1-\sigma_Z)} - \frac{(\tilde{q}^2-1)}{2h}\tilde{k}, \tag{37a}$$

$$L \equiv \left(Q\frac{\sigma_K}{1-\sigma_Z}\tilde{k}^{\frac{\sigma_K}{1-\sigma_Z}-1} - \frac{(\tilde{q}^2-1)}{2h} - \mu_1\tilde{q}\right)(k_0-\tilde{k}), \tag{37b}$$

and Q is defined in (30a).

Acknowledgment The constructive suggestions of an anonymous referee are gratefully acknowledged. Schubert's research was supported by funds of the Free University of Bozen-Bolzano. Turnovsky's research was supported in part by the Castor endowment at the University of Washington.

References

Bardhan P, Lewis S (1970) Models of growth with imported inputs. Economica 37:373–385

Barro RJ (1997) Determinants of economic growth: a cross-country empirical study. MIT Press, Cambridge, MA

Barro RJ (2003) Determinants of economic growth in a panel of countries. Ann Econ Finance 4:231–274

Barsky RB, Kilian L (2004) Oil and the macroeconomy since 1970s. J Econ Perspect 18:115–134

Bean CR (1986) The terms of trade, labour supply and the current account. Econ J 96:38–46

Becker T, Mauro P (2006) Output drops and the shocks that matter. IMF Working Paper No. 06/172

Bhandari JS, Turnovsky SJ (1984) Materials price increases and aggregate adjustment in an open economy. Eur Econ Rev 25:151–182

Bruno M, Sachs J (1982a) Energy and resource allocation: a dynamic model of the Dutch disease. Rev Econ Stud 49:845–859

Bruno M, Sachs J (1982b) Input price shocks and the slowdown in economic growth: the case of UK manufacturing. Rev Econ Stud 49:679–705

Corden WM (1975) A framework for analyzing the implications of the rise in oil prices. In: Rybczynski T (ed) The economics of the oil crisis. Holmes and Meier, New York

Eicher TS, Schubert SF, Turnovsky SJ (2008) Dynamic effects of terms of trade shocks: the impact on debt and growth. J Int Money Finance

Eicher TS, Turnovsky SJ (1999) International capital markets and non-scale growth. Rev Int Econ 7:171–188

Findlay R, Rodriguez AC (1977) Intermediate imports and macroeconomic policy under flexible exchange rates. Can J Econ 10:208–217

Golub S (1983) Oil prices and exchange rates. Econ J 93:576–593

Grounder R, Bartleet M (2007) Oil price shocks and economic growth: evidence for New Zealand, 1989–2006. NZ Association of economists, Christchurch

Harberger AC (1950) Currency depreciation, income, and the balance of trade. J Polit Econ 58: 47–60

Hayashi F (1982) Tobin's marginal q, average q: a neoclassical interpretation. Econometrica 50:213–224

Huang KXD, Meng Q (2007) The Harberger–Laursen–Metzler effect under capital market imperfections. J Int Money Finance 26:1001–1015

Ikeda S (2001) Weakly non-separable preferences and the Harberger–Laursen–Metzler effect. Can J Econ 34:290–307

Jones CI (1995a) R & D based models of economic growth. J Polit Econ 103:759–784

Jones CI (1995b) Time series tests of endogenous growth models. Q J Econ 110:495–527

Kandil M (2006) On the transmission of exchange rate fluctuations to the macroeconomy: contrasting evidence for developing and developed countries. J Int Trade Econ Dev 15:101–127

Kose MA (2002) Explaining business cycles in small open economies: how much do world prices matter?. J Int Econ 56:299–327

Krugman P (1983) Oil and the dollar. In: Bhandari J, Putnam B (eds) Economic interdependence and flexible exchange rates, MIT Press, Cambridge, MA

Laursen S, Metzler LA (1950) Flexible exchange rates and the theory of employment. Rev Econ Stat 32:281–299

Marion N (1984) Nontraded goods, oil price increases and the current account. J Int Econ 16:29–44

Marion N, Svensson LEO (1984) Adjustments to expected and unexpected oil price changes. Can J Econ 17:15–31

Matsuyama K (1988) Terms-of-trade, factor intensities and the current account in a life-cycle model. Rev Econ Stud 55:247–262

Mendoza EG (1995) The terms of trade, the real exchange rate, and economic fluctuations. Int Econ Rev 36:101–137

Obstfeld M (1980) Intermediate imports, the terms of trade and the dynamics of the current account. J Int Econ 10:461–480

Obstfeld M (1982) Aggregate spending and the terms of trade: Is there a Laursen–Metzler effect? Q J Econ 97:251–270

Otto G (2003) Terms of trade shocks and the balance of trade: there is a Harberger–Laursen–Metzler effect. J Int Money Finance 22:155–184

Persson T, Svensson LEO (1985) Current account dynamics and the terms of trade: Harberger–Laursen–Metzler two generations later. J Polit Econ 93:43–65

Romer PM (1986) Increasing returns and long-run growth. J Polit Econ 94:1002–1038

Sachs J (1983) Energy and growth under flexible exchange rates. In: Bhandari J, Putnam B (eds) Economic interdependence and flexible exchange rates, MIT Press, Cambridge, MA

Sachs J, Cooper RN, Fischer S (1981) The current account and macroeconomic adjustment in the 1970s. Brookings Papers Econ Activity 1:201–268

Schubert SF, Turnovsky SJ (2002) The dynamics of temporary policies in a small open economy. Rev Int Econ 10:604–622

Sen P (1991) Imported input price and the current account in an optimizing model without capital mobility. J Econ Dyn Control 15:91–101

Sen P, Turnovsky SJ (1989) Deterioration of the terms of trade and capital accumulation: a re-examination of the Laursen–Metzler effect. J Int Econ 26:227–250

Serven L (1999) Terms-of-trade shocks and optimal investment: another look at the Laursen–Metzler effect. J Int Money Finance 18:337–365

Svensson LEO (1984) Oil prices, welfare and the trade balance. Q J Econ 99:649–672

Svensson LEO, Razin A (1983) The terms of trade and the current account: The Harberger–Laursen–Metzler effect. J Polit Econ 91:97–125

Turnovsky SJ (1996) Fiscal policy, growth, and macroeconomic performance in a small open economy. J Int Econ 40:41–66

Turnovsky SJ, Chattopadhyay P (2003) Volatility and growth in developing economies: some numerical results and empirical evidence. J Int Econ 59:267–295

Multiplicity and Stability of Equilibrium in Trade Models with Durable Goods

Eric Bond(✉) and Robert Driskill

Abstract We examine dynamic stability in Shimomura's durable-goods model of trade when there are multiple steady-state equilibria. In the case we examine, there are three such equilibria, corresponding to the three equilibria in Marshall's famous "shoelace" diagram. The two extreme equilibria are always characterized by saddlepath stability. The interior equilibrium may be a source, a sink, or a center, depending on the value of the intertemporal elasticity of substitution. Finally, we show that there is a unique equilibrium that is the limit of the equilibrium of a finite-horizon version of the model as the horizon goes to infinity.

1 Introduction

A classic result in static international trade theory concerns the conditions under which a two good trade model will have a unique trading equilibrium. The possibility of multiple equilibria is epitomized by the famous "shoelace" diagram of Marshall, which shows offer curves for two countries that generate three different world prices that are consistent with equilibrium in world markets. Associated with the result is the Marshall–Lerner condition for market stability, which shows that the highest and the lowest of these three prices will be stable, but the middle price is unstable under a Walrasian price adjustment process. The source of instability in the static model is the income effects in demand. When the exporting country has a higher marginal propensity to consume its export good than does the importing country, then the aggregate excess demand curve can be upward sloping in the neighborhood of the equilibrium.[1]

[1]See Jones (1961) for an overview and extension.

E. Bond
Department of Economics, Vanderbilt University, VU Station B #351819, 2301 Vanderbilt Place, Nashville, Tennessee 37235, USA, e-mail: eric.w.bond@vanderbilt.edu

T. Kamihigashi and L. Zhao (eds.) *International Trade and Economic Dynamics – Essays in Memory of Koji Shimomura.*

In this chapter we address the question of multiplicity and dynamic stability in the model of trade with a durable good developed by Shimomura (1993). Our analysis is motivated by Shimomura's subsequent analysis (Shimomura (2004)), which showed that the model could have multiple steady states when the durable good was inferior in the importing country. Furthermore, he showed that one of these steady states could exhibit dynamic indeterminacy.[2] However, his analysis neither did provide general conditions on preferences that would give rise to multiple steady states nor did it indicate whether the existence of multiple steady states would necessarily imply the existence of dynamic indeterminacy. In Bond and Driskill (2007), we addressed the former question and showed that if the consumption good is not inferior, then a sufficient condition for it to be a unique steady state is that the exporter's marginal propensity to consume be no higher than that in the importing country. Thus, the configuration of income effects that is sufficient to ensure uniqueness of equilibrium in the static model is also sufficient for the uniqueness of the steady-state equilibrium when one of the goods is durable. In this chapter we consider the example where the preferences fail for this sufficient condition for uniqueness, and address the question of whether multiple steady states can arise when neither good is inferior and whether the existence of multiple steady states implies the presence of dynamic indeterminacy.

Our results indicate that multiple steady-state equilibria can arise in cases where neither good is inferior in either country. We also show that the dynamic stability of these steady states will depend on the intertemporal elasticity of substitution. When each country has an infinite intertemporal elasticity of substitution and there are three equilibria, each of the extreme equilibria will exhibit saddlepath stability. The "middle" equilibrium will be unstable, in the sense that it is a "source" and all potential price paths will lead away from this equilibrium for initial stocks of the durable good in the neighborhood of the steady-state equilibrium. In this case, the results from the dynamic model are similar to those obtained in the static model, in that the unstable equilibrium is flanked by (saddlepath) stable equilibria.[3] However, the behavior in the neighborhood of the middle steady-state equilibrium price is sensitive to the value chosen for the intertemporal elasticity of substitution. For values sufficiently low, the middle equilibrium becomes a "sink" and there is dynamic indeterminacy. In contrast, the extreme equilibria are saddle points for all values of the intertemporal elasticity of substitution.

We also examine whether the dynamic model can provide a selection criterion for choosing among "stable" equilibria. In the static model, there is no criterion for choosing between the extreme equilibrium prices when there are multiple equilibria, because both satisfy the stability criterion. However, Karp and Paul (2003) have noted that dynamic elements of a model can be used to restrict the range of initial

[2] Doh et al. (2007) show that indeterminacy can also arise in a discrete time model. Their example also involves the durable good being inferior in the importing country.

[3] Unlike the static model, though, trajectories that start in the neighborhood of the middle steady-state do not end up at one of the extreme equilibria, but rather "escape" along an unbounded path.

conditions for which there exist multiple equilibria.[4] We follow this approach by using the criterion of selecting the equilibrium that is the limit of the equilibria of the finite horizon model. We show that the finite horizon equilibrium will be unique in this model, which leads to the selection of the equilibrium where the price of the durable good is relatively low.

Section 2 of this chapter presents the general version of a model of trade with a durable good and summarizes some of the properties of this model. Section 3 characterizes the steady-state equilibrium of our example in which each country has marginal propensity to consume its export good of unity, and provides an example in which there are multiple steady states. Section 4 examines the dynamics of this model, and shows how the dynamic behavior is affected by changes in the intertemporal elasticity of substitution. Section 5 applies the finite horizon selection criterion to the model, and Section 6 offers some concluding remarks.

2 The Model

As in Bond and Driskill (2007) and Shimomura (2004), we assume a continuous-time two-country two-sector model in which in each country one sector produces a durable consumption good and the other sector a nondurable consumption good. In the home (foreign) country, a representative agent derives instantaneous utility from consumption of a quantity C (C^*) of the nondurable consumption good and a quantity A (A^*) of the durable. The home (foreign) representative agent receives an endowment ω_C (ω_C^*) of the nondurable good and an endowment ω_A (ω_A^*) of the durable. The durable good depreciates at exponential rate δ. There is no international borrowing or lending. The relative price of the nondurable good in world markets at time t is denoted by $p(t)$, and domestic prices in each country will equal the world price due to the assumed absence of transport costs and trade barriers. Given a path $p(t)$, each representative agent maximizes the present discounted value of instantaneous utility. That is, we assume the home-country agent solves the following problem:

$$\max_C \int_0^\infty U(C,A)\,\mathrm{e}^{-\rho t}\,\mathrm{d}t$$

subject to

$$\dot{A} = \omega_A + p(\omega_C - C) - \delta A. \tag{1}$$

The current-value Hamiltonian is

$$H = U(A,C) + \lambda\{\omega_A + p(\omega_C - C) - \delta A\},$$

[4] See, for example, Matsuyama (1991) and Krugman (1991).

where λ is the current-value costate variable. The first-order conditions for the home-country representative agent are thus

$$U_C = p\lambda, \tag{2}$$

$$\dot{\lambda} = \lambda(\rho+\delta) - U_A. \tag{3}$$

The foreign agent solves the analogous problem, and thus has analogous first-order conditions.

The world market-clearing condition for the nondurable good is

$$C + C^* = \omega_C + \omega_C^*. \tag{4}$$

The world stock of the durable good evolves as

$$\dot{A} + \dot{A}^* = \omega_A + \omega_{A^*}^* - \delta(A + A^*). \tag{5}$$

A steady state in this model will be a world price p such that (1)–(5) are satisfied, with $\dot{\lambda} = \dot{\lambda}^* = \dot{A} = \dot{A}^* = 0$. In solving this problem, it is convenient to define steady state excess demand functions $m_i(p)$, $i = A, C$; $m_{i^*}^*(p)$, $i^* = A^*, C^*$, which represent the excess demand function for good i (i^*) that satisfies (1)–(3), with $\dot{\lambda} = \dot{\lambda}^* = \dot{A} = \dot{A}^* = 0$. Letting $m_i^*(p)$ denote the corresponding steady state demand functions for the foreign country, it then follows that a steady-state equilibrium for the world economy will satisfy $m_i(p) + m_{i^*}^*(p) = 0$.

The properties of these excess demand functions can be used to yield the following result (proven in Bond and Driskill (2007)), which yields a principle of comparative advantage for the steady state equilibrium and a sufficient condition for uniqueness.

Proposition 1. *If good C is not inferior in either country, then*

1. *There exist a unique home (foreign) autarky price $p\,(p^*)$ satisfying $m_C(p) = 0$ $(m_{C^*}^*(p^*) = 0)$*
2. *There exists at least one steady-state world price, and the country with the lower autarky price of good C will be the exporter in the steady state equilibrium*
3. *A sufficient condition for uniqueness is that the marginal propensity to consume good C in the exporting country be no higher than that in the importing country*

The uniqueness of the autarky equilibrium follows from the fact that the steady state excess demand functions will be continuous and must be negatively sloped at any p satisfying $m_C(p) = 0$. Since world steady state excess demand will then necessarily be positive (negative) for prices below (above) that of the country with the lower (higher) autarky price, the steady state pattern of trade must be predicted by a comparison of the autarky prices.

Part (3) indicates that a necessary condition for these to exist in multiple equilibria is that the exporting country has a higher marginal propensity to consume its exportable than does the importing country. This result is the same as that occurs in a static trade model, and arises for the same reason. An increase in the relative price of a good results in substitution away from the good in all countries, but also transfers income from the importing country to the exporting country. When substitution effects are small and the difference in marginal propensities to consume is large, an increase in price can actually increase the excess demand for the good.

Proposition 1 provides results on the number of equilibria, but it does not have anything to say about the dynamics in the neighborhood of the equilibrium. In the static model, a Walrasian price dynamic is added that results in the characterization of any equilibrium price at which the aggregate demand function is upward sloping as being unstable. This also means that any unstable equilibrium will be bounded by stable equilibria in the static model. In contrast to the ad hoc nature of price adjustment in the static model, the system of differential equations describing the motion of the stocks of the durable goods and the evolution of the costate variable provide a natural dynamic to examine the stability of equilibrium in the model with durable goods. A natural question to ask in this setting is what determines the "stability" of the dynamic model. Do the slopes of excess demand functions at the steady state provide information about the local behavior of the system at a steady state? What role does the intertemporal elasticity of substitution, a factor that is ignored in static models, play in determining dynamic behavior?

Our interest is in exploring the dynamic properties of this model when there are multiple equilibria. Proposition 1 establishes that to find such cases, we need to consider models in which the exporting country has a higher marginal propensity to consume its export good. Our examples below focus on the case in which each country has a marginal propensity to consume the export good of unity. What we show with these examples is the existence of a somewhat robust result: with three steady-state equilibria, the local dynamics around the two nonadjacent equilibria are characterized by saddlepath stability, while the interior equilibrium local dynamics exhibit a wide variety of characteristics, ranging from unstable to stable periodic solutions, depending upon parameter values. This implies that there are always two saddlepath-stable trajectories, each approaching a different steady state for any initial condition. In addition, when local dynamics around the interior steady-state equilibrium exhibit damped cyclical trajectories, then there are in addition an infinite number of trajectories that approach this interior steady state for a set of initial conditions sufficiently close to the steady-state value of the domestic stock of the durable associated with the interior equilibrium.

We also show an associated robust result: there exists a unique equilibrium path for an arbitrary initial condition that is the limit of a finite-horizon analogue to the model.

3 Examples

We now construct examples to illustrate these possibilities. First we demonstrate the conditions under which we are assured of three equilibria. We then investigate the dynamic properties associated with these cases.

3.1 Existence of Multiple Steady States

3.1.1 The Foreign Country Offer Curve

The general two-country model leads to a dynamic system with three state variables. We follow the insight of Shimomura (2004) in reducing the dimensionality of the problem by assuming quasi-linear preferences for the instantaneous utility function of the foreign country's representative agent. In particular, we assume

$$U^*(t) = A^*(t) + \beta_0 C^*(t) - \frac{\beta}{2}(C^*(t))^2, C^* \leq \frac{\beta_0}{\beta,}, \beta > 0, \beta_0 > 0.$$

The first-order conditions for the foreign country representative agent are thus

$$U^*_{C^*} = p\lambda^*,$$
$$\dot{\lambda}^* = \lambda^*(\rho + \delta) - U^*_{A^*}.$$

Because $U^*_{C^*} = 1$, the only value of λ^* consistent with a stable solution is

$$\lambda^*(t) = \frac{1}{\rho + \delta}. \quad (6)$$

The constancy of λ^*, the shadow-price of A^*, is the key implication of quasi-linearity, and it facilitates a significant simplification of the problem.

Substituting the assumed specific functional forms into these first-order conditions and rearranging, we have

$$-m^*_{A^*} = [(\rho + \delta)(\beta_0 - \beta\omega^*_{C^*})] - \beta(\rho + \delta)(m^*_{C^*})^2 \equiv \phi^*(m^*_{C^*}), \quad (7)$$

where $m^*_{A^*}$ and $m^*_{C^*}$ are the net import functions for the durable good and the consumption good, respectively. That is

$$m^*_{A^*} = \dot{A}^* - \omega^*_{A^*} + \delta A^*,$$
$$m^*_{C^*} = C^* - \omega^*_{C^*}.$$

This is the foreign country's offer curve. For purposes of our example, assume

$$(\beta_0 - \beta\omega^*_{C^*}) > 0.$$

Then, $-m^*_{A^*}$ achieves a maximum value of

$$-m^*_{A^*\max} = \frac{1}{4}\left[\frac{\beta_0 - \beta\omega^*_{C^*}}{\beta}\right].$$

Furthermore, $-m^*_{A^*} = 0$ when $m^*_{C^*} = \frac{\beta_0 - \beta\omega^*_{C^*}}{\beta}$. The offer curve is depicted in Fig 1.

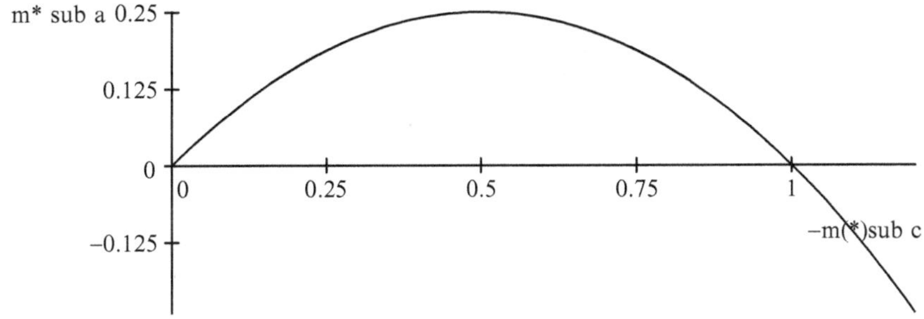

Fig. 1 Foreign country offer curve

3.1.2 The Home-Country Steady-State Offer Curve

The home country's representative agent is assumed to have preferences represented by the following instantaneous utility function:

$$U = \frac{\{C + \alpha_0 A - \frac{\alpha}{2}A^2\}^{1-\gamma}}{1-\gamma}, A < \frac{\alpha_0}{\alpha}, \alpha > 0, \alpha_0 > 0, \gamma > 0, \gamma \neq 1, \tag{8}$$

where γ is the inverse of the intertemporal elasticity of substitution. This agent maximizes the present discounted value of utility, subject to the constraints

$$p = \frac{m_A}{-m_C},$$
$$\dot{A} = \omega_A + m_A - \delta A.$$

First-order conditions are

$$\left\{C + \alpha_0 A - \frac{\alpha}{2}A^2\right\}^{-\gamma} = \lambda p, \tag{9}$$

$$\dot{\lambda} = \lambda(\rho + \delta) - \left\{C + \alpha_0 - \frac{\alpha}{2}A^2\right\}^{-\gamma}(\alpha_0 - \alpha A). \tag{10}$$

Setting all time derivatives to zero, we derive the home-country steady-state offer curve as

$$-m_C = m_A\left(\frac{\alpha_0\delta - \alpha\omega_A}{(\rho+\delta)\delta}\right) - \frac{\alpha}{(\rho+\delta)\delta}(m_A)^2 \equiv \phi(m_A). \tag{11}$$

Assume $(\alpha_0\delta - \alpha\omega_A) > 0$. When $m_A = \frac{\alpha_0\delta - \alpha\omega_A}{\alpha}$, $-m_C = 0$. Furthermore, when $m_A = \frac{\alpha_0\delta - \alpha\omega_A}{2\alpha}$, $\phi(m_A)$ obtains its maximum value of

$$-m_{C\max} = \frac{(\alpha_0\delta - \alpha\omega_A)^2}{4\alpha\delta(\rho+\delta)}.$$

Note that this steady-state offer curve is independent of the intertemporal elasticity-of-substitution parameter, γ. This parameter, though, will have important implications for the dynamic analysis.

3.1.3 Steady-State Equilibria

It is straightforward to specify parameter values such that the two steady-state offer curves form the classic "shoelace" diagram with three distinct equilibria. Such a case is depicted in Fig. 2. For example, such a set of parameter values is

$$\delta = .2,\ \beta_0 = 2.4,\ \beta = 1,\ \alpha_0 = 6,\ \alpha = 3,$$
$$\omega_C = 5,\ \omega_A = (1/(16)),\ \omega^*_{C^*} = .1,\ \omega^*_{A^*} = 1.$$

Associated equilibrium steady-state prices are

$$p_1 = .0810705;$$
$$p_2 = .139386;$$
$$p_3 = .285544.$$

As noted, traditional analysis of this case of multiple equilibria invoked the concept of Walrasian stability to show that the two extreme equilibria were stable while the interior one was unstable. With one durable good, though, the model is truly dynamic, and we can investigate the dynamic stability properties of these equilibria in both local and global terms.

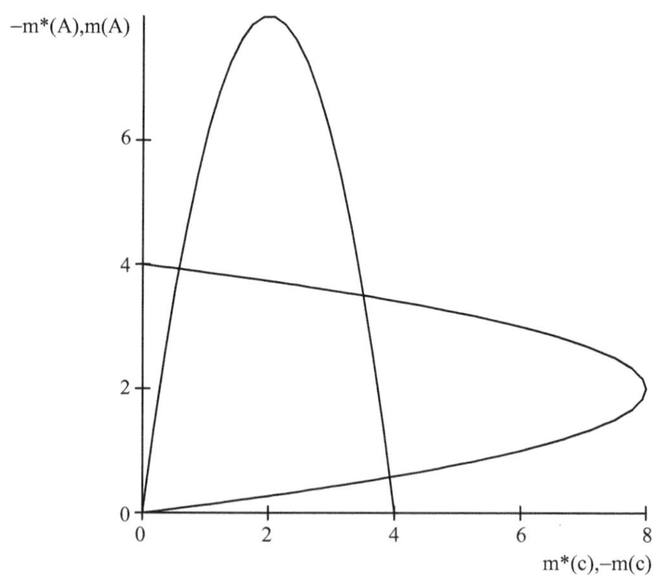

Fig. 2 Multiple steady-state equilibria

Throughout the remainder of our analysis, we assume parameter values are such that there exists three steady-state equilibria.

4 Dynamic Analysis

The foreign country first-order conditions and the market-clearing conditions for the nondurable lead to the following relationship between p, the relative price of the nondurable, and C, the home-country consumption of the nondurable:

$$\omega_C - C = \frac{-p}{\beta(\rho+\delta)} + \frac{\beta_0}{\beta} - \omega^*_{C^*}. \tag{12}$$

The first-order condition (9) and condition (12) together imply a relationship between C, A, and λ:

$$C = \Omega(A, \lambda).$$

This, in turn, when combined with (9) again, implies that p is a function of just A and λ:

$$p = \lambda^{-1}\left\{\Omega(A,\lambda) + \alpha_0 A - \frac{\alpha}{2}A^2\right\}^{-\gamma}.$$

Hence, the two dynamic equations governing the evolution of A and λ are given as

$$\begin{aligned} \dot{A} = \omega_A &- \frac{\lambda^{-2}\left\{\Omega(A,\lambda) + \alpha_0 A - \frac{\alpha}{2}A^2\right\}^{-2\gamma}}{\beta(\rho+\delta)} \\ &+ \lambda^{-1}\left\{\Omega(A,\lambda) + \alpha_0 A - \frac{\alpha}{2}A^2\right\}^{-\gamma}\left(\frac{\beta_0}{\beta} - \omega^*_{C^*}\right) - \delta A, \end{aligned} \tag{13}$$

$$\dot{\lambda} = \lambda(\rho+\delta) - U(A, \Omega(A,\lambda)). \tag{14}$$

This nonlinear coupled system of differential equations can be analyzed numerically for specific parameter values, the results of which will be reported shortly. But insights can be gained from considering the special case of $\gamma = 0$.

With $\gamma = 0$, the dynamic system simplifies to

$$\dot{A} = \omega_A + \lambda^{-1}\left(\frac{-\lambda^{-1}}{\beta(\rho+\delta)} + \frac{\beta_0}{\beta} - \omega^*_{C^*}\right) - \delta A,$$

$$\dot{\lambda} = \lambda(\rho+\delta) - \alpha_0 + \alpha A.$$

The $\dot{\lambda} = 0$ locus is a downward-sloping straight line in the (λ,A) plane. Denote the $\dot{A} = 0$ locus as $A = \Phi(\lambda)$. This function is continuous for $\lambda > 0$ and has the properties

$$\lim_{\lambda\to 0} \Phi(\lambda) = -\infty,$$

$$\lim_{\lambda\to\infty} \Phi(\lambda) = 0.$$

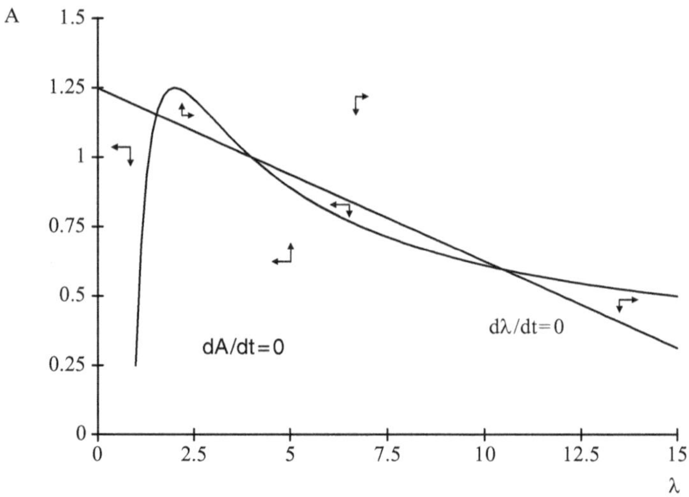

Fig. 3 Phase plane

Finally, note that

$$\frac{\partial \dot{A}}{\partial A} = -\delta < 0, \ \frac{\partial \dot{\lambda}}{\partial \lambda} = \rho + \delta > 0, \ \frac{\partial \dot{\lambda}}{\partial A} = \alpha > 0.$$

Thus, the phase diagram for this system is as depicted in Fig. 3.

The key feature of this phase diagram is the relative slopes of the two loci at the three critical points: at the critical points associated with the smallest and largest critical values of λ, the slope of the $\dot{\lambda} = 0$ locus is steeper than the slope of the $\dot{A} = 0$ locus, while at the middle critical point, the magnitudes of these slopes are reversed. We exploit this feature to analyze local dynamics in the neighborhoods of the critical points.

To investigate these local dynamics, we consider the linearized system around a critical point:[5]

$$\dot{\lambda} = a_{11}\lambda + a_{12}A + K_1,$$
$$\dot{A} = a_{21}\lambda + a_{22}A + K_2,$$

where

$$a_{11} = \rho + \delta, \ a_{12} = \alpha,$$
$$a_{21} = \left[-\left(\frac{\beta_0}{\beta} - \omega^*_{C^*} \right) (\bar{\lambda}_i)^{-2} + \left(\frac{1}{\beta(\rho + \delta)} \right) (\bar{\lambda}_i)^{-3} \right],$$
$$a_{22} = -\delta, \qquad i = 1, 2, 3,$$

[5] We use "critical point" (sometimes referred to as a singular point) interchangeably with the less formal terminology that identifies such points as "steady states."

and where, without loss of generality, we denote the values of λ associated with the critical points as $\bar{\lambda}_1$, $\bar{\lambda}_2$, and $\bar{\lambda}_3$, with $\bar{\lambda}_1 < \bar{\lambda}_2 < \bar{\lambda}_3$. The characteristic roots of this linearized system, denoted as θ_1 and θ_2, satisfy

$$\theta_1 + \theta_2 = a_{11} + a_{22} = \rho,$$
$$\theta_1 \theta_2 = a_{11}a_{22} - a_{21}a_{12} = -\delta(\rho+\delta) - \alpha f(\bar{\lambda}_i),$$

where

$$f(\bar{\lambda}_i) \equiv \left[-\left(\frac{\beta_0}{\beta} - \omega_{C^*}^{*} \right) (\bar{\lambda}_i)^{-2} + \left(\frac{1}{\beta(\rho+\delta)} \right) (\bar{\lambda}_i)^{-3} \right].$$

Because of the properties of the $\dot{A} = 0$ and $\dot{\lambda} = 0$ loci, we have the following proposition:

Proposition 2. *For the case in which $\gamma = 0$, local dynamics in the neighborhood of the critical points associated with critical point values $\bar{\lambda}_1$ and $\bar{\lambda}_3$ are characterized by saddlepath stability, while in the neighborhood of the critical point associated with critical point value $\bar{\lambda}_2$, the local dynamics are characterized by unstable trajectories.*

Proof. We know that at the two nonadjacent critical points, the slope of the $\dot{\lambda} = 0$ locus is greater (less steep) than the slope of the $\dot{A} = 0$ locus. This implies

$$(-a_{21}/a_{22}) < (-a_{11}/a_{12}).$$

Given the known algebraic signs of a_{11}, a_{12}, and a_{22}, this implies

$$a_{12}a_{21} > a_{11}a_{22}.$$

Thus, the determinant is negative at these two points, and one characteristic root is positive and the other negative. At the interior critical point, the slopes are reversed, and this implies the determinant is positive. Furthermore, the trace is positive, so the real parts of both roots are positive. □

This implies that for any initial condition $A_0 = A(0)$, there exist two stable equilibria, each associated with an initial value $\lambda(0)$, one on the stable arm of the saddlepath through the critical point $(\bar{\lambda}_1, \bar{A}_1)$ and one on the stable arm of the saddlepath through the critical point $(\bar{\lambda}_3, \bar{A}_3)$. Of course, each of these equilibria converges to a different steady state. A depiction of these multiple stable paths is shown in Fig. 4.

The middle critical point, as noted, is unstable. Some possibilities about the global dynamics associated with trajectories that start near to this critical point can be inferred from the phase diagram. For example, a trajectory, which must spiral outward in some neighborhood of the source, can eventually straighten out and move in a southeastern direction. Other possibilities will be explored later with the use of more specific examples.

Although the steady-state equilibrium prices are not affected by the value of the intertemporal elasticity of substitution, the dynamic behavior in the neighborhood

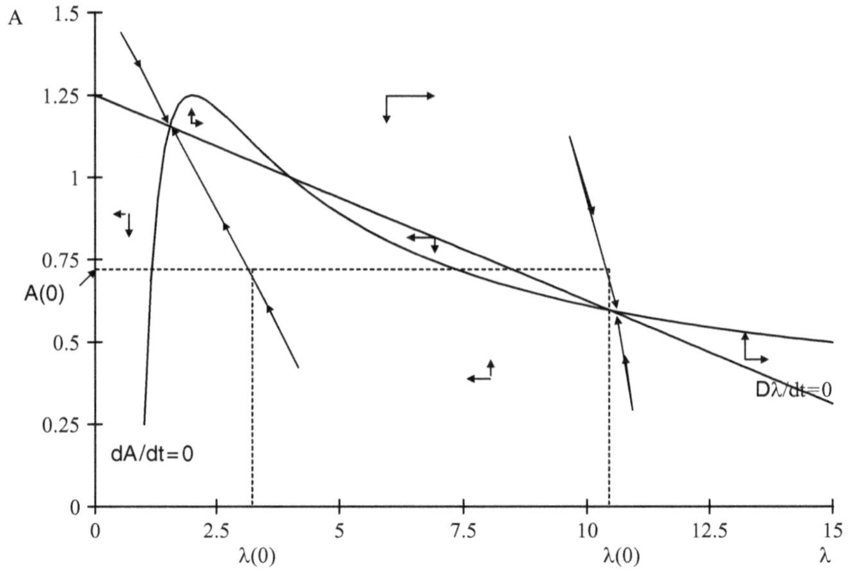

Fig. 4 Multiple stable paths

of the steady state will be influenced by the value of γ. The reason for this can be seen by referring to the components of the trace of this system:

$$\frac{\partial \dot{\lambda}}{\partial \lambda} = \rho + \delta - U_{AC}\frac{\partial C}{\partial \lambda},$$
$$\frac{\partial \dot{A}}{\partial A} = -\delta + \frac{\partial \left(p(\omega_C - C)\right)}{\partial A}.$$

If $\gamma = 0$, the level of home consumption is unaffected by λ and the values of p and C are unaffected by A. Therefore, the trace will equal $\rho > 0$ and the system will exhibit dynamic instability at the middle price where the determinant is positive. If $\gamma > 0$, an increase in λ will raise U_A because $U_{AC} < 0$ and C is decreasing in λ. Similarly, it can be shown that the value of home exports of C will be decreasing in A so that the trace will be less than ρ for $\gamma > 0$. For the particular parameter values we examine here, the value of the trace is monotonically decreasing in γ and will equal 0 at $\gamma \approx .5$. Although the sign of the trace varies with the level of γ in our numerical example, the value of the determinant does not. This means that the extreme steady states will continue to have a negative determinant, yielding saddlepath stability for all values of γ.

For the interior critical point price, the trace and determinant are both positive for γ less than the value at which the trace equals 0. For these values of the intertemporal elasticity of substitution, the middle equilibrium point is a source and the system exhibits unstable behavior in the neighborhood of this critical point. However, for γ exceeding the value at which the trace is negative, the determinant is positive, and so the interior critical point is a sink. At the value of γ at which the trace equals 0, the

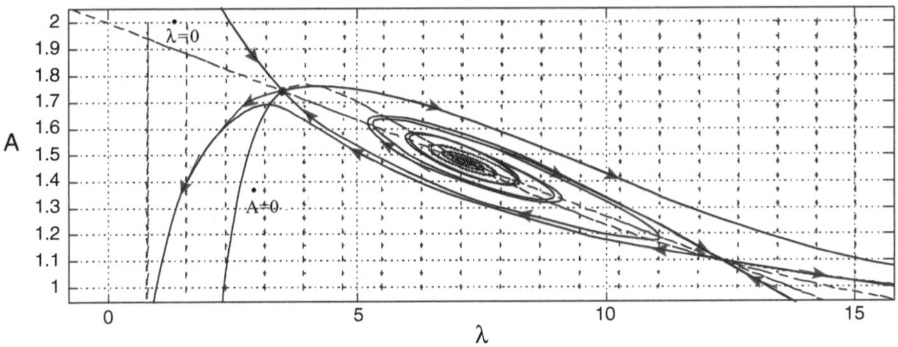

Fig. 5 Spiral paths from a source

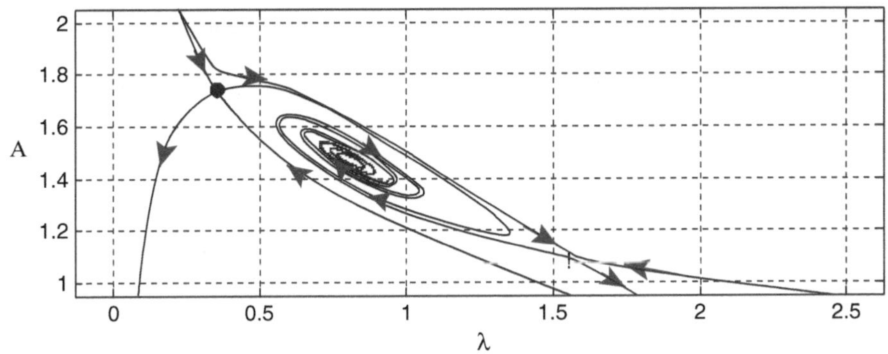

Fig. 6 Spiral paths into a sink

interior equilibrium is a center. The interesting feature here is that when this critical point is a center or a sink, we have indeterminacy. That is, for any initial condition A_0, there will be an infinite number of equilibrium trajectories, either cycling around the interior critical point or asymptotically spirally into it.[6]

A depiction of a spiral path is shown in Fig. 5. What is also interesting here is that, for this case, the stable arm of the saddlepath for the critical point $(\bar{\lambda}_3,\bar{A}_3)$ is one of the spiral paths that originate at the middle source. Thus, for any initial condition value of A that falls "close" to the value at the interior critical point, there are multiple equilibrium paths, all starting at different points on the same spiral saddlepath trajectory, which asymptotically approach the critical point $(\bar{\lambda}_3,\bar{A}_3)$. Also note that the unstable arm of the saddlepath associated with $(\bar{\lambda}_3,\bar{A}_3)$ is the stable arm of the saddlepath that approaches $(\bar{\lambda}_1,\bar{A}_1)$.

A depiction of a spiral path around a sink is depicted in Fig. 6. In this case, one of the unstable arms of the saddlepath originating at critical point $(\bar{\lambda}_3,\bar{A}_3)$ spirals into the sink that is critical point.

---

[6] Shimomura (2004) also found indeterminacy around the interior critical point in his model.

5 A Refinement

This model is an infinite-horizon dynamic perfect foresight model. As noted in Driskill (2006), in such models only one of the multiple equilibria may be the limit of a unique finite-horizon equilibrium as the horizon tends to infinity. The basic idea, observed by Tsutsui and Mino (1990) and Karp (1996), is that infinite-horizon perfect-foresight dynamic models are always "short" one boundary condition.

Some intuition for this result is found in a parable recounted by Shell (1971) of a hotelier with an infinite number of available rooms. In the parable, a traveler arrived and asked for a room. The hotelier responded that he was all booked, but he could make room by moving the guest in room No. 1 to room No. 2, the guest in room No. 2 to room No. 3, and so on.

In infinite-horizon dynamic perfect foresight models, the equilibrium price or shadow value is analogous to the traveler: a different initial value can be accommodated by changing the ensuing infinite sequence of prices. This feature does not arise in a finite-horizon formulation, in which an additional boundary condition arises from first-order conditions associated with terminal values of variables. We show that this is the case in this model: there is a unique solution that is the limit of the equilibrium of the finite-horizon analogue of the model.

Consider the finite-horizon analogue for the home-country representative agent:

$$\max_{C} \int_{0}^{T} U(C,A)\,\mathrm{e}^{-\rho t}\,\mathrm{d}t,$$

subject to

$$\dot{A} = \omega_A + p(\omega_C - C) - \delta A.$$

The additional first-order condition not present in the infinite-horizon model is that $A(T)\lambda(T) = 0$. That is, either the stock of the durable good or its shadow value must be zero at the end of the horizon.[7] The dynamic equations (13) and (14) that describe the evolution of the variables through time are unaffected.

The other key feature of our model that leads to this turnpike result is the existence of a saddlepath associated with the critical point $(\bar{\lambda}_1,\bar{A}_1)$; the critical point closest to the vertical axis in the (λ,A) plane at $\dot{\lambda} = 0$. Because the coupled differential equations (13) and (14) are autonomous, one and only one trajectory in the phase plane goes through every point in the plane. Thus, the stable arm of the saddlepath that goes through critical point $(\bar{\lambda}_1,\bar{A}_1)$ is a separatrix that bifurcates the plane. Hence, for any initial value A_0, the only possible equilibrium trajectories that can reach $A(T) = 0$ or $\lambda(T) = 0$ in finite time are those that start to the left of this stable arm.

---

[7] It may be worth noting that the transversality condition for the infinite-horizon problem is not equivalent to this first-order condition: taking the limit of a first-order condition and using it to solve for an equilibrium does not insure that you will replicate what happens when you use the finite-horizon first-order condition to obtain an equilibrium the limit of which is then taken.

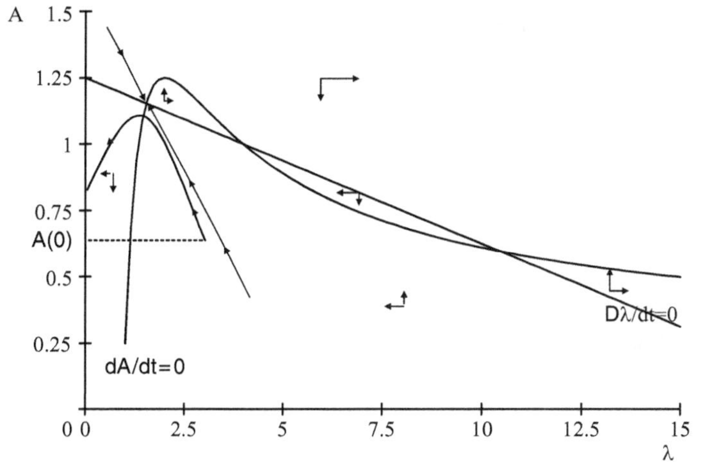

Fig. 7 Finite horizon trajectories

Now consider what must happen as $T \rightarrow \infty$. As the horizon lengthens, the time it takes to traverse an equilibrium trajectory must increase. This can only happen as the trajectory gets closer and closer to the stable arm of the saddlepath. Such paths spend more time in the neighborhood of the critical point, where $\dot{\lambda}$ and $\dot{A}$ are small.

All this can be summarized in the following proposition:

Proposition 3. *The unique limit of the finite-horizon solution is the stable arm of the saddlepath that goes through the critical point* $(\bar{\lambda}_1, \bar{A}_1)$.

This is depicted in Fig 7.

6 Conclusion

This chapter was motivated in part by a desire to analyze stability in multiple-equilibria trading models in which structural dynamics were introduced by the assumption of a durable good. In a result reminiscent of the traditional static analyses in which two nonadjacent equilibria were Walrasian stable, we find that the non-adjacent equilibria in this dynamic model exhibit saddlepath stability. The existence of saddlepath stability at two separate equilibria means that, for arbitrary initial conditions on the stock of the durable good, there are two distinct dynamic paths, one for each steady-state equilibria, both of which converge to their respective steady states. And like in the traditional static analysis, we did find examples in which these stable nonadjacent equilibria surround an unstable interior equilibrium. In these examples, the interior steady-state equilibrium is a source for the dynamic system and generates trajectories leading from its neighborhood in expanding spirals.

In contrast to the static analysis, though, the stability properties of the interior equilibrium depend in critical ways upon the parameters that describe the dynamic aspects of the model. In particular, the value of the elasticity of intertemporal substitutability determines whether this interior equilibrium is a source, a center, or a sink. For high values, the interior equilibrium is a source, and all trajectories that begin in its neighborhood eventually lead to unbounded values of the shadow price of the durable good. For a low enough value, it is a center, surrounded by periodic trajectories. For values even lower, it is a sink, and all trajectories that begin in its neighborhood spiral inward, converging to this interior steady state. Thus, for the case of a sufficiently low value of the intertemporal elasticity of substitution, the interior equilibrium has local dynamics characterized by indeterminacy: for an initial stock of the durable good sufficiently close to this interior equilibrium, there exist an infinite number of equilibrium paths all of which converge to the associated steady state.

A natural question to ask is the extent to which these results generalize to other assumptions regarding preferences. We have examined the robustness of these results by considering a variant of the model with CES preferences in each country that is parameterized to generate multiple steady-state equilibria. The results are similar in that the nonadjacent equilibria are saddle points and the middle equilibrium may be a source or a sink depending on the elasticity of substitution. We have not established a general result establishing that having multiple steady states is necessary for indeterminacy to arise, but these results are suggestive.

The global dynamic properties of the model, though, permit application of a selection criterion that eliminates all but one of these multitude of possible equilibrium paths. In particular, only one equilibrium path, the stable arm of the saddlepath that goes through the steady-state equilibrium associated with the smallest steady-state value of the durable good, is the limit as the horizon goes to infinity of the equilibrium path of the unique finite-horizon equilibrium path. This "turnpike" result is due in part to the requirement that at the end of a finite horizon, the value of the durable good must be zero.[8] Views about whether such a selection criterion is a fruitful approach to the problem of multiple equilibria are not unanimous, of course.

Finally, we should note that all of these results on indeterminacy are dependent on the assumption that there is no capital market. That is, as shown in Bond and Driskill (2007), all equilibria are saddlepath-stable when there are perfect capital markets.

References

Bond EW, Driskill R (2007) Income effects, wealth effects, and multiple equilibria in trade models with durable goods. Vanderbilt University, mimeo

Doh J, Iwasa K, Shimomura K (2007) Indeterminacy in a free-trade world. J Differ Equ Appl 13:135–149

[8] In the durable goods monopolist literature, this characteristic has been used by Kahn (1985), for example, as a device for constructing the backward-induction equilibrium of the model.

Driskill R (2006) Multiple equilibria in dynamic rational expectations models: a critical review. Eur Econ Rev 50:171–210

Jones RW (1961) Stability conditions in international trade: a general equilibrium analysis. Int Econ Rev 2:199–209

Karp L, Paul T (2003) Friction and the multiplicity of equilibria. Department of Agricultural and Resource Economics, Working paper no. 960, University of California, Berkeley; http://are.Berkeley.edu/karp/

Karp L (2006) Depreciation Erodes the Coarse Conjecture. European Economic Review 40:473–490

Kahn C (1985) The durable goods monopolist and consistency with increasing costs. Econometrica 54:275–294

Krugman PR (1991) History versus expectations. Q J Econ 104:651–667

Matsuyama K (1991) Increasing returns, industrialization, and indeterminacy of equilibrium. Q J Econ 104:617–650

Shell K (1971) Notes on the economics of infinity. J Polit Econ 79:1002–1011

Shimomura K (1993) Durable consumption goods and the pattern of international trade. In: Herberg H, Long NV (eds) Trade, welfare, and economic policies: Essays in honor of Murray C. Kemp, Michigan University Press

Shimomura K (2004) Indeterminacy in a dynamic general equilibrium model of international trade. In: Boldrin M, Chen BL, Wang P The development process of rapidly growing economies: From theory to empirics. Edward Elgar, Cheltenham, UK

Tsutsui S, Mino K (1990) Nonlinear strategies in dynamic duopolistic competition with sticky prices. J Econ Theory 52:136–151

Import Tariffs and Growth in a Model with Habits[1]

Been-Lon Chen(✉), Shun-Fa Lee, and Koji Shimomura

Abstract This chapter studies the long-run relationship between tariffs and economic growth in a two-country AK growth model. We find that a sufficiently high tariff can increase or decrease economic growth and depends on the levels of productivity coefficients in both countries. Moreover, the Ricardian theorem of comparative advantage is sustained in the long-run equilibrium and local indeterminacy emerges in the case of incomplete specialization under milder conditions compared with conventional literature.

1 Introduction

This analysis studies the relationship between tariffs and economic growth in an endogenous growth framework in which countries trade with each other and consumption in one country affect household's utility in another country. While most existing studies find a negative relationship between import tariffs and the rate of economic growth, there are findings of an ambiguous or even positive relationship.

[1] The authors are grateful to Hong Hwang, Tsechien Hsu, Kenji Fujikawa, and especially Henry Wan, and participants at the Conference on Globalization, International Trade and Economic Dynamics in Memory of Koji Shimomura, held on November 22–24, Kobe University, Japan, for valuable comments and suggestions. Part of the research was conducted while Chen was visiting professor at Washington University in St. Louis, whose hospitality, provided especially by the department chair, Ping Wang, is gratefully acknowledged. This chapter is dedicated to and in memory of late Professor Koji Shimomura, a prolific economist, a dedicated teacher and a truthful friend.

B.-L. Chen
Institute of Economics, Academia Sinica, Taiwan, and Department of Economics, Washington University in St Louis, USA, e-mail: bchen@econ.sinica.edu.tw

T. Kamihigashi and L. Zhao (eds.) *International Trade and Economic Dynamics – Essays in Memory of Koji Shimomura.*

In existing theoretical work most studies maintain that tariffs slow down economic growth (Jones and Manuelli 1990; Easterly and Rebelo 1993; Osang and Pereira 1996; Ben-David and Loewy 1998; Naito 2006a). However, others hold different points of view. In a R&D model, for example, Grossman and Helpman (1990) argued that the relationship between tariffs and economic growth is ambiguous, depending on how the fraction of resources to the R&D sector is affected. A similar argument has been made in a R&D model by Rivera-Batiz and Romer (1991).[2] Where growth is driven by resource accumulation, existing chapters also obtain both a positive and a negative relationship between tariffs and relationships (Naito 2005, 2006b).

In empirical findings, while most chapters documented a negative relationship between tariff rates and economic growth (Lee 1993; Harrison 1996; and Edwards 1992), Rodriguez and Rodrik (2001) and Sala-i-Martin (1997) contended that the relationship is not robust. Indeed, Yanikkaya (2003) has found a positive relationship using cross-country data over the period of 1970–1997. Moreover, O'Rourke (2000) and Irwin (2002) reported a positive relationship between tariffs and economic growth in the late nineteenth and early twentieth century, as opposed to the otherwise consensus of a negative relationship in the Post-War era. Recently, Clements and Williamson (2004) have confirmed that high tariffs were associated with fast growth before World War II, but with slow growth thereafter.

We build a dynamic trade model in a two-country (Home and Foreign), two-output (pure consumption and investment goods) Ricardian framework with capital accumulation as the source of economic growth, as opposed to R&D as the source of economic growth in the Grossman and Helpman (1990) and Rivera-Batiz and Romer (1991) model. In this chapter, we use AK technologies in production. The choice is made in order to differentiate the role of physical capital accumulation from the human capital accumulation as a source of economic growth.[3] A special feature of our model is to incorporate time nonseparable preferences; we introduce the endogenous rate of time preference and the average living standard in the foreign country as benchmark consumption.

A growing body of empirical evidence using country or cross-country data has confirmed the importance of time nonseparable preferences.[4] In particular, extensive literature on asset pricing and real business cycles lends further credit to the level of benchmark consumption being a significant determinant of consumption behavior.[5] Habit-forming consumers dislike large and rapid cuts in consumption. While the endogenous rate of time preference equalizes the marginal products of capital to the

[2] Rivera-Batiz and Romer (1991) show that the growth rate is a nonmonotone function of the tariff rate, where it first declines as the tariff rate rises from zero and then rises after a positive critical tariff rate: the growth rate in the free trade regime is never reached.

[3] If human capital accumulation is introduced, there is a nontradable, third sector that produces pure investment goods. The resulting model gains few insights but adds a lot of analytical complication.

[4] See Van de Stadt et al. (1985) using data in the Netherlands, Osborn (1988) using data in the U.K., and Fuhrer and Klein (1998) using data in the G-7 countries.

[5] See Abel (1990), Constantinides (1990), and Campbell and Cochrane (1999) on asset pricing and Ljungqvist and Uhlig (2000) and Boldrin et al. (2001) on real business cycles.

subjective rate of discount across countries in order to avoid sudden capital flight following a shock, the average living standard results in a large premium to hold risky assets that might force a rapid cut in consumption.

Despite the evidence supporting the relevance of benchmark consumption levels for current consumption decisions, no attempts have been made to introduce time nonseparable preferences into endogenous growth literature in an open economy framework. Recently, this approach has been pursued by Carroll et al. (2000), Fisher and Hof (2000), Alonso-Carrera et al. (2005), and Chen (2006) in an endogenous growth, closed-economy framework.[6] Our model may be considered as an extension of these works to an open-economy framework. In particular, we investigate the effects of tariffs on the trade patterns and the sustainable rate of economic growth that have never been studied in the existing work.

Our primary findings may be summarized as follows. First, the Ricardian theorem of comparative advantage holds in the two-country world even if the preferences are different across countries. Second, in the case of incomplete specialization, local indeterminacy emerges under milder conditions, as compared to Drugeon (1998) and Nishimura and Shimomura (2006). Third, in the case of complete specialization, the relationship between tariffs and economic growth is ambiguous. When the Home country specializes in the investment (respectively, consumption) goods, a sufficiently higher rate of tariffs on the consumption (respectively, investment) goods reverses the trade pattern in the long run and decreases economic growth when the productivity coefficient of the investment goods in the Home (respectively, Foreign) country is larger than the threshold. However, economic growth is increased when the productivity coefficient of the investment goods in the Home (respectively, Foreign) country is smaller and in the Foreign (respectively, Home) country is larger than the threshold. Finally, tariffs increase (respectively, decrease) the long-run welfare in the Home country when it specializes in the investment (respectively, consumption) goods.

Intuitively, the effects of a tariff on economic growth work through its effect on the difference between the interest rate and the rate of time preference. The import tariff raises the price of the imported goods in the Home country, attracting more resources into this sector. As a result of a higher demand for capital, the interest rate is increased in the Home country. However, the international price of the imported goods is reduced by augmented output supply, thereby decreasing the demand for capital and the interest rate in the Foreign country. Higher domestic and lower foreign interest rates indicate that the ratio of Home to Foreign consumption increases (respectively, decreases) when the Home country is specialized in investment (respectively, consumption) goods, resulting in a higher (respectively, lower) rate of time preference in the Home country. Moreover, the change in the interest rates in the Home and Foreign countries depends on the productivity level in the investment goods sector. When the productivity level of the investment goods in the Home (respectively, Foreign) country is higher than the threshold, the increase

[6] In contrast, there is a number of studies in a bounded growth framework. Examples include Dupor and Liu (2003), Alonso-Carrera et al. (2004, 2006), and Liu and Turnovsky (2005), among others.

in the interest rate is smaller than the increase in the rate of time preference. As a result, economic growth is lower. When the productivity level of the investment goods in the Home (respectively, Foreign) country is smaller than the threshold and in the Foreign (respectively, Home) country is larger than the threshold, the former makes the interest rate increase more, whereas the latter makes the rate of time preference increase less. As a result, the rate of economic growth is increasing in tariffs.

Finally, the reason for the effect on long-run welfare is simple. The long-run welfare in the Home country is increasing in the ratio of consumption between the Home and Foreign country. When the Home country specializes in the investment (respectively, consumption) goods, tariffs on the imported consumption (respectively, investment) goods increase (respectively, decrease) the ratio of consumption between the Home and Foreign country in the long run, thereby increasing (respectively, decreasing) long-run welfare in the Home country.

The structure of the chapter is as follows. In Sect. 2, we set up the basic model. In Sect. 3, we analyze the balanced growth path (BGP) and the transitional dynamics. In Sect. 4, we study the relationship between the import tariff policy and economic growth. In Sect. 5, we investigate the welfare effect of tariffs. Finally, some concluding remarks are made in Sect. 6.

2 The Basic Model

2.1 Firms

There are two sectors in each country: a pure consumption good and a pure investment good sector; both use only capital, k_i.[7] The capital may be thought of as a composite of various types of physical and human capital as outlined in Rebelo (1991). Following the Oniki and Uzawa tradition, we assume that while the two goods are tradable, capital stock is not internationally mobile. The production function of good i is denoted as

$$y_i = a_i k_i, \quad i = 1, 2. \tag{1}$$

where $i = 1$ (respectively, 2) corresponds to the consumption (respectively, investment) good. The full employment conditions are

$$k = k_1 + k_2, \tag{2}$$

where k is the total capital stock.

---

[7] With only one consumption good, the quadratic utility form used in existing studies can be relaxed.

The first-order conditions for Home country's representative competitive firm are

$$pa_1 = r, \tag{3a}$$

$$a_2 = r, \tag{3b}$$

where p is the price of consumption good in terms of the investment good; r is the interest rate, and thus the net rental rate of capital if we assume that there is no depreciation of capital.

There are two countries in the world, Home and Foreign countries, which may have different production technologies and preferences. Suppose the Foreign country has a similar production structure to those in (1) and (2). Denote the variables with an asterisk as in the Foreign country. Then this is a Ricardian model, which means that the trade pattern is determined by comparative advantage. Thus, we classify into three types of the trade pattern.

Case 1. $a_1/a_2 = a_1{}^*/a_2{}^*$.

This is the case of incomplete specialization with each country producing both goods. Conditions (3) imply that both p and r are constant, that is, $p = a_2/a_1$ and $r = a_2$.

Case 2. $a_1/a_2 < a_1{}^*/a_2{}^*$.

Complete specialization arises in this case. The Home country only produces and exports the investment goods and imports the consumption goods that is produced solely by the Foreign country; hence, $k_1 = 0$, $k_2 = k$, $k_1^* = k^*$, and $k_2^* = 0$. Therefore, conditions (3) indicates that $r = a_2$ and $r^* = a_1^* p$.

Case 3. $a_1/a_2 > a_1^*/a_2^*$.

In this case, the trade pattern is reversed and thereby $k_1 = k$, $k_2 = 0$, $k_1^* = 0$, and $k_2^* = k^*$. Thus, conditions (3) indicates that $r = a_1 p$ and $r^* = a_2^*$.

In sum, combining (2) and (3), we obtain

$$\begin{cases} k = k_1, k_2 = 0; & k^* = k_2^*, k_1^* = 0; & r = a_1 p; & r^* = a_2^*; & a_2/a_1 < p < a_2^*/a_1^*; \\ k = k_1 + k_2; & k^* = k_1^* + k_2^*; & r = a_2; & r^* = a_2^*; & p = a_2/a_1; \\ k = k_2, k_1 = 0; & k^* = k_1^*, k_2^* = 0; & r = a_2; & r^* = a_1^* p; & a_2/a_1 > p > a_2^*/a_1^*; \end{cases} \tag{4}$$

$$\text{if} \quad \begin{array}{l} a_1/a_2 > a_1^*/a_2^* \\ a_1/a_2 = a_1^*/a_2^*. \\ a_1/a_2 < a_1^*/a_2^* \end{array}$$

2.2 Households

The representative household earns factor income with $k(0)$ units of capital endowed initially. The household's budget constraint is

$$\dot{k} = rk - pc, \tag{5}$$

where c is consumption.

The felicity of the representative agent is $u(c, c^*)$, where c^* is the average consumption level in the foreign country, a consumption externality. The felicity allows for the idea that the representative household cares about his living standard relative to the average living standard in the Foreign country. We assume that $u(c, c^*)$ is increasing and concave in c. Moreover, we assume that $u(c, c^*)$ is decreasing in c^*. The assumption is similar to the one made in Abel (1990), Dupor and Liu (2003), and Chen and Hsu (2007) in which an individual is "keeping up with the Joneses."

The above model fits in the reality better for countries in their neighborhood. Suppose there are two countries, Japan and Taiwan. In trade, Japan specializes in investment goods and Taiwan in consumption goods. Fashions, food, and other consumption activities in both Japan and Taiwan are likely to affect each other in many perspectives. In this case, our model may shed light on the interactions and trade between countries like Japan and Taiwan.

The representative agent maximizes the discounted sum of the lifetime felicity, with discount factor X. The discount factor changes in the following way:

$$\dot{X} = -\rho(u)X. \tag{6}$$

Following Uzawa (1968), we call $\rho(u)$ the time preference function and consider

Assumption 1. $0 < \rho(0) < a_2$ and $\rho(u) > 0, \rho'(u) > 0, \rho''(u) > 0, \rho(u) - u\rho'(u) > 0$ for all $u > 0$.

We use the following form for the felicity,

$$u(c, c*) = u\left(\frac{c}{c*}\right). \tag{7}$$

While the above form is consistent with the assumption of a positive and decreasing marginal utility in c and a decreasing utility in c^*, let us make some remarks. In Abel (1990), Gali (1994), Chen (2007) and others, the form $u[\frac{c}{(c*)^\gamma}]$ is used, where $0 < \gamma \leq 1$. Our form is a special case of this class of felicity that takes the extreme case at $\gamma = 1$. The reason for choosing $\gamma = 1$ is due to the endogenous rate of time preference in an open economy with perpetual growth as follows.

In a two-country dynamic Heckscher–Ohlin model by Baxter (1992), the responses to taxes and other shocks are very dramatic and not continuous. Chen et al. (2008) finds that introducing an endogenous rate of time preference avoids such a problem and assures continuous responses. In a recent study with endogenous rates of time preference, Palivos et al. (1997) showed that the rate of time preference must be constant along a BGP. Given that the rate of time preference is monotone in the felicity, the only way to guarantee a constant rate of time preference along a BGP is $\gamma = 1$. Moreover, our form (7) is consistent with the recent study on endogenous rates of time preference by Drugeon (1998) that shows that the homogeneity of degree zero with respect to an individual consumption and the living standard is a necessary condition for the existence of a BGP.[8] Thus, although our function form is restrictive, it is necessary in order to assure a BGP. Nevertheless, when we introduce the distortionary tariff policy, the consumption ratio in a BGP could deviate from unity.

Let $z \equiv c/c^*$. We make the following standard assumptions for the felicity in (7).

Assumption 2. $u(0) = 0, u'(z) > 0, u''(z) < 0, [u'(z)z]/u(z) < 1$.

If we denote λ and μ as the co-state variables of k and X, the Hamiltonian of the household optimization problem is

$$\Im = u\left(\frac{c}{c^*}\right)X + \lambda\{rk - pc\} + \mu\{-\rho(u)X\}.$$

The necessary conditions for optimality are

$$u'\left(\frac{c}{c^*}\right)\left[1 - \mu\rho'\left(u\left(\frac{c}{c^*}\right)\right)\right] = \frac{\lambda pc^*}{X}, \tag{8a}$$

$$\frac{\dot{\lambda}}{\lambda} = -r, \tag{8b}$$

$$\frac{\dot{\mu}}{\mu} = \rho\left(u\left(\frac{c}{c^*}\right)\right) - \frac{1}{\mu}u\left(\frac{c}{c^*}\right), \tag{8c}$$

with the two transversality conditions $\lim_{t\to\infty} \lambda k = 0$ and $\lim_{t\to\infty} \mu X = 0$.

While condition (8a) equates the marginal utility of consumption to the marginal cost of foregone savings, conditions (8b and 8c) are Euler equations for capital and the discount, respectively.

3 Two-Country World Market Equilibrium

In a trade paper of world equilibrium with K countries by Wan and Majumdar (1980), their technology is loglinear and includes a linear technology as a special case. Under the condition that the utility is loglinear, their model indicates that the fraction of output spent on home goods will be fixed over time. Our long-run equilibrium shares a similar feature.

The world commodity market-clearing condition for the consumption goods is

$$c + c^* = a_1k_1 + a_1^*k_1^*. \tag{9}$$

Once (9) is satisfied, the world market for the investment goods is automatically cleared.

---

[8] In a recent chapter, Drugeon (1998) introduces endogenous discounting that is increasing in consumption and decreasing in the living standard in a society, measured by the average consumption in the society. Our formulation is consistent with Drugeon (1998) in that the discounting is decreasing in average foreign living standards.

3.1 Transformation of the Economic System

To analyze the equilibrium, it is necessary to transform the equilibrium conditions with perpetual growth into a system with stationary variables. Denote $m \equiv pc/k, m^* \equiv pc^*/k^*$, $v_1 = k_1/k$, $v_2 = k_2/k$, $v_1^* = k_1^*/k^*$, and $v_2^* = k_1^*/k^*$. In what follows we briefly explain the transformation.

First, (8c) in terms of the transformed variables and its counterpart for the Foreign country are

$$\frac{\dot{\mu}}{\mu} = \rho(u(z)) - \frac{1}{\mu}u(z), \tag{10a}$$

$$\frac{\dot{\mu}^*}{\mu^*} = \rho^*(u(\frac{1}{z})) - \frac{1}{\mu^*}u^*(\frac{1}{z}). \tag{10b}$$

Next, differentiating (8a) and its foreign counterpart, with (8b), (10a), and (10b) yields

$$\frac{\dot{c}}{c} = \frac{1}{\chi(z)}\left\{r - \rho(u(z)) - [1-\chi(z)]\frac{\dot{c}^*}{c^*} - \frac{\dot{p}}{p} - \frac{\rho'(u(z))[\mu\rho(u(z)) - u(z)]}{1-\mu\rho'(u(z))}\right\}, \tag{11a}$$

$$\frac{\dot{c}^*}{c^*} = \frac{1}{\chi^*(z)}\left\{r^* - \rho^*(u^*(\frac{1}{z})) - [1-\chi^*(z)]\frac{\dot{c}}{c} - \frac{\dot{p}}{p} - \frac{\rho^{*\prime}(u^*(\frac{1}{z}))[\mu^*\rho^*(u^*(\frac{1}{z})) - u^*(\frac{1}{z})]}{1-\mu^*\rho^{*\prime}(u^*(\frac{1}{z}))}\right\}, \tag{11b}$$

where $\chi(z) \equiv \sigma(z) + \frac{\mu\rho'(u(z))}{1-\mu\rho'(u(z))}\psi(z) > 0$, in which $\sigma(z) \equiv \frac{-u''(z)z}{u'(z)} > 0$ denotes the reciprocal of the intertemporal elasticity of substitution in the Home country and $\psi(z) \equiv \frac{\rho''(u(z))u'(z)z}{\rho'(u(z))} > 0$, the elasticity of the marginal time preference rate with respect to z in the Home country. Similarly, $\chi^*(z) \equiv \sigma^*(z) + \frac{\mu^*\rho^{*\prime}(\frac{1}{z})}{1-\mu^*\rho^{*\prime}(\frac{1}{z})}\psi^*(z) > 0$, $\sigma^*(z) \equiv \frac{-u^{*\prime\prime}(\frac{1}{z})}{u^{*\prime}(\frac{1}{z})z}$, and $\psi^*(z) \equiv \frac{\rho^{*\prime\prime}(\frac{1}{z})u^{*\prime}(\frac{1}{z})}{\rho^{*\prime}(\frac{1}{z})z}$ are the corresponding counterparts in the Foreign country, respectively.

Then, if we substitute $\frac{\dot{p}}{p}$ in (11a) into (11b), we obtain

$$\frac{\dot{z}}{z} = \frac{1}{\chi(z)+\chi^*(z)-1}\left\{r - \rho(u(z)) - r^* + \rho^*(u^*(\frac{1}{z})) - \frac{\rho'(u(z))[\mu\rho(u(z)) - u(z)]}{1-\mu\rho'(u(z))} + \frac{\rho^{*\prime}(u^*(\frac{1}{z}))[\mu^*\rho^*(u^*(\frac{1}{z})) - u^*(\frac{1}{z})]}{1-\mu^*\rho^{*\prime}(u^*(\frac{1}{z}))}\right\}. \tag{12}$$

Moreover, (5) is rewritten as

$$\frac{\dot{k}}{k} = r - m. \tag{13}$$

Using (11a)–(13), we obtain

$$\frac{\dot{m}}{m} = \chi^*(z)\frac{\dot{z}}{z} + r^* - \rho^*(u^*(\frac{1}{z})) - \frac{\rho^{*\prime}(u^*(\frac{1}{z}))[\mu^*\rho^*(u^*(\frac{1}{z})) - u^*(\frac{1}{z})]}{1-\mu^*\rho^{*\prime}(u^*(\frac{1}{z}))} - r + m, \tag{14a}$$

$$\frac{\dot{m}^*}{m^*} = -\chi(z)\frac{\dot{z}}{z} + r - \rho(u(z)) - \frac{\rho'(u(z))[\mu\rho(u(z)) - u(z)]}{1 - \mu\rho'(u(z))} - r^* + m^*. \tag{14b}$$

Further, multiplying (9) by p/c^* the world market-clearing condition may be rewritten as

$$z + 1 = p\left(\frac{a_1 z v_1}{m} + \frac{a_1^* v_1^*}{m*}\right). \tag{15}$$

Finally, the full employment conditions and the first-order conditions for the firm summarized in (4) can now be rewritten as follows:

$$\begin{cases} v_1 = v_2^* = 1; & v_2 = v_1^* = 0; & r = a_1 p; & r^* = a_2^*; & a_2/a_1 < p < a_2^*/a_1^*; \\ v_1 + v_2 = 1; & v_1^* + v_2^* = 1; & r = a_2; & r^* = a_2^*; & p = a_2/a_1; \\ v_2 = v_1^* = 1; & v_1 = v_2^* = 0; & r = a_2; & r^* = a_1^* p; & a_2/a_1 > p > a_2^*/a_1^*; \end{cases} \tag{16}$$

$$\text{if} \quad \begin{matrix} a_1/a_2 > a_1^*/a_2^* \\ a_1/a_2 = a_1^*/a_2^*. \\ a_1/a_2 < a_1^*/a_2^* \end{matrix}$$

Equations (10a), (10b), (12), and (14a)–(16) are the transformed equilibrium system. The system determines the equilibrium paths of the twelve control variables, z, m, m^*, μ, μ^*, p, v_1, v_2, v_1^*, v_2^*, r, and r^*.

3.2 Balanced Growth Path

We now analyze the equilibrium in a steady state. A steady state is a perfect foresight equilibrium with a BGP under which z, m, m^*, μ, μ^*, p, v_1, v_2, v_1^*, v_2^*, r, and r^* are constant, and thus $\dot{z}/z = \dot{m}/m = \dot{m}^*/m^* = \dot{p}/p = \dot{\mu}/\mu = \dot{\mu}^*/\mu^* = 0$. Denote $\tilde{z}, \tilde{m}, \tilde{m}^*, \tilde{\mu}, \tilde{\mu}^*, \tilde{p}, \tilde{v}_1, \tilde{v}_2, \tilde{v}_1^*, \tilde{v}_2^*, \tilde{r}$, and $\tilde{r}^*$ as the values in a BGP. Then, they are determined by the following relationships:

$$\rho[u(\tilde{z})]\tilde{\mu} - u(\tilde{z}), \tag{17a}$$

$$\rho^*[u^*(\frac{1}{\tilde{z}})]\tilde{\mu}^* = u^*(\frac{1}{\tilde{z}}), \tag{17b}$$

$$\tilde{r} - \rho[u(\tilde{z})] = \tilde{r}^* - \rho^*[u^*(\frac{1}{\tilde{z}})], \tag{17c}$$

$$\tilde{r}^* - \rho^*[u^*(\frac{1}{\tilde{z}})] = \tilde{r} - \tilde{m}, \tag{17d}$$

$$\tilde{r} - \rho[u(\tilde{z})] = \tilde{r}^* - \tilde{m}^*, \tag{17e}$$

$$\tilde{z} + 1 = \tilde{p}\left(\frac{a_1 \tilde{z} \tilde{v}_1}{\tilde{m}} + \frac{a_1^* \tilde{v}_1^*}{\tilde{m}*}\right), \tag{17f}$$

$$1 = \tilde{v}_1 + \tilde{v}_2, \; 1 = \tilde{v}_1^* + \tilde{v}_2^*, \tag{17g}$$

$$\begin{cases} \tilde{v}_2 = \tilde{v}_1^* = 0, & \text{if } a_1/a_2 > a_1^*/a_2^*, \\ \tilde{p} = \frac{a_2}{a_1} = \frac{a_2^*}{a_1*}, & \text{if } a_1/a_2 = a_1^*/a_2^*, \\ \tilde{v}_1 = \tilde{v}_2^* = 0, & \text{if } a_1/a_2 < a_1^*/a_2^*, \end{cases} \tag{17h}$$

$$\tilde{r} = \begin{cases} a_1\tilde{p} \geq a_2, & \text{if } a_1/a_2 \geq a_1^*/a_2^*, \\ a_2 \geq a_1\tilde{p}, & \text{if } a_1/a_2 \leq a_1^*/a_2^*, \end{cases} \quad \tilde{r}^* = \begin{cases} a_2^* \geq a_1^*\tilde{p}, & \text{if } a_1/a_2 \geq a_1^*/a_2^*, \\ a_1^*\tilde{p} \geq a_2^*, & \text{if } a_1/a_2 \leq a_1^*/a_2^*. \end{cases} \tag{17i}$$

Three cases are examined in order to analyze the existence of BGP.

Case 1. $a_1/a_2 = a_1^*/a_2^*$ (Incomplete specialization.)

First, (17h) and (17i) indicate that $\tilde{p} = a_2/a_1, \tilde{r} = a_2$, and $\tilde{r}^* = a_2^*$ and are all constant. Substituting them in (17c) yields

$$a_2 - \rho[u(\tilde{z})] = a_2^* - \rho^*[u^*(\frac{1}{\tilde{z}})], \tag{18a}$$

which determines a unique $\tilde{z}$ under Assumptions 1 and 2.

Next, if we substitute $\tilde{z}$ in (17a), (17b), (17d), and (17e), $\tilde{\mu}, \tilde{\mu}^*, \tilde{m}$, and $\tilde{m}^*$ are determined uniquely, respectively. Finally, if we substitute in $\tilde{z}, \tilde{m}$, and $\tilde{m}^*$, the three relationships in (17f) and (17g) need to determine the four endogenous variables: $\tilde{v}_1, \tilde{v}_2, \tilde{v}_1^*$, and $\tilde{v}_2^*$. Multiplicity of BGPs thus emerges. Given a set of values for $\tilde{v}_1$ and $\tilde{v}_1^*$, then $\tilde{v}_2$ and $\tilde{v}_2^*$ can be uniquely determined by the two relationships in (17g).

Using (17f), the set of values for $\tilde{v}_1$ and $\tilde{v}_1^*$ is determined by

$$(\tilde{v}_1, \tilde{v}_1^*) = \left\{ (\tilde{v}_1, \tilde{v}_1^*) | \tilde{z} + 1 = \tilde{p}\left(\frac{a_1\tilde{z}\tilde{v}_1}{\tilde{m}} + \frac{a_1^*\tilde{v}_1^*}{\tilde{m}*} \right) \right\}.$$

It is obvious that there is a continuum of BGPs, indexed by $\tilde{v}_1$. For each $\tilde{v}_1$, there exists a unique $\tilde{v}_1^*$ that satisfies the equilibrium condition in the above expression. As the choice of the value of $\tilde{v}_1$ in (0,1) is free, there is a continuum of BGPs. The results indicate that any combination of incomplete specialization that satisfies the market-clearing conditions in the two countries is a long-run equilibrium. As both $\tilde{v}_1 > \tilde{v}_1^*$ and $\tilde{v}_1 < \tilde{v}_1^*$ could emerge, the long term trade patterns are thus indeterminate for these two countries.

Case 2. $a_1/a_2 < a_1^*/a_2^*$. (Complete specialization.)

In this case, the Home country completely specializes in the production of and export of investment goods, while the Foreign country completely specializes in and exports consumption goods.

Substituting (17h) and (17g) in (17f), we obtain $a_1\tilde{p}/(\tilde{z}+1) = \tilde{m}^*$. This relationship, together with (17c), (17e), and (17i) yields

$$a_2 - \rho(u(\tilde{z})) = \rho^*\left(u^*\left(\frac{1}{\tilde{z}}\right)\right)\tilde{z}. \tag{18b}$$

The left hand side of (22) is decreasing in $\tilde{z}$ and the right hand side of (18b) is increasing in $\tilde{z}$ under Assumptions 1 and 2.[9] Thus, (18b) determines a unique $\tilde{z}$. Then, variables $\tilde{r}$, $\tilde{r}^*$, $\tilde{\mu}$, $\tilde{\mu}^*$, $\tilde{m}$, and $\tilde{m}^*$ are uniquely determined by the other equations. In particular, $\tilde{v}_1 = \tilde{v}_2^* = 0$ and $\tilde{v}_2 = \tilde{v}_1^* = 1$. Using (17i), the equilibrium relative price of the consumption goods in the long run is therefore uniquely determined as $\tilde{p} = \tilde{r}^*/a_1^*$.

Case 3. $a_1/a_2 > a_1^*/a_2^*$. (Complete specialization.)

In this case, the Home country completely specializes in the production of and exports of consumption goods, while the Foreign country completely specializes in and exports investment goods.

First, we use (17c), (17d), (17f), (17h), and (17i) to obtain

$$a_2^* - \rho^*[u^*(\frac{1}{\tilde{z}})] = \frac{\rho[u(\tilde{z})]}{\tilde{z}}. \tag{18c}$$

Assumptions 1 and 2 assure the existence of a unique $\tilde{z}$. Then, other variables are determined in the fashion similar to the way used in Case 2. The equilibrium relative price of the consumption goods is $\tilde{p} = \tilde{r}/a_1$.

We should mention that in a BGP, the rates of economic growth for consumption and income are equal. The long-run rate of economic growth is determined as follows:

In a BGP, $\frac{\dot{p}}{p} = 0$, and moreover, (17a) and (17b) indicate $\tilde{\mu} = u/\rho$ and $\tilde{\mu}^* = u^*/\rho^*$. Substituting these relationships in (11a) and (11b), the economic growth rates in the two countries are, respectively,

$$\frac{\dot{c}}{c} = \frac{1}{\chi(z)}\left\{r - \rho(u(z)) - [1-\chi(z)]\frac{\dot{c}^*}{c^*}\right\}, \tag{19a}$$

$$\frac{\dot{c}^*}{c^*} = \frac{1}{\chi^*(z)}\left\{r - \rho(u(z)) - [1-\chi(z)]\frac{\dot{c}}{c}\right\}. \tag{19b}$$

Then, if we substitute $\frac{\dot{c}^*}{c^*}$ in (19b) into (19a), we obtain

$$\frac{\dot{c}}{c} = \frac{\chi^*}{[\chi + \chi^* - 1]}\left\{r - \rho - \frac{1-\chi}{\chi^*}(r^* - \rho^*)\right\}.$$

Using (17c), we then obtain

$$\frac{\dot{c}}{c} = r - \rho[u(z)]. \tag{20a}$$

[9] $\frac{\partial}{\partial z}\left(\rho^*\left(u^*\left(\frac{1}{\tilde{z}}\right)\right)\tilde{z}\right) = \rho^* - u^*\rho^{*\prime}\left(\frac{u^{*\prime}}{u^*\tilde{z}}\right) > 0$, and $\frac{\partial}{\partial z}\left(\frac{\rho(u(z))}{z}\right) = \frac{-[\rho - u\rho'(u'z/u)]}{z^2} < 0$, under Assumption 1 and 2.

In a similar fashion, we obtain

$$\frac{\dot{c}^*}{c^*} = r^* - \rho^*[u^*(\frac{1}{z})]. \tag{20b}$$

To summarize the results analyzed above, we obtain

Proposition 1. *Under AK technologies and Assumptions 1 and 2, the Ricardo theorem of comparative advantage holds in the two-country world even if the preferences are different across countries.*

Remark 1. In a two-country endogenous growth model with a Ricardian technology, the price of consumption is determined by the technology. Thus, the trade pattern is not affected by the household's preferences and behavior, but may be changed by the distortion to the firm's behavior. Thus, output taxes or import tariffs may affect the trade pattern.

Remark 2. When the two countries have the same technologies, the *factor price equalization theorem* holds in the case of incomplete specialization, in which $r = a_2 = a_2^* = r^*$, but fails to hold in the case of complete specialization with the exception only when the following conditions are met.

$$\begin{cases} r \equiv [a_2^* - \rho^*(u^*(\frac{1}{\tilde{z}}))](1+\tilde{z}) = a_2^* \equiv r^*, & \text{if } a_1/a_2 > a_1^*/a_2^*. \\ r \equiv a_2 = [a_2 - \rho(u(\tilde{z}))](\frac{1+\tilde{z}}{\tilde{z}}) \equiv r^*, & \text{if } a_1/a_2 < a_1^*/a_2^*. \end{cases}$$

3.3 Local Dynamics

In this section, we analyze the local dynamics. We only study the situation when both countries are incomplete specialization, that is, under Case 1 where $a_1/a_2 = a_1^*/a_2^*$.

It is obvious that the dynamic system is recursive: while (10a), (10b), (12), (14a), and (14b) simultaneously govern the dynamics of z, m, m^*, μ, and μ^*, the dynamics of other variables are easily determined by substituting these variables into other equations. In equilibrium, the equilibrium values for z, m, m^*, μ, and μ^*, together $\tilde{p}$, $\tilde{r}$ and$\tilde{r}^*$, are unique along a BGP, but there is a continuum of equilibrium values for $\tilde{v}_1, \tilde{v}_2, \tilde{v}_1^*$, and $\tilde{v}_2^*$. We consider

Condition D. $\sigma + \dfrac{\mu\rho'}{1-\mu\rho'}\psi > 1$ and $\sigma^* + \dfrac{\mu^*\rho^{*\prime}}{1-\mu^*\rho^{*\prime}}\psi^* > 1.$

Condition D requires a sufficiently small intertemporal elasticity of substitution; namely, a sufficiently large value of σ. This condition is plausibly met.[10]

[10] In general σ is larger than 1. For example, Ogaki and Reinhart (1998) estimated the value using the US data and obtained $\sigma \in [2.22, 3.125]$. Yogo (2004) used cross-country data and uncovered $\sigma > 2$ across eleven developed countries which was smaller than $\sigma > 5$ he estimated for the U.S. economy.

If we apply linear Taylor expansion of (10a), (10b), (12), (14a), and (14b) near the unique $(\tilde{\mu}, \tilde{\mu}^*, \tilde{z}, \tilde{m}, \tilde{m}^*)$, we obtain

$$\begin{pmatrix} \dot{\mu} \\ \dot{\mu}^* \\ \dot{z} \\ \dot{m} \\ \dot{m}^* \end{pmatrix} = \begin{pmatrix} \rho & 0 & b_{13} & 0 & 0 \\ 0 & \rho^* & b_{23} & 0 & 0 \\ b_{31} & b_{32} & 0 & 0 & 0 \\ b_{41} & b_{42} & 0 & \tilde{m} & 0 \\ b_{51} & b_{52} & 0 & 0 & \tilde{m}^* \end{pmatrix} \begin{pmatrix} \mu - \tilde{\mu} \\ \mu^* - \tilde{\mu}^* \\ z - \tilde{z} \\ m - \tilde{m} \\ m^* - \tilde{m}^* \end{pmatrix}, \tag{21}$$

where $b_{13} = -u'(1-\mu\rho') < 0$, $b_{23} = \frac{u^{*\prime}}{z^2}(1-\mu^*\rho^{*\prime}) > 0$, $b_{31} = \frac{-\rho'\rho z}{(\chi+\chi^*-1)(1-\mu\rho')} < 0$, $b_{32} = \frac{\rho^{*\prime}\rho^* z}{(\chi+\chi^*-1)(1-\mu^*\rho^{*\prime})} > 0$, $b_{41} = \frac{-\chi^* m\rho'\rho}{(\chi+\chi^*-1)(1-\mu\rho')} < 0$, $b_{42} = \frac{-m(\chi-1)\rho^{*\prime}\rho^*}{(\chi+\chi^*-1)(1-\mu^*\rho^{*\prime})} < 0$, $b_{51} = \frac{-\rho'\rho m^*(\chi^*-1)}{(\chi+\chi^*-1)(1-\mu\rho')} < 0$, and $b_{52} = \frac{-m^*\chi\rho^{*\prime}\rho^*}{(\chi+\chi^*-1)(1-\mu^*\rho^{*\prime})} < 0$.
Under Condition D, we obtain $b_{13} < 0, b_{23} > 0, b_{31} < 0, b_{32} > 0, b_{41} < 0, b_{42} < 0, b_{51} < 0$, and $b_{52} < 0$.

Notice that the system in (21) includes only variables that may jump instantaneously and does not involve any state variables whose values are predetermined. As a result, on the one hand, there exists a unique equilibrium path toward the BGP if the number of eigenvalues with negative real parts for the Jacobean matrix on the right hand side of (21) is zero. On the other hand, if the number of eigenvalues with negative real parts is larger than or equal to one, then there exists a continuum of equilibrium paths toward the BGP.

Denote by J the Jacobean matrix in (21), by θ the corresponding eigenvalues, and by I an identity matrix of order 5. The eigenvalues are then determined by

$$\Omega(\theta) \equiv |J - \theta I| = (\tilde{m} - \theta)(\tilde{m}^* - \theta)\Gamma(\theta) = 0,$$

where $\Gamma(\theta) = \{-\theta^3 + (\rho+\rho^*)\theta^2 - (\rho\rho^* - b_{13}b_{31} - b_{23}b_{32})\theta - (b_{13}b_{31}\rho^* + b_{23}b_{32}\rho)\}$. It is clear to see that two of the five eigenvalues are positive: $\theta_1 = \tilde{m} > 0$ and $\theta_2 = \tilde{m}^* > 0$. The remaining three roots, denoted by θ_3, θ_4, and θ_5, are determined by $\Gamma(\theta)$. Using the result that

$$\Gamma(0) \equiv \theta_3\theta_4\theta_5 = -(b_{13}b_{31}\rho^* + b_{23}b_{32}\rho) < 0,$$

there are either one or three roots with negative real parts. When there are three roots with negative real parts, the dynamic equilibrium path toward the BGP is local indeterminacy.

To summarize,

Proposition 2. *Under Condition D, suppose that the two countries in the world have technologies with identical comparative advantage, that is,* $a_1/a_2 = a_1^*/a_2^*$. *Then, the BGP is locally indeterminate.*

Our result may be compared with that of Nishimura and Shimomura (2006), which finds the emergence of local indeterminacy in the neighborhood of a steady state in a similar two-country trade model with bounded growth.[11] The local indeterminacy in our model with unbounded growth is established with weaker requirements. Our model shares with that of Nishimura and Shimomura (2006) in the use of an AK technology that is similar to a Leontief technology. Different from these authors, we use an implicit functional form for the felicity by assuming only one kind of consumption goods. As a result, the emergence of local indeterminacy in our model requires neither a particular factor intensity ranking nor specific restrictions on parameters, except for a sufficiently small intertemporal elasticity of substitution. However, there is an external effect in the felicity in our model emerging from the consumption standard in the Foreign country that is absent in Nishimura and Shimomura (2006). Because of the external effect, restrictive conditions necessary to obtain indeterminacy in Nishimura and Shimomura (2006) are not required in our model.

The external effect is reminiscent of the consumption externalities in a closed-economy, unbounded growth model by Drugeon (1998). By assuming an agent's rate of time preference that is decreasing in the consumption standard measured by average consumption, Drugeon (1998) finds the emergence of local indeterminacy. Like Drugeon (1998), the rate of time preference is decreasing in the consumption externalities in our model. Yet, different from Drugeon (1998), the felicity is decreasing in the consumption externalities in our model. As a result, the consumption externalities may be likely to offset the possibilities of the emergence of local indeterminacy via the negative effect on the felicity. Because of the open economies in our model, the emergence of local indeterminacy does not require the former effect to dominate the latter effect.

4 Import Tariff and Growth

In this section, we examine the long-run relationship between import tariffs and growth. To simplify the analysis, we assume two countries identical in every aspect, except for the technologies. As a result, $\rho^*(u^*(\frac{1}{Z}))=\rho(u(\frac{1}{Z}))$. As the case of incomplete specialization (Case 1) involves a continuum of BGPs, our comparative-static analysis is conducted under the case of complete specialization (Cases 2 and 3) that has a unique BGP.

4.1 Home Country Specializes in the Investment Goods

This is under Case 2 in Sect. 3.2, in which $a_1/a_2 < a_1^*/a_2^*$, and thereby, the Home country exports the investment goods and imports the consumption goods.

[11] In Nishimura and Shimomura (2006), the emergence of local indeterminacy requires that (a) the technology be of a Leontief-type and the explicit utility form be quadratic, (b) the consumption good be more labor intensive than the investment good, and (c) parameter values for technology and preference are restricted.

Suppose that the government in the Home country imposes an ad-valorem import tariff on the consumption goods with the amount of tariff revenues transferring to the households in a lump-sum fashion.[12] The government budget constraint is

$$T = sp_{\mathrm{T}}(c - y_1), \tag{22a}$$

where $s \geq 0$ is the tariff rate of the imports, p_{T} is the international price of the consumption goods under the tariff policy, and T is the transfer payment.[13] In what follows, a variable with subscript T is used to denote the variable under the tariff regime, while a variable with subscript F is used to denote the variable under the free trade regime.

As the Home country completely specializes in investment goods, $y_1 = 0$ and (20a) becomes $T = sp_{\mathrm{T}}c$. Now, $p_{\mathrm{T}}(1+s)$ is the Home country's domestic prices of the pure consumption good. Thus, the flow budget constraint of the household is

$$\dot{k} = rk - p_{\mathrm{T}}(1+s)c + T. \tag{22b}$$

Note that $m = p(1+s)c/k$ when $(1+s)a_1/a_2 > a_1^*/a_2^*$. In a BGP, equilibrium system (17) remains the same, except for (17f), (17h), and (17i) that now become

$$\begin{cases} \tilde{z}+1 = \tilde{p}_{\mathrm{T}}\left(\dfrac{(1+s)a_1\tilde{z}\tilde{v}_1}{\tilde{m}} + \dfrac{a_1^*\tilde{v}_1^*}{\tilde{m}^*}\right), & \text{if } (1+s)a_1/a_2 \geq a_1^*/a_2^*, \\ \tilde{z}+1 = \tilde{p}_{\mathrm{T}}\left(\dfrac{a_1\tilde{z}\tilde{v}_1}{\tilde{m}} + \dfrac{a_1^*\tilde{v}_1^*}{\tilde{m}^*}\right), & \text{if } (1+s)a_1/a_2 \leq a_1^*/a_2^*, \end{cases} \tag{17f$'$}$$

$$\begin{cases} \tilde{v}_2 = \tilde{v}_1^* = 0, & \text{if } (1+s)a_1/a_2 > a_1^*/a_2^*, \\ \tilde{p}_{\mathrm{T}} = \dfrac{a_2}{(1+s)a_1} = \dfrac{a_2^*}{a_1^*}, & \text{if } (1+s)a_1/a_2 = a_1^*/a_2^*, \\ \tilde{v}_1 = \tilde{v}_2^* = 0, & \text{if } (1+s)a_1/a_2 < a_1^*/a_2^*, \end{cases} \tag{17h$'$}$$

$$\tilde{r} = \begin{cases} a_1 p_{\mathrm{T}}(1+s) \geq a_2, & \text{if } (1+s)a_1/a_2 > a_1^*/a_2^*, \\ a_2 \geq a_1\tilde{p}_{\mathrm{T}}(1+s), & \text{if } (1+s)a_1/a_2 \leq a_1^*/a_2^*, \end{cases}$$

$$\tilde{r}^* = \begin{cases} a_2^* \geq a_1^*\tilde{p}_{\mathrm{T}}, & \text{if } (1+s)a_1/a_2 \geq a_1^*/a_2^*, \\ a_1^*\tilde{p}_{\mathrm{T}} \geq a_2^*, & \text{if } (1+s)a_1/a_2 \leq a_1^*/a_2^*. \end{cases} \tag{17i$'$}$$

---

[12] The results under a specific import tariff are qualitatively similarly to those of an ad-valorem import tariff, but the analysis under an ad-valorem import tariff is simpler. We thus focus on the analysis of the effects of an ad-valorem import tariff.

[13] From a mathematic point of view, otherwise imported goods under free trade may become exported goods under the tariff, which may change to an export subsidy. We thank a referee to point out this possibility. Here, in this chapter we would lie to focus only on tariffs and not on an export subsidy. Our choice is based on a practice as a tariff policy is used often in many countries and is still acceptable by the World Trade Organization (WTO). An export subsidy, in contrast, is not acceptable by the WTO, albeit it is theoretically interesting.

To analyze the impacts of import tariffs on economic growth in a BGP, we compare the economic growth rate under tariff with the rate under free trade. Denote $\hat{s} \equiv \frac{a_1*/a_2*}{a_1/a_2} - 1$. Apparently, $\hat{s} > 0$ in the case under study.

First, if $s < \hat{s}$, then $(1+s)a_1/a_2 < a_1^*/a_2^*$, and thereby, the trade pattern is not changed. The rate of economic growth depends upon the value of $\tilde{z}$ along the BGP. As $\tilde{z}$ is not affected, the rate of economic growth is unchanged.

Second, if $s > \hat{s}$, then $(1+s)a_1/a_2 > a_1^*/a_2^*$. As a result, the trade pattern is reversed. The economy changes from the importer to the exporter of the consumption and imports the investment goods. The tariff is on the imports of consumption goods, but the Home country imports the investment goods after the tariff policy is enforced. As a consequence, the Home country does not have any tariff revenues, and thus, the transfer payment is zero in the long-run equilibrium.

To investigate the effect of the tariff policy on the interest rate, we note from (17i) that under the free trade regime $\tilde{r}_F = a_2$ and $\tilde{r}_F^* = a_1^* \tilde{p}_F$. Because of the tariff policy, there is an excess of supply of the consumption goods in the world market at $\tilde{p}_F$, making the world-market clearing price lower, $\tilde{p}_T < \tilde{p}_F$. Thus, after the policy is enforced, (17i′) indicates that $\tilde{r}_T = a_1 \tilde{p}_T (1+s) > a_2$ and $a_1^* \tilde{p}_F > \tilde{r}_T^* = a_2^* > a_1^* \tilde{p}_T$. Therefore, while the interest rate in the Home country is raised under the tariff regime, that is, $\tilde{r}_T > \tilde{r}_F$, the interest rate in the Foreign country is lowered under the tariff regime, that is, $\tilde{r}_T^* < \tilde{r}_F^*$. As a result, (17c) suggests $\tilde{z}_T > \tilde{z}_F$. Moreover, (18b) indicates that

$$\tilde{z}_F \gtreqless 1, \text{ if } a_2 \lesseqgtr 2\rho(u(1)), \tag{23a}$$

while (18c) indicates that

$$\tilde{z}_T \gtreqless 1, \quad \text{if } a_2^* \lesseqgtr 2\rho(u(1)). \tag{23b}$$

We are ready to examine the effect of the tariff policy on economic growth. Under free trade, from (17i) and (20a), the economic growth rate is equal to $g_F(z) = a_2 - \rho(u(z))$, which using (18b) is rewritten as

$$g_F(\tilde{z}_F) \equiv \rho\left(u\left(\frac{1}{\tilde{z}_F}\right)\right)\tilde{z}_F. \tag{24a}$$

Under the tariff regime, in contrast, the economic growth rate in the Home country is $g_T = a_1 \tilde{p}_T (1+s) - \rho(u(z))$, which using (17c), (17d), and (17f′) is rewritten as

$$g_T(\tilde{z}_T) \equiv \rho(u(\tilde{z}_T))/\tilde{z}_T. \tag{24b}$$

Under Assumptions 1 and 2, g_F is increasing in $\tilde{z}_F$, while g_T is decreasing in $\tilde{z}_T$. Moreover, loci g_F and g_T intersect at $\tilde{z}_F = \tilde{z}_T = 1$ (Fig. 1).

1. $a_2 \geq 2\rho(u(1))$.
   In this case, (23a) indicates that the ratio of Home to Foreign consumption is $\tilde{z}_F \geq 1$ under free trade (see point F_1 in Fig. 1). Recall that the import tariff policy leads to a higher ratio of Home to Foreign consumption, that is, $\tilde{z}_T > \tilde{z}_F$

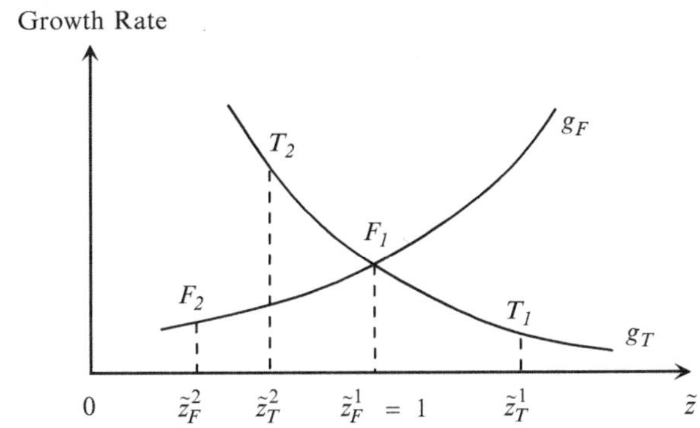

Fig. 1 Growth rates $(a_1/a_2 < a_1^*/a_2^*)$

Table 1 Import Tariff and Growth Rate $(a_1/a_2 < a_1^*/a_2^*)^\dagger$

Import tariffs	Conditions	Variation of growth rate
$s < \hat{s} \equiv \frac{a_1^* a_2}{a_1 a_2^*} - 1$	–	Unchanged
	$a_2 \geq 2\rho[u(1)]$	Lower
$s > \hat{s} \equiv \frac{a_1^* a_2}{a_1 a_2^*} - 1$	$a_2 < 2\rho[u(1)] \leq a_2^*$	Higher
	a_2 and $a_2^* < 2\rho[u(1)]$	Ambiguous

†The utility and the time preference rates are the same in the two countries

(say at Point T_1 in Fig. 1). As a result, $g_T(\tilde{z}_T) < g_F(\tilde{z}_F)$. The rate of economic growth is lower under the tariff regime.

2. $a_2 < 2\rho(u(1))$.
   In this case, $\tilde{z}_F < 1$ exists under free trade according to (23a). Under the tariff regime, $\tilde{z}_T > \tilde{z}_F$. It is possible that economic growth is higher under the tariff regime, depending upon the relative magnitude between a_2^* and $2\rho(u(1))$.

   2.1 If $a_2^* \geq 2\rho(u(1))$, (23b) indicates that $\tilde{z}_T \leq 1$. As $\tilde{z}_T > \tilde{z}_F$, it indicates $\tilde{z}_F < \tilde{z}_T \leq 1$ (see F_2 for free trade and T_2 for the tariff regime in Fig. 1). As a result, growth rate is increased under the tariff regime.
   2.2 If $a_2^* < 2\rho(u(1))$, (23b) suggests that $\tilde{z}_T > 1$, say at T_1 in Fig. 1. As a result, it must be $\tilde{z}_F < 1 < \tilde{z}_T$. In this situation, the economic growth is ambiguous after the tariff. Therefore, the growth effect is ambiguous in this case.

We summarize the results in these different cases in Table 1.

The effects on economic growth can be understood by the effect of the tariff policy on the interest rate relative to the rate of time preference in the Home country a la (17c). The import tariff makes the price of consumption goods higher in the Home country, thereby attracting more resources into this sector. As a result of higher demand for capital, the interest rate is increased in the Home country. However, the international price of the consumption goods is reduced by augmented output supply, thereby decreasing the demand for capital and the interest rate in the Foreign country. As the result of higher domestic interest rates and lower foreign interest rates, (17c) indicates that the ratio of Home to Foreign consumption is increased and the rate of time preference in the Home country is increasing, $\rho'(u(\tilde{z}_{\mathrm{T}}))u'(\tilde{z}_{\mathrm{T}}) > 0$. So, the economic growth rate, $\tilde{r}_{\mathrm{T}} - \rho(u(z))$, is ambiguous.

In particular, the change in the interest rates is $\Delta\tilde{r}_{\mathrm{T}} = a_1\tilde{p}_{\mathrm{T}}(1+s) - a_2 > 0$ and $\Delta\tilde{r}^*_{\mathrm{T}} = a^*_2 - a^*_1\tilde{p}_{\mathrm{F}} < 0$. If a_2 is sufficiently large so that $a_2 \geq 2\rho(u(1))$, then the increase in $\Delta\tilde{r}_{\mathrm{T}} > 0$ is smaller than the increase in $\rho'(u(\tilde{z}_{\mathrm{T}}))u'(\tilde{z}_{\mathrm{T}}) > 0$; hence, the economic growth rate $\tilde{r} - \rho(u(z))$ is reduced. Alternately, if a_2 is small, such that $a_2 < 2\rho(u(1))$, then the increase in $\Delta\tilde{r}_{\mathrm{T}} > 0$ is large. Moreover, from (17c), the increment of z depends on the magnitude of $\Delta\tilde{r}^*_{\mathrm{T}}$. If a^*_2 is sufficiently large, such that $a^*_2 \geq 2\rho(u(1))$, the foreign interest rate decreases less and so does the increment of z. This causes the domestic time preference rate to increase less. Thus, $\tilde{r}_{\mathrm{T}} - \rho(u(z))$ increases in equilibrium, making economic growth higher. However, if a^*_2 is sufficiently small, such that $a^*_2 < 2\rho(u(1))$, the foreign interest rate decreases more and so does the increment of z. This higher domestic time preference rate leads to an ambiguous sign of $\tilde{r}_{\mathrm{T}} - \rho(u(z))$.

To summarize the results,

Proposition 3. *Suppose that the felicity and the rate of time preference be identical initially across countries. Let* $\hat{s} \equiv \frac{a_1*/a_2*}{a_1/a_2} - 1 > 0$, *so the Home country imports the consumption goods. Then, the effect of imposing the tariff rate s on the imports of the consumption goods is as follows.*

1. *If* $s < \hat{s}$, *nothing is affected;*
2. *If* $s > \hat{s}$, *the trade pattern is reversed in the long run, and the Home country has a higher ratio of Home to Foreign consumption and*
   a. *lower economic growth when* $a_2 \geq 2\rho(u(1))$;
   b. *higher economic growth when* $a_2 < 2\rho(u(1)) \leq a^*_2$;
   c. *ambiguous economic growth when* $a_2 < 2\rho(u(1))$ *and* $a^*_2 < 2\rho(u(1))$.

4.2 Home Country Specializes in the Consumption Goods

This is Case 3 in Sect. 3.2, in which $a_1/a_2 > a^*_1 a^*_2$, and thereby, the Home country exports the consumption goods and imports the investment goods.

Suppose now that the government in the Home country imposes an import tariff on the investment goods. Then, the government budget constraint is

$$T = \tau(\dot{k} - y_2), \tag{25a}$$

where $\tau \geq 0$ is the rate of tariff.

As the Home country completely specializes in the production of consumption goods, $y_2 = 0$ and (25a) becomes $T = \tau\dot{k}$. Now $(1+\tau)$ is the domestic prices of the pure investment goods in the Home country. Thus, the flow budget constraint of the household in (5) now turns into

$$\dot{k} = \frac{1}{1+\tau}(rk - p_{\mathrm{T}}c + T). \tag{25b}$$

Similarly, let $m = pC/[(1+\tau)k]$ when $a_1/[a_2(1+\tau)] < a_1^*/a_2^*$. As a result, the equilibrium conditions (17) in a BGP remain the same except for (17c), (17e), (17g), (17h), and (17i) that now become, respectively,[14]

$$\frac{\tilde{r}}{1+\tau} - \rho(u(\tilde{z})) = \tilde{r}^* - \rho^*(u^*(\frac{1}{\tilde{z}})), \tag{17c''}$$

$$\frac{\tilde{r}}{1+\tau} - \rho(u(\tilde{z})) = \tilde{r}^* - \tilde{m}^*, \tag{17e''}$$

$$\begin{cases} \tilde{z}+1 = \tilde{p}_{\mathrm{T}}\left(\dfrac{a_1\tilde{z}\tilde{v}_1}{\tilde{m}} + \dfrac{a_1^*\tilde{v}_1^*}{\tilde{m}^*}\right), & \text{if } a_1/[a_2(1+\tau)] \geq a_1^*/a_2^*, \\ \tilde{z}+1 = \tilde{p}_{\mathrm{T}}\left(\dfrac{a_1\tilde{z}\tilde{v}_1}{(1+\tau)\tilde{m}} + \dfrac{a_1^*\tilde{v}_1^*}{\tilde{m}*}\right), & \text{if } a_1/[a_2(1+\tau)] \leq a_1^*/a_2^*, \end{cases} \tag{17f''}$$

$$\begin{cases} \tilde{v}_2 = \tilde{v}_1^* = 0, & \text{if } a_1/[a_2(1+\tau)] > a_1^*/a_2^*, \\ \tilde{p}_{\mathrm{T}} = \frac{(1+\tau)a_2}{a_1} = \frac{a_2^*}{a_1*}, & \text{if } a_1/[a_2(1+\tau)] = a_1^*/a_2^*, \\ \tilde{v}_1 = \tilde{v}_2^* = 0, & \text{if } a_1/[a_2(1+\tau)] < a_1^*/a_2^*, \end{cases} \tag{17h''}$$

$$\tilde{r} = \begin{cases} a_1\tilde{p}_{\mathrm{T}} \geq (1+\tau)a_2, \text{if } a_1/[a_2(1+\tau)] \geq a_1^*/a_2^*, \\ (1+\tau)a_2 \geq a_1\tilde{p}_{\mathrm{T}}, \text{if } a_1/[a_2(1+\tau)] \leq a_1^*/a_2^*, \end{cases}$$

$$\tilde{r}^* = \begin{cases} a_2^* \geq a_1^*\tilde{p}_{\mathrm{T}}, & \text{if } a_1/[a_2(1+\tau)] \geq a_1^*/a_2^*, \\ a_1^*\tilde{p}_{\mathrm{T}} \geq a_2^*, & \text{if } a_1/[a_2(1+\tau)] \leq a_1^*/a_2^*. \end{cases} \tag{17i''}$$

The effects of the tariff policy depends on the rate of the tariff relative to the threshold $\hat{\tau} \equiv \frac{a_1/a_2}{a_1*/a_2*} - 1 > 0$. As in Sect. 4.1, if it is smaller than the threshold, the comparative advantage is not changed and so is trade patterns. The marginal return of capital, that is, $r/(1+\tau)$, is changed and so is z. In light of (17c″), (17d), (17e″), and (17f″), then $\tilde{z}$ is determined by

$$(1+\tau)\rho(u(\tilde{z})) = (\tilde{z}-\tau)\left[a_2^* - \rho^*\left(u^*\left(\frac{1}{\tilde{z}}\right)\right)\right]. \tag{26}$$

In an economy with a positive growth rate in the two countries, the existence of $\tilde{z}$ is ensured by a sufficiently small tariff, $\tau < \tilde{z}$, and the slope of left hand side in (26) is smaller than that of right hand side, that is, $(1+\tau)\rho'u' < [a_2^* - \rho^*] + (z-\tau)\rho^{*\prime}u^{*\prime}/z^2$. In this case, it is easy to prove that $\tilde{z}$ increases as a higher tariff.

---

[14] The necessary conditions in (8a) and (8b) now become $u'(\frac{c}{c*})[1-\mu\rho'(u(\frac{c}{c*}))] = \frac{\lambda p_T c*}{X(1+\tau)}$ and $\frac{\dot{\lambda}}{\lambda} = -\frac{r}{1+\tau}$.

Moreover, time preference rate in Foreign is lowered and then the rate of economic growth in the Foreign country is raised. In a BGP, the rate of economic growth in the Home country is equal to that in the Foreign country (17c″) and hence the rate of economic growth in the Home country is also raised.

Alternatively, if the rate of tariff is larger than the threshold, the comparative advantage is distorted sufficiently, so the comparative advantage is changed. Then, the Home country produces the investment goods and imports the consumption goods in the long run. In equilibrium, there is no tariff revenue. Moreover, the domestic interest rate is reduced but the foreign interest rate is raised. As a result, z decreases. As in Sect. 4.1, the effect on economic growth depends upon the magnitude of the productivity coefficients relative to the time preferences rate in both countries evaluated at an identical level of consumption. The results are summarized in Fig. 2 and Table 2.

To summarize the results in this subsection,

Proposition 4. *Suppose that the felicity and the rate of time preference be identical initially across countries. Let* $\hat{\tau} \equiv \frac{a_1/a_2}{a_1*/a_2*} - 1 > 0$*, so the Home country imports the investment goods. Then, the effects of imposing the tariff rate* τ *on the imports of the investment goods are as follows.*

(i) If $\tau < \hat{\tau}$*, the Home country has a higher ratio of Home to Foreign consumption and economic growth*

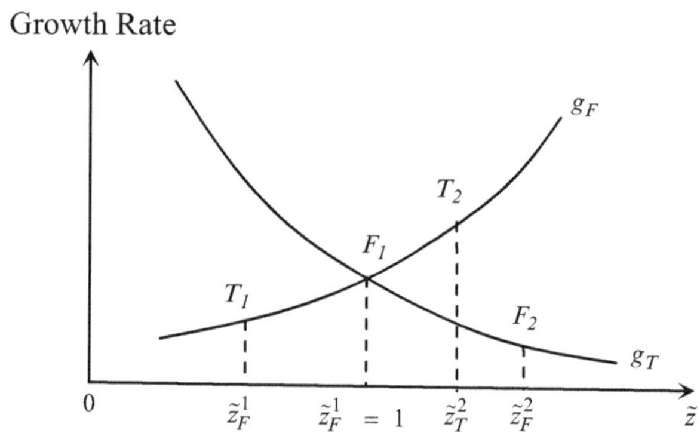

Fig. 2 Growth rates $(a_1/a_2 > a_1^*/a_2^*)$

Table 2 Import Tariff and Growth Rate $(a_1/a_2 > a_1^*/a_2^*)^\dagger$

Import tariffs	Conditions	Variation of growth rate
$\tau < \hat{\tau} \equiv \frac{a_1 a_2^*}{a_1^* a_2} - 1$	–	Higher
	$a_2^* \geq 2\rho[u(1)]$	Lower
$\tau > \hat{\tau} \equiv \frac{a_1 a_2^*}{a_1^* a_2} - 1$	$a_2^* < 2\rho[u(1)] \leq a_2$	Higher
	a_2 and $a_2^* < 2\rho[u(1)]$	Ambiguous

† The preferences and time preference rates are assumed to be the same between two countries

(ii) If $\tau > \hat{\tau}$, the trade pattern is reversed in the long run, and the Home country has a smaller ratio of Home to Foreign consumption and

a. Lower economic growth when $a_2^* \geq 2\rho(u(1))$
b. Higher economic growth when $a_2^* < 2\rho(u(1)) \leq a_2$
c. Ambiguous economic growth when $a_2 < 2\rho(u(1))$ and $a_2^* < 2\rho(u(1))$

5 Import Tariff and Welfare

Finally, we turn to examine the relationship between tariffs and welfare in the long run. In a BGP, the representative agent's lifetime utility in the Home country is

$$U = \int_0^\infty u(\tilde{z})\,\mathrm{e}^{-\rho(u(\tilde{z}))t}\,\mathrm{d}t = \frac{u(\tilde{z})}{\rho(u(\tilde{z}))}.$$

This indicates that the long-run welfare is increasing in $\tilde{z}$ [15] Changes in the welfare depend on the goods the Home country imports.

Under Case 2, in which the Home country specializes in the investment goods, the consumption goods are imported. Tariffs s on the imports of the consumption goods lead to a higher $\tilde{z}$ in the long run if $s > \hat{s}$. As a result, the tariffs increase the long-run welfare in the Home country if $s > \hat{s}$.

In contrast, under Case 3, in which the Home country specializes in the consumption goods, the investment goods are imported. Tariffs on the imports of the investment goods result in a lower $\tilde{z}$ in the long run if $\tau > \hat{\tau}$, It follows that the tariffs decrease the long-run welfare in the Home country if $\tau > \hat{\tau}$,

To summarize the relationship between tariffs and welfare in the long run, we obtain

Proposition 5. *Let a_1/a_2 <(respectively, >) a_1^*/a_2^*. Then, a tariff on the imports of the consumption (respectively, investment) goods raises (respectively, reduces) the long-run welfare in the Home country if the tariff reverses the trade pattern.*

6 Conclusion

While most existing documents find a negative relationship between the import tariffs and the rate of economic growth, there are studies finding an ambiguous, or even positive, relationship. This chapter builds a two-country, two-output trade model and studies the relationship between tariffs and economic growth in an endogenous growth framework. The AK technologies are used to differentiate the role of physical capital accumulation from the human capital accumulation as a source

[15] According to Assumption 1, $\frac{\mathrm{d}U}{\mathrm{d}\tilde{z}} = \frac{u'[\rho - \rho' u]}{\rho^2} > 0$.

of economic growth. The choice leads to Ricardian technologies; yet, the Ricardian theorem of comparative advantage holds in the two-country world even if the preferences are different across countries.

A special feature of our model is to incorporate time nonseparable preferences. A growing body of empirical evidence using country or cross-country data has confirmed the importance of time nonseparable preferences. We introduce the endogenous rate of time preference. An extensive literature on asset pricing and real business cycles lends further credit to the level of benchmark consumption being a significant determinant of consumption behavior. We incorporate the average living standard in the foreign country as benchmark consumption. We find that in the case of incomplete specialization, local indeterminacy arises in the neighborhood of a BGP.

We examine the relationship between tariffs and economic growth in the case of complete specialization. We find an ambiguous relationship. In particular, when the Home country specializes in the investment (respectively, consumption) goods, a sufficient higher rate of tariffs on the consumption (respectively, investment) goods reverses the trade pattern in the long run and decreases economic growth when the productivity coefficient of the investment goods in the Home (respectively, Foreign) country is larger than the threshold. However, economic growth is increased when the productivity coefficient of the investment goods in the Home (respectively, Foreign) country is smaller and in the Foreign (respectively, Home) country is larger than the threshold. Finally, tariffs increase (respectively, decrease) the long-run welfare in the Home country when it specializes in the investment (respectively, consumption) goods.

Finally, we discuss some avenues of the study. First, although we have analyzed dynamic stability properties, we only characterize the long-run relationship between tariffs and economic growth. The reason is that only few existing studies are conducted in a two-country endogenous growth model and all these chapters focused on trade patters and economic growth in the long run.[16] None of these chapters studied the long-run relationship between tariffs and economic growth that is investigated in this current study. Nevertheless, it is of importance to study the dynamic relationship between tariffs and economic growth. This is an avenue of further research.

Second, to simplify the model, we consider two countries of a similar size, so our analysis is focused on the case of complete specialization. Alternatively, if there is a country whose size is sufficiently large, in a Ricardian model one of the two countries may be incompletely specialized, especially during the transition. It is interesting to extend our model to the direction with a sufficiently large country and study the implication on the relationship between tariffs and economic growth.

Third and finally, in this chapter we only investigate tariff policies and do not consider export subsidy policies. It is possible that imported goods under free trade may become the exported good under the tariff; thus, a tariff policy may eventually change to an export subsidy. This provides an avenue for further research.

[16] Notable chapters are by Bond et al. (2003), Farmer and Lahiri (2005, 2006), and Doi et al. (2007), which built on the Lucas (1988) framework.

References

Abel AB (1990) Asset prices under habit formation and catching up with the Joneses. Am Econ Rev (Papers Proc) 80:38–42

Alonso-Carrera J, Caballe J, Raurich X (2004) Consumption externalities, habit formation and equilibrium efficiency. Scand J Econ 106:231–251

Alonso-Carrera J, Caballe J, Raurich X (2005) Growth, habit formation, and catching-up with the Jones. Eur Econ Rev 49:1885–1891

Alonso-Carrera J, Caballe J, Raurich X (2006) Welfare implications of the interaction between habits and consumption externalities. Int Econ Rev 47:557–571

Alvarenz-Cuadrado F, Monteiro G, Turnovsky S (2004) Habit formation, catching up with the Joneses, and economic growth. J Econ Growth 9:47–80

Ben-David D, Loewy MB (1998) Free trade, growth, and convergence. J Econ Growth 3:143–170

Baxter M (1992) Fiscal policy, specialization, and trade in the two-sector model: the returns to Ricardo. J Polit Econ 100:713–744

Boldrin M, Christiano LJ, Fisher JDM (2001) Habit persistence, asset Returns, and the business cycle. Am Econ Rev 91:149–165

Bond E, Trask E, Wang P (2003) Factor accumulation and trade: dynamic comparative advantage with endogenous physical and human capital. Int Econ Rev 44:1041–1060

Campbell JY, Cochrane JH (1999) By force of habit: a consumption-based explanation of aggregate stock market behavior. J Polit Econ 107:205–251

Carroll CD, Overland JR, Weil DN (2000) Saving and growth with habit formation. Am Econ Rev 90:341–355

Chen BL (2007) Multiple BGPs in a growth model with habit persistence. J Money Credit Bank 39:25–48

Chen BL, Hsu M (2007) Admiration is a source of indeterminacy. Econ Lett 95:96–103

Chen BL, Nishimura K, Shimomura K (2008) Time preference and two-country trade. Int J Econ Theory 4:29–52

Clements MA, Williamson JG (2004) Why did the tariff-growth correlation change after 1950. J Econ Growth 9:5–46

Constantinides GM (1990) Habit formation: a resolution of the equity premium puzzle. J Polit Econ 98:519–543

Doi K, Nishimura K, Shimomura K (2007) A two-country dynamic model of international trade and endogenous growth: multiple balanced growth paths and stability. J Math Econ 47:390–419

Dupor B, Liu WF (2003) Jealousy and equilibrium overconsumpiton. Am Econ Rev 93:423–428

Drugeon JP (1998) A model with endogenously determined cycles, discounting and growth. Econ Theory 12:349–369

Easterly W, Rebelo S (1993) Fiscal policy and economic growth. J Monetary Econ 32:417–458

Edwards S (1992) Trade orientation, distortions and growth in developing countries. J Dev Econ 39:31–57

Farmer R, Lahiri A (2005) A two-country model of endogenous growth. Rev Econ Dyn 8:68–88

Farmer R, Lahiri A (2006) Economic growth in an interdependent world economy. J Econ 116:969–990

Fisher WH, Hof FX (2000) Relative consumption, economic growth and taxation. J Econ 72:241–262

Fuhrer JC, Klein MW (1998) Risk habits: on risk sharing, habit formation and interpretation of international consumption correlation. NBER Working Paper No. 6735

Gali J (1994) Keeping up with the Joneses: consumption externalities, portfolio choice and asset prices. J Money Credit Bank 26:1–8

Grossman GM, Helpman E (1990) Comparative advantage and long-run growth. Am Econ Rev 80:796–815

Harrison A (1996) Openness and growth: a time series, cross-country analysis for developing countries. J Dev Econ 48:419–447

Irwin DA (2002) Interpreting the tariff-growth correlation of the late nineteenth century. NBER Working Paper Series, No. 8739

Jones LE, Manuelli R (1990) A convex model of equilibrium Growth. J Polit Econ 98:1008–1037

Lee JW (1993) International trade, distortions, and long-run economic growth. IMF Staff Papers 40:299–328

Liu WF, Turnovsky S (2005) Consumption externalities, production externalities, and long-run macroeconomic efficiency. J Publ Econ 89:1097–1129

Ljungqvist L, Uhlig H (2000) Tax policy and aggregate demand management under catching up with Joneses. Am Econ Rev 90:356–66

Naito T (2005) Revenue-neutral environmental tariff reform, growth, and welfare. Rev Int Econ 13:985–996

Naito T (2006a) Tariff and tax reform: dynamic implications. J Int Econ 68:504–517

Naito T (2006b) Growth, revenue, and welfare effects of tariff and tax reform: win–win–win strategies. J Publ Econ 90:1263–1280

Nishimura K, Shimomura K (2006) Indeterminacy in a dynamic two-country model. Econ Theory 29:307–324

Ogaki M, Reinhart CM (1998) Measuring intertemporal substitution: the role of durable goods. J Polit Econ 106:1078–1098

O'Rourke KH (2000) Tariffs and growth in the late nineteenth century. Econ J 110:456–483

Osang T, Pereira A (1996) Import tariffs and growth in a small open economy. J Publ Econ 60: 45–71

Osborn DR (1988) Seasonality and habit persistence in a life cycle model of consumption. J Appl Econometrics 3:255–266

Rivera-Batiz LA, Romer PM (1991) International trade with endogenous technological change. Eur Econ Rev 35:971–1004

Rodriguez F, Rodrik D (2001) Trade policy and economic growth: a skeptic's guide to the cross-national evidence. In: Bernanke BS, Rogoff K (eds) NBER macroeconomics annual 2000. MIT Press, Cambridge

Sala-i-Martin XX (1997) I just ran two million regressions. Am Econ Rev 87:178–183

Uzawa H (1968) Time preference, the consumption function, and optimum asset holdings. In: Wolfe JN (ed) Value, capital, and growth. papers in honor of Sir John Hicks, Chap. 21. University Press, Edinburgh, pp 485–504

Wan HY, Majumdar M (1980) Trade under temporary equilibrium: evolution in a loglinear world. J Int Trade 10:37–62

Van de Stadt H, Kapteyn A, van de Geer S (1985) The relativity of utility: evidence from panel data. Rev Econ Stat 67:179–187

Yanikkaya H (2003) Trade openness and economic growth: a cross-country empirical investigation. J Dev Econ 72:57–89

Yogo M (2004) Estimating the elasticity of intertemporal substitution when instruments are weak. Rev Econ Stat 86:797–810

Preference Structure and Volatility in a Financially Integrated World

Kazuo Mino

Abstract This chapter investigates a two-country model of capital accumulation with country-specific production externalities. The main concern of our discussion is to explore the presence of equilibrium indeterminacy in an open economy setting. In contrast to the existing studies on equilibrium indeterminacy in small-open economies, the present chapter demonstrates that opening up international trade and financial interactions between two counties does not necessarily enhance the possibility of indeterminacy of equilibrium. It is shown that the results depend heavily upon not only the degree of external increasing returns but also the preference structures.

1 Introduction

The equilibrium business cycle theory based on indeterminacy and sunspots has claimed that economic fluctuations caused by extrinsic uncertainty tend to be more prominent in open economies than in closed economies. For example, inspecting a small-open economy version of the two-sector model studied by Benhabib and Farmer (1996), Weder (2001) concludes that the small-open economy requires a lower degree of external increasing returns to yield indeterminacy of equilibrium than the closed economy counterpart. Similarly, Aguiar-Conraria and Wen (2005), Lahiri (2001), and Meng and Velasco (2003, 2004) also demonstrate that perfect capital mobility may enhance indeterminacy of equilibrium for small-open economies.[1] The main reason for this results is that in the small-open economies, the

[1] Meng and Velasco (2003, 2004) study two-sector dependent economy models with sector-specific externalities in which investment goods are not traded. Lahiri (2001) examines a two-sector endogenous growth model with capital mobility.

K. Mino
Graduate School of Economics, Osaka University, 1-7 Machikaneyama, Toyonaka, Osaka 560-0043, Japan, e-mail: mino@econ.osaka-u.ac.jp

T. Kamihigashi and L. Zhao (eds.) *International Trade and Economic Dynamics – Essays in Memory of Koji Shimomura.*

interest rate is fixed in the world financial market, so that consumption behaves as if the utility function were linear. Since a high elasticity of intertemporal substitutability in consumption serves as a cause of indeterminacy, the small-open economies tend to be more volatile than the closed economies with the same technologies and preferences.

The purpose of this chapter is to examine whether the volatility of open economies emphasized by the existing studies mentioned above will hold in the world economy model as well. Since the world economy is a closed economy with heterogeneous agents, the present chapter may be considered a study on the relationship between heterogeneity and indeterminacy.[2] The analytical framework of this chapter is a two-good, two-country model of capital accumulation with external increasing returns. We assume that these two countries trade consumption goods. In addition, it is assumed that agents in both countries can access to the perfect international bond market. Given such a setting, we compare the indeterminacy conditions in the autarky equilibrium with those in the world economy.[3]

Our main finding is that, as opposed to the results established in the small-open economy models, the global economy does not necessarily exhibit a higher possibility of indeterminacy. In particular, if the preference structures of both countries satisfy additive separability between consumption goods and labor, then opening up international transactions will not enhance the possibility of indeterminacy. Furthermore, even if we assume a more general form of utility function, we do not find unambiguous results, indicating that the world economy holds indeterminacy under weaker restrictions on technology and preferences than the closed economies.

It is to be noted that the main concern of this chapter is closely related to a seminal contribution by Nishimura and Shimomura (2002a) who study equilibrium indeterminacy of a world economy with free trade of commodities. Nishimura and Shimomura (2002b) utilize the standard neoclassical growth model with production externalities in the Heckscher–Ohlin setting where consumption as well as investment goods are freely traded but there is no financial interactions between the home and the foreign countries. They find that indeterminacy conditions for a closed economy may generate multiple equilibria in the world economy as well.[4] Our study reconsiders the same issue in the context of a two-country version of the real business cycle model with production externalities and free capital mobility.

The rest of the chapter is organized as follows. Section 2 sets up the base model. Section 3 specifies functional forms involved in the model and explores

---

[2] In a different context, Ghiglino and Olszak-Duquenne (2005) also consider the relation between heterogeneity of agents and equilibrium indeterminacy in a closed economy model of economic growth with production externalities.

[3] In the open-macroeconomics literature, we have not seen any study on indeterminacy in a two-country model. As for a general discussion concerning the effect of financial integration on macroeconomic volatility, see, e.g., Evans and Hnatkovska (2006).

[4] Nishimura and Shimomura (2006) examine the possibility of equilibrium indeterminacy in a dynamic Heckscher–Ohlin model of a world economy in the absence of production externalities. Indeterminacy in their model comes from the fact that intertemporal trade between the home and foreign countries is prohibited.

indeterminacy conditions under alternative assumptions on the utility functions. Section 4 concludes the chapter.

2 The Analytical Framework

2.1 Structure of the Model

There are two countries: country 1 and country 2. Each country produces a country-specific, single good. We assume that country 1 specializes in good x and country 2 specializes in good y. Each good can be either consumed or invested for physical capital accumulation. We assume that the imported goods can be consumed, but they cannot be used as investment goods. In addition, agents in each country cannot access to the direct ownership of the foreign capital stock. However, the agents in both counties may access to the perfect international bond market, so that they can freely lend to or borrow from each other. Since the international bond market is assumed to be perfect, the uncovered interest parity ensures that the nominal interest rates in both countries are equalized in each moment.[5] Although our assumption that imported goods cannot be used for investment is restrictive, it is helpful to determine the level of real investment in each country without introducing additional assumptions such as the presence of adjustment costs of investment.

2.1.1 Production

The production technology of each country is described by

$$z_i = f^i\left(k_i, l_i, \bar{k}_i, \bar{l}_i\right), \quad i = 1, 2, \tag{1}$$

where z_i, k_i, and l_i, respectively, denote the output, capital, and labor input of country i. In addition, $\bar{k}_i$ and $\bar{l}_i$ express external effects associated with the social levels of capital and labor in country i. It is assumed that function $f^i(\cdot)$ is homogeneous of degree 1 in k_i and l_i and that it increases with $\bar{k}_i$ and $\bar{l}_i$. This means that while the private technology under given level of external effects satisfies constant returns, the social technology exhibits increasing returns to scale with respect to the aggregate levels of capital and labor. We assume that those external effects are country specific, so that there are no international spillovers of production technologies.

The commodity markets in both countries are competitive. Firms maximize their instantaneous profits under given levels of external effects. Hence, letting r_i and w_i

[5] The structure of the base model is close to the two-country model examined by Turnovsky (1997, Chap. 7). Since Turnovsky (1997) does not assume the presence of external increasing returns, indeterminacy of equilibrium is not the issue in his argument. Baxter and Crucini (1995) use a similar model in their study on international real business cycles.

be the real interest rate and the real wage rate in country i, they, respectively, equal the net marginal product of capital and the marginal product of labor:

$$r_i = f_k^i\left(k_i, l_i, \bar{k}_i, \bar{l}_i\right) - \delta_i,$$

$$w_i = f_l^i\left(k_i, l_i, \bar{k}_i, \bar{l}_i\right), \quad i = 1, 2.$$

where $\delta_i \in (0,1)$ denotes the depreciation rate of capital.

2.1.2 Households

The number of households in each country is normalized to one. The objective function of the representative household in country i is a discounted sum of utilities such that

$$U_i = \int_0^\infty u^i\left(x_i, y_i, l_i\right) \mathrm{e}^{-\rho t} \mathrm{d}t, \quad \rho > 0, \quad i = 1, 2,$$

where x_i and y_i denote the consumption of x and y goods in country i. By our assumption, y_1 is exported from country 2 to country 1 and x_2 is exported from country 1 to country 2. The instantaneous utility is assumed to be increasing in x_i and y_i and decreasing in labor l_i. The standard concavity assumption is imposed on $u^i(\cdot)$. We assume that the households in both countries may have different utility functions but their discount rates are the same rate of ρ.[6]

The flow budget constraint for the households in each country is given by

$$\dot{\omega}_i = r_i \omega_i + w_i l_i - m_i, \quad i = 1, 2, \tag{2}$$

where ω_i is the real asset holding and m_i is the real consumption expenditure. For notational convenience, ω_i, w_i, and m_i are expressed in terms of the good country i produces. Thus, if p denotes the price of good y in terms of good x, the consumption spending in both countries is, respectively, given by

$$m_1 = x_1 + p y_1, \quad m_2 = \frac{x_2}{p} + y_2.$$

The real asset ω_i consists of capital stock k_i and the foreign bond holding b_i. Therefore, we define

$$\omega_i = k_i + b_i, \quad i = 1, 2.$$

where b_1 and b_2 are evaluated in terms of x good and y good, respectively.

The household maximizes U_i subject to (2) and the initial holding of ω_i by controlling consumption levels and labor supply. We impose the no-Ponzi-game condition, and hence the following intertemporal budget constraint is satisfied as well:

---

[6] This assumption is introduced only for notational simplicity.

$$\omega_i(0) + \int_0^\infty \exp\left(-\int_0^t r_i(s)\,ds\right) w_i(t)\, l_i(t)\,dt$$
$$= \int_0^\infty \exp\left(-\int_0^t r_i(s)\,ds\right) m_i(t)\,dt, \quad i = 1, 2.$$

2.1.3 Market Equilibrium Conditions

Since physical capital stocks are not traded, the market equilibrium conditions for the commodity markets are

$$z_1 = x_1 + x_2 + \dot{k}_1 + \delta_1 k_1, \tag{3}$$

$$z_2 = y_1 + y_2 + \dot{k}_2 + \delta_2 k_2. \tag{4}$$

The world financial market is assumed to be perfect. This means that the uncovered interest parity yields

$$r_1 = r_2 + \frac{\dot{p}}{p}. \tag{5}$$

The international borrowing and lending in the world economy should be balanced in each moment, implying that the equilibrium condition for the bond market is

$$b_1 + p b_2 = 0. \tag{6}$$

Note that the homogeneity of production functions gives $z_i = r_i k_i + w_i l_i$ $(i = 1, 2)$. Hence, in view of (3), (4), and $\omega_i = k_i + b_i$, the flow budget constraints in (2) present the dynamic equations of b_1 and b_2 as follows:

$$\dot{b}_1 = r_1 b_1 + x_2 - p y_1, \tag{7}$$

$$\dot{b}_2 = r_2 b_2 + y_1 - \frac{x_2}{p}. \tag{8}$$

Equations (7) and (8), respectively, describe the current accounts of country 1 and country 2.[7]

[7] We assume that the solvency conditions for international lending and borrowing are satisfied. Namely, the following hold:

$$b_1(0) + \int_0^\infty \exp\left(-\int_0^t r_1(s)\,ds\right) x_2(t)\,dt = \int_0^\infty \exp\left(-\int_0^t r_1(s)\,ds\right) p(t)\, y_1(t)\,dt,$$

$$b_2(0) + \int_0^\infty \exp\left(-\int_0^t \left[r_2(s) + \frac{\dot{p}(s)}{p(s)}\right] ds\right) y_1(t)\,dt = \int_0^\infty \exp\left(-\int_0^t \left[r_2(s) + \frac{\dot{p}(s)}{p(s)}\right] ds\right) \frac{x_2(t)}{p(tto)}\,dt.$$

2.1.4 Perfect-Foresight Competitive Equilibrium

To sum up, the perfect-foresight competitive equilibrium (PFCE) of the world economy is defined in the following manner.

Definition 1. The PFCE of the world economy is established if the following conditions are satisfied:

(i) The firms maximize instantaneous profits under given levels of external effects, $\bar{k}_i$ and $\bar{l}_i$.
(ii) The households maximize their discounted sum of utilities under given sequences of prices, $\{r_i(t), w_i(t), p(t)\}_{t=0}^{\infty}$.
(iii) Commodity markets clear and the bond market is in equilibrium.
(iv) The uncovered interest parity condition (5) is satisfied.
(v) External effects satisfy consistency conditions, i.e., $\bar{k}_i = k_i$ and $\bar{l}_i = l_i$.

In what follows, we analyze the corresponding planning economy rather than the decentralized system displayed above.

2.2 A Pseudo-Planning Problem

When inspecting the equilibrium dynamics of the world economy, it is convenient to consider the following pseudo-planning problem:

$$\max \int_0^{\infty} \left[\mu_1 u^1(x_1, y_1, l_1) + \mu_2 u^2(x_2, y_2, l_2)\right] \mathrm{e}^{-\rho t} \mathrm{d}t, \quad \mu_i > 0, \quad \mu_1 + \mu_2 = 1$$

subject to

$$\dot{k}_1 = f^1\left(k_1, l_1, \bar{k}_1, \bar{l}_1\right) - x_1 - x_2 - \delta_1 k_1, \tag{9}$$

$$\dot{k}_2 = f^2\left(k_2, l_2, \bar{k}_2, \bar{l}_2\right) - y_1 - y_2 - \delta_2 k_2, \tag{10}$$

and given initial levels of $k_1(0)$ and $k_2(0)$. A positive constant μ_i denotes a weight on the utility in country i. Taking the sequences of external effects, $\{\bar{k}_1(t), \bar{l}_1(t), \bar{k}_2(t), \bar{l}_2(t)\}_{t=0}^{\infty}$, as given, the planner solves this problem by selecting the optimal levels of l_i, x_i, and y_i $(i = 1, 2)$.

The Hamiltonian function for the planning problem can be set as

$$\begin{aligned} H = {} & \mu_1 u^1(x_1, y_1, l_1) + \mu_2 u^2(x_2, y_2, l_2) \\ & + q_1\left[f^1\left(k_1, l_1, \bar{k}_1, \bar{l}_1\right) - x_1 - x_2 - \delta_1 k_1\right] \\ & + q_2\left[f^2\left(k_2, l_2, \bar{k}_2, \bar{l}_2\right) - y_1 - y_2 - \delta_2 k_2\right], \end{aligned}$$

where q_i represents the shadow value of k_i. The necessary conditions for an optimum are

$$\mu_i u^i_{x_i}(x_i, y_i, l_i) = q_1, \quad i = 1, 2, \tag{11}$$

$$\mu_i u^i_{y_i}(x_i,y_i,l_i) = q_2, \quad i=1,2, \tag{12}$$

$$\mu_i u^i_{l_i}(x_i,y_i,l_i) = q_i f^i_{l_i}\left(k_i,l_i,\bar{k}_i,\bar{l}_i\right), \quad i=1,2, \tag{13}$$

$$\dot{q}_i = q_i\left[\rho+\delta_i - f^i_{k_i}\left(k_i,l_i,\bar{k}_i,\bar{l}_i\right)\right], \quad i=1,2, \tag{14}$$

together with (9), (10), and the transversality conditions:

$$\lim_{t\to\infty} e^{-\rho t} q_i k_i = 0, \quad i=1,2. \tag{15}$$

Inserting $\bar{k}_i = k_i$ and $\bar{l}_i = l_i$ into the optimal conditions, we find that the necessary conditions for an optimum of this pseudo-planning problem completely characterize PFCE conditions of the world economy defined above.

Lemma 1. *If μ_1 and μ_2 are appropriately selected, the necessary conditions for an optimum for the planning problem and the PFCE in the world economy are identical.*

Proof. See Appendix 1. □

Due to this fact, we can focus on the dynamic behavior of the pseudo-planning economy when examining the competitive equilibrium dynamics of the world economy.

2.3 Dynamic Systems

The necessary conditions for the planning problem may be summarized as a complete dynamic system with respect to the state variables, k_1 and k_2, and the costate variables, q_1 and q_2. The structure of the dynamic system is sensitive to the specification of the preference structure. First, consider the general case where the instantaneous utility functions are nonseparable ones. In this case, by use of (11) and (12), consumption demand x_i and y_i may be expressed as functions of q_1, q_2, and k_i. Substituting those functions into (13) and assuming that $\bar{k}_i = k_i$ and $\bar{l}_i = l_i$, we find that l_i depends on q_1, q_2, and k_i. Therefore, the equilibrium levels of x_i, y_i, and l_i are written as

$$x_i = x^i(k_i,q_1,q_2), \quad y_i = y^i(k_i,q_1,q_2), \quad l_i = l^i(k_i,q_1,q_2), \quad i=1,2.$$

Substituting those into (9), (10), and (14), the complete dynamic system may be written as

$$\dot{k}_1 = z^1(k_1,q_1,q_2) - x^1(k_1,q_1,q_2) - x^2(k_2,q_1,q_2) - \delta_1 k_1,$$

$$\dot{k}_2 = z^2(k_2,q_1,q_2) - y^1(k_1,q_1,q_2) - y^2(k_2,q_1,q_2) - \delta_2 k_2,$$

$$\dot{q}_i = q_i\left[\rho - r^i(k_i,q_1,q_2)\right], \quad i=1,2,$$

where

$$z^i(k_i,q_1,q_2) \equiv f^i\left(k_i,l^i(k_i,q_1,q_2),k_i,l_i(k_i,q_1,q_2)\right),$$

$$r^i(k_i,q_1,q_2) \equiv f_k\left(k_i,l^i(k_i,q_1,q_2),k_i,l^i(k_i,q_1,q_2)\right) - \delta_i.$$

Next, assume that the utility function is additively separable between consumption and labor in such a way that

$$u^i(x_i,y_i,l_i) = \phi^i_{\mathrm{c}}(x_i,y_i) + \phi^i_{\mathrm{L}}(l_i). \tag{16}$$

Then, it is easy to see that x_i and y_i depend only on q_1 and q_2 alone, while $z^i(\cdot)$ and $r^i(\cdot)$ involve only k_i and q_i:

$$\dot{k}_1 = z^1(k_1,q_1) - x^1(q_1,q_2) - x^2(q_1,q_2) - \delta_1 k_1,$$

$$\dot{k}_2 = z^2(k_2,q_2) - y^1(q_1,q_2) - y^2(q_1,q_2) - \delta_2 k_2,$$

$$\dot{q}_i = q_i\left[\rho + \delta_i - r^i(k_i,q_i)\right], \quad i = 1,2.$$

Finally, consider the case in which the utility function is additively separable for each argument, i.e.,

$$u^i(x_i,y_i,l_i) = \phi^i_X(x_i) + \phi^i_Y(y_i) + \phi^i_{\mathrm{L}}(l_i). \tag{17}$$

As demonstrated by Turnovsky (1997, Chap. 7), this assumption simplifies the dynamic system substantially: consumption demand for x goods depends on q_1 alone and that for y good depends on q_2 alone. Thus, the dynamic system is described by

$$\dot{k}_1 = z^1(k_1,q_1) - x^1(q_1) - x^2(q_1) - \delta_1 k_1,$$

$$\dot{k}_2 = z^2(k_2,q_2) - y^1(q_2) - y^2(q_2) - \delta_2 k_2,$$

$$\dot{q}_i = q_i\left[\rho + \delta_i - r^i(k_i,q_i)\right], \quad i = 1,2.$$

Note that this system consists of two independent subsystems with respect to (k_1,q_1) and (k_2,q_2). Therefore, while the current account depends on the foreign variables (see (7) and (8)), consumption and investment decisions in each country are not interdependent each other even in the financially integrated world. Since the most general case will not produce tractable results in the base model, we focus on the second and the third cases when examining exogenous growth models in the next section.

3 Equilibrium Dynamics

3.1 Specification

To obtain concrete results about determinacy of equilibrium, we now specify the production and the utility functions as the forms that have been frequently employed in the literature on indeterminacy and sunspots in the real business cycle models. The production function of each country is

$$z_i = k_i^{a_i} l_i^{1-a_i} \bar{k}_i^{\alpha_i - a_i} \bar{l}^{\beta_i + a_i - 1}, \quad 0 < a_i < 1, \quad \alpha_i, \beta_i > 0, \quad \alpha_i + \beta_i > 1.$$

Accordingly, imposing $\bar{k}_i = k_i$ and $\bar{l}_i = l_i$, we obtain the social production function in each country as follows:

$$z_i = k_i^{\alpha_i} l_i^{\beta_i}, \quad i = 1, 2. \tag{18}$$

In what follows, we assume that $0 < \alpha_i < 1$, so that capital externalities are not so large that unbounded growth is possible. The rate of return to capital and the real wage rate are, respectively, given by

$$r_i = f_k^i - \delta_i = a_i k_i^{\alpha_i - 1} l_i^{\beta_i} - \delta_i, \quad i = 1, 2, \tag{19}$$

$$w_i = f_l^i = (1 - a_i) k_i^{\alpha_i} l_i^{\beta_i - 1}, \quad i = 1, 2. \tag{20}$$

The utility function is assumed to be additively separable between consumption and labor. More specifically, the instantaneous utility of the households in country i is given by

$$u^i(x_i, y_i, l_i) = \begin{cases} \dfrac{\left(x_i^{\theta_i} y_i^{1-\theta_i}\right)^{1-\sigma_i} - 1}{1 - \sigma_i} - \dfrac{l_i^{1+\gamma_i}}{1+\gamma_i}, & 0 < \theta_i < 1, \quad \gamma_i > 0, \quad \sigma_i > 0, \\ \theta_i \ln x_i + (1-\theta_i) \ln y_i - \dfrac{l_i^{1+\gamma_i}}{1+\gamma_i}, & \text{for } \sigma_i = 1. \end{cases}$$

Given those specifications, the optimal conditions (11), (12), (13), and (14) are, respectively, written as the following equations:

$$\mu_i \theta_i x_i^{\theta_i(1-\sigma_i)-1} y_i^{(1-\theta_i)(1-\sigma_i)} = q_1, \quad i = 1, 2, \tag{21}$$

$$\mu_i (1 - \theta_i) x_i^{\theta_i(1-\sigma_i)} y_i^{(1-\theta_i)(1-\sigma_i)-1} = q_2, \quad i = 1, 2, \tag{22}$$

$$\mu_i l_i^{\gamma_i} = (1 - a_i) k_i^{\alpha_i} l_i^{\beta_i - 1} q_i, \quad i = 1, 2, \tag{23}$$

and

$$\dot{q}_i = q_i \left(\rho + \delta_i - a_i k_i^{\alpha_i - 1} l_i^{\beta_i}\right), \quad i = 1, 2. \tag{24}$$

3.2 Indeterminacy with Logarithmic Utility Functions

We first examine the case where the utility function has a log-additive form in consumption. Ever since Benhabib and Farmer (1994), this specification has been most popular in the studies on indeterminacy and sunspots in the real business cycle settings. In this case $\sigma_1 = \sigma_2 = 1$, and hence the consumption demand functions become

$$x_i = \frac{1}{\mu_i \theta_i q_1}, \quad y_i = \frac{1}{\mu_i (1-\theta_i) q_2}, \quad i = 1,2. \tag{25}$$

As pointed out in Sect. 3.1, the demand functions for each good depend on its own price alone. In view of (22), we obtain

$$l_i = \left[\frac{1-a_i}{\mu_i}\right]^{1/(\gamma_i+1-\beta_i)} k_i^{\alpha_i/(\gamma_i+1-\beta_i)} q_i^{1/(\gamma_i+1-\beta_i)}, \quad i = 1,2. \tag{26}$$

This states that the effects of changes in capital and commodity price on the equilibrium level of labor input depend on the sign of $\gamma_i + 1 - \beta_i$. If the external effect of labor is small enough to satisfy $\gamma_i + 1 > \beta_i$, then the employment level is positively related to q_i and k_i. If $\gamma_i + 1 < \beta_i$, the labor employment decreases with q_i and k_i.

By use of (9), (10), and (24)–(26), we obtain a complete dynamic system with logarithmic utility functions as follows:

$$\dot{k}_1 = A_1 k_1^{\alpha_1(\gamma_1+1)/(\gamma_1+1-\beta_1)} q_i^{\beta_1/(\gamma_1+1-\beta_1)} - \left[\frac{1}{\theta_1\mu_1} + \frac{1}{\theta_2\mu_2}\right]\frac{1}{q_1} - \delta_1 k_1, \tag{27}$$

$$\dot{k}_2 = A_2 k_2^{\alpha_2(\gamma_2+1)/(\gamma_2+1-\beta_2)} q_2^{\beta_2/(\gamma_2+1-\beta_2)} - \left[\frac{1}{(1-\theta_1)\mu_1} + \frac{1}{(1-\theta_2)\mu_2}\right]\frac{1}{q_2} - \delta_2 k_2, \tag{28}$$

$$\dot{q}_1 = q_1 \left[\rho + \delta_1 - a_1 A_1 k_1^{[\alpha_1(\gamma_1+1)/(\gamma_1+1-\beta_1)]-1} q_1^{\beta_1/(\gamma_1+1-\beta_1)}\right], \tag{29}$$

$$\dot{q}_2 = q_2 \left[\rho + \delta_2 - a_2 A_2 k_2^{[\alpha_2(\gamma_2+1)/(\gamma_2+1-\beta_2)]-1} q_2^{\beta_2/(\gamma_2+1-\beta_2)}\right], \tag{30}$$

where

$$A_i = \left[\frac{1-a_i}{\mu_i}\right]^{\beta_i/(\gamma_i+1-\beta_i)}, \quad i = 1,2.$$

In the steady-state equilibrium, k_i and q_i stay constant over time. Given our specification of functional forms and given the parameter values, μ_1 and μ_2, it is easy to see that the steady-state equilibrium is uniquely determined. Letting k_i^* and q_i^* be the steady-state values of capital stocks and prices; the dynamic system linearized at the steady state is written as

$$\begin{bmatrix}\dot{k}_1\\ \dot{k}_2\\ \dot{q}_1\\ \dot{q}_2\end{bmatrix} = \begin{bmatrix} h_{11} & 0 & h_{13} & 0\\ 0 & h_{22} & 0 & h_{24}\\ h_{31} & 0 & h_{33} & 0\\ 0 & h_{42} & 0 & h_{44}\end{bmatrix}\begin{bmatrix} k_1 - k_1^*\\ k_2 - k_2^*\\ q_1 - q_1^*\\ q_2 - q_2^*\end{bmatrix},$$

where $h_{11} = \partial \dot{k}_1 / \partial k_1$, $h_{13} = \partial \dot{k}_1 / \partial q_1$, etc., all of which are evaluated by the steady-state values of k_i^* and q_i^*. Denote the eigenvalue of the coefficient matrix given above by λ. Then, the characteristic equation of the coefficient matrix in the above linear system is given by the following:

$$\left[\lambda^2 - (h_{11} + h_{33})\lambda + h_{11}h_{33} - h_{13}h_{31}\right] \times \left[\lambda^2 - (h_{11} + h_{33})\lambda + h_{22}h_{44} - h_{24}h_{42}\right] = 0. \tag{31}$$

Note that in view of the steady-state condition, $a_i A_i k_i^{[\alpha_i(\gamma_i+1)/(\gamma_i+1-\beta_i)]-1} q_i^{\beta_i/(\gamma_i+1-\beta_i)} = \rho + \delta_i$, we obtain

$$\begin{aligned} h_{ii} &= A_1 \frac{\alpha_i(\gamma_i + 1)}{\gamma_i + 1 - \beta_i} k_1^{[\alpha_1(\gamma_1+1)/(\gamma_1+1-\beta_1)]-1} q_i^{\beta_1/(\gamma_1+1-\beta_1)} - \delta_1 \\ &= \frac{\gamma_i + 1}{\gamma_i + 1 - \beta_i}\left[\rho + \frac{\delta_i \beta_i}{\gamma_i + 1}\right], \quad i = 1, 2, \end{aligned}$$

implying that

$$\operatorname{sign} h_{ii} = \operatorname{sign}(\gamma_i + 1 - \beta_i), \quad i = 1, 2.$$

We also see that when $\gamma_i + 1 - \beta_i > 0$, it holds that h_{13}, h_{31}, h_{24}, $h_{42} > 0$ and h_{33}, $h_{44} < 0$. As a result, we find that if $\gamma_i + 1 - \beta_i > 0$, then (31) has two positive and two negative real roots. The presence of two-dimensional stable manifold around the steady state means that the initial levels of jump variables q_1 and q_2 can be uniquely determined. Therefore, we obtain the following result.

Proposition 1. *If the utility function is additively separable between domestic and imported good, and production technologies of both countries satisfy* $\gamma_i + 1 - \beta_i > 0$ $(i = 1, 2)$*, then the steady state of the world economy is determinate.*

In contrast, if $\gamma_i + 1 < \beta_i$ $(i = 1, 2)$, it holds that h_{11}, h_{22}, h_{13}, $h_{24} < 0$ and h_{31}, h_{33}, h_{42}, $h_{44} > 0$. Thus, it is possible to have the following inequalities:

$$\begin{aligned} h_{11} + h_{33} < 0, &\quad h_{11} + h_{33} < 0, \\ h_{11}h_{33} - h_{13}h_{31} > 0, &\quad h_{22}h_{44} - h_{24}h_{42} > 0. \end{aligned}$$

If this is the case, (31) have four roots with negative real parts, implying that there are a continuum of converging paths near the steady state. Hence, the steady state of the world economy is at least locally indeterminate. If $\gamma_1 + 1 > \beta_1$ and $\gamma_2 + 1 < \beta_2$, then the steady state of country 2 will be indeterminate, but country 1 has a locally determinate steady state. Since fluctuations of country 2 will not affect investment and price in country 1, opening up international trade and financial integration does not alter the dynamic behavior of each economy.

In addition, our specification yields that volatility in country 2 does not fluctuate the current account of country 1 either. To see this, we should note that, as shown in Appendix 1, the relative price p in the market economy is proportional to the ratio of shadow values of capital, q_2/q_1. Given this fact, from (25), the current account of country 1 is described by

$$\begin{aligned}\dot{b}_1 &= r^1(k_1,q_1)b_1 + x_2(q_1) - \frac{q_2\mu_2}{q_1\mu_1}y_1(q_2)\\ &= a_1A_1k_1^{[\alpha_1(\gamma_1+1)/(\gamma_1+1-\beta_1)]-1}q_1^{\beta_1/(\gamma_1+1-\beta_1)}b_1 + \frac{1}{\mu_2\theta_2 q_1} - \frac{\mu_2}{\mu_1^2(1-\theta_1)q_1}.\end{aligned}$$

What is noteworthy is that the current account of country 1 depends on k_1 and q_1 alone. Therefore, even if the equilibrium trajectory of country 2 is indeterminate, so that q_2 exhibits volatility, the imported good y in terms of good x is independent of the behavior of q_2.[8] The current account of country 1 is affected by sunspot-driven expectations only when the autarkic equilibrium of country 1 is indeterminate. In sum, we have shown:

Proposition 2. *If the utility functions of both countries are logarithmic in consumption goods, then the possibility of indeterminacy will not be enhanced by international trade and financial integration. Indeterminacy in one country will not spillover to the other country in any respect.*

Obviously, this proposition depends on the fact that the utility function is of a log-linear form. If the additively separable utility function takes a general form of (16), the dynamic equation of foreign bond holding of country 1 is given by $\dot{b}_1 = r^1(k_1,q_1)b_1 + x_2(q_1) - \frac{q_2\mu_2}{q_1\mu_1}y_1(q_2)$, so that q_2 directly affects the country 1's current account. In this case, even though (k_1,q_1) converge to their steady-state values on a unique stable saddle path, q_2 may fluctuate in response to sunspot-driven expectations change in country 2. Thus, the current account of country 1 is volatile as well, while all the other real variables in country 1 exhibit stable behavior in the transition toward the steady-state equilibrium of the world economy.

3.3 Indeterminacy with CES Utility Functions

When $\sigma_i \neq 1$ so that the utility function of each country has a CES form in the felicity of consumption, (21) and (22) yield the following consumption demand functions:

$$x_i = \Delta_x^i q_1^{[(1-\acute{\sigma}_i)(1-\theta_i)-1]/\sigma_i} q_2^{-[(1-\sigma_i)(1-\theta_i)]/\sigma_i} - \delta_1 k_1, \quad i=1,2, \tag{32}$$

$$y_i = \Delta_y^i q_1^{\{[(1-\sigma_i)(1-\theta_i)-1]/\sigma_i\}+1} q_2^{-[(1-\sigma_i)(1-\theta_i)/\sigma_i]-1} - \delta_2 k_2, \quad i=1,2, \tag{33}$$

[8] If this is the case, comparative dynamics analysis by Turnovsky (1997, Chap. 7) that assumes determinacy of equilibrium should be re-examined.

where

$$\Delta_x^i = \frac{1}{\mu_i \theta_i} \left(\frac{\theta_i}{1-\theta_i} \right)^{(1-\sigma_i)(1-\theta_i)} > 0,$$

$$\Delta_y^i = \frac{1}{\mu_i \theta_i} \left(\frac{\theta_i}{1-\theta_i} \right)^{(1-\sigma_i)(1-\theta_i)+1} > 0.$$

We see that the own price effect is always negative, while the effects of foreign price on consumption demand for the home good depend on the sign of $1-\sigma_i$. If $\sigma_i > 1$, the substitution effect dominates, so that a rise in the foreign price increases in consumption demand for the home goods. Conversely, if $\sigma_i < 1$, a higher foreign good price lowers demand for the home goods.

The dynamic equations in the case of nonseparable utility between x_i and y_i are thus given by

$$\begin{aligned} \dot{k}_1 = {} & A_1 k_1^{\alpha_1(\gamma_1+1)/(\gamma_1+1-\beta_1)} q_i^{\beta_1/(\gamma_1+1-\beta_1)} \\ & - \sum_{i=1,2} \Delta_x^i q_1^{[(1-\acute{\sigma}_i)(1-\theta_i)-1]/\sigma_i} q_2^{-(1-\sigma_i)(1-\theta_i)/\sigma_i} - \delta_1 k_1, \end{aligned} \tag{34}$$

$$\begin{aligned} \dot{k}_2 = {} & A_2 k_2^{\alpha_2(\gamma_2+1)/(\gamma_2+1-\beta_2)} q_2^{\beta_2/(\gamma_2+1-\beta_2)} \\ & - \sum_{i=1,2} \Delta_y^i q_1^{\{[(1-\sigma_i)(1-\theta_i)-1]/\sigma_i\}+1} q_2^{-[(1-\sigma_i)(1-\theta_i)/\sigma_i]-1} - \delta_2 k_2, \end{aligned} \tag{35}$$

together with (27) and (28).

Inspecting the dynamic system derived above, we find that if the closed economies hold determinacy of equilibrium, opening up international trade will not enhance volatility. More formally, we obtain the following result.

Proposition 3. *Suppose that $\gamma_i + 1 - \beta_i > 0$ for $i = 1$ and 2, so that the steady state in the autarkic equilibrium of both countries is locally determinate. Then, the competitive equilibrium of the world economy is locally determinate for any values of σ_i (> 0).*

Proof. See Appendix 2. □

In this model, the price of foreign good affects capital formation of the home country only through consumption demand. Proposition 3 indicates that such an interaction between the two countries may not enhance the possibility of indeterminacy. Therefore, in this case, globalization would not produce fluctuations due to extrinsic uncertainty in self-fulfilling expectations. On the contrary, globalization may be a "stabilizing factor," as the following proposition demonstrates.

Proposition 4. *Suppose that country 1 holds indeterminacy in the autarkic equilibrium, while country 2 satisfies determinacy condition, i.e., $\gamma_2 + 1 > \beta_2$. Then, if the own price effects in the consumption demand functions dominate their crossprice effects, the world economy may establish determinacy of equilibrium.*

Proof. See Appendix 3. □

The intuitive interpretation of this result may be stated as follows. From (23), we obtain

$$\frac{\mu_1 l_1^{\gamma_1}}{q_1} = (1-a_1)\, k_1^{\alpha_1} l_1^{\beta_1 - 1}.$$

Given the price q_1 and capital k_1, the left-hand side of the above equation expresses labor supply curve and the right-hand side is the labor demand curve in country 1. If country 1 is a closed economy, then $\gamma_1 + 1 < \beta_1$ is a necessary condition for local indeterminacy around the steady state. As discussed by Benhabib and Farmer (1994), in this case the labor demand curve has a positive slope and it is steeper than the labor supply curve.

Now, suppose that country 1 initially stays at the steady state. Then, if the household anticipates a reduction in price q_1, the labor supply curve shifts up, implying that labor employment and production increase. Since a lower price raises the domestic demand for x goods, such an increase in consumption demand may be consistent with a rise in production. This means that the initial anticipation of a lower price will be self-fulfilling. In the world economy, the mechanism that may generate indeterminacy is essentially the same as that in the close economy. If the households in the world anticipated a decrease in q_1, the consumption demand for x goods increases. This again makes the labor supply curve in country 1 shifts up, which raises the production level of x. However, in the case of world economy, a lower q_1 increases the export for country 2 as well as the domestic consumption demand. If such a demand effect is large enough, a rise in employment in country 1 is insufficient to satisfy the newly created consumption demand. In this case, the initial anticipation cannot be self-fulfilled. Therefore, the equilibrium is determinate even though labor externalities are sufficiently large to satisfy $\gamma_1 + 1 < \beta_1$.

3.4 A Remark on the Steady-Sate Equilibrium

Since we have allowed free international lending and borrowing, there exists a continuum of steady-state distribution of capital stocks between the two countries. When the equilibrium path is uniquely determined, which steady state is realized depends on the initial distribution of capital stocks. To see this, remember that the stability analysis shown above assumes that the weights for the felicity of each country, μ_1 and μ_2, are exogenously given. Since the steady-state values of k_i and q_i depend on the magnitudes of μ_1 and μ_2, the long-run wealth and income distributions between two countries are sensitive to the planner's choice of μ_i. As Appendix 1 shows, in the competitive economy, the relation between the relative price p and the shadow values of wealth of each country is represented by the following condition:

$$p = \mu \frac{v_2}{v_1}.$$

Here, v_i is the costate variable associated with the wealth ω_i in the household's optimization problem and μ denotes a positive constant. Since the relative price between x and y goods equals the relative shadow values in the planning problem, it holds that $p = q_2/q_1$. This means that if we set $\mu = \mu_2/\mu_1$ and $q_i = \mu_i v_i$ $(i = 1,2)$, then the relationship between the shadow values in the competitive and the planning economies are clarified. Thus, as well as in the planning economy, the steady-state values of capital and consumption in the competitive system also depend on the choice of μ.

If the dynamic system of the planning economy satisfies determinacy of equilibrium, then, under given levels of initial capital stocks $k_1(0)$ and $k_2(0)$, there is a unique converging path that leads the economy to a particular steady state corresponding to specific levels of μ_1 and μ_2 $(=1-\mu_1)$. That is, a choice of the initial distribution of capital simultaneously determines the values of μ_i and the steady-state equilibrium associated with these levels of μ_i. Therefore, if we set $\mu = \mu_2/\mu_2$ and if we choose the same initial distribution of capital stocks as that in the planning economy, both planning and competitive economies follow exactly the same path and reach the identical steady-state equilibrium.

In the presence of equilibrium indeterminacy of the world economy, we cannot establish the one-to-one correspondence between the initial position and the steady-state equilibrium mentioned above. Therefore, the same initial distribution of capital between the two countries may yield different long-run distributions of capital depending on the expectations formation of households in both countries. In other words, there is a continuum of the initial distribution of capital that leads to the same steady state corresponding to a particular value of μ $(=\mu_2/\mu_1)$.

4 Conclusion

The central message of this chapter is that the relation between indeterminacy of equilibrium and openness of the economy is sensitive not only to production technologies but also to preference structure. By use of a two-country model with financial integration, we have examined whether or not financial interactions and international trade enhance the possibility of indeterminacy. We have found that, as opposed to the results shown by the existing studies on small-open economies, opening up international transactions does not necessarily yield a higher possibility of indeterminacy. On the contrary, in some cases globalization may serve as a "stabilizing factor," in the sense that the equilibrium path of the world economy can be determinate even though the autarky equilibrium of each country is indeterminate. Since our finding depends heavily upon the model structure we use in the chapter, it may not be appropriate to claim that the global economy is in general less volatile than closed economies. However, our analysis has suggested that the relation between the expectations-driven fluctuations and openness of the economy may not be so straightforward as the small-open economy models demonstrate, if we consider the general equilibrium of the world economy.

Appendix 1

Proof of Lemma 1

First, consider the optimization behavior of the households in country i. The Hamiltonian function for the household's problem is

$$H_i = u^i(x_i, y_i, l_i) + v_i(r_i\omega_i + w_i l_i - m_i), \quad i = 1, 2,$$

where $m_1 = x_1 + py_1$ and $m_2 = x_2/p + y_2$. The necessary conditions for the optimization problems are summarized as follows:

$$u_x^1(x_1, y_1, l_1) = v_1, \quad u_x^2(x_2, y_2, l_2) = v_2/p, \tag{36}$$

$$u_y^1(x_1, y_1, l_1) = pv_1, \quad u_y^2(x_2, y_2, l_2) = v_2, \tag{37}$$

$$u_l^i(x_i, y_i, l_i) = v_i w_i, \quad i = 1, 2, \tag{38}$$

$$\dot{v}_i/v_i = \rho - r_i, \quad i = 1, 2, \tag{39}$$

$$\lim_{t \to \infty} v_i e^{-\rho t} \omega_i = 0, \quad i = 1, 2. \tag{40}$$

Using the nonarbitrage condition (5) and (33), we obtain

$$\frac{\dot{p}}{p} = r_1 - r_2 = \frac{\dot{v}_2}{v_2} - \frac{\dot{v}_1}{v_1}.$$

This shows that the relation between the relative price p and the marginal utility of capital v_i must satisfy

$$p = \mu \frac{v_2}{v_1}, \tag{41}$$

where μ is a positive constant. From (30), μ satisfies

$$\mu = \frac{u_x^1(x_2, y_2, l_2)}{u_x^2(x_1, y_1, l_1)}.$$

Thus, if the economy involves a steady state in which each variable stays constant over time, substituting the steady-state values of x_i, y_i, and l_i into the above equation determines the magnitude of μ.

From (30), (31), and (41), we obtain

$$\frac{u_y^1}{u_x^1} = \frac{u_y^2}{u_x^y} = p = \mu \frac{v_2}{v_1}, \quad \frac{u_x^2}{u_x^1} = \frac{u_y^2}{u_y^1} = \frac{v_2}{v_1 p} = \mu. \tag{42}$$

Now, remember that the optimal conditions (11) and (12) for the planning problem yield

$$\frac{u_y^1}{u_y^1} = \frac{q_1}{q_2} = \frac{u_y^2}{u_x^2}, \quad \frac{u_x^2}{u_y^1} = \frac{u_y^2}{u_y^2} = \frac{\mu_1}{\mu_2}. \tag{43}$$

Therefore, if we set $q_1/q_2 = p$ and $\mu_1/\mu_2 = \mu$, (42) and (43) receptively correspond to (11) and (12) for the planning problem, so that the optimal conditions for the consumption decisions in the market economy and those in the planning economy are exactly the same. In addition, the optimal conditions for labor supply (32) are identical to (13) in the planning problem and the commodity market equilibrium conditions (3) and (4) are described by (9) and (10), repetitively.

Finally, the solvency conditions for international lending and borrowing require that

$$\lim_{t\to\infty} b_1(t)\exp\left(-\int_0^t r_1(t)\,\mathrm{d}s\right) = \lim_{t\to\infty} b_2(t)\exp\left(-\int_0^t r_2(s)\,\mathrm{d}s\right) = 0.$$

Thus, the transversality conditions (40) give $\lim_{t\to\infty} \mathrm{e}^{-\rho t} v_{it} k_{it} = 0\ (i = 1,2)$. Since we may set $q_i = \mu_i v_i$, conditions in (40) are equivalent to (15) for the planning problem.

Appendix 2

Proof of Proposition 3

The dynamic behavior of the closed economy is described by

$$\dot{k}_i = k_i^{\alpha_i(\gamma_i+1)/(\gamma_i+1-\beta_i)} q_i^{\beta_i/(\gamma_i+1-\beta_i)} - \frac{1}{q_i} - \delta_i, \tag{44}$$

$$\dot{q}_i = q_i \left[\rho + \delta_i - a_i k_i^{[\alpha_i(\gamma_i+1)/(\gamma_i+1-\beta_i)]-1} q_i^{\beta_i/(\gamma_i+1-\beta_i)}\right]. \tag{45}$$

Linearizing (34) and (35) at the steady-state equilibrium, it is easy to see that the trace of the coefficient matrix equals to ρ (>0). On the other hand, the coefficient matrix of the linearized system of (27), (28), (34), and (35) is given by

$$\Lambda(\lambda) = \begin{vmatrix} \lambda - h_{11} & 0 & -h_{13} & -h_{14} \\ 0 & \lambda - h_{22} & -h_{23} & -h_{24} \\ -h_{31} & 0 & \lambda - h_{33} & 0 \\ 0 & -h_{42} & 0 & \lambda - h_{44} \end{vmatrix} = 0,$$

where $h_{13} = \partial x_1/\partial q_1 + \partial x_2/\partial q_1$, $h_{14} = \partial x_1/\partial q_1 + \partial x_2/\partial q_1$, $h_{23} = \partial y_1/\partial q_1 + \partial y_2/\partial q_1$, and $h_{24} = \partial y_1/\partial q_2 + \partial y_2/\partial q_2$. All of the elements are evaluated at the steady state. The characteristic equation is thus written as

$$\Lambda(\lambda) = \left[\lambda^2 - (h_{11} + h_{33})\lambda + h_{11}h_{33} - h_{13}h_{31}\right] \times \left[\lambda^2 - (h_{22} + h_{44})\lambda + h_{22}h_{44} - h_{24}h_{42}\right] - h_{14}h_{23}h_{31}h_{42} = 0. \tag{46}$$

Given our assumptions, if $h_{14} = h_{23} = 0$, then $\Lambda(\lambda) = 0$ has two positive and two negative roots. Thus, if the number of negative roots of $\Lambda(\lambda) = 0$ is higher than

3 for $h_{14} \neq 0$ and $h_{23} \neq 0$, then the steady state of the world economy is locally indeterminate. Note that

$$\Lambda(0) = (h_{11}h_{33} - h_{13}h_{31})(h_{22}h_{44} - h_{24}h_{42}) - h_{14}h_{23}h_{31}h_{42},$$

$$\Lambda'(0) = -(h_{11} + h_{33})(h_{22}h_{44} - h_{24}h_{42}) - (h_{22} + h_{44})(h_{11}h_{33} - h_{13}h_{31}).$$

As well as the closed system, if $\gamma_i + 1 > \beta_i$ $(i = 1,2)$ holds, $h_{11} + h_{33} > 0$ and $h_{22} + h_{44} > 0$. In addition, the saddle-point properties of the closed economies mean that $h_{22}h_{44} - h_{24}h_{42} < 0$ and $h_{11}h_{33} - h_{13}h_{31} < 0$. Hence, $\Lambda'(0) > 0$ and $\Lambda(0) > 0$ for $h_{14} = h_{23} = 0$. This shows that $\Lambda'(\lambda) = 0$ has two positive and one negative roots. This means that when $h_{14} = h_{23} = 0$, regardless of the sign of $h_{14}h_{23}h_{31}h_{42}$, the characteristic equation $\Lambda(\lambda) = 0$ has at most two negative roots.

Appendix 3

Proof of Proposition 4

Since country 1 has an indeterminate steady state and country 2 has a determinate one, (36) involves three negative and one positive roots when $h_{14} = h_{23} = 0$. Namely, $\Lambda(0)$ in Appendix 2 has a negative value if $h_{14} = h_{23} = 0$. Observe that $\Lambda(0)$ can be written as

$$\begin{aligned}\Lambda(0) = {} & h_{11}h_{22}h_{33}h_{44} - h_{11}h_{42}h_{24}h_{33} - h_{31}h_{13}h_{22}h_{44} \\ & + h_{31}h_{42}(h_{13}h_{24} - h_{14}h_{23}).\end{aligned}$$

Under our assumption, $\gamma_1 + 1 < \beta_1$ and $\gamma_2 + 1 > \beta_2$, it holds that $h_{31} > 0$ and $h_{42} > 0$. Therefore, if

$$h_{13}h_{24} - h_{14}h_{23} < 0, \tag{47}$$

then $\Lambda(0)$ may have a positive sign. If this is the case, it is easy to see that the characteristic equation has two positive and two negative roots, so that the steady state of the world economy is determinate. Condition (37) is equivalent to

$$\left(\sum_{i=1,2}\frac{\partial x_i}{\partial q_1}\right)\left(\sum_{i=1,2}\frac{\partial y_i}{\partial q_2}\right) - \left(\sum_{i=1,2}\frac{\partial x_i}{\partial q_2}\right)\left(\sum_{i=1,2}\frac{\partial y_i}{\partial q_1}\right) > 0,$$

which states that the own price effects on consumption demand dominate the crossprice effects.

Acknowledgments I gratefully acknowledge many years of fruitful discussion with Koji Shimomura on dynamic economic theory that has been very helpful in writing this chapter. I thank Hideyuki Adachi, Eric Bond, Ben Heijdra, Yoshiyasu Ono, and Tamotsu Nakamura for their useful comments on earlier versions of Mino (2007) on which the present chapter partially depends. I also thank a referee of this chapter for helpful comments.

References

Aguiar-Conraria L, Wen Y (2005) Foreign trade and equilibrium indeterminacy. Working Paper 2005-041A, Federal Reserve Bank of St. Louis

Baxter M, Crucini MJ (1995) Business cycles and the asset structure of foreign trade. Int Econ Rev 36:821–854

Benhabib J, Farmer REA (1994) Growth and indeterminacy. J Econ Theory 63:19–41

Benhabib J, Farmer REA (1996) Indeterminacy and sector-specific externalities. J Monetary Econ 37:397–419

Evans MD, Hnatkovska V (2006) Financial integration, macroeconomic volatility and welfare (unpublished)

Farmer REA, Lahiri A (2005) A two-country model of endogenous growth. Rev Econ Dyn 8:68–88

Farmer REA, Lahiri A (2006) Economic growth in an interdependent world economy. Econ J 116:969–990

Ghiglino C, Olszak-Duquenne M (2005) On the impact of heterogeneity on indeterminacy. Int Econ Rev 46:171–188

Lahiri A (2001) Growth and equilibrium indeterminacy: the role of capital mobility. Econ Theory 17:197–208

Meng Q, Velasco A (2003) Indeterminacy in a small open economy with endogenous labor supply. Econ Theory 22:661–669

Meng Q, Velasco A (2004) Market imperfections and the instability of open economies. J Int Econ 64:503–519

Mino K (2001a) Indeterminacy in two-sector endogenous growth models with leisure. Econ Lett 62:311–317

Mino K (2001b) Indeterminacy and endogenous growth with social constant returns. J Econ Theory 97:203–222

Mino K (2007) Financial integration and volatility in a two-country world (unpublished)

Nishimura K, Shimomura K (2002a) Indeterminacy in a dynamic small open economy. J Econ Dyn Control 27:271–281

Nishimura K, Shimomura K (2002b) Trade and indeterminacy in a dynamic general equilibrium model. J Econ Theory 105:249–259

Nishimura K, Shimomura K (2006) Indeterminacy in a dynamic two-country model. Econ Theory 29:307–324

Obstfeld M, Rogoff K (1996) Foundations of international macroeconomics. MIT, Cambridge, MA

Pelloni A, Waldmann R (1998) Stability properties of a growth model. Econ Lett 61:55–60

Turnovsky S (1997) International macroeconomic dynamics. MIT, Cambridge, MA

Weder M (2001) Indeterminacy in a small open economy Ramsey model. J Econ Theory 98: 339–356

Wen Y (2001) Understanding self-fulfilling rational expectations equilibria in real business cycle models. J Econ Dyn Control 25:1221–1240

Part IV
Macroeconomic Dynamics

Efficient Fiscal Policy Restrictions in a Monetary Union

Costas Azariadis(✉) and Raphael W.K. Lam

Abstract We study the interactions of monetary and fiscal policies in the context of a monetary union. Tensions over fiscal policies have become one of the key issues in the operation in the European Union. We analyze restrictions on public debt in a monetary union in which a patient central bank plays a one-shot Stackelberg game against a number of impatient fiscal authorities in a simple environment without uncertainty. The noncooperative outcome of this game is excessive borrowing relative to the planning optimum. This will drive up the inflation target as the central bank attempts to minimize the impact of higher yields on borrowing member nations.

Fiscal borrowing constraints on member nations improve economic coordination by bringing public deficits more in line with household desires, in turn reducing the pressure on the central bank to inflate its way to lower real yields. We show, in particular, that there exist fiscal constraints supporting the cooperative allocation as a Stackelberg equilibrium.

1 Introduction

The early success of the economic and monetary union (EMU) since 1999 is now a matter of public record, and the euro has gained widespread international acceptance. However, tensions over fiscal policies of member nations have cast doubts on future of the euro and of the EMU. Larger members like Germany and France are unwilling to accept any serious interference with their sovereignty over national fiscal policy and tend to ignore the restrictions imposed by the stability pact. What will be the impact of Germany and France continuing to ignore the fiscal restrictions imposed by the European Stability and Growth Pact? The Dutch government

C. Azariadis
Department of Economics, Washington University in St. Louis, and Federal Reserve Bank of St. Louis, St. Louis, MO 63130, USA, e-mail: azariadi@artsci.wustl.edu

T. Kamihigashi and L. Zhao (eds.) *International Trade and Economic Dynamics – Essays in Memory of Koji Shimomura.*

is cautious on the decision by France and Germany to ride roughshod over the euro's stability pact rules on budget deficits. Is the Dutch government correct in insisting that *all* member nations have to adhere these restrictions at all times? This chapter provides efficiency arguments for defining public debt limits in a simple monetary union in which consumption smoothing is not an important consideration for any decision maker.

The efficiency argument, simply stated, is that fiscal constraints operating on all member nations serve to internalize the negative externality caused by an individual nation's fiscal deficit on the *common* borrowing cost of all member states. If one or more members are allowed to ignore these constraints, then the outcome is socially inefficient for the entire group. Discretionary national policies are, thus, the main reason for economic inefficiency.

To be specific, we will demonstrate that the Dutch government correctly objects to German and French deficits. To do so, we envision an environment in which the public sector deficit of any member nation causes a *pecuniary externality* for all other members by raising the average costs of loans in the monetary union. This externality is particularly relevant if fiscal authorities are less patient than the representative household or the common central bank. National fiscal authorities are willing to borrow excessively against their own future income. In this situation, the central bank is forced to raise its target rate of inflation and distort real economic activity, in an attempt to contain the upward pressure of real interest rates. When the member nations in the monetary union set deficits noncooperatively, the central bank is forced to choose between low inflation and low real yields. If the common central bank decides to have both, as the households would desire, it has to coordinate fiscal policies more efficiently. *Fiscal constraints turn out to be a substitute for policy coordination*: they limit the national governments from going into excessive debt, control the pecuniary externality from fiscal competition, and provide incentives for the central bank to choose an inflation target that strikes the right balance between real economic activity and real costs of capital.

It is worth noting that the argument *against* debt limits is based on the need to smooth consumption against uninsurable idiosyncratic (i.e., country-specific) risks. Member nations that must deal with severe negative income shocks need to borrow beyond the agreed limits in the monetary union for a certain periods and repay loans with future income. We assume that all agents are risk neutral in this chapter.

Chari and Kehoe (2002, 2003) are the closest chapters related to ours. They study the design of monetary unions and argue that the time-inconsistency problem in monetary policy leads to free riding in the setting of fiscal policies. Our chapter shares this problem because, in our setting, there are noncooperative fiscal authorities, competitive households, and a benevolent monetary authority that chooses inflation. In the Chari–Kehoe framework, the free-rider problem occurs when the actions of fiscal authorities affect the common inflation rate and therefore the payoffs to individual member nations.

Our chapter is also related to the literature on the interactions of fiscal policy with monetary policy, including Giovannini and Spaventa (1991), Uhlig (2002), Cooper and Kempf (2004), and Dixit and Lambertini (2003). In particular, Cooper and Kempf (2004) and Uhlig (2002) study fiscal policies in the context of a monetary union. They emphasize the potential gains from commitment for a common central bank in a monetary union. These studies find that a lack of commitment and free-rider problems tend to reduce the social gains from setting up the monetary union. On the other hand, Dixit and Lambertini (2003) emphasize differences in the objectives or preferences between monetary and fiscal authorities. They consider a model that the two authorities have different inflation and output targets in a static framework. Cooper and Kempf (2004) explore the presence of this tradeoff and find that there will be no welfare improvement from a monetary union alone if national shocks are weakly correlated. Fiscal interventions by member nations, combined with a common monetary policy, are equivalent to a commitment on monetary policy. In equilibrium, this type of monetary union will be welfare improving for any correlation of shocks.

There are two key issues here. The first issue is whether the conduct of fiscal policy by any national fiscal authority creates an externality on other nations. External effects like free-rider problems may induce the monetary union to reach some optimal cooperative outcomes that are not feasible in a noncooperative environment. The second issue is to examine the channels of the externality. In the model of Chari and Kehoe (2002), the actions of individual fiscal authorities affect the common inflation rate, and thus affect the payoffs of other nations. On the other hand, our chapter focuses on what happens to borrowing costs. Borrowing by individual fiscal authorities may push up interest costs for all member nations in a monetary union.

Given these external effects of driving up the common inflation rate or the cost of borrowing, the noncooperative equilibrium may not be socially optimal. We consider simple fiscal constraints with a borrowing limit and find that, by carefully choosing the constraints, the social optimum can be decentralized in a noncooperative environment.

This chapter is organized as follows. Section 2 describes the economic environment and defines noncooperative equilibria and social optimum. Sections 3 and 4 show that an optimum allocation of resources can be achieved as a competitive equilibrium only through the use of fiscal constraints. Conclusions and policy implications are discussed in Sect. 5.

2 Environment

We consider a monetary union with a common independent central bank and $i = 1,\ldots,N$ member states/nations. Each state or nation has a great deal of independence in setting fiscal policies, subject to mild restrictions. All nations share a central monetary authority which sets a single monetary policy, and a common inflation rate, for all member states of the union. The monetary union tends to impose certain restrictions on borrowing by member states. Chari and Kehoe (2002) suggest that fiscal constraints prevent a free-ride problem from arising in monetary unions of forward-looking agents. In their model, individual fiscal policies affect the common inflation rate and thus indirectly the payoff to other governments. A change in individual fiscal policies alters agents' expectation of future inflation across the member states and thus changes all current actions.

This section presents a simple model of differences in payoffs to analyze the interactions between fiscal and monetary policies in the context of monetary union. We study an exchange economy that consists of a number of impatient national fiscal authorities, $i = 1, \ldots, N$, and a patient common central bank. Time extends for two periods denoted as $t = 1, 2$.

2.1 Fiscal Authorities and Households

Each nation consists of an autarkic household with pretax endowment income $w_i = (y_1^i, y_2^i(\pi))$. The index i is used interchangeably to denote the fiscal authority (FA) and the representative household in each member nation. Endowments are exogenous in the first period and decreasing functions of the inflation rate in the second period.[1] This means that inflation in our simple environment imposes a deadweight loss on real output, i.e.,

$$y_2'(\pi) < 0 \quad \text{and} \quad y_2''(\pi) < 0 \quad \forall i \text{ and } \pi \geq 0.$$

This assumption is consistent with a progressive income tax system in which brackets are not indexed to inflation. As prises rise, individuals are pushed into higher brackets and higher marginal tax rates, which cause bigger deadweight losses and less output.

For simplicity, we assume that the households have a common linear utility function:

$$U^i = c_1^i + \beta c_2^i, \quad \beta > 0.$$

Each national fiscal authority has a payoff similar to that of households with a lower discount factor δ:

$$V^i = c_1^i + \delta c_2^i, \quad \beta > \delta > 0.$$

In other words, fiscal authorities are less patient than individual households because politicians have a planning horizon equal to an electoral cycle while households plan for an entire life cycle. For example, Drazen (2000) states:"First, both empirically and theoretically, a monetary-based PBC (political business cycle) model, either for manipulating aggregate economic activity via monetary surprises before an election or for explaining partisan effects after an election by inducing inflation surprises, is less than fully convincing. Second, there appears to be a strong role for fiscal policy in many countries and in the U.S. over certain time periods. This suggests basing

[1] The first-period endowment is assumed to be exogenous for simplicity. It may also be written as a function of an anticipated inflation rate. This will not change the results in our subsequent analysis. In particular, we can always normalize the first-period endowment and express the second-period endowment as the growth rate of the economy.

PBC models on fiscal rather than monetary policy." A similar assumption is used in Vuletin (2006). This discrepancy between β and δ creates a disagreement over what actions are best for households and for fiscal authorities. We assume that each fiscal authority $i = 1,\ldots,N$ pays a subsidy b^i to households at $t = 1$, levies a tax τ^i at $t = 2$ which repays the debt with interest in the second period. Fiscal policy is then the vector (b^i, τ^i). We define $b^{-i} = (b^1, b^2, \ldots, b^{i-1}, b^{i+1}, \ldots, b^N)$ to denote the borrowing by all nations other than nation i. Budget constraints for the households are as follows:

$$\begin{aligned} c_1^i &= y_1^i + b^i, \\ c_2^i &= y_2^i(\pi) - \tau^i, \end{aligned}$$

where $b^i > 0$ indicates the borrowing or subsidy by fiscal authority i. Households have no access to any foreign loan market.

Two key assumptions in our model are that national fiscal authorities face a common cost of borrowing, which they do not take as given. We assume that fiscal authorities have some monopsony power in the international loan market, which means that they must contend with an upward-sloping loan supply schedule. A second basic assumption is that the cost of capital is the same for all member nations. The data pages of the weekly *The Economist* newspaper show that the yield on short-term government bonds is exactly the same for all EMU members; 10-year bond yields are within 15 basis points. In particular, we suppose that the cost of borrowing is low if average borrowing per nation is at or below a critical value $B(\pi)$, which depends on the common inflation rate, otherwise it is higher for all borrowing in excess of that threshold value. In particular, we write the household after-tax endowment as $\tilde{w}^i = (y_1^i + b^i, y_2^i(\pi) - \tau^i)$ where the amount of loan repayment is

$$\begin{aligned} \tau^i &= R_{\mathrm{L}} B(\pi) + R_{\mathrm{H}} \left(\tfrac{1}{N}\textstyle\sum_{i=1}^N b^i - B(\pi)\right) && \text{if } \textstyle\sum_{i=1}^N b^i > NB(\pi) \\ &= R_{\mathrm{L}} b^i && \text{if } \textstyle\sum_{i=1}^N b^i \le NB(\pi). \end{aligned} \tag{1}$$

In this expression, R_{H} and $R_{\mathrm{L}} < R_{\mathrm{H}}$ are the high and low yields on loans, respectively.

Equation (1) says that the Fisher equation fails: moderate inflation lowers the real loan yield, partly because loans are unindexed at low inflation rates. This channel weakens progressively as the inflation rate picks up. In general, we suppose that the borrowing limit $B(\pi)$ is an increasing concave function of the inflation rate. Thus, the central bank can use inflation to lower the average real cost of loans to member nations, but inflation matters more at low levels than at high ones.[2] If the debt is below the borrowing limit $B(\pi)$, the nation will borrow at a lower cost of capital R_{L}; otherwise, any amount beyond the limit will be subject to a higher interest cost at R_{H}.

[2] In this chapter, we assume that the borrowing limit depends only on the common inflation rate set by the monetary union. In other words, all nations face the same borrowing limit $B^i(\pi) = B(\pi)\ \forall i$. The borrowing limit may be better perceived as a ratio of borrowing to total output, to be in line with the constraint imposed on members of the European Union.

Each fiscal authority chooses only b^i taking as given all other b^i, the interest costs $(R_{\mathrm{L}}, R_{\mathrm{H}})$, and the common inflation rate π. The free-rider problem considered in Chari and Kehoe (2002) also exists in this setting: any excessive borrowing from a particular nation will drive up the interest costs to all other member nations, taking the inflation rate as given. Excessive borrowing changes the intertemporal marginal rate of substitution and reduces the resources available for consumption in an exchange economy.

2.2 The Central Bank

We assume that the common monetary authority has a social welfare function identical to the one of households in the member nations, with a weight assigned on each nation in the monetary union. This means that the central bank chooses the common inflation rate that maximizes the welfare function:

$$W(\pi) = \sum_{i=1}^{N} \lambda^i U^i = \sum_{i=1}^{N} \lambda^i \left[c_1^i + \beta c_2^i\right],$$

for fixed weights $\lambda^i \geq 0$.

We sum up and interpret some technical assumptions on the endowment and the borrowing limits before defining the equilibrium. The functions $(y_2^i(\pi), B(\pi))$ are monotone in π for any given $\pi \in [0, \bar{\pi}]$. In particular:

- Inflation distorts real output, i.e., $y_2^i(\pi)$ is decreasing and concave in π for all $\pi \geq 0$.
- Inflation reduces the cost of borrowing by raising the borrowing limit, i.e., $B(\pi)$ is increasing and concave in π for all $\pi \in [0, \bar{\pi}]$.
- Negative inflation is not distortive of real output, and any inflation higher than $\bar{\pi}$ does not affect the cost of borrowing:

$$y_2'(\pi) = B'(\pi) = 0 \quad \text{for all} \quad \pi \geq \bar{\pi} \text{ and } \pi < 0.$$

- There are two levels of yields on loans $(R_{\mathrm{H}}, R_{\mathrm{L}})$ such that the households face a lower yield R_{L} if aggregate borrowing is within the limit $B(\pi)$; otherwise, any excess amount beyond the limit will be charged with a higher yield R_{H}. We assume that

$$R_{\mathrm{H}} > 1/\beta > R_{\mathrm{L}} > 1/\delta.$$

This condition implies that each fiscal authority is so impatient that it cares only about current consumption and borrows against all future income. The households in each nation will do the same if the borrowing limit is so large that households earn a low yield on their loans. On the other hand, if households face a tight borrowing limit, they will choose to be at the kink of their budget set. In that case, households will consume in both periods.

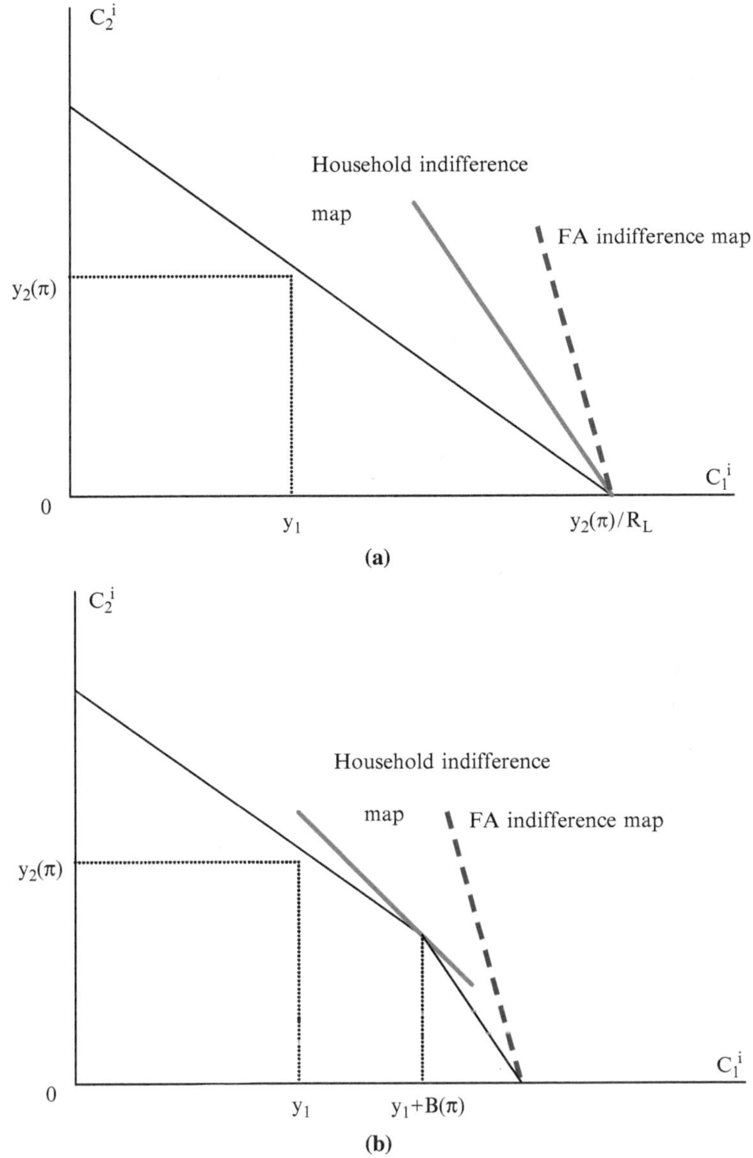

Fig. 1 (**a**) Slack credit market: $y_2(\pi) - R_L B(\pi) \leq 0$ and (**b**) Tight credit market: $y_2(\pi) - R_L B(\pi) > 0$

Figure 1 illustrates the last assumption in the two cases defined by $y_2(\pi) - R_L B(\pi) \leq 0$ and $y_2(\pi) - R_L B(\pi) > 0$. Given (π, R_L, R_H), the fiscal authority and the household choose the same consumption vector in the former case, but different ones in the latter case.

3 Social Optimum and Equilibria

We define equilibria and optima for the policy vectors $(b^1, \ldots, b^N, \pi)$. First, we consider a noncooperative equilibrium of the Stackelberg type with the central bank being the leader. The fiscal authorities in each nation choose the amount borrowed at the given inflation rate, while the common central bank chooses the inflation rate given the best response of fiscal authorities to the common inflation rate.

Definition 1. An unconstrained Nash equilibrium is a vector $(b^1, \ldots, b^N, \tau^1, \ldots, \tau^N, \pi)$ with the following properties:

(i) Each fiscal authority chooses (b^i, τ^i) to maximize $V_i = y_1^i + b^i + \delta(y_2^i - \tau^i)$ subject to the budget constraint (1) and to $y_1^i + b^i \geq 0$ and $y_2^i(\pi) - \tau^i \geq 0$ for a given (b^{-i}, τ^{-i}, π).

(ii) The central bank chooses a common inflation rate π to maximize the social welfare function:

$$W(\pi) = \sum_{i=1}^{N} \lambda^i U^i = \sum_{i=1}^{N} \lambda^i [y_1^i + b^i + \beta(y_2^i(\pi) - \tau^i)]$$

subject to $y_1^i + b^i \geq 0$ and $y_2^i(\pi) - \tau^i \geq 0$ for given $(b^1, \ldots, b^N)$ and $(\tau^1, \ldots, \tau^N)$.

(iii) The goods market clears at every period, i.e., $c_1^i = y_1^i + b^i$ and $c_2^i = y_2^i(\pi) - \tau^i$. In the case of fiscally constrained Nash equilibrium, there is an additional constraint on fiscal authorities.

(iv) $b^i \leq X^i \; \forall i$, where X^i is exogenously imposed.

We may derive the best response function for each fiscal authority and the central bank. Given the assumptions on time preference, it is clear that the fiscal authority will borrow against all future income $y_2^i(\pi) = \tau^i \; \forall i$, regardless of the inflation rate chosen by the central bank. So, the best response function for each fiscal authority is to choose $b^i = y_2^i(\pi)/R$, where R is defined according to (1). In this sense, the social welfare function of the central bank is reduced to $W(\pi) = \sum_{i=1}^{N} \lambda^i [y_1^i + b^i]$, which is not a function of inflation rate π. This means that the central bank has no power of optimization with its inflation instrument, and the best response function for the central bank is not well defined. The unconstrained Nash equilibrium consists of a policy vector $(b^1, \ldots, b^N, \pi)$ such that each fiscal authority borrows the entire present value of its own future income but the inflation rate is not well defined.

Definition 2. An unconstrained Stackelberg equilibrium with the monetary authority moving first consists of a policy vector $(b^1, \ldots, b^N, \tau^1, \ldots, \tau^N, \pi)$ with the following properties:

(i) Each fiscal authority chooses (b^i, τ^i) to maximize $V^i = y_1^i + b^i + \delta(y_2^i - \tau^i)$ subject to the budget constraint (1), $y_1^i + b^i \geq 0$, and $y_2^i(\pi) - \tau^i \geq 0$ for a given (b^{-i}, τ^{-i}, π).

(ii) The central bank chooses a common inflation rate π to maximize the social welfare function:

$$W(\pi) = \sum_{i=1}^{N} \lambda^i U^i = \sum_{i=1}^{N} \lambda^i [y_1^i + b^i + \beta(y_2^i(\pi) - \tau^i)]$$

subject to $y_1^i + b^i \geq 0$ and $y_2^i(\pi) - \tau^i \geq 0$ and taking as given the best response (b^i, τ^i) of each fiscal authority to the inflation choice π.

(iii) The goods market clears at every period, i.e., $c_1^i = y_1^i + b^i$ and $c_2^i = y_2^i(\pi) - \tau^i$.
In case of fiscally constrained Stackelberg equilibrium, there is an additional constraint.

(iv) $b^i \leq X^i \; \forall i$, where X^i is exogenously imposed.

The case of Stackelberg equilibrium is different from Nash equilibrium. The best response of the central bank on the strategies from fiscal authorities is well defined. The inflation rate chosen ($\hat{\pi}$) maximizes the social welfare function taking fiscal responses as given. That means

$$\hat{\pi} \in \arg\max_{\pi} \sum_{i=1}^{N} \lambda^i [y_1^i + b^i + \beta(y_2^i(\pi) - \tau^i)].$$

(b^i, τ^i) are best response of fiscal authority i to π, X_i, and all other policies (b^{-i}, τ^{-i}). In addition, we define the cooperative social optimum among all fiscal authorities and the central bank.

Definition 3. An optimum allocation is a cooperative choice of the policy vector $(b^1, \ldots, b^N, \tau^1, \ldots, \tau^N, \pi)$ that maximizes the social welfare function $W(\pi) = \sum_{i=1}^{N} \lambda^i U^i = \sum_{i=1}^{N} \lambda^i [y_1^i + b^i + \beta(y_2^i(\pi) - \tau^i)]$ subject to the budget constraint (1), $y_1^i + b^i \geq 0$, and $y_2^i(\pi) - \tau^i \geq 0$ for all member nations.

Note that in the optimal allocation, the weighted household utility in the monetary union is maximized given the cooperative choice of the policy vector $(b^1, \ldots, b^N, \tau^1, \ldots, \tau^N, \pi)$. However, this outcome is generally unachievable in a noncooperative equilibrium because fiscal authorities discount future consumption more heavily than households. This discrepancy creates a wedge between the goals of fiscal authorities and those of the central bank. Since the central bank shares the same utility function as the households, the socially optimal allocation is the outcome chosen by the central bank if it was in charge of all policies, including both the fiscal and the monetary side.

Without much loss of generality, we restrict our analysis to symmetric equilibria in which the households and fiscal authorities are the same across nations. Each one has the same endowment process, time preference and therefore chooses the same amount borrowed from the international credit market, i.e., $b^i = b$. Furthermore, we analyze "equal-treatment" optima where each country has the same weight $\lambda^i = \lambda$ in the social welfare function. The notation i indicating each nation is dropped from the variables in the equal-treatment optimal allocation. From Definition 2, the policy vector in a symmetric equal-treatment optimum consists of (b, τ, π) that maximizes

$$W(b, \pi) = y_1 + b + \beta[y_2(\pi) - \tau]$$

subject to

$$\begin{aligned} b &\geq -y_1, \quad \tau \leq y_2(\pi), \\ \tau &= R_\mathrm{L} b \quad &&\text{if} \quad b \leq B(\pi) \\ &= R_L B(\pi) + R_\mathrm{H}(b - B(\pi)) \quad &&\text{if} \quad b > B(\pi). \end{aligned}$$

It is easy to see from Fig. 1b that the optimal consumption puts the household at the kink in its budget set, i.e.,

$$\begin{aligned} c_1 &= y_1 + B(\pi), \\ c_2 &= y_2 - R_\mathrm{L} B(\pi). \end{aligned}$$

Therefore, the optimal choice for inflation rate is

$$\pi^* \in \arg\max_{\pi} W^*(\pi), \quad \text{where} \quad W^*(\pi) \equiv y_1 + \beta y_2(\pi) + (1 - \beta R_\mathrm{L}) B(\pi). \tag{2}$$

Note that the first term $y_2(\pi)$ in $W^*(\pi)$ is decreasing in π, while the second term $B(\pi)$ is increasing in π from above. By the technical assumptions listed earlier, we also know that $W^*(\pi)$ is a concave function with a positive derivative at inflation rate $\pi = 0$ and a negative derivative at $\pi = \bar{\pi}$. Hence, there exists a unique $\pi^* \in (0, \bar{\pi})$ that maximizes $W(\pi)$. That π^* is the optimum rate of inflation. An optimum puts the consumers at the kink of the budget set defined for $\pi = \pi^*$. At that kink, we have

$$(b^*, \pi^*, R^*) = (B(\pi^*), \pi^*, R_\mathrm{L}). \tag{3}$$

The key question is whether the socially optimal allocation is achievable in a decentralized setting. A quick comparison indicates that the optimal allocation (b^*, π^*, R^*) is different from the Nash equilibrium in Definition 1 simply because $R = R_\mathrm{H}$ at any Nash equilibrium. In Sect. 4, we will examine if adding fiscal constraints in a Stackelberg equilibrium helps to achieve the optimal allocation.

4 Equilibrium Without Fiscal Constraints

4.1 The Credit Market Is Not Tight

Suppose first that $y_2(\pi) \leq R_\mathrm{L} B(\pi)$ or equivalently that $\pi \in [\pi^\mathrm{C}, \bar{\pi})$, where $y_2(\pi^\mathrm{C}) = R_\mathrm{L} B(\pi^\mathrm{C})$ as shown in Fig. 2. In this case, the amount borrowed is less than the present value of future income, and the fiscal authority can borrow at the low interest yield. The credit market is slack with a sufficiently large borrowing limit $B(\pi)$. As shown in Fig. 1a, the budget set at any symmetric equilibrium does not have a kink and therefore we can state the amount borrowed in a simple form:

$$b = y_2(\pi) = R_\mathrm{L} < B(\pi). \tag{4}$$

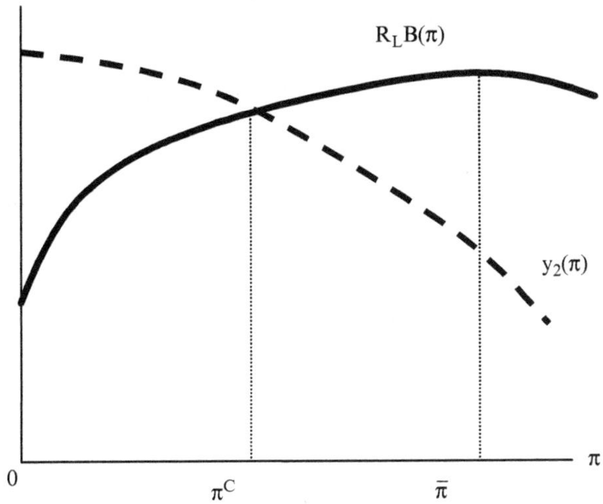

Fig. 2 Critical inflation rates

From the diagram, it is clear that the best response of the fiscal authority coincides with the household choice in the Stackelberg equilibrium. At the low interest yield R_L, both the household and the fiscal authority will borrow against all the future income $y_2(\pi)$ and consume in the current period. Equation (4) indicates that the consumption choices are

$$c_1 = y_1 + y_2(\pi)/R_L, \quad c_2 = 0.$$

The result is based on our linear utility for both household and fiscal authority, and the assumption that $1/\beta > R_L > 1/\delta$. The household wants to borrow as much as possible at the low interest yield, while the fiscal authority always wants to borrow against all future income regardless of the interest yield. We can also derive the payoffs to the symmetric fiscal authority and the central bank, respectively, as follows:

$$\begin{aligned}
\text{FA}: \quad V(\pi) &= c_1^i + \delta c_2^i \\
&= y_1 + y_2(\pi)/R_L, \\
\text{MA}: \quad W(\pi) &= \sum_{i=1}^{N} \lambda^i [c_1^i + \beta c_2^i] \\
&= y_1 + y_2(\pi)/R_L \\
&\leq y_1 + B(\pi) \quad \text{for} \quad \pi \in [\pi^C, \bar{\pi}].
\end{aligned} \tag{5}$$

The central bank achieves maximal payoff at the lowest feasible value of π in the interval $[\pi^C, \bar{\pi}]$, i.e., at $\pi = \pi^C$.

4.2 The Credit Market Is Tight

Suppose next that inflation rate $\pi \in [0, \pi^{\mathrm{C}})$ is sufficiently low to have $y_2(\pi) - R_{\mathrm{L}}B(\pi) > 0$. In this scenario, the budget set has a interior kink at $B(\pi)$ and the credit market is relatively tight with a borrowing cost higher than R_{L}. Figure 1 shows that there is a divergence between the choice of the households and the fiscal authorities in this case. In a symmetric equilibrium, the fiscal authority always wants to borrow as much as possible against all future income. Its best response is to have zero future consumption regardless of the interest yield, because $R_{\mathrm{H}} > R_{\mathrm{L}} > 1/\delta$. We work out the best response on the amount borrowed from the international credit market:

$$b = \frac{y_2(\pi) + (R_{\mathrm{H}} - R_{\mathrm{L}})B(\pi)}{R_{\mathrm{H}}},$$

which implies the consumption vector:

$$c_1 = y_1 + \frac{y_2(\pi) + (R_{\mathrm{H}} - R_{\mathrm{L}})B(\pi)}{R_{\mathrm{H}}}, \quad c_2 = 0.$$

On the other hand, the household's optimal choice is always at the kink position given $R_{\mathrm{H}} > 1/\beta > R_{\mathrm{L}}$. The household wants to borrow up to the limit $B(\pi)$ at the low interest yield R_{L}. The payoff to the household in the symmetric Stackelberg equilibrium is identical to the central bank payoff, i.e.,

$$\begin{aligned} W(\pi) &= \sum_{i=1}^{N} \lambda^i [c_1^i + \beta c_2^i] \\ &= y_1 + \frac{y_2(\pi) + (R_{\mathrm{H}} - R_{\mathrm{L}})B(\pi)}{R_{\mathrm{H}}}. \end{aligned} \tag{6}$$

We obtain different payoffs to the central bank at the social optimum (2), at an equilibrium with a slack credit market (5), and at an equilibrium with a tight credit market (6). The three different payoffs to the central bank allow us to compare the alternative allocations and measure the deviation of the decentralized scenario from the social optimum. We can write them as follows:

- The social optimal when the planner chooses the amount borrowed b is

$$W^*(\pi) \equiv y_1 + \beta y_2(\pi) + (1 - \beta R_{\mathrm{L}})B(\pi).$$

- The Stackelberg equilibrium with the fiscal authority choosing b in a slack credit market is

$$W(\pi) = y_1 + y_2(\pi)/R_{\mathrm{L}} \quad \text{if} \quad \pi \geq \pi^{\mathrm{C}}.$$

- The Stackelberg equilibrium with the fiscal authority choosing b in a tight credit market is

$$W(\pi) = y_1 + \frac{y_2(\pi) + (R_{\mathrm{H}} - R_{\mathrm{L}})B(\pi)}{R_{\mathrm{H}}} \quad \text{if} \quad 0 < \pi < \pi^{\mathrm{C}}.$$

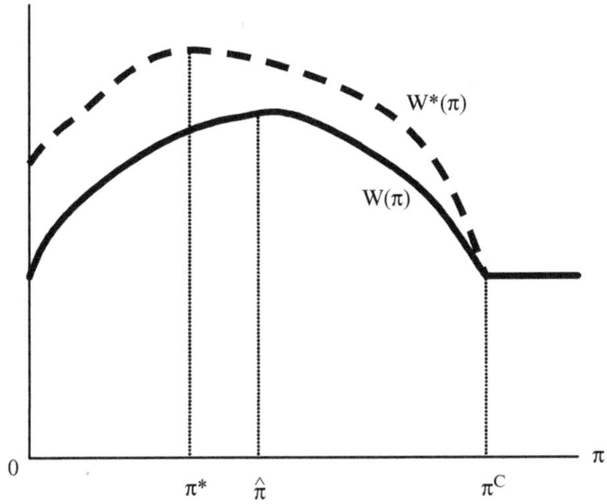

Fig. 3 Social welfare functions

The deviation of the central bank's payoff from the socially optimal allocation can be obtained by

$$\begin{aligned} W^*(\pi) \quad W(\pi) &- (1-\beta R_L)\left[B(\pi) - \tfrac{y_2(\pi)}{R_L}\right] && \text{if} \quad \pi \in [\pi^C, \bar{\pi}] \\ &= \left(\beta - \tfrac{1}{R_H}\right)[y_2(\pi) - R_L B(\pi)] && \text{if} \quad \pi \in [0, \pi^C). \end{aligned}$$

From these expressions, we can easily prove that $W^*(\pi) - W(\pi) > 0$ for all inflation rates $\pi \in [0, \bar{\pi}]$. The unconstrained symmetric Stackelberg equilibrium arrives at different inflation choices and payoffs to the central bank from those of the equal-treatment optimum.

Figure 3 graphs the social welfare function at different inflation rates. The optimal inflation rate π^* is lower than the symmetric Stackelberg equilibrium at $\hat{\pi}$. The two functions coincide after the critical inflation rate π^C because fiscal authorities and households choose the same outcomes at inflation rates beyond π^C. Therefore, we have the following proposition.

Proposition 1. *The optimal equal-treatment inflation rate π^* is lower than the unconstrained symmetric Stackelberg equilibrium $\hat{\pi}$.*

Proof. We prove this by contradiction. Let $\pi^* > \hat{\pi}$. Then by previous assumption, it follows that $B'(\pi^*) < B'(\hat{\pi})$ as $B(\cdot)$ is a concave increasing function in inflation. Then, using the first-order condition, we have

$$\begin{aligned} y_2'(\pi) + (1/\beta - R_L)B'(\pi^*) = 0, \\ y_2'(\pi) + (1/\beta - R_L)B'(\hat{\pi}) = 0, \end{aligned}$$

and conclude that $y_2'(\hat{\pi}) < y_2'(\pi^*)$. This in turn implies $\hat{\pi} > \pi^*$ which is a contradiction to the above. □

Next, we describe the policy vector and the interest yield that support the two important allocations. First, at the equal-treatment optimum, we have

$$\begin{aligned}
\pi^* &\in \arg\max_{\pi} W^*(\pi), \\
R^* &= R_{\mathrm{L}}, \\
b^* &= B(\pi^*), \\
c_1^* &= y_1 + B(\pi^*), \\
c_2^* &= y_2(\pi^*) - R_{\mathrm{L}} B(\pi^*).
\end{aligned}$$

Lastly, the unconstrained symmetric Stackelberg equilibrium satisfies

$$\begin{aligned}
\hat{\pi} &\in \arg\max_{\pi} W(\pi), \\
\hat{R} &= R_{\mathrm{H}}, \\
\hat{b} &= \frac{y_2(\hat{\pi}) + (R_{\mathrm{H}} - R_{\mathrm{L}})B(\hat{\pi})}{R_{\mathrm{H}}}, \\
\hat{c}_1^* &= y_1 + \hat{b}, \\
\hat{c}_2^* &= 0.
\end{aligned}$$

5 Equilibrium with Fiscal Constraints

We saw in Sect. 4 that the social optimum and the unconstrained Stackelberg equilibrium are different in terms of inflation targets (π^* vs. $\hat{\pi}$), interest yield (R_{L} vs. R_{H}), and consumption allocations. In particular, if the fiscal authorities and the central bank do not cooperate, the difference in objectives will cause deviations from the social optimum. We regard the case where the fiscal authorities are less patient than the central bank as just an illustrative example. Additional discrepancies may occur if disagreements exist on the value of public goods, or the value of commitment. Then, a natural question is whether the monetary union can adopt policies that can move the Stackelberg equilibrium closer to the social optimum.

The example illustrated above indicates the fiscal authorities tend to borrow against future income. In the extreme case, the fiscal authorities borrow against all future income to pay for current consumption. This section examines if some fiscal constraints imposed by a constitutional mandate help to move the decentralized economy toward the social optimum. By carefully choosing borrowing constraints, a monetary union may be able to achieve the social optimum as a decentralized Stackelberg equilibrium.

It is straightforward to see this in our symmetric setting. The cooperative outcome is achieved at a borrowing limit $X^i(\pi) = B(\pi)$. Then, the best response for each fiscal authority is to borrow up to the limit $B(\pi)$ that coincides with the optimal outcome from the viewpoint of the household and central bank. We can write down the constrained symmetric equilibrium as follows.

Definition 4. A constrained Stackelberg equilibrium with the monetary authority moving first consists of a policy vector $(b^1,\ldots,b^N,\pi)$ with the following properties:

(i) Each fiscal authority chooses b^i to maximize $V^i = y_1^i + b^i + \delta(y_2^i - \tau^i)$ subject to the budget constraint (1), the fiscal constraint $b^i \leq X^i$, and $y_1^i + b^i \geq 0$, $y_2^i(\pi) - \tau^i \geq 0$ for a given (b^{-i}, X^i, π).
(ii) The central bank chooses a common inflation rate π to maximize the social welfare function $W(\pi) = \sum_{i=1}^N \lambda^i U^i = \sum_{i=1}^N \lambda^i [y_1^i + b^i + \beta(y_2^i(\pi) - \tau^i)]$ subject to budget constraint (1), $y_1^i + b^i \geq 0$, and $y_2^i(\pi) - \tau^i \geq 0$, and taking as given the best response functions of all fiscal authorities.
(iii) The goods market clears at every period, i.e., $c_1^i = y_1^i + b^i$ and $c_2^i = y_2^i(\pi) - \tau^i$.

When the fiscal constraint X^i is the same as the borrowing limit $B(\pi)$, we can easily write down the equilibrium outcomes and payoffs of the fiscal authorities and the central bank. The fiscal authority borrows up to the limit $\tilde{b} = B(\pi)$ and enjoys the low interest yield $\tilde{R} = R_{\mathrm{L}}$. The fiscal constraint is satisfied in the monetary union as $\sum_{i=1}^N b^i \leq NB(\pi)$. The central bank chooses the inflation rate at $\tilde{\pi} = \pi^*$ and gets the same payoff as in the equal-treatment optimum. So, the fiscal constraints can be viewed as a decentralization mechanism to reach the social optimum defined in Sect. 4.

Fiscal constraints prevent the fiscal authorities of member nations from acting in ways that raise the cost of borrowing above R_{L}, thus allowing the central bank to pursue a lower inflation target to minimize the distortions from inflation. This conclusion relies on the greater impatience of the fiscal authorities and will hold in considerably broader circumstances than the simple framework studied in this chapter. The result does not depend on the assumed linearity of the utility function, the specification of credit demand schedules, the autarkic nature of households, or the finite time horizon.

Recent European experience shows that large member nations in a monetary union like France and Germany have a tendency to ignore the fiscal constraints in adverse circumstances as they attempt to smooth consumption. We may extend our framework to incorporate idiosyncratic shocks in our environment. The key issue seems to be one of mechanism design: how a monetary union strikes a balance between consumption smoothing and incentives to adhere to limits on fiscal deficits in the face of nation-specific shocks.

6 Conclusions

In a simple currency union with linear payoffs, perfect certainty and a finite economic horizon, we have explored how fiscal constraints serve the policy aims of a patient central bank as it deals with the impatient fiscal authorities of member nations. By limiting public debt, fiscal constraints ease the burden on the central bank to keep real interest rates from rising too much, allowing the central bank to lower its inflation target and minimize the economic harm from inflation.

The logic of this argument seems to be robust to the particular assumptions made in our model economy, with two possible exceptions: idiosyncratic income shocks and limited enforcement. Uniform, across-the-board restrictions on deficits and public debt like those envisioned in the European Union Stability Pact limit the ability of fiscal authorities to smooth idiosyncratic shocks to national income by taking long positions in international asset markets. The temptation to ignore agreements on debt limits is strongest when large economies like Germany and France face economic adversity.

Should the European Union scrap the Stability Pact? This chapter cannot claim to provide an answer. To provide a reliable answer, we would need concave payoffs that value smooth consumption, and market incompleteness that makes smoothing hard to attain. But we do have a suggestion on how to enforce whatever fiscal limits are found to be in the best interests of European households. Instead of threatening deviant nations with fines that will prove inadequate or hard to collect, the European Commission should leave the job of enforcing the Stability Pact provisions to the central bank. When the European Central Bank builds up substantial positions in the public debt of member nations, it will have the ability to reward those who observe fiscal constraints and punish those who do not, by repatriating most of the interest income it collects from the former and withholding all interest from the latter.

Acknowledgment A preliminary draft of this chapter was prepared for the conference "Five Years of the Euro: Successes and New Challenges," organized by Federal Reserve Bank of Dallas and the University of Texas at Austin, with the support of the Delegation of the European Commission, May 14–16, 2004. Support from the Program for Dynamic Economics at UCLA and the Center for Dynamic Economics at Washington University is gratefully acknowledged as are comments from an anonymous referee.

References

Chari V, Kehoe P (2002) Time consistency and free-riding in a monetary union. Fed Reserve Bank Minneap Staff Report 308 (forthcoming in J Money Credit Banking)

Chari V, Kehoe P (2003) On the desirability of fiscal constraints: a monetary union. Fed Reserve Bank Minneap Staff Report 330

Cooper R, Kempf H (2004) Overturning Mundell: fiscal policy in a monetary union. Rev Econ Stud 71:371–396

Dixit A, Lambertini L (2003) Interactions of commitment and discretion in monetary and fiscal policies. Am Econ Rev 93:1522–1542

Drazen A (2000) The political business cycle after 25 years. In: Bernanke B, Rogoff R (eds) NBER macroeconomics annual 2000. MIT, Cambridge, MA

Giovannini A, Spaventa L (1991) Fiscal rules in the European monetary union: a no-entry clause. CEPR Discussion Paper 516, London

Uhlig H (2002) One money, but many fiscal policies in Europe: what are the consequences? Humboldt University, Berlin (unpublished)

Vuletin G (2006) Exchange rate regimes and fiscal discipline: the role of capital controls. Working Paper, University of Maryland

The Effects of Factor Taxation in Dynamic Economies with Externalities and Endogenous Labor Supply

Daisuke Amano, Jun-ichi Itaya(✉), and Kazuo Mino

Abstract This chapter examines the long-run effects of factor income and expenditure taxes in an infinitely lived representative agent growth model that allows both for production externalities and endogenous labor supply. The novelty of this analysis is that it investigates how the long-run impacts of these taxes are affected by the indeterminacy of equilibria, mainly the result of nonseparable preferences between consumption and leisure. We show that the tax effects on steady-state welfare – as well as the steady-state levels of consumption, capital, and employment – are all negative, regardless of whether the steady state is determinate or indeterminate in the standard neoclassical growth model. When the model displays endogenous growth, the distortionary taxes are growth and welfare enhancing. This holds in both the determinate steady state, where the labor supply curve features an unconventional slope, and the indeterminate steady state, where it displays a conventional slope.

1 Introduction

In this chapter, we examine the long-run effects of three types of tax instruments accompanied by compensating lump-sum transfers: capital income taxes, labor income taxes, and consumption taxes. The analysis allows for both endogenous labor supply and production externalities in an infinitely lived representative agent growth model. We show that the long-run effects of these taxes (i.e., the effects on steady-state capital, consumption, labor supply, welfare, and the growth rate of the economy) are significantly affected by the emergence of indeterminate equilibrium caused by nonseparable preferences between consumption and leisure, coupled with production externalities, when the model generates sustained endogenous growth.

J. Itaya
Graduate School of Economics and Business Administration, Hokkaido University, Sapporo 060-0809, Japan, e-mail: itaya@econ.hokudai.ac.jp

T. Kamihigashi and L. Zhao (eds.) *International Trade and Economic Dynamics – Essays in Memory of Koji Shimomura.*

The dynamic effects of taxation have been studied in various growth models using the framework of an intertemporally optimizing representative agent. In the standard neoclassical growth model, where physical capital is the only factor that can be accumulated (henceforth, we refer to this model as an *exogenous* growth model, in the sense that long-run growth is determined by exogenous variables such as the rate of time preference, population growth, etc.), both capital and labor income taxes reduce the steady-state level of income, but have no effect on the net return to capital and thus no growth effect in the long run (see, e.g., Turnovsky 1982; Becker 1985; Sinn 1987; Judd 1987). On the other hand, the literature on endogenous growth models has reexamined the long-run effects of factor income taxation in a framework where both capital and labor (human capital) are reproducible factors under constant returns-to-scale accumulation technology (see, e.g., Pecorino 1993; Devereux and Love 1994; Milesi-Ferretti and Roubini 1998). This literature shows that both labor and capital income taxes generally reduce the long-run growth rate. Indeed, these two distortionary taxes effectively act as a tax on human and nonhuman capital incomes, respectively, thereby generating a disincentive to the accumulation of both types of capital.

These findings have been derived using standard versions of exogenous and endogenous growth models where the dynamic equilibrium path is uniquely determined. However, recent advances in macroeconomics have highlighted the importance of self-fulfilling prophecies, such as "sunspots" and "animal spirits," in explaining economic fluctuations. Models of the indeterminacy of converging paths provide a useful vehicle to account for the business cycle and other macroeconomic phenomena without needing to rely on random shocks to economic fundamentals. In particular, the nonuniqueness of equilibrium can arise straightforwardly in dynamic general equilibrium settings once the assumptions of perfectly competitive markets and constant returns-to-scale are dropped. Although several authors investigate how the presence of fiscal or monetary policy alters the likelihood of indeterminacy (e.g., Guo and Lansing 1998), few studies in this area have explored the policy implications for indeterminacy, despite the fact that the emergence of indeterminacy may potentially and drastically change its implications.

Drawing on both strands, the present chapter investigates how the emergence of indeterminacy affects the long-run impacts of taxes in both exogenous and endogenous growth models. In our models, both with and without endogenous growth, indeterminate steady-state equilibria are mainly caused, as in Bennett and Farmer's (2000) model, by the assumption of nonseparable utility between consumption and leisure. In view of Samuelson's correspondence principle, one may reasonably expect that the dynamic behavior of such a growth model in the neighborhood of a steady state will be linked to its comparative statics properties. More specifically, since the Jacobian matrix of the dynamic system evaluated at a steady state would be of opposite sign, depending on whether the steady state is determinate or indeterminate, the long-run comparative statics properties may be reversed if indeterminacy occurs. If this conjecture is correct, the long-run effects of taxation may be significantly affected by the emergence of indeterminacy.

In the existing literature, Pelloni and Waldmann (2000) is mostly closely related to our study. This chapter considers the effects of taxes combined with various forms of government expenditure in an endogenous growth model featuring the indeterminacy of equilibrium paths. Our model differs from Pelloni and Waldmann's (2000) model in five important ways. First, unlike their tax experiment, we consider three types of taxation: a capital income tax, a labor income tax, and a consumption tax, all of which are accompanied by compensating lump-sum transfers. This method of analysis is very common in the literature on dynamic tax effects, partly because of analytical convenience, but also because it intends to isolate the pure incentive effect of the tax by nullifying the negative income effect. Owing to this virtue, this decomposition method serves to highlight the efficiency aspects of taxation. Second, we compare the long-run effects of taxation in exogenous and endogenous growth models, retaining the same isoelastic utility and Cobb–Douglas production functions, but differentiating the degree of capital externality. Such a comparison enables one to clarify the essential role of endogenous growth in the context of dynamic tax analysis. Third, we allow the Frisch labor supply curve to slope downward. Since Pelloni and Waldmann (2000) have used the model with nonseparable, strictly concave preferences, this important extension is left unexplored. In particular, Pelloni and Waldmann (2000) show that if the market equilibrium is indeterminate, capital income taxes increase the balanced growth rate. This somewhat paradoxical finding conveys the impression that the adverse effects of distortionary taxes will be overturned if the indeterminacy of equilibrium occurs. Our exercises show that this may not always be the case.

Fourth, we investigate how the degree of production externalities or increasing returns at the aggregate level affects the long-run impacts of taxation. This aspect received little attention in Pelloni and Waldmann (2000) and related work. Ignoring productivity spillovers where they exist may lead to the substantial underestimation of the actual impacts of tax changes. Accordingly, larger degrees of externalities may *quantitatively* alter the long-run impacts, as well as the welfare implications of tax policy, indicated by traditional tax analysis. Fifth, for analytical convenience, Pelloni and Waldmann (2000) assume that there are no pre-existing taxes. This means that a tax increase is just the introduction of a new tax, setting all other taxes to zero. Put differently, and in their words, Pelloni and Waldmann's (2000) analysis is inappropriate for examining the effects of real-world taxes that are far from "small" ones. This point is also made by Vandendorpe and Friedlaender (1976) as well as others in the tax incidence literature. In our analysis, we allow for pre-existing taxes.

Section 2 first describes the behavior of households, firms, and the government in an exogenous growth model where the long-run growth rate is exogenously given. The section then investigates the stability properties of the model. Section 3 derives the effects of factor income and expenditure taxes on steady-state capital, consumption, employment, and welfare. Section 4 constructs an endogenous growth version of the basic model by increasing only the parameter value representing the magnitude of capital externalities so as to eliminate diminishing returns to capital. Section 5 analyzes the growth and welfare effects of these taxes along a balanced growth path. Section 6 concludes the chapter. Some mathematical derivations are given in the appendices.

2 The Model

2.1 Firms

There is a continuum of identical competitive firms in the economy, with the total number normalized to one. The representative firm i produces output using a constant returns-to-scale Cobb–Douglas technology:

$$Y_i = K_i^a L_i^b X, \quad a+b=1, \tag{1}$$

where K_i and L_i are the capital stock and the labor hours employed by firm i, respectively. The term X represents the productive externalities taken as given by each firm. Following Benhabib and Farmer (1994), we further specify these externalities as

$$X = K^{\alpha-a} L^{\beta-b}, \; a < \alpha \leq 1, \; b < \beta < 1, \text{ and } \alpha+\beta > 1, \tag{2}$$

where K and L represent the aggregate stock of capital and the aggregate labor hours, respectively.[1] In a symmetric equilibrium, all firms take the same action such that for all i, $Y_i = Y$, $K_i = K$, and $L_i = L$. Substituting (2) into (1), we can obtain the following social production technology:

$$Y = K^{\alpha} L^{\beta}. \tag{3}$$

We analyze separately two cases where $\alpha < 1$ and $\alpha = 1$. The first case corresponds to an exogenous growth model, while the second case corresponds to an endogenous growth model in which the capital externalities are strong enough to generate sustained endogenous growth.[2]

Given these external effects, competitive firms maximize their profits, thus yielding

$$r = a(Y/K) = aK^{\alpha-1}L^{\beta}, \tag{4a}$$
$$w = b(Y/L) = bK^{\alpha}L^{\beta-1}, \tag{4b}$$

where r and w denote the pretax rates on the return to capital and the real wage, respectively.

---

[1] Benhabib and Farmer (1994) show that the assumption $\beta > 1$ is needed to deliver an indeterminate steady state. However, this assumption is difficult to reconcile with empirical facts, as pointed out in a number of recent empirical studies. One of the reasons we adopt nonseparable utility here is to avoid such criticism.

[2] When $\alpha > 1$, growth is explosive and thus we do not analyze this case.

2.2 Households with Nonseparable Preferences

There is a unit measure of identical infinitely lived households, each of which maximizes its lifetime utility:

$$\int_0^{\infty} \frac{[cV(l)]^{1-\sigma}-1}{1-\sigma} \mathrm{e}^{-\rho t} \mathrm{d}t, \tag{5}$$

where $V(l) \equiv (1-l)^{\chi}$, c and l are, respectively, the individual's consumption and hours worked, σ (>0 but $\sigma \neq 1$) denotes the inverse of the intertemporal elasticity of substitution in consumption, and ρ (>0) is the subjective rate of time preference.[3] Also, $1-\chi(1-\sigma)$ expresses the inverse of the *effective* intertemporal elasticity of substitution in leisure.[4] When σ tends to 1, by continuity, the instantaneous utility function reduces to $\ln[cV(l)]$.

The budget constraint faced by the representative household is given by

$$\dot{k} = (1-\tau_{\mathrm{w}})wl + (1-\tau_{\mathrm{k}})(r-\delta)k + z - (1+\tau_{\mathrm{c}})c, \quad k(0) \text{ given}, \tag{6}$$

where δ and z are the depreciation rate and transfer payments that are rebated to households in a lump-sum fashion, respectively. The variables τ_{k}, τ_{w}, and τ_{c} represent the tax rates applied to capital income, labor income, and consumption, respectively.

The current-value Hamiltonian function can be written as

$$H(c,l,k,\lambda) \equiv \frac{[c(1-l)^{\chi}]^{1-\sigma}-1}{1-\sigma} + \lambda[(1-\tau_{\mathrm{w}})wl + (1-\tau_{\mathrm{k}})(r-\delta)k + z - (1+\tau_{\mathrm{c}})c],$$

where λ represents the shadow price of capital holdings. The first-order conditions for this problem are given by

$$\left(c(1-l)^{\chi}\right)^{-\sigma}(1-l)^{\chi} - \lambda(1+\tau_{\mathrm{c}}) = 0, \tag{7a}$$

$$-\left(c(1-l)^{\chi}\right)^{-\sigma} c\chi(1-l)^{\chi-1} + \lambda(1-\tau_{\mathrm{w}})w = 0, \tag{7b}$$

$$\dot{\lambda} - \rho\lambda = -\lambda(1-\tau_{\mathrm{k}})(r-\delta), \tag{7c}$$

together with the given initial level of capital stock k_0 and the transversality condition $\lim_{t\to\infty} \mathrm{e}^{-\rho t}\lambda(t)k(t) = 0$.

---

[3] Alternatively, we may assume that $V(l) \equiv \exp[-l^{1+\gamma}/(1+\gamma)]$, which has been used by Bennett and Farmer (2000). It can be verified that our essential results remain valid.

[4] Hintermaier (2003) points out that since the instantaneous utility function in (5) displays a strictly concave property when $\sigma > \chi/(1+\chi)$, the Frisch labor supply curve is positively sloped. In contrast, we allow for a *quasiconcave* instantaneous utility function, so that the parameter σ takes any nonnegative value. In this case, the slope of the Frisch labor supply curve may be negative; see footnote 6 for further details.

Since we have assumed that the instantaneous utility function in (5) is quasi-concave, we need to check whether the solution to the household's optimization problem given by (7a), (7b), and (7c) is also sufficient for maximization. To show this, we make use of Proposition 8 of Arrow and Kurz (1970, p. 49) in that a sufficient condition for maximization is that the maximized Hamiltonian $H^*(k,\lambda) \equiv \max_{c,l} H(c,l,k,\lambda)$ is concave for k given λ, where the functions $c(\lambda)$ and $l(\lambda)$ can be obtained by solving (7a) and (7b), respectively, given λ. Since the functions $c(\lambda)$ and $l(\lambda)$ depend on λ but not on k, the maximized Hamiltonian function $H^*(k,\lambda)$ associated with our household's optimization problem is linear in k given λ, and hence concave in k. As a result, the sufficient condition for maximization is satisfied.

To focus on the problem in hand, we rule out a market for government bonds and expenditures. As stated earlier, we conduct a tax analysis in such a way that the government's flow budget should be balanced at each point in time through adjusting the size of transfer payments to households when the government changes each of the tax parameters.[5] Its flow budget constraint is thus expressed by

$$Z = \tau_{\mathrm{w}} wL + \tau_{\mathrm{k}}(r-\delta)K + \tau_{\mathrm{c}}C, \tag{8}$$

where Z stands for total transfers to households.

3 Steady-State Tax Incidence

Since we focus on a symmetric perfect-foresight equilibrium, households know the future paths of factor prices and taxes as well as transfer payments when they decide how much to consume, work, and invest over their lifetime. In this equilibrium, the aggregate consistency condition requires that $k = K$, $c = C$, $l = L$, and $z = Z$.

Dividing (7b) by (7a) and taking into account (4b) results in

$$\chi \frac{c}{1-l} = \frac{b(1-\tau_{\mathrm{w}})}{1+\tau_{\mathrm{c}}} k^{\alpha} l^{\beta-1}. \tag{9}$$

This condition requires that the marginal rate of substitution between consumption and leisure should be equated to the real wage rate adjusted for the consumption and wage taxes at each point in time. Combining (9) with (7a), we can rewrite the functions $c(\lambda)$ and $l(\lambda)$ as $c(k,\lambda,\tau_{\mathrm{c}},\tau_{\mathrm{w}})$ and $l(k,\lambda,\tau_{\mathrm{c}},\tau_{\mathrm{w}})$, respectively.

[5] Such a transfer scheme can be straightforwardly implemented in exogenous growth models. In an endogenous growth model, however, because all state variables grow indefinitely at a positive constant rate along a balanced growth path, we have to adjust the compensated lump-sum transfers so as to keep the ratio of the scale of the government budget to the level of GDP constant along a balanced growth path when each of the taxes is changed.

Substitution of $c(k,\lambda,\tau_c,\tau_w)$ and $l(k,\lambda,\tau_c,\tau_w)$ into (6) and (7c), together with (4a), (4b), and (8), yields

$$\dot{k} = k^{\alpha} l(k,\lambda,\tau_c,\tau_w)^{\beta} - c(k,\lambda,\tau_c,\tau_w) - \delta k, \tag{10a}$$

$$\dot{\lambda} = \lambda[\rho - (1-\tau_k)\{ak^{\alpha-1} l(k,\lambda,\tau_c,\tau_w)^{\beta} - \delta\}]. \tag{10b}$$

Taking a linear approximation of (10a) and (10b) around the steady state, we have

$$\begin{bmatrix} \dot{k} \\ \dot{\lambda} \end{bmatrix} = \begin{bmatrix} \alpha\hat{k}^{\alpha-1}\hat{l}^{\beta} + \hat{k}^{\alpha}\beta\hat{l}^{\beta-1}l_k - c_k - \delta & \hat{k}^{\alpha}\beta\hat{l}^{\beta-1}l_{\lambda} - c_{\lambda} \\ -\hat{\lambda}(1-\tau_k)a(\alpha-1)\hat{k}^{\alpha-2}\hat{l}^{\beta} - \hat{\lambda}(1-\tau_k)a\hat{k}^{\alpha-1}\beta\hat{l}^{\beta-1}l_k & -\hat{\lambda}(1-\tau_k)a\hat{k}^{\alpha-1}\beta\hat{l}^{\beta-1}l_{\lambda} \end{bmatrix} \begin{bmatrix} \hat{k}-k \\ \hat{\lambda}-\lambda \end{bmatrix}, \tag{11}$$

where c_j and l_j $(j = k,\lambda)$ represent the partial derivatives with respect to the argument j and the notation ^ denotes the steady-state value of the corresponding variable. The steady-state values of c and k satisfy the following steady-state conditions:

$$\hat{k}^{\alpha} l(\hat{k},\hat{\lambda},\tau_c,\tau_w)^{\beta} = c(\hat{k},\hat{\lambda},\tau_c,\tau_w) + \delta\hat{k}, \tag{12a}$$

$$\frac{\rho}{1-\tau_k} + \delta = a\hat{k}^{\alpha-1} l(\hat{k},\hat{\lambda},\tau_c,\tau_w)^{\beta}. \tag{12b}$$

To identify the qualitative nature of the model's dynamics, we should investigate the signs of the determinant and the trace of the matrix appearing on the right-hand side of (11). The determinant of the Jacobian matrix, denoted by $R(\hat{l})$, is given by

$$R(\hat{l}) \equiv [\rho + (1-\tau_k)\delta](1-\alpha)\frac{\Delta(\hat{l})^{-1}}{1-\hat{l}}\frac{\hat{c}}{\hat{k}}, \tag{13}$$

where

$$\Delta(\hat{l}) \equiv \sigma\left[\beta - 1 - \frac{\hat{l}}{1-\hat{l}}\right] + (1-\sigma)\chi\frac{\hat{l}}{1-\hat{l}} = \sigma\left[\beta - 1 - \left(1 + \frac{\sigma-1}{\sigma}\chi\right)\frac{\hat{l}}{1-\hat{l}}\right].$$

It follows from (13) that $\text{sign}[R(\hat{l})] = \text{sign}[\Delta(\hat{l})]$. This means that if $\Delta(\hat{l}) < 0$, then the system has a saddle-point property, whereas if $\Delta(\hat{l}) > 0$, then indeterminacy arises, provided that the trace of the Jacobian matrix

$$\frac{\rho}{1-\tau_k} - \Delta(\hat{l})^{-1}\left(\frac{\rho}{1-\tau_k} + \delta\right)Q(\hat{l})$$

is negative, where

$$Q(\hat{l}) \equiv (\sigma-1)\left[\beta - \chi\frac{\hat{l}}{1-\hat{l}}\left\{1 - \alpha\delta\left(\frac{\rho}{1-\tau_k} + \delta\right)^{-1}\right\}\right] + \frac{\alpha-a}{a}\frac{\sigma}{1-\hat{l}} + \beta\tau_k.$$

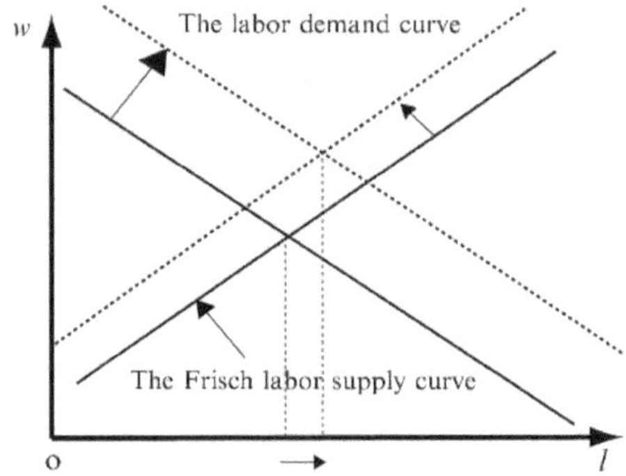

Fig. 1 The labor demand curve and the Frisch labor supply curve cross with "normal" slopes (i.e., $\Delta(\hat{l}) < 0$)

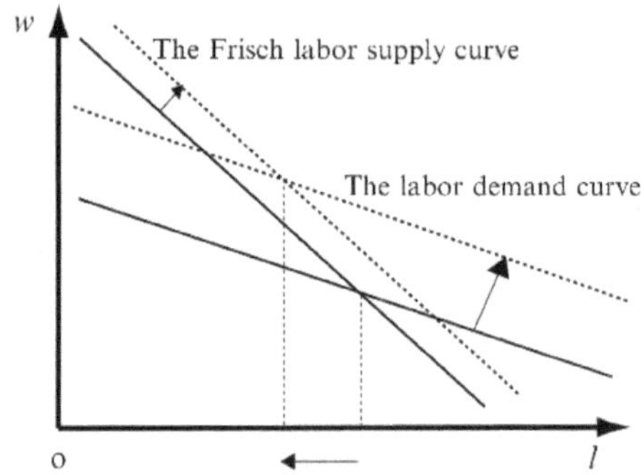

Fig. 2 The labor demand curve and the Frisch labor supply curve cross with the "wrong" slopes (i.e., $\Delta(\hat{l}) > 0$)

As shown, the sign of $\Delta(\hat{l})$ reflects the relative slope of the labor demand and Frisch labor supply curves.[6] Either when the Frisch labor supply curve is positively sloped as illustrated in Fig. 1 or when the Frisch labor supply curve is negatively sloped but its slope is less steep than the labor demand curve (we may say that the labor demand and Frisch labor supply curves cross with "normal" slopes), then $\Delta(\hat{l}) < 0$.

On the other hand, if the Frisch labor supply curve is steeper than the labor demand curve, as illustrated in Fig. 2 (i.e., the labor demand and Frisch labor supply curves cross with the "wrong" slopes), then $\Delta(\hat{l}) > 0$.

[6] According to Bennett and Farmer (2000), the Frisch labor supply curve is the labor supply as a function of the real wage, holding the marginal utility of consumption constant. By taking the logarithm of both sides of (7b) and substituting (9) for c in the resultant expression, the resulting curve can be expressed by $\log w = [-1+(1-\sigma)\chi/\sigma]\log(1-\hat{l}) - (1/\sigma)\ln\lambda + \text{const}$. The slope of the Frisch labor supply curve evaluated at the steady state is given by $[1+(\sigma-1)\chi/\sigma][\hat{l}/(1-\hat{l})] \lesseqgtr 0$, while the slope of the labor demand curve is $\beta - 1 < 0$. It should also be noted that assumption $\beta < 1$ implies that the determinant condition for indeterminacy (13) (i.e., $\Delta(\hat{l}) > 0$) is met only when $\sigma < 1$.

Totally differentiating (12a) and (12b) and rearranging, we obtain the long-run effects of changes in the respective taxes as follows:

$$\frac{\mathrm{d}\hat{k}}{\mathrm{d}\tau_k} = -\frac{\hat{k}}{1-\tau_k}\frac{\rho}{\rho+(1-\tau_k)\delta}\frac{1}{1-\alpha}\left[\beta(1-\hat{l})\frac{\delta\hat{k}}{\hat{c}}+1\right] < 0, \tag{14a}$$

$$\frac{\mathrm{d}\hat{c}}{\mathrm{d}\tau_k} = -\frac{\hat{c}}{1-\tau_k}\frac{\rho}{\rho+(1-\tau_k)\delta}\frac{1}{1-\alpha}\left[\beta(1-\hat{l})\frac{\delta\hat{k}}{\hat{c}}+(\alpha\hat{k}^{\alpha-1}\hat{l}^{\beta}-\delta)\frac{\hat{k}}{\hat{c}}\right] < 0, \tag{14b}$$

$$\frac{\mathrm{d}\hat{l}}{\mathrm{d}\tau_k} = -\frac{\hat{l}}{1-\tau_k}\frac{\rho}{\rho+(1-\tau_k)\delta}(1-\hat{l})\frac{\delta\hat{k}}{\hat{c}} < 0, \tag{14c}$$

$$\frac{\mathrm{d}j}{\mathrm{d}\tau_c} = -\frac{j}{1+\tau_c}\frac{\beta}{1-\alpha}(1-\hat{l}) < 0, \quad j=\hat{k},\hat{c}, \tag{14d}$$

$$\frac{\mathrm{d}\hat{l}}{\mathrm{d}\tau_c} = -\frac{\hat{l}}{1+\tau_c}(1-\hat{l}) < 0, \tag{14e}$$

$$\frac{\mathrm{d}j}{\mathrm{d}\tau_w} = -\frac{j}{1-\tau_w}\frac{\beta}{1-\alpha}(1-\hat{l}) < 0, \quad j=\hat{k},\hat{c}, \tag{14f}$$

$$\frac{\mathrm{d}\hat{l}}{\mathrm{d}\tau_w} = -\frac{\hat{l}}{1-\tau_w}(1-\hat{l}) < 0. \tag{14g}$$

It is immediately clear from (14a)–(14g) not only that the factor $\Delta(\hat{l})$ does not appear in all of the above expressions, but also that the steady-state effects of changes in the respective taxes on the long-run capital stock, consumption, and labor supply (i.e., employment) are all *negative*. More specifically, the long-run effects of the taxes do not hinge on whether the steady state is determinate or indeterminate in the present exogenous growth model (or equivalently, whether the labor demand and Frisch labor supply curves may cross with the "normal" or the "wrong" slopes). In addition, since the parameter σ does not appear in (14a)–(14g), the effects of the taxes are *qualitatively* and *quantitatively* unaffected by the (*pure*) intertemporal substitution parameter σ. In other words, in the class of CES utility functions, the effects of the taxes remain the same, irrespective of whether the utility function is separable (i.e., $\sigma = 1$) or nonseparable (i.e., $\sigma \neq 1$). This is mainly because under homothetic utility, the consumption–leisure choice dictated by (9) is independent of σ.[7]

In summary, we have the following proposition.

Proposition 1. *(i) An increase (decrease) in each of capital income, labor income, and consumption taxes decreases (increases) the steady-state levels of capital,*

[7] It should also be remarked that these properties may not be robust under more general preferences, as shown in Appendix 1. According to Appendix 1, it appears that the effect of the capital income tax (i.e., (33)) also depends on the sign of the determinant of the Jacobian matrix evaluated at the steady state, i.e., the stability property of the steady state.

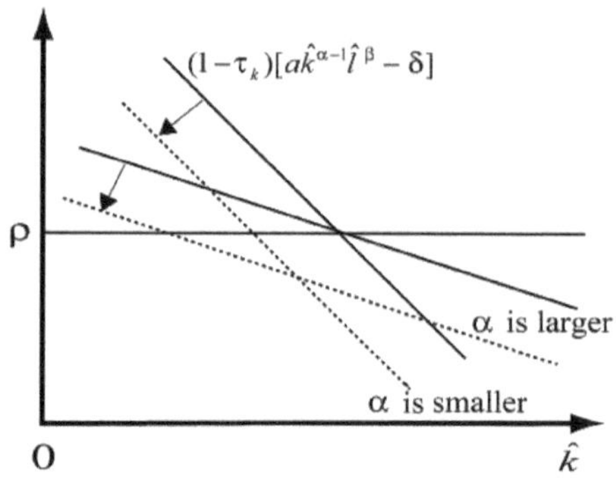

Fig. 3 The effect of an increase in the capital income tax on the long-run capital stock

consumption, and employment, regardless of whether the steady state is determinate or indeterminate.

(ii) As the capital and/or labor externalities become larger, so do the effects of the respective taxes on capital and consumption in absolute value, but the effects of the respective taxes on employment remain unaffected.

(iii) The magnitudes of the elasticity of intertemporal substitution in consumption have no effect on capital, consumption, and employment.

The reason why the long-run effects of the taxes on capital stock and consumption are in magnitude positively associated with the degree of production externalities can best be explained with Fig. 3. As α becomes larger, the long-run capital demand curve $(1-\tau_k)[a\hat{k}^{\alpha-1}\hat{l}^{\beta}-\delta]$ will be flatter (i.e., more elastic with respect to $\hat{k}$), while the long-run capital supply curve represented by the horizontal line at ρ remains unchanged. Since an increase in the capital income tax τ_k shifts the capital demand curve to the left owing to the decreased net return on capital, the resulting decrease in the demand for capital $\hat{k}$ will be larger with α, as shown in Fig. 3. On the other hand, as β becomes larger, the long-run capital demand curve becomes more responsive to variations in $\hat{l}$ caused by the tax changes, and thus the effects on $\hat{c}$ and $\hat{k}$ will be more negative.

The long-run effects of the taxes are uninfluenced by the stability properties of the steady state. This is because of both the infinitely elastic long-run supply curve of capital (i.e., the horizontal line at ρ) and the homogeneous property of the Cobb–Douglas production function. Indeed, by manipulating (12a) and (12b), the long-run rental capital market equilibrium condition can boil down to

$$\rho = (1-\tau_k)\left[a\left(\frac{\hat{c}}{\hat{k}}+\delta\right)-\delta\right], \tag{15}$$

which reveals that (15) solely determines the ratio $\hat{c}/\hat{k}$. Combining (12a) with (9) results in

$$\chi\frac{\hat{l}}{1-\hat{l}} = \frac{b(1-\tau_w)}{1+\tau_c}\left[1+\delta\frac{\hat{k}}{\hat{c}}\right], \tag{16}$$

which reveals that the steady-state level of employment responds to any tax changes independently of different values of α or β. Given the ratio $\hat{c}/\hat{k}$ determined by (15), an increase in τ_c or τ_w always lowers the long-run level of employment $\hat{l}$ through (16), regardless of whether the steady state is determinate or indeterminate. The resulting reduction in $\hat{l}$ depresses the marginal product of capital, thereby shifting the long-run capital demand curve to the left. This movement causes $\hat{k}$ and thus $\hat{c}$ to fall, while leaving the ratio $\hat{c}/\hat{k}$ invariant.

Furthermore, we investigate the tax effects on the lifetime utility of the representative agent (5) evaluated at the steady state, i.e., $[(\hat{c}(1-\hat{l})^{\chi})^{1-\sigma}-1]/(1-\sigma)\rho$ (denoted by W_{ss}). Differentiating W_{ss} with respect to each tax rate and using (12a) and (14a)–(14g), we obtain

$$\frac{dW_{ss}}{d\tau_k}=\frac{1}{\rho}[\hat{c}(1-\hat{l})^{\chi}]^{1-\sigma}\frac{1-\hat{l}}{1-\tau_k}\frac{\rho}{\rho+(1-\tau_k)\delta}\frac{\delta\hat{k}}{\hat{c}}$$
$$\times\left[-\frac{\beta}{1-\alpha}+\chi\frac{\hat{l}}{1-\hat{l}}-\frac{1}{(1-\alpha)(1-\hat{l})}\frac{\alpha\hat{k}^{\alpha-1}\hat{l}^{\beta}-\delta}{\delta}\right]<0, \tag{17a}$$

$$\frac{dW_{ss}}{d\tau_c}=\frac{1}{\rho}[\hat{c}(1-\hat{l})^{\chi}]^{1-\sigma}\frac{1-\hat{l}}{1+\tau_c}\left[-\frac{\beta}{1-\alpha}+\chi\frac{\hat{l}}{1-\hat{l}}\right]<0, \tag{17b}$$

$$\frac{dW_{ss}}{d\tau_w}=\frac{1}{\rho}[\hat{c}(1-\hat{l})^{\chi}]^{1-\sigma}\frac{1-\hat{l}}{1-\tau_w}\left[-\frac{\beta}{1-\alpha}+\chi\frac{\hat{l}}{1-\hat{l}}\right]<0. \tag{17c}$$

The negative sign of (17a)–(17c) can be verified by the following inequalities:

$$-\frac{\beta}{1-\alpha}+\chi\frac{\hat{l}}{1-\hat{l}}<-\frac{b}{1-a}+\frac{b(1-\tau_w)\hat{k}^{\alpha}\hat{l}^{\beta}}{(1+\tau_c)\hat{c}}=\frac{-(1+\tau_c)\hat{c}+(1-\tau_w)w\hat{l}}{1+\tau_c}<0,$$

where the first inequality follows from the inequalities $a<\alpha$ and $b<\beta$ coupled with (9), while the last inequality follows from (6) (noting that $b=1-a$). An increase in any tax reduces the labor supply, thereby improving welfare. However, it also decreases output and thus consumption owing to the decreased labor supply, thereby depressing welfare. Although these two effects on welfare work in opposite directions, (17a)–(17c) reveal that the latter negative consumption effect on welfare unambiguously dominates the former positive effect through leisure. We may, therefore, conclude that there is no tied relationship between the stability properties of the steady state and the welfare effects.

Proposition 2. *The effects of the respective taxes on steady-state welfare are all negative. Moreover, the negative effects strengthen with the magnitude of production externalities.*

As explained below, Proposition 2 is consistent with the findings of Chamley (1986) and Mino (2001), who discuss optimal capital income taxation in exogenous growth models. Chamley (1986) finds that in the absence of spillover effects, the long-run distortionary taxes should eventually be eliminated, while Mino (2001) shows that in the presence of positive production externalities, the capital income tax should be negative in the steady state (i.e., capital should be subsidized). These findings are consistent with Proposition 2 in that irrespective of whether such externalities are present, higher rates of distortionary taxes unambiguously depress social welfare. Moreover, since it follows from (15) and (16) that the steady-state level of employment is independent of the degree of externalities, larger degrees of increasing returns (i.e., $\alpha + \beta$) tend to magnify the detrimental effects of distortionary taxation on welfare. This is because, as the degree of increasing returns becomes greater, the negative impact of the distortionary taxes on output is reinforced through (12a), thereby leading to a further reduction in consumption, but leaving the level of employment intact. This reinforced negative effect of capital income taxation on welfare is the other side of the coin to Mino's (2001) *negative* optimal capital income tax rate.

4 The Case of Endogenous Growth

In this section, we consider the case where the economy follows a balanced growth equilibrium path (called a BGE path). The model is identical to the basic model presented in Sect. 2 except for setting $\alpha = 1$, which is needed to generate sustained growth. Note also that when $\alpha = 1$, the Jácobian $R(\hat{l})$ vanishes so that the dynamics of the resulting model becomes one dimensional.

Taking the time derivative of the logarithm of (7a) and substituting (7c) into the resultant expression, we obtain

$$\frac{\dot{c}}{c} = -\frac{1-\sigma}{\sigma}\frac{\chi}{1-l}\dot{l} + \frac{(1-\tau_k)\left(al^{\beta} - \delta\right) - \rho}{\sigma}, \tag{18}$$

where noting $r = al^{\beta}$. Equations (9) and (10a), together with $\alpha = 1$, are, respectively, rewritten as follows:

$$\frac{c}{k} = \frac{b(1-\tau_w)}{1+\tau_c}\frac{l^{\beta-1}(1-l)}{\chi} \tag{19a}$$

and

$$\frac{\dot{k}}{k} = l^{\beta} - \frac{c}{k} - \delta. \tag{19b}$$

Equations (18), (19a), and (19b) together completely characterize the dynamics of the present endogenous growth model.[8]

Before proceeding to the comparative statics exercises, we need to check the stability of the BGE in the model. To do this, we subtract (19b) from both sides of (18), together with (19a),

[8] Along the BGE, the transversality condition is given by $\lim_{t\to\infty} k_0 c_0^{-\sigma}(1-\hat{l})^{(1-\sigma)\chi} e^{-[\rho-(1-\sigma)g]t} (1+\tau_c)^{-1} = 0$, which is equivalent to the condition that $\rho > g(1-\sigma)$, where k_0 and c_0 are the initial levels of capital and consumption, respectively.

$$\frac{\dot{c}}{c} - \frac{\dot{k}}{k} = -\frac{1-\sigma}{\sigma}\frac{\chi}{1-l}\dot{l} + N(l), \tag{20}$$

where

$$N(l) \equiv \frac{(1-\tau_{\mathrm{k}})\left(al^{\beta}-\delta\right)-\rho}{\sigma} - l^{\beta} + \frac{b(1-\tau_{\mathrm{w}})}{1+\tau_{\mathrm{c}}}\frac{l^{\beta-1}(1-l)}{\chi} + \delta.$$

By taking the time derivative of the logarithm of (19a), on the other hand, we find

$$\frac{\dot{c}}{c} - \frac{\dot{k}}{k} = \left[\beta - 1 - \frac{l}{1-l}\right]\frac{\dot{l}}{l}. \tag{21}$$

Equating (21) with (20) and rearranging, we finally obtain

$$\frac{\dot{l}}{l} = \sigma\frac{N(l)}{\Delta(l)}. \tag{22}$$

Since the BGE path is characterized by a situation where both c and k (and w) grow at the same rate (denoted by g), l remains constant (hence $\dot{l}=0$). As a result, the BGE level of employment $\hat{l}$ is obtained by setting $N(\hat{l})=0$:

$$\frac{(1-\tau_{\mathrm{k}})\left(a\hat{l}^{\beta}-\delta\right)-\rho}{\sigma} = \hat{l}^{\beta} - \frac{h(1-\tau_{\mathrm{w}})}{1+\tau_{\mathrm{c}}}\frac{\hat{l}^{\beta-1}(1\ \ \hat{l})}{\chi} - \delta. \tag{23}$$

Since $\dot{l}$ in (22) depends only on l, not on k, to know the stability properties of the BGE, we only have to identify the sign of $\mathrm{d}\dot{l}/\mathrm{d}l$ evaluated at $\hat{l}$. Differentiating the right-hand side of (22) with respect to $\hat{l}$ yields

$$\frac{\mathrm{d}(\dot{l}/l)}{\mathrm{d}l} = \sigma\frac{N'(\hat{l})\Delta(\hat{l}) - N(\hat{l})\Delta'(\hat{l})}{[\Delta(\hat{l})]^2} = \sigma\frac{N'(\hat{l})}{\Delta(\hat{l})}, \tag{24}$$

where noting $N(\hat{l})=0$ and

$$N'(\hat{l}) \equiv \left[\frac{(1-\tau_{\mathrm{k}})a}{\sigma} - 1\right]\beta\hat{l}^{\beta-1} + \frac{b(1-\tau_{\mathrm{w}})}{1+\tau_{\mathrm{c}}}\frac{\hat{l}^{\beta-2}(1-\hat{l})}{\chi}\left[\beta - 1 - \frac{\hat{l}}{1-\hat{l}}\right]. \tag{25}$$

The sign of (24) is in general undetermined because of the ambiguous signs of both $\Delta(\hat{l})$ and $N'(\hat{l})$. Further inspection of (24) reveals that if both $\Delta(\hat{l})$ and $N'(\hat{l})$ are of the same sign, then $\mathrm{d}\dot{l}/\mathrm{d}l > 0$, and thus the fixed point $\hat{l}$ is a repeller; consequently, the BGE is locally determinate. In contrast, if $\Delta(\hat{l})$ and $N'(\hat{l})$ are of opposite signs, then $\mathrm{d}\dot{l}/\mathrm{d}l < 0$, and thus the fixed point $\hat{l}$ is an attractor; hence, the BGE is locally indeterminate.

In Figs. 4–7, the graph of (23) is drawn and shows that the curves corresponding to the left- and right-hand sides of (23) both slope upward (see Appendix 2). The intersection of these curves gives the common growth rate of consumption and capital on the vertical axis and the BGE level of labor supply on the horizontal axis.

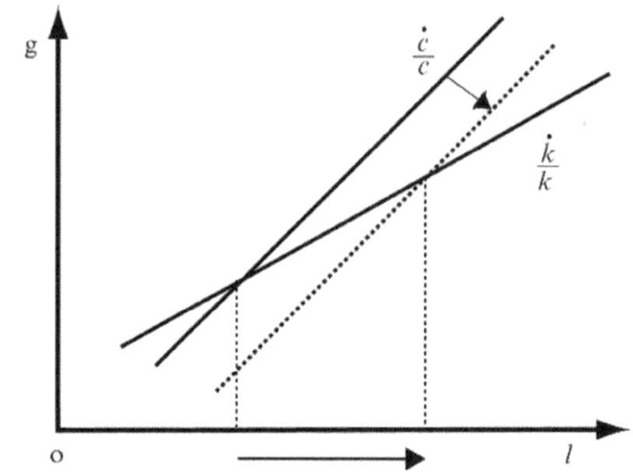

Fig. 4 The effect of an increase in the capital income tax if $N'(\hat{l}) > 0$

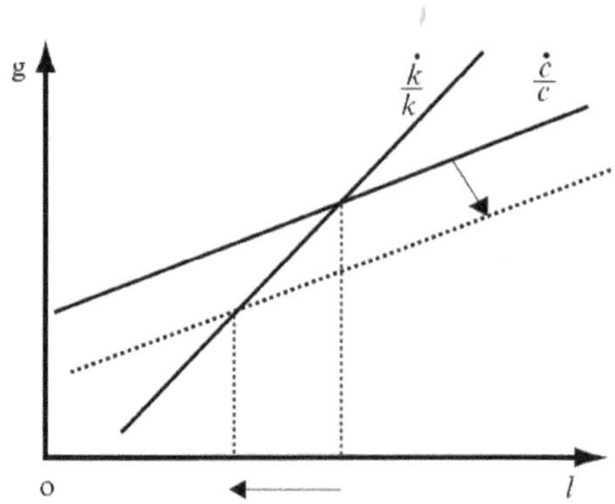

Fig. 5 The effect of an increase in the capital income tax if $N'(l) < 0$

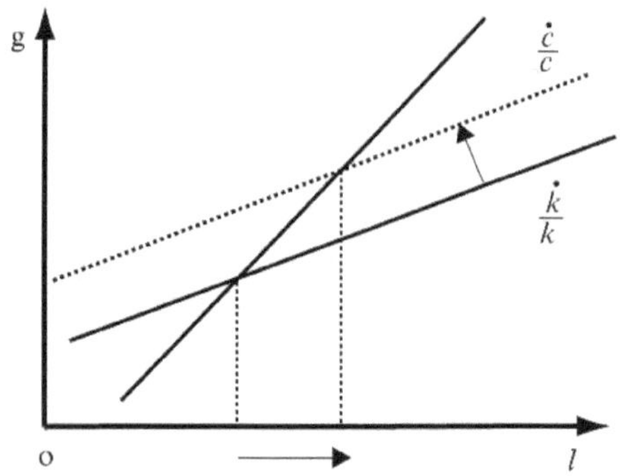

Fig. 6 The effect of an increase in the consumption tax (or the labor income tax) if $N'(l) > 0$

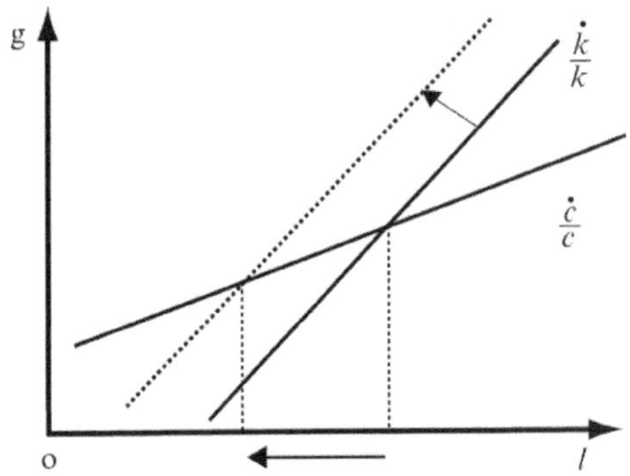

Fig. 7 The effect of an increase in the consumption tax (or the labor income tax) if $N'(l) < 0$

As shown in Appendix 2, $N'(\hat{l}) > 0$ graphically implies that at the fixed point $\hat{l}$, the curve $\dot{k}/k$ cuts the $\dot{c}/c$ curve from above as illustrated in Figs. 4 and 6, whereas $N'(\hat{l}) < 0$ implies the opposite, as illustrated in Figs. 5 and 7. Taken together, we have the following.

Proposition 3. *When the labor demand and Frisch labor supply curves cross with "normal" slopes (i.e., $\Delta(\hat{l}) < 0$), a BGE is locally indeterminate if $N'(\hat{l}) > 0$, while it is locally determinate if $N'(\hat{l}) < 0$. When the labor demand and Frisch labor supply curves cross with the "wrong" slopes (i.e., $\Delta(\hat{l}) > 0$), the results are reversed.*

This proposition allows us to identify the two possible conditions for the emergence of an indeterminate BGE, namely, the signs of $\Delta(\hat{l})$ and $N'(\hat{l})$. This stands in sharp contrast to the exogenous growth model presented in Sect. 2, since in the exogenous growth model the likelihood of indeterminacy hinges solely on the sign of $\Delta(\hat{l})$ (recall $\text{sign}[R(\hat{l})] = \text{sign}[\Delta(\hat{l})]$). Moreover, Pelloni and Waldmann (2000) assume strict concavity of the utility function, and thereby rule out a case where the labor demand and Frisch labor supply curves cross with the "wrong" slope (i.e., $\Delta(\hat{l}) > 0$). As a result, in Pelloni and Waldmann's (2000) model, the stability properties of the BGE are governed solely by the sign of $N'(\hat{l})$. By contrast, in our endogenous growth model, which allows for quasiconcave preferences, the relative slope of the demand and supply curves in the labor market gives another condition for generating indeterminacy, in addition to the sign of $N'(\hat{l})$.

5 A Balanced Growth Path Incidence

In this section, we examine the growth effects of taxes along the BGE path of the endogenous growth model presented in Sect. 4. Since in endogenous growth models consumption and capital stock both grow indefinitely, we cannot compute the *level* effects of the tax changes on these real variables. Instead, we first study the tax effects on employment and thus on the economy's growth rate along the BGE path. Armed with these results, we compute the welfare effects of the respective taxes along the BGE path. This allows for a comparison of the tax effects in the exogenous and endogenous growth models.

Totally differentiating (23) with respect to each tax rate and manipulating yields

$$\frac{d\hat{l}}{d\tau_k} = \frac{a\hat{l}^{\beta} - \delta}{\sigma} \left[N'(\hat{l})\right]^{-1}, \tag{26a}$$

$$\frac{d\hat{l}}{d\tau_c} = \frac{\hat{l}^{\beta-1}(1-\hat{l})}{\chi} \frac{b(1-\tau_w)}{(1+\tau_c)^2} \left[N'(\hat{l})\right]^{-1}, \tag{26b}$$

$$\frac{d\hat{l}}{d\tau_w} = \frac{\hat{l}^{\beta-1}(1-\hat{l})}{\chi} \frac{b}{1+\tau_c} \left[N'(\hat{l})\right]^{-1}. \tag{26c}$$

It is immediately shown that the effect of a change in each tax rate on the BGE level of employment is governed only by the sign of $N'(\hat{l})$ rather than whether the BGE is determinate or indeterminate. It is also important to note that the qualitative and quantitative impacts of the taxes are sensitively influenced by the value of σ, unlike the exogenous growth model presented in Sect. 2. This difference stems from the fact that the parameter σ does not vanish in the balanced growth rate of consumption (18) coupled with $\dot{l} = 0$, unlike the steady-state conditions (9), (12a), and (12b) in the exogenous growth model which do *not* contain the parameter σ.

After substitution of (19a) for c/k in (19b), setting $g \equiv \dot{k}/k$ and differentiating the resultant expression with respect to each tax rate yields

$$\frac{dg}{d\tau_k} = \left[\beta\frac{\hat{l}}{1-\hat{l}}\chi - \frac{b(1-\tau_w)}{1+\tau_c}\left(\beta - 1 - \frac{\hat{l}}{1-\hat{l}}\right)\right] \frac{\hat{l}^{\beta-2}(1-\hat{l})}{\chi}\frac{d\hat{l}}{d\tau_k}, \tag{27a}$$

$$\frac{dg}{d\tau_c} = \frac{1-\tau_k}{1+\tau_c}\frac{a\beta\hat{l}^{2(\beta-1)}}{\sigma}\frac{1-\hat{l}}{\chi}\frac{b(1-\tau_w)}{1+\tau_c}\left[N'(\hat{l})\right]^{-1}, \tag{27b}$$

$$\frac{dg}{d\tau_w} = \frac{1-\tau_k}{1-\tau_w}\frac{a\beta\hat{l}^{2(\beta-1)}}{\sigma}\frac{1-\hat{l}}{\chi}\frac{b(1-\tau_w)}{1+\tau_c}\left[N'(\hat{l})\right]^{-1}. \tag{27c}$$

It is immediate that the effects of the respective taxes on the growth rate have the same signs as $d\hat{l}/d\tau_j$ $(j = k, c, w)$ (i.e., $N'(\hat{l})$), respectively.

A higher capital income tax shifts the $\dot{c}/c$ curve downward, while leaving the $\dot{k}/k$ curve unchanged. When $N'(\hat{l}) > 0$, the new BGE will be located to the northeast of the previous intersection, featuring higher employment and a higher growth rate of the economy, as shown in Fig. 4. At the initial level of employment $\dot{k}/k > \dot{c}/c$, the ratio c/k will decline. The sustained increase in k causes the labor demand curve to shift to the right, while the sustained increase in c causes the Frisch labor supply curve to shift upward (see Figs. 1 and 2).[9] Since the growth rate of k is greater than that of c, the rightward movement of the labor demand curve is bigger than the

[9] More precisely, since both c and k are growing at a common positive rate along the BGE path, the labor demand and supply curves illustrated in Figs. 1 and 2 keep moving up, so that the real wage rate continues to rise, while leaving the BGE level of employment unchanged.

leftward movement of the labor supply curve, as shown in Fig. 1. Thus, employment ends up rising as long as the labor demand and Frisch labor supply curves cross with "normal slopes" (i.e., $\Delta(\hat{l}) < 0$). This movement is thus consistent with the new BGE featuring higher employment, so that employment gradually rises to the new BGE level. Hence, it is stable and thus locally indeterminate. In contrast, when the labor demand and Frisch labor supply curves cross with the "wrong" slopes (i.e., $\Delta(\hat{l}) > 0$), employment falls, in spite of the large increase in labor demand, as shown in Fig. 2. This movement of employment induces the economy to depart from the new BGE. Hence, the new BGE is unstable and thus locally determinate. Accordingly, when the tax is unexpectedly increased in this economy, employment must instantaneously jump to its new BGE level.

Conversely, when $N'(\hat{l}) < 0$, the new BGE will be located to the southwest of the previous intersection; in Fig. 5, this entails lower employment and a lower growth rate. Furthermore, since at the initial level of employment $\dot{k}/k > \dot{c}/c$, the ratio c/k will decline. When $\Delta(\hat{l}) < 0$, employment rises for the same reason outlined above. This movement induces the economy to depart from the new BGE. As a result, employment should immediately jump to the new BGE level, and thus the new BGE is locally determinate. When $\Delta(\hat{l}) > 0$, employment falls and thus gradually approaches the new BGE level; hence, it is locally indeterminate.

When the consumption tax (or the labor income tax) is increased, and accompanied by compensating lump-sum transfers, consumption becomes more expensive relative to leisure, thus inducing a substitution away from the demand for consumption to leisure. When $N'(\hat{l}) > 0$, the induced fall in the ratio c/k moves up the curve $\dot{k}/k$, which is implied by (19b), while leaving the curve $\dot{c}/c$ unchanged, as shown in Fig. 6. Consequently, the new BGE entails higher employment and a higher growth rate. When $\Delta(\hat{l}) < 0$ ($\Delta(\hat{l}) > 0$), labor supply falls but employment gradually rises (immediately jumps) to the new BGE level, and thus the new BGE is locally indeterminate (determinate). Conversely, when $N'(\hat{l}) < 0$, although the dynamic movement of l toward the new BGE is still uncertain depending on the sign of $\Delta(\hat{l})$, an increase in τ_c or τ_w unambiguously has a negative impact on employment and thus on the growth rate along the BGE path (see Fig. 7). Thus, we have the following.

Proposition 4. *(i) When the labor demand and Frisch labor supply curves cross with "normal" slopes, an increase in each of the respective taxes increases (decreases) the BGE level of employment along with the balanced growth rate, if and only if the BGE is locally indeterminate (determinate).*

(ii) When the labor demand and Frisch labor supply curves cross with the "wrong" slopes, an increase in each of the respective taxes increases (decreases) the BGE level of employment along with the balanced growth rate, if and only if the BGE is locally determinate (indeterminate).

To compare the *growth effects* of the taxes in the endogenous growth model with their *level effects* presented in the exogenous growth model, we examine the welfare effects along the BGE path in response to changes in the respective taxes. The level of welfare along the BGE path denoted by W_{BG} is obtained by substituting (19a) into c in (5) and manipulating:

$$W_{\mathrm{BG}} \equiv \frac{1}{1-\sigma}\left[\frac{\{c_0(1-\hat{l})^{\chi}\}^{1-\sigma}}{\rho-g(1-\sigma)}-\frac{1}{\rho}\right], \tag{28}$$

where c_0 $(=k_0 b(1-\tau_{\mathrm{w}})\,\hat{l}^{\beta-1}(1-\hat{l})/[\chi(1+\tau_{\mathrm{c}})])$ is the endogenously determined initial level of consumption situated in the BGE path. Differentiating the right-hand side of (28) with respect to each tax rate results in

$$\frac{\mathrm{d}W_{\mathrm{BG}}}{\mathrm{d}\tau_j}=\Gamma(\hat{l})^{-\sigma}\frac{(\mathrm{d}\Gamma(\hat{l})/\mathrm{d}\tau_j)[\rho-g(1-\sigma)]+\Gamma(\hat{l})(\mathrm{d}g/\mathrm{d}\tau_j)}{[\rho-g(1-\sigma)]^2}, \quad j=k,c,w, \tag{29}$$

where $\Gamma(\hat{l})\equiv c_0(1-\hat{l})^{\chi}$. Appendix 3 demonstrates that $\mathrm{d}W_{\mathrm{BG}}/\mathrm{d}\tau_j$ (for $j=k,c,w$) have the signs of $\mathrm{d}\hat{l}/\mathrm{d}\tau_j$ (i.e., $N'(\hat{l})$), respectively. Therefore, we have the following proposition.

Proposition 5. *(i) When the labor demand and Frisch labor supply curves cross with "normal" slopes, an increase in each of the respective taxes increases (decreases) welfare along the BGE path if and only if the BGE is locally indeterminate (determinate).*

(ii) When the labor demand and Frisch labor supply curves cross with the "wrong" slopes, an increase in each of the respective taxes increases (decreases) welfare along the BGE path if and only if the BGE is locally determinate (indeterminate).

Propositions 4 and 5 are a straightforward generalization of Propositions 2 and 3 in Pelloni and Waldmann (2000) in the following sense. First, Pelloni and Waldmann (2000) restrict their analysis to the case where the labor demand and Frisch labor supply curves cross with "normal" slopes, while we also analyze the case where these curves cross with the "wrong" slopes. Unlike Pelloni and Waldmann (2000), our generalized results suggest that the long-run outcomes of distortionary taxation are no longer uniquely tied to the stability properties of the economy. Accordingly, Pelloni and Waldmann's (2000) paradoxical result may occur, even in the determinate steady state of our endogenous growth model. Second, although Pelloni and Waldmann's (2000) results are derived in an economy where there are no pre-existing taxes, Propositions 4 and 5 in our analysis reveal that their results continue to hold, even in an economy with pre-existing distortionary taxes. In fact, Pelloni and Waldmann (2000) only analyze the first-order welfare effect, and thus ignore the excess burden associated with pre-existing taxes. Accordingly, Pelloni and Waldmann's (2000) analysis tends to underestimate the welfare losses (or gains). Nevertheless, Proposition 5 reveals that the welfare effects of capital income taxation as derived by Pelloni and Waldmann (2000) remain valid. Furthermore, our Propositions 4 and 5 differ from those in Uchijima (2005). Using a similar model, Uchijima (2005) shows that the growth and welfare effects of tax changes do not hinge on whether the BGE is locally indeterminate or determinate. Since Uchijima's

(2005) analytical focus lies in the global stability properties of the BGE, he imposes more stringent conditions to ensure its global uniqueness compared to our local analysis. This difference distinguishes Uchijima's (2005) comparative statics results from ours.

Propositions 4 and 5 appear counterintuitive, probably because the conventional view is that tax substitution from nondistortionary taxes (such as lump-sum taxes) to distortionary taxes usually has an adverse effect on welfare. In contrast, such a tax substitution may improve welfare in the present endogenous growth model. This is partly because the change in the growth rate of the economy (i.e., consumption and capital) plays a dominant role in determining the ultimate effect on welfare, but also because the response of employment to the tax changes, which is positively associated with the growth rate, rests on the relative slopes of the labor demand and supply curves. Hence, when the tax increase enhances the growth rate of consumption, the growth-promoting effect on welfare tends to outweigh the negative effect of the increased labor supply on welfare.

6 Concluding Remarks

This chapter investigates the relationship between the long-run effects of factor income and expenditures taxes and stability properties (i.e., whether the steady state is determinate or indeterminate) in an infinite-horizon, representative agent growth model with endogenous labor supply. The stability properties of the model characterized by the CES utility and Cobb–Douglas production functions do not matter for long-run tax analysis so long as the model displays exogenous growth, whereas the stability properties matter if endogenous growth is displayed. Moreover, in the former, all taxes unambiguously depress economic activity, whereas in the latter these taxes may potentially stimulate economic activity. In either of the determinate and indeterminate steady states of the endogenous growth model analyzed here, the tax increase may promote growth and improve welfare. This contrasts with Pelloni and Waldmann's (2000) result in that only the indeterminate steady state delivers such a counterintuitive outcome. We may conclude not only that these "paradoxical" results emerge only in the endogenous growth model, but also that the one-to-one relationship between the stability properties of the model and its comparative statics results is broken, at least in an economy structured by CES preferences and Cobb–Douglas technology.

Admittedly, all of the results in this chapter depend on the specification of the model. As noted by King et al. (1988), the functional form of the instantaneous utility function assumed is the most general form compatible with balanced growth and stationary labor supply. The specification of the utility and production functions we employ here could be justified by this restriction. Nevertheless, since it appears that the choice of functions is crucial in determining the long-run impacts of taxes, as implied in Appendix 1, examining the dynamic tax effects under other functional forms is valuable to assess the robustness of our results.

Appendix 1

Consider the economy whose dynamics are characterized as follows:

$$\dot{k} = f(k,l) - c - \delta k, \tag{30}$$
$$\dot{\lambda}/\lambda = \rho - (1-\tau_{\mathrm{k}})\left[r(k,l) - \delta\right], \tag{31}$$

where $f(\cdot)$ represents the social production function and the remaining variables are identical to those in the text. Taking a linear approximation around the steady state yields

$$\begin{bmatrix} \dot{k} \\ \dot{\lambda} \end{bmatrix} = \begin{bmatrix} f_k + f_l l_k - c_k - \delta & f_l l_\lambda - c_\lambda \\ -\hat{\lambda}(1-\tau_{\mathrm{k}})(f_{kk} + f_{kl} l_k) & -\hat{\lambda}(1-\tau_{\mathrm{k}}) f_{kl} l_\lambda \end{bmatrix} \begin{bmatrix} \hat{k} - k \\ \hat{\lambda} - \lambda \end{bmatrix}. \tag{32}$$

We carry out the comparative statics exercises with respect to, say, the capital income tax τ_{k}:

$$\partial\hat{k}/\partial\tau_{\mathrm{k}} = \rho\,(f_l l_\lambda - c_\lambda)\,\lambda/(1-\tau_{\mathrm{k}})\,|J|, \tag{33}$$

where $|J|$ is the determinant of the Jacobian matrix appearing on the right-hand side of (32). Inspection of (33) reveals that we need more information to identify the exact relationship between the sign of $|J|$ and the effect of capital income taxation on the long-run capital stock. If the sign of $f_l l_\lambda - c_\lambda$ remains unchanged when the sign of $|J|$ changes, there is a one-to-one relationship between the sign of $|J|$ and the effect of the capital income tax. Nevertheless, it may or may not be true depending on the further specification of the model in the case of *exogenous* growth model.

Appendix 2

Since the slope of the $\dot{c}/c$ curve is given by $\sigma^{-1}[(1-\tau_{\mathrm{k}})(a\hat{l}^{\beta} - \delta) - \rho]$ along a BGE path (recall (18)), we differentiate it with respect to $\hat{l}$, thus yielding

$$\sigma^{-1}(1-\tau_{\mathrm{k}})\,a\beta\hat{l}^{\beta-1} > 0, \tag{34}$$

which implies that the $\dot{c}/c$ curve is positively sloped. As to the $\dot{k}/k$ curve, substituting (19a) into (19b), we differentiate the resultant expression with respect to $\hat{l}$ to obtain

$$\beta\hat{l}^{\beta-1} - \frac{b(1-\tau_{\mathrm{w}})}{1+\tau_{\mathrm{c}}}\frac{\hat{l}^{\beta-2}(1-\hat{l})}{\chi}\left[\beta - 1 - \frac{\hat{l}}{1-\hat{l}}\right] > 0. \tag{35}$$

This implies that the $\dot{k}/k$ curve is also positively sloped.

Moreover, since the right-hand side of (25) can be rearranged as

$$N'(\hat{l}) = \frac{(1-\tau_{\mathrm{k}})\,a\beta\hat{l}^{\beta-1}}{\sigma} - \left[\beta\hat{l}^{\beta-1} - \frac{b(1-\tau_{\mathrm{w}})}{1+\tau_{\mathrm{c}}}\frac{\hat{l}^{\beta-2}(1-\hat{l})}{\chi}\left(\beta - 1 - \frac{\hat{l}}{1-\hat{l}}\right)\right], \tag{36}$$

(34) and (35) together imply that the first and second terms on the right-hand side of (36) represent the slopes of the $\dot{c}/c$ curve and the $\dot{k}/k$ curve, respectively. Hence, it can be shown that when $N'(\hat{l}) > 0$, the $\dot{c}/c$ curve has a steeper upward slope compared with the $\dot{k}/k$ curve, and vice versa.

Appendix 3

Since the denominator of (29) is positive, the sign of (29) is determined according to its numerator:

$$(\mathrm{d}\Gamma(\hat{l})/\mathrm{d}\tau_j)\,[\rho - g(1-\sigma)] + \Gamma(\hat{l})\,(\mathrm{d}g/\mathrm{d}\tau_j) \quad \text{for} \quad j = k, c, w. \tag{37}$$

Recalling $\Gamma(\hat{l}) \equiv c_0(1-\hat{l})^{\chi} = k_0 b\,(1-\tau_{\mathrm{w}})\,(1-\hat{l})^{1+\chi}\hat{l}^{\beta-1}/\,[\chi\,(1+\tau_{\mathrm{c}})]$, we differentiate $\Gamma(\hat{l})$ with respect to τ_{k} to obtain

$$\frac{\mathrm{d}\Gamma(\hat{l})}{\mathrm{d}\tau_{\mathrm{k}}} = \left[\beta - 1 - \frac{\hat{l}}{1-\hat{l}}(1+\chi)\right]\frac{\Gamma(\hat{l})}{\hat{l}}\frac{\mathrm{d}\hat{l}}{\mathrm{d}\tau_{\mathrm{k}}}. \tag{38}$$

Substituting (23), (19a), and (19b) into ρ and g in the expression $\rho - g(1-\sigma)$, respectively, results in

$$\rho - g(1-\sigma) = (1-\tau_{\mathrm{k}})\,(a\hat{l}^{\beta} - \delta) - \left[\hat{l}^{\beta} - \frac{b\,(1-\tau_{\mathrm{w}})}{1+\tau_{\mathrm{c}}}\frac{\hat{l}^{\beta-1}(1-\hat{l})}{\chi} - \delta\right]. \tag{39}$$

We substitute (27a), (38), and (39) into (37) to obtain

$$\left[\left\{\beta - 1 - \frac{\hat{l}}{1-\hat{l}}(1+\chi)\right\}\left\{(1-\tau_{\mathrm{k}})\,(a\hat{l}^{\beta} - \delta) - \left(\hat{l}^{\beta} - \frac{b\,(1-\tau_{\mathrm{w}})}{1+\tau_{\mathrm{c}}}\frac{\hat{l}^{\beta-1}(1-\hat{l})}{\chi} - \delta\right)\right\}\right.$$
$$\left. + \left\{\beta\frac{\hat{l}}{1-\hat{l}}\chi - \frac{b\,(1-\tau_{\mathrm{w}})}{1+\tau_{\mathrm{c}}}\left(\beta - 1 - \frac{\hat{l}}{1-\hat{l}}\right)\right\}\frac{\hat{l}^{\beta-1}(1-\hat{l})}{\chi}\right]\frac{\Gamma(\hat{l})}{\hat{l}}\frac{\mathrm{d}\hat{l}}{\mathrm{d}\tau_{\mathrm{k}}}.$$

Further rearrangement gives rise to

$$= \left[\left\{\beta - 1 - \frac{\hat{l}}{1-\hat{l}}(1+\chi)\right\}\left\{-\hat{l}^{\beta}(1-a) - \tau_{\mathrm{k}}(a\hat{l}^{\beta} - \delta)\right\}\right.$$
$$\left. + \hat{l}^{\beta-2}\left\{\beta - \frac{b\,(1-\tau_{\mathrm{w}})}{1+\tau_{\mathrm{c}}}\right\}\right]\frac{\Gamma(\hat{l})}{\hat{l}}\frac{\mathrm{d}\hat{l}}{\mathrm{d}\tau_{\mathrm{k}}}. \tag{40}$$

Since $\beta - 1 - [(1+\chi)\hat{l}/(1-\hat{l})] < 0$ and $\beta - [b\,(1-\tau_{\mathrm{w}})\,/\,(1+\tau_{\mathrm{c}})] > 0$, all terms within the square brackets of (40) are positive. As a result, the signs of (37) and thus

$dW_{BG}/d\tau_k$ depend only on that of $d\hat{l}/d\tau_k$ (i.e., $N'(\hat{l})$). In an analogous manner, we can show that

$$\text{sign}\left[\frac{dW_{BG}}{d\tau_j}\right] = \text{sign}\left[\frac{d\hat{l}}{d\tau_j}\right] = \text{sign}\left[N'(\hat{l})\right] \quad \text{for} \quad j = c, w.$$

Acknowledgment The authors would like to thank Etsuo Shioji, Taro Akiyama, Tetsugen Haruyama, and seminar participants at Hokkaido University, Yokohama National University, and the University of Glasgow for their helpful comments on an earlier version of this chapter. The financial support of a Grant-in-Aid for Scientific Research, Ministry of Education, Science and Culture (#16530117) is also gratefully acknowledged. The usual disclaimer applies.

References

Arrow KJ, Kurz M (1970) Public investment, the rate of return, and optimal fiscal policy. The Johns Hopkins University Press, Baltimore

Becker RA (1985) Capital income taxation and perfect foresight. J Public Econ 26:147–167

Benhabib J, Farmer REA (1994) Indeterminacy and increasing returns. J Econ Theory 63:19–41

Bennett RJ, Farmer REA (2000) Indeterminacy with non-separable utility. J Econ Theory 93:118–143

Chamley C (1986) Optimal taxation of capital income in general equilibrium with infinite lives. Econometrica 54:607–622

Devereux MB, Love DRF (1994) The effects of factor taxation in a two-sector model of endogenous growth. Can J Econ 27:509–536

Guo J-T, Lansing KJ (1998) Indeterminacy and stabilization policy. J Econ Theory 82:481–490

Hintermaier T (2003) On the minimum degree of returns to scale in sunspot models of the business cycle. J Econ Theory 110:400–409

Judd KL (1987) The welfare cost of factor taxation in a perfect-foresight model. J Polit Econ 95:675–709

King RG, Plossser CI, Rebelo ST (1988) Production, growth and business cycles. I. The basic neoclassical model. J Monetary Econ 21:195–232

Milesi-Ferretti GM, Roubini N (1998) On the taxation of human and physical capital in models of endogenous growth. J Public Econ 70:237–254

Mino K (2001) Optimal taxation in dynamic economies with increasing returns. Jpn World Econ 13:235–253

Pecorino P (1993) Tax structure and growth in a model with human capital. J Public Econ 52:251–271

Pelloni A, Waldmann R (2000) Can waste improve welfare? J Public Econ 77:45–79

Sinn HW (1987) Capital income taxation and resource allocation. North-Holland, Amsterdam

Turnovsky SJ (1982) The incidence of taxes: a dynamic macroeconomic analysis. J Public Econ 18:161–194

Uchijima T (2005) Taxes and indeterminacy. Yokohama Ichiritsu University Ronso (in Japanese) 57:21–102

Vandendorpe AL, Friedlaender AF (1976) Differential incidence in the presence of initial distorting taxes. J Public Econ 6:205–229

Status Seeking and Bubbles[1]

Takashi Kamihigashi

Abstract This chapter examines the possibility of stock market bubbles in a deterministic variant of the Lucas (Econometrica 46:1429–1445, 1978) asset pricing model in which utility depends on status in addition to consumption. Status is formulated first as the ratio of the individual level of wealth to the average level of wealth in the economy, and second as the difference of the individual level and the average level. It is shown that in the first case, bubbles are ruled out by the transversality condition, whereas in the second case, bubbles are possible because all increasing price paths satisfying the Euler equation also satisfy the transversality condition.

1 Introduction

It is popularly believed that stock market bubbles have a significant effect on real activity. The Great Depression after the Wall Street Crash of 1929 and Japan's "lost decade" after the bursting of the Japanese bubble in the early 1990s are well-known examples. Although these and other episodes suggest that stock market bubbles are an important macroeconomic issue, there are very few representative agent models in which stock market bubbles arise. This is mainly because bubbles are ruled out by the transversality condition in standard models (Kamihigashi 1998, 2001).[2]

[1] This chapter is dedicated to the memory of Koji Shimomura. Koji was interested in the effects of status seeking on growth and trade in his last years. This chapter studies the effect of status seeking on the possibility of bubbles.

[2] See Brunnermeier (2008) and Iraola and Santos (2008) for surveys on bubbles in various frameworks.

T. Kamihigashi
RIEB, Kobe University, Rokkodai, Nada, Kobe 657-8501, Japan,
e-mail: tkamihig@rieb.kobe-u.ac.jp

T. Kamihigashi and L. Zhao (eds.) *International Trade and Economic Dynamics – Essays in Memory of Koji Shimomura.*

One of the mechanisms that can potentially break the tie between the transversality condition and the absence of bubbles is status seeking. In the economic literature, an individual's status is often formulated as a function of his own level of wealth and the average level of wealth in the economy (Bakshi and Chen 1996; Futagami and Shibata 1998; Long and Shimomura 2004; Hu and Shimomura 2007).[3] If individuals wish to maintain their status, they have an incentive to keep up with average wealth. If their wealth consists of shares of stocks, this means that they have an incentive to keep their shares even when the stock prices become higher than the fundamental values. This would make bubbles more likely to arise under status seeking. To our knowledge, however, the effect of status seeking on the possibility of bubbles has not been explored yet. The purpose of this chapter is to examine this effect.

This study is closely related to Kamihigashi (2008), where it was shown that stock market bubbles are possible if utility depends on the individual's wealth, provided that the marginal utility of wealth does not decline to zero as wealth goes to infinity.[4] In this chapter, we focus on the case in which utility depends on both individual wealth and average wealth.[5]

We study a deterministic variant of the Lucas (1978) asset pricing model in which utility depends on status in addition to consumption. We formulate status first as the ratio of individual wealth to average wealth, and second as the difference of individual wealth and average wealth.[6] We show that in the first case, bubbles are ruled out by the transversality condition, whereas in the second case, bubbles are possible because all increasing price paths satisfying the Euler equation also satisfy the transversality condition.

Intuitively, bubbles are possible when the incentive to keep up with average wealth remains strong no matter how large individual wealth and average wealth may be. This is true in the second case since the marginal utility of individual wealth remains constant along any equilibrium path. In the first case, by contrast, the marginal utility of individual wealth declines to zero asymptotically along any unboundedly increasing price path. Therefore, if the stock price keeps increasing indefinitely, the effect of status seeking disappears asymptotically, which in turn rules out increasing price paths in equilibrium.

The rest of the chapter is organized as follows. Section 2 presents the general model and gives definitions of bubbles and fundamental values. Section 3 studies the case in which status is formulated as the ratio of individual wealth to average

---

[3] Status can also be formulated as the individual level of wealth alone (see Bakshi and Chen 1996; Zou 1998).

[4] The argument for this result is similar to that used by Obstfeld and Rogoff (1986) to construct a parametric example of a money-in-the-utility-function model in which hyperdeflations are possible; see Buiter and Sibert (2007) for a recent treatment.

[5] Hence, the model here is similar to the exchange economy studied in Kamihigashi (2008) except that utility depends on average wealth. Accordingly, there is some overlap between this chapter and Kamihigashi (2008).

[6] These two cases and the case studied in Kamihigashi (2008) roughly correspond to the three cases analyzed by Bakshi and Chen (1996).

wealth. Section 4 studies the case in which status is formulated as the difference of individual wealth and average wealth. Section 5 concludes the chapter.

2 The General Model

Consider an economy in which there is only one asset, or "stock," and there are many homogeneous individuals each of whom faces the following maximization problem:

$$\max_{\{c_t,w_t,s_t\}_{t=0}^{\infty}} \quad \sum_{t=0}^{\infty} \beta^t [u(c_t,w_t,W_t)] \tag{1}$$

$$\text{s.t.} \quad c_t + w_t = (p_t + d)s_{t-1}, \tag{2}$$

$$w_t = p_t s_t, \tag{3}$$

$$c_t, s_t \geq 0, \tag{4}$$

$$s_{-1} = 1 \text{ given}, \tag{5}$$

where $\beta \in (0,1)$ is the discount factor, c_t is the consumption in period t, w_t is the individual's wealth in period t, W_t is the average level of wealth in the economy, p_t is the price of the stock in period t, s_t is shares of the stock held at the end of period t, and $d > 0$ is the dividend per share, which is assumed to be constant over time.

The model here is similar to the Lucas (1978) asset pricing model except that utility depends on w_t and W_t in addition to c_t. In this section, status is not explicitly formulated; two explicit formulations are considered in Sects. 3 and 4. Throughout this chapter, we assume the following.

Assumption 1. $u : \mathbb{R}_+^3 \to [-\infty,\infty)$ is continuous, continuously differentiable in the first two arguments on $\mathbb{R}_{++}^3$, strictly increasing and concave in the first two arguments, and decreasing in the last argument.

The Euler equation and the transversality condition are given by

$$[u_1(c_t,w_t,W_t) - u_2(c_t,w_t,W_t)]p_t = \beta u_1(c_{t+1},w_{t+1},W_{t+1})(p_{t+1}+d), \tag{6}$$

$$\lim_{t\uparrow\infty} \beta^t [u_1(c_t,w_t,W_t) - u_2(c_t,w_t,W_t)]p_t s_t = 0. \tag{7}$$

The Euler equation (6) is necessary for interior optimal paths. Since the nonnegativity constraints (4) are never binding in equilibrium by (8) and (9) below, the Euler equation is necessary for equilibrium paths. The two conditions (6) and (7) combined are sufficient for optimal paths (e.g., Stokey and Lucas 1989). The transversality condition (7) is necessary if, e.g., u is bounded (e.g., Kamihigashi 2002), as assumed in Sect. 3.

An *equilibrium* of this economy is defined as a set of nonnegative paths $\{c_t,w_t,s_t,p_t,W_t\}_{t=0}^{\infty}$ such that (a) given $\{p_t,W_t\}$, $\{c_t,w_t,s_t\}$ solves the maximization problem (1)–(5); (b) the good and stock markets clear in each period t:

$$c_t = d, \tag{8}$$
$$s_t = 1; \tag{9}$$

and (c) the rational expectations condition holds in each period t:

$$w_t = W_t. \tag{10}$$

It follows from (3), (9), and (10) that in equilibrium,

$$w_t = W_t = p_t. \tag{11}$$

If $p_t \leq 0$, individuals wish to increase s_t indefinitely to receive an indefinite amount of dividend payment in period $t+1$. Since this cannot happen in equilibrium, we have in equilibrium

$$p_t > 0. \tag{12}$$

We define a *steady state* as a price level $p > 0$ such that the set of paths $\{c_t, w_t, s_t, p_t, W_t\}_{t=0}^{\infty}$ given by $p_t = p$, (8), (9), and (11) for all $t \geq 0$ is an equilibrium. Since any constant price path satisfies the transversality condition (7) with (8)–(11), any stationary solution of the Euler equation (6) is a steady state.

To define bubbles formally, let

$$R_{t+1} = \frac{u_1(d, p_t, p_t) - u_2(d, p_t, p_t)}{\beta u_1(d, p_{t+1}, p_{t+1})}, \tag{13}$$
$$q_{t+1} = \frac{1}{R_{t+1}}. \tag{14}$$

Note that R_{t+1} is the (implicit) gross interest rate in equilibrium and q_{t+1} is its inverse. From (6) and (14), p_t can be written successively as

$$\begin{aligned}
p_t &= q_{t+1}d + q_{t+1}p_{t+1} && (15)\\
&= q_{t+1}d + q_{t+1}q_{t+2}d + q_{t+1}q_{t+2}p_{t+2} && (16)\\
&= q_{t+1}d + q_{t+1}q_{t+2}d + q_{t+1}q_{t+2}q_{t+3}d + q_{t+1}q_{t+2}q_{t+3}p_{t+3} && (17)\\
&\vdots && (18)\\
&= \sum_{j=1}^{J}\left(\prod_{i=1}^{j} q_{t+i}\right)d + \left(\prod_{i=1}^{J} q_{t+i}\right)p_{t+J} && (19)\\
&= \sum_{j=1}^{\infty}\left(\prod_{i=1}^{j} q_{t+i}\right)d + \lim_{J\uparrow\infty}\left(\prod_{i=1}^{J} q_{t+i}\right)p_{t+J}. && (20)
\end{aligned}$$

The above limit exists since the sum in (19) is increasing in J and thus the second term in (19) is decreasing in J. Define

$$p_t^{\mathrm{f}} = \sum_{j=1}^{\infty} \left(\prod_{i=1}^{j} q_{t+i} \right) d, \tag{21}$$

$$p_t^{\mathrm{b}} = \lim_{J \uparrow \infty} \left(\prod_{i=1}^{J} q_{t+i} \right) p_{t+J}. \tag{22}$$

Note that p_t^{f} is the present discounted value of the dividend stream. We call p_t^{f} the *fundamental value* and p_t^{b} the *bubble*. Now, p_t can be written as

$$p_t = p_t^{\mathrm{f}} + p_t^{\mathrm{b}}. \tag{23}$$

If $p > 0$ is a steady state, and if q and p^{f} are the corresponding values of q_t and p_t^{f}, then from (15) and (21),

$$p = \frac{q}{1-q} d = p^{\mathrm{f}}. \tag{24}$$

Hence, there is no bubble in any steady state.

3 The Ratio w/W as Status

This section focuses on the case in which status is formulated as the ratio of individual wealth to average wealth. More specifically, we assume that utility depends on consumption and this ratio.

Assumption 2. There exists a bounded function $v : \mathbb{R}_+^3 \to \mathbb{R}$ such that

$$u(c, w, W) = v(c, w/W) \tag{25}$$

for all $c, w, W \geq 0$.

The boundedness condition can be relaxed with additional work. Under the above assumption, we have

$$u_1(d, p_t, p_t) = v_1(d, 1), \tag{26}$$

$$u_2(d, p_t, p_t) = \frac{v_2(d, 1)}{p_t}. \tag{27}$$

For $i = 1, 2$, define

$$\mu_i = v_i(d, 1). \tag{28}$$

Then, the Euler equation (6) and the transversality condition (7) are written in equilibrium as

$$\mu_1 p_t - \mu_2 = \beta \mu_1 (p_{t+1} + d), \tag{29}$$

$$\lim_{t \uparrow \infty} \beta^t (\mu_1 p_t - \mu_2) = 0. \tag{30}$$

As mentioned in Sect. 2, the above two conditions are necessary and sufficient for equilibrium paths.

Note that (29) can be written as

$$p_{t+1} = \beta^{-1} p_t - \theta, \tag{31}$$

where

$$\theta = \frac{\mu_2}{\beta \mu_1} + d. \tag{32}$$

The following result establishes the uniqueness of an equilibrium.

Proposition 1. *Let Assumptions 1 and 2 hold. There exists a unique steady state p^*, which is given by*

$$p^* = \frac{\beta\theta}{1-\beta}. \tag{33}$$

Furthermore, there exists a unique equilibrium path $\{p_t\}$, which is given by $p_t = p^*$ for all $t \geq 0$.

Proof. It is easy to see that the unique stationary solution to (31) is given by (33). Hence, p^* as defined in (33) is the unique steady state.

Let $\{p_t\}$ be a strictly positive price path satisfying (31). Using (31) iteratively, we have

$$\begin{aligned} p_t &= \beta^{-1} p_{t-1} - \theta && (34)\\ &= \beta^{-2} p_{t-2} - \theta(1+\beta^{-1}) && (35)\\ &= \beta^{-3} p_{t-3} - \theta(1+\beta^{-1}+\beta^{-2}) && (36)\\ &\;\;\vdots && (37)\\ &= \beta^{-t} p_0 - \theta(1+\beta^{-1}+\cdots+\beta^{-t+1}). && (38) \end{aligned}$$

Therefore,

$$\begin{aligned} \beta^t p_t &= p_0 - \theta\beta(1+\beta+\cdots+\beta^{t-1}) && (39)\\ &\to p_0 - p^* \text{ as } t \uparrow \infty. && (40) \end{aligned}$$

Thus, the transversality condition (30) holds if and only if $p_0 = p^*$. The proposition now follows. □

Note from (27) that the marginal utility of individual wealth, $u_2(d, p_t, p_t)$, decreases to zero as p_t grows indefinitely. Thus, the effect of status seeking decreases to zero when p_t keeps rising unboundedly. This is the main reason why such price paths cannot be supported by the effect of status seeking here. Since p^* equals the fundamental value in steady state by (24), bubbles are impossible in the present case.

4 The Difference $w - W$ as Status

This section focuses on the case in which status is formulated as the difference of individual wealth and average wealth. More specifically, we assume that utility depends on consumption and this difference.

Assumption 3. There exists a function $v : \mathbb{R}_+ \times \mathbb{R} \to \mathbb{R}$ such that

$$u(c, w, W) = v(c, w - W) \tag{41}$$

for all $c, w, W \geq 0$.

Under this assumption, $u_i(d, p_t, p_t)$ for $i = 1, 2$ does not depend on t:

$$u_i(d, p_t, p_t) = v_i(d, 0) \equiv \mu_i. \tag{42}$$

It follows that R_t and q_t do not depend on t either:

$$R = \frac{\mu_1 - \mu_2}{\beta \mu_1}, \quad q = \frac{1}{R}. \tag{43}$$

To have $R > 0$, we need to assume the following.

Assumption 4. $v_1(d, 0) > v_2(d, 0)$.

The Euler equation (6) and the transversality condition (7) reduce in equilibrium to

$$p_t = q(p_{t+1} + d), \tag{44}$$

$$\lim_{t \uparrow \infty} \beta^t [\mu_1 - \mu_2] p_t = 0. \tag{45}$$

As mentioned in Sect. 2, these two conditions are sufficient and the Euler equation (44) is necessary for equilibrium paths.

It follows from (44) that the fundamental value is constant for any price path and is given by

$$p^{\mathrm{f}} = \frac{q}{1 - q} d. \tag{46}$$

Note that (44) can be written as

$$p_{t+1} = R p_t - d. \tag{47}$$

See Fig. 1 for an example of a price path satisfying this equation.

Proposition 2. *Let Assumptions 1, 3, and 4 hold. There exists a unique steady state, which is equal to p^{f}. Furthermore, there exists a continuum of equilibria. In particular, for each $p \geq p^{\mathrm{f}}$, there exists a unique equilibrium price path $\{p_t\}$ with $p_0 = p$. If $p_0 = p^{\mathrm{f}}$, then $p_t = p^{\mathrm{f}}$ for all $t \geq 0$. If $p_0 > p^{\mathrm{f}}$, then $\{p_t\}$ is strictly increasing and satisfies* $\lim_{t \uparrow \infty} p_t = \infty$. *There exists no equilibrium price path $\{p_t\}$ with $p_0 < p^{\mathrm{f}}$.*

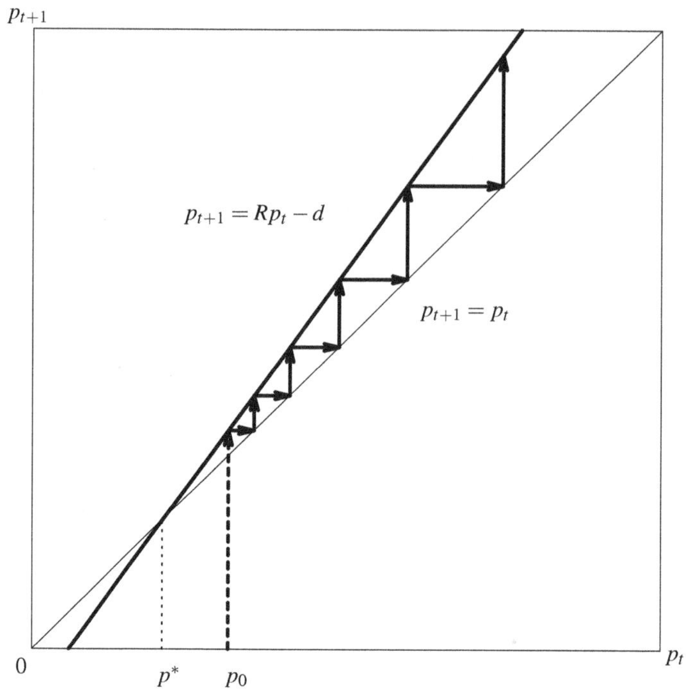

Fig. 1 Price dynamics in case $u(c,w,W) = v(c,w-W)$

Proof. Since p^{f} is the unique stationary solution of the Euler equation (44), it is the unique steady state.

Let $\{p_t\}$ be a strictly positive price path satisfying (47). It is easy to see from Fig. 1 that we must have $p_0 \geq 0$. To establish the proposition, it suffices to verify the transversality condition (45) for any $p_0 \geq 0$.

Note from (47) that for $t \geq 1$,

$$p_t = Rp_{t-1} - d < Rp_{t-1} \leq R^t p_0. \tag{48}$$

Therefore, for $t \geq 1$,

$$\beta^t p_t < \beta^t R^t p_0. \tag{49}$$

The right-hand side converges to 0 because by (43),

$$\beta R = \frac{\mu_1 - \mu_2}{\mu_1} < 1. \tag{50}$$

It follows that the transversality condition (45) holds. □

Note from (42) that the marginal utility of individual wealth, $u_2(d, p_t, p_t)$, remains constant along any price path (as long as $w_t = W_t$). This along with the Euler equation (44) implies that the gross growth rate of p_t is always strictly smaller than

$1/\beta$, so that any increasing price path satisfying the Euler equation also satisfies the transversality condition (45). Hence, any such path is supported as an equilibrium. The difference between $1/\beta$ and the gross growth rate of p_t is due to status seeking.

Intuitively, in the present case, individuals have a strong incentive to keep up with average wealth no matter how large it may be, since their status is equally sensitive to changes in their own wealth regardless of the level of average wealth. Therefore, once a bubble arises, an unboundedly increasing price path becomes self-fulfilling: everyone keeps up with it because everyone else does.

5 Concluding Remarks

In this chapter, we have examined the possibility of stock market bubbles in a deterministic variant of the Lucas (1978) asset pricing model in which utility depends on status. We have shown that bubbles are impossible if status is formulated as the ratio of individual wealth to average wealth. On the other hand, bubbles are possible if status is formulated as the difference of individual wealth and average wealth.

It should be mentioned that bubbles have no welfare effect here even if they arise, since utility remains constant in any equilibrium. This is because in the cases considered here, individual wealth and average wealth cancel out in equilibrium. If this were not true, bubbles would have a welfare effect. The possibility of bubbles in such cases can be dealt with along the lines of Kamihigashi (2008).

References

Bakshi GS, Chen Z (1996) The spirit of capitalism and stock-market prices. Am Econ Rev 86:133–157

Brunnermeier, Markus K. “bubbles.” The New Palgrave Dictionary of Economics. Second Edition. Eds. In: Steven N. Durlauf and Lawrence E. Blume. Palgrave Macmillan, 2008. The New Palgrave Dictionary of Economics Online. Palgrave Macmillan. 08 August 2008 ⟨http://www.dictionaryofeconomics.com/article?id=pde2008_S000278⟩ doi:10.1057/9780230226203.0168

Buiter WH, Sibert AC (2007) Deflationary bubbles. Macroecon Dyn 11:431–454

Futagami K, Shibata A (1998) Keeping one step ahead of the Joneses: status, the distribution of wealth, and long run growth. J Econ Behav Org 36:109–126

Hu Y, Shimomura K (2007) Status-seeking, catching-up, and comparative statics in a dynamics Hechsher–Ohlin model. Rev Dev Econ 11:258–274

Iraola, Miguel A. and Manuel S. Santos. “speculative bubbles.” The New Palgrave Dictionary of Economics. Second Edition. Eds. In: Steven N. Durlauf and Lawrence E. Blume. Palgrave Macmillan, 2008. The New Palgrave Dictionary of Economics Online. Palgrave Macmillan. 08 August 2008 ⟨http://www.dictionaryofeconomics.com/article?id=pde2008_S000205⟩ doi:10.1057/9780230226203.1589

Kamihigashi T (1998) Uniqueness of asset prices in an exchange economy with unbounded utility. Econ Theory 12:103–122

Kamihigashi T (2001) Necessity of transversality conditions for infinite horizon problems. Econometrica 69:995–1012

Kamihigashi T (2002) A simple proof of the necessity of the transversality condition. Econ Theory 20:427–433

Kamihigashi T (2008) The spirit of capitalism, stock market bubbles, and output fluctuations. Int J Econ Theory 4:3–28

Long NV, Shimomura K (2004) Relative wealth, status-seeking, and catching-up. J Econ Behav Org 53:529–542

Lucas RE Jr (1978) Asset prices in an exchange economy. Econometrica 46:1429–1445

Obstfeld M, Rogoff K (1986) Ruling out divergent speculative bubbles. J Monetary Econ 17:349–362

Stokey N, Lucas RE Jr (1989) Recursive methods in economic dynamics. Harvard University Press, Cambridge, MA

Zou H (1998) The spirit of capitalism, social status, money, and accumulation. J Econ 68:219–233

On the Role of the Rate of Time Preference in Macroeconomics: A Survey

Koichi Hamada(✉) and Yosuke Takeda

Abstract This chapter surveys the literature on the role of the rate of time preference in macroeconomics. The tradition of Böhm-Bawerk (The positive theory of capital, MacMillan, London, 1891) and Fisher (The theory of interest, MacMillan, New York, NY, 1930) to contemplate on nature and causes of time discount was distilled by Samuelson (1937) in his elegant formulation of the discounted utility (DU) model, which almost dominated the profession for a long time. As noted by Koopmans (Econometrica 28:287–309, 1960) and Ramsey (Econ J 38:543–559, 1928), time consistency is a key postulate required for the DU formulation. Following Stroz (Rev Econ Stud 23:165–180, 1955), Phelps and Pollak (Rev Econ Stud 35:185–199, 1968) and Laibson (Q J Econ 112:443–477, 1997) explored a game-theoretic situation where the present self has a conflict with the future selves. Laibson's hyperbolic discounting, motivated by the psychological and experimental findings that people tend to discount the immediate future more than the distant one, opens up a wide perspective in macroeconomics. Also, large accumulation of international debts can be attributed to the difference in time discount rates among nations.

Homage to Koji Shimomura by Koichi Hamada

My encounter with Koji Shimomura started in the autumn of 2000 when he appeared in my office at Yale, thanks to the exchange agreement between the Research Institute of Economics and Business (RIEB) at Kobe University and the Economic Growth Center at Yale. I was puzzled by the question if the typical form of free trade agreement (FTA) without any compensatory tariff reductions or transfers to the rest of the world would always deteriorate the welfare of the rest of the world. In a few days, he transformed my old-fashioned approach into a full-fledged expenditure–revenue framework.

K. Hamada
Yale University, New Haven, CT 06520-8269, USA

T. Kamihigashi and L. Zhao (eds.) *International Trade and Economic Dynamics – Essays in Memory of Koji Shimomura.*

From January 2001, I was assigned to be a head of the Economics and Social Research Institute (ESRI) in the Japanese government, and my research into this issue was virtually interrupted for 2 years. In my next meeting with him at Kobe in 2003, he almost reproduced his framework to enlighten my old-fashioned approach that I repeated in the seminar. From that time, we started the intensive collaboration for our paper entitled "Can a preferential trade agreement benefit the welfare of the rest of the world?"

At the same time, alas!, he told me of his eternal illness. Even after that, I wonder how many scholars gathered from all over the world in Kobe to benefit from his unbelievably clear and hardworking brain that kept working in spite of his illness. Of course, I was one of them.

My another coauthor Masahiro Endoh and I waited for Koji to complete our manuscript into crystal clear analytical style. This was interrupted by his hospitalization and was not done completely, but his analytical insight was everywhere in the completed chapter (Endoh et al. 2008).

The messages in the chapter are as follows. In a two commodity world where the goods are normal, a formation of a preferential trade agreement (PTA) that is mutually agreeable to the member countries and without any tariff (income) concessions to the neighbor countries certainly deteriorate the neighbor's welfare, unless one of the member countries is an entrepôt (or a transient port). On the other hand, if one of them is an entrepôt, then the neighbor countries will definitely benefit from a formation of a PTA. Under the Armington assumption that precludes the existence of an entrepôt, the above result will carry through for N-commodity case provided that the goods are substitutes.

I had an inclination to seek such results as to imply that most PTAs without outside compensations will harm the welfare of neighbors. They do not contradict the Kemp–Wan theorem at all because outside compensations to outsider countries are precluded. Koji, perhaps as a brilliant student of Murray Kemp, seemed to look for such results that warrant the Pareto-efficient PTA formation exists. A major part of my last conversation with Koji at the Kobe University Hospital was on this aspect of the model.

This was not all our academic conversations in our last meeting. He would like to turn to the field of international finance and to ask for my advice, he said. He found that the long-run state of a growing world economy would not necessarily be the state that the net debt or credit would converge to zero. I answered, rather plainly, without knowing that would become our last conversation, that his intuition was right and probably understood by most of the profession. I added that we have to create a formulation with certain microeconomic foundation to make such models useful and interesting. I should have been more encouraging and embracing.

About a month later, I was asked by the Peterson Institute for International Economics in Washington, DC to present a chapter on the recent current account of Japan, with a short notice of 1 month. Distinguished members of the Institute including its President, Fred Bergsten, and John Williamson held the idea that actual levels of exchange rates may often diverge from the equilibrium level so widely that a country should take a policy that adjusts the exchange rate to the equilibrium exchange rate. The equilibrium exchange rate is the real equilibrium exchange rate that equates the current account in equilibrium, or at least within a range that may accommodate the normal flow of capital between countries. Hardly anybody has shown, however, what are the normal flows of capital between countries in a growing world economy. This led me to explore a microeconomic foundation of capital movements, particularly liberating the assumption of the identical rate of time preference among individuals or nations. I have found that the economies in the growing world will approach the long-run stage similar to what Koji Shimomura stated in his last conversations to me, i.e., as the nonvanishing debt–indebtedness situation in a growing economy.

Koji's guidance gave me remarkable insights in our collaboration. I wish he would continue to guide me by his invisible hand from heaven!

1 Introduction

> In the Sung Dynasty in China, a human had to save food expenses for monkeys. He gave them three nuts at dawn and four at dusk. Monkeys got furious. Next day he gave monkeys four nuts at dawn and three nuts at dusk. Monkeys jumped with joy.

This story is usually given as a moral example showing how stupid monkeys are. We would rather interpret it, however, as the manifestation of true monkey nature or even of true human nature. Having a time preference is a natural tendency for a human as for an animal. In fact, as will be seen, the state with substantial borrowing and lending in a growing world economy is closely related to the difference in the rates of time preference among agents constituting the world economy. To commemorate Koji Shimomura's deep interest in economic dynamics and the long-run debt credit pattern, and to lay the ground work for our analysis of microfoundation of international indebtedness, in this chapter, we would like to review the current literature on rates of time preference.

The concept of time preference is old enough to have been known since Rae (1834), who preceded in discussing the subject before the well-known dispute between Eugen von Böhm-Bawerk and Irving Fisher. In their exchanges of arguments, their attention was focused upon psychological determinants of time preference. Fisher (1930), for instance, listed as such determinants, "self-control," "habit," "concern for the lives of other persons," and "fashion."

Such an interest in the psychological factors for time preference greatly changed, since a provocative work of Samuelson (1937). Samuelson proposed a clear formulation of intertemporal decision makings over consumption profiles, in a form of the so-called discounted utility (DU) model. Over a finite or infinite horizon, a person's cardinal instantaneous utility functional is integrated though being discounted with a constant rate. Samuelson considered the model as neither normatively nor descriptively valid for practical intertemporal decision makings. Contrary to the Samuelson's manifest reservation about the validity of the discounted utility model in practice, the simplicity and the elegance has made it the standard for our economists. This does not mean, however, a constant and exogenously determined rate of time preference is the reality.

Time preference itself is a psychological and ethical concept concerning human beings. In an epoch-making work of macroeconomics, Ramsey (1928) indeed justified a zero rate of time preference by saying "we do not discount later enjoyments in comparison with earlier ones, a practice which is ethically indefensible." By the same token, almost all the serious economic analyses, including Koopmans (1960) that explored building axioms for the discounted utility model, inevitably become tangent on ethics, psychology, or philosophy. In Friedman (1957), there are also the pragmatic yet similar assumptions to Ramsey that "eliminate some of the usual reasons assigned for time preference, in particular the possibility that the consumer unit will not live to engage in consumption in subsequent years, or that equally satisfactory consumer goods will not for one reason or another be available then as now" (p. 12). Moreover, the recent contribution of quasihyperbolic discounting function has been motivated by some experimental results in psychology.

To have a general perspective in the area of time preference and to promote researches in this classical field that involves philosophical thinking, in this chapter, we review the implications of the time preference in macroeconomics emphasizing theoretical aspects more than related empirical aspects. We pay a particular attention to the models of economic growth, and life-cycle savings and wealth distribution. The reason that we limit our area to macroeconomics proper is that there is a growing literature in economics and finance on some empirical puzzles, such as "retirement consumption puzzle" (Bernheim et al. 2001). By limiting our objectives to chapters in macroeconomics, we hope to be able to give a coherent view of the work dealing with on the role of time preference in macroeconomics. This chapter thus attempts to review the literature on the role of time preference in macroeconomics, either old or new. As will be seen, a new area concerning the rate of time preference, rather than the conventional discounted utility formulation, seems to be now fermenting in macroeconomic theory.

The structure of this chapter is as follows. Section 2 presents for a heuristic purpose a couple of fundamental findings to prepare the later discussion. Section 3 describes macroeconomic models where the rate of time preference is either endogenously determined or dependent on time distance from the present. Section 4 mentions some empirical evidences on rate of time preference, in either estimation studies or experimental ones. Section 5 discusses our own contributions on the rates of time preference as determinants of international indebtedness. Finally, Sect. 6 concludes with a short account of possible directions for the future research.

2 Preliminaries

2.1 Axioms for Discounted Utility Model

It would be a natural question, for a mathematical economist with deep philosophical insight, to ask what kind of axioms on consumer preferences is necessary or sufficient for the existence of the discounted utility formulation in macroeconomics. Koopmans (1960) postulated some axioms of a utility functional of programs with an infinite time horizon. For a program for an infinite future ${}_1x \equiv (x_1, x_2, \ldots) \equiv (x_1, {}_2x)$, the conditions Koopmans supposed are as follows.

Axiom 1 (Continuity) *Continuity of a utility functional.*

Axiom 2 (Sensitivity) *Sensitivity property for existence of first-period consumption vectors x_1, x_1' such that $U(x_1, {}_2x) > U(x_1', {}_2x)$ for any subsequent consumptions ${}_2x$.*

Another axiom is

Axiom 3 (Aggregation by periods) *Aggregation by periods that for all x_1, $x_1', {}_2x, {}_2x'$, $U(x_1, {}_2x) \geqq U(x_1', {}_2x)$ implies $U(x_1, {}_2x') \geqq U(x_1', {}_2x')$ and $U(x_1, {}_2x) \geqq U(x_1, {}_2x')$ implies $U(x_1', {}_2x) \geqq U(x_1', {}_2x')$.*

It makes possible a form $U(x) = V(u_1(x_1), U_2({}_2x))$ of utility functional, where aggregate utility $U(x)$ is expressed as a *(time) aggregator* function $V(u_1, U_2)$ defined in immediate utility $u_1(x_1)$ and prospective one $U_2(\cdot)$. The fourth axiom below guarantees the form of utility functional $U(x) = V(u_1(x_1), U({}_2x))$.

Axiom 4 (Stationarity) *Stationarity such that $U(x_1, {}_2x) \geqq U(x_1, {}_2x')$ if and only if $U_2({}_2x) \geqq U_2({}_2x')$.*

Finally, Koopmans supposed

Axiom 5 (Extreme program) *Extreme programs ${}_1\underline{x}, {}_1\overline{x}$ satisfying $U({}_1\underline{x}) \leqq U({}_1x) \leqq U({}_1\overline{x})$ for any ${}_1x$.*

Defining the "impatience condition" as

$$\Phi(U) \equiv V(u_1, V(u_2, U)) - V(u_2, V(u_1, U)) > 0 \quad \text{when} \quad u_1 > u_2, \tag{1}$$

Koopmans (1960) showed that under the Axioms 1–5, the impatience condition is met in a finite time horizon. What is more important for us, Koopmans added another axiom similar to Axiom 3 (aggregation by periods). The additional one is

Axiom 6 (Period independence) *Period independence such that for all x_1, x_2, ${}_3x$, x_1', x_2', and ${}_3x'$, $U(x_1, x_2, {}_3x) \geqq U(x_1', x_2', {}_3x)$ implies $U(x_1, x_2, {}_3x') \geqq U(x_1', x_2', {}_3x')$ and $U(x_1, x_2, {}_3x) \geqq U(x_1', x_2, {}_3x')$ implies $U(x_1, x_2', {}_3x) \geqq U(x_1', x_2', {}_3x')$.*

The addition of independence makes possible a utility functional of the discounted utility model that Samuelson (1937) proposed, such that $U({}_1x) = \sum_{t=1}^{\infty} \alpha^{t-1} u(x_t)$ where aggregate utility is a discounted sum of all future immediate utilities with a constant discount rate α. Thus, Koopmans showed an axiomatic basis for the discounted utility model.

Throughout the arguments below, we mention which axioms matter when we change the formulation of discounted utility model.

2.2 The Ramsey Problem of Optimal Savings

As a famous example of using the discounted utility model for analyzing optimal savings, we present a model of Ramsey (1928) to illustrate the interaction of time preference and macroeconomic behavior. Ramsey was a pioneer to the series of questions now known as optimal economic growth, life-cycle savings, and wealth distribution.

The Ramsey problem in a continuous-time formulation is as follows. Consider an infinite horizon economy producing one kind of output from a single capital stock. Output can be either consumed or invested. We denote the capital stock and the consumption rate at time t by k_t and c_t, respectively. The production function $f(k_t) : [0,\infty) \longmapsto \mathbb{R}$ is continuous, twice continuously differentiable and strictly concave. We also assume $f(0) = 0$ and the Inada condition $\lim_{k \longrightarrow 0} f'(k) = \infty$. The objective function of the representative consumer is to maximize the discounted utility over the infinite horizon, such as $\int_0^\infty u(c_t)\mathrm{e}^{-\rho t}\mathrm{d}t$, where the utility function $u : [0,\infty) \longmapsto \mathbb{R}$, subject to a resource constraint $\mathrm{d}k_t/\mathrm{d}t = f(k_t) - c_t$, and given k_0. The discount rate is assumed to be constant ρ over time. Note that the Ramsey problem of optimal savings is a simple example of the discounted utility model that was formulated in Samuelson (1937).

Ramsey applied the calculus of variations to the problem, where the present-value Hamiltonian is $H_t = u(c_t) + \lambda_t(f(k_t) - c_t)$. The first-order conditions with respect to consumption, the adjoint equation, and the transversality condition are, respectively,

$$\frac{\mathrm{d}H_t}{\mathrm{d}c_t} = \frac{\mathrm{d}u(c_t)}{\mathrm{d}c_t} - \lambda_t = 0, \tag{2}$$

$$\frac{\mathrm{d}\lambda_t}{\mathrm{d}t} - \rho\lambda_t = -\frac{\mathrm{d}H_t}{\mathrm{d}k_t} = -\lambda_t \frac{\mathrm{d}f(k_t)}{\mathrm{d}k_t}, \tag{3}$$

and

$$\lim_{t \longrightarrow \infty} \lambda_t k_t \mathrm{e}^{-\rho t} = 0. \tag{4}$$

Associated with the transversality condition (4), the two differential equations of the capital stock and the consumption solve the Ramsey problem:

$$\frac{\mathrm{d}k_t}{\mathrm{d}t} = f(k_t) - c_t, \tag{5}$$

$$\frac{\mathrm{d}c_t}{\mathrm{d}t} = -\left(\frac{\mathrm{d}f(k_t)}{\mathrm{d}k_t} - \rho\right) \frac{\frac{\mathrm{d}u(c_t)}{\mathrm{d}c_t}}{\frac{\mathrm{d}^2u(c_t)}{\mathrm{d}c_t^2}}. \tag{6}$$

The solution path guarantees the "quasi-Golden rule" in a steady state named by Phelps (1961), toward which the saddle-point path converges under the assumptions above.

As in case of many authors following Ramsey, we assume a competitive market for capital, so that the marginal rate of return $f'(k_t)$ is equal to real interest rate at date t denoted by r_t. For later references, we present possible reduced forms of the Ramsey problem in cases of the isoelasticity or log-utility function.

The instantaneous utility function exhibits a constant elasticity of marginal utility: $u(c) = \frac{c^{1-\theta}-1}{1-\theta}$ for $\theta > 0$. Then, the Euler equation is reduced to $\frac{\frac{dc_t}{dt}}{c_t} = \frac{\frac{df(k_t)}{dk_t}-\rho}{\theta}$. Hence, the consumption growth rate is $\frac{\frac{dc_t}{dt}}{c_t} = \frac{r_t-\rho}{\theta}$. Among the isoelasticity utility functions, we may take the logarithmic case where the elasticity is equal to unity ($\theta = 1$), $u(c) = \log c$, which results in the consumption growth rate $\frac{\frac{dc_t}{dt}}{c_t} = r_t - \rho$. Then, from the resource constraint $\frac{dk_t}{dt} = f(k_t) - c_t = r_t k_t - c_t$ and the formula on consumption growth rate, we have a relation $c_t = \rho k_t$ which represents the marginal propensity to consume out of wealth. With the log utility where income and substitution effects of interest rates exactly cancel out, the marginal propensity to consume out of wealth is equal to the discount rate. This insight was rediscovered, after the development of growth theory, by Cass (1965) and Koopmans (1965).

The production function exhibits a linear transformation: $f(k) = Ak$ for $A > 0$. Then, a marginal rate of return is a constant A, not a time-varying variable. With the linear production function, the Euler equation is reduced with the consumption growth rate equal to a constant, either $(A-\rho)/\theta$ or $A-\rho$ depending on the isoelasticity or the log-utility function to be chosen.

3 Time Preference in Macroeconomics

The Ramsey model provided a prototype of optimal saving models. With respect to the discounted utility model (also, its axiomatic basis and the application to optimal savings), we introduce a few alternative models to the discounted utility model in terms of economic growth and life-cycle savings. In this section, the examples are confined to theoretical chapters.

3.1 Endogenous Time Preferences

3.1.1 Psychological Time

Uzawa (1968) pioneered a theory of "endogenous time preference," by considering a dependence of time preference on the utility level of present and future consumption. As already argued "Poverty bears down heavily on all portions of a man's expected life. But it increases the want for immediate income even more than it increases the want for future income," Fisher (1930) considered the rate of time preference to depend on the utility level negatively, so that a poor living standard increases the rate of time preference. Uzawa, on the other hand, observed that rich countries like the United States save less and formulated that the rate of time preference increases if an individual is richer. In our commonsense language, this can be interpreted that a fat cat becomes lazy. This assumption assures the stability of growth model as well. Let us denote the rate of time preference from the present to time t as $\Delta_{0,t}, t = 1, 2, \ldots$ for discounting utility stream $u_t, t = 1, 2, \ldots$ at a planning period 0. Then, the aggregate utility U is equal to $U = u_0 + \frac{u_1}{1+\Delta_{0,1}} + \frac{u_2}{1+\Delta_{0,2}} + \cdots$, so that the rate of time preference $\Delta_{0,t}$ depends on the entire time profile of utility stream, $\Delta_{0,t} = \Delta_{0,t}(u_0, u_1, \ldots)$.

Just as Koopmans relied on the independence ((3) and (6)) axioms and the stationarity axiom (postulate (4)), Uzawa constrained the structure of time preference by postulate. First, the rate of time preference $\Delta_{0,t}$ for time t utility is independent of the utility levels occurring after time t. That is, we obtain $\Delta_{0,t} = \Delta_{0,t}(u_0, u_1, \ldots, u_t)$. The independence leads to $\Delta_{s,t} = \Delta_{s,t}(u_s, u_{s+1}, \ldots, u_t)$ whenever $s < t$. Second, the discounting function is "independent of the manner in which discounting is done," particularly requiring $1 + \Delta_{0,t} = (1 + \Delta_{0,s})(1 + \Delta_{s,t})$ for $0 < s < t$. These two independence assumptions correspond to the Koopmans' (1968) postulate (3) and (6). Finally, the structure of time preference remains invariant through the entire period, which means an increase in the rate of time preference applying to period $t-1$ and t utility, $\frac{1+\Delta_{0,t}(u_0,u_1,\ldots,u_t)}{1+\Delta_{0,t-1}(u_0,u_1,\ldots,u_{t-1})} = 1 + \Delta_{t-1,t}(u_{t-1}, u_t) = 1 + \delta(u_{t-1}, u_t)$ with a certain function δ. The last assumption in Uzawa (1968) is analogous to the Koopmans' stationarity postulate (4).

Based upon these assumptions on rate of time preference, Uzawa formulates an intertemporal optimization of the representative consumer living forever. Using the same notations as are used in the Ramsey problem,

$$\max_{\{c,k\}} U = \int_0^\infty u_t \mathrm{e}^{-\Delta_t} \mathrm{d}t, \tag{7a}$$

$$\text{s.t.} \quad \frac{\mathrm{d}k_t}{\mathrm{d}t} = f(k_t) - c_t, \tag{7b}$$

$$\text{given } k_0. \tag{7c}$$

Here, the difference between Uzawa (1968) and the Ramsey problem is in that Uzawa postulated the endogenous rate of time preference satisfying the following properties $\frac{\mathrm{d}\Delta_t}{\mathrm{d}t} = \delta(u_t)$, $\delta(u_t) > 0$, $\delta'(u_t) > 0$, $\delta''(u_t) > 0$, $\delta(u_t) - \delta'(u_t)u_t > 0$ for all $u > 0$. The last assumption on the convexity of the discount rate function implies that between two stationary consumption streams providing the same utility u, the consumer with time preference growing with a constant rate $\delta(u)$ would prefer the one with higher instantaneous utility, since the assumption guarantees

$$\frac{\mathrm{d}\left[\int_0^\infty u \mathrm{e}^{-\delta(u)t} \mathrm{d}t\right]}{\mathrm{d}u} = \frac{\mathrm{d}\left[\frac{u}{\delta(u)}\right]}{\mathrm{d}u} = \frac{\delta(u) - \delta'(u)u}{[\delta(u)]^2} > 0.$$

The maximization problem can be solved with the same technique as in the Ramsey problem, except for applying a transformation of *physical* time into the rate of time preference called "psychological time" by Uzawa. Utilizing the definition of time preference $\mathrm{d}\Delta_t/\mathrm{d}t = \delta(u_t)$, the objective function U can be transformed into

$$\int_0^\infty u_t e^{-\Delta_t} dt = \int_0^\infty \frac{u}{\delta(u)} e^{-\Delta} d\Delta,$$

where we take Δ as the independent variable instead of time t. The resource constraint is also turned to $dk/d\Delta = (f(k) - c)/\delta(u)$. Taking a costate variable $\lambda(\Delta)$ associated with the Hamiltonian in the transformed problem yields $\frac{\frac{d\lambda(\Delta)}{d\Delta}}{\lambda(\Delta)} = \frac{\delta(u)-r}{\delta(u)}$, where a variable r denotes a competitive rate of interest assumed to be constant through time at the marginal productivity of capital. Substituting the equation into the first-order condition, we have

$$\frac{dc}{d\Delta} = \frac{r - \delta - \delta' u'(f(k) - c)}{\delta\left(\frac{u'\delta''(u+u'(f(k(-c))))}{\delta - u\delta'} - \frac{u''}{u'}\right)}.$$

The differential equation and the other $dk/d\Delta = (f(k) - c)/\delta(u)$ determine an existence of saddle-point path converging to a stationary point.

Lucas and Stokey (1984) also work with a similar model to Uzawa (1968) by using a recursive but nonadditively time-separable preference and derive sufficient conditions for the existence of a unique stationary point. One problem exists with such a endogenous time preference that depends on utility. That is, there is no rationale for Uzawa's assumption on time preference function $\delta'(u_t) > 0$, which means that a higher consumption at time t increases the discount factor to the utilities after time t. Though the assumption is required in the model for stability, the implication itself should be empirically tested, since it seems natural as Fisher said, to be the case that the rich are more likely to be patient.

3.1.2 Future-Oriented Capital

Besides Uzawa (1968), there are a few models based on endogenous time preference. Among them, we introduce a model of "future-oriented capital" by Becker and Mulligan (1997). While in Uzawa (1968) the time preference function depends on utility and therefore consumption flows, Becker and Mulligan (1997) model presents the time preference function that depends on efforts and time called "future-oriented capital" for easily helping image formation and scenario simulation in the process of anticipation. This subtle concept of capital is motivated by some historical remarks in Böhm-Bawerk and Fisher. We can see for instance:

> Indeed, to have any effect on the future, we must form a double series of anticipations. We must be able to form a mental picture of what will be the state of our wants, needs, feelings, at any particular point of time. And we must be able to form another set of anticipations as to the fate of those measures which we take at the moment with a view to the future. (Böhm-Bawerk 1891, p. 244)

Such anecdotes suggest that patience seems to be associated with culture and poverty, as well as income, development, and education. These factors reflect the psychological arguments on time preference in the age of the classical economics, especially before development of the discounted utility model by Samuelson (1937). People are required to invest efforts and time to become "rational" by overcoming their endowed imperfect ability to imagine the future.

Becker and Mulligan (1997) present a finite horizon model where the representative consumer with the length of life T maximizes aggregate utility $V = \sum_{t=0}^{T} \beta(S)^t u(c_t)$ subject to the intertemporal budget constraint $\sum_{t=0}^{T} R_t c_t + pS = A_0$, with respect to consumption profile $\{c_t\}_{t=0}^{T}$ and initial investments S for the future-oriented capital. It is assumed that the price of the investment for patience p is the same for every individual and independent of wealth or endowed patience, and that the internal rate factor defined as a product $R_t = \Pi_{\tau=0}^{t}(1+r_\tau)$ of rate of return r_t for $\tau = 1,\ldots,t$ is exogenous for the consumer. What is crucial in the model is that the time-invariant discount factor $\beta(S)$ satisfies $\beta(S) > 0$, $\beta'(S) \geq 0$, and $\beta''(S) \leqq 0$ for all S. As a rationale for the properties, it is assumed that to increase their appreciation of the future, people spend resources on being able to imagine future pleasures as in a less remote picture. More resources spent on imagination increase the propinquity of future pleasures. The resources also become less and less effective in decreasing the future remoteness. The endowed discount factor $\beta(0) < 1$ reflects an imperfectness of imagination ability.

The maximization with this formulation yields the first-order conditions with respect to the consumption and the capital investment. One of the first-order conditions is the familiar condition that the marginal utility of consumption adjusted by a discount factor and the internal rate factor must be equal to the marginal utility of wealth λ_0. The latter condition is specific to the model and written as $\beta'(S)\sum_{t=1}^{T} t\beta(S)^{t-1}u(c_t) = \lambda_0 = u'(c_0)$, where the left-hand side of the marginal benefit of patience investment must be equal to the right-hand side of the marginal utility of wealth. The condition for the patience investment generates complementarity between time preference and future utility under the assumptions on $\beta(S)$. An increase in future utilities raises the advantage of low discount on the future. The implication coincides with some empirical findings, such as drug use, heavy drinking, and other addictions.

More interesting for us, the model implies some intragenerational inequality of wealth and consumption. Persons who are richer with more assets would be more patient than persons with fewer assets. Thus, the rich choose to be more patient, rather than they intrinsically are, than the poor. As a result, inequality of wealth and consumption within a cohort should rise as the cohort members get aged, which is the empirical finding of Deaton and Paxson (1994) in the US, UK, and Taiwan. The result, however, depends on an assumption that the price p of the future-oriented capital S is given as constant regardless of wealth levels.

We are interested in the growth process of the world economy. Assuming the constant price of p, this work has the following implication. Contrary to the assumption in Uzawa (1968), if the rich have an incentive for becoming more patient, the patience price p for the rich may be higher than for the poor. Then, the intratemporal inequality in wealth and consumption could be less conspicuous than the extent observed in Deaton and Paxson (1994).

3.2 Time-Varying Time Preference

3.2.1 Time Inconsistency

While both Uzawa (1968) and Becker and Mulligan (1997) focus on the endogeneity of time preference rates, they treated the world where the consistency of preferences prevails through the planning horizon.

There is, however, economic literature that draws upon a psychological finding that rate of time preference differs in calendar time or "time distance." In that sense, for instance optimal saving plans for the present self would not be optimal for the later self. The dependence on time distance brings about intertemporal time inconsistency. According to the calendar time when each chapter was published on this theme, we look at a few older chapters on the intertemporal dynamic inconsistency of an individual agent, and in Sect. 3.2.2 we will explain some new results in recent years.

A classical chapter by Stroz (1955) was the first contribution to a formal modeling of the time consistency problem. Following Pigou (1920), Stroz (1955) pointed out a phenomenon that he called a person's "spend-thriftiness myopia." An individual has a myopic tendency to resist delaying consumption in the near future. Stroz (1955) assumed that the discount factor applied to a future utility should depend on the time distance τ from the present date t. A consumer with an initial wealth A_0 at time $t = 0$ wishes to maximize the aggregate utility functional $\int_0^T \lambda(t)u(c_t)\mathrm{d}t$, subject to the resource constraint $\int_0^T c_t \mathrm{d}t = A_0$. The discount rate $\lambda(\tau)$ depends on time distance τ. Similar to the Ramsey problem, the calculus of variations yields the first-order condition

$$\frac{\frac{\mathrm{d}\lambda(t)}{\mathrm{d}t}}{\lambda(t)} = -\frac{\frac{\mathrm{d}\left(\frac{\mathrm{d}u(c_t)}{\mathrm{d}c_t}\right)}{\mathrm{d}t}}{\frac{\mathrm{d}u(c_t)}{\mathrm{d}c_t}}$$

for $0 \leq t \leq T$. This equation says that the discounted marginal utility of consumption should be the same for all dates in an ex ante meaning. However, there occurs an ex post time inconsistency problem that at a later date $\tau > 0$ than the planning date $\tau = 0$, the consumer maximizes $\int_0^T \lambda(t-\tau)u(c_t)\mathrm{d}t$ with respect to $\{c_t\}_{t=0}^T$, subject to $\{c_t\}_{t=0}^{\tau}$ given and $\int_\tau^T c_t \mathrm{d}t = A_0 - \int_0^\tau c_t \mathrm{d}t$. Similarly, the first-order condition becomes

$$\frac{\frac{\mathrm{d}\lambda(t-\tau)}{\mathrm{d}t}}{\lambda(t-\tau)} = -\frac{\frac{\mathrm{d}\left(\frac{\mathrm{d}u(c_t)}{\mathrm{d}c_t}\right)}{\mathrm{d}t}}{\frac{\mathrm{d}u(c_t)}{\mathrm{d}c_t}}$$

for $\tau \leq t \leq T$. This ex post best plan is entirely different from the ex ante optimal condition. If the consumption plan is to be re-evaluated continuously, actual behavior is given by a locus of the best plans $\{c_t\}_{t=\tau}^T$ evolving as date τ proceeds from 0 to T.

Stroz (1955) suggested a "harmony" case when an individual who continuously re-evaluates his/her consumption plans follows the originally optimal plan itself. In such a harmony case, for all dates τ, both

$$\frac{\frac{d\lambda(t)}{dt}}{\lambda(t)} = -\frac{\frac{d\left(\frac{du(c_t)}{dc_t}\right)}{dt}}{\frac{du(c_t)}{dc_t}}$$

and

$$\frac{\frac{d\lambda(t-\tau)}{dt}}{\lambda(t-\tau)} = -\frac{\frac{d\left(\frac{du(c_t)}{dc_t}\right)}{dt}}{\frac{du(c_t)}{dc_t}}$$

should coincide with each other. The necessary and sufficient condition for the consistency of choice is that the discount function is to follow a logarithmic constant rate of change, i.e., $\lambda(\tau) = \rho^{\tau}$ for a constant ρ.

However, except in the harmony case, the consumer who faces time inconsistency over the entire period may probably resort to ex ante strategies for avoiding the inconsistency. Stroz (1955) considered two possible strategies for the intrapersonally inconsistent consumer, the precommitment and the consistent planning. Precommitment strategy is possibly an option to avoid our tendency toward procrastination. Unpleasant things which the present ourselves want to do sometime in the future would be put off till later dates. To avoid temptation and actually to do the task, we are willing to pay a price to precommitment future actions. Though precommitment strategy in Stroz (1955) is concerned with the consumption plan for the consumer with time preference depending on time distance, the logic seems to be similar to Becker and Mulligan (1997), where the discount function itself depends on the investments of future-oriented capital as a precommitment device.

The other strategy of consistent planning is more interesting to us, since here the discounted utility model can be implied as a specific example of the harmony case. To solve a consistent planning achieving the best plan $\{c_t^*\}_{t=0}^{T}$ in the model, Stroz (1955) considered the following problem. The consumer at date τ maximizes $\int_0^{\tau} \lambda(t-\tau)u(c_t^*)dt + \int_{\tau}^{\tau+\Delta\tau} \lambda(t-\tau)u(c_t)dt + \int_{\tau+\Delta\tau}^{T} \lambda(t-\tau)u(c_t^*)dt$, with respect to $\{c_t\}_{t=\tau}^{\tau+\Delta\tau}$, subject to the constraint $\int_{\tau}^{\tau+\Delta\tau} c_t dt = A_0 - \int_0^{\tau} c_t^* dt - \int_{\tau+\Delta\tau}^{T} c_t^* dt$. The first-order condition says

$$\frac{\frac{d\lambda(t-\tau)}{dt}}{\lambda(t-\tau)} = -\frac{\frac{d\left(\frac{du(c_t)}{dc_t}\right)}{dt}}{\frac{du(c_t)}{dc_t}}$$

for $\tau \leq t < \tau + \Delta\tau$, so that as $\Delta\tau \to 0$, the maximum condition gets

$$\frac{\frac{d\lambda(0)}{dt}}{\lambda(0)} = -\frac{\frac{d\left(\frac{du(c_t)}{dc_t}\right)}{dt}}{\frac{du(c_t)}{dc_t}}$$

for every date t. This condition can be reduced to the harmony case where the discount function is of a geometric form $e^{d\lambda(0)/dt} = k$ a constant. The case results in the discounted utility model.

Stroz's insight on the myopic nature of human beings introduced an example of varying rate of time preference and later opened up a whole subject of time inconsistency in decision making.

3.2.2 Quasihyperbolic Discounting

Imperfect Altruism

Phelps and Pollak (1968) also addressed the time inconsistency with a special attention to a game-theoretic situation between the present and future selves. Instead of Koopmans' (1960) stationarity postulate or Ramsey's (1928) perfect altruism, Phelps and Pollak (1968) presented a framework reflecting both myopia and imperfect altruism with discount factor of utility. Their aggregate utility is represented as $U = u(c_0) + \alpha\delta u(c_1) + \alpha^2\delta u(c_2) + \cdots$, with $0 < \delta < 1$ and $0 < \alpha < 1$. The constant parameters α and δ represent myopia and imperfect altruism, respectively. Both of two parameters consist of the discount factor function $\alpha^t\delta$ applied to utility of the consumption at date t. Note that perfect altruism means $\delta = 1$, as in the Ramsey problem. It is shown that except for the perfect altruism, the present self chooses as a first-best solution a smaller saving ratio than the future saving ratio that the present self would wish the future one to select.

Golden Eggs

The discount function proposed by Phelps and Pollak (1968) is now called "quasihyperbolic discounting" and frequently used in psychological experiments as well as in economics. This name came from its proximity to generalized hyperbolic function, though strictly speaking it is quasigeometric. Focusing upon the quasihyperbolic discounting, Laibson (1997) showed that illiquid assets such as housing, social security wealth or "children" provide a form of yet imperfect commitment to mitigate the intrapersonal time inconsistency problem. Illiquid assets have the same property as the goose that laid golden eggs. The bonus system in Japan is another example of institutional device to improve overtime efficiency.

In the Laibson (1997) model, a consumer with such a quasihyperbolic discounting makes consumption and savings decisions in discrete time $t \in \{1, 2, \ldots, T\}$. He or she is born with both exogenous endowments of liquid x_0 and illiquid assets z_0, and one unit of labor. Every time period t, at the beginning of the period, the consumer faces a budget constraint $c_t \leq y_t + R_t x_{t-1}$, receiving both labor income y_t for inelastically providing one unit of labor and a gross return $R_t = 1 + r_t$ for liquid asset savings x_{t-1} chosen at the end of time period $t-1$. The net return r_t for liquid assets x_{t-1} is assumed to be the same rate for illiquid asset holdings z_{t-1} decided at the end of period $t-1$, for simplicity. With the budget constraint, the consumer chooses current consumption c_t. At the end of the period, then the consumer chooses new allocations for liquid x_t and illiquid assets z_t, subject to a budget constraint $y_t + R_t x_{t-1} - c_t + R_t z_{t-1} = x_t + z_t$ for $x_t \geq 0$ and $z_t \geq 0$. In the model, it is crucially assumed that an illiquid asset requires us to initiate a sale one period before its actual proceeds are received. At time t, the consumer maximizes the aggregate utility function

$$U_t = E_t\left[u(c_t) + \alpha \sum_{\tau=1}^{T-t} \delta^\tau u(c_{t+\tau})\right].$$

There occurs a time inconsistency problem between preferences at different time periods. Using the quasihyperbolic discounting, it is shown that at time t the marginal rate of substitution for the decision maker at time 1, after period t, $u'(c_{t+1})/\delta u'(c_{t+2})$ between two periods $t+1$ and $t+2$, does not coincide with the marginal rate of substitution for the decision maker at time $t+1$, $u'(c_{t+1})/\alpha\delta u'(c_{t+2})$, unless the myopia parameter $\alpha = 1$.

In a dynamic game with time inconsistency between a sequence of temporal selves, Laibson (1997) showed that under a certain restricting condition on labor income process, a unique subgame perfect equilibrium strategy exists. The equilibrium strategy satisfies some plausible properties. First, the consumption and asset allocation strategy is "resource exhausting" in that for all the paths for the feasible history, the joint path is characterized by $x_T = z_T = 0$. Second, the Euler equation is satisfied for the current period t self. Third, when marginal utility enjoyed by the descendant self is strictly too higher than one of the current self, the liquidity constraint of the current self must be binding $c_t = y_t + R_t x_{t-1}$. Fourth and fifth, if consumption level of the descendant selves is expected to be higher (lower) relative to what the current self prefers them to be, then the current self will limit (enhance) the descendant's liquidity as much as possible, $x_t = 0$ ($z_t = 0$).

What is interesting in the "golden eggs" model is that it provides an explanation to comovement between consumption and income. In the standard theory for the consumption–income comovement, a buffer-stock theory of savings (Carroll 1992), impatient consumers with high discount rates hold little wealth for a precautionary savings motive and choose optimal consumption path, so that consumption and income move together over the life cycle. As an alternative explanation to the buffer-stock savings theory, the golden eggs model suggests that the consumer at the equilibrium faces a binding liquidity constraint $c_t = y_t + R_t x_{t-1}$ every moment, which is not exogenously given but self-imposed. When a given labor income y_t is expected to be high, the $t-1$ self limits the liquidity of the t self as much as possible by choosing smaller x_{t-1}. However, what the $t-1$ self can do is to deny the t self's access to assets held, not including the access to labor income at time t. It means that predictable movements in income will tend to be reflected in movements in consumption. Unlike in the buffer-stock savings model, the explanation of the consumption–income comovement does not depend on how high the discount rate of the consumers is. In equilibrium, decisions to dissave out of illiquid assets do not depend on the parameter α. This is because the t self cannot consume the illiquid assets immediately, so that it does not consider tradeoffs between consumptions today and tomorrow, and instead it does consider the tradeoffs between $t+1$ period and after-$(t+1)$.

Ramsey Meets Laibson

Following Laibson (1997), Barro (1999) considered possible hypotheses for empirically testing the quasihyperbolic discounting in the literature of economic growth. Barro (1999) cited a paragraph in Ramsey (1928) as follows:

> In assuming the rate of discount constant, I [mean that] the present value of an enjoyment at any future date is to be obtained by discounting it at the rate ρ. ... This is the only assumption we can make, without contradicting our fundamental hypothesis that successive generations are actuated by the same system of preferences. For if we had a varying rate of discount – say a higher one for the first fifty years – our preference for enjoyments in 2000 A.D. over those in 2050 A.D. would be calculated at the lower rate, but that of the people alive in 2000 A.D. would be at the higher. (Ramsey 1928, p. 553)

As it says, Ramsey understood the time inconsistency problem in face of time-varying rate of time preference. Speculating the probable understanding by Ramsey, Barro (1999) tried to show an observational equivalence between the neoclassical growth model and the quasihyperbolic discounting model as constructed by Phelps and Pollak (1968) and Laibson (1997).

Barro (1999) confines the model into a case of log utility with nonlinear production functions, because log utility leads to a reduced form of solution, but linear technology degenerates transitional dynamics due to a constant rate of return. In his model, the aggregate utility function at period τ is $U_\tau = \int_\tau^\infty u(c_t)\mathrm{e}^{-[\rho(t-\tau)+\phi(t-\tau)]}\mathrm{d}t$, where in addition to the standard exponential factor $\mathrm{e}^{-\rho(t-\tau)}$ with a constant discount rate ρ, a discount function $\phi(t-\tau) \geq 0$ captures dependence of time preference on time distance $t-\tau$ at period τ. The discount function should be considered to satisfy $\phi'(v) \geq 0$, $\phi''(v) \leq 0$, and $\lim_{v\to\infty} \phi'(v) = 0$. The production function is, on the other hand, usual in the neoclassical growth model given by $y = f(k)$. Barro discusses first a case under commitment, and then one without commitment.

In the log-utility case with commitment, the consumption growth rate becomes $\frac{\mathrm{d}c_t/\mathrm{d}t}{c_t} = r_t - \rho - \phi'(t-\tau)$ for $t > \tau$. The difference from the Ramsey problem is the term $\phi'(t-\tau)$, where the instantaneous rate of time preference $\rho + \phi'(t-\tau)$ at period t is higher than the Ramsey problem and declines toward ρ as the time distance $t-\tau$ approaches to ∞. The Euler equation is given for an arbitrarily chosen time period τ, so there are no rationales that a commitment opportunity arises suddenly at the time τ. Suppose that commitment would have existed in the infinitely distant past. Then, current and all future consumptions would have been already determined and the current period τ should have been minus infinity. As a result, since the time distance in the discount function becomes infinity, the instantaneous rate of time preference $\rho + \phi'(t-\tau)$ would have been ρ for all $t \geq 0$. The conjecture can apply to transitional dynamics as well as stationary state in the quasihyperbolic discounting model. Hence in the presence of commitment, the model coincides with the Ramsey problem.

Next, Barro (1999) addresses the other case without any commitment. Without commitment devices, the consumer has to figure out how its current decision c_τ affects its asset holdings and how the change in asset positions influences the descendants' consumption decisions later. Relying on a perturbation method similar to used in Stroz (1955) where solving a time-consistent solution reduced to the "harmony case," Barro (1999) showed an observational equivalence of the quasi-hyperbolic discounting model with log utility and no commitment, to the Ramsey problem.

Suppose that the consumer chooses a constant flow c_τ over a short discrete interval $[\tau, \tau+\varepsilon]$. Then, the aggregate utility at the date τ,

$$U_\tau = \int_\tau^{\tau+\varepsilon} \log c_t \mathrm{e}^{-[\rho(t-\tau)+\phi(t-\tau)]} \mathrm{d}t + \int_{\tau+\varepsilon}^{\infty} \log c_t \mathrm{e}^{-[\rho(t-\tau)+\phi(t-\tau)]} \mathrm{d}t$$

is approximated by

$$U_\tau \approx \varepsilon \log c_\tau + \int_{\tau+\varepsilon}^{\infty} \log c_t \mathrm{e}^{-[\rho(t-\tau)+\phi(t-\tau)]} \mathrm{d}t.$$

The effect of the current decision c_τ on the asset holdings and the effects of the change in asset positions on the descendants' consumption decisions later should be separately considered. From the consumer's budget constraint $\mathrm{d}k_t/\mathrm{d}t = r_t k_t + w_t - c_t$, where factor prices r_t and w_t are competitively determined, at the period $\tau+\varepsilon$, there obtains $k_{\tau+\varepsilon} \approx k_\tau(1+\varepsilon r_\tau) + \varepsilon w_\tau - \varepsilon c_\tau$. So, $\mathrm{d}k_{\tau+\varepsilon}/\mathrm{d}c_\tau = -\varepsilon$. As for the other effects, from a conjecture that in case of log utility the marginal propensity to consume out of wealth is constant as in the Ramsey problem, the consumption level c_t is proportional to wealth k_t, i.e., $c_t = \lambda k_t$ for some constant $\lambda > 0$. Because of the consumption growth rate $r_\tau - \lambda$ at time τ, we have $\log c_t = \log c_{\tau+\varepsilon} + \int_{\tau+\varepsilon}^{t} r_v \mathrm{d}v - \lambda[t-(\tau+\varepsilon)]$ for any $t \geq \tau+\varepsilon$. Substituting this relation into the aggregate utility, there obtains

$$U_\tau \approx \varepsilon \log c_\tau + \int_{\tau+\varepsilon}^{\infty} \log c_t \mathrm{e}^{-[\rho(t-\tau)+\phi(t-\tau)]} \mathrm{d}t \tag{7d}$$

$$\approx \varepsilon \log c_\tau + \log c_{\tau+\varepsilon} \int_{\tau+\varepsilon}^{\infty} \mathrm{e}^{-[\rho(t-\tau)+\phi(t-\tau)]} \mathrm{d}t + \cdots, \tag{7e}$$

where the residual does not depend on the consumption path. Defining $\Omega \equiv \int_0^\infty \mathrm{e}^{-[\rho v+\phi(v)]} \mathrm{d}v$, we can derive the marginal effects of c_τ on U_τ that should be zero in optimum, i.e.,

$$\frac{\mathrm{d}U_\tau}{\mathrm{d}c_\tau} \approx \frac{\varepsilon}{c_\tau} + \frac{\Omega}{c_{\tau+\varepsilon}} \frac{\mathrm{d}c_{\tau+\varepsilon}}{\mathrm{d}k_{\tau+\varepsilon}} \frac{\mathrm{d}k_{\tau+\varepsilon}}{\mathrm{d}c_\tau} = 0.$$

Since $c_\tau = c_{\tau+\varepsilon}/\Omega\lambda$ as ε tends to zero and consequently, $\lambda = 1/\Omega$ exists and verifies the conjecture of $c_t = \lambda k_t$ for some constant $\lambda > 0$. Note that $\lambda = \rho$ in a specific case of $\phi(v)$ for all v that corresponds to the Ramsey problem.

Further, Barro (1999) specified forms of the discount function in two ways. One is the continuous-time version of the discrete one in Laibson (1997) with a threshold value $V > 0$, $\phi(v) = 0$ for $0 \leq v \leq V$, $\phi(v) = -\log\beta$ for $v > V$. β is a constant satisfying $0 < \beta \leq 1$. The discount function leads to $\Omega = [1-(1-\beta)\mathrm{e}^{-\rho V}]/\rho$, which as V tends to infinity, $\Omega = 1/\rho$, i.e., the Ramsey case. If $\rho V \ll 1$, Ω goes to β/ρ, so that $\lambda = \rho/\beta$. However, obviously the discount function has a discrete jump at $v = V$. The other way of discount function is smooth, $\phi'(v) = be^{-\gamma v}$ for $b = \phi'(0) \geq 0$ and $\gamma > 0$. This means $\phi(v) = \frac{b}{\gamma}(1 - e^{-\gamma v})$ with a boundary condition $\phi(0) = 0$. In this case, $\Omega = e^{-b/\gamma} \int_0^\infty e^{-\rho v + (b/\gamma)e^{-\gamma v}} dv$. In any case, instead of rate of time preference ρ in the Ramsey problem, the effective rate of time preference λ replaces in the quasihyperbolic discounting model. The constancy of both rates λ and ρ means that we cannot distinguish between the Ramsey and the Laibson model. Thus, there exists an observational equivalence between them.

Invisible vs. Visible Hands

As a final example in this section, we introduce a welfare analysis of the quasihyperbolic discounting model by Krusell, Kuruscu, and Smith (2002; hereafter KKS). Their motivation is welfare analysis of the market mechanism compared with social planner allocation in the quasihyperbolic discounting model without commitment. Since except for the time-varying discount function, their model addresses a frictionless Ramsey problem, it is generally admitted that market mechanism and social planner can achieve the same first-best allocation. Surprisingly, their model concludes whenever there is a time inconsistency or preference reversals, a benevolent social planner cannot deliver the same consumption allocation as does a laissez-faire market mechanism, and the planned economy does strictly worse in terms of the welfare than the competitive economy.

KKS (2002) suppose time-consistent Markov equilibria in a model where they specify a log utility $u(c) = \log c$ and the Cobb–Douglas production functions $f(k) = Ak^\alpha$. In a recursive competitive equilibrium, we have two state variables: one for the individual's own capital holdings k and the other for aggregate capital holdings $\bar{k}$ reflecting prices in the economy. A recursive competitive equilibrium is defined as a decision rule $g(k,\bar{k})$, a value function $V(k,\bar{k})$, pricing functions $r(\bar{k})$ and $w(\bar{k})$, and a law of motion for aggregate capital $\bar{k}' = G(\bar{k})$, such that:

1. Given $V(k,\bar{k})$, $g(k,\bar{k})$ solves the maximization problem $V_0(k,\bar{k}) = \max_{k'} \log(r(\bar{k})k + w(\bar{k}) - k') + \beta\delta V(k',\bar{k}')$, where $V(k,\bar{k}) = \log(r(\bar{k})k + w(\bar{k}) - g(k,\bar{k})) + \delta V(g(k,\bar{k}),\bar{k}')$.
2. Given $g(k,\bar{k})$, $V(k,\bar{k})$ satisfies the functional equation $V(k,\bar{k}) = \log(r(\bar{k})k + w(\bar{k}) - g(k,\bar{k})) + \delta V(g(k,\bar{k}),\bar{k}')$.
3. Firms maximize profits at $r(\bar{k}) = f'(\bar{k})$ and $w(\bar{k}) = (1-\alpha)f(\bar{k})$.
4. The current self's decision is consistent with the law of motion for aggregate capital $g(\bar{k},\bar{k}) = G(\bar{k})$.

The recursive competitive equilibrium is given by a reduced-form solution of

$$g(k,\bar{k}) = \frac{\beta\delta}{1-(1-\beta)\delta} r(\bar{k})k,$$

$$V(k,\bar{k}) = a + \frac{\alpha - 1}{(1-\alpha\delta)(1-\delta)} \log\bar{k} + \frac{1}{1-\delta} \log\left(k + \frac{(1-\alpha)(1-(1-\beta)\delta)}{\alpha(1-\delta)}\bar{k}\right),$$

and

$$G(\bar{k}) = \frac{\alpha\beta\delta}{1-(1-\beta)\delta} A\bar{k}^{\alpha}.$$

As Barro (1999) does, KKS (2002) also show an observational equivalence of the aggregate allocation between time-inconsistent preference without commitment and the exponential preference, the latter of which coincides with the case of time-inconsistent preference with commitment.

On the other hand, KKS (2002) suppose a planning economy where the social planner is a consumer representative who faces the same time inconsistency problem as the consumer does. The crucial difference between the competitive market economy and the social planning one is that the consumer takes prices as given in the competitive market, whereas the planner has a resource constraint. The difference reduces the state variables in the planning economy, where the aggregate state $\bar{k}$ reflecting prices should be redundant. The planning economy consists of a fixed-point solution $\tilde{h}(k) = h(k)$ for all k, satisfying $V_0(k) = \max_{k'} u(f(k) - k') + \beta\delta V(k')$, where $V(k) = u(f(k) - h(k)) + \delta V(h(k))$. The reduced-form solution is

$$\tilde{h}(k) = \frac{\beta\delta}{1-\alpha(1-\beta)\delta} \alpha A k^{\alpha}$$

and

$$V(k) = a + \frac{\alpha - 1}{(1-\alpha\delta)(1-\delta)} \log k.$$

Comparing these two solutions, KKS (2002) find that whenever $\alpha < 1$, the competitive equilibrium differs from the social planner equilibrium. Note that when $\alpha = 1$, the Cobb–Douglas function corresponds to a linear production economy with a constant rate of return. Without any variations in the factor prices $r(\bar{k})$ and $w(\bar{k})$, the aggregate state $\bar{k}$ would become redundant for the consumer in the competitive market, which is in the same situation as in the planning economy.

When $\alpha < 1$, the effect of the social planner's decision to save is acknowledged as a decreasing return to savings, while in the competitive market the effects of the individual savings are given as negligible for price takers. Due to the difference between the social planning and the competitive market, with an excessive short-run impatience $\beta < 1$ where future selves are undersaving, the consumer saves more than the planner does; with excessive short-run patience $\beta > 1$ where too much savings are held by the future selves, the consumer saves less than the planner.

What is most important in KKS (2002) is the welfare comparison. They conclude the competitive economy results in strictly higher welfare than the planning economy does, when $\beta \neq 1$ and $\alpha < 1$. The result should be clearer in the Euler equation for each of the planner or the competitive economy. For the social planner,

$$u'(c_t) = \beta\delta u'(c_{t+1}) \left(f'(k_{t+1}) + \left(\frac{1}{\beta} - 1 \right) h'(k_{t+1}) \right),$$

where

$$\widetilde{h}(k) = \frac{\beta\delta}{1-\alpha(1-\beta)\delta}\alpha A k^{\alpha}.$$

For the consumer with excessive short-run impatience $\beta < 1$, every unit of savings for preventing overconsumption decreases consumption at next period by the marginal propensity to save $h'(k_{t+1})$. The term $\left(\frac{1}{\beta}-1\right)h'(k_{t+1})$ is then an additional return to savings at time t, with decreasing returns with respect to k if $\alpha < 1$. As for the competitive economy, the Euler equation becomes

$$u'(c_t) = \beta\delta u'(c_{t+1})\left(f'(k_{t+1}) + \left(\frac{1}{\beta}-1\right)g_1'(k_{t+1},k_{t+1})\right),$$

where

$$g(k,\bar{k}) = \frac{\beta\delta}{1-(1-\beta)\delta}\alpha A \bar{k}^{\alpha-1}k$$

is a linear function in k. The term $\left(\frac{1}{\beta}-1\right)g_1'(k_{t+1},k_{t+1})$ is an additional constant return to savings. Because of the difference in the return to savings between two economies, when $\beta < 1$, the competitive equilibrium consumer benefits from savings than does the planner, leading to welfare enhancing. When $\beta > 1$, the negative return to savings deteriorates more the welfare of the planner than one of the consumer.

4 Empirical Evidence

We have discussed a number of interesting theoretical articles on the roles of time preference in macroeconomics. The theoretical significance of time preference covers the roles concerned with economic growth, life-cycle savings, wealth distribution, welfare, and so forth. In spite of the significance, however, there have been only limited numbers of empirical studies of econometric estimation. In contrast, there are many records of psychological experiments. Since time preference should be a psychological concept concerned with human beings, it makes sense that economics should respect those psychological findings. Here, we review some empirical evidence on time preference, which has been explored with both econometric and psychological approaches.

4.1 Estimation

Ogaki and Atkeson (1997) directly test the effects of wealth on rate of time preference assumed in Fisher (1930) and Uzawa (1968), as well as the wealth effect on intertemporal elasticity of substitution, using data for total, food, and nonfood consumptions in the Indian villages.

The statistical model is motivated by a permanent-income model in complete contingent markets. A household h has an isoelastic utility $u(c_h) = [(c_h - \gamma)^{1-\alpha} - 1]/(1-\alpha)$, where a parameter γ represents the subsistence level of consumption. The intertemporal elasticity of substitution

$$\sigma_h \equiv -\frac{u'(c_h)c_h}{u''(c_h)} = \frac{1}{\alpha}\left(1 - \frac{\gamma}{c_h}\right).$$

Note that if the subsistence level is positive, i.e., $\gamma > 0$, the intertemporal elasticity of substitution is higher for richer households than for poorer ones.

He or she maximizes the utility function in complete contingent markets where the state contingency claims for the history vector of the economy $e_t \equiv (s_0, s_1, \ldots, s_t)$ consisting from a state s_τ of the world each period $\tau = 1, 2, \ldots, t$. The price of the contingent claim is expressed as $R[t-1, e(t-1), e(t)]$ which is the gross real rate of return of the state-contingent claim for the history $e(t)$ at period t given the previous history $e(t-1)$. The transition probability from state $e(t-1)$ to $e(t)$ is denoted by $\Pr(e(t)|e(t-1))$. Then, a household h maximizes $U_h = \sum_{t=0}^{T}\sum_{e(t)}(\beta_h)^t \Pr(e(t)|e(0))u(c_h(t, e(t)))$ subject to a lifetime budget constraint $\sum_{t=0}^{T}\sum_{e(t)}\prod_{\tau=0}^{t} R[\tau-1, e(\tau-1), e(\tau)]^{-1} c_h(t, e(t)) \leq W_h$, where a variable W_h means an initial wealth of the household h.

Note that the discount rate β_h is assumed to be different across households but constant over time for each household. This crucial assumption greatly simplifies the empirical estimation, though unable to empirically explore the time-varying time preference.

The first-order condition for the maximization in case of an isoelastic utility is

$$\left(\frac{c_h(t, e(t)) - \gamma}{c_h(t+1, e(t+1)) - \gamma}\right)^{-\alpha} = \beta_h R[t, e(t), e(t+1)].$$

The theoretical model treats measurement errors sensitive to estimation result, particularly in using data of the less developed economy like the Indian villages. It assumes a multiplicative measurement error $\varepsilon_h^{\mathrm{m}}(t)$ in a relation to measured consumption $c_h^{\mathrm{m}}(t, e(t))$ as $c_h^{\mathrm{m}}(t, e(t)) - \gamma = [c_h(t, e(t)) - \gamma]\varepsilon_h^{\mathrm{m}}(t)$, where the measurement errors $\varepsilon_h^{\mathrm{m}}(t)$ of positive values might be serially correlated but independent across households. It also assumes another measurement error in a proxy y_h^{c} for permanent income as following $\ln \beta_h = \beta_0 + \beta_1 y_h^{\mathrm{c}} + \varepsilon_h^{\mathrm{c}}$, where the error is assumed to be independent across households. Combining these equations yields a statistical model of household consumption growth to estimate:

$$\ln(c_h(t+1, e(t+1)) - \gamma) - \ln(c_h(t, e(t)) - \gamma) = \phi(t) + b_y y_h^{\mathrm{c}} + \upsilon_h(t),$$

where

$$\phi(t) = \frac{1}{\alpha}(\ln R[t, e(t), e(t+1)] + \beta_0), \quad b_y = \frac{\beta_1}{\alpha},$$
$$\upsilon_h(t) = \ln \varepsilon_h^{\mathrm{m}}(t+1) \ln \varepsilon_h^{\mathrm{m}}(t) + \frac{1}{\alpha}\varepsilon_h^{\mathrm{c}}.$$

The statistical model encompasses some cases concerning time preference or intertemporal elasticity of substitution. First, consider a case in which the subsistence level of consumption $\gamma = 0$ and the error term $\upsilon_h(t) = 0$. Then, if the parameter $b_y = \beta_1/\alpha$ is positive due to the wealth-varying rate of time preference, then the mean growth rate of consumption will be higher for richer households than for poorer ones.

Second, take another case where $b_y = 0$ and $\upsilon_h(t) = 0$. Then, the consumption growth is given by

$$\frac{c_h(t+1, e(t+1))}{c_h(t, e(t))} = \mathrm{e}^{\phi(t)} + \frac{\gamma(1 - \mathrm{e}^{\phi(t)})}{c_h(t, e(t))}.$$

It suggests that if the parameter for the subsistent level $\gamma > 0$ and a constant $\phi(t)$ is positive, i.e., $\phi(t) > 0$, then the consumption growth rate of households with higher consumption level will be higher than the growth rate with the lower level of consumption. If $\gamma > 0$ and $\phi(t) < 0$, the consumption growth rate of households with higher consumption level shrinks faster than that with lower consumption level. The conjecture means that if $\gamma > 0$ which indicates the wealth-varying intertemporal elasticity of substitution, the volatility in the consumption growth rate is larger for richer households than for poorer ones.

Ogaki and Atkeson (1997) estimate the statistical model with the generalized method of moment (GMM), associated with some orthogonality conditions. They can neither find evidences against a hypothesis $b_y = 0$ nor find estimates of γ significantly positive. The result is robust with the three choices of total, food, or nonfood consumption, denying that the consumption growth mean is significantly different between poor and rich households, while the volatility is larger for rich households than for poor ones. Thus, Ogaki and Atkeson (1997) suggest that the rate of time preference is constant across households' wealth levels, while the intertemporal elasticity of substitution increases with the wealth levels. As the authors admitted, however, there is another possibility of interpreting their empirical results in terms of incomplete markets with borrowing constraints on households. Also, their finding on the constant rate of time preference in the Indian village data contradicts with the empirical evidence by Lawrance (1991) who applied a similar method to Ogaki and Atkeson (1997), using the US Panel Study of Income Dynamics (PSID) data. Assuming a constant intertemporal elasticity of substitution, Lawrance (1991) suggests empirical evidences that richer households in the US have higher discount rates (equivalently, lower rates of time preference), after controlling for race, education, and age and family compositions.

4.2 Experiments

Frederick, Loewenstein, and O'Donoghue (2002; hereafter FLO) comprehensively review literatures on the time preference, with special attention to the experiments from a viewpoint of psychology. The procedure for measuring discount rates is divided into two categories (1) field studies, "in which discount rates are inferred from economic decisions that people make in their ordinary life" and (2) experimental studies, "in which people are asked to evaluate stylized intertemporal prospects involving real or hypothetical outcomes." The experimental studies on time preference are exemplified by an elicitation from respondents' answers to such a question as "which would you prefer: $100 today or $150 one year from today?" FLO (2002) define discount factor as $\delta \equiv 1/(1+\rho)$, where ρ is a discount rate. Summarizing the estimates of the discount factor elicited in the previous literature, FLO (2002) point out three tendencies of the experimental researches. First, "there is tremendous variability in the estimates (the corresponding implicit annual discount rates range from -6% to infinity)." Second, "there is no evidence of methodological progress: the range of estimates is not shrinking over time." Third, "high discounting predominates, as most of the data points imply the rate of time preference well below unity, the value that represents equal weighting of present and future."

It may be premature to evaluate rightly the achievement of those attempts to liberalize the rate of discount from the tight DU framework. At least, that these attempts have made the consumption theory to be relatively free from the rigid formulation is welcome. They reveal the distance between real intertemporal choice and the elegant mathematical formulation of traditional theory of consumers. We are glad that psychologists, sociologists, behavioral economists, and neuroscientists are starting to enlighten the structure of human behavior toward time discount. Economists should be open to any criticisms that the standard formulation does not capture the essential features of human behavior that have been studied in other sciences (as a most recent review from economic, psychological, and neuroscience perspectives, see Berns et al. 2007).

4.3 *Counter-Critiques of Varying Time Preference*

On the other hand, it is unfair not to mention the counter arguments against these new interdisciplinary approaches. Thus, we will introduce two critiques against the psychological and experimental studies. One is an unpublished yet often referred chapter by Mulligan (1996) that casts doubts upon the quasihyperbolic discounting. The other critique is Joseph Schumpeter lecture at the European Economic Association by Rubinstein (2001), which concerns the role of experimental economics, and his own alternative to the quasihyperbolic discounting in interpreting experimental results.

4.3.1 Wealth Maximizer or Not

Mulligan (1996) considers a typical monetary experiment seen in some researches as follows. Question 1: "Would you like $10 today or $15 tomorrow?" and Question 2: "Would you like $10 in 100 days or $14 in 101 days?" Usual quasihyperbolic discounters could take the $10 in Question 1 and the $14 in Question 2. Mulligan then poses a simple question to proponents of quasihyperbolic discounting, "Do your hyperbolic discounters maximize wealth?"

> If the answer is "yes," and hyperbolic discounters can trade in a market, then they will answer Questions 1 and 2 to maximize wealth. If the interest rate (inclusive of all relevant transactions costs) is greater than 50%, the wealth maximizer chooses the $10 today because $10 today can, with interest, produce more than $15 tomorrow. If the interest rate is less than 50%, the wealth maximizer chooses the $15 tomorrow.

We should note that since the "exponential" discounters with the constant rate of time preference are also wealth maximizers, they should answer Questions 1 and 2 "in the same way as the wealth-maximizing hyperbolic discounter(s)." So, we cannot elicit quasihyperbolic discounting from Questions 1 and 2.

Otherwise if the answer is no, suppose due to their preference reversals, nonwealth-maximizing hyperbolic discounters might open to the following sequence of deals in "Dutch books." First, "Deal 1: ask the hyperbolic discounters to promise to pay you $10 in 100 days in exchange for $14 in 101 days." According to the Question 2, the nonwealth maximizers will do so. Second, "Deal 2: after 100 days have passed, collect your $10; offer the hyperbolic discounters $10 today in exchange for $15 tomorrow; and pay the $10." According to the Question 1, the hyperbolic discounters will accept the offer. When the 101st day arrives, "collect the $15 promised in Deal 2 and pay the $14 promised in Deal 1."

The Dutch books make you $1 every time. Nonwealth-maximizing hyperbolic discounters do not search for a cheaper Dutch booker, so that any Dutch bookers do not have to compete with each other for the attention of a hyperbolic discounter. Exchange between wealth maximizers and nonwealth-maximizing hyperbolic discounters can only lead to the exploitation of the latter.

Based upon results of these experiments, Mulligan (1996) concludes:

> It is illogical to use experimental evidence from psychological literature to support the hyperbolic discounting hypothesis unless one is willing to accept one of two propositions (a) hyperbolic discounters do not trade in markets or (b) hyperbolic discounters have no wealth. Neither of these propositions is compatible with an interesting economic analysis, so it is illogical to use the experimental results to defend hyperbolic discounting in economic analysis.

4.3.2 Alternative to Quasihyperbolic Discounting

Rubinstein (2001) discusses in a casual way quasihyperbolic discounting where psychological experiments have motivated a new theory. Consider the following questions Rubinstein actually experimented. "Q1: you can receive the amount of money indicated according to one of the two following schedules: A April 1, $1000; July 1, $1000; October 1, $1000; December 1, $1000 or B March 1, $997; June 1, $997; September 1, $997; November 1, $997." "Q2: you have to choose between A receiving $1000 on December 1 and B receiving $997 on November 1."

The hyperbolic discounting predicts that every subject choosing B in Q2 will choose B in Q1. That is because if a subject chooses B in Q2, then he or she is ready to sacrifice \$3 to advance the payment by 1 month, and he would find the \$3 sacrifice worthwhile to advance any one of the other three scheduled payments by 1 month. However, the actual experiment results say that only 34% chose B in Q1 while 54% of the subjects chose B in Q2.

To explain an anomaly for hyperbolic discounting, Rubinstein adopts an alternative of the similarity-based approach. The object of choice is of the form (x,t), where x is a prize received with a delay of t unit of time. In comparing two pairs (x,t) and (y,s), it is presupposed that we go through a three-stage procedure as follows:

Stage 1. The decision maker looks for dominance: if x is better than y and $t < s$, then a pair (x,t) is preferred to (y,s).
Stage 2. The decision maker looks for similarities between x and y and between t and s. If he or she finds similarity in one dimension, it determines its preference between the two pairs using the other dimension without similarity.
Stage 3. If the first two stages were not decisive, the choice is made using a different criterion.

Applying the similarity-based approach to the experiment above, Rubinstein explains as follows:

> In Q1 many subjects viewed the alternative as a paired sequence of dates and \$ amounts. The manipulation of subjects' behavior in this experiment was accomplished by triggering the similarity relation with regard to the sequence of dates. ... Many subjects preferred A over B ... since they viewed the sequence of dates (April 1, July 1, October 1, December 1) to be similar to the sequence (March 1, June 1, September 1, November 1) while they found the sequence of payments (\$1000, \$1000, \$1000, \$1000) less similar to (\$997, \$997, \$997, \$997) than \$1000 was to \$997.

Rubinstein finally points out, "the problem is that experimental findings do not justify the selection of one of the infinite number of functional forms which are consistent with them." As a result, "the basic procedural element which undermines the constant discounting model also undermines hyperbolic discounting."

Dialogues between the traditional and those who promote experiments as well as psychological approach are extremely useful. It will take more investigations and experiments to settle the dispute.[1]

5 Different Rates of Time Preference in the Theory of Capital Movements

So far, the topic of different or varying rate of time preference was discussed in rather philosophical or theoretical domain, or with respect to microeconomic household behavior – such as usury, forced savings, bonus scheme, and procrastination. Below, we would like to report an application to international economics by Cheng,

[1] As Solow once said, "Indeed the billiard board is crooked, but this is the only board in town." Whoever wants to introduce a change in paradigm has to convince the public that his/her new board is genuine.

Hamada, and Kamihigashi (2008; hereafter CHK). The research follows the spirit of Shimomura as indicated in the foreword of this chapter.

First, international investment behavior is discussed as the current account problem in a framework of trade theory. The imbalances in the current account generate the international credit and indebtedness. Second, however, capital movements can be analyzed as the equating process in the rate of return to capital, which Murray Kemp pioneered a long time ago. Moreover, international capital movements are regarded as the consequences of the process of overtime smoothing of consumption path among nations. In practice as seen in the IMF, this phenomenon was approached following the approach of trade balances, and policy discussions center on the need to alter the real exchange rate. The purpose of CHK is, however, to explore the implication of accumulation behavior for the determinant of international capital movements. In spite of the observation of large capital flows in the present world and in spite of the urge to give microfoundation to international economics (Obstfeld and Rogoff 1995), the literature for the economic explanation of large flows of capital movements is very limited. In particular, though capital movements are closely related to intertemporal behavior, the link of capital movements to rates of time preference was thoroughly studied only by a few pioneering works, notably by Buiter (1981) in a overlapping generation model. CHK formulate it with regard to the different rates of time preference among nations and among individuals who live in nations.[2]

CHK construct a simple framework of international capital movements that would explain the long-run tendency of international indebtedness among countries in the world. In a two-person differential game with identical production function, identical stationary labor force, and different rates of time preference, CHK have found that the stationary state of the Nash equilibrium exhibits a substantial credit of the more patient country. Unless rates of exogenous growth or the rates of time preference are different, there exists no stationary long-run equilibrium with a nonzero per-capita debt in this Nash formulation of two-country optimal growth. The magnitude of net international borrowing of a country depends on (1) the difference between the average rate of time preference of the individuals in the country and the average rate of time preference of the individuals in the world, (2) the scale of the economy measured by numbers of individuals, and (3) the scale of the world market.

Moreover, the CHK framework can be extended to a differential game version of the optimal saving model with multiple agents – a model that has essentially much in common to the model explored by Sorger (2008). CHK argue, contrary to the conventional views, that the situation with large discrepancies between creditors and debtors can be considered as a reasonable consequence of intertemporal

---

[2] In a framework analyzed in Hamada (1966), capital movements are explained solely by the intertemporal saving–investment process and trade flows are assumed to accommodate this intertemporal choice. In the actual world economy, both this kind of intertemporal choice and trade activities are working interactively but at the same time in a consistent manner. Hamada (1966) considered a two-country model given the assumption that saving ratios in the two countries are exogenously given. CHK give, instead, a microeconomic foundation to the savings behavior.

accumulation behavior of nations and individuals who possess different rates of time preference. Flows of capital movements are explained by the difference between macroeconomic variables of relevant countries, such as labor growth rate, technological growth rate, saving ratios, and underlying rates of time preference.

In fact, this is a differential game formulation, in terms of two players and in a simplified form of the Ramsey–Cass–Koopmans optimal growth problem analyzed by Sorger (2008). The formulation of CHK is simplified than his in a few ways. For example, the constant labor supply is assumed here, while in his formulation it comes as a conclusion. The competitive rental and wage formation is also assumed here, while in his formulation it is derived. Moreover, Sorger (2008) gives the following reason justifying this game-theoretic or oligopolistic saving behavior formulated here against the conventional wisdom that the accumulation behavior is determined by purely instantaneous rate of returns to capital and the rate of time preference. If rates of time preference differ across agents, then the agent with the lowest time discount rate will own the total capital in the long run. It is unconceivable that he or she, somebody like George Soros, will take the rate of return to capital as a given constant. He or she must take into account impacts of his or her action on the rate of returns.

CHK show, in the model with a representative agent for each country, that the world economy under free capital mobility will converge to the stationary state, where the rate of return to capital is equated to the average rate of time preference. However, the stationary per-capita borrowing of a less patient country (or lending of a more patient country) is different from zero except for coincidence and equal to the difference in the rates of time preference divided by the second derivative of production function. Though a difference in the rates of time preference is a necessary condition for the nontrivial value of the stationary international debt, it is shown that even a slight difference in the rates of time preference creates a large value of international debt or credit.

The result of CHK would be a good rationale for asserting that the current account balance or the absence of net indebtedness in the stationary state is not the norm but a strong assumption about the similarity of the rates of time preference between countries. As is also indicated above, in the mutually optimizing model with the Ricardian equivalence, the government spending would not affect the stationary value of indebtedness. Fiscal policies could be only a temporally remedy for the indebtedness in the short run.

6 Concluding Remarks

We have reviewed in this chapter the role of time preference in macroeconomic models. We covered some ground of psychological and experimental studies but, because of the limitation of space, we delegated these to surveys in special fields. Even from this short survey, the readers would understand that research free from the rigid formulation of the straightforward DU model is as if we would open the Pandora's box.

The axiomatic approach by Koopmans (1960) always serves as a reference point to assess the various approach to time preference. After more than half a century, the Ramsey formulation remains the prototype of associating capital accumulation behaviors with the rate of time preference. We have seen, among other development, many interesting new consequences of deviating our interest from the DU model in:

1. Making the rate of preference dependent upon the utility level
2. Making the capacity to preview the future as a part of human capital to which one can invest
3. Making the rate of time preference dependent upon the distance between the planning time and the occurrence time
4. Assuming agents constituting the economy diverse rates of time preference

In particular, case 3 creates additional problems of time inconsistency or the game between the present self and the future selves, and case 4 can be applied to the analysis of international capital movements.

References

Barro RJ (1999) Ramsey meets Laibson in the neoclassical growth model. Q J Econ 114:1125–1152

Becker GS, Mulligan CB (1997) The endogenous determination of time preference. Q J Econ 112:729–758

Bernheim D, Skinner J, Weinberg S (2001) What accounts for the variation in retirement wealth among households? Am Econ Rev 91:832–857

Berns GS, Laibson D, Loewenstein G (2007) Intertemporal choice – toward an integrative framework. Trends Cogn Sci 11:482–488

Böhm-Bawerk EV (1891) The positive theory of capital. Smart WA (transl.). MacMillan, London

Buiter WH (1981) Time preference and international lending and borrowing in an overlapping-generations model. J Polit Econ 89:769–797

Carroll CD (1992) The buffer-stock theory of saving: some macroeconomic evidence. Brook Pap Econ Act 2:61–156

Cass D (1965) Optimum growth in an aggregative model of capital accumulation. Rev Econ Stud 32:233–240

Cheng X, Hamada K, Kamihigashi T (2008) Toward a microfoundation of the theory of capital movements (in progress)

Deaton A, Paxson C (1994) Intertemporal choice and inequality. J Polit Econ 102:437–467

Endoh M, Hamada K, Shimomura K (2008) Can a preferential trade agreement benefit the neighbors without compensating them? Econ Growth Cent Discuss Pap 961

Fisher I (1930) The theory of interest. MacMillan, New York, NY

Frederick S, Loewenstein G, O'Donoghue T (2002) Time discounting and time preference: a critical review. J Econ Lit 40:351–401

Friedman M (1957) A theory of the consumption function. Princeton University Press, Princeton

Hamada K (1966) Economic growth and long-term international capital movements. Yale Econ Essays 6:49–96

Koopmans TC (1960) Stationary ordinal utility and impatience. Econometrica 28:287–309

Koopmans TC (1965) On the concept of optimal economic growth. In: The econometric approach to development planning. Pontif. Acad. Sc. Scripta Varia 28:225–300
Krusell P, Kuruscu B, Smith AA Jr (2002) Equilibrium welfare and government policy with quasi-geometric discounting. J Econ Theory 105:42–72
Laibson D (1997) Golden eggs and hyperbolic discounting. Q J Econ 112:443–477
Lawrance EC (1991) Poverty and the rate of time preference: evidence from panel data. J Polit Econ 99:54–77
Lucas RE, Stokey NL (1984) Optimal growth with many consumers. J Econ Theory 32:139–171
Mulligan CB (1996) A logical economist's argument against hyperbolic discounting. Mimeo
Obstfeld M, Rogoff K (1995) Exchange rate dynamics redux. J Polit Econ 103:624–660
Ogaki M, Atkeson A (1997) Rate of time preference, intertemporal elasticity of substitution, and level of wealth. Rev Econ Stat 79:564–572
Phelps ES (1961) The golden rule of accumulation. Am Econ Rev 51:638–642
Phelps ES, Pollak R (1968) On second-best national saving and game-equilibrium growth. Rev Econ Stud 35:185–199
Pigou AC (1920) The economics of welfare. MacMillan, London
Rae J (1834) The sociology theory of capital, reprinted edn. MacMillan, London
Ramsey FP (1928) A mathematical theory of saving. Econ J 38:543–559
Rubinstein A (2001) A theorist's view of experiments. Eur Econ Rev 45:615–628
Samuelson P (1937) A note on measurement of utility. Rev Econ Stud 4:155–161
Sorger G (2007) Strategic saving decisions in the infinite-horizon model. Econ Theory 36:353–377
Stroz RH (1955) Myopia and inconsistency in dynamic utility maximization. Rev Econ Stud 23:165–180
Uzawa H (1968) Time preference, the consumption function, and optimum asset holdings. In: Wolfe JN (ed) Value, capital, and growth: papers in honour of Sir John Hicks. The University of Edinburgh Press, Edinburgh

Characterization of Equilibrium Paths in a Two-Sector Economy with CES Production Functions and Sector-Specific Externality[1]

Miki Matsuo, Kazuo Nishimura(✉), Tomoya Sakagami, and Alain Venditti

Abstract In this chapter, we study a two-sector CES economy with sector-specific externality as described by Nishimura and Venditti (J Difference Equ Appl 10:1153–1169, 2004). We characterize the equilibrium paths in the case that allows negative externality as that equlibrium paths were not explicitly discussed by Nishimura and Venditti. We show how the degree of externality affects the local behavior of the equilibrium path around the steady state.

1 Introduction

This chapter characterizes the local behavior of the equilibrium paths around the steady state in a two-sector model with CES production functions and sector-specific externality. It is well known that externalities may cause indeterminate equilibrium paths in an infinite horizon model. Benhabib and Farmer (1994) have shown that indeterminacy could occur in a one-sector growth model with both externality and increasing returns. In their model, the production function has constant returns to scale from the private perspective, while it has increasing returns to scale from the social perspective. Since then, there have been many chapters about the existence of indeterminate equilibria in dynamic general equilibrium models. However, until Benhabib and Nishimura (1998, 1999), most of the literature dealt with models in which the production function has increasing returns to scale from the social perspective. They proved indeed that indeterminacy may arise in a continuous time economy in which the production functions from the social perspective have constant returns to scale. Benhabib et al. (2002) then studied a discrete-time two-sector

[1] This chapter is dedicated to Koji Shimomura. We miss Koji who was a very good friend and a distinguished economist.

K. Nishimura
Institute of Economic Research, Kyoto University, Japan, e-mail: nishimura@kier.kyoto-u.ac.jp

T. Kamihigashi and L. Zhao (eds.) *International Trade and Economic Dynamics – Essays in Memory of Koji Shimomura.*

model with sector-specific external effects. They assumed that each sector has a Cobb–Douglas production function with positive sector-specific externalities, which are a special case of CES functions, and there is an infinitely lived representative agent with a linear utility function. Under these assumptions, they provided conditions in which indeterminacy may occur even if the production functions have decreasing returns to scale from the social perspective. Nishimura and Venditti (2004) consider a CES economy with sector-specific external effects and partial depreciation of capital. They study the interplay between the elasticity of capital–labor substitution and the rate of depreciation of capital, and its influence on the local behavior of the equilibrium paths in the neighborhood of the steady state.

In this chapter, we study the Nishimura and Venditti (2004) model, focussing on the external effect of the capital–labor ratio in the pure capital good sector and characterize the equilibrium paths in the case that allows negative externality. That particular scenario was not explicitly discussed by Nishimura and Venditti. We assume indeed that the externality is given by the capital stock per capita. Such a formulation then implies that for a given level of capital, the externality from labor is negative. We demonstrate that the degree of externality affects the local behavior of the equilibrium path around the steady state.

In Sect. 2 we describe the model. We discuss the existence of a steady state and give the local characterization of the equilibrium paths around the steady state in Sect. 3. Section 4 contains some concluding comments.

2 The Model

We consider a two-sector model with an infinitely lived representative agent. We assume that its single period linear utility function is given by

$$u(c_t) = c_t.$$

We assume that the consumption good, c, and the capital good, y, are produced with a CES technology.

$$c_t = \left[\alpha_1 K_{ct}^{-\rho_c} + \alpha_2 L_{ct}^{-\rho_c}\right]^{-\frac{1}{\rho_c}}, \tag{1}$$

$$y_t = \left[\beta_1 K_{yt}^{-\rho_y} + \beta_2 L_{yt}^{-\rho_y} + e_t\right]^{-\frac{1}{\rho_y}}, \tag{2}$$

where $\rho_c, \rho_y > -1$, and e_t represents the time-dependent externality in the investment good sector. Let the elasticity of capital–labor substitution in each sector be $\sigma_c = \frac{1}{1+\rho_c} \geq 0$ and $\sigma_y = \frac{1}{1+\rho_y} \geq 0$. We assume that the externalities are as follows:

$$e_t = b\overline{K}_{yt}^{-\rho_y} - b\overline{L}_{yt}^{-\rho_y}, \tag{3}$$

where $b > 0$, and $\overline{K}_y$ and $\overline{L}_y$ represents the economy-wide average values. The representative agent takes these economy-wide average values as given.

Definition 1. We call $y = \left[\beta_1 K_y^{-\rho_y} + \beta_2 L_y^{-\rho_y} + e\right]^{-\frac{1}{\rho_y}}$ the production function from the private perspective, and $y = \left[(\beta_1 + b)K_y^{-\rho_y} + (\beta_2 - b)L_y^{-\rho_y}\right]^{-\frac{1}{\rho_y}}$ the production function from the social perspective.

In the rest of the chapter, we assume that $\alpha_1 + \alpha_2 = \beta_1 + \beta_2 = 1$. Thus, if $\hat{\beta}_1 = \beta_1 + b$ and $\hat{\beta}_2 = \beta_2 - b$, then $\hat{\beta}_1 + \hat{\beta}_2 = 1$.

Remark 1. Notice that the externality (3) may be expressed as follows

$$e = b\overline{L}_y^{-\rho_y}\left[\left(\frac{\overline{K}_y}{\overline{L}_y}\right)^{-\rho_y} - 1\right]. \tag{4}$$

Now consider the production function from the social perspective as given in Definition 1. Dividing both sides by L_y, we get denoting $k_y = K_y/L_y$ and $\tilde{y} = y/L_y$

$$\tilde{y} = \left[(\beta_1 + b)\, k_y^{-\rho_y} + (\beta_2 - b)\right]^{-\frac{1}{\rho_y}}. \tag{5}$$

From (4) and (5) we derive that the externality is given in terms of the capital–labor ratio in the investment good sector. This implies that for a given level of capital $\overline{K}_y$, the externality from labor $\overline{L}_y$ is negative.

The aggregate capital is divided between sectors,

$$k_t = K_{ct} + K_{yt},$$

and the labor endowment is normalized to one and divided between sectors,

$$L_{ct} + L_{yt} = 1.$$

The capital accumulation equation is

$$k_{t+1} = y_t.$$

Thus capital depreciates completely in one period. To simplify the formulation, we assume that both technologies are characterized by the same properties of substitution, that is, $\rho_c = \rho_y = \rho$.

The consumer optimization problem is given by

$$\begin{aligned}
\max \quad & \sum_{t=0}^{\infty} \delta^t \left[\alpha_1 K_{ct}^{-\rho} + \alpha_2 L_{ct}^{-\rho}\right]^{-\frac{1}{\rho}} \\
s.t. \quad & y_t = \left[\beta_1 K_{yt}^{-\rho} + \beta_2 L_{yt}^{-\rho} + e_t\right]^{-\frac{1}{\rho}}, \\
& 1 = L_{ct} + L_{yt}, \\
& k_t = K_{ct} + K_{yt},
\end{aligned}$$

$$y_t = k_{t+1},$$
$$k_0, \ \{e_t\}_{t=0}^{\infty} \ \text{given}, \tag{6}$$

where $\delta \in (0,\ 1)$ is the discount factor. p_t, r_t, and w_t, respectively, denote the price of capital goods, the rental rate of the capital goods, and the wage rate of labor at time $t \geq 0$.[2] For any sequences $\{e_t\}_{t=0}^{\infty}$ of external effects that the representative agent considers as given, the Lagrangian at time $t \geq 0$ is defined as follows:

$$\mathscr{L}_t = \left[\alpha_1 K_{ct}^{-\rho} + \alpha_2 L_{ct}^{-\rho}\right]^{-\frac{1}{\rho}} + p_t\left[\left(\beta_1 K_{yt}^{-\rho} + \beta_2 L_{yt}^{-\rho} + e_t\right)^{-\frac{1}{\rho}} - k_{t+1}\right]$$
$$+ r_t\left(k_t - K_{ct} - K_{yt}\right) + w_t\left(1 - L_{ct} - L_{yt}\right). \tag{7}$$

Then the first order conditions derived from the Lagrangian are as follows:

$$\frac{\partial \mathscr{L}_t}{\partial K_{ct}} = \alpha_1\left(\frac{c_t}{K_{ct}}\right)^{1+\rho} - r_t = 0, \tag{8}$$

$$\frac{\partial \mathscr{L}_t}{\partial L_{ct}} = \alpha_2\left(\frac{c_t}{L_{ct}}\right)^{1+\rho} - w_t = 0, \tag{9}$$

$$\frac{\partial \mathscr{L}_t}{\partial K_{yt}} = p\beta_1\left(\frac{y_t}{K_{yt}}\right)^{1+\rho} - r_t = 0, \tag{10}$$

$$\frac{\partial \mathscr{L}_t}{\partial L_{yt}} = p\beta_2\left(\frac{y_t}{L_{yt}}\right)^{1+\rho} - w_t = 0. \tag{11}$$

From the above first order conditions, we derive the following equation,

$$\left(\frac{\alpha_1/\alpha_2}{\beta_1/\beta_2}\right) = \left(\frac{K_{ct}/L_{ct}}{K_{yt}/L_{yt}}\right)^{1+\rho}. \tag{12}$$

If $\alpha_1/\alpha_2 > (<) \beta_1/\beta_2$, then the consumption (capital) good sector is capital intensive from the private perspective.

For any value of (k_t, y_t), solving the first order conditions with respect to K_{ct}, K_{yt}, L_{ct}, and L_{yt} gives inputs as functions of capital stock at time t and $t+1$, and external effect, namely,

$$K_{ct} = K_c\left(k_t, y_t, e_t\right), \ \ L_{ct} = L_c\left(k_t, y_t, e_t\right),$$
$$K_{yt} = K_y\left(k_t, y_t, e_t\right), \ L_{yt} = L_y\left(k_t, y_t, e_t\right).$$

For any given sequence $\{e_t\}_{t=0}^{\infty}$, we define the efficient production frontier as follows:

$$T\left(k_t, k_{t+1}, e_t\right) = \left[\alpha_1 K_c\left(k_t, y_t, e_t\right)^{-\rho} + \alpha_2 L_c\left(k_t, y_t, e_t\right)^{-\rho}\right]^{-\frac{1}{\rho}}.$$

---

[2] We normalize the price of consumption goods to one.

Using the envelope theorem, we derive the equilibrium prices.[3]

$$T_2(k_t, k_{t+1}, e_t) = -p_t, \tag{13}$$

$$T_1(k_t, k_{t+1}, e_t) = r_t. \tag{14}$$

Next we solve the intertemporal problem (6). In this model, the lifetime utility function becomes

$$U = \sum_{t=0}^{\infty} \delta^t T(k_t, k_{t+1}, e_t).$$

From the first order conditions with respect to k_{t+1}, we obtain the Euler equation

$$T_2(k_t, k_{t+1}, e_t) + \delta T_1(k_{t+1}, k_{t+2}, e_{t+1}) = 0. \tag{15}$$

The solution of (15) also has to satisfy the following transversality condition

$$\lim_{t \to +\infty} \delta^t k_t T_1(k_t, k_{t+1}, e_t) = 0. \tag{16}$$

We denote the solution of this problem $\{k_t\}_{t=0}^{\infty}$. This path depends on the choice of the sequence $\{e_t\}_{t=0}^{\infty}$. If the sequence $\{e_t\}_{t=0}^{\infty}$ satisfies

$$e_t = bK_y(k_t, y_t, e_t)^{-\rho} - bL_y(k_t, y_t, e_t)^{-\rho}, \tag{17}$$

then $\{\hat{k}_t\}_{t=0}^{\infty}$ is called an equilibrium path.

Definition 2. $\{k_t\}_{t=0}^{\infty}$ is an equilibrium path if $\{k_t\}_{t=0}^{\infty}$ satisfies (15), (16), and (17).

Solving (17) for e_t, we derive e_t as a function of $(k_t,\ k_{t+1})$, namely $e_t = \hat{e}(k_t, k_{t+1})$. Let us substitute $\hat{e}(k_t, k_{t+1})$ in (13) and (14) and define the equilibrium prices as

$$p_t = p_t(k_t, k_{t+1}),$$

$$r_t = r_t(k_t, k_{t+1}).$$

Then the Euler equation (15) evaluated at $\{k_t\}_{t=0}^{\infty}$ is

$$-p(k_t, k_{t+1}) + \delta r(k_{t+1}, k_{t+2}) = 0. \tag{18}$$

3 Steady State and Local Stability Properties

Definition 3. A steady state is defined by $k_t = k_{t+1} = y_t = k^*$ and is given by the solution of $T_2(k^*, k^*, e^*) + \delta T_1(k^*, k^*, e^*) = 0$ with $e^* = \hat{e}(k^*, k^*)$.

---

[3] See Takayama (1997, pp. 160–165) for the envelope theorem. Using the envelope theorem, we get $\frac{\partial \mathscr{L}_t}{\partial k_t} = \frac{\partial T}{\partial k_t}$ and $\frac{\partial \mathscr{L}_t}{\partial k_{t+1}} = \frac{\partial T}{\partial k_{t+1}}$. This is equivalent to (13) and (14).

In the rest of the chapter, we assume the following restriction on parameters' values that guarantees all the steady state values are positive.

Assumption 1. The parameters δ, β_1, b, and ρ satisfy

$$(\delta\beta_1)^{\frac{-\rho}{1+\rho}} < \beta_1 + b.$$

From the proof given in Nishimura and Venditti (2004), we can obtain the steady state value.

Proposition 1. *In this model, there exists a unique stationary capital stock k^* such that*

$$k^* = \left\{1 + \left(\frac{\alpha_1\beta_2}{\alpha_2\beta_1}\right)^{\frac{-1}{1+\rho}} (\delta\beta_1)^{\frac{-1}{1+\rho}} \left[1 - (\delta\beta_1)^{\frac{1}{1+\rho}}\right]\right\}^{-1} \left[\frac{1-\hat{\beta}_1(\delta\beta_1)^{\frac{-\rho}{1+\rho}}}{\hat{\beta}_2}\right]^{\frac{1}{\rho}}. \quad (19)$$

To study the local behavior of the equilibrium path around the steady state k^*, we linearize the Euler equation (15) at the steady state k^* and obtain the following characteristic equation:

$$\delta T_{12}\lambda^2 + [\delta T_{11} + T_{22}]\lambda + T_{21} = 0,$$

or

$$\delta\lambda^2 + \left[\delta\frac{T_{11}}{T_{12}} + \frac{T_{22}}{T_{12}}\right]\lambda + \frac{T_{21}}{T_{12}} = 0. \quad (20)$$

As shown in Nishimura and Venditti (2004), the expressions of the characteristic roots are as follows:

Proposition 2. *The characteristic roots of (20) are*

$$\lambda_1 = \frac{1}{(\delta\beta_2)^{\frac{1}{1+\rho}}\left[\left(\frac{\beta_1}{\beta_2}\right)^{\frac{1}{1+\rho}} - \left(\frac{\alpha_1}{\alpha_2}\right)^{\frac{1}{1+\rho}}\right]}, \quad (21)$$

$$\lambda_2(b) = \frac{(\delta\beta_2)^{\frac{1}{1+\rho}}\left[\frac{\beta_1+b}{\beta_1}\left(\frac{\beta_1}{\beta_2}\right)^{\frac{1}{1+\rho}} - \frac{\beta_2-b}{\beta_2}\left(\frac{\alpha_1}{\alpha_2}\right)^{\frac{1}{1+\rho}}\right]}{\delta}.$$

The roots of the characteristic equation determine the local behavior of the equilibrium paths. The sign of λ_1 is determined by factor intensity differences from the private perspective.[4]

Remark 2. The capital/labor ratio externality, that is, the negative labor externality, implies that the characteristic root $\lambda_2(b)$ in Proposition 2 is larger than the corresponding characteristic root from Nishimura and Venditti (2004).

[4] If $\alpha_2\beta_1 - \alpha_1\beta_2 > 0$, the capital good sector is capital intensive from the private perspective.

We now characterize the equilibrium paths in this model. In particular, we can show that the local behavior of the equilibrium path around the steady state changes according to the degree of external effect in the capital good sector.

Definition 4. A steady state k^* is called locally indeterminate if there exists $\varepsilon > 0$ such that for any $k_0 \in (k^* - \varepsilon, k^* + \varepsilon)$, there are infinitely many equilibrium paths converging to the steady state.

As there is one predetermined variable, the capital stock, local indeterminacy occurs if the stable manifold has two dimensions, that is, if the two characteristic roots are within the unit circle. We also present conditions for local determinacy (saddle-point stability) in which there exists a unique equilibrium path. Such a configuration occurs if the stable manifold has one dimension, that is, if one root is outside the unit circle while the other is inside.

When the investment good is capital intensive, local indeterminacy cannot occur. However, depending on the size of the externality, saddle-point stability or total instability may occur.

Proposition 3. *Suppose that the capital good sector is capital intensive from the private perspective, that is, $\alpha_2\beta_1 > \alpha_1\beta_2$. The following cases hold:*

(1) *If $\rho \in (-1,0)$, there is $b(\delta) > \beta_2$ such that the steady state is a saddle point for $b \in [0, b(\delta))$ and is totally unstable for $b > b(\delta)$.*
(2) *If $\rho = 0$, the steady state is a saddle point for $b \in [0, \beta_2)$ and is totally unstable for $b > \beta_2$.*
(3) *If $\rho > 0$, there exists $0 < \delta_2 < 1$ and $0 < b(\delta) < \beta_2$ such that when $\delta \in (\delta_2, 1)$, the steady state is a saddle point for $b < b(\delta)$ and is totally unstable for $b > b(\delta)$. When $\delta \in (0, \delta_2)$, the steady state is totally unstable.*

Proof. Notice that $\lambda_1 > 0$ and define $\delta_1 \equiv \beta_2^{-1}\left[(\beta_1/\beta_2)^{\frac{1}{1+\rho}} - (\alpha_1/\alpha_2)^{\frac{1}{1+\rho}}\right]^{-1-\rho} > 1$.[5] From this we obtain $\lambda_1 = (\delta_1/\delta)^{\frac{1}{1+\rho}} > 1$ for any $\delta \in (0,1)$. Since $(\beta_1 + b)/\beta_1 > 1$ and $(\beta_2 - b)/\beta_2 < 1$, $\lambda_2(b)$ is always positive. Thus $\lambda_2(b)$ is an increasing function of b. For $b = 0$, we get $\lambda_2(0) = \delta^{-\frac{\rho}{1+\rho}}\delta_1^{-\frac{1}{1+\rho}}$ and for $b = \beta_2$, we have $\lambda_2(\beta_2) = (\delta\beta_1)^{\frac{-\rho}{1+\rho}}$.

(1) If $-1 < \rho < 0$, $0 < \lambda_2(0) < 1$, and $\lambda_2(\beta_2) < 1$. Therefore, there is $b(\delta) > \beta_2$ such that $0 < \lambda_2(b) < 1$ for $b \in (0, b(\delta))$, and $\lambda_2(b) > 1$ for $b > b(\delta)$.
(2) If $\rho = 0$, $0 < \lambda_2(0) = \delta_1^{-1} < 1$, and $\lambda_2(\beta_2) = 1$. Therefore, $\lambda_2(b) < 1$ for $b < \beta_2$ and $\lambda_2(b) > 1$ for $b > \beta_2$.
(3) If $\rho > 0$, $0 < \lambda_2(0) < 1$ for $\delta_2 < \delta < 1$ and $\lambda_2(0) > 1$ for $\delta \in (0, \delta_2)$ with $\delta_2 = \delta_1^{-\frac{1}{\rho}}$. Moreover $\lambda_2(\beta_2) > 1$. Therefore, if δ lies in $(\delta_2, 1)$, there is $b(\delta) \in (0, \beta_2)$ such that $\lambda_2(b) < 1$ for $b \in (0, b(\delta))$ and $\lambda_2(b) > 1$ for $b > b(\delta)$. If δ lies in $(0, \delta_2)$, then $\lambda_2(0) > 0$ and $\lambda_2(\beta_2) > 1$, and therefore $\lambda_2(b) > 1$ for all $b > 0$. □

[5] Note that $\delta_1 = \alpha_2\left[(\alpha_2\beta_1)^{\frac{1}{1+\rho}} - (\alpha_1\beta_2)^{\frac{1}{1+\rho}}\right]^{-1-\rho} > \frac{\alpha_2}{(\alpha_2\beta_1)} = \frac{1}{\beta_1} > 1$.

Remark 3. Consider the production function from the social perspective as given in Definition 1 and recall from (5) that we can express it as follows:

$$\tilde{y} = \left[(\beta_1 + b)k_y^{-\rho_y} + (\beta_2 - b)\right]^{-\frac{1}{\rho_y}}. \tag{22}$$

According to $b \gtrless \beta_2$, the following inequality holds: for any $\eta > 1$,

$$\begin{aligned}\left[(\beta_1 + b)(\eta k_y)^{-\rho} + (\beta_2 - b)\right]^{-\frac{1}{\rho}} &\gtrless \left[(\beta_1 + b)(\eta k_y)^{-\rho} + \eta^{-\rho}(\beta_2 - b)\right]^{-\frac{1}{\rho}} \\ &= \eta\left[(\beta_1 + b)k_y^{-\rho} + (\beta_2 - b)\right]^{-\frac{1}{\rho}}.\end{aligned}$$

If b is larger than β_2, the function $\tilde{y}$ exhibits increasing returns. If b is smaller than β_2, the function $\tilde{y}$ exhibits decreasing returns. Note that larger values of b contribute to have total instability.

Next we present our results assuming that the capital good is labor-intensive from the private perspective, that is, $\alpha_2\beta_1 - \alpha_1\beta_2 < 0$. This case results in local indeterminacy. By rewriting (21), the characteristic roots are

$$\begin{aligned}\lambda_1 &= -\frac{1}{(\delta\beta_2)^{\frac{1}{1+\rho}}\left[\left(\frac{\alpha_1}{\alpha_2}\right)^{\frac{1}{1+\rho}} - \left(\frac{\beta_1}{\beta_2}\right)^{\frac{1}{1+\rho}}\right]}, \\ \lambda_2(b) &= -\frac{(\delta\beta_2)^{\frac{1}{1+\rho}}\left[\frac{\beta_2-b}{\beta_2}\left(\frac{\alpha_1}{\alpha_2}\right)^{\frac{1}{1+\rho}} - \frac{\beta_1+b}{\beta_1}\left(\frac{\beta_1}{\beta_2}\right)^{\frac{1}{1+\rho}}\right]}{\delta}.\end{aligned} \tag{23}$$

To get $\lambda_1 \in (-1,0)$, we need, however, to suppose a slightly stronger condition than simply ensuring the capital good sector to be labor-intensive from the private perspective. The capital intensity difference $\alpha_1\beta_2 - \alpha_2\beta_1$ needs to be large enough and the discount factor has to be close enough to 1.

Proposition 4. *Assume that* $(\alpha_1\beta_2)^{\frac{1}{1+\rho}} - (\alpha_2\beta_1)^{\frac{1}{1+\rho}} > \alpha_2^{\frac{1}{1+\rho}}$ *and* $\delta \in (\delta_3, 1)$, *with* $\delta_3 = \beta_2^{-1}\left[(\beta_1/\beta_2)^{\frac{1}{1+\rho}} - (\alpha_1/\alpha_2)^{\frac{1}{1+\rho}}\right]^{-1-\rho} < 1$. *Then the following cases hold:*

(1) *If* $\rho \in (-1,0)$, *there exist* $\underline{b}(\delta) \in (0, \beta_2)$ *and* $\overline{b}(\delta) > \beta_2$ *such that the steady state is a saddle point for* $b \in (0, \underline{b}(\delta)) \cup (\overline{b}(\delta), +\infty)$ *and is locally indeterminate for* $b \in (\underline{b}(\delta), \overline{b}(\delta))$.
(2) *If* $\rho = 0$, *the steady state is a saddle point for* $b \in (0, \beta_2 - 2\alpha_2) \cup (\beta_2, +\infty)$ *and is locally indeterminate for* $b \in (\beta_2 - 2\alpha_2, \beta_2)$.
(3) *If* $\rho > 0$, *there are* $\underline{b}(\delta)$ *and* $\overline{b}(\delta)$ *in* $(0, \beta_2)$ *such that the steady state is a saddle point for* $b \in (0, \underline{b}(\delta)) \cup (\overline{b}(\delta), +\infty)$ *and is locally indeterminate for* $b \in (\underline{b}(\delta), \overline{b}(\delta))$.

Proof. If $(\alpha_1\beta_2)^{\frac{1}{1+\rho}} - (\alpha_2\beta_1)^{\frac{1}{1+\rho}} > \alpha_2^{\frac{1}{1+\rho}}$ and $\delta \in (\delta_3, 1)$, then $-1 < \lambda_1 < 0$. The size of $\lambda_2(b)$ is determined in the following way. Recall that $\lambda_2(b)$ is increasing in b. For $b = 0$, $\lambda_2(0) = 1/\delta\lambda_1 < -1$ by the above hypothesis and for $b = \beta_2$, $\lambda_2(\beta_2) = (\delta\beta_1)^{\frac{-\rho}{1+\rho}}$.

(1) If $-1 < \rho < 0$, $\lambda_2(\beta_2) < 1$. Therefore, there exist $\underline{b}(\delta) \in (0, \beta_2)$ and $\overline{b}(\delta) > \beta_2$ such that $\lambda_2 < -1$ for $b \in (0, \underline{b}(\delta))$, $-1 < \lambda_2 < 1$ for any $b \in (\underline{b}(\delta), \overline{b}(\delta))$ and $\lambda_2 > 1$ for any $b > \overline{b}(\delta)$.
(2) If $\rho = 0$, $\lambda_2(\beta_2) = 1$. Therefore, $\lambda_2(b) < -1$ for $b \in (0, \beta_2 - 2\alpha_2)$, $-1 < \lambda_2(b) < 1$ for $b \in (\beta_2 - 2\alpha_2, \beta_2)$, and $\lambda_2(b) > 1$ for $b > \beta_2$.
(3) If $\rho > 0$, $\lambda_2(\beta_2) > 1$. Therefore, there exist $\underline{b}(\delta)$ and $\overline{b}(\delta)$ in $(0, \beta_2)$, such that $\lambda_2(b) < -1$ for $b \in (0, \underline{b}(\delta))$, $-1 < \lambda_2(b) < 1$ for $b \in (\underline{b}(\delta), \overline{b}(\delta))$, and $\lambda_2(b) > 1$ for $b > \overline{b}(\delta)$. □

Notice that intermediary values for b are necessary to get local indeterminacy. Indeed, values of b that are too small or too large imply saddle-point stability.

Remark 4. In Proposition 4 we consider restrictions implying that the first characteristic root λ_1 is negative and larger than -1. These restrictions also imply that the second characteristic root is such that $\lambda_2(0) < -1$. As the characteristic root $\lambda_2(b)$ is an increasing function of b, a large enough (but not too large) amount of externalities ensures the existence of local indeterminacy. Building on Remark 2, we also derive that local indeterminacy is more likely in our framework than in that of Nishimura and Venditti (2004) in the sense that their framework requires a larger amount of externalities.

Next we still assume that capital goods are labor-intensive from the private perspective with $\alpha_2\beta_1 - \alpha_1\beta_2 < 0$, but we make λ_1 an unstable root, that is, $\lambda_1 < -1$. Two cases need to be considered: $(\alpha_1\beta_2)^{\frac{1}{1+\rho}} - (\alpha_2\beta_1)^{\frac{1}{1+\rho}} > \alpha_2^{\frac{1}{1+\rho}}$ and $\delta \in (0, \delta_3)$, as well as $(\alpha_1\beta_2)^{\frac{1}{1+\rho}} - (\alpha_2\beta_1)^{\frac{1}{1+\rho}} < \alpha_2^{\frac{1}{1+\rho}}$.

Proposition 5. *Suppose that the capital good sector is labor-intensive from the private perspective and let* $\delta_4 = \beta_2^{\frac{1}{\rho}} \left[(\beta_1/\beta_2)^{\frac{1}{1+\rho}} - (\alpha_1/\alpha_2)^{\frac{1}{1+\rho}}\right]^{\frac{1+\rho}{\rho}}$.

(1) *If* $(\alpha_1\beta_2)^{\frac{1}{1+\rho}} - (\alpha_2\beta_1)^{\frac{1}{1+\rho}} > \alpha_2^{\frac{1}{1+\rho}}$ *and* $\delta \in (0, \delta_3)$, *the following results hold:*
  (a) *Let* $\rho \in (-1, 0)$. *If* $\delta \in (0, \delta_4)$, *then there exist* $\underline{b}(\delta) \in (0, \beta_2)$ *and* $\overline{b}(\delta) > \beta_2$ *such that the steady state is a saddle point for* $b \in (\underline{b}(\delta), \overline{b}(\delta))$ *and is totally unstable for* $b \in (0, \underline{b}(\delta)) \cup (\overline{b}(\delta), +\infty)$. *If* $\delta \in (\delta_4, \delta_3)$, *then there exists* $\overline{b}(\delta) > \beta_2$ *such that the steady state is a saddle point for* $b \in (0, \overline{b}(\delta))$ *and is totally unstable for* $b > \overline{b}(\delta)$.
  (b) *Let* $\rho = 0$. *Then the steady state is a saddle point for* $b \in (\beta_2 - 2\alpha_2, \beta_2)$ *and is totally unstable for* $b \in (0, \beta_2 - 2\alpha_2) \cup (\beta_2, +\infty)$.
  (c) *Let* $\rho > 0$. *Then there exist* $\underline{b}(\delta), \overline{b}(\delta) \in (0, \beta_2)$ *such that the steady state is a saddle point for* $b \in (\underline{b}(\delta), \overline{b}(\delta))$ *and is totally unstable for* $b \in (0, \underline{b}(\delta)) \cup (\overline{b}(\delta), +\infty)$.

(2) *If* $(\alpha_1\beta_2)^{\frac{1}{1+\rho}} - (\alpha_2\beta_1)^{\frac{1}{1+\rho}} < \alpha_2^{\frac{1}{1+\rho}}$, *the following results hold:*

- *(a) Let* $\rho \in (-1,0)$. *Then there exists* $\overline{b}(\delta) > \beta_2$ *such that the steady state is saddle point for* $b \in \left(0,\overline{b}(\delta)\right)$ *and totally unstable for* $b > \overline{b}(\delta)$.
- *(b) Let* $\rho = 0$. *Then the steady state is saddle point for* $b \in (0,\beta_2)$ *and totally unstable for* $b > \beta_2$.
- *(c) Let* $\rho > 0$. *If* $\delta \in (0,\delta_4)$, *then there exist* $\underline{b}(\delta) \in (0,\beta_2)$ *and* $\overline{b}(\delta) > \beta_2$ *such that the steady state is saddle point for* $b \in \left(\underline{b}(\delta),\overline{b}(\delta)\right)$ *and totally unstable for* $b \in (0,\underline{b}(\delta)) \cup (\overline{b}(\delta),+\infty)$. *If* $\delta \in (\delta_4,1)$, *then there exists* $\overline{b}(\delta) > \beta_2$ *such that the steady state is saddle point for* $b \in \left(0,\overline{b}(\delta)\right)$ *and totally unstable for* $b > \overline{b}(\delta)$.

Proof. We assume here that $\lambda_1 < -1$. Recall that $\lambda_2(b)$ increases with b. Moreover, for $b = 0$, we get $\lambda_2(0) = -\delta^{-\frac{\rho}{1+\rho}}\delta_3^{-\frac{1}{1+\rho}}$, with δ_3 as defined in Proposition 4, and for $b = \beta_2$, we get $\lambda_2(\beta_2) = (\delta\beta_1)^{\frac{-\rho}{1+\rho}}$. We easily get $\lambda_2(0) \in (-1,0)$ if and only if $\delta^\rho > \delta_3^{-1}$. As shown above, two cases have to be considered:

(1) Let $(\alpha_1\beta_2)^{\frac{1}{1+\rho}} - (\alpha_2\beta_1)^{\frac{1}{1+\rho}} > \alpha_2^{\frac{1}{1+\rho}}$ and $\delta \in (0,\delta_3)$ with $\delta_3 < 1$.

- (a) When $-1 < \rho < 0$, we get $\lambda_2(\beta_2) < 1$ and $\lambda_2(0) < -1$ if and only if $\delta < \delta_3^{-\frac{1}{\rho}} \equiv \delta_4$. It follows then that $\delta_4 < \delta_3$ as $\delta_3^{-\frac{1+\rho}{\rho}} < 1$. We conclude that $\lambda_2(0) < -1$ if $0 < \delta < \delta_4$, while $\lambda_2(0) > -1$ if $\delta \in (\delta_4,\delta_3)$. Therefore, if δ lies in $(0,\delta_4)$, there exist $\underline{b}(\delta) \in (0,\beta_2)$ and $\overline{b}(\delta) > \beta_2$ such that $\lambda_2(b) < -1$ for $b \in (0,\underline{b}(\delta))$, $-1 < \lambda_2(b) < 1$ for $b \in \left(\underline{b}(\delta),\overline{b}(\delta)\right)$, and $\lambda_2(b) > 1$ for $b > \overline{b}(\delta)$. If δ lies in (δ_4,δ_3), there exists $b(\delta) > \beta_2$ such that $-1 < \lambda_2(b) < 1$ for $b \in (0,b(\delta))$ and $\lambda_2(b) > 1$ for $b > b(\delta)$.
- (b) If $\rho = 0$, $\lambda_2(0) < -1$, and $\lambda_2(\beta_2) = 1$. Therefore, $-1 < \lambda_2(b) < 1$ for $b \in (\beta_2 - 2\alpha_2, \beta_2)$ and $\lambda_2(b) > 1$ for $b \in (0,\beta_2 - 2\alpha_2)$ or $b > \beta_2$.
- (c) If $\rho > 0$, then $\delta_4 > \delta_3$ and thus $\lambda_2(0) < -1$ for any $\delta \in (0,\delta_3)$. Moreover $\lambda_2(\beta_2) > 1$. Therefore, there exist $\underline{b}(\delta)$ and $\overline{b}(\delta)$ in $(0,\beta_2)$ such that $\lambda_2(0) < -1$ for $b \in (0,\underline{b}(\delta))$, $-1 < \lambda_2(b) < 1$ for $b \in \left(\underline{b}(\delta),\overline{b}(\delta)\right)$, and $\lambda_2(0) > 1$ for $b > \overline{b}(\delta)$.

(2) Let $(\alpha_1\beta_2)^{\frac{1}{1+\rho}} - (\alpha_2\beta_1)^{\frac{1}{1+\rho}} < \alpha_2^{\frac{1}{1+\rho}}$. In this case we have $\delta_3 > 1$.

- (a) When $-1 < \rho < 0$, $\lambda_2(\beta_2) < 1$. Moreover, we get $\delta^\rho > 1 > \delta_3^{-1}$ so that $\lambda_2(0) > -1$. Then there exists $\overline{b}(\delta) > \beta_2$ such that $-1 < \lambda_2(b) < 1$ for $b \in \left(0,\overline{b}(\delta)\right)$, and $\lambda_2(b) > 1$ for $b > \overline{b}(\delta)$.
- (b) If $\rho = 0$, $-1 < \lambda_2(0) < 0$ and $\lambda_2(\beta_2) = 1$. Therefore, $-1 < \lambda_2(b) < 1$ for $b \in (0,\beta_2)$ and $\lambda_2(b) > 1$ for $b > \beta_2$.
- (c) If $\rho > 0$, then $\lambda_2(0) > -1$ if and only if $\delta > \delta_3^{-\frac{1}{\rho}} \equiv \delta_4$, with $\delta_4 < 1$ and thus $\lambda_2(0) < -1$ for any $\delta \in (0,\delta_4)$. Moreover $\lambda_2(\beta_2) > 1$. Therefore, if δ lies in $(0,\delta_4)$, then there exist $\underline{b}(\delta) \in (0,\beta_2)$ and $\overline{b}(\delta) > \beta_2$ such that $\lambda_2(b) < -1$ for $b \in (0,\underline{b}(\delta))$, $-1 < \lambda_2(b) < 1$ for $b \in \left(\underline{b}(\delta),\overline{b}(\delta)\right)$, and

$\lambda_2(b) > 1$ for $b > \overline{b}(\delta)$. If δ lies in $(\delta_4, 1)$, there exists $b(\delta) > \beta_2$ such that $-1 < \lambda_2(b) < 1$ for $b \in (0, b(\delta))$ and $\lambda_2(b) > 1$ for $b > b(\delta)$. □

Notice that the impact of b on the local stability properties of the steady state depends on the value of the discount factor δ. If δ is not too small, larger values of b contributes to total instability as in Proposition 3 (see cases 1-a) with $\delta \in (\delta_4, \delta_3)$ and 2-c) with $\delta \in (\delta_4, 1)$ in Proposition 5). On the contrary, if δ is close enough to zero, local instability is obtained for low enough and large enough values of b.

4 Concluding Remarks

In this chapter we have characterized the local dynamics of the equilibrium paths depending on the size of the external effects b. We have shown that when the investment good is capital intensive, large values of b contributes to total instability. When the consumption good is capital intensive, the effect of b on the local dynamics of the equilibrium path is more complex. If the capital intensity difference is large enough, local indeterminacy occurs for intermediary values of b while saddle-point stability is obtained when b is low enough or large enough. If the capital intensity difference is small, local indeterminacy cannot occur and the role of b depends on the size of the discount factor. When the discount factor is not too low, larger values of b again contributes to total instability. However, when the discount factor is close enough to zero, total instability is also obtained for small values of b. In this case indeed, saddle-point stability requires intermediary values of b.

In this chapter, we have assumed that both sectors have the same elasticity of capital–labor substitution. It would be interesting to study the characterization of the equilibrium paths by introducing heterogeneity.

Acknowledgments We thank an anonymous referee for useful comments. This chapter has been revised while Alain Venditti was visiting the Institute of Economic Research of Kyoto University. He thanks Professor Kazuo Nishimura and all the staff of the Institute for their kind invitation.

References

Benhabib J, Farmer R (1994) Indeterminacy and increasing returns. J Econ Theory 20:19–41

Benhabib J, Nishimura K (1998) Indeterminacy and sunspots with constant returns. J Econ Theory 81:58–96

Benhabib J, Nishimura K (1999) Indeterminacy arising in multisector economies. Jpn Econ Rev 50:485–506

Benhabib J, Nishimura K, Venditti A (2002) Indeterminacy and cycles in two-sector discrete-time model. Econ Theory 20:217–235

Nishimura K, Venditti A (2004) Capital depreciation, factor substitutability and indeterminacy. J Difference Equations Appl 10:1153–1169

Takayama A (1997) Mathematical economics, 2nd edn. Cambridge University Press, Cambridge

Tobin's "Keynesian Models of Recessions and Depression" Revisited

Partha Sen

Abstract I look at an exogenous decrease in the desire to save in a two-sector-two-period overlapping generations model, where the consumption good is capital-intensive and the elasticities of substitution in production are "small." It is shown that there is a Keynesian-type multiplier at work, even though the model is a competitive one with full employment (and inelastic labor supply). It is reminiscent of Tobin (Am Econ Rev 65:195202, 1975) who had shown 30 years ago that Keynesian results could be obtained with (short run) Marshallian dynamics (albeit in an ad-hoc model).

1 Introduction

It is almost 30 years since James Tobin's chapter "Keynesian Models of Recession and Depression" (Tobin (1975)) appeared. In that chapter, Tobin, following a suggestion by Milton Friedman, showed that Keynesian conclusions followed naturally if we appended a "Marshallian" (short-run) dynamic adjustment to a standard macro model. If, per contra, the dynamics was of the "Walrasian" variety, classical results followed. The framework that Tobin used was, of course, a standard work-horse of that era – an IS-LM-Phillips Curve model. Tobin's basic insight seems to have been forgotten since.

In the last two decades, various authors have sought to provide microfoundations for macroeconomics. While macroeconomists of a classical persuasion tend to prefer a competitive framework, those who want to provide Keynesian economics with microeconomic underpinnings prefer a noncompetitive (usually a monopolistically competitive) framework. In an imperfectly competitive framework (and/or in

P. Sen
Delhi School of Economics, Delhi University, Delhi, India

T. Kamihigashi and L. Zhao (eds.) *International Trade and Economic Dynamics – Essays in Memory of Koji Shimomura.*

a model with increasing returns to scale), it is possible to obtain a multiplier-type relationship[1] and policy intervention can (under certain circumstances) improve the welfare of all individuals.[2]

There is, however, near-unanimity (the qualification "near" is probably redundant) that a multiplier cannot be obtained in a competitive model. On the one hand, in the words of an influential survey (Matsuyama 1995): "...the standard neoclassical paradigm, exemplified by Arrow and Hahn (1971), emphasizes the self-adjusting mechanisms of market forces with its efficient resource allocation. As different activities compete for scarce resources, expansion of one activity comes only at the expense of others, which tends to dampen any perturbation to the system." (p. 702). And, on the other hand: "The departure from perfect competition means that the firm, faced with downward sloping demands, sets prices above marginal cost.... Aggregate demand management could be effective in stimulating aggregate economic activity as well as raising the welfare of the economy." (p. 703).

In this chapter, I revisit Tobin's insight but in an optimizing setting. I show that it is possible to obtain a multiplier – that is reminiscent of the text-book Keynesian-cross diagram – in a perfectly competitive optimizing model. This is done in a two-sector overlapping generation model, where the consumption good is capital-intensive and the elasticities of substitution between inputs in both sectors are "low" – the latter assumption is equivalent to assuming that the short run dynamics is of the Marshallian variety.[3] The model satisfies the usual conditions for dynamic efficiency, viz. the rate of interest exceeds the population growth rate.[4] The new equilibrium path does not Pareto-dominate the initial equilibrium, but *may* improve the welfare of all those individuals who "contribute" to the increase in aggregate demand (i.e., all generations barring the initially old).

The model is described in the next section and the aggregate demand experiment is introduced. In section 3, I provide an example with Leontief technologies, while section 4 looks at the case with non-zero elasticities of substitution in production. Finally, in section 5 there are some concluding comments.

---

[1] A multiplier arises when the resulting increase in output is greater than the initial increase in expenditure – below this initial increase is due to a decline in the rate of time preference.

[2] See, for instance, Blanchard and Kiyotaki (1987), Gali (1994), Mankiw (1988), Kiyotaki (1988), Startz (1984, 1989), Heijdra (1998), and Weitzman (1982); for surveys see Dixon and Rankin (1994), Matsuyama (1995), and Solow (1998).

[3] There is some empirical justification for both our capital intensity and low elasticities of substitution assumptions. On capital intensities, see, for example, Takahashi et al. (2004), who found that the Japanese investment goods sector is more labor-intensive (since 1975). The authors have calculated the capital-intensities for the two sectors for the UK, the US, and Germany and found the investment good to be labor-intensive. Buffie (2001) summarizes time series studies as having obtained elasticities in production of around 0.5.

[4] See Abel et al. (1989), Buiter (1981), Matsuyama (1991), and Shell (1971) for discussions on the possibility of over-accumulation in two-period overlapping generations models.

2 The Model

The (closed) economy consists of overlapping generations of individuals or households with two-period lives. Each household supplies one unit of labor in the first period of its life, and in the second period consumes the saving from the first period plus the return on these savings. No household is altruistically linked to any future generations, that is, there are no bequests or inheritances. The population is constant – the size of the population is assumed to be two, the size of each generation is unity. Agents have perfect foresight. We study the properties of the model by log-linearizing it around the initial steady state.

The representative household born in time period t maximises the following logarithmic utility function[5]

$$U_t = \log C_t^t + (1+\rho)^{-1} \log C_{t+1}^t, \quad t = 0 \ldots -2, -1, 0, 1, 2, \ldots, \tag{1a}$$

where C_{t+1}^i is the consumption in period $t+i$ of a household born in t and $\rho > 0$ is the rate of time preference.

Its lifetime budget constraint is

$$W_t = C_t^t + (1+r_{t+1})^{-1} C_{t+1}^t, \tag{1b}$$

where W_t is the wage rate in time period t and r_{t+1} is the own interest rate on one period consumption loans between t and $t+1$.

This yields

$$C_t^t = [(1+\rho)/(2+\rho)] W_t \tag{2a}$$

and

$$C_{t+1}^t = [(1+r_{t+1})/(2+\rho)] W_t. \tag{2b}$$

The savings and indirect utility functions are given by (where m is a constant),

$$S_t \equiv W_t - C_t^t - (2+\rho)^{-1} W_t, \tag{3}$$

$$V_t = V(W_t, 1+r_{t+1}) = m + [(2+\rho)\log W_t + \log(1+r_{t+1})]/(1+\rho). \tag{4}$$

Note that savings in time period t do not depend on any variable in time period $t+1$ (e.g., the expected return on capital in $t+1$). This makes the model's dynamics scalar, that is, it can be represented by a single difference equation (7).

The production side of the economy is represented by two cost-equal-to-price equations. The consumption good (C) and the investment good (I) are produced under conditions of constant returns to scale using the two inputs, capital (K) and

[5] Galor (1992) (Sect. 6) and Azariadis (1993) (example 13.5) use the two-sector overlapping generations model with logarithmic utility.

labor (L). All inputs are mobile between sectors instantaneously. Capital is assumed to depreciate completely in the process of production.[6]

$$a_{LC}W_t + a_{KC}R_t = 1, \tag{5a}$$

$$a_{LI}W_t + a_{KI}R_t = p_t, \tag{5b}$$

where a_{ij} is the requirement of the ith input ($i = K, L$) in the production of the jth good ($j = C, I$), p is the relative price of the investment good in terms of the numeraire good C, and R is the gross return on capital. Since we assume capital depreciates completely in the process of production, in equilibrium: $(1 + r_{t+1}) = R_{t+1}/p_t$. The a_{ij}'s are functions of the relative factor prices unless the technologies are Leontief (as in Sect. 3).

There are two goods markets (for C and I) and two factor markets (for K and L). By Walras' Law, if three of these are in equilibrium in any period, then so is the fourth one. We thus have (the aggregate demand shock is introduced below in (9))

$$a_{LC}C_t + a_{LI}I_t = 1, \tag{6a}$$

$$a_{KC}C_t + a_{KI}I_t = k_t, \tag{6b}$$

$$p_tI_t = (2+\rho)^{-1}W_t. \tag{6c}$$

Equations (6a)–(6c) are the market-clearing conditions for the labor, capital, and investment goods markets, respectively. The variable C_t is the production of the consumption good, I_t is the output of the investment good, and k_t is the capital stock (all are per worker magnitudes in time period t).

Finally, the dynamics of the economy is represented by the difference equation

$$k_{t+1} = I_t. \tag{7}$$

Appendix 1 shows that we can solve (6a) and (6b) to get $I_t = I(p_t, k_t)$. Substituting this in (6c) we can solve $p_t = p(k_t)$.[7] Equation (7) can then be linearized around the steady state and written as

$$\mathrm{d}k_{t+1} = \{(\partial I/\partial p)(\partial p/\partial k) + (\partial I/\partial k)\}\mathrm{d}k_t. \tag{8a}$$

Stability requires

$$-1 \le \mathrm{d}k_{t+1}/\mathrm{d}k_t = (\eta_{Ip}\eta_{pk} + \eta_{Ik}) \le 1, \tag{8b}$$

where $\mathrm{d}k_{t+i} \equiv k_{t+i} - k$ is the deviation of the $t+i$ period capital per worker from its steady state value (a variable's steady state value is denoted without a time sub-

---

[6] This is for analytical convenience only. Dropping this requires capital gains on the sale of capital to be part of the return to holding of capital. That leaves the steady state, where there are no capital gains, unaffected.

[7] This is explained at length in the paragraphs following (9).

script). An η_{ij} is the elasticity of variable i with respect to j – these are given in Appendix 1.

The expression for η_{pk} will play a crucial role in obtaining the results that we do in this chapter, so we turn to a detailed discussion of this expression. Equation (6c) can be differentiated logarithmically to obtain

$$\hat{W}_t = \hat{p}_t + \hat{I}_t + \Gamma$$

or (using (27a), (29a), and (29c))

$$(\eta_{Wp} - 1 - \eta_{Ip})\hat{p}_t = \eta_{Ik}\hat{k}_t. \tag{9}$$

If the consumption good is capital-intensive, $\eta_{Wp} > 1$ and $\eta_{Ik} < 0$ (from the Stolper–Samuelson theorem and the Rybczinski theorem, respectively). The term $\Psi \equiv (\eta_{Wp} - 1 - \eta_{Ip})$ measures the contribution of a change in price to excess demand for the investment good, ceteris paribus. The demand for capital goods is given by the elasticity of supply of savings η_{Wp}, while the elasticity of the supply responsiveness of investment goods (measured in units of consumption) is given by $1 + \eta_{Ip}$. We assume that $\Psi > 0$, that is, the (upward-sloping) demand curve for investment is more responsive to a price change than the supply curve (also upward-sloping) – the short-run dynamics is of the Marshallian-type ($\Psi < 0$ is the Walrasian case).[8]

In Fig. 1, the II curve is drawn depicting p.I(p,k) and the SS curve for $S\eta W(p)/[(2+\rho)]$ – ignore the broken lines for now. With p on the horizontal axis,

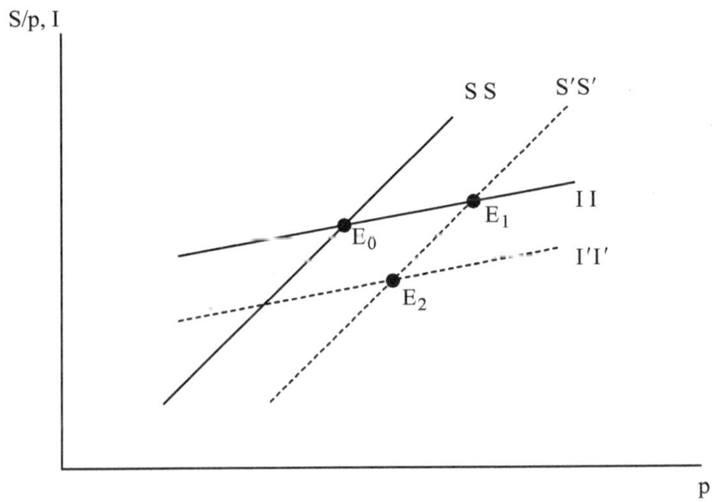

Fig. 1 Marshallian Dynamics

[8] Note our interpretation of demand and supply for capital is at variance with what might be the natural interpretation of these terms in a one good dynamic model. There savings are taken to be the supply of capital and k_{t+1}, the next period's capital stock, constitutes the demand for it (see, e.g., Diamond (1965), Galor and Polemarchakis (1986) and Persson (1985) for such a usage).

when the II curve is flatter than the SS curve, we have Marshallian dynamics. Note that if we had output on the horizontal axis, we would get back the Keynesian-cross diagram (in its saving equals investment variant).

With our capital intensity and short run dynamics assumptions, (9) gives $\eta_{pk} \equiv \hat{p}/\hat{k} = \eta_{Ik}/\Psi < 0$, i.e., because of the assumed Marshallian dynamics there is negative relationship between p and k in any period.

3 An Exogenous Decrease in Desired Saving with Leontief Technologies

It would be enormously helpful for expository purposes to start off with the case where the elasticities of substitution in production are zero.[9]

With Leontief technologies in both sectors, the stability requirement (see (8b)) is now (with $\eta_{Ip} = 0$) $-1 < \eta_{Ik} < 0$, which, in turn, requires $\lambda_{KC} > 2\lambda_{LC}$ (where λ_{ij} is the share of sector j in the total employment of input I, e.g., $\lambda_{KC} \equiv a_{KC}C/k$).[10]

Consider a decrease in desired saving, for example, an increase in the rate of time preference, ρ. What does this do to national income, wages etc.? Is it true that in the new equilibrium the increase in income, if at all, comes at the expense of other activities? It is obvious that in the absence of unemployment of some resource (or, more generally, with elastic factor supplies), the scale of some activities would be reduced, as those of others are increased. The question is then whether this precludes the presence of a multiplier-type relationship?

If the economy were initially in a steady state, the economy jumps straight to a new steady state following a change in (the composition of) aggregate demand. To see this note that in (5a), (5b), (6a), and (6b), now the a_{ij}'s are constants (i.e., do not depend on factor prices). From (6a) and (6b), I_t and C_t are determined in any period, given k_t. If we start from a steady state, then $I = k$ (from (7)). So, from (6a), (6b), and (7), we determine the values of k, I, and C. These are invariant to a change in desired saving.

Recalling, from (27a), $W_t = W(p_t)$ and from (29a) and (29c) (with Leontief technologies), $I_t = I(k_t)$. With k_1 predetermined (and equal to the initial steady state value, if the system starts from a steady state), we have from (9) (with both $\eta_{Ip} = 0, \hat{k} = 0$)

$$\hat{W} = \hat{p} + \mathrm{d}A/S, \tag{9'}$$

where $\mathrm{d}A \equiv [S/(2+\rho)]\mathrm{d}\rho$ is the increase in aggregate demand in terms of the numeraire.

---

9 Calvo (1978) was the first one, to the best of my knowledge, to use a two-sector overlapping generations model with Leontief technologies.

10 Note if technologies are Leontief, stability is ruled out if the consumption good is labor-intensive.

Thus (below θ_{ij} is the share of the ith input in the jth sector price, for example, $\theta_{LI} \equiv a_{LI} \cdot W/p$ and $\Delta \equiv \theta_{LC} - \theta_{LI}$; see Appendix 1 for details),

$$\hat{p}/\mathrm{d}A = -\Delta/(\theta_{KI}S), \tag{10a}$$

$$\hat{W}/\mathrm{d}A = \theta_{KC}/(\theta_{KI}S), \tag{10b}$$

$$\mathrm{d}W/\mathrm{d}A = \theta_{KC}(2+\rho)/\theta_{KI} > 2, \tag{10b$'$}$$

$$\hat{R}/\mathrm{d}A = -\theta_{LC}/(\theta_{KI}S) < 0. \tag{10c$'$}$$

Now, the GDP (denoted by Q) is given by the identity

$$Q \equiv C + pI.$$

So, $\mathrm{d}Q = pI\hat{p}$ (by the envelope theorem)

$$\mathrm{d}Q/\mathrm{d}A = -\Delta/\theta_{KI} > 0. \tag{11}$$

In (11), $\mathrm{d}Q/\mathrm{d}A$ is "likely" to be greater than unity since $(-\Delta/\theta_{KI})$ is "likely" to be greater than unity (the stability condition requires good C to be sufficiently capital intensive) – for the parameter values in Appendix 1, $\mathrm{d}Q/\mathrm{d}A$ is 1.5. Note both W and, possibly, Q increase by more than the initial increase in demand due to a decline in the desire to save – this is, what I refer to as a "multiplier" (see Footnote 1).

Given these, the utility of generation 0 (the initially old)

$$\mathrm{d}V_0 = k\mathrm{d}R = -(R/p)(\theta_{LC}/\theta_{KI})\mathrm{d}A < 0. \tag{12}$$

And those of the subsequent generations is given by ($R/p > 1$ is the dynamic efficiency condition – see Appendix 2 for a derivation)

$$\mathrm{d}V = [V_W((R/p) - 1)\theta_{LC}/(p\theta_{KI})]\mathrm{d}A > 0, \tag{13}$$

where $V_W = (2+\rho)/((1+\rho)W)$.

We can sum this up as Proposition 1:

Proposition 1. *If the technologies in both the sectors are Leontief and the economy is initially in a steady-state, then an exogenous decrease in saving takes the economy to a new steady instantaneously with a lower R/p, and higher W and Q. There is a multiplier effect on W, and possibly Q. As a consequence, the old (generation 0) lose, but everyone else is better off, if the economy is dynamically efficient.*

The intuition for the multiplier process is that, given Leontief technologies and starting off from a steady state, k, and hence I, are fixed. Savings have to finance this given amount of I. This, in turn, fixes S/p. If now the rate of time preference increases, wages have to increase to generate the given amount of real savings (in terms of the I good). This requires p to increase, which raises Q. The rise in W increases welfare of generation 1 onwards, iff $R/p >\ 1$ (i.e., the interest rate was above the population growth rate). The increased W is accompanied by a fall in R

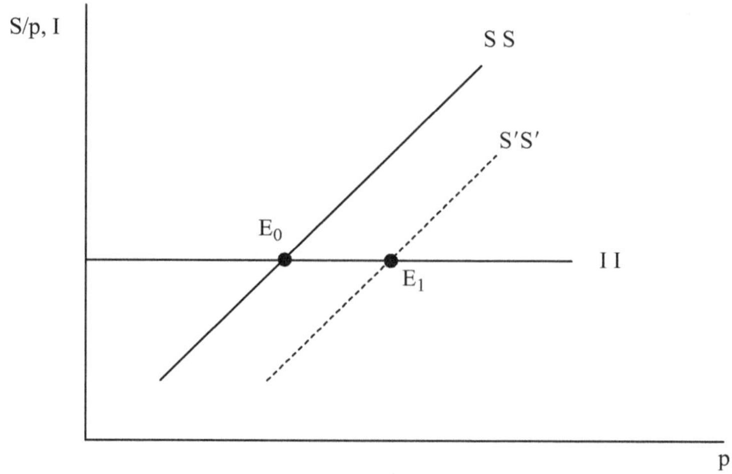

Fig. 2 A Fall in Desired Saving

that causes V_0 to fall. Note that all the action is coming from a change in relative prices – the real quantities, C, I, and k, do not change. Also note that Rybczinski Theorem – a veritable Pandora's box in two sector models – plays no role in the results obtained.

In Fig. 2, the initial equilibrium is at E_0. An autonomous decline in desired saving moves the SS line down to S_1S_1. The new equilibrium is at E_1 – the price of investment goods increases from p_0 to p_1.

A brief point about the perceived difference between Keynesian and classical models is in order here. It is often mentioned that classical models (including the Solow growth model) do not have an independent investment function. In this section, we have seen that in a completely neoclassical setting, we can have an independent investment function that is dictated by technology. Hence, it is not surprising that we get results that one normally associates with Keynesian models.[11]

4 The Multiplier with Nonzero Elasticities of Substitution

With nonzero elasticities of substitution in production, there are two changes: (1) the value of static multiplier changes because $\eta_{Ip} > 0$; and (2) there is nondegenerate dynamics – one implication of this is that even with dynamic efficiency not all generation (barring generation 0, of course) may gain. I discuss what happens in periods 1, 2 and the steady state, leaving the details of the dynamics for Appendix 3.

[11] Robert Solow, in correspondence with the author, has queried whether the presence of a multiplier makes it a "Keynesian model." I would say that it is a competitive model with properties one expects in a Keynesian model.

Rewrite (9′) as follows

$$\hat{W}_1 = \hat{p}_1 + \hat{I}_1 + (\mathrm{d}A/S). \tag{14}$$

As before, $W_t = W(p_t)$, but now $I_t = I(p_t, k_t)$. With k_1 predetermined, we have (remember $\Psi \equiv (\eta_{Wp} - 1 - \eta_{Ip})$)

$$\hat{p}_1/\mathrm{d}A = 1/(S\Psi), \tag{15a}$$

$$\hat{W}_1/\mathrm{d}A = -\theta_{KC}/(\Delta S\Psi), \tag{15b}$$

$$\mathrm{d}W_1/\mathrm{d}A = -\theta_{KC}(2+\rho)/(\Delta\Psi) > 2, \tag{15c}$$

$$\hat{R}_1/\mathrm{d}A = \theta_{LC}/(\Delta S\Psi) < 0. \tag{15d}$$

The only change from the Leontief technologies case is that now the price change also elicits a supply response in the investment goods market.

The change in GNP ($Q \equiv C + p.I$) in period 1 is given by

$$\mathrm{d}Q_1/\mathrm{d}A = pI\hat{p}_1/\mathrm{d}A = 1/\Psi > 0. \tag{16}$$

Note that both W_1 and Q_1 rise by more than in the Leontief case (for the assumed parameter values in Appendix 1, $\mathrm{d}Q_1/\mathrm{d}A$ is 2.5 approximately, compared to 1.5 in the Leontief case). This is because the term in the denominator $\Psi \equiv (-\theta_{KI}/\Delta) - \eta_{Ip} < (-\theta_{KI}/\Delta)$.[12]

The changes in the next period (i.e., period 2) are given by

$$\hat{k}_2 = \hat{I}_1 = \eta_{Ip}\hat{p}_1 = [\eta_{Ip}/(S\Psi)]\mathrm{d}A > 0, \tag{17a}$$

$$\hat{p}_2 = [(1 + \eta_{Ip}\eta_{Ik}\Psi^{-1})/(S\Psi)]\mathrm{d}A, \tag{17b}$$

$$\hat{W}_2 = -[\theta_{KC}(1 + \eta_{Ip}\eta_{Ik}\Psi^{-1})/(\Delta S\Psi)]\mathrm{d}A, \tag{17c}$$

$$\hat{R}_2 = [\theta_{LC}(1 + \eta_{Ip}\eta_{Ik}\Psi^{-1})/(\Delta S\Psi)]\mathrm{d}A. \tag{17d}$$

Note, that if $\eta_{Wp} - 1 - \eta_{Ip}(1 - \eta_{Ik}) < 0$, that is, if $-\eta_{Ik}\eta_{Ip} > \Psi$, then $\hat{p}_2 < 0$ and $\hat{W}_2 < 0$. In this case, the direct effect of the increased demand (i.e., $\mathrm{d}A/S$) is outweighed by the decline in investment caused by increased capital accumulation (remember the investment good is labor-intensive).

If the initial equilibrium was at E_0 in Fig. 1, the change in the rate of time preference shifts the SS curve down (the dashed line S_1S_1), with the period 1 equilibrium at E_1. In period 2, as capital is accumulated, the II curve shifts down to I_1I_1, with the new equilibrium E_2 to the left of E_1 (and possibly to the left of E_0).

[12] $\Psi > 0$ implies $(-\theta_{KI}/\Delta)(1-\varepsilon_I) - \lambda_{LC}\varepsilon_I/(\Delta\Omega) > 0$, while $\mathrm{d}Q_1/\mathrm{d}A$ requires $(-\theta_{KI}/\Delta)(1 - \varepsilon_I) < 1 + \lambda_{LC}\varepsilon_I/(\Delta\Omega)$.

The new steady state of the economy is obtained (by solving (6c) and (7) together).

$$\Psi \hat{p} = \eta_{Ik}\hat{k} + (1/S)\mathrm{d}A, \tag{19}$$

$$\hat{k} = \eta_{Ip}\hat{p} + \eta_{Ik}\hat{k}. \tag{20}$$

And, so

$$\hat{p}/\mathrm{d}A = 1/[\Xi S], \tag{21a}$$

$$\hat{W}/\mathrm{d}A = (-\theta_{KC})/[\Xi S\Delta] > 0, \tag{21b}$$

$$\hat{R}/\mathrm{d}A = (\theta_{LC})/[\Xi S\Delta] < 0, \tag{21c}$$

$$\hat{k}/\mathrm{d}A = \eta_{Ip}/\{(1-\eta_{Ik})\Xi S\} > 0, \tag{21d}$$

$$\mathrm{d}Q/\mathrm{d}A = 1/[\Xi] > 0, \tag{21e}$$

where $\Xi \equiv \eta_{Wp} - 1 - \eta_{Ip}(1-\eta_{Ik})^{-1} \geq \Psi$

Since $\Xi \geq \Psi$, the long run increases in p, W, and Q are smaller than the corresponding ones in the short run – this is due to a crowding-in of capital, which lowers investment, ceteris paribus.[13] Startz (1989), in a monopolistically competitive model, had obtained a similar result and had attributed this to an entry of new firms and the consequent whittling away of profits. In Baxter and King (1993), however, the long run fiscal multiplier exceeds the short run one because of crowding-in of capital (see also Turnovsky and Sen (1991) for a crowding-in of capital in an open economy framework). This is because in an optimal growth model, in the steady state the rate of time preference has to equal the marginal product of capital. If labor supply increases (due to, e.g., increased (lump sum) taxation), there is a crowding-in of capital to enable the capital-labor ratio to go back to its previous value.

Turning to the welfare effects

$$\mathrm{d}V_0 = k_1\mathrm{d}R_1/\mathrm{d}A = Rk\hat{R}_1/\mathrm{d}A = (R/p)\theta_{LC}.(\Delta\Psi)^{-1}\mathrm{d}A < 0, \tag{22}$$

$$\begin{aligned}\mathrm{d}V_1/\mathrm{d}A &= [(2+\rho)(\hat{W}_1/\mathrm{d}A) + (\hat{R}_2/\mathrm{d}A) - (\hat{p}_1/\mathrm{d}A)]/(1+\rho),\\ &= \{(2+\rho)(-\theta_{KC}\Delta^{-1}) - 1 + (1+\eta_{Ik}\eta_{Ip}\Psi^{-1})\theta_{LC}\Delta^{-1}\}/((1+\rho)\Psi S) > 0,\end{aligned} \tag{23}$$

(this expression is positive, because compared to the (steady state) welfare change with Leontief technologies, we have a positive term $(\eta_{Ik}\eta_{Ip}\theta_{LC})(\Psi\Delta)^{-1} > 0$).

And the steady state utility change is given by

$$\mathrm{d}V/\mathrm{d}A = -V_W[((R/p)-1)S(\hat{R}/\mathrm{d}A)] > 0 \tag{24}$$

The change in long run welfare is lower compared to the short run because as capital gets crowded in, some of the increased aggregate demand disappears – in Fig. 1, the II line shifts down – thereby checking the increase in wages and the fall in the interest rate. As long as the economy is dynamically efficient, the wage effect dominates, though (see Appendix 2).

[13] As mentioned above, even in period 2 the wage rate and output could fall if $(-\eta_{Ik}\eta_{Ip}) > \Psi$.

The dynamics of prices is summarized in Appendix 3. Equation (33) is the basic dynamic equation governing the evolution of $\hat{p}_t$. Equation (34) is the solution to this difference equation. Equations (35) and (36), respectively, give us the initial condition and the steady state values. Equation (37) is the root of the equation. Equation (38) gives the general expression for welfare.

The solution to the difference (33) given in (34) gives us some understanding about the possible reasons why the wage rate may fall in period 2 and with it the welfare of generation 2. Also note that the steady state welfare rises, so that the possible decline in welfare happens, if at all, only during the transition. To see this

$$\hat{p}_{t+1}/\mathrm{d}A = ((\Psi S)^{-1} - (\Xi S)^{-1})\Theta^{t} + (S\Xi)^{-1}. \tag{25}$$

Since, the initial change in $\hat{p}_t$ is greater than its steady state value (since $\Psi < \Xi$), that is, $\hat{p}_1$ overshoots its long-run value and in the odd periods following the shock (i.e., periods 2,4,6,....) this positive gap gets multiplied by a negative number Θ^i, where i is the period since the shock (Θ is the root of the difference equation). In these periods, there is a negative effect of capital accumulation on investment (and on prices and wages). There is a positive effect through $\hat{p}(= (S\Xi)^{-1})$ in all periods. In the initial stages the negative effect could dominate, while as i becomes larger the negative effect dies out and the steady state effects of the fall in desired savings on price, wages, output, and welfare is expansionary.

I summarize the discussion in this section in Proposition 2:

Proposition 2. *If there are positive elasticities of substitution – Marshallian dynamics puts an upper bound on these – and the economy is initially in a steady-state, then an exogenous decrease in saving takes the economy to a new steady with a lower R/p, and higher W and Q. As a consequence, the old (generation 0) lose, but everyone else is better off, if the economy is dynamically efficient. During the initial phase of the adjustment process, which is cyclical, there could be other losers.*

5 Conclusions

Revisiting Tobin's insight that in a model with Marshallian dynamics one can obtain Keynesian results, I looked for a multiplier-type expression in a two-sector overlapping generations model. Here in a perfectly competitive model with maximizing agents, I showed that Keynesian-type multipliers, reminiscent of the Keynesian-cross, can indeed be obtained. A decline in the saving propensity can cause wages and output to increase – since a given amount of investment, ceteris paribus, has to be financed, savings, and hence wages, increase. However, unlike macroeconomic models with monopolistic competition, the new equilibrium path is not Pareto-superior compared to the initial one – at least one generation loses along the new equilibrium path.

Appendix 1

Equations (4) and (5) yield by logarithmic differentiation (see Atkinson and Stiglitz (1980), Chap. 6 for details)

$$\theta_{LC}\hat{W}_t + \theta_{KC}\hat{R}_t = 0, \tag{26a}$$

$$\theta_{LI}\hat{W}_t + \theta_{KI}\hat{R}_t = \hat{p}_t, \tag{26b}$$

where θ_{ij} is the share of the ith input in the jth sector price (e.g., $\theta_{LI} \equiv a_{LI}.W/p$) and a hat over a variable denotes a percentage change.

From (26a) and (26b), we can solve for $\hat{W}_t$ and $\hat{R}_t$ in terms of $\hat{p}_t$. We thus have

$$\eta_{Wp} \equiv \hat{W}_t/\hat{p}_t = -\theta_{KC}/\Delta, \tag{27a}$$

$$\eta_{Rp} \equiv \hat{R}_t/\hat{p}_t = \theta_{LC}/\Delta, \tag{27b}$$

where $\Delta \equiv \theta_{LC} - \theta_{LI} = \theta_{KI} - \theta_{KC}$ and η_{ij} is the (partial) elasticity of variable i with respect to j. From (27a) and (27b), we see that η_{Wp} and η_{Rp} depend on capital intensities. Given our assumption that the consumption good is capital-intensive, $\Delta < 0$. And hence by the Stolper–Samuelson theorem, $\eta_{Wp} > 1, \eta_{Rp} < 0$.

Similarly by logarithmically differentiating (6a)–(6c) we have

$$\lambda_{LC}\hat{C}_t + \lambda_{LI}\hat{I}_t = [\hat{W}_t - \hat{R}_t][\lambda_{LC}\theta_{KC}\varepsilon_C + \lambda_{LI}\theta_{KI}\varepsilon_I], \tag{28a}$$

$$\lambda_{KC}\hat{C}_t + \lambda_{KI}\hat{I}_t = \hat{k}_t - [\hat{W}_t - \hat{R}_t][\lambda_{KC}\theta_{LC}\varepsilon_C + \lambda_{KI}\theta_{LI}\varepsilon_I], \tag{28b}$$

$$\hat{p}_t + \hat{I}_t = \hat{W}_t, \tag{28c}$$

where λ_{ij} is the share of sector j in the total employment of input i and ε_j is the elasticity of substitution between inputs in the jth industry.

From (28a) and (28b), we have the Rybczinski effects (which depend on assumed capital intensities)

$$\eta_{Ik} \equiv \hat{I}_t/\hat{k}_t = \lambda_{LC}/\Omega < 0, \tag{29a}$$

$$\eta_{Ck} \equiv \hat{C}_t/\hat{k}_t = -\lambda_{LI}/\Omega > 0, \tag{29b}$$

where $\Omega \equiv \lambda_{LC} - \lambda_{KC} < 0$ (by assumption).

From (28a) and (28b), we have the supply elasticities (which are independent of capital intensities)

$$\eta_{Ip} \equiv \hat{I}_t/\hat{p}_t = \{\lambda_{LC}\lambda_{KC}\varepsilon_C + (\lambda_{LC}\lambda_{KI}\theta_{LI} + \lambda_{KC}\lambda_{LI}\theta_{KI})\varepsilon_I\}/(\Delta\Omega) > 0, \tag{29c}$$

$$\eta_{Cp} \equiv \hat{C}_t/\hat{p}_t = -\{\lambda_{LI}\lambda_{KI}\varepsilon_I + (\lambda_{LC}\lambda_{KI}\theta_{KC} + \lambda_{KC}\lambda_{LI}\theta_{LC})\varepsilon_C\}/(\Delta\Omega) < 0. \tag{29d}$$

If we substitute for $\hat{W}_t$, from (27a) into (28c), we can solve (28a), (28b), and (28c) for $\hat{C}_t, \hat{I}_t$, and $\hat{p}_t$ in terms of $\hat{k}_t$. In particular,

$$\eta_{pk} \equiv \hat{p}_t/\hat{k}_t = \eta_{Ik}/\Psi = (-\lambda_{LC}\Delta)[\theta_{KI}\Omega + \{\lambda_{LC}\lambda_{KC}\varepsilon_C + (\lambda_{LC}\lambda_{KI}\theta_{LI} + \lambda_{KC}\lambda_{LI}\theta_{KI})\varepsilon_I\}]^{-1}, \quad (30)$$

where $\Psi \equiv \eta_{Wp} - 1 - \eta_{Ip}$.

The stability condition for (7) in the text requires

$$-1 \leq \mathrm{d}k_{t+1}/\mathrm{d}k_t = (\eta_{Ip}\eta_{pk} + \eta_{Ik}) \equiv \Theta \leq 1. \quad (31)$$

Thus, if the model is stable with $\eta_{pk} < 0$, the convergence is cyclical. The condition for stability turns out to be

$$[\theta_{KI}(\lambda_{KC} - 2\lambda_{LC}) - \{\lambda_{LC}\lambda_{KC}\varepsilon_C + (\lambda_{LC}\lambda_{KI}\theta_{LI} + \lambda_{KC}\lambda_{LI}\theta_{KI})\varepsilon_I\}]/(\Delta\Omega) > 0. \quad (32)$$

The condition in (32) is more stringent than for $\hat{p}/\hat{k} < 0$ in (30) – the term multiplying θ_{KI} is $\lambda_{KC} - 2\lambda_{LC}$ instead of $\lambda_{KC} - \lambda_{LC}$. Consider the following numerical example: $\lambda_{LC} = 0.15, \lambda_{KC} = 0.8, \theta_{LI} = 0.8, \theta_{LC} = 0.5, \varepsilon_I = \varepsilon_C = 0.4$. We have both $\hat{p}/\hat{k} < 0$ and $-1 < \mathrm{d}k_{t+1}/\mathrm{d}k_t < 0$.

Appendix 2

In the steady state, if we have the general utility function $U(C^1C^2)$, then the indirect utility function is

$V(W, R/P)$ (which is derived from $U(W-S, S(R/p))$, where S is chosen optimally).

$\mathrm{d}V = V_W\mathrm{d}W + V_R\mathrm{d}R/P$. Note $V_W = U_1 > 0, V_R = SU_2$

$\mathrm{d}V = V_W\left(\mathrm{d}W + S(R/p)^{-1}d(R/p)\right)$, because

$U_1 = (R/p)U_2 \quad = V_W\left(I\mathrm{d}p - k\mathrm{d}R + S(R/p)^{-1}\mathrm{d}(R/p)\right)$

(from $W + Rk = C + pI$ and the envelope theorem implies $\mathrm{d}W + k\mathrm{d}R = I\mathrm{d}p$)

$$= V_W\left(k\mathrm{d}p - k\mathrm{d}R + S(R./p)^{-1}(\frac{\mathrm{d}R}{p} - \frac{R}{p^2}\mathrm{d}p)\right)$$

$$= V_W\left(k\mathrm{d}p - \frac{S}{R/P}\frac{R}{p^2}\mathrm{d}p + \frac{S}{R/P}\frac{\mathrm{d}R}{p} - k\mathrm{d}R\right)$$

because the first two terms in the previous line cancel out (i.e., $k = I = S/p$), we have $\mathrm{d}V = V_W S(1 - (R/p))\hat{R}$ – this appears as (17) and (24) in the text.

Appendix 3

$$\hat{p}_{t+1} = \eta_{Ik}(\eta_{Wp} - 1)\Psi^{-1}\hat{p}_t + (1 - \eta_{Ik})(S\Psi)^{-1}\mathrm{d}A, \quad (33)$$

$$\hat{p}_{t+1} = ((S\Psi)^{-1} - \hat{p})\{\eta_{Ik}\Psi^{-1}(\eta_{Wp} - 1)\}^t + \hat{p} \quad t = 0, 1, 2, \ldots, \quad (34)$$

$$\hat{p}_1 = (S\Psi)^{-1}\mathrm{d}A, \tag{35}$$

$$\hat{p} = (1-\eta_{Ik})\{(\eta_{Wp}-1)(1-\eta_{Ik})-\eta_{Ip}\}^{-1}S^{-1}\mathrm{d}A > 0, \tag{36}$$

$$-1 < \Theta \equiv \eta_{Ik}(\eta_{Wp}-1)\Psi^{-1} < 0, \tag{37}$$

$$\begin{aligned}\mathrm{d}V_t &= [S^{-1}\{(2+\rho)\theta_{KC}\Delta^{-1}-1\}(\hat{p}_t/\mathrm{d}A)+\theta_{LC}\Delta^{-1}(\hat{p}_{t+1}/\mathrm{d}A)]\mathrm{d}A,\\ &= [(-S\Delta)^{-1}\{(2+\rho)\theta_{KC}+\Delta-\Theta\theta_{LC}\}\{(\hat{p}_1/\mathrm{d}A)-(\hat{p}/\mathrm{d}A)\}\Theta^{t-1}\\ &\quad+\{(2+\rho)\theta_{KC}+\Delta-\theta_{LC}\}\{(\hat{p}/\mathrm{d}A)]\mathrm{d}A \quad t=1,2,\ldots.\end{aligned}$$

Acknowledgment A previous version of this chapter was presented at IRES (Louvain-la-Neuve), ECARES (ULBruxelles), and the University of Dundee. I am grateful to Raouf Boucekine, David de la Croix, Robert Solow and, especially, Philippe Weil for helpful discussion and comments. Thanks are also due to Janet Yellen (who introduced me to the literature) and (the late) James Tobin with whom I had the pleasure of discussing some of these issues many months ago.

References

Abel A, Mankiw NG, Summers LH, Zeckhauser R (1989) Assessing dynamic efficiency. Rev Econ Studies 56:1–19

Arrow KJ, Hahn FH (1971) General competitive analysis. Holden-Day, San Fransisco

Atkinson AB, Stiglitz JE (1980) Lectures in Public Economics. McGraw Hill, New York

Azariadis C (1993) Intertemporal Macroeconomics. Basil Blackwell, Oxford

Baxter M, King RG (1993) Fiscal policy in general equilibrium. Am Econ Rev 83:315–334

Blanchard OJ, Kiyotaki N (1987) Monopolistic competition and effects of aggregate demand. Am Econ Rev 77:647–666

Buffie E (2001) Trade Policy in Developing Countries. Cambridge University Press, Cambridge, UK

Buiter WH (1981) Time preference and international lending and borrowing in an overlapping generations model. J Political Econ 89:769–797

Calvo G (1978) On the indeterminacy of interest rates and wages with perfect foresight, *Journal of Economic Theory*, 19, 321–337.

Diamond PA (1965) National debt in a neoclassical growth model. Am Econ Rev 55:1126–1150

Dixon HD, Rankin N (1994) Imperfect competition and macroeconomics: A survey. Oxford Econ Papers 46:177–199

Gali J (1994) Monopolistic Competition, business cycles and the composition of aggregate demand J Econ Theory 63:73–96

Galor O (1992) A two-sector overlapping generations model: a characterization of the dynamical system. Econometrica 60:1351–1386

Galor O, Polemarchakis HM (1986) Intertemporal equilibrium and the transfer paradox. Rev Econ Studies 54:147–156

Heijdra B (1998) Fiscal policy multiplier: the role of monopolistic competition, scale economies and intertemporal labour substitution. Int Econ Rev 38:659–696

Kiyotaki N (1988) Multiple expectational equilibria under monopolistic competition Quarterly J Econ 103:695–703

Mankiw NG (1988) Imperfect competition and the Keynesian cross. Econ Lett 26:7–14

Matsuyama K (1991) Immiserizing growth in Diamond's overlapping generations model: a geometrical exposition. Int Econ Rev 32:251–262

Matsuyama K (1995) Complementarities and cumulative processes in models of monopolistic competition. J Econ Lit 33:701–729
Persson T (1985) Deficits and intergenerational welfare in an open economy. J Int Econ 19:67–84
Shell K (1971) Notes on the economics of infinity. J Political Econ 79:1002–1011
Solow RM (1998) Monopolistic Competition and Macroeconomic Theory. Cambridge University Press, Cambridge, UK
Startz R (1984) Prelude to macroeconomics. Am Econ Rev 74:881–892
Startz R (1989) Monopolistic competition as a foundation for Keynesian macroeconomic models. Quarterly J Econ 104:737–752
Tobin J (1975) Keynesian models of recession and depression. Am Econ Rev 65:195–202
Turnovsky SJ, Sen P (1991) Fiscal policy, the current account and debt in an open economy. Oxford Econ Papers 43:1–28
Takahashi H, Mashiya K, Sakagami T (2004) The capital-intensity reversal in the post-war Japanese economy – Why did Japan grow so fast during 1955–1975? Meiji Gakuin University, Mimeo
Weitzman ML (1982) Increasing returns and the foundation of unemployment theory. Econ J 92:787–804

Inflation Dynamics and the Cross-Sectional Distribution of Prices in the E.U. Periphery[1]

Constantina Kottaridi, Diego Méndez-Carbajo(✉), and Dimitrios D. Thomakos

Abstract We explore the connection between inflation and its higher-order moments for three economies in the periphery of the European Union (E.U.), Greece, Portugal, and Spain. Motivated by a micro-founded model of inflation determination, along the lines of the hybrid New Keynesian Phillips curve, we examine whether and how much the cross-sectional skewness in producer prices affects the path of inflation. We develop our analysis with the perspective of economic integration/inflation harmonization (in the E.U.) and discuss the peculiarities of these three economies. We find evidence of a strong positive relation between aggregate inflation and the distribution of relative-price changes for all three countries. A potentially important implication of our results is that, if the cross-sectional skewness of prices is directly related to aggregate inflation, not only the direction but also the magnitude of a nominal shock would influence output and inflation dynamics. Moreover, the effect of such a shock could be received asymmetrically, even when countries share a common currency.

1 Introduction

Evidence of a significant statistical relationship between inflation and the higher cross-sectional moments (variance and skewness) of the distribution of prices is amply available in the literature. On the basis of Vining's and Elwertowski's (1976)

[1] We thank the anonymous referee for very useful comments that improved the content of the chapter, and Kostas Papandreou for providing us with the industry-level Greek data. Any errors are our responsibility.

D. Méndez-Carbajo
Department of Economics, Illinois Wesleyan University. P.O. Box 2900, Bloomington, IL 61702, USA, e-mail: dmendez@iwu.edu

T. Kamihigashi and L. Zhao (eds.) *International Trade and Economic Dynamics – Essays in Memory of Koji Shimomura.*

seminal chapter, different lines of research have examined both the existence of this relationship and its origins.[2]

Attention has been concentrated toward the study of the relationship between inflation and its second higher moment,[3] although recently the exploration of the relationship between inflation and its third higher moment has gained momentum. Ball and Mankiw (1995) and Balke and Wynne (2000) have built on previous work by Batchelor (1981), Blejer (1983), and Mizon et al. (1990) to study the nature of this relationship. Although the existence of this empirical regularity has been reported under a variety of circumstances for a number of different countries,[4] its categorization as a macroeconomic stylized fact has been questioned by the work of Bryan and Cecchetti (1999a) and, in some measure, by Verbrugge (1999).

Bryan and Cecchetti (1999a) have argued that the observed positive correlation between the mean and the cross-sectional skewness of price changes suffers from small-sample bias. Using Monte Carlo experiments, they claim to be able to fully account for the correlation present in the data as a result of the mentioned bias, concluding that when price-change distributions are asymmetrical on average, there will be a small-sample bias in the mean-variance correlation. In such a case, one of the stylized facts in the literature of aggregate price behavior would turn out to be the result of defective statistical analysis. The response to this argument by Ball and Mankiw (1999) and Verbrugge (1999) has been twofold. On the one hand, they criticize the construction of the Monte Carlo experiments for failing to capture the true nature of the cross-sectional sampling involved in the construction of a measure of aggregate inflation. On the other hand, they argue that the use of monthly data will sidestep the small-sample bias. Since our analysis employs monthly PPI data, Verbugge's (1999) caveat will fit our research. We will not attempt to settle this issue as Bryan and Cecchetti (1999b) continue to discuss it; however, our results are rather robust for the three countries we analyze and continue to hold both at the individual country level and at a panel level, respectively.

The question of the origin of this correlation between inflation and its higher order moments is also open to debate. The most frequently cited Neo-Keynesian argument, invoking the existence of menu costs to justify the apparent sluggishness of the relative price adjustment processes, has been questioned by Balke and Wynne (2000). These authors argue that technology shocks are, instead of menu costs, responsible for this empirical regularity.

Our analysis is motivated by the argument that adjustments to a firm's price schedule can be costly.[5] Borrowing from the large body of existing literature, see

---

[2] For an early extensive literature review see Marquez and Vining (1984) and, more recently, see Golob (1993).

[3] Fischer (1981) and Fischer (1982), for example, are frequently cited studies on the relationship bewteen inflation and the variance of price changes.

[4] Vining and Elwertowski (1976), Ball and Mankiw (1995), and Balke and Wynne (2000) for the United States; Dopke and Pierdzioch (2003) for Germany; Amano and Macklem (1997) for Canada; De Abreu Lourenco and Gruen (1995) for Australia.

[5] The literature is abundant in the formalization of these costs. See Friedman and Hahn (1990), Chaps. 11 and 19, for a detailed discussion of these models and an extensive literature review.

for example Driffill et al. (1990), we can describe the price-adjustment process as follows. Firms face a cost when adjusting their nominal prices to changes in relative prices. Therefore, a monopolistically competitive firm would change its nominal prices infrequently and only when the magnitude of the required price adjustment equals or exceeds the menu cost. Heterogeneity in menu costs across industries[6] facing a common price shock or, instead, industry-specific price shocks will promote adjustments of disparate magnitude in relative price levels. In other words, an indicator of the asymmetry of nominal price shocks is likely to contain valuable information regarding the magnitude of the change in the mean value of inflation.

Under a framework of analysis that follows that of Ball and Mankiw (1995), our main contention in this chapter is that we expect positive relative price shocks to be positively related to contemporary inflation, while negatively related to future inflation. We examine this claim by studying the relationship between aggregate inflation and the cross-sectional distribution of relative-price changes in the context of three economies in the periphery of the European Union (E.U.), Greece, Spain, and Portugal. Their similar economic traits and their parallel historical process of admission into the E.U. make a comparative analysis of these three countries particularly interesting. We offer a brief overview in Sect. 2 of this chapter. In our analysis, we employ an expanded hybrid New Keynesian Phillips curve model, augmented by the presence of contemporaneous and lagged skewness as suggested by the theory. To preview our results, we find strong empirical evidence in all three countries, supporting the hypothesis connecting aggregate inflation with its third cross-sectional moment. Our results are very robust across a variety of different specifications and offer additional material for discussing issues such as inflation convergence in the context of the E.U. In addition, they have important implications for the new member states of the E.U. as well as for prospective members, such as Bulgaria, Romania, and Turkey. To the extent that nominal rigidities, perhaps in the form of menu costs, are prevalent in these countries, the impact of a common monetary policy on their price-adjustment processes is likely to be significantly different from that experienced by older E.U. members.[7]

The remainder of the chapter is organized as follows. In Sect. 2, we offer a brief overview of the historical economic developments in Greece, Portugal, and Spain. In Sect. 3, we give an outline of the theoretical motivation and empirical model that we use for our analysis. In Sect. 4, we summarize and discuss our data and offer a first glimpse into the skewness-inflation relationship. In Sect. 5, we discuss our estimation results. Section 6 has some concluding remarks and suggestions for further research. Figures and tables are to be found at the end of the chapter.

[6] Dhyne et al. (2006) found that in the E.U. the most frequently adjusted retail prices are those of energy and unprocessed food items; processed food, nonenergy industrial goods, and services change less frequently.

[7] See Dhyne et al. (2006) for an extended discussion of the potential reasons behind nominal rigidities across selected European countries.

2 Greece, Portugal, and Spain: A Brief Overview

Greece, Portugal, and Spain were late additions (in this order) to the pre-Euro European Union. Both the Spanish and Portuguese applications were finally accepted in 1977, within four months of one another; the Greek application was reactivated in 1974. In all these countries, slow and difficult political transitions from authoritarian regimes to full-fledged democracy hampered their admission to the European common market. At the time of admission (Greece in 1981, Spain and Portugal in 1986), their per capita GDP was at the bottom of the income distribution in Europe: in 1986, Spain and Greece barely exceeded 70% of the average of the 12 members and Portugal trailed with 60%.[8] In addition, they displayed significant positive inflation differentials (with respect to inflation in the core E.U. countries[9]): these were 10% for Greece, 6% for Portugal and Spain, on the basis of the consumer price index.

During the following decade, much faster economic growth than the E.U. core helped to close part of the income gap for Spain and Portugal, while Greece receded. Remarkably, this growth was achieved while adhering strictly to the Maastricht treaty, which set stringent conditions for participation in the European Monetary Union.[10] Between 1994 and 1997, Portugal and Spain drove their budget deficits and debt levels to parity with the rest of the Union. Austerity came late to the Greek economy, and the country was not included in the first wave of Euro members. With regards to price behavior, the convergence criteria reduced the inflation differentials between the periphery and the core: in Spain and Portugal to less than 1%, in Greece to 5%. These would be all-time minimums and encompass the first years of our sample period.

At the time of the launching of the Euro, January of 1999, the periphery had closed in on the core's income levels: Portuguese per capita income was 74% of the E.U. average; Spain's was 83%, and Greece's 66% – regaining some of the ground lost in the last decade. Paradoxically, this stage of the process of European monetary unification marked the end of the low inflation period for Spain and Portugal. When, after two years of stringent economic reforms, Greece joined the Euro with the second wave of E.U. countries in 2001, its inflation rate exceeded the Euro zone's average by only 1.2%. Simultaneously, Spanish and Portuguese inflation differentials were on the rise, above the core's average by 1.5 and 3% points, respectively.

The physical introduction of the Euro accompanied the process of real income per capita convergence for Greece and Spain, while during this time Portugal receded. By 2005, Spain had reached 90% of the EU-15 average, while Greece exceeded 76%; Portugal shrank to 66%. The Greek fast expansion widened the

[8] All figures of per capita income are from the European Commission.

[9] The core countries in the exchange rate mechanism (ERM) and later the European Monetary Union (EMU) are widely considered to be Germany, France, and Austria. Despite faster growth between 1996 and 2000 in the periphery, per capita GDP per hour of work in 2001 was only 63% of the core's value.

[10] Detailed accounts of the convergence process, toward achieving the Maastricht criteria, abound; see for example Detragiache and Hamann (1999).

inflation gap to 2.7% points, while the Spanish economy registered inflation rates 1.2% points above the Euro-zone average. Only the 2001–2002 contraction in the Portuguese economy brought inflation rates to full parity.

The fact that during the last two decades inflation rates in these three countries of the EU periphery have remained consistently above the Euro-zone average presents a much-debated question.[11] By studying the dynamic characteristics of inflationary processes in Portugal, Spain, and Greece,[12] employing a hybrid New Keynesian Phillips curve and incorporating a measure of price dispersion as a potential signal of asymmetric nominal shocks we believe that we contribute to this ongoing discussion.

3 Theoretical and Empirical Framework

In this section, we present in brief a standard formulation of the hybrid New Keynesian Phillips curve, sometimes referred to as the structural inflation equation. Then we integrate the measure of inflation skewness as one of its building blocks.

As in Calvo (1983), we assume that nominal individual prices are not subject to continuous revisions. The price-setting monopolistically competitive firms face adjustment costs that make these frequent price changes unfeasible.[13] As a result, only a fraction χ of all firms would revise their nominal prices at time t. The process of price adjustment will then depend on (a) the difference between the current and desired price level[14] and (b) the gap between the actual and desired firm markup. This yields the familiar expression[15]:

$$p_t^* = p_t + \alpha y_t, \tag{1}$$

where p_t^* is the desired price level, p_t is the actual price level, and by normalizing potential output to zero, y_t is the output gap at time t. Unless the magnitude of the price revisions exceeds, the adjustment cost nominal prices are left unchanged. In terms of inflation rates, $\pi_t = \Delta p_t$, (1) can be expressed as:

$$\pi_t = \beta y_t + E(\pi_{t+1}|F_t), \tag{2}$$

[11] Although this chapter does not aim to compare the inflation dynamics in the E.U. periphery to those of the E.U. core per se, Busetti et al. (2006) document periods of inflation convergence and divergence between these two regions during 1980 and 2005.

[12] Garganas and Tavlas (2001) provide a detailed analysis on inflation performance during the post 1975 period for Greece.

[13] Even if individually small, these adjustment costs can generate significant aggregate nominal price rigidities. See Akerlof and Yellen (1985) and Mankiw (1985).

[14] All references to levels are for the natural logarithms of the corresponding variables.

[15] Since marginal cost rises with increased demand, monopolistically competitive firms would like to increase their prices when the economy expands. In other words, the gap between the actual and desired firm markups is usually expressed as the output gap, the difference between actual output and its natural rate.

where $\beta > 0$ and is determined[16] by both χ and α and $E(\pi_{t+1}|F_t)$ is the expectation conditional on time-t information of inflation.

In the above formulation inflation expectations $E(\pi_{t+1}|F_t)$ play a significant role in the determination of inflation. However, there is no independent role for lagged inflation. Multiple authors argue for the inclusion in the structural inflation equation of either past values of inflation or a combination of forward-looking and backward-looking elements. The choice of the proxy variable, which adequately captures the inflationary pressures of the output gap, is also subject to extensive debate. Traditional proxies of the output gap employ detrended computations of GDP and the unemployment rate, as well as multiple incarnations of the nonaccelerating inflation rate of unemployment (NAIRU). More recently, an aggregate measure of the real marginal cost, also referred to as the labor income share, has gained momentum in the literature.[17]

For example, Gali et al. (2001) consider the following variation of the traditional staggered contract model for the European Union:

$$\pi_t = \gamma_b \pi_{t-1} + \lambda mc_t + \gamma_f E\left(\pi_{t+1}|F_t\right), \tag{3}$$

where mc_t is the real marginal cost, computed as the labor income share, and λ is the discounted fraction of firms which in any given period can reset their prices and choose them optimally (i.e. on the basis of expected future marginal costs).[18] Common labor and business practices, such as wage and price indexation, represent examples of backward-looking behavior in price setting. We argue that in all three cases examined past inflation, π_{t-1}, is a candidate proxy for inflation expectations.[19] At the same time, and in order to check the robustness of this assumption, we estimate, along the lines of Gali et al. (2001), a hybrid new Phillips curve incorporating both past inflation and forward looking inflation expectations. Gali et al. have shown that in the Euro area inflation dynamics display a strong forward-looking component. Although both sample periods coincide between comparisons, works are limited because we employ different measures of inflation and to their lack of individual Euro area country-level estimates.

---

[16] See Calvo (1983) or Mankiw and Reis (2002) for the algebraic derivation of this coefficient.

[17] Rudd and Whelan (2007) offer a critical, and exceedingly accessible, review of recent contributions to this topic, as well as several others regarding the use of rational expectations sticky-price models to capture inflation dynamics.

[18] The fraction of firms able to reset prices but following a suboptimal rule of thumb consider the average of newly adjusted prices last period plus an adjustment for expected inflation, based on lagged inflation. Gali et al. (2001) estimate a closed form of this hybrid new Phillips curve for the European Union (1970–1998) and find that forward-looking behavior is dominant.

[19] For Spain: see Alvarez and Hernando (2005) for an extensive discussion of the pricing behavior of retailing firms, and Dolado et al. (2000) and Sobczak (1998) for applications of this approach. For Portugal: see Martins (2006) for a survey-based analysis of firms' pricing behavior, and Angeloni et al. (2003) for a discussion of the implications of this behavior on monetary transmission. Although no such study is available for Greece works focused on inflation persistence, monetary policy and exchange rate regimes belong to: Hondroyiannis and Lazaretou (2004), Hall and Zonzilos (2000), Alogoskoufis, Lee and Philippopoulos (1998), and Lazaretou (1995).

As mentioned earlier, the parameterization of the output gap has recently added new candidate measures.[20] Although the fact that the counter cyclical behavior of the labor share of income complicates the theoretical argument justifying its use as a measure of marginal cost, Gali et al. (2005) argue that its empirical contribution is robust.[21] At the same time, traditional measures of the output gap perform very well in conventional econometric estimation. We do not attempt to settle this issue here and choose to employ an instrument uniformly defined across the three economies object of our study.

The gap between the actual unemployment rate and the NAIRU is a widely used robust approximation to the output gap and therefore a good candidate for this study. Camba and Radriguez (2003) show that in the E.U. case such a measure performs well relative to other candidate measures. At the same time, Estrada et al. (2000) find that the usefulness of the NAIRU when discussing Spanish macroeconomic policy is very limited, and that the NAIRU is indeed closely matched by actual unemployment.[22] On the basis of their findings, we will proxy the output gap, y_t, by measures of the unemployment rate, u_t: an expansion (an incipient positive output gap) will be associated with a fall in the overall unemployment rate; a contraction (an incipient negative output gap) will be associated with a rise in the overall unemployment rate.

Putting them all together, a stylized, compact econometric representation of such a hybrid New Keynesian Phillips curve widely present in the literature could then be given as:

$$\pi_t = c^* + \gamma_b \pi_{t-1} + \gamma_g u_t + \gamma_f E\left(\pi_{t+1} | F_t\right) + \varepsilon_t^* \tag{4}$$

with ε_t^* an appropriately defined exogenous price shock.

Our contribution starts with (4) and adds to it various measures of the cross-sectional distribution of relative price changes and a couple of control variables. The inclusion of additional variables in such *a structural* inflation equation is not explictly warranted by the theory; it is, however, guided by the arguments in Ball and Mankiw (1995) and can be seen as a theoretically motivated test for the marginal predictive ability of the cross-sectional distribution of relative prices. We thus explore the association between inflation and its higher moments by focusing on the relationship between aggregate PPI inflation and the skewness in relative-price changes, which we denote by s_t^{π} and define in the next secition. Note that the existing literature indistinctively employs weighted and unweighted measures

[20] See Rudd and Whelan (2007) for a discussion of the use of the labor income share as a proxy of the output gap. See Orphanides et al. (1999) for a discussion of the traditional operational definitions of the output gap: the difference between the current unemployment rate and the NAIRU and the difference between actual GDP and an estimation of potential GDP.

[21] Among other issues, these authors parry the claims of (a) Linde (2005) regarding how estimating a hybrid New Keynesian Phillips curve with full information maximum likelihood (FIML) yields results superior to the Generalized Method of Moments (GMM) and (b) Sbordone (2005) who proposes a two-step minimum distance estimation procedure to test whether *expected* future marginal costs drive inflation.

[22] Estrada et al. (2000) compute and compare several empirical definitions of the NAIRU and conclude (p. 26) that all but one of the NAIRU estimates shows a time-pattern in five-year subperiods that is quite similar to the observed unemployment.

and obtains almost identical results. In all our empirical models, the dependent variable is the (appropriately defined) PPI-based monthly or annual inflation rate π_t. As noted, on the right-hand side, we have variables describing the distribution of relative-price changes. To capture the dynamic features of the price adjustment process, and in accordance with the model of (4), we include lagged inflation and lagged skewness terms. The most generic equation that we estimate then takes the following form:

$$\gamma_b(L)\,\pi_t = c + \gamma_g u_t + \gamma_f E(\pi_{t+1}|F_t) + \beta_s(L)s_t^{\pi} + \beta_v v_t + x_t\beta_x + \varepsilon_t + \theta\varepsilon_{t-q}, \quad (5)$$

where $\gamma_b(L) = 1 - \sum_{j=1}^{p}\gamma_{bj}L^j$ is a polynomial in the lag operator L for inflation; $\beta(L) = \beta_0 + \beta_1 L$ takes into account current and lagged skewness; v_t is the cross-sectional standard deviation of inflation, also defined in the next section. Finally, x_t is an oil-inflation based control that we add to check for robustness, after the estimation of the main equations. The model error can take the form of a moving average when forward looking expectations are included in the model and takes the value $q = 1$ or $q = 12$.

We perform our analysis with the following specifications (and corresponding parameter restrictions):

- Without including inflation expectations $E(\pi_{t+1}|F_t)$ and unemployment; we thus have $\gamma_f = \gamma_g = \theta = 0$; we estimate the corresponding model twice, once by least squares (LS) and once by two stage least squares (2SLS) to account for possible endogeneity problems from the presence of the contemporaneous skewness and standard deviation variables.
- With inflation expectations but without unemployment; we thus have $\gamma_g = 0$; we estimate the model by 2SLS.
- With inflation expectations and unemployment (full model); we estimate the model again by 2SLS.

2SLS estimation is performed using lags of the dependent and explanatory variables as instruments. The number of instruments is kept to a minimum to account for possible problems with weak instruments (see later). We use heteroskedasticity-consistent standard errors to assess significance for the estimated parameters. After estimation, we perform a test for the long-run effect of skewness, namely a test for the hypothesis $H_0 : \beta_0 + \beta_1 = 0$, and also a variety of residual diagnostic tests, including tests for residual autocorrelation, conditional heteroscedasticity, normality and functional (miss)specification.

Finally, an important issue is the potential problem of "weak instruments." There is a growing literature about this problem, especially in the context of forward-looking models like the one we employ. Related references include Stock and Wright (2000), Hahn and Hausman (2002), Ma (2002), Stock et al. (2002), and Mavroeidis (2004). There are two methods that one can pursue: either test for the problem of weak instruments or follow some method of inference able to handle the problem. As our results appear to be quite robust across countries and equation specifications, we decided to follow the first method of testing the null hypothesis of weak instruments. Stock and Yogo (2003, 2005) propose the use of the Gragg and Donald (1993) statistic as an appropriate testing tool when the occurrence of weak instruments is suspected. The test statistic is the smallest estimated eigenvalue of the following covariance matrix:

$$\mathbf{G}_T = \widehat{\Sigma}_v^{-1/2} \mathbf{Y}^{\perp\prime} \mathbf{P_Z} \mathbf{Y}^{\perp} \widehat{\Sigma}_v^{-1/2}, \tag{6}$$

where the component matrices are residuals matrices that remove the influence of the exogenous/predetermined variables and the instruments **X**, **Z** from the right-hand side endogenous variables **Y**.[23] The limiting distribution of the minimum eigenvalue of $\mathbf{G}_T$ is found under different assumptions, and here we use the vari-

Table 1 Distributional descriptive statistics

	Monthly inflation	Monthly cross-sectional std. deviation	Monthly cross-sectional skewness	Annual inflation	Annual cross-sectional std. deviation	Annual cross-sectional skewness	Unem-ployment
GREECE							
Mean	0.26	1.31	0.88	3.41	5.10	0.80	10.91
Maximum	2.37	4.26	5.63	9.38	8.06	5.14	12.76
Minimum	−1.36	0.62	−6.28	−1.17	3.11	−2.17	9.18
Std. dev.	0.65	0.62	2.69	2.33	1.23	1.66	0.91
Skewness	0.45	2.33	−0.60	0.50	0.08	0.67	−0.00
Kurtosis	4.19	10.25	2.81	2.52	2.25	2.87	2.27
Normality	0.01	0.00	0.05	0.08	0.31	0.03	0.46
Observations	96	96	96	96	96	96	70
PORTUGAL							
Mean	0.22	1.24	0.74	2.54	5.50	0.80	5.86
Maximum	2.29	3.58	6.07	15.57	13.46	6.00	8.00
Minimum	−2.24	0.40	−7.29	−7.64	2.32	−3.82	3.70
Std. dev.	0.72	0.55	3.10	4.26	2.28	2.28	1.37
Skewness	0.17	1.63	−0.19	0.59	1.34	0.07	−0.21
Kurtosis	4.07	6.56	2.10	4.52	5.18	2.24	1.49
Normality	0.03	0.00	0.06	0.00	0.00	0.20	0.00
Observations	139	139	139	128	128	128	136
SPAIN							
Mean	0.21	0.95	0.47	2.21	5.04	0.87	15.05
Maximum	1.47	2.97	4.80	6.41	12.61	4.43	23.85
Minimum	−1.05	0.24	−4.81	−2.22	1.84	−3.56	8.39
Std. dev.	0.39	0.47	2.64	2.25	2.23	2.37	4.94
Skewness	0.24	1.19	−0.22	0.18	1.21	−0.15	0.41
Kurtosis	3.59	5.27	1.82	1.93	4.45	1.63	1.64
Normality	0.19	0.00	0.01	0.03	0.00	0.01	0.00
Observations	138	138	138	127	127	127	138

Notes: The row "Normality" gives the *p*-value of the Jarque-Bera test for normality in the marginal distribution of the series.

[23] See Stock and Yogo (2005) for detailed information about the construction of these matrices and their relationship with the model's reduced form.

ant that relates the number of endogenous regressors, the number of instrumental variables, and the desired maximal bias relative to LS (the aforementioned authors list critical values for up to 30% maximal bias). Table 1 in Stock and Yogo (2005) gives related critical values for a combination of the above quantities at the 5% level of significance but we find more informative to report, besides the test statistic value, the estimated maximal bias relative to LS. We refer the reader to Stock and Yogo (2005) for more details of this test statistic.[24]

4 Data and Descriptive Statistics

Our data were obtained from the respective statistical service agencies of the three countries we examine. We have data on the components of the producer price index (PPI) as well as the index itself, and data on unemployment for sample periods when they are consistently available.

These sample sizes are almost identical, starting from 1995 and ending in 2003 for Greece and 2006 for Portugal and Spain. However, the data differ in the classification digits for the components of the PPI: for Greece we have data for 4-digit classification, for Portugal we have data for 3-digit classification, and for Spain we have data for 2-digit classification. Our choices were dictated by reasons of data consistency and availability. For all three countries, there were frequent revisions, before 1995, both in base years and methods of aggregations and reporting on the components of the PPI. Unemployment data were available on a quarterly frequency for Portugal and Spain but for Greece it was consistently available only after 1998. The unemployment data for all three countries were interpolated to monthly frequency using a cubic spline method.[25]

For all the countries, the same procedure was followed in constructing the two measures of the cross-sectional distribution of relative prices, standard deviation, and skewness. The industry-level data were arranged in a $T \times N$ matrix, of $t = 1,2,\ldots,T$ months and $j = 1,2,\ldots,N$ industries per month. The definition of the cross-sectional moments we use is given in the following equation:

$$v_t^2 = \frac{1}{N}\sum_{j=1}^{N}(\pi_{tj} - \bar{\pi}_t), \quad s_t^{\pi} = \frac{1}{N}\sum_{j=1}^{N}\left(\frac{\pi_{tj} - \bar{\pi}_t}{v_t}\right)^3, \tag{7}$$

where π_{tj} is the (monthly or annual) inflation of the jth sector for month t and $\bar{\pi}_t = N^{-1}\sum_{j=1}^{N}\pi_{tj}$ is the corresponding cross-sectional mean inflation of the jth

[24] An important aspect of this class of tests is that they are strictly applicable in linear IV-type models (so they are appropriate to use in our context) but was originally designed under an assumption of i.i.d. errors. However, our rejection of the null hypothesis of weak instruments is quite strong in almost all equations and, as Stock and Yogo (2005) note, this is an indication that there is no real problem with our estimation results.

[25] The cubic spline matched the last monthly observation within a quarter to the corresponding actual quarterly observation. Further details about our data are available on request.

sector. Assuming that the industries are uncorrelated for every month in our sample, the above equation provides us with consistent estimators of the degree of dispersion and asymmetry in the distribution of producer prices. Finally, monthly and annual PPI inflation were computed using the standard formula $\pi_t = \log(P_t/P_{t-k}) \times 100$, for $k = 1, 12$.

In Figs. 1–3, we have a visual representation of our data series for all three countries: Greece, Portugal, and Spain. These figures contain the monthly and annual inflation rates, the corresponding cross-sectional monthly and annual standard deviations and skewness of the PPI and, finally, unemployment. In Tables 1 and 2, we present some distributional and temporal descriptive statistics for all these series.

Figure 1 shows the monthly and annual PPI inflation and the PPI skewness series for Greece. As usual, the path of monthly inflation exhibits less persistence than the path of annual inflation, a stylized fact also captured in Table 2.[26] Annual inflation and the cross-sectional skewness move almost together, falling until the late 1990s and then increasing before "stabilizing" after 2001. The average inflation rates for the whole period are 0.26% (monthly) and 3.41% (annually), respectively. It is noteworthy that skewness turned from positive to negative in the period (of about) 1996–1998 and then sharply increased to positive again. The evidence in the literature points out to the deflationary impact of the convergence criteria set by the Maastricht treaty. Afterwards, and even within a common currency framework, such stringent macroeconomic constraints were missing. The contemporaneous correlation between monthly and annual inflation and skewness is 43 and 63%, respectively, suggesting that there is some substantial linear dependence between them. Estimating two simple linear regressions of monthly and annual inflation on the cross-sectional skewness we obtain the following results:

$$\text{Greece - Monthly PPI Inflation}\, \pi_t = 0.20 + 0.09 s_t^{\pi}, \quad R^2 = 18.58\% \tag{8a}$$

$$\text{Greece - Annual PPI Inflation}\, \pi_t = 2.70 + 0.90 s_t^{\pi}, \quad R^2 = 40.33\% \tag{8b}$$

The estimated coefficients are significant at the 1% level, for both equations,[27] lending some initial support to the potential relationship between inflation and its third moment. The finding that 20% (40%) of the variability of monthly (annual) inflation can be potentially explained by its cross-sectional skewness is remarkable and agrees with the original predictions of Ball and Mankiw (1995).

In Fig. 2, we have the monthly and annual PPI inflation and the PPI skewness series for Portugal. As before, the path of monthly inflation exhibits less persistence

[26] We note that for all countries annual inflation exhibits strong persistence at low lags but it decays rapidly, in contrast to unit-root nonstationary behavior. Although we provide p-values for a standard unit root test that do not reject the null of nonstationarity, we believe that a target variable like inflation cannot be characterized as a behavior like a random walk. In addition, the low power of unit root tests combined with policy interventions suggests that we should treat the results of such tests with some caution.

[27] For all simple regressions reported in this section, significance is based on either heteroskedasticity or heteroskedasticity-autocorrelation consistent standard errors. Results from 2SLS estimation are similar and available on request.

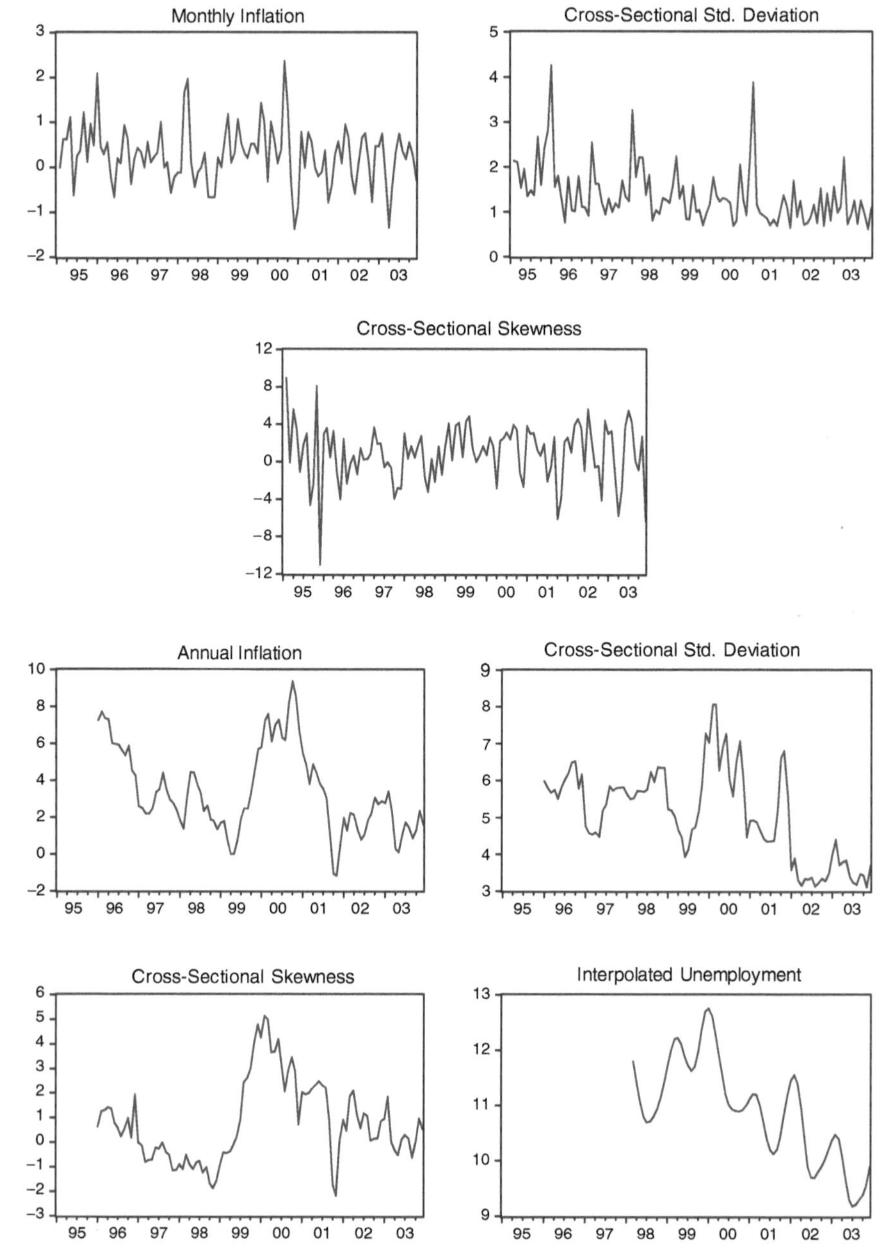

Fig. 1 Monthly and annual inflation, cross-sectional standard deviation and skewness and unemployment for Greece

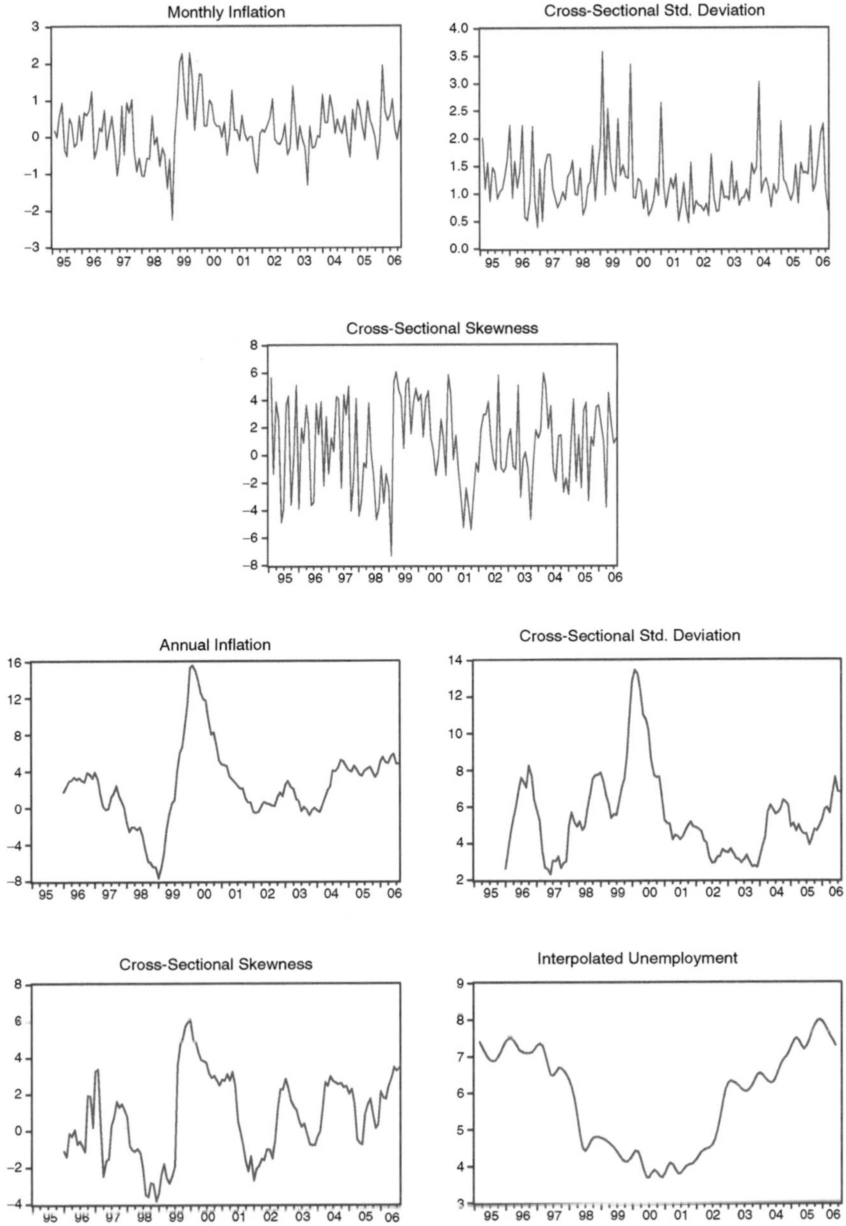

Fig. 2 Monthly and annual inflation, cross-sectional standard deviation and skewness and unemployment for Portugal

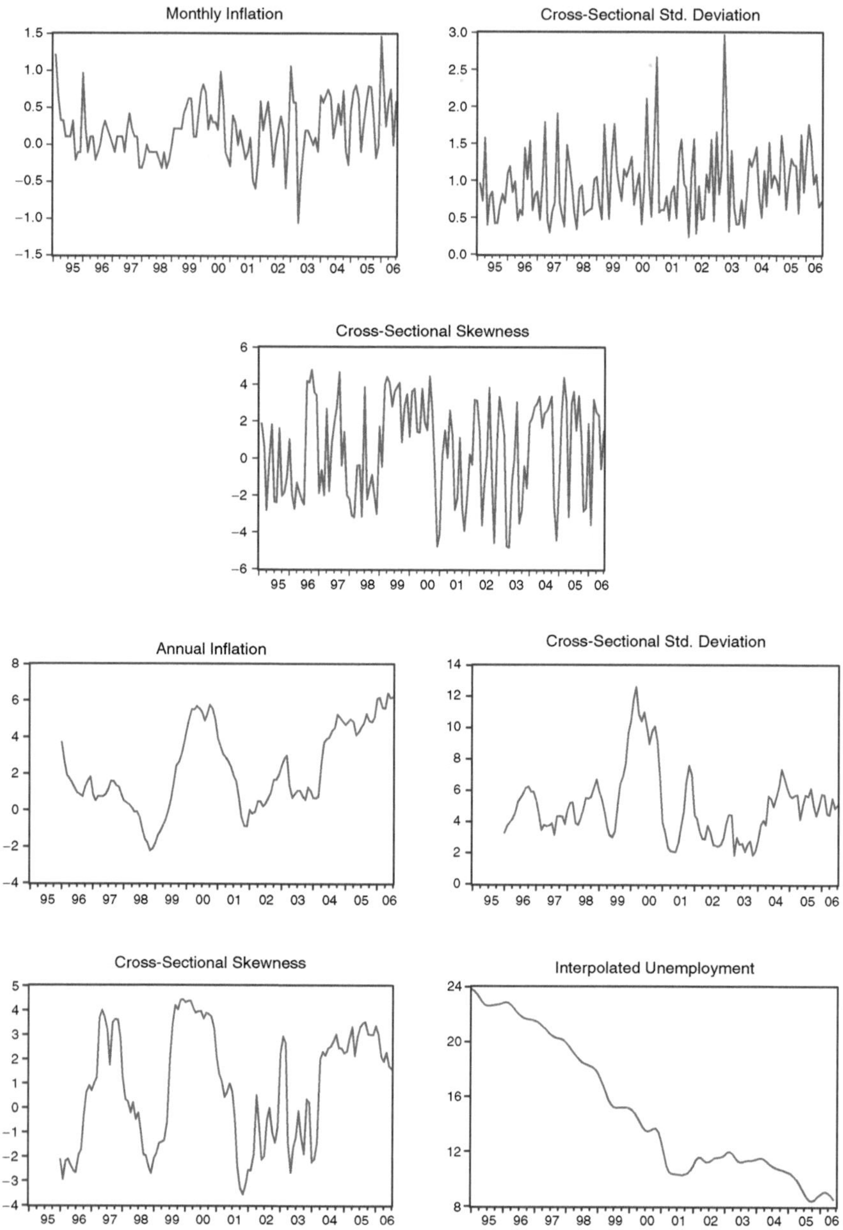

Fig. 3 Monthly and annual inflation, cross-sectional standard deviation and skewness and unemployment for Spain

Table 2 Temporal descriptive statistics

	Monthly inflation	Monthly cross-sectional std. deviation	Monthly cross-sectional skewness	Annual inflation	Annual cross-sectional std. deviation	Annual cross-sectional skewness
GREECE						
r(1)	0.29	0.31	0.03	0.91	0.86	0.89
r(12)	0.07	0.26	0.05	−0.24	0.00	0.12
r(24)	0.00	0.20	0.04	−0.14	0.20	−0.37
ADF	0.00	0.00	0.00	0.13	0.24	0.19
PORTUGAL						
r(1)	0.43	0.08	0.22	0.97	0.95	0.89
r(12)	0.10	0.19	0.03	−0.11	0.11	−0.21
r(24)	−0.03	0.02	0.10	−0.42	−0.14	−0.28
ADF	0.00	0.00	0.00	0.18	0.06	0.03
SPAIN						
r(1)	0.44	0.09	0.41	0.94	0.92	0.91
r(12)	0.07	0.01	0.02	−0.03	−0.02	−0.26
r(24)	0.01	0.07	−0.07	−0.19	−0.08	−0.14
ADF	0.00	0.00	0.00	0.48	0.04	0.09

Notes:
The rows labeled "r(h)" give the sample hth order autocorrelation of the series.
The rows labeled ADF give the p-value of the Augmented Dickey-Fuller test for a unit root.
The 5% standard error of the sample autocorrelations is: 0.19 for Greece, 0.17 for Portugal/Spain.

than the path of annual inflation. Similarities with the case of Greece are patent, although there are differences in magnitude. For example, the rise in annual inflation after 1999 is over two times that of Greece's (Greece peaks at about 7% while Portugal peaks at about 16%); the Portuguese average inflation rates for the whole period are 0.22% (monthly) and 2.54% (annually), respectively. Additionally, during the sample period Portuguese inflation is more volatile: in terms of historical standard deviations Portugal registers 0.72% vs. 0.65% in Greece for monthly inflation and 4.26% vs. 2.23% in Greece for annual inflation. Finally, the contemporaneous correlation between Portuguese monthly and annual inflation and their corresponding skewness measures is 62% and 82%, respectively. These figures amply exceed the corresponding Greek values of 43% and 63%. Estimating, as before, two simple linear regressions of monthly and annual inflation on the corresponding skewness measures we obtain the following results:

$$\text{Portugal - Monthly PPI Inflation } \pi_t = 0.11 + 0.14 s_t^{\pi}, \quad R^2 = 38.36\% \tag{9a}$$

$$\text{Portugal - Annual PPI Inflation } \pi_t = 1.31 + 1.54 s_t^{\pi}, \quad R^2 = 67.64\% \tag{9b}$$

The estimated coefficients are again significant at the 1% level, and the R-squared values are higher than in the case of Greece, suggesting an even stronger link between inflation and its third moment. The fit for the annual inflation equation is the strongest between the three countries under consideration.

Finally, in Fig. 3, we have the graphical representation of the Spanish series. As expected, the path of monthly inflation exhibits less persistence than the path of annual inflation. As the third member of the EU periphery, the evolution of Spanish inflation is quite similar to those of Greece and Portugal. Again, differences in magnitude and timing are remarkable. For example, after the sharp increase in 1999 and 2000, annual inflation drops and then starts increasing again, instead of "stabilizing" as in the case of Greece and Portugal. Also note that unemployment falls with a definite downward trend from 1995 onwards – in contrast with the rise of Portugal's unemployment after 2000. However, the average unemployment rate for Spain is three times that of Portugal.[28] The average inflation rates for the whole period are 0.21% (monthly) and 2.21% (annually), respectively, almost identical to those of Portugal. In contrast with Portugal, the historical standard deviation of inflation for Spain is lower and closer to that of Greece with 0.39% (monthly) and 2.25% (annually), respectively. Finally, the contemporaneous correlation between monthly and annual inflation and skewness is 67% and 72%, respectively. Estimating, as before, two simple linear regressions of monthly and annual inflation on the cross-sectional skewness, we obtain the following results:

$$\text{Spain - Monthly PPI Inflation}\,\pi_t = 0.16 + 0.10 s_t^{\pi},\, R^2 = 44.84\% \qquad (10a)$$

$$\text{Spain - Annual PPI Inflation}\,\pi_t = 1.62 + 0.69 s_t^{\pi},\, R^2 = 52.11\% \qquad (10b)$$

The estimated coefficients are significant at the 1% level and the fit for the monthly inflation equation is the highest among the three countries.

In the next section, we present our estimation results for the generic model of (5) and discuss the implications of our findings, which are strongly supportive of the simple regressions presented above.

5 Estimation Results and Discussion

The core estimation results, on the basis of the model of (5), appear in Tables 3–9. We present the coefficient estimates along with their significance, the fit of each model, a number of residual diagnostics, and the test statistic on the basis of (6) on the null hypothesis of weak instruments. Also, the long-run effect of skewness on inflation is tested and reported. When using 2SLS, our instrument lists include past values of (monthly or annual) inflation, the relevant standard deviation and skewness measures, and unemployment. The structure of Tables 3–8 is the same: they contain four column panels that correspond to the four different model combinations we consider. These are, in column order: (1) the model without forward looking

[28] As large as this disparity in unemployment rates may seem, particularly for neighboring countries, Castillo et al. (1998) found that both countries experienced similar shocks to their unemployment rates from the 1980s onwards. We will follow Blanchard and Jimeno (1995) in approaching the treatment of this question with "humility" and follow their example by leaving this intellectual challenge to others.

Table 3 Estimation results for Greece – monthly inflation

Explanatory variables	Model 1 OLS	Model 2 2SLS	Model 3 2SLS w/FI	Model 4 Phillips curve
Forward inflation (+1)			0.81***	0.71***
			(0.27)	(0.16)
Lagged inflation (−1)	0.33***	0.33***	0.63***	0.66***
	(0.12)	(0.13)	(0.11)	(0.12)
Lagged inflation (−2)	−0.17**	−0.16*	−0.08	−0.18**
	(0.08)	(0.10)	(0.10)	(0.09)
Current skewness	0.09***	0.12**	0.10**	0.05*
	(0.02)	(0.06)	(0.04)	(0.03)
Lagged skewness (−1)	−0.005	0.004	−0.09***	−0.06**
	(0.02)	(0.02)	(0.02)	(0.03)
Current std. dev.	0.21	0.38*	−0.08	−0.21
	(0.15)	(0.20)	(0.10)	(0.17)
Unemployment				−0.03
				(0.04)
Moving average			−0.55*	−0.61***
			(0.33)	(0.20)
Observations	105	102	101	67
R-squared	0.35	0.30	0.36	0.52
F-test	0.00	0.00	0.00	0.00
s.e.e.	0.54	0.55	0.54	0.46
Long-run effect of skewness	0.00	0.08	0.94	0.74
Ljung-Box(12) test	0.97	0.97	0.92	0.69
Normality test	0.32	0.00	0.31	0.11
ARCH(12)	0.24	0.53	0.38	0.61
RESET(1) test	0.66	0.15	1.00	1.00
GT test	n.a.	7.84	7.00	1.42
(≈max. bias relative to OLS at 5% significance)	n.a.	11.3%	12.5%	40%

Notes: Heteroskedasticity consistent std. errors in parentheses below the estimates; *, ** and *** denote significance at the 10%, 5%, and 1% level, respectively.
F-test gives the p-value for the joint significance of the explanatory variables.
s.e.e. is the standard error of estimation.
Long-run effect of skewness gives the p-value of the Wald test for the null hypothesis that the sum of the coefficients of current and lagged skewness is zero.
Ljung-Box(24) test gives the *p*-value of the corresponding test for residual autocorrelation using 24 lags.
Normality test gives the *p*-value of the Jarque-Bera test for residual normality.
ARCH(24) test gives the p-value of the corresponding test for residual conditional autoregressive heteroskedasticity using 12 lags.
RESET(1) test gives the p-value of Ramsey's test for misspecification using one fitted term.
GT test gives the test value from the Gragg and Donald (1993) minimum eigenvalue statistic for the null hypothesis of weak instruments as proposed by Stock and Yogo (2005).

expectations and unemployment, estimated by LS; (2) the same model estimated by 2SLS; (3) the model with forward looking expectations but without unemployment, estimated by 2SLS; (4) the hybrid Phillips curve model with both forward looking expectations and unemployment, estimated by 2SLS.

Table 4 Estimation results for greece – annual inflation

Explanatory variables	Model 1 OLS	Model 2 2SLS	Model 3 2SLS w/ FI	Model 4 Phillips curve
Forward inflation (+1)			0.41***	0.41***
			(0.09)	(0.08)
Lagged inflation (−1)	1.07***	1.07***	0.76***	0.78***
	(0.09)	(0.08)	(0.08)	(0.08)
Lagged inflation (−2)	−0.22**	−0.21**	−0.13*	−0.18***
	(0.09)	(0.10)	(0.07)	(0.06)
Current skewness	0.71***	0.79***	0.66**	0.53***
	(0.09)	(0.30)	(0.27)	(0.17)
Lagged skewness (−1)	−0.59***	−0.67**	−0.65***	−0.49***
	(0.10)	(0.29)	(0.23)	(0.14)
Current std. dev.	0.14***	0.13**	−0.001	0.09
	(0.05)	(0.06)	(0.06)	(0.07)
Unemployment				−0.21 **
				(0.08)
Moving average			−0.15	−0.37**
			(0.19)	(0.19)
Observations	94	91	90	67
R-squared	0.93	0.93	0.96	0.98
F-test	0.00	0.00	0.00	0.00
s.e.e.	0.60	0.61	0.47	0.40
Long-run effect of skewness	0.00	0.00	0.82	0.00
Ljung-Box(12) test	0.25	0.33	0.72	0.17
Normality test	0.64	0.80	0.98	0.74
ARCH(12)	0.61	0.64	0.84	0.99
RESET(1) test	0.64	0.20	1.00	1.00
GT test	n.a.	7.10	6.84	5.86
(≈max. bias relative to OLS at 5% significance)	n.a.	12.3%	12.7%	14.1%

Notes: See Table 3.

The results of our estimations for Greece are presented in Tables 3 and 4. Table 3 summarizes the results for monthly inflation and Table 4 for annual inflation. When considering monthly inflation, the signs of the estimated coefficients of contemporaneous and lagged skewness are as anticipated by the theory suggested by Ball and Mankiw (1995): positive for contemporaneous skewness and negative for lagged skewness. The coefficients of contemporaneous skewness in three out of four cases are significant at the 5% level or above, while it is interesting to note that the coefficients of lagged skewness are significant only when forward looking inflation is included in the model (columns 3 and 4). Since lagged skewness is not significant in the first two models, we do not consider its impact on the long-run effects for these models. For models 3 and 4, our estimation does not indicate the existence of a significant long-run effect of the third moment on inflation and the corresponding statistic does not reject the null hypothesis of zero long-run effect.

Table 5 Estimation results for Portugal – monthly inflation

Explanatory variables	Model 1 OLS	Model 2 2SLS	Model 3 2SLS w/FI	Model 4 Phillips curve
Forward inflation (+1)			0.38***	0.38***
			(0.08)	(0.10)
Lagged inflation (−1)	0.18**	0.17	0.70***	0.56***
	(0.08)	(0.13)	(0.13)	(0.19)
Lagged inflation (−2)	0.06	0.11	−0.02	0.002
	(0.07)	(0.07)	(0.08)	(0.06)
Current skewness	0.12***	0.15***	0.15***	0.14***
	(0.02)	(0.05)	(0.05)	(0.03)
Lagged skewness (−1)	0.02	−0.001	−0.16***	−0.12**
	(0.01)	(0.02)	(0.04)	(0.05)
Current std. dev.	0.26***	0.64*	−0.04	0.04
	(0.09)	(0.33)	(0.08)	(0.08)
Unemployment				−0.002
				(0.008)
Moving average			−0.90***	−0.85**
			(0.21)	(0.35)
Observations	137	134	129	128
R-squared	0.49	0.39	0.54	0.60
F-test	0.00	0.00	0.00	0.00
s.e.e.	0.52	0.58	0.54	0.48
Long-run effect of skewness	0.00	0.01	0.00	0.00
Ljung-Box(12) test	0.54	0.08	0.60	0.54
Normality test	0.00	0.00	0.81	0.25
ARCH(12)	0.92	0.89	0.98	0.77
RESET(1) test	0.09	0.36	0.00	0.00
GT test	n.a.	7.74	3.32	3,50
(≈max. bias relative to OLS at 5% significance)	n.a.	11.4%	23.1%	22.2%

Notes: See Table 3.

Lagged inflation is always highly significant (in all cases at the 1% level), and there is ample evidence of both strong persistence and mean reversion, with lagged inflation alternating signs between lag one and lag two. Forward inflation also enters significantly into the estimating equation and the magnitude of the respective coefficient is higher than that of the coefficient of the first lag of inflation. Finally, unemployment in the hybrid model in column 4 does not enter significantly. Only in this last case, the G_T statistic points towards weakly defined instruments by yielding a value that exceeds the maximal bias (30%) for which critical values were computed by Stock and Yogo (2005).

The results for annual inflation for Greece, in Table 4, are much stronger and robust as far as the effects of skewness are concerned. Now both contemporaneous and lagged skewness appear with the expected signs and are strongly significant. Remarkably, the long-run effect of skewness is consistently present, even when lagged inflation is used; it only disappears in model 3 when forward looking

Table 6 Estimation results for Portugal – annual inflation

Explanatory variables	Model 1 OLS	Model 2 2SLS	Model 3 2SLS w/FI	Model 4 Phillips curve
Forward inflation (+1)			0.33***	0.33***
			(0.08)	(0.06)
Lagged inflation (−1)	1.33***	1.35***	0.80***	0.81***
	(0.08)	(0.11)	(0.12)	(0.10)
Lagged inflation (−2)	−0.43***	−0.44***	−0.17**	−0.18***
	(0.07)	(0.10)	(0.07)	(0.06)
Current skewness	0.48***	0.43*	0.38**	0.33**
	(0.05)	(0.22)	(0.16)	(0.16)
Lagged skewness (−1)	−0.35***	−0.32*	−0.29**	−0.24*
	(0.07)	(0.18)	(0.14)	(0.14)
Current std. dev.	0.07	0.05	0.02	0.01
	(0.04)	(0.04)	(0.03)	(0.03)
Unemployment				−0.001
				(0.03)
Moving average			−0.36**+	−0.37**+
			(0.15)	(0.16)
Observations	126	124	112	111
R-squared	0.98	0.98	0.99	0.99
F-test	0.00	0.00	0.00	0.00
s.e.e.	0.67	0.67	0.46	0.45
Long-run effect of skewness	0.01	0.14	0.06	0.09
Ljung-Box(12) test	0.20	0.16	0.29	0.15
Normality test	0.00	0.00	0.07	0.59
ARCH(12)	0.03	0.06	0.02	0.02
RESET(1) test	0.27	0.37	0.00	0.00
GT test	n.a.	11.02	8.87	8.58
(≈max. bias relative to OLS at 5% significance)	n.a.	8.31%	10.0%	10.4%

Notes: See Table 3. The + sign denotes a 12-order moving average.

inflation is included and enters again when incorporating unemployment in model 4. Regarding the lagged and forward inflation, we report highly significant coefficients. Now, lagged inflation enters with higher values than forward inflation. Finally, unemployment enters with the expected (negative) sign and is significant.[29]

The results for Portugal, presented in Tables 5 and 6, are similar to the results for Greece, albeit with higher degrees of significance when considering monthly inflation. In this case, the long-run effect of skewness is always present, even when incorporating forward inflation in the equations. The estimates obtained from the annual inflation data show, again more strongly and consistently, the

[29] Gali and Gertler (1999) showed that the sum of the backward and forward-looking parameters could be smaller than or equal to unity depending on how strongly or weakly price-setting firms discount future prices. In this chapter, for simplicity, we consider an implicit discount factor of one. The results for Greece indicate that the sum of these estimates is equal to unity cannot be rejected for both annual and monthly models. The same result applied to Portugal and Spain as well.

Table 7 Estimation results for Spain – monthly inflation

Explanatory variables	Model 1 OLS	Model 2 2SLS	Model 3 2SLS w/FI	Model 4 Phillips curve
Forward inflation (+1)			0.40**	0.53***
			(0.17)	(0.13)
Lagged inflation (−1)	0.32***	0.28**	0.58***	0.60***
	(0.08)	(0.14)	(0.14)	(0.10)
Lagged inflation (−2)	−0.10	−0.10	−0.08	−0.13*
	(0.07)	(0.09)	(0.11)	(0.07)
Current skewness	0.09***	0.13**	0.10*	0.06**
	(0.01)	(0.06)	(0.06)	(0.03)
Lagged skewness (−1)	−0.02*	−0.03	−0.08**	−0.05**
	(0.01)	(0.02)	(0.03)	(0.02)
Current std. dev.	0.02	0.06	0.05	0.03
	(0.08)	(0.19)	(0.07)	(0.04)
Unemployment				0.000
				(0.002)
Moving average			−0.63*	−0.71**
			(0.37)	(0.30)
Observations	136	134	131	131
R-squared	0.52	0.48	0.57	0.65
F-test	0.00	0.00	0.00	0.00
s.e.e.	0.27	0.28	0.25	0.23
Long-run effect of skewness	0.00	0.00	0.08	0.53
Ljung-Box(12) test	0.71	0.76	0.92	0.98
Normality test	0.00	0.00	0.86	0.48
ARCH(12)	0.96	0.81	0.62	0.77
RESET(1) test	0.28	0.16	1.00	0.01
GT test	n.a.	8.70	5.61	5.58
(≈max. bias relative to OLS at 5% significance)	n.a.	10.3%	15.1%	15.2%

Notes: See Table 3.

contemporaneous and lagged effects of cross-sectional skewness on relative prices. However, unemployment does not enter significantly in the monthly or in the annual inflation models. Also, although the long-run effect of skewness is present, it appears more strongly in Greece than in Portugal.

The results for Spain appear in Tables 7 and 8, and are similar to the results for Portugal and Greece. Therefore, we will focus our discussion on the annual inflation data. Past inflation values influence current inflation levels in a very similar order of magnitude in both Spain and Portugal.[30] Unemployment also enters significantly, as

[30] The literature indicates that producer prices are revised more frequently than consumer prices; see Alvarez and Hernando (2005) for a discussion of the Spanish case. Adjustments of consumer prices take twice as long in the EU than in the USA: both Gali et al. (2000) and Dhyne et al. (2006) estimate an average adjustment period in Europe between four and six quarters. Nevertheless, there is great variability within the EMU: according to Cecchetti and Debelle (2006), CPI inflation persistence is higher in Italy than in Finland by an order of magnitude of almost 30.

Table 8 Estimation results for Spain – annual inflation

Explanatory variables	Model 1 OLS	Model 2 2SLS	Model 3 2SLS w/FI	Model 4 Phillips curve
Forward inflation (+1)			0.36***	0.32***
			(0.07)	(0.06)
Lagged inflation (−1)	1.28***	1.32***	0.80***	0.71***
	(0.07)	(0.09)	(0.13)	(0.10)
Lagged inflation (−2)	−0.32***	−0.35***	−0.16**	−0.15**
	(0.06)	(0.08)	(0.07)	(0.07)
Current skewness	0.29***	0.22***	0.18***	0.18***
	(0.05)	(0.09)	(0.07)	(0.06)
Lagged skewness (−1)	−0.25***	−0.20***	−0.16***	−0.09**
	(0.03)	(0.08)	(0.06)	(0.04)
Current std. dev.	0.02*	0.01	0.00	0.02
	(0.01)	(0.01)	(0.01)	(0.01)
Unemployment				−0.04**
				(0.01)
Moving average			−0.55***+	−0.56***+
			(0.16)	(0.16)
Observations	125	124	111	111
R-squared	0.98	0.98	0.99	0.99
F-test	0.00	0.00	0.00	0.00
s.e.e.	0.33	0.34	0.21	0.18
Long-run effect of skewness	0.09	0.33	0.23	0.01
Ljung-Box(12) test	0.16	0.08	0.06	0.55
Normality test	0.12	0.09	0.00	0.01
ARCH(12)	0.38	0.40	0.27	0.77
RESET(1) test	0.54	0.74	0.00	0.00
GT test	n.a.	14.23	12.54	12.29
(≈max. bias relative to OLS at 5% significance)	n.a.	6.56%	7.38%	7.52%

Notes: See Table 3. The + sign denotes a 12-order moving average.

in Greece. We find some noteworthy differences in the magnitudes of the estimated coefficients of contemporaneous and lagged skewness among Spain, Portugal, and Greece. This last country exhibits the highest estimated effect of skewness on inflation while Portugal and Spain's estimates have almost half the magnitude of those of Greece. This can be a sign of an "idiosyncratic" response of the Greek economy to changes in the cross-sectional distribution of prices and, possibly, a sign of common shocks that underlie relative price changes in Portugal and Spain.[31]

[31] This finding may signal an idiosyncratic feature of the price-setting process in Greece, where firms may consider more relevant the nominal price adjustments across industries than the past (or future) realizations of aggregate inflation. In that light, Greek firms would not be as backward, or forward, looking as their Portuguese and Spanish counterparts but rather "lateral-looking". Unfortunately, there is no study, to our knowledge, that discusses the price setting behavior of Greek firms.

Table 9 Estimation results with oil inflation + panel – annual inflation

Explanatory variables	Greece Phillips curve	Portugal Phillips curve	Spain Phillips curve	Panel Phillips curve
Forward inflation (+1)	0.30***	0.47***	0.37***	0.31***
	(0.03)	(0.05)	(0.04)	(0.05)
Lagged inflation (−1)	0.98***	0.68***	0.86***	0.86***
	(0.07)	(0.11)	(0.09)	(0.10)
Lagged inflation (−2)	−0.28***	−0.14**	−0.23***	−0.19***
	(0.04)	(0.07)	(0.05)	(0.06)
Current skewness	0.35***	0.13**	0.08***	0.44***
	(0.07)	(0.06)	(0.03)	(0.07)
Lagged skewness (−1)	−0.32***	−0.13**	−0.08***	−0.21***
	(0.07)	(0.05)	(0.03)	(0.05)
Current std. dev.	0.13***	0.01	0.00	0.07**
	(0.03)	(0.01)	(0.00)	(0.04)
Unemployment	−0.23***	0.01	−0.00	−0.12**
	(0.04)	(0.02)	(0.00)	(0.05)
Change in oil inflation	0.01***	−0.01***	−0.00	
	(0.00)	(0.00)	(0.00)	
Moving average	−0.76***	−0.47**	−0.77***	
	(0.15)	(0.20)	(0.16)	
R-squared	0.99	0.99	0.99	0.34
F-test	0.00	0.00	0.00	n.a.
s.e.e.	0.32	0.40	0.18	0.64
Long-run effect of skewness	0.30	0.82	0.99	0.00
Ljung-Box(12) test	0.69	0.04	0.00	n.a.
Normality test	0.59	0.60	0.28	0.00
ARCH(12)	0.54	0.09	0.06	n.a.
RESET(1) test	0.00	1.00	0.00	n.a.

Notes: See Table 3.

An important feature of the price-setting process that stands out in all the models we consider is that our skewness estimates appear to be "dynamically consistent," in the sense that besides finding a positive relationship between contemporaneous skewness and inflation, we strongly register a negative relationship between current inflation and lagged skewness. This expected relationship was pointed out by Ball and Mankiw (1995) but could not be identified in their data set for U.S. economy from 1949 to 1989. Its robust presence here, regardless of whether the economy in question is experiencing continuous inflation (i.e., Spain) or a protracted deflation (i.e., Portugal),[32] is suggestive of its potential validity as an "inflation regularity" – at least in the three-country context we consider here.

We consider two extensions to the previously considered models and report them collectively in Table 9. First, we include the change in annual oil inflation as a control variable in the annual inflation hybrid models. The results on lagged and forward

[32] Aucremanne et al. (2002) also identify this dynamic feature of the skewness-inflation relationship but in the case of Belgium, they find that the long-run effect is negative and effectively zero.

inflation and contemporaneous and lagged skewness are unaffected by the inclusion of this additional variable. Second, we pool our data and form a three-country panel equation similar to the hybrid model we had before (but without the oil variable and the moving average). We estimate this panel equation using the generalized method of moments with dynamic instruments (that include also the instruments used in the single country equations). The results are surprisingly robust: contemporaneous and lagged skewness enter with the anticipated, dynamically consistent, signs and are strongly significant. In addition, unemployment now enters with the expected negative sign and is significant as well.

Summarizing, our estimation results are strongly supportive of the theory expounded in Ball and Mankiw (1995) about the effects of the cross-sectional third moment of inflation on relative price changes. We find a significant presence of current and lagged skewness as a determinant of current inflation, even after controlling for a number of variables that enter in more traditional inflation equations (lagged and forward inflation, the cross-sectional standard deviation, unemployment, and oil inflation). Our results continue to hold when we pool our data together and consider the effect of skewness on the three countries simultaneously.

6 Conclusions

In this chapter, we explore the connection between inflation and its higher-order moments (skewness) for three peripheral E.U. countries Greece, Portugal, and Spain along the lines of the menu cost theory of price rigidities in product markets. Our work is among the relatively few studies that appeared in previous literature that explore this topic using a similar approach. We contribute to this line of research by examining three economies that may be emulated by the new E.U. member states or candidate member states, such as Bulgaria, Romania, or Turkey, with regard to the effects of monetary and antiinflationary policies they pursue within the context of the E.U.

Employing an augmented version of the hybrid New Keynesian Phillips curve and monthly data on producer prices, we find a robust short-run impact of the skewness of observed relative prices on aggregate inflation in line with the Ball and Mankiw (1995). Our results are in accordance with the predictions of the menu cost models and importantly, they go beyond the contemporaneous mean-skewness correlation and are "dynamically consistent."

The main policy implications of our analysis regard the impact that an asymmetric distribution of prices would have on the transmission of monetary policy. When the cross-sectional skewness of prices is directly related to aggregate inflation not only the direction but also the magnitude of a nominal shock would influence output and inflation dynamics. Peersman (2004) has found some evidence that the same monetary policy shocks have different effects across E.M.U. countries (e.g., a stronger price response in Spain and Italy than in Austria and the Netherlands). His "puzzling result" may be the result of an incomplete characterization of the process of inflation dynamics. We propose the inclusion of the cross-sectional skewness of relative prices in the hybrid New Keynesian Phillips curve as a more complete characterization of the process of price adjustments in the periphery of the E.M.U.

Although our results are quite robust for the three countries examined here, it is important to look to a larger group of countries if we want to check whether the effects of skewness on inflation are truly an "empirical regularity." Enlarging our sample to include countries from the E.U.-15 and E.U.-25 groups as well as using OECD countries and data of a lower (e.g. quarterly) frequency appears to be a fruitful extension of our research.

References

Akerlof G, Yellen J (1985) A near-rational model of the business cycle, with wage and price inertia. Q J Econ 100(5):823–838

Alogoskoufis G, Lee DH, Philippopoulos A (1998) Exchange rate regimes, political parties and the inflation-unemployment tradeoff: evidence from Greece. Open Econ Rev 9:39–51

Alvarez L, Hernando I (2005) The price setting behaviour of Spanish firms: evidence from survey data. Banco de España, Working Paper 538

Amano R, Macklem R (1997) Menu costs, relative prices, and inflation: evidence for Canada. Bank of Canada Working Paper 97

Angeloni I, Kashyap A, Mojon B (2003) Monetary policy transmission in the euro area. Cambridge University Press, Cambridge

Aucremanne L, Brys G, Hubert M, Rousseeuw P, Struyf A (2002) Inflation, relative prices and nominal rigidities. Bank of Belgium Working Paper 20

Balke N, Wynne M (2000) An equilibrium analysis of relative price changes and aggregate inflation. J Monet Econ 45:269–292

Ball L, Mankiw N (1995) Relative-price changes as aggregate supply shocks. Q J Econ 110:161–193

Ball L, Mankiw N (1999) Interpreting the correlation between inflation and the skewness of relative prices: a comment. Rev Econ Stat 81:197–198

Batchelor R (1981) Aggregate expectations under the stable laws. J Econometrics 61:199–210

Blanchard O, Jimeno J (1995) Structural unemployment: Spain versus Portugal. Am Econ Rev 85(2):212–218

Blejer M (1983) On the anatomy of inflation, the variability of relative commodity prices in Argentina. J Money Credit Bank 15:469–482

Bryan M, Cecchetti S (1999a) Inflation and the distribution of price changes. Rev Econ Stat 81:188–196

Bryan M, Cecchetti S (1999b) Inflation and the distribution of price changes: rejoinder. Rev Econ Stat 81:203–204

Busetti F, Forni L, Harvey A, Venditti F (2006) Inflation convergence and divergence within the European Monetary Union. European Central Bank, Working Paper Series 574

Calvo G (1983) Staggered prices in a utility-maximizing framework. J Monet Econ 12:383–398

Camba-Mendez G, Rodriguez-Palenzuela D (2003) Assessment criteria for output gap estimates. Econ Model 20(3):529–562

Castillo S, Dolado J, Jimeno-Serrano J (1998) A tale of two neighbour economies: labour market dynamics in Spain and Portugal. CEPR Discussion Papers 1954

Cecchetti S, Debelle G (2006) Inflation persistence: does it change? Econ Pol 46:311–341

De Abreu Lourenco R, Gruen D (1995) Price stickiness and inflation. Reserve Bank of Australia Research Discussion Paper 9502

Detragiache E, Hamann J (1999) Exchange Rate-Based Stabilization in Western Europe: Greece, Ireland, Italy, and Portugal. Contemp Econ Policy 17(3):358–369

Dhyne E, Alvarez LJ, Le Bihan H, Veronese G, Dias D, Hoffmann J, Jonker N, Lunnemann P, Rumler F, Vilmunen J (2006) Price changes in the Euro area and the United States: Some facts from individual consumer price data. J Econ Perspect 20(2):171–192

Dolado JJ, Lopez-Salido JD, Vega JL (2000) Unemployment and inflation persistence in Spain, are there Phillips trade-offs? Spanish Econ Rev 2:267–291

Dopke J, Pierdzioch C (2003) Inflation and the skewness of the distribution of relative price changes, empirical evidence for Germany. Jahrbucher fur Nationalokonomie und Statistik 223(2):136–158

Driffill J, Mizon G, Ulph A (1990) Costs of inflation. In: Friedman BM, Hahn FH. (eds) Handbook of monetary economics. North-Holland, New York, pp 1013–1066

Estrada A, Hernando I, López-Salido JD (2000) Measuring the NAIRU in the Spanish economy. Banco de España, Working Paper 0009

Fischer S (1981) Relative shocks, relative price variability, and inflation. Brookings Papers on Economic Activity 1981:381–431

Fischer S (1982) Relative price variability and inflation in the United States and Germany. Eur Econ Rev 18:171–196

Friedman B, Hahn F (eds) (1990) Handbook of monetary economics, vols. 1 and 2. Elsevier, New York

Gali J, Gertler M (1999) Inflation dynamics: a structural econometric analysis. J Monet Econ 44(2):195–222

Gali J, Gertler M, Lopez-Salido JD (2001) European inflation dynamics. Eur Econ Rev 45(7):1237–1270

Gali J, Gertler M, Lopez-Salido JD (2005) Robustness of the estimates of the hybrid new Keynesian Phillips curve. J Monet Econ 52(6):1107–1118

Garganas N, Tavlas G (2001) Monetary regimes and inflation performance: the case of Greece. In: Bryant R, Garganas NC, Tavlas GS (eds) Greece's economic performance and prospects. Brookings Istitution, Washington DC, pp 43–96

Golob J (1993) Inflation, inflation uncertainty, and relative price variability: a survey. Federal Reserve Bank of Kansas City, Research Working Paper 93–15

Hahn J, Hausman J (2002) A new specification test for the validity of instrumental variables. Econometrica 70:163–189

Hall S, Zonzilos N (2000) The determination of wage and price inflation in Greece: an application of modern cointegration techniques. Centre for International Macroeconomics Discussion Paper No 2000–06

Hondroyiannis G, Lazaretou S (2004) Inflation persistence during periods of structural change: an assessment using Greek data. European Central BankWorking Paper Series No 370/June 2004

Lazaretou S (1995) Inflation and real exchange rate behaviour under alternative nominal excange rate regimes: the Greek experience of 1877–1936. Greek Econ Rev 36:1–21

Linde J (2005) Estimating new-Keynesian Phillips curves: a full information maximum likelihood approach. J Monet Econ 52(6):1135–1149

Ma A (2002) GMM estimation of the New Phillips Curve. Econ Lett 76:411–417

Mankiw G (1985) Small menu costs and large business cycles: a macroeconomic model of monopoly. Q J Econ 100(2):529–538

Mankiw G, Reis R (2002) Sticky information versus sticky prices: a proposal to replace the new Keynesian Phillips curve. Q J Econ 117(4):1295–1328

Marquez J, Vining D (1984) Inflation and relative price behavior: a survey. In: Ballabon M (ed) Economic perspectives: An annual survey of economics, vol 3. Harwood Academics, New York, pp 1–56

Martins F (2006) The pricing behaviour of Portuguese firms: evidence from survey data. Bank of Portugal Working Paper 4–06

Mavroeidis S (2004) Weak identification of forward-looking models in monetary economics. Oxford Bull Econ Stat 66:609–635

Mizon G, Safford J, Thomas S (1990) The distribution of consumer price changes in the United Kingdom. Economica 57:249–262

Orphanides A, Porter R, Reifschneider D, Tetlow R, Finan F (1999) Errors in the measurement of the output gap and the design of monetary policy. Board of Governors of the Federal Reserve System, Finance and Economics Discussion Paper 1994–45

Peersman G (2004) The transmission of monetary policy in the euro area: are the effects different across countries? Oxford Bull Econ Stat 66(3):285–308

Rudd J, Whelan K (2007) Modeling inflation dynamics: a critical review of recent research. J Money Credit Bank 39(Supplement):155–170

Sbordone A (2005) Do expected future marginal costs drive inflation dynamics? J Monet Econ 52(6):1183–1197

Stock J, Wright J (2000) GMM with weak identification. Econometrica 55:703–708

Stock J, Yogo M (2003) Asymptotic distributions of instrumental variables statistics with many weak instruments. Manuscript, Harvard University

Stock J, Yogo M (2005) Testing for weak instruments in linear IV regression. In: Andrews D, Stock J (eds) Identification and inference for econometric models: essays in honor of Thomas Rothenberg. Cambridge University Press, England, pp 80–108

Stock J, Wright J, Yogo M (2002) A survey of weak instruments and weak identification in generalized method of moments. J Bus Econ Stat 20:518–529

Verbrugge R (1999) Cross-sectional inflation asymmetries and core inflation: a comment on Bryan and Cecchetti. Rev Econ Stat 81:199–202

Vining D, Elwertowski T (1976) The relationship between relative prices and the general price level. Am Econ Rev 66:699–708

Macro Dynamics and Labor-Saving Innovation: US vs. Japan

Ryuzo Sato and Tamaki Morita(✉)

Abstract This article deals with the empirical analysis of the economic growth of the United States and Japan from 1970 to 2005. Following our analysis in "Quantity or Quality: The Impact of Labor-Saving Innovation on US and Japanese Growth Rates, 1960–2004" (March 2007), we applied the same method to a different data series to confirm our previous findings. As with the previous work, the results shown in this chapter support our view that Japan's declining population can be compensated for by additional quality improvement of the existing labor force.

1 Introduction

The contrast between the population changes in the United States and Japan has recently become more distinct. Japanese population growth has slowed and is expected to continuously decline, while the population in US reached 3 billion in 2006 and is expected to continue to expand due to subsequent immigration.

A recent study by Sato and Morita (2007), (hereinafter "previous study") attempted to determine whether population changes severely affect economic growth. Extracting the "labor-saving innovation" from the economic growth led to the conclusion that it is not the "quantity," but the "quality" of growth that matters. By dividing conventional total factor productivity (TFP) into "labor efficiency" and "capital efficiency," we pointed out that improved labor efficiency would compensate for the shrinking of the labor force in the near future.

We begin by reviewing the previous study's key points.

- The novel contribution of the previous study, accruing from those of Sato and Ramachandran (1987) and Sato (1970), was that we analyzed not only how the

T. Morita
National Graduate Institute for Policy Studies (GRIPS) 7-22-1, Roppongi, Minato-ku, Tokyo 162-0835, Japan, e-mail: morita@grips.ac.jp

T. Kamihigashi and L. Zhao (eds.) *International Trade and Economic Dynamics – Essays in Memory of Koji Shimomura.*

TFP had increased or decreased, but also analyzed separately the efficiency of capital and the efficiency of labor. The result of the analysis allowed us to make a policy proposal that in order to raise TFP growth, we have to consider how and how much the efficiency of either or both of capital and labor must be increased. Merely knowing TFP is generally considered sufficient for economic analysis. However, our comparison of the two countries showed that because each country's composition of TFP is fundamentally different, knowing only total efficiency would not suffice.

- To analyze the efficiency of capital and labor, we need to know the production function or the elasticity of (factor) substitution, which is the summary index of the production function. Our growth analysis used the concept of elasticity of substitution and applied the concept to the data of the two countries.
- After the theoretical explanations, we conducted the estimation using both countries' macro data. The data were taken from 1960 to 2004 and then divided into two periods: Period I (1960–1989) and Period II (1990–2004). Period II for Japan includes the lost decade, while that for US is often described as the new economy. The analysis on Period II was particularly effective in highlighting the characteristics of each economy.
- We contrasted the difference in the economic structures of Japan and US by comparing the rate of factor-augmenting technical progress. The source of Japan's economic growth was quality improvement – rather than quantity increase – of population and labor force. In contrast, for US, what supported its economic growth was quantity increase – rather than quality improvement – of population and labor force. Our investigation revealed that whether or not the capital and labor are efficiently used has a strong impact on economic growth.
- Overall, we discovered that Japan's high growth in Period I was not so much due to the increase of the population, but to improved labor efficiency. Japan's stagnation, too, was explained not by the population decrease or shortage of effective demands, but by the slowdown of the improvement of labor efficiency. Broadly defined innovation has been and will be the engine of the development and growth of the Japanese economy. Thus, Japan does not have to be pessimistic about the effect of the declining birth rate on the economy.
- We also tested the equilibrium condition to determine each economy's performance. In Japan, the actual value of output per effective labor has been much higher than the equilibrium value of output per effective labor. Japanese capital stock has grown very fast, but it was not utilized to increase the economy's total income (GDP). In Period I, especially before the first oil crisis in 1973, an extremely high rate of investment accumulated Japanese physical stock at a very rapid pace, which supported the country's miraculous economic growth. As for US, the actual value of output per effective labor is very close to the equilibrium value of output per effective labor, and the actual output in each period was just below the optimal output. The growth rate of effective capital and effective labor, and the economic growth rate, were balanced in both Period I and Period II.

Our study differs from other studies in that we did not define TFP as pure technology shock. As Solow (1957) originally did, we consider any kind of shift in production function as technical change.

Although our result that Japanese TFP declined in the 1990s is close to the finding of Hayashi and Prescott (2002), we assumed the constant elasticity of substitution (CES) function instead of the Cobb-Douglas function as they have done. To exclude the possibility that the TFP may reflect change in the degrees of scale economy, we carefully chose CES, and found that the CES function with biased technical change fits well to actual economic growth. With the observation that capital efficiency is not equal to labor efficiency, we are able to avoid the case that TFP reflects the change in the degrees of scale economy.

Another point of difference between our study and previous ones is that we did not purify the Solow residuals by controlling imperfect competition, factor utilization, and reallocation effects, as Kawamoto (2005) has done. For the purpose of dividing TFP, we dared to minimize the cumulative adjustment error in TFP itself. Some adjustments will be made in our subsequent studies to clarify the nature of the technical change defined by Solow.

In this chapter, we apply the same methods to more specific data on US and Japan in order to confirm the characteristics of the countries' macro-dynamics described in the previous study. This time, the production series Y is represented by net domestic product (NDP) instead of gross domestic product (GDP), which was used in the previous study. This change allows us to more directly find the income shares of capital and labor, and enables us to omit the effect of "consumption of fixed capital," which amounts to as much as about 20% of Japan's GDP and about 10% of US GDP. We selected strictly "private-nonagricultural" sectors for all the series, including Japan's net stock. Because of data constraints, we use data from a slightly shorter range of years (1970–2005).

2 The Data

The three major differences between the data used here and that used in the previous study are listed below.

1. As a series of an economy's output, Y, the real net domestic product, is taken instead of the real gross domestic product.
2. The public sector and the agricultural sector are excluded from all the series.
3. Instead of OECD data, the countries' own official data are carefully selected and adjusted to improve comparability between US and Japan.

We implemented the first change because we needed a more income-oriented value of the shares of capital and labor – the estimation of biased technical progress depends largely upon them. In addition, omitting "consumption of fixed capital" helped us to observe how new value is added to each economy. Because of these

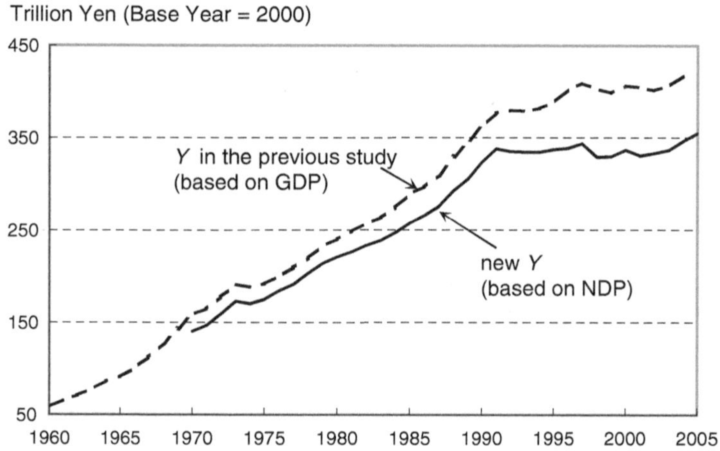

Fig. 1a Comparison of the Series Y: Japan

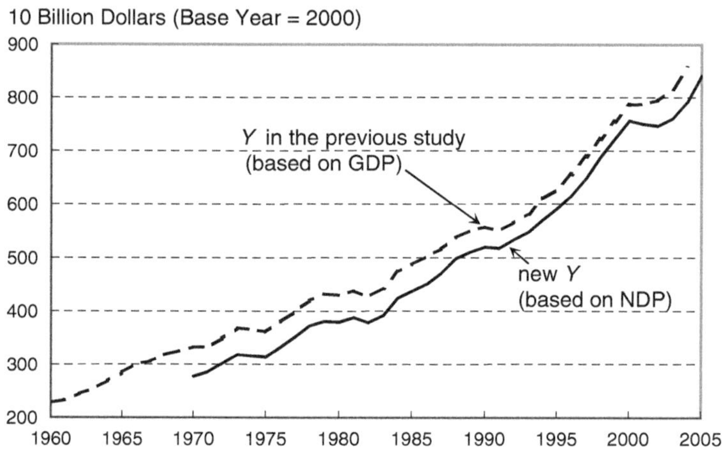

Fig. 1b Comparison of the Series Y: US

changes in the data, mostly influenced by the first change, the series Y of each country is generally lower than that in the previous work, as is depicted in Fig. 1a (Japan) and Fig. 1b (US).

The average relative shares of capital and labor differed considerably as well, and the labor share is smaller here. For example, take average labor share α after 1990. In Japan, it was formerly 75.17%, but in the new series, it was calculated as 72.07%. In US, it also declined from 67.61% to 61.97%. The new series describe more accurately how the newly added income each year is distributed to capital and labor. Precise comparison is shown in Table 1a (Japan) and Table 1b (US).

Table 1 Average relative share of input factors

	New data (%)			Previous data (%)		
	1970–2005	1970–1989	1990–2005	1960–2004	1960–1989	1990–2004
a. Japan						
Average relative share of capital α	31.54	34.42	27.93	29.34	31.60	24.82
Average relative share of labor β	68.46	65.58	72.07	70.66	68.40	75.17
Total	100	100	100	100	100	100
b. US						
Average relative share of capital α	37.62	37.30	38.03	31.33	30.80	32.39
Average relative share of labor β	62.38	62.70	61.97	68.67	69.20	67.61
Total	100	100	100	100	100	100

Notes: α and β are calculated as period averages of $\alpha(t) = r(t)K(t)/Y(t)$ and $\beta(t) = w(t)L(t)/Y(t)$

3 Neutrality Tests

Before estimating the production function using the new data, we have to confirm whether the selected series in both countries are appropriate for the analysis of the biased technical change.

The production function with biased technical change can be expressed as (1), in an aggregative economy under the neo-classical constant returns to scale technology, where at each year t, one output ($Y(t)$) is produced by two factor inputs, capital ($K(t)$) and labor ($L(t)$).

$$Y(t) = F\left[A(t)K(t),\ B(t)L(t)\right], \tag{1}$$

where $A(t)$ and $B(t)$ are efficiencies of capital and labor, respectively.

We followed the method used in the previous study and conducted two tests: one on whether the elasticity of factor substitution is unity, and another on whether the production function is Hicks-neutral. The results are shown in Tables 2 and 3.

In Table 2, if the three variables converge to one, i.e.,

$$\bar{R}(z/w) = \bar{R}(y/r) = \bar{R}(x/\omega) = 1,$$

where r = return to capital, w = wage rate of labor, $x = L/K, y = Y/K, z = Y/L, \omega = r/w$, and $R(y/r) = (\dot{y}/y)/(\dot{r}/r)$, the elasticity of factor substitution σ in (1) is on average equal to unity.[1] The results show that the three variables are not equal, and

[1] The reason is explained in Sato and Morita (2007).

Table 2 Average elasticity of substitution method results

	Japan	United States
$\bar{R}(z/w)$	0.7036 (1.1309)	0.9467 (1.2583)
$\bar{R}(y/r)$	0.6691 (0.7857)	0.5688 (0.9303)
$\bar{R}(x/\omega)$	0.5643 (0.8060)	0.2544 (1.2390)

Notes: Standard deviation is in parentheses. Extreme 1–3 data are excluded in each series

Table 3 Hicks-neutrality test results

	Japan	United States
Average $\dot{T}/T$	0.74%	1.07%
α	0.3154	0.3762
β	0.6846	0.6238
Equation (2) Regression Results	$\frac{\bar{w}}{w} = -0.0008 + 0.6859 \frac{\bar{k}}{k}$ (−0.21) (11.18) Adj $R^2 = 0.7849$	$\frac{\bar{w}}{w} = -0.0116 + 0.1103 \frac{\bar{k}}{k}$ (6.24) (−1.00) Adj $R^2 = -0.0003$
	Estimated $\dot{T}/T$ −0.08%	Estimated $\dot{T}/T$ 1.66%
	Estimated σ 0.4598	Estimated σ −3.4107
Equation (3) Regression Results	$\frac{\bar{r}}{r} = 0.0160 - 1.044 \frac{\bar{k}}{k}$ (1.22) (−4.97) Adj $R^2 = 0.4109$	$\frac{\bar{r}}{r} = 0.0245 - 1.3241 \frac{\bar{k}}{k}$ (3.87) (−5.02) Adj $R^2 = 0.4156$
	Estimated $\dot{T}/T$ 1.60%	Estimated $\dot{T}/T$ 2.45%
	Estimated σ 0.6557	Estimated σ 0.4711

not even close to unity. Hence, the production functions cannot be Cobb-Douglas type.

Table 3 presents the results of the following regression:

$$\frac{\dot{w}}{w} = \frac{\dot{T}}{T} + \frac{\alpha}{\sigma}\frac{\dot{k}}{k} \tag{2}$$

$$\frac{\dot{r}}{r} = \frac{\dot{T}}{T} - \frac{\beta}{\sigma}\frac{\dot{k}}{k}. \tag{3}$$

T is the index of technical change in the production function with Hicks-neutral technical change ($Y(t) = T(t)F\left[K(t), L(t)\right]$), which is equivalent to TFP. If the relationships of (2) and (3) simultaneously hold, and $\dot{T}/T$ in the two equations are equal in each country, then the country's production function is Hicks-neutral. The results suggest, however, that the relationships hardly hold because the estimated variables are not significant, and the estimated two $\dot{T}/T$ differ greatly in each country. This leads to our judgment that the technical change in each country is not Hicks-neutral, and it should be estimated with biased technical change.

4 Estimates of Production Functions

4.1 Method

In accordance with the detailed explanation in Sato and Morita (2007), we take four steps in the estimation of the production functions with biased technical change for Japan and US.

Step 1

Estimation of Hicks-neutral technical progress

First, we calculate $\dot{T}/T$ in each year t, using

$$\frac{\dot{T}(t)}{T(t)} = \frac{\dot{z}(t)}{z(t)} - \alpha(t)\frac{\dot{k}(t)}{k(t)}, \tag{4}$$

where $z = Y/L, \quad k = K/L$.

Step 2

Deriving average elasticity of substitution σ^N

Next, we estimate the average elasticity of substitution. To analyze the efficiency of capital and labor, we need to know the elasticity of (factor) substitution, which is the summary index of the production function. As Sato and Beckmann (1968) and Rose (1968) discovered, the elasticity of substitution plays a critical role in the analysis of the efficiency of each input factor. Here, we estimate it under the assumption of Hicks-neutral technical progress, σ^N, by the following definition:

$$\sigma^N(t) = \frac{\mathrm{d}\left(\frac{K(t)}{L(t)}\right) / \left(\frac{K(t)}{L(t)}\right)}{\mathrm{d}\left(\frac{w(t)}{r(t)}\right) / \left(\frac{w(t)}{r(t)}\right)} = \frac{\frac{\dot{K}(t)}{K(t)} - \frac{\dot{L}(t)}{L(t)}}{\frac{\dot{w}(t)}{w(t)} - \frac{\dot{r}(t)}{r(t)}}.$$

Step 3

Estimation of CES functions with Hicks-neutral technical change

Our data contains no trends of σ correlating with the values k or time t. Thus, we assume the constant elasticity of substitution (CES) production function and determine how σ^N fits the actual data. Before we directly estimate the production function with biased technical change, we estimate the function with Hicks-neutral technical change so that we can compare the fittedness of the two kinds of estimated production functions.

With Hicks-neutral technical change, the CES function should take the form of

$$Y^N(t) = T(t)\left[\alpha K(t)^{-\rho^N} + \beta L(t)^{-\rho^N}\right]^{-1/\rho^N}, \tag{5}$$

where $\sigma^N = 1/(1+\rho^N)$. $T(t)$ is assumed to grow at a constant rate during a period, which is given as the average of each $\dot{T}(t)/T(t)$ estimated in (4). We also assume the income shares of factors α and β are constant throughout the period, and we apply period averages of observed α and β.

Step 4

Estimation of CES functions with biased technical change

Finally, we estimate the CES function with biased technical change. Sato (1970) argued that theoretically, the elasticity of substitution of biased technical change has to be stated as (6)

$$\sigma^{\mathrm{B}} = \frac{\mathrm{d}\left(\frac{AK}{BL}\right) / \left(\frac{AK}{BL}\right)}{\mathrm{d}\left(\frac{\partial F/\partial BL}{\partial F/\partial AK}\right) / \left(\frac{\partial F/\partial BL}{\partial F/\partial AK}\right)}, \tag{6}$$

because when technical progress is nonneutral, the value of the elasticity itself is influenced by the efficiencies of capital and labor. However, because we cannot observe σ^{B} directly, we use σ^N as a proxy of σ^{B}, and we substitute the estimates of elasticity σ^N intoσ in (7) and (8) to derive $\dot{A}/A$ and $\dot{B}/B$,[2]

$$\frac{\dot{A}(t)}{A(t)} = \frac{\sigma(t)\frac{\dot{r}(t)}{r(t)} - \left(\frac{\dot{Y}(t)}{Y(t)} - \frac{\dot{K}(t)}{K(t)}\right)}{\sigma(t)-1}. \tag{7}$$

$$\frac{\dot{B}(t)}{B(t)} = \frac{\sigma(t)\frac{\dot{w}(t)}{w(t)} - \left(\frac{\dot{Y}(t)}{Y(t)} - \frac{\dot{L}(t)}{L(t)}\right)}{\sigma(t)-1}. \tag{8}$$

Then, the production function becomes

$$Y^{\mathrm{B}}(t) = \left[\alpha\left(A(t)K(t)\right)^{-\rho^N} + \beta\left(B(t)L(t)\right)^{-\rho^N}\right]^{-1/\rho^N}. \tag{9}$$

Estimated $Y^{\mathrm{B}}(t)$ summarizes our model. It represents both the form of the production function and the biasedness of technical change.

4.2 Simulation Results

In this subsection, we present the estimated values of actual Y, Y^N and Y^{B}. In Fig. 2 (Japan) and Fig. 3 (US), CES production functions with Hicks-neutral technical change Y^N are plotted with thick gray lines. CES production functions with biased technical change Y^{B} are shown by thin lines with markers.

Estimated data from 1970 to 2005 are shown in Panel 1 of each figure, and in Panel 2, the data are divided into two at the year 1990, so that Y^N and Y^{B} in 1990

[2] Equations (7) and (8) are derived in Sato (1970).

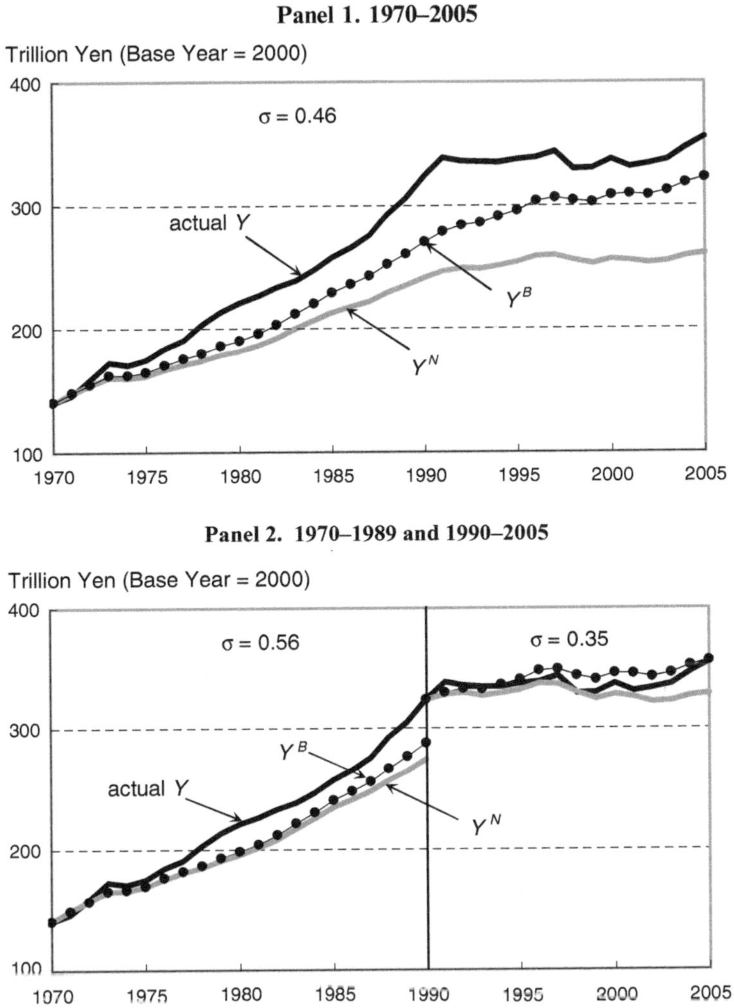

Fig. 2 Estimated output of Japan

start from the actual Y in the year. Generally, Y^N deviate from actual Y, and Y^{B} fit better than do Y^N. This supports our view that the economies of both Japan and US experienced biased technical growth. It suggests that estimation of TFP does not suffice to diagnose economic performance or to prescribe any policy for either of these countries.

We should note one point here. In Fig. 2, Panel 2, the Y^N and Y^{B} in period 1970–1989 seem to be very close. One may conjecture that this similarity occurs because $\dot{A}/A \simeq \dot{B}/B \simeq \dot{T}/T$. Actually, though, as shown in the next subsection, estimated capital efficiency growth $\dot{A}/A$ was negative, and labor efficiency growth $\dot{B}/B$ was positive, and was much larger than $\dot{T}/T$. In this case Y^N and Y^{B} coincidentally appeared to be close.

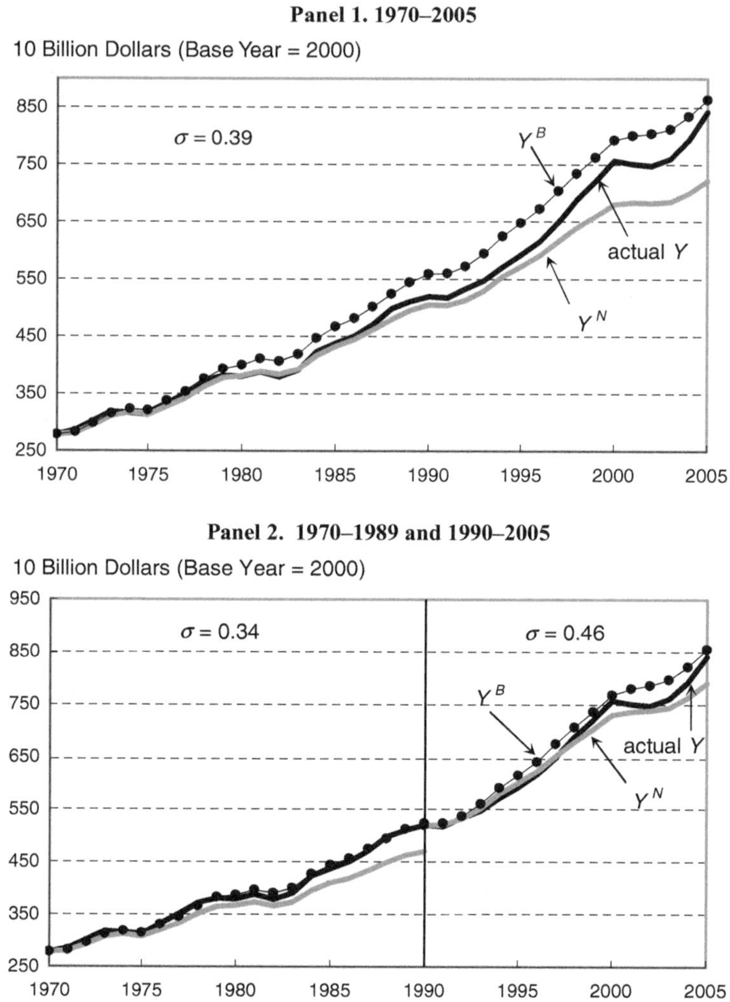

Fig. 3 Estimated output of the United States

4.3 Biased Technical Change of Japan and the United States

During the estimation process, in Step 1, we get some important values that explain economic dynamics of both countries. Table 4 lists the period average values for some of the variables.

The table compares the new data with those in the previous study, so we can observe not only the periodic change but also the effect of excluding "consumption of fixed capital" and of strictly selecting the private-nonfarm sector.

In Japan's case, when we compare the new and previous data, the exclusion of the high-growth decade (1960s) due to data constraints strongly affected the growth

Table 4 Growth rate of Hicks-neutral technical change and other factors

	New data (%)			Previous data (%)		
	1970–2005	1970–1989	1990–2005	1960–2004	1960–1989	1990–2004
a. Japan						
Growth rate of output $\dot{Y}/Y$	2.72	4.20	0.97	4.65	6.35	1.03
Growth rate of Hicks-neutral technical change $\dot{T}/T$	0.74	0.99	0.44	2.13	2.91	0.45
Growth rate of capital $\dot{K}/K$	5.15	7.45	2.41	7.32	9.25	3.18
Growth rate of labor $\dot{L}/L$	0.35	0.86	−0.27	0.28	0.56	−0.31
Growth rate of output per labor $\dot{z}/z$	2.36	3.31	1.23	4.35	5.76	1.34
b. US						
Growth rate of output $\dot{Y}/Y$	3.25	3.29	3.20	3.08	3.05	3.13
Growth rate of Hicks-neutral technical change $\dot{T}/T$	1.07	0.76	1.44	1.07	0.90	1.43
Growth rate of capital $\dot{K}/K$	3.11	3.55	2.59	3.31	3.58	2.72
Growth rate of labor $\dot{L}/L$	1.58	1.88	1.23	1.39	1.49	1.19
Growth rate of output per labor $\dot{z}/z$	1.64	1.38	1.95	1.66	1.54	1.92

rate of output and other variables. Nevertheless, in comparisons from the 1990s, the differences clearly show the effect of the change of data source. From the 1990s onwards, capital growth in the new data is 2.4% and 0.77% point lower than that in the previous data. This explains how the consumption of fixed capital affected the Japanese economy.

Among those variables, there is a well-known and important relationship:

$$\frac{\dot{Y}(t)}{Y(t)} = \frac{\dot{T}(t)}{T(t)} + \alpha(t)\frac{\dot{K}(t)}{K(t)} + \beta(t)\frac{\dot{L}(t)}{L(t)}, \tag{10}$$

which is equivalent to (4). Table 5 shows the period average values of each term in (10), in percentage contribution rates.

In Japan, capital $(\alpha \cdot (\dot{K}/K))$ was the largest contributor to the economic growth. Capital investment, though excluding the consumption of fixed capital, still supported about 70% of economic growth during 1990–2005. In this period, capital and technical change compensated for the decline of labor $(\beta \cdot (\dot{L}/L))$.

Table 5 Relative contributions to economic growth by technical change and factor inputs

	New data (%)			Previous data (%)		
	1970–2005	1970–1989	1990–2005	1960–2004	1960–1989	1990–2004
a. Japan						
$\frac{\dot{T}}{T}/\frac{\dot{Y}}{Y}$	27.11	23.55	45.35	45.76	45.87	44.30
$\left(\alpha\frac{\dot{K}}{K}\right)/\frac{\dot{Y}}{Y}$	59.64	61.13	69.32	46.14	46.05	76.90
$\left(\beta\frac{\dot{L}}{L}\right)/\frac{\dot{Y}}{Y}$	8.74	13.49	−19.66	4.30	6.03	−22.60
Statistical adjustment	4.52	1.84	4.99	3.80	2.05	1.41
Total	100	100	100	100	100	100
b. US						
$\frac{\dot{T}}{T}/\frac{\dot{Y}}{Y}$	32.87	23.09	44.82	34.80	29.58	45.69
$\left(\alpha\frac{\dot{K}}{K}\right)/\frac{\dot{Y}}{Y}$	36.02	40.20	30.81	33.65	36.11	28.15
$\left(\beta\frac{\dot{L}}{L}\right)/\frac{\dot{Y}}{Y}$	30.34	35.82	23.71	31.09	33.73	25.71
Statistical adjustment	0.77	0.90	0.65	0.46	0.58	0.45
Total	100	100	100	100	100	100

Notes: To apply actual data to the theory, we have to approximate differentiation by difference. Thus the weighted sum of the increase of each factor is not equal to the growth rate. We show such discrepancy as "statistical adjustment"

In US, the three variables contributed almost evenly to the growth on average. In the period 1990–2005, the TFP growth rate (1.44% per annum) explains about 45% of the growth, which suggests productivity improvement during the period.

Once σ is determined in Step 3, the growth rates of capital and labor efficiencies can be estimated in Step 4. The results are shown in Table 6. In both countries $\sigma < 1$ and $\dot{A}/A < \dot{B}/B$, so both countries are experiencing what Hicks (1932) originally defined as "labor-saving innovation.[3]"

We should also mention here that T, A, and B are related as follows:

$$\frac{\dot{T}(t)}{T(t)} \equiv \alpha(t)\frac{\dot{A}(t)}{A(t)} + \beta(t)\frac{\dot{B}(t)}{B(t)} \qquad (11)$$

This is a simplified version of (13) in Sato and Morita (2007). The values of each item in (11) are presented in Table 7.

[3] Definition of the labor-saving innovation also appears in Sato and Morita (2007).

Table 6 Growth rate of biased technical change

	New data (%)			Previous data (%)		
	1970–2005	1970–1989	1990–2005	1960–2004	1960–1989	1990–2004
a. Japan						
Growth rate of Hicks-neutral technical change $\dot{T}/T$	0.74	0.99	0.44	2.13	2.91	0.45
Estimated elasticity of substitution $\sigma_{\mathrm{AVG}}^{N}$	0.46	0.56	0.35	0.57	0.63	0.50
Growth rate of capital efficiency $\dot{A}/A$	−1.24	−1.04	−0.93	−1.61	−1.63	−1.36
Growth rate of labor efficiency $\dot{B}/B$	1.65	1.77	1.00	3.86	5.11	1.01
b. US						
Growth rate of Hicks-neutral technical change $\dot{T}/T$	1.07	0.76	1.44	1.07	0.90	1.43
Estimated elasticity of substitution $\sigma_{\mathrm{AVG}}^{N}$	0.39	0.34	0.46	0.46	0.51	0.38
Growth rate of capital efficiency $\dot{A}/A$	−0.04	−0.30	0.20	−0.41	−0.59	0.08
Growth rate of labor efficiency $\dot{B}/B$	1.74	1.40	2.18	1.74	1.56	1.97

Table 7 Relative contributions to Hicks-neutral technical change by biased technical change

	New data (%)			Previous data (%)		
	1970–2005	1970–1989	1990–2005	1960–2004	1960–1989	1990–2004
a. Japan						
$\left(\alpha\frac{\dot{A}}{A}\right)/\frac{\dot{Y}}{Y}$	−53.16	−36.33	−59.03	−22.18	−17.67	74.09
$\left(\beta\frac{\dot{B}}{B}\right)/\frac{\dot{Y}}{Y}$	153.48	117.29	164.11	128.14	119.97	167.09
Statistical adjustment	−0.32	19.04	−5.08	−5.95	−2.30	7.00
Total	100	100	100	100	100	100
b. US						
$\left(\alpha\frac{\dot{A}}{A}\right)/\frac{\dot{Y}}{Y}$	−1.33	−14.74	5.22	−11.96	−20.18	1.86
$\left(\beta\frac{\dot{B}}{B}\right)/\frac{\dot{Y}}{Y}$	101.32	115.74	94.14	111.44	119.80	92.95
Statistical adjustment	0.01	−1.00	0.64	0.52	0.38	5.19
Total	100	100	100	100	100	100

Notes: See the notes of Table 5

In Japan, the $\dot{A}/A$ was on average negative throughout the period, according to the results in the previous study. Considering these results, we presumed one of the reasons for this negative value could be a relatively large amount of "consumption of fixed capital" (approximately one fifth of the GDP). However, even when we excluded the factor, the results did not change significantly. The $\dot{A}/A$ in 1990–2005 is a scant 0.43% point higher than the previous result, but is still negative.

From 1990, despite the decline of labor (−0.27%, Table 4), the labor efficiency grew at 1% per annum (Table 6), which contributed 164.11% to TFP. In other words, the labor efficiency growth compensated for the decline of labor. We emphasized this point in the previous study, and it is still persuasive with the new data.

In US, both experiments showed the $\dot{A}/A$ to be slightly positive from the 1990s. This change from that in the period 1970–1989, together with the increase in $\dot{B}/B$, is a key to the rapid TFP growth in 1990–2005. We presume the possibility that it could be a structural change relating to the "new economy."

The contribution rate of capital efficiency growth $\alpha \cdot (\dot{A}/A)$ turned positive but remains low. It may be interesting to point out that if this contribution rate does not grow much in the future, we will be able to judge the US technical change to be more like Harrods-neutral.

4.4 Stability Under Biased Technical Change

In the economy with biased technical change defined as (1), the stability condition should be as in (12).

$$\left(\frac{\dot{\bar{Y}}}{\bar{Y}}\right)^* = \left(\frac{\frac{d}{dt}(AK)}{AK}\right)^* = \left(\frac{\frac{d}{dt}(BL)}{BL}\right)^*, \tag{12}$$

where $\bar{Y}$ = output after technical change, AK = effective capital, and BL = effective labor.

The precise explanation of (12) is presented in Sato and Morita (2007). Here we would like to determine whether the economies of Japan and US satisfy this condition. We show the growth rate of AK, BL, and the economic growth rate in Table 8.

We can see that in Japan, compared with the economic growth rate, the growth rate of effective capital was higher and that of effective labor was lower. Consequently, the effective capital growth is twice as high as the effective labor growth. Thus, the Japanese economy's growth path is far from balanced. In contrast, in US, the growth rate of each factor is almost even, especially during the period 1970–1989. By estimating the capital and labor efficiency, we can clearly observe how much Japan needs to raise its labor efficiency in the era of the shrinking labor force.

Table 8 Growth rate of *AK*, *BL*, and *Y*

	New data			Previous data		
	1970–2005	1970–1989	1990–2005	1960–2004	1960–1989	1990–2004
a. Japan						
Growth rate of effective capital $\frac{\frac{d}{dt}(AK)}{AK}$	3.90%	6.41%	1.48%	5.71%	7.62%	1.82%
Growth rate of effective labor $\frac{\frac{d}{dt}(BL)}{BL}$	2.00%	2.63%	0.74%	4.14%	5.66%	0.70%
Growth rate of output $\dot{Y}/Y$	2.72%	4.20%	0.97%	4.65%	6.35%	1.03%
$\frac{\dot{Y}}{Y}/\frac{\frac{d}{dt}(AK)}{AK}$	0.70	0.65	0.66	0.82	0.83	0.56
$\frac{\dot{Y}}{Y}/\frac{\frac{d}{dt}(BL)}{BL}$	1.36	1.60	1.32	1.12	1.12	1.46
$\frac{\frac{d}{dt}(AK)}{AK}/\frac{\frac{d}{dt}(BL)}{BL}$	1.95	2.44	2.01	1.38	1.35	2.60
b. US						
Growth rate of effective capital $\frac{\frac{d}{dt}(AK)}{AK}$	3.08%	3.25%	2.79%	2.90%	2.99%	2.80%
Growth rate of effective labor $\frac{\frac{d}{dt}(BL)}{BL}$	3.32%	3.29%	3.41%	3.13%	3.05%	3.16%
Growth rate of output $\dot{Y}/Y$	3.25%	3.29%	3.20%	3.08%	3.05%	3.13%
$\frac{\dot{Y}}{Y}/\frac{\frac{d}{dt}(AK)}{AK}$	1.06	1.01	1.15	1.06	1.02	1.12
$\frac{\dot{Y}}{Y}/\frac{\frac{d}{dt}(BL)}{BL}$	0.98	1.00	0.94	0.98	1.00	0.99
$\frac{\frac{d}{dt}(AK)}{AK}/\frac{\frac{d}{dt}(BL)}{BL}$	0.93	0.99	0.82	0.93	0.98	0.89

5 Summary and Conclusion

We have confirmed the findings in Sato and Morita (2007) by using more specific data – the nonfarm-private sector's net domestic product (NDP) – instead of gross domestic product (GDP). As our neutrality tests confirmed, the new series in both countries were also appropriate for the analysis of biased technical change. We illustrated that the estimations of production functions with biased technical change fit better to actual output than those with Hicks-neutral technical change.

To compare the new results with the previous results for Japan, the differences are as follows:

- The economic growth rate and some other new series during 1970–2005 and 1970–1989 differ considerably from the previous series. Most of the differences are explained by the exclusion of the data for the 1960s owing to data constraints. The strong influence of the data (or lack thereof) for the 1960s indicates that the extremely high growth in that decade too strongly affected the analysis of 1960–2004 or 1960–1989 in the previous study.
- In 1990–2005, capital growth was lower in the new series, which suggests that the increase of "consumption of fixed capital" affected the growth rate. Excluding it, in the new data, the growth rate of capital efficiency in 1990–2005 was still negative, but its degree was smaller. It follows that the contribution of effective capital to the economic growth went up with the better capital efficiency. The new data more clearly shows the role of newly accumulated capital.
- Estimated elasticity of substitution in 1990–2005 was lower in the new data.

The results common to the two studies regarding Japan are:

- The Japanese growth rate was backed by both capital growth and growth of labor efficiency throughout the observation periods.
- The Japanese economy remains far from the steady state. It is highly possible that the economy will autonomously adjust itself eventually.

Our findings that labor efficiency supported the growth of the Japanese economy (and its decline in the second period) seems to have some relevance to the study of Kobayashi and Inaba (2006). They applied the business cycle accounting developed by Chari et al. (2007) to find that among the four wedges to the economy (efficiency, labor, investment, and government wedges), labor wedges were a major contributor to the recession in the 1990s in Japan. That labor wedge may have caused the decline in the labor efficiency observed in our analysis. We would like to investigate the causes of such changes in factor efficiency in our future study.

For US, there is just one major difference between the new results and the previous results: the estimated elasticity of substitution was lower in 1970–1989, but higher in 1990–2005.

The results common to the two studies regarding US are the following:

- In contrast to Japan, no effects of the exclusion of the 1960s data were found for US, except the value of elasticity of substitution. The two studies in general showed closely corresponding results despite the difference in the period. The reason why only the elasticity differs should be investigated in future studies.
- Capital efficiency turned positive in 1990–2005, which hints that there may have been a technical change that may relate to the so-called new economy.
- The US economy has been in the steady state since the 1960s.

In conclusion, what has our application of the theory of biased technical change revealed? The US economy has been in the steady state, but the Japanese economy is far from it. Because the ratio of the growth rate of effective capital to the growth rate of effective labor is too high in Japan, two possible processes could enable the country to reach the steady state. One is negative adjustment – decline of effective capital, which may lower the rate of steady-state growth. The other is positive adjustment – increase of effective labor, which may realize higher steady-state growth. According to our studies, Japan has continuously improved labor efficiency until it was able to compensate for the decline of labor. As its labor force continues to shrink, Japan should make a perpetual effort to raise labor efficiency with a view to avoiding the negative type of adjustment.

Data Appendix

Japan

Y: "Net domestic product" excluding "agriculture, forestry and fishing, plus producers of government services," deflated by GDP Deflator

(Department of National Accounts, Economic and Social Research Institute, Cabinet Office, Government of Japan, *Annual Report on National Accounts*)

K: "Tangible fixed assets" excluding "dwellings" (net stock, real) multiplied by the ratio of "private sector" in "producing assets" (gross stock, nominal)

(Department of National Accounts, Economic and Social Research Institute, Cabinet Office, Government of Japan, *Annual Report on National Accounts*) multiplied by the ratio of "gross capital stock by industry, total minus agriculture, forestry and fishing" (gross stock, real)

(Department of National Accounts, Economic and Social Research Institute, Cabinet Office, Government of Japan, *Annual Report on Gross Capital Stock of Private Enterprises*)

L: "Hours worked per employee" multiplied by "number of private employees" excluding "agriculture"

(The Japan Institute for Labor Policy and Training, *Roudou Toukei Deeta Kensaku Sisutemu* (Search System for Labor Statistics), http://stat.jil.go.jp/, and Statistics and Information Department, Ministry of Health, Labor and Welfare, *Monthly Labor Survey*)

w: "Compensation of employees" excluding "agriculture, forestry and fishing, and producers of government services" deflated by GDP deflator

(Department of National Accounts, Economic and Social Research Institute, Cabinet Office, Government of Japan, *Annual Report on National Accounts*) divided by labor force (L)

United States

Y: "National income without capital consumption adjustment by industry, private" excluding "agriculture" (National Income and Product Accounts Tables, Bureau of Economic Analysis, U.S. Department of Commerce, http://www.bea.gov/national/nipaweb/Index.asp)

K: "Current-cost net stock of private nonresidential fixed assets by industry group and legal form of organization, private" excluding "farms" deflated by "chain-type quantity indexes for net stock of private nonresidential fixed assets by industry group and legal form of organization" (Fixed Asset Tables, Bureau of Economic Analysis, U.S. Department of Commerce, http://www.bea.gov/national/FA2004/SelectTable.asp#S6)

L: "Average weekly hours of production and nonsupervisory workers on private nonfarm payrolls" multiplied by 52 weeks multiplied by "employees on private nonfarm payrolls" (Employment, Hours, and Earnings from the Current Employment Statistics survey, Bureau of Labor Statistics, U.S. Department of Labor, http://www.bls.gov/ces/home.htm)

w: "Compensation of employees by industry, private industries" excluding "farms" deflated by GDP deflator (National Income and Product Accounts Tables, Bureau of Economic Analysis, U.S. Department of Commerce, http://www.bea.gov/national/nipaweb/Index.asp) divided by labor force (L)

Acknowledgment We thank the anonymous referee for useful comments. We also thank Professor Donna Amoroso and Ms. Patricia Decker at GRIPS for their editorial assistance. This chapter is partly supported by Grant-in-Aid for Scientific Research (19830020).

References

Chari VV, Kehoe PJ, McGrattan ER (2007) Business cycle accounting. Econometrica 75(3):781–836

Hayashi F, Prescott EC (2002) The 1990s in Japan: a lost decade. Rev Econ Dyn 5:206–235

Hicks JR (1932, 2nd edn in 1963) The theory of wages. Macmillan, London

Kawamoto T (2005) What do the purified Solow residuals tell us about Japan's lost decade? Monetary Econ Stud 23(1):113–148

Kobayashi K, Inaba M (2006) Business cycle accounting for the Japanese economy. Jpn World Econ 18:418–440

Rose H (1968) The condition for factor-augmenting technical change. Econ J 78(312):966–971

Sato R (1970) The estimation of biased technical progress and the production function. Int Econ Rev 11:179–208. Reprinted in Sato R, Growth theory and technical change, The selected essays of Ryuzo Sato, Vol 1, Economists of the twentieth century series, Edward Elgar Publishing, 1996, Ch 12

Sato R, Beckmann MJ (1968) Neutral inventions and production functions, Rev Econ Stud 35(1):57–66. Reprinted in R Sato, Growth theory and technical change, The selected essays of Ryuzo Sato, Vol 1, Economists of the twentieth century series, Edward Elgar Publishing, 1996, Ch 11

Sato R, Morita T (2007) Quantity or quality: the impact of labor-saving innovation on US and Japanese growth rates, 1960–2004. CIRJE Discuss Pap, CIRJE-F-483, The University of Tokyo. COE Discuss Pap Ser, COE-DP F-168, Research Center for the Relationship between Market Economy and Non-Market Institutions, The University of Tokyo. Work Pap Ser, N-07, The Center for Japan-U.S. Business and Economic Studies, Leonard N. Stern School of Business, New York University

Sato R, Ramachandran R (1987) Factor price variation and the Hicksian hypothesis: a microeconomic model. Oxford Econ Pap 39:343–356. Reprinted in Sato R, Growth theory and technical change, The selected essays of Ryuzo Sato, Vol 1, Economists of the twentieth century series, Edward Elgar Publishing, 1996, Ch 15

Solow R (1957) Technical change and the aggregate production function. Rev Econ Stat 39(3):312–320

Part V
Compensation, Entrepreneurship, and Price Leadership

Entrepreneurship, Organization Capital, and the Evolution of the Firm[1]

Atsushi Oshima and B. Ravikumar, and Raymond Riezman(✉)

Abstract We view the entrepreneur as an agent who possesses human capital in the form of specific skills or talents. When she starts a firm, her human capital is essential to the firm and it has substantial private value. The entrepreneur transforms her human capital over time into what we call "organization capital." This organization capital can be sold as part of the firm, and so the dynamic process of transforming specific human capital into organization capital means that the value of the firm increases over time.

1 Introduction

The study of how and why firms get started has a rich tradition in the economics literature. Knight (1971) views an entrepreneur as someone who accepts production risk in exchange for the authority to direct other factors of production; this view is essentially static and helps identify entrepreneurial activity with the risk characteristics of the population. Kihlstrom and Laffont (1979) view an entrepreneur as someone who bears risk and receives the reward for the risk. Schumpeter (1949) thinks of the entrepreneur as someone who transforms inventions and discoveries into commercially viable processes. Baumol (1986, 1990 and Holmes and Schmitz (1990) focus on the entrepreneur's role in adapting new technology to create new products.

Our theory of the entrepreneur differs from previous theories in one important aspect: we view the entrepreneur as an *organizer* of production who transforms a specific, nontradable capital into a general, tradable capital. The entrepreneur is an agent who possesses human capital in the form of specific skills or talents. When she

[1] We dedicate this chapter to the memory of Koji Shimomura.

R. Riezman
Department of Economics, University of Iowa, Iowa, e-mail: raymond-riezman@uiowa.edu

T. Kamihigashi and L. Zhao (eds.) *International Trade and Economic Dynamics – Essays in Memory of Koji Shimomura.*

starts a firm, her human capital is essential to the firm. If there were no information or incentive problems, then she could write a contract that would result in her supplying her human capital fully and the firm's value would be close to her private value.[2] However, since human capital cannot be sold or, in many instances, efficiently contracted over, the actual value is substantially lower than her private value. The entrepreneur solves this problem by transforming her human capital into what we call "organization capital." The organization capital can be sold as part of the firm, so that the dynamic process of transforming human capital into organization capital means that the value of the firm increases over time. By this process, the entrepreneur uses her specific human capital to accumulate general, tradable assets.

The process of using human capital to create organization capital is the focus of our analysis. We define organization capital to be information, specific to the firm, which allows the firm to transform technological know-how and factors of production into products and services it can sell in the market. The organization capital is thus embodied in the firm and has value.

The dynamic optimization problem faced by the entrepreneur is as follows. The entrepreneur's time weighted by her human capital is used directly in the production process to produce output and is also used to produce organization capital. Organization capital is an imperfect substitute for human capital in the production process. The entrepreneur must, therefore, decide how much time to devote to current production, how much to devote to build organization capital, which earns a return in the future, and how much leisure to consume. Given the leisure-work decision, the entrepreneur trades off creating more organization capital now, which means that the firm has substantial value sooner, against using that human capital for current production, which generates income in the current period. The solution to this dynamic optimization problem pins down the evolution of organization capital over time and the rate at which the value of the firm grows. As the firm evolves over time, the entrepreneur transforms her human capital, a specific, nontradable asset, into a general asset that is tradable in the market.

We develop and solve a very simple model of the evolution of the firm, which yields a number of results. First, we show that the entrepreneur devotes a lot of time in the initial stages to create organization capital but decreases her time as the firm evolves. We show that the stock of organization capital increases at a decreasing rate. Finally, we show that the value of the firm (the value without the entrepreneur) increases over time, gets closer to entrepreneur's value, but is always below the entrepreneur's value (which includes the entrepreneur's efforts to increase organization capital).

Our idea of organization capital as accumulated knowledge embodied in the firm is similar to the type of capital considered by Marshall (1930). In related work, Rosen (1972) and, more recently, Atkeson and Kehoe (2005) develop models in which the firm produces organization capital and output as a bundle. In contrast, in our model there is a trade-off – the entrepreneur has to divide her time between production of output and creation of organization capital. In Prescott and Visscher

[2] See Wu (1989) for a background on why no one may be willing to hire entrepreneurs.

(1980), the organization capital is embodied in the firm's workers. In such models, the difference between the value of the firm to the entrepreneur and others is likely to be small. In our model, the organization capital is embodied in the firm and hence, the difference between the value of the firm to the entrepreneur and to outsiders depends upon how important the entrepreneur is to the future of the firm.

2 Model

This is a model of one firm in a competitive market. An entrepreneur produces a product and sells it at a fixed price. For convenience we assume that this price is one. The entrepreneur hires labor, l, on the spot market at a wage, w, and produces output using her human capital, h, and organization capital, k, along with the labor. The human capital is relatively specific on several dimensions; it may be specific to the product being produced, the location where it is produced, etc. The organization capital is an imperfect substitute for human capital in the production process.

Define τ_t^p to be the fraction of time the entrepreneur devotes to the production process in period t. Profit at time t, x_t, is then given by

$$x_t = F(k_t, \tau_t^p h, l_t) - wl_t,$$

where $F(\cdot)$ is increasing, strictly concave, and homogeneous of degree one. We have assumed that the entrepreneur's human capital h and the market wage w are constant over time.

The entrepreneur is also responsible for creating organization capital. The entrepreneur spends τ_t^k of her time producing organization capital. The stock of organization capital depends on how much time the entrepreneur devotes in creating it as well as how much is carried over from previous period. The following equation describes the evolution of the stock of organization capital:

$$k_{t+1} - g(\tau_t^k h, k_t).$$

Loosely speaking, h represents the specific human capital that is essential to start the firm. In this case, h may represent knowledge of how to convert a blueprint into a new commercial product. Without h there is no product to produce. While knowledge of computer hardware, programming, networks, etc. is a tradeable asset, knowledge of how to transform this into a marketable product is not. The entrepreneur not only performs this transformation, but also converts the specific human capital into a tradeable asset. She does so by making herself gradually inessential over time. In this process, she faces an intertemporal trade-off: her current consumption is enhanced by devoting more time to the production process, but her future consumption will be enhanced if she devotes more time in creating organization capital.

The entrepreneur maximizes the sum of discounted utility over profits and leisure. We normalize the total amount of time available in a period to be *one*.

Assume that the entrepreneur's utility function is logarithmic and that her subjective discount factor is β. Her problem is to choose τ^p, τ^k, and l each period in order to maximize her discounted lifetime utility. Formally, the infinite horizon problem faced by the entrepreneur is

$$\max \sum_{t=0}^{\infty} \beta^t \left\{ \phi \ln \left(F(k_t, \tau_t^p h, l_t) - w l_t \right) + (1-\phi) \ln \left(1 - \tau_p^p - \tau_t^k \right) \right\}$$
$$\text{subject to, } \forall t \geq 0:$$
$$k_{t+1} = g(k_t, \tau_t^k h),$$
$$k_0 > 0 \text{ given.}$$

Notice that her problem does not explicitly depend on the time period once we know the beginning-of-period stock of organization capital. This helps us cast her infinite horizon optimization problem as the following dynamic program:

$$V(k) = \max\ \phi \ln \left(F(k, \tau^p h, l) - wl \right) + (1-\phi) \ln \left(1 - \tau^p - \tau^k \right) + \beta V(k')$$
$$\text{subject to } k' = g(k, \tau^k h),$$

where $V(k)$ is the (endogenous) value of the entrepreneur's objective when she currently has k units of organization capital, τ^p, τ^k, and l are current choices of the entrepreneur's time for production, time for organization capital accumulation, and labor, and k' is the next period's chosen level of organization capital.

It is easy to show that there exists a unique function $V(\cdot)$ that solves the above Bellman's functional equation (see Alvarez and Stokey (1998)). Furthermore, $V(\cdot)$ is increasing, concave, and differentiable. These properties of $V(\cdot)$ imply that the choice variables τ^p, τ^k, l, and k' are all stationary functions of k, that is, while the values of τ, l, and k' change over time, the function describing the values does not.

The first order conditions are

$$\tau^p : \phi \frac{F_2(k, \tau^p h, l) h}{F(k, \tau^p h, l) - wl} = (1-\phi) \frac{1}{1 - \tau^p - \tau^k}, \tag{1}$$

$$\tau^k : (1-\phi) \frac{1}{1 - \tau^p - \tau^k} = \beta V'(k') g_2(k, \tau^k h) h, \tag{2}$$

$$l : F_3(k, \tau^p h, l) = w. \tag{3}$$

The Envelope theorem implies that

$$V'(k) = \phi \frac{F_1(k, \tau^p h, l)}{F(k, \tau^p h, l) - wl}. \tag{4}$$

Combining (2) and (4) gives us

$$(1-\phi)\frac{F_2(k,\tau^p h,l)}{F(k,\tau^p h,l)-wl} = \beta\phi\frac{F_1(k',\tau^{p'} h,l')}{F(k',\tau^{p'} h,l')-wl'}g_2(k,\tau^k h). \tag{5}$$

Thus, (1), (3), and (5) describe the economy.

2.1 Value of Organization Capital

Since we emphasize the role of the entrepreneur as one of transforming specific nontradable human capital into tradable organization capital, it would be interesting to know the valuation of the enterprise with and without the entrepreneur. Our model suggests that the discounted sum of utilities is the value of the enterprise to the entrepreneur. The value to the entrepreneur with k_t units of organization capital in period t is

$$V(k_t) = \max\sum_{s=t}^{\infty}\beta^{s-t}\left[\phi\ \ln\left(F(k_s,\tau_s^p h,l_s)-wl_s\right)+(1-\phi)\ln\left(1-\tau_s^p-\tau_s^k\right)\right]$$
$$\text{subject to } k_{s+1} = g(k_s,\tau_s^k h).$$

We can also compute the discounted sum of utilities without the entrepreneur's time but with the organization capital; this we call the value of the firm without the entrepreneur or the value of the firm. To compute the value at any point in time, we set the level of organization capital equal to the entrepreneur's chosen level at the time and then calculate the discounted sum of utilities. Since $h=0$, $k_{t+1}=g(k_t,0)$, and $x_t = F(k_t,0,l_t)-wl_t$.

The value of a firm with k units of organization capital but without the entrepreneur's human capital would be

$$\widehat{V}(k_t) = \max\sum_{s=t}^{\infty}\beta^{s-t}\left[\phi\ \ln\left(F(k_s,0,l_s)-wl_s\right)+(1-\phi)\ln(1)\right]$$
$$\text{subject to } k_{s+1} = g(k_s,0).$$

We next calibrate the model to see how it behaves and do some simple comparative static exercises.

3 Calibration

We adopt a particular functional form for the production function and law of motion of organization capital.

$$F(k,\tau^p h,l) = [\mu(\tau^p h)^\rho+(1-\mu)k^\rho]^{\frac{\alpha}{\rho}}l^{1-\alpha},$$
$$k' = [\mu(\tau^k h)^\rho+(1-\mu)(k)^\rho]^{\frac{1}{\rho}}.$$

Given these functional forms, (1), (3), and (5) become

$$\phi \frac{\mu(\tau^p h)^\rho}{\tau^p[\mu(\tau^p h)^\rho + (1-\mu)k^\rho]} = (1-\phi)\frac{1}{1-\tau^p-\tau^k}, \tag{6}$$

$$l = b(w)[\mu(\tau^p h)^\rho + (1-\mu)k^\rho]^{\frac{1}{\rho}}, \tag{7}$$

$$\begin{aligned} \frac{1-\phi}{\phi} \frac{1}{\mu(\tau^p h)^\rho + (1-\mu)k^\rho} \left(\frac{\tau^p}{\tau^k}\right)^{\rho-1} \\ = \beta \frac{1}{\mu(\tau^k h)^\rho + (1-\mu)(k)^\rho} \frac{(1-\mu)(k')^{\rho-1}}{\mu(\tau^{p'} h)^\rho + (1-\mu)k'^\rho}. \end{aligned} \tag{8}$$

We next use these equations to compute a numerical solution to the model.

We have a number of technology parameters:

μ – Ratio of investment in organization capital to the stock of organization capital
ρ – Substitutability of investment with existing organization capital
α – Profit to output ratio
h – Stock of human capital
Z – Total factor productivity
w – Wage rate

and preference parameters:

ϕ – Weight indicating preference for leisure
β – Discount rate.

The calibration strategy is the following. We first fix the level parameters h, Z, and w. The levels of these are arbitrary so we set $h = 3$, $Z = 3$, and $w = 1$. β is set to a standard value, 0.96, which typically implies a real interest rate of 4%. We set $\rho = 0.95$. This means that investment in organization capital is a close substitute for existing organization capital. We use the "Survey of Private Enterprise" to compute the value of profit–output ratio, $\alpha = 0.732$. Output is defined to be net profit + wage payments. We calculate the profit–output ratio of manufacturing, wholesale, retail, and service industries from 1980 to 2005 in Japan. Using GDP share, we take the weighted average of these industries in each year and then take the average over the entire sample period.

Finally, we determine ϕ and μ. We jointly calibrate these two parameters to match the steady state hours worked and steady state investment to capital ratio. We calculate the steady state hours worked as follows. Since we have normalized the time available to the entrepreneur as 1, we take the average weekly hours worked in Japan during 1980–2005 and divide by 112 (16 h each day times 7 days). The fraction is 0.368.[3] Our steady state investment is $\mu^{\frac{1}{\rho}} \tau^k h$. We calculate the capital stock with the perpetual inventory method.[4] We set the initial capital stock to be

[3] Source: Monthly Labor Survey issued the Ministry of Labor.

[4] Investment data source is "Annual Report on National Accounts" issued by Department of National Accounts, ESRI.

the same as that in Hayashi and Prescott (2002). This calcualtion yields the average investment to capital ratio in Japan from 1980 to 2005 to be 0.1332. The reason we set organization capital investment to organization capital ratio as the same as the one with physical capital is because of the research by Corrado et al. (2006). They found that intangible investment to tangible investment ratio in the United States during 1990s is 1.1. With these targets we find that $\phi = 0.4264$ and $\mu = 0.1473$.

The calculated parameters imply the following steady state values of the variables:

K^*	1.100
L^*	0.691
τ^{k*}	0.367
τ^{p*}	0.000
$\tau^{k*} + \tau^{p*}$	0.367
$V(K^*)$	0.214
Y^*	2.577
X^*	0.147
X^*/K^*	0.133
π^*/Y^*	0.732

4 Benchmark Results

Next, using the approximated value function and policy functions, we simulate the model for 25 years. The initial level of organization capital is 0.01. Organization capital takes 19 periods to reach 99% level of the steady state, which is 1.1 (see Fig. 1). For the first few periods, an entrepreneur devotes more than 50% of her time endowment for work (production + organization capital formation). As Fig. 2 shows, she spends 58% of her time for work in the second period, which is quite similar to the one reported in the "Survey of New Entrepreneurs' Activity" in 2002 issued by National Life Finance Corporation (an entrepreneur uses 55% of her time for work).

In contrast, growth in labor (Fig. 3) in the first four periods is much larger than the one reported in the same survey (Model: 553%, Data: 71%). As shown in Fig. 4, average growth of profit in 25 years is 9.8%, which is also larger than the data (2.8% from 1980 to 2005) reported in the National Accounts.[5]

In the benchmark case, the entrepreneur stops working at production activities after two periods. Furthermore, time for capital accumulation is concave. When the level of organization capital is low, the entrepreneur needs to work. However, once she reaches a certain level of organization capital, she stops working on production

[5] Source: Profit of Private unincorporated enterprizes in "Annual Report on National Accounts" issued by Department of National Accounts, ESRI.

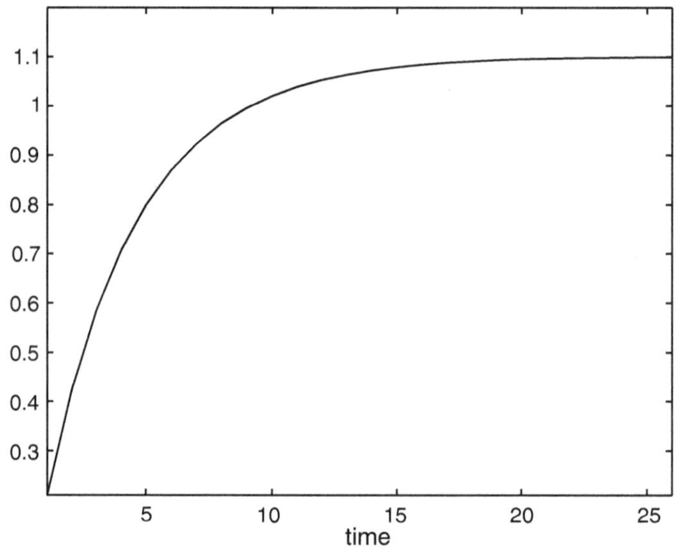

Fig. 1 Evolution of organization capital

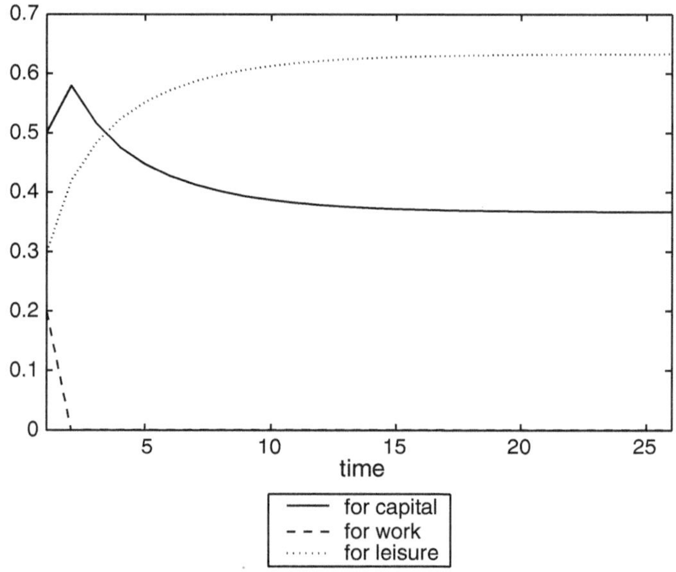

Fig. 2 Evolution of time allocation by the entrepreneur

and also begins to reduce the time spent on organization capital formation. Figure 5 shows that the value of the firm to the entrepreneur as well as the value of the firm without the entrepreneur increases over time. The gap between the values narrows, but it does not seem to converge to zero.

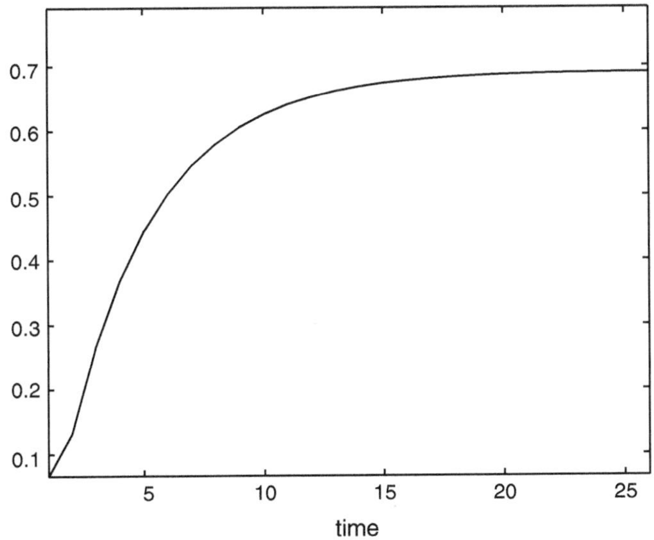

Fig. 3 Evolution of labor hired by the entrepreneur

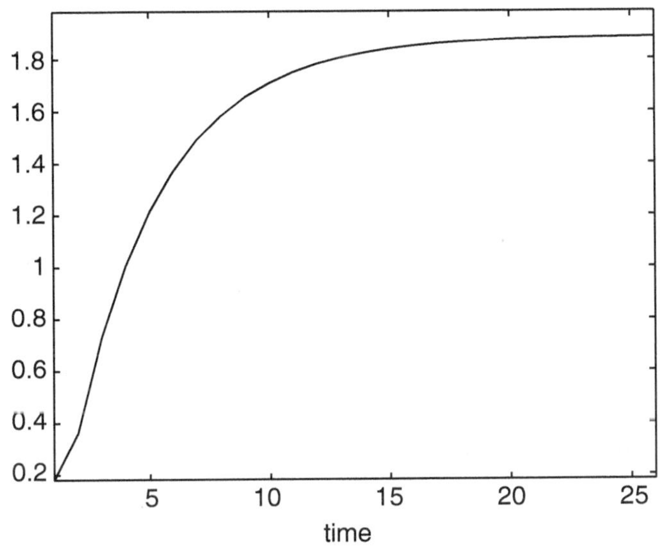

Fig. 4 Evolution of profit

5 Comparative Statics

We do some simple comparative static exercises to examine the effect of changes in ρ, μ ϕ, and h. We first look at lower values of ρ, $\rho = 0.90$, and $\rho = 0.85$. Decreases in ρ decreases the steady state level of investment, employment, and value of the

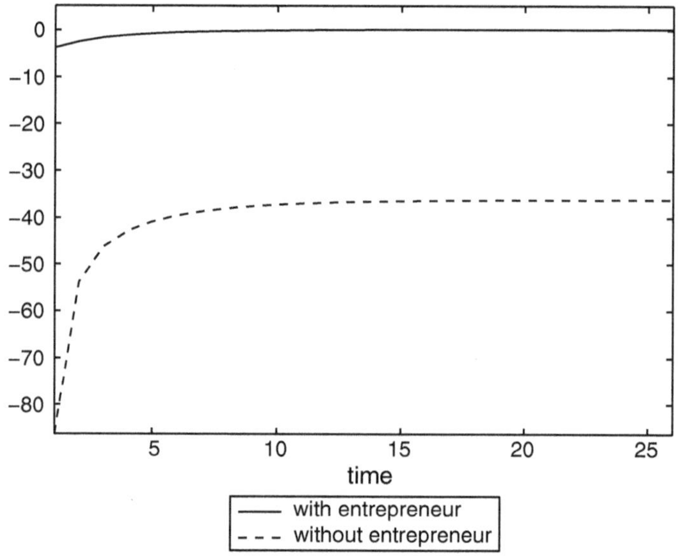

Fig. 5 Evolution of the values of the firm

firm. In the simulation, decreases in ρ increases growth of profit. Second, we look at what happens if investment in organization capital is a larger percentage of the stock of organization capital ($\mu = 0.3$ and $\mu = 0.5$). μ has a strong impact on the steady state level of organization capital, but the change is not monotone in μ. Increasing μ from the benchmark value to 0.3 raises the steady state organization capital. But, when μ increases from 0.3 to 0.5, the steady state level of organization capital decreases markedly. Third, we consider a lower and a higher value of ϕ ($\phi = 0.3$ and $\phi = 0.55$). When the entrepreneur cares more about income relative to leisure she works more. Both steady state hours devoted to organization capital and hours worked towards production increase as ϕ goes up. Thus, the firm grows faster as ϕ rises. Finally, we analyze the effect of human capital ($h = 2$ and $h = 4$). On the one hand, the steady state level of organization capital and the number of employees increase as the level of human capital increases. On the other hand, change in human capital does not affect the steady state time allocation. The impact of the level of human capital on the marginal benefits of time for production and investment are exactly the same in the steady state so that the steady state time allocation is independent of h. Because of our production function, labor demand is increasing function of $h\tau^p$. Since τ^p does not change in the steady state, increasing h increases the number of employees. Also, the steady state level of organization capital is increasing in $h\tau^k$. Therefore, it increases as h increases.

6 Concluding Comments

In developing a theory of start-up firms or entrepreneurship, we focus on the role of organization capital. The entrepreneur is able to transform her human capital into a marketable asset, which we call organization capital, by building an effective business organization, thereby making herself inessential over time. This organization capital can be used by the entrepreneur to generate future streams of profits and create value.

Our view is that organization capital plays an important role in determining the value of a firm. When firms are sold, the price the firm sells for reflects future profitability. But what is it that the buyer is actually buying? Our view is that besides the physical assets when you buy a business you are in large part purchasing the organization capital.

Our model implies that the firm increases organization capital at a decreasing rate. Labor demand by the firm (and profits) also increases at a decreasing rate. This means that the value of a firm increases at a decreasing rate.

We think this framework will be useful in analyzing the behavior of multinational firms. For example, consider a multinational firm that wants to take advantage of cheap inputs available in another country. It could choose to operate a plant in that country, enter into a joint venture with a local firm, or contract out to a local firm. Our model suggests that their choice of mode of entry into this market will be affected by the way organization capital is created by the multinational firm.

There are many important issues that we have not dealt with at this point, such as the extent to which organization capital is embodied in people, whether organization capital can be purchased and transferred to other uses and to what extent organization capital is a public good. We leave these issues for future research.

Appendix: Data Sources

Harada (2003)

This chapter, written in Japanese, analyzes working hours of entrepreneurs who had set up their business 3–7 years before 2002 (so they started their business between 1995 and 1999). He collected data by questionnaires. The sample size is 755. He asked the survey participants,

Could please answer the number of weekly hours that you think you use for your business? For your information, one week is 24 h × 7 days = 168 h.[6]

According to his survey, the average number of hours worked in a week is 66. About 87% of the entrepreneurs in the sample work more than 41 h a week, 63% work more

[6] English translation from Japanese.

than 61 h a week. This is about 18 h longer than the average weekly working hours of full-time employees.[7]

National Life Finance Cooperation

Hours worked

"Survey of New Entrepreneurs' Activities" in 2002 reports the average daily working hours of an entrepreneur who started his business between April and September in 2000. The interviews were done in August 2002. The average business length in the sample is 14.8 months. Thus, the sample is restricted to fairly new entrepreneurs.

The report shows that a new entrepreneur works 10.4 h a day on average. About 15% of the entrepreneurs in the sample work more than 13 h a day. Entrepreneurs working less than 6 h a day are only 4.2% of the sample. Furthermore, the number of holidays taken in a month is 4.3 on average. This means that the new entrepreneurs work 6 days a week. Using these facts, the average weekly hours worked would be about 62.4 h, which is pretty close to the results in Harada (2003).[8] Therefore, we could say that a typical entrepreneur in Japan works much longer than other types of workers when her business is in early stage.

There is another interesting feature in the statistics of entrepreneurs' holidays. About 11% of the sample do not take holidays at all. The share of an entrepreneur who takes less than 3 days in a month is 23.5%. About a quarter of a new entrepreneurs work 7 days a week at some points during a month. This tells us that entrepreneurs' time endowment could be very different from the usual employees' one.

Employees

"Panel Survey of New Entrepreneurs' Activities" in 2005 documents the number of workers in the firms from 2001 to 2004. They interview the companies starting in 2001. The average number of workers (including entrepreneurs themselves) increases from 4.1 to 6.3.[9] These numbers tell us that the employment would increase about 53% in 4 years.

There is another source of information on the number of workers employed by entrepreneurs. "Survey of New Entrepreneurs' Activities" in 2003 keeps track of the number of workers at the time the entrepreneur started her business, and the number when the NLFC surveyed, from 1991 to 2003. The average lag is 15 months. Hence, the NLFC has data about how many additional workers an entrepreneur hires 15 months after she started up her business. The average growth rate of workers in the first 15 months between 1991 and 2003 is 28%.

---

[7] See "Labor Force Survey" issued by the Ministry of International Affairs and communications.

[8] However, the samples in Harada (2003) started their business 1–7 years earlier.

[9] The sample number is 849.

References

Alvarez F, Stokey NL (1998) Dynamic programming with homogeneous functions. J Econ Theory 82:167–189
Atkeson A, Kehoe PJ (2005) Modeling and measuring organization capital. J Political Econ 113(5):1026–1053
Baumol WJ (1986) Productivity growth, convergence, and welfare: what the long-run data show. Am Econ Rev 76(5):1072–1086
Baumol WJ (1990) Entrepreneurship: productive, unproductive, and destructive. J Political Econ 98(5):893–921
Corrado CA, Hulten CR, Sichel DE (2006) Intangible capital and economic growth. NBER Working Paper, No. 11948
Harada N (2003) Kigyouka no roudoujikan. JCER Discussion Paper, No. 85 (in Japanese)
Hayashi F, Prescott EC (2002) The 1990s in Japan: a lost decade. Rev Econ Dyn 5(1):206–235
Holmes TJ, Schmitz JA (1990) A theory of entrepreneurship and its application to the study of business transfers. J Political Econ 98(2):265–294
Kihlstrom R, Laffont JJ (1979) A general equilibrium theory of the firm based on risk aversion. J Political Econ 87(4):719–748
Knight FH (1971) Risk, uncertainty and profit. University of Chicago Press, Chicago
Marshall A (1930) Principles of economics: an introductory volume, 8th edn. Macmillan, London
Prescott EC, Visscher M (1980) Organization capital. J Political Econ 88(3):446–461
Rosen S (1972) Learning by Experience as Joint Production. Quarterly J Econ 86(3):366–382
Schumpeter JA (1949) The theory of economic development. Harvard University Press, Cambridge
Wu SY (1989) Production, entrepreneurship and profit. Basil Blackwell, New York

On Yano's Price Leadership Game[1]

Makoto Yano(✉) and Takashi Komatsubara

Abstract Yano (2001) has constructed a game of endogenous price leadership for a homogeneous product with two firms and different technologies and demonstrated that the state in which the technologically superior firm acts as a price leader is a Nash equilibrium (a superior leader equilibrium). This study extends the original framework of Yano (2001) and spells out technical details so as to fully characterize the Nash equilibria in that framework. We demonstrate the existence of a strong presumption in favor of the emergence of a superior leader equilibrium.

1 Introduction

In his recent book, Yano (2001) has constructed a game of endogenous price leadership for a homogeneous product with two firms and different technologies and demonstrated that the state in which the technologically superior firm acts as a price leader is a Nash equilibrium (a superior leader equilibrium). In that book, however, whether or not the state in which the technologically inferior firm acts as a price leader can also be a Nash equilibrium (an inferior leader equilibrium) has been left as an open question. It has turned out that this question is not at all obvious; one complication making the question difficult is a technical ambiguity in Yano's description of the model. By using a completely different specification, Yano and Komatsubara (2006) show that superior and inferior leader equilibria coexist, but that it is difficult to eliminate the inferior leader equilibrium by a purely noncooperative method of equilibrium selection.

[1] This chapter is dedicated to the late Professor Koji Shimomura, whose insights and productivity have always inspired us all. A technological difference, on which our study focuses, were one of the issues that Koji found to be important; see, for example, Kikuchi and Shimomura (2007). We are grateful to an anonymous referee for useful comments.

M. Yano
Kyoto University, Kyoto, Japan

T. Kamihigashi and L. Zhao (eds.) *International Trade and Economic Dynamics – Essays in Memory of Koji Shimomura.*

This study returns to the original framework of Yano (2001) and spells out technical details so as to fully characterize the Nash equilibria in that framework. Confirming that Yano's superior leader equilibrium in fact exists, we demonstrate that the inferior leader equilibrium, if exists, can be eliminated by the standard method of the iterated elimination of weakly dominated strategies (see Fudenberg and Tirole (1991)). This demonstrates the existence of a strong presumption in favor of the emergence of a superior leader equilibrium.

Yano (2001), as well as this study, incorporates a game theoretic framework to the pioneering work of Ono (1978), in which endogenous price leadership is characterized by means of the technological difference between two firms.[2] In doing so, Yano adopts the extended game with observable delay of Hamilton and Slutsky (1990).[3] Assuming that a firm can sell an amount smaller than the demand that it faces, this study follows the original specification of Ono (1978).

The organization of this study is as follows: In Sect. 2 we explain the basic structure of the model. In Sect. 3 we examine the determination of price leadership.

2 Basic Structure of the Model

The model of this study follows Yano's two-period duopoly model. There are two firms, which produce a homogeneous product. Let $C_i(y)$ be firm i's total cost function satisfying $C_i(0) = 0$. Firm i's marginal cost, which is denoted by $C_i'(y)$, is U-shaped. One firm's marginal cost curve lies below the other firm's curve. The former firm is referred to as the technologically superior firm (S); the latter firm is referred to as the technologically inferior firm (I). That is to say, $C_S'(y) < C_I'(y)$.

There are two periods. Following Hamilton and Slutsky (1990), Yano (2001) assumes that each firm simultaneously chooses its role (leader or follower) in the first period. If the two firms choose different roles in the first period, they engage in Stackelberg price competition in the second period, in which the leader firm sets its price first and, after seeing the price, the follower firm sets its price. If the two firms choose the same role in the first period, they engage in Bertrand price competition in the second period, in which each firm sets its price simultaneously.

A firm sells the optimal quantity within the demand that it faces. Let M_i $(i = S, I)$ be a function of price such that

$$M_i(p_i) = \max C_i'^{-1}(p_i),\ p_i > c_i, \tag{1}$$

[2] In addition to Ono (1978), a number of studies have examined endogenous price leadership in a homogeneous product market in the existing literature; see Deneckere and Kovenock (1992), Yano (2001), Tasnádi (2003), Dastidar and Furth (2005), Yano and Komatsubara (2006), and Zhu and Wu (2007). Amir and Stepanova (2006) focus on a differentiated product market and relate endogenous price leadership to a technological difference. Also see van Damme and Hurkens (2004).

[3] Deneckere and Kovenock (1992) adopt a slightly different specification and characterize endogenous price leadership by means of the capacity difference between two firms.

where $C_i'^{-1}$ is the inverse of firm i's marginal cost function and c_i is its shutdown price. Firm i sells the minimum of its demand and $M_i(p_i)$ if p_i is higher than c_i. Otherwise, it sells no product.

For the sake of explanation, denote as D the market demand for the product; it is strictly decreasing and continuous on $(0,\infty)$. Let p_i' be the price p such that $D(p) = M_i(p)$ and $p_i^{1/2}$ be the price p such that $D(p)/2 = M_i(p)$. By assumption, it holds that $p_i' > p_i^{1/2}$. It follows from $C_S'(y) < C_I'(y)$ that $p_I' > p_S'$ and $p_I^{1/2} > p_S^{1/2}$. Let p_i^M be firm i's monopoly price, satisfying

$$p_i^M = \arg\max_p \,[pD(p) - C_i(D(p))].$$

Yano (2001) assumes $p_i^M \geq p_i' + 1$ and $p_i^{1/2} \geq c_i + 1$.

2.1 Stackelberg Price Competition

Think of the case in which a Stackelberg price game is played in the second period. Following Yano (2001), the leader's expectation of its demand is different from that of the follower.

Let firm j $(j = S, I)$ be the leader and firm i $(\neq j)$ be the follower. Firm i's demand is as follows: If firm i sets its price above that of firm j, firm i's demand is equal to zero. If firm i sets its price below or equal to that of firm j, firm i's demand is equal to the market demand. In short, firm i expects that if it sets its price at p_i, its demand is given by

$$D_i(p_i; p_j) = \begin{cases} 0 & \text{if } p_i > p_j \\ D(p_i) & \text{if } p_i \leq p_j, \end{cases} \tag{2}$$

provided that firm j sets its price at p_j. To reconstruct Yano's Stackelberg equilibrium, it is crucial to assume that firm i obtains the entire market demand if it sets the same price as firm j.

With this expectation, firm i sets its price p_i and sells the optimal quantity within the demand that it faces at that price, p_i. Following Yano (2001), we assume that firm i sets its price $p_i = p_j$ or $p_i \in (0, p_j - 1] \cup [p_j + 1, \infty)$, given firm j's price p_j. This assumption implies that if firm i chooses to set a price different from that of firm j, its price must be different from that of firm j at least by one penny.

Firm i's optimal price depends on firm j's price; it is represented by the best-response correspondence. Recall that c_i is firm i's shutdown price. Following Yano (2001), we assume that if $p_j \leq c_i$, firm i sets its price above p_j and sells no product. If $p_j > c_i$ and if firm i is indifferent between setting $p_i = p_j$ and setting $p_i \neq p_j$, firm i sets $p_i = p_j$. Define $\tilde{p}_i^M$ in $(p_i^M, p_i^M + 1)$ such that

$$\tilde{p}_i^M D(\tilde{p}_i^M) - C_i(D(\tilde{p}_i^M)) = (\tilde{p}_i^M - 1)D(\tilde{p}_i^M - 1) - C_i(D(\tilde{p}_i^M - 1)).$$

The price setting of firm i (the follower) is summarized as follows:

Lemma 1. *In Stackelberg price competition in which firm j is the leader and firm $i(\neq j)$ is the follower, firm i's optimal price depends on p_j and its best-response correspondence is given by*

$$P_i(p_j) = \begin{cases} p_i^M & \text{if } p_j \geq p_i^M + 1 \\ p_j - 1 & \text{if } \tilde{p}_i^M < p_j < p_i^M + 1 \\ p_j & \text{if } c_i < p_j \leq \tilde{p}_i^M \\ [p_j + 1, \infty) & \text{if } p_j \leq c_i, \end{cases} \tag{3}$$

where p_j is firm j's price.

Proof. If $p_j \leq c_i$, (3) follows directly from the assumption introduced before this lemma. If $p_j \geq p_i^M + 1$, it is optimal for firm i to set its monopoly price. This implies the first expression on the right hand side of (3).

Take the case in which $c_i < p_j < p_i'$. If firm i sets $p_i = p_j$, it obtains the market demand. By the definition of p_i', it sells $M_i(p_j)$. If firm i sets $p_i = p_j - 1$, it obtains the market demand. By the definition of p_i', it sells $M_i(p_j - 1)$. It is clear that firm i's profit is larger in the case in which it sets $p_i = p_j$. Hence, firm i sets $p_i = p_j$ (it sells $M_i(p_j)$).

Take the case in which $p_i' \leq p_j < p_i' + 1$. If firm i sets $p_i = p_j$, it obtains the market demand. By the definition of p_i', it sells the quantity demanded. If firm i sets $p_i = p_j - 1$, it obtains the market demand. By the definition of p_i', it sells $M_i(p_j - 1)$. Because, by assumption, $p_i^M \geq p_i' + 1$, firm i's profit is larger in the case in which it sets $p_i = p_j$. Hence, firm i sets $p_i = p_j$ (it sells $D(p_j)$).

Take the case in which $p_i' + 1 \leq p_j < p_i^M + 1$. Either if firm i sets $p_i = p_j$ or if it sets $p_i = p_j - 1$, it obtains the market demand and sells the quantity demanded. By the definition of $\tilde{p}_i^M$, if $p_i' + 1 \leq p_j < \tilde{p}_i^M$, firm i sets $p_i = p_j$ (it sells $D(p_j)$). If $p_j = \tilde{p}_i^M$, by assumption, firm i sets $p_i = p_j$ (it sells $D(p_j)$). If $\tilde{p}_i^M < p_j < p_i^M + 1$, firm i sets $p_i = p_j - 1$ (it sells $D(p_j - 1)$). □

Firm j (the leader) expects that it obtains a residual demand. The demand for firm j is summarized as follows:

Lemma 2. *In Stackelberg price competition in which firm j is the leader and firm $i(\neq j)$ is the follower, firm j's demand is given by*

$$D_j^{\mathrm{L}}(p_j) = \begin{cases} 0 & \text{if } p_j \geq p_i' \\ D(p_j) - M_i(p_j) & \text{if } c_i < p_j < p_i' \\ D(p_j) & \text{if } p_j \leq c_i, \end{cases} \tag{4}$$

where p_j is firm j's price.

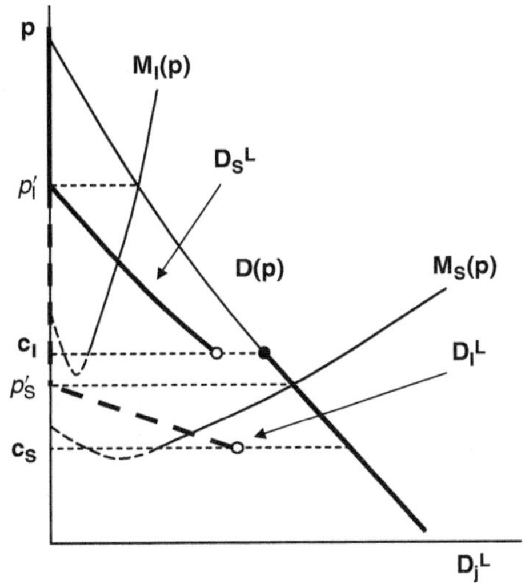

Fig. 1 A leader's demand

Proof. It is clear from Lemma 1. □

Figure 1 illustrates $D_j^{\mathrm{L}}(p_j)$, $j = S, I$. Firm j sells the quantity that is equal to

$$Q_j^{\mathrm{L}}(p_j) = \min\{D_j^{\mathrm{L}}(p_j), M_j(p_j)\},$$

which depends on firm j's price, p_j. Firm j chooses p_j so as to maximize its profit, which is given by

$$p_j Q_j^{\mathrm{L}}(p_j) - C_j(Q_j^{\mathrm{L}}(p_j)).$$

In Stackelberg price competition in which firm S is the leader, firm S has the following two choices. In the case in which firm S sets a price p_{S} above c_{I} but below p'_{I}, it can obtain a residual demand. Denote by $\hat{\pi}_{\mathrm{S}}$ firm S's maximum profit in this case. That is, it satisfies

$$\hat{\pi}_{\mathrm{S}} = \max_{c_{\mathrm{I}} < p_{\mathrm{S}} < p'_{\mathrm{I}}} [p_{\mathrm{S}}(D(p_{\mathrm{S}}) - M_{\mathrm{I}}(p_{\mathrm{S}})) - C_{\mathrm{S}}(D(p_{\mathrm{S}}) - M_{\mathrm{I}}(p_{\mathrm{S}}))].$$

In the case in which firm S sets a price below or equal to c_{I}, it can obtain the market demand. Denote by $\check{\pi}_{\mathrm{S}}$ firm S's maximum profit in this case. That is, it satisfies

$$\check{\pi}_{\mathrm{S}} = \max_{p_{\mathrm{S}} \leq c_{\mathrm{I}}} [p_{\mathrm{S}} D(p_{\mathrm{S}}) - C_{\mathrm{S}}(D(p_{\mathrm{S}}))].$$

Each firm's equilibrium profit is characterized as follows:

Lemma 3. *In the Stackelberg equilibrium in which firm S is the leader, let* $\pi_{\mathrm{S}}^{\mathrm{L}}$ *be firm S's profit and* $\pi_{\mathrm{I}}^{\mathrm{F}}$ *be firm I's profit. If* $\hat{\pi}_{\mathrm{S}} > \check{\pi}_{\mathrm{S}}$*, firm S's price is higher than* c_{I} *but lower than* p'_{I}*, and it holds that*

$$\pi_S^L = \hat{\pi}_S \ \ and \ \ \pi_I^F > 0. \tag{5}$$

If $\hat{\pi}_S < \check{\pi}_S$*, firm S's price is lower than or equal to* c_I*, and it holds that*

$$\pi_S^L = \check{\pi}_S \ \ and \ \ \pi_I^F = 0. \tag{6}$$

If $\hat{\pi}_S = \check{\pi}_S$*, either* (5) *or* (6) *holds.*

Proof. Take the case in which $\hat{\pi}_S > \check{\pi}_S$. In this case, firm *S*'s price is higher than c_I but lower than p_I', and it holds that $\pi_S^L = \hat{\pi}_S$. By Lemma 1, firm *I* sets the same price as firm *S*'s price. By the definition of c_I, it holds that $\pi_I^F > 0$.

Take the case in which $\hat{\pi}_S < \check{\pi}_S$. In this case, firm *S*'s price is lower than or equal to c_I, and it holds that $\pi_S^L = \check{\pi}_S$. By Lemma 1, firm *I* sets a price above firm *S*'s price, and it holds that $\pi_I^F = 0$.

In the case in which $\hat{\pi}_S = \check{\pi}_S$, it is clear that either (5) or (6) holds. □

Following Yano (2001), we focus on the case in which the technological difference between the two firms is large. That is, we assume the following:

Assumption 1. $p_S' \leq c_I$.

Under this assumption, each firm's equilibrium profit in Stackelberg price competition in which firm *I* is the leader is characterized as follows:

Lemma 4. *In the Stackelberg equilibrium in which firm I is the leader, let* π_S^F *be firm S's profit and* π_I^L *be firm I's profit. Then, it holds that*

$$\pi_S^F \geq 0 \ \ and \ \ \pi_I^L = 0. \tag{7}$$

Proof. Let p_I be firm *I*'s price. Take the case in which $p_I < p_S'$. By Lemma 2, firm *I* obtains a demand. By Assumption 1, $p_I < p_S'$ implies $p_I < c_I$. By the definition of c_I, firm *I* sells no product. Take the case in which $p_I \geq p_S'$. By Lemma 2, firm *I* obtains no demand. Hence, it holds that $\pi_I^L = 0$. Moreover, it is clear that $\pi_S^F \geq 0$. □

In the equilibrium firm *I*'s profit is zero. This implies that firm *I*'s optimal price is not determined uniquely. Moreover, because firm *S*'s profit depends on firm *I*'s price, it is not uniquely determined either.

2.2 Bertrand Price Competition

Next, think of the case in which a Bertrand price game is played in the second period. Following Yano (2001), assume that if the two firms set identical prices, each firm will face half of the market demand. Moreover, each firm believes that if it raises its price in that state, it will lose its demand completely. If the firm lowers its price, it will face the entire market demand. In short, firm i ($i = S, I$) expects that if it sets its price at p_i, its demand is given by

$$D_i(p_i;p_j) = \begin{cases} 0 & \text{if } p_i > p_j \\ D(p_i)/2 & \text{if } p_i = p_j \\ D(p_i) & \text{if } p_i < p_j, \end{cases} \tag{8}$$

provided that firm j ($\neq i$) sets its price at p_j.[4] With this expectation, firm i sets its price p_i and sells the optimal quantity within the demand that it faces at that price, p_i.

Firm i's optimal price depends on firm j's price; it is represented by the best-response correspondence. Assume that there exists a price t_i in $(p_i^{1/2}, p_i')$ such that

$$t_iD(t_i)/2 - C_i(D(t_i)/2) = (t_i - 1)M_i(t_i - 1) - C_i(M_i(t_i - 1)).$$

Under this assumption, the price setting of firm i is summarized as follows:

Lemma 5. *In Bertrand price competition, firm i's optimal price depends on p_j and its best-response correspondence is given by*

$$P_i(p_j) = \begin{cases} p_i^M & \text{if } p_j \geq p_i^M + 1 \\ p_j - 1 & \text{if } t_i < p_j < p_i^M + 1 \\ p_j & \text{if } c_i < p_j \leq t_i \\ [p_j + 1, \infty) & \text{if } p_j \leq c_i, \end{cases} \tag{9}$$

where p_j is firm j's price.

Proof. Take the case in which $p_j \leq c_i$. By assumption, firm i sets a price higher than or equal to $p_j + 1$.

Take the case in which $c_i < p_j \leq c_i + 1$. If firm i sets $p_i = p_j$, it obtains half of the market demand. Because, by assumption, $c_i + 1 \leq p_i^{1/2}$, it holds that $p_j \leq p_i^{1/2}$. By the definition of $p_i^{1/2}$, it sells $M_i(p_j)$ and obtains a positive profit. If firm i sets $p_i = p_j - 1$, it obtains the market demand. It, however, holds that $p_i \leq c_i$. By the definition of c_i, firm i sells no product and obtains no profit. Hence, in this case, firm i sets $p_i = p_j$.

Take the case in which $c_i + 1 < p_j < p_i^{1/2}$. If firm i sets $p_i = p_j$, it obtains half of the market demand. By the definition of $p_i^{1/2}$, it sells $M_i(p_j)$. If firm i sets $p_i = p_j - 1$, it obtains the market demand. Because $p_i^{1/2} < p_i'$, $p_j < p_i^{1/2}$ implies $p_j - 1 < p_i'$. By the definition of p_i', firm i sells $M_i(p_j - 1)$. Since $M_i(p_j)$ is larger than $M_i(p_j - 1)$, firm i sets $p_i = p_j$ in this case.

Take the case in which $p_i^{1/2} \leq p_j < p_i' + 1$. If firm i sets $p_i = p_j$, it obtains half of the market demand. By the definition of $p_i^{1/2}$, it sells the quantity demanded. In this case, firm i's profit is given by

$$p_jD(p_j)/2 - C_i(D(p_j)/2).$$

[4] Dastidar (1995) adopts this specification with the assumption that a firm must satisfy the entire demand that it faces. In that case, unlike in the present study, the subjective demand that a firm believes always coincides with the objective demand.

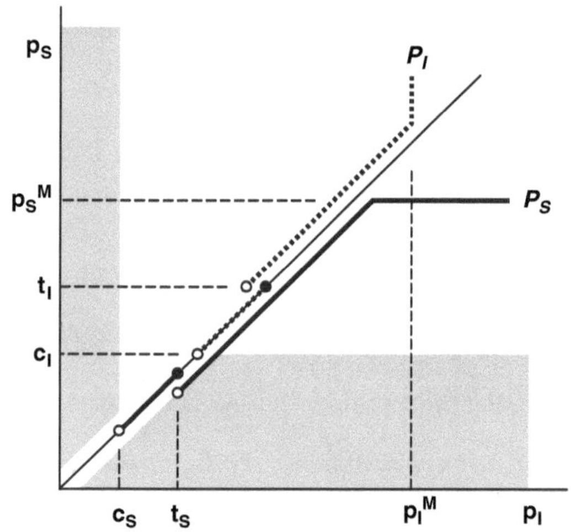

Fig. 2 The Bertrand equilibrium

If firm i sets its price $p_i = p_j - 1$, it obtains the market demand. By the definition of p_i', it sells $M_i(p_j - 1)$. In this case, its profit is given by

$$(p_j - 1)M_i(p_j - 1) - C_i(M_i(p_j - 1)).$$

If $p_i^{1/2} \leq p_j < t_i$, firm i sets $p_i = p_j$ and sells $D(p_j)/2$. If $p_j = t_i$, by assumption, firm i sets $p_i = t_i$ and sells $D(t_i)/2$. If $t_i < p_j < p_i' + 1$, firm i sets $p_i = p_j - 1$ and sells $M_i(p_j - 1)$.

Take the case in which $p_i' + 1 \leq p_j < p_i^M + 1$, where p_i^M is firm i's monopoly price. If firm i sets $p_i = p_j$, it sells $D(p_j)/2$. If firm i sets $p_i = p_j - 1$, it sells $D(p_j - 1)$. It is clear that firm i's profit is larger in the case in which it sets $p_i = p_j - 1$. Hence, firm i sets $p_i = p_j - 1$.

Take the case in which $p_j \geq p_i^M + 1$. In this case, it is optimal for firm i to set its monopoly price. □

Figure 2 illustrates the two firms' best-response correspondences. The Bertrand equilibrium is a pair of prices such that the two firms' best-response correspondences intersect. Under Assumption 1, the Bertrand equilibrium is characterized as follows:

Lemma 6. *The set of Bertrand equilibrium prices is given by*

$$\{(p_S, p_I) : p_I = p_S + 1,\ t_S - 1 < p_S \leq c_I\}. \tag{10}$$

In the Bertrand equilibrium, let π_S^B be firm S's profit and π_I^B be firm I's profit. Then, it holds that

$$\pi_S^B > 0 \ \textit{and} \ \pi_I^B = 0. \tag{11}$$

Proof. By the definition of t_S, $t_S < p'_S$. By Assumption 1, $t_S < p'_S$ implies $t_S < c_I$. From Fig. 2, the set of Bertrand equilibrium prices is given by (10). Moreover, it is clear that (11) holds. □

Because the two firms' best-response correspondences intersect below the 45-degree line, firm *I* obtains no demand and firm *S* obtains the market demand in the Bertrand equilibrium.[5]

3 Price Leadership

In the first period, each firm simultaneously chooses its role. If firm *S* chooses $x_S = L$ (leader) and firm *I* chooses $x_I = F$ (follower), firms *S* and *I* engage in Stackelberg price competition in which firm *S* is the leader and obtain profits π_S^L and π_I^F, respectively. If firm *S* chooses $x_S = F$ and firm *I* chooses $x_I = L$, firms *S* and *I* engage in Stackelberg price competition in which firm *I* is the leader and obtain profits π_S^F and π_I^L, respectively. Either if both firms choose $x_S = x_I = L$ or if both firms choose $x_S = x_I = F$, firms *S* and *I* engage in Bertrand price competition and obtain profits π_S^B and π_I^B, respectively.

Firm *S*'s profit is characterized as follows:

Lemma 7. *If* $\hat{\pi}_S > \check{\pi}_S$, $\pi_S^L > \pi_S^B$. *If* $\hat{\pi}_S < \check{\pi}_S$, $\pi_S^L \geq \pi_S^B$. *Moreover,* $\pi_S^F \geq 0$.

Proof. By the definition of $\check{\pi}_S$, it is clear that $\check{\pi}_S \geq \pi_S^B$. By Lemma 3, if $\hat{\pi}_S > \check{\pi}_S$, $\pi_S^L = \hat{\pi}_S$. This implies $\pi_S^L > \pi_S^B$. By Lemma 3, if $\hat{\pi}_S < \check{\pi}_S$, $\pi_S^L = \check{\pi}_S$. This implies $\pi_S^L \geq \pi_S^B$. Lemma 4 implies $\pi_S^F \geq 0$. □

Firm *I*'s profit is characterized as follows:

Lemma 8. *If* $\hat{\pi}_S > \check{\pi}_S$, $\pi_I^F > 0$. *If* $\hat{\pi}_S < \check{\pi}_S$, $\pi_I^F = 0$. *Moreover,* $\pi_I^L = \pi_I^B = 0$.

Proof. It is clear from Lemmas 3, 4, and 6. □

The game in the first period is summarized in Table 1. The next theorem shows that the state in which firm *S* acts as a price leader is a Nash equilibrium.

Table 1 Price leadership

S, I	*L*		*F*	
L	π_S^B	$\pi_I^B(=0)$	$\pi_S^L(\geq \pi_S^B)$	$\pi_I^F(\geq 0)$
F	π_S^F	$\pi_I^L(=0)$	π_S^B	$\pi_I^B(=0)$

[5] Following Yano (2001), this study does not require that the market demand is completely absorbed in the equilibrium. This guarantees the existence of the Bertrand equilibrium. If we exclude states in which the market demand is not completely absorbed from the equilibrium, the Bertrand equilibrium may not exist.

Theorem 1 (superior leader equilibrium). *Strategy profile* $(x_S, x_I) = (L, F)$ *is a Nash equilibrium.*

Proof. By Lemma 7, $\pi_S^L \geq \pi_S^B$. By Lemma 8, $\pi_I^F \geq \pi_I^B$. Hence, $(x_S, x_I) = (L, F)$ is a Nash equilibrium. □

In the general setting above, a superior leader equilibrium may coexist with an inferior leader equilibrium, in which firm S chooses $x_S = F$ and firm I chooses $x_I = L$. The inferior leader equilibrium can, however, be eliminated with an additional assumption by the iterated elimination of weakly dominated strategies.

Theorem 2. *Suppose* $\hat{\pi}_S > \check{\pi}_S$. *Then, strategy profile* $(x_S, x_I) = (F, L)$ *is eliminated by the iterated elimination of weakly dominated strategies.*

Proof. We can eliminate firm I's L because it is weakly dominated. Once we eliminate firm I's L, we can eliminate firm S's F. □

Because both $\hat{\pi}_S$ and $\check{\pi}_S$ are endogenous variables, it is desirable to derive a sufficient condition on the structure of the model that guarantees the hypothesis of the above theorem ($\hat{\pi}_S > \check{\pi}_S$). Towards this end, define

$$\bar{\pi}_S = c_I D(c_I) - C_S(D(c_I)).$$

The next corollary follows directly from Theorem 2.

Corollary 1 (elimination of the inferior leader equilibrium). *Suppose* $\hat{\pi}_S > \bar{\pi}_S$ *and* $p_S^M \geq c_I$. *Then, strategy profile* $(x_S, x_I) = (F, L)$ *is eliminated by the iterated elimination of weakly dominated strategies.*

The hypothesis of Theorem 2 ($\hat{\pi}_S > \check{\pi}_S$) is crucial in formulating the first-stage game in a straight-forward fashion. In the case of $\hat{\pi}_S < \check{\pi}_S$, it is necessary to introduce an additional structure in order to set up the first-stage game. This is because, in that case, the return to firm I would become zero in every entry of the return matrix. This implies that firm I would have no incentive to choose its role in the first period.

In the case of $\hat{\pi}_S < \check{\pi}_S$, as is noted above, firm I is indifferent with respect to the choice of its role. Therefore, it is possible to think of a new game in which firm S chooses the roles of both S and I in the first period in such a way that firm S maximizes its profit. The solution to this modified game is characterized as follows:

Proposition 1. *Suppose* $\hat{\pi}_S < \check{\pi}_S$. *Selling no product in the second period, firm I is indifferent with respect to the choice of its role. If firm S is allowed to choose the roles of both S and I, two types of equilibria may arise. That is, firm S chooses* $(x_S, x_I) = (L, F)$ *if* $\pi_S^L > \pi_S^F$ *and* $(x_S, x_I) = (F, L)$ *if* $\pi_S^L < \pi_S^F$.

Proof. It is easy to prove that either $\pi_S^L > \pi_S^F$ or $\pi_S^L < \pi_S^F$ is possible. □

References

Amir R, Stepanova A (2006) Second-mover advantage and price leadership in Bertrand duopoly. Game Econ Behav 55:1–20

Dastidar KG (1995) On the existence of pure strategy Bertrand equilibrium. Econ Theor 5:19–32

Dastidar KG, Furth D (2005) Endogenous price leadership in a duopoly: Equal products, unequal technology. Int J Econ Theor 1:189–210

Deneckere RJ, Kovenock D (1992) Price leadership. Rev Econ Stud 59:143–162

Fudenberg D, Tirole J (1991) Game theory. The MIT Press, Cambridge

Hamilton JH, Slutsky SM (1990) Endogenous timing in duopoly games: Stackelberg or Cournot equilibria. Game Econ Behav 2:29–46

Kikuchi T, Shimomura K (2007) Monopolistic competition with cross-country technological differences and international trade. Jpn World Econ 19:236–247

Ono Y (1978) The equilibrium of duopoly in a market of homogeneous goods. Economica 45:287–295

Tasnádi A (2003) Endogenous timing of moves in an asymmetric price-setting duopoly. Portuguese Econ J 2:23–35

van Damme E, Hurkens S (2004) Endogenous price leadership. Game Econ Behav 47:404–420

Yano M (2001) Applications of microeconomics (in Japanese, Mikuro keizaigaku no ouyou). Iwanami Shoten, Tokyo

Yano M, Komatsubara T (2006) Endogenous price leadership and technological differences. Int J Econ Theor 2:365–383

Zhu Q, Wu X (2007) Endogenous price leader: A geometric interpretation. Mimeo

Vilfredo Pareto's Principle of Compensation[1]

Murray C. Kemp

Abstract Pareto proposed his well-known Principle of Compensation in 1894. However, a debate is still active concerning Pareto's own interpretation of the Principle. Did he mean that compensation should be hypothetical (feasible but not necessarily carried out) or should be carried out? It is here argued, against views to the contrary, that Pareto had in mind, the second alternative.

1 Introduction

In 1894, Vilfredo Pareto proposed his well-known Principle of Compensation as a condition to be satisfied by any politically-devised program of economic reform; and, in later years, the Principle has been interpreted also in a context of natural disturbances.[2] After seventy years of intermittent debate, however, economists still have not been able to agree on the precise interpretation of the Principle intended by Pareto. Some believe that Pareto intended that a change in policy should be approved by economists only if compensation of the losers is both feasible and approved by the government. Others hold that he intended that a change in policy should be approved by economists, if compensation of the losers is feasible even if it is not intended and is therefore merely hypothetical. Intertwined with the strands of that historical debate are the strands of a quite distinct ethical debate concerning

[1] Chapter prepared for the Conference on Globalization, International Trade, and Economic Dynamics – In Memory of Koji Shimomura, held at Kobe University, November 22–24, 2007. I acknowledge with gratitude many helpful conversations with Binh Tran-Nam and useful comments from an anonymous referee.

[2] The latter interpretation, almost certainly would have been rejected by Pareto himself.

M.C. Kemp
University of New South Wales, Sydney, NSW 2052, Australia,
e-mail: murraykemp@bigpond.com

T. Kamihigashi and L. Zhao (eds.) *International Trade and Economic Dynamics – Essays in Memory of Koji Shimomura.*

the relative merits of hypothetical and actual compensation. It is highly desirable that the long historical debate be settled; then the focus of debate might shift to the ethical desirability of compensation in each of its forms and in each feasible situation.[3]

Pareto's own discussion of the Principle is contained in just two paragraphs of his well-known article published in 1894; the paragraphs will be reproduced in Sect. 2. Later statements in his 'Mathematical Theory of International Trade' (1895), in the *Cours* (1896–1897: Volume II, Sects. 721–723), and in the *Manuel* (1909: Chap. 6 and Sects. 89–129 of the Appendix) added little information; and Pareto's correspondence with Walras, about the 1894 article [Jaffé (1965: Volume II, 605–612)] added no new information. In his later sociological writing [Pareto (1913, 1923)], Pareto added nothing to his discussion of 1894; nor did he withdraw any part of it.

There seems to have been very little discussion of the Principle by Italian economists (or by French and German economists), even in the years immediately after 1894.[4] The debate, already referred to, was initiated in England much later, in the years immediately preceding World War II, and since then has been conducted almost entirely in English. In 1939, Nicholas Kaldor and John Hicks each published a chapter in the *Economic Journal* supporting the Principle of Hypothetical Compensation.[5] After the War, in a salute to Pareto on the centenary of his birth, Joseph Schumpeter (1949: 163) referred to Pareto as 'the patron saint of the

[3] My thoughts on that topic have developed over many years in joint work with Henry Wan; see Kemp and Wan (1993, 1999) and Wan (1997).

[4] Enrico Barone (1908) acknowledged his general indebtedness to 'that solitary thinker of Céligny' but did not mention Pareto (1894) and did not address the question posed in the present note.

[5] Kaldor (1939: 550) argued that economists should speak in favor of a change in policy, if compensation of the losers is feasible – implicitly, even if the government is not expected to undertake full compensation.

> "In all cases ... where a certain policy leads to an increase in physical productivity, and thus of aggregate real income, the economist's case for the policy is quite unaffected by the question of the comparability of individual satisfactions; since in all such cases it is *possible* to make everybody better off than before or at any rate to make some people better off without making anybody worse off. There is no need for the economist to prove – as indeed he never could prove – that as the result of the adoption of a certain measure nobody in the community is going to suffer. In order to establish his case [in favor of the measure], it is quite sufficient for him to show that even if all those who suffer as a result are fully compensated for their loss, the rest of the community will still be better off than before. Whether the landlords, in the free-trade case, should in fact be given compensation or not, is a political question on which the economist, *qua* economist, could hardly pronounce an opinion. The important fact is that, in the argument in favor of free trade, the fate of the landlords is wholly irrelevant: Since the benefits of free trade are by no means destroyed even if the landlords are fully reimbursed for their losses."

Hicks (1939) provided essentially the same message as Kaldor but was quite explicit that economists should support projects if complete compensation is feasible, whatever the likely attitude of the government to compensation. Towards the end of his life, Hicks reprinted his chapter without retraction; see Hicks (1981: 59–77).

"New Welfare Economics"' as founded by Kaldor and Hicks.[6] Later again, John Chipman (1976: 92–93) asserted that '... Pareto's argument contains the essence of the New Welfare Economics launched by Hicks forty-five years later.' In the opinion of Murray Kemp and Paul Pezanis–Christou (1999: 441), however, Schumpeter and Chipman have seriously misrepresented Pareto: '... in the cited chapter, Pareto argued to the contrary, that in the formulation of economic policy, compensation should be considered only if it is carried out.' In support to their conclusion, Kemp and Pezanis–Christou reviewed Pareto's formulation of the Principle and explained why, in their opinion, Pareto had in mind actual compensation. Their reasoning, like Pareto's own, will be summarized in Sect. 2. The latest contribution to the debate has been provided by Chipman (2006). In his new essay, Chipman responds to the comments of Kemp and Pezanis–Christou on his earlier chapter. In Sect. 3, I shall set out his argument in detail and provide reasons for judging it to be inadequate.

2 Analysis: Pareto, Interpreted by Kemp and Pezanis–Christou[7]

Pareto focused on an economy, perhaps small and open but in any case facing given commodity and factor prices and with a Ministry of Production, which experiments with small adjustments to a production coefficient a_s in a particular industry. After an adjustment to a_s, the Ministry notes the maximum amount (in terms of a numeraire) that household i can give up without being on balance worse off than before the change; let us denote the maximum by $\lambda_i(a_s)$. If the sum of these amounts over households, $\sum_i \lambda_i(a_s)$, is positive then, Pareto argued, it is possible by means of lump sum inter-household transfers to make all households better off than before the change; that is, it is possible to find a scheme of lump sum compensation that brings about a Pareto improvement.[8] There may be many such schemes. Pareto assumed that there exists a value of a_s, say $a_s{}^*$, such that $\sum_i \lambda_i(a_s{}^*) = 0$.

The position taken by Kaldor and Hicks may be compared with the mature position taken by Pareto in the second edition of his *Trattato di Sociologia Generale* (1923):

> "When the community stands at a point, Q, that it can leave with resulting benefits to all individuals, procuring greater enjoyments for all of them, it is obvious that from the economic standpoint it is advisable not to stop at that point but to move on from it as far as the movement away from it is advantageous to all. When, then, the point P, where that is no longer possible, is reached, it is necessary, as regards the advisability of stopping there or going on, to resort to other considerations foreign to economics – to decide on grounds of ethics, social utility, or sacrifice. From the strictly economic standpoint, as soon as the community has reached a point P it has to stop." (Quotation from the English translation of the *Trattato* (1935: 1466–1467).)

There is no evidence in their pre-war articles that either Kaldor or Hicks had read Pareto's fundamental contribution of 1894 or his *Trattato*.

[6] The term "new welfare economics" was introduced by Hicks (1939: 698).

[7] Inevitably, given my desire to offer a complete account of Pareto's reasoning, Sect. 2 reproduces material from Kemp and Pezanis–Christou (1999).

[8] Whether Pareto succeeded in establishing this proposition need not concern us.

Pareto's two key paragraphs may now be reproduced in full, in terms of our present notation and with commodity A serving as numeraire. Pareto's equation (7), mentioned in the second paragraph, defines the λs.[9]

> If all the λs are positive, every individual makes a gain in *utility* and we shall say *elliptically* that there is an increase in social utility. It will be desirable in that case to increase a_s, by da_s, for all members of society. Similarly, if all the λs are negative, each individual will suffer a loss in utility and we shall say *elliptically* that there is a decrease in social utility. In that case it will be desirable not to increase a_s but rather to decrease it by da_s. And so one will proceed in one way or another as long as all the λs have the same sign. But, when we reach the point at which some are positive and others negative, we shall not be able to proceed further because we shall be favoring some individuals at the expense of others. When a_s increases by da_s, if some λs are positive and others negative, this means that the utility enjoyed by certain individuals increase and that of others decrease. It is not possible to establish a compensation among these various utilities since they are reckoned in different units.
>
> Expressions (7) on the contrary all represent quantities of commodity A, the other commodities thus being expressed in the same unit. Letting ζ be the sum of the positive λs and σ that of the negative λs, if $\zeta - \sigma$ is positive, we can take as much of commodity A from the individuals for whom the λs are positive (the others being reckoned in A) as is needed to bring the negative λs back to zero, and there will still be a residual. Hence, society considered as a whole will have made a gain. This gain can be distributed among all members of the society, or among only some. This is a question which I shall not now examine; it is enough to point out the existence. Hence it will be desirable to increase a_s, by da_s, and only later to examine how to distribute that residual. When should we stop increasing a_s? Precisely when we have $\zeta - \sigma = 0$; because proceeding still further, when $\zeta - \sigma$ becomes negative, it would no longer be possible to take away so and so much of the commodity from those for whom the λs are positive to compensate the individuals for whom the λs are negative. Society as a whole would therefore undergo a loss and no longer a gain.
>
> [Pareto (1894: 60)].[10]

In the first, of these two paragraphs, Pareto made it clear that, if some λs were positive and others negative, he would not be prepared to say that social utility had increased or decreased. It follows that when in the second paragraph, Pareto stated that '... if $\zeta - \sigma$ is positive, ... society considered as a whole will have made a gain,' it must be understood that the negative λs have been forced up to zero by precisely compensatory lump sum transfers, so that distribution of the *gain* means

[9] Pareto's equation (7) is simply

$$\left(\frac{\partial r_{ia}}{\partial a_s} + p_b \frac{\partial r_{ib}}{\partial a_s} + p_c \frac{\partial r_{ic}}{\partial a_s} + \ldots\right) \mathrm{d}a_s = \lambda_i$$

where, for example, r_{ib} is the consumption by individual i of commodity B, p_b is the price of B in terms of the numeraire A and the subscript i runs over the set of all consumers.

[10] An English translation, prepared by John Cairncross and revised by John Chipman, will appear in the second volume of *Collected chapters of Vilfredo Pareto in Mathematical and Quantitative Economics*, to be edited by J.S. Chipman for the American Economic Association and published by the Academic Press. This quotation is from the Cairncross–Chipman translation. I am grateful to Academic Press for permission to quote from the translation. The reader should note that the quoted paragraphs make sense only if either σ is redefined as the sum of the absolute values of the negative λs or $\zeta - \sigma$ is replaced by $\zeta + \sigma$. It is clear to me that the error is of Pareto, not that of the translators.

distribution of the *residual*. Any other understanding of the passage must be based on the assumption that, in composing the second paragraph, Pareto had forgotten what he had said in the first.

Pareto's argument is couched in terms of infinitesimal changes in a_s. However, he clearly had in mind a sequence of small changes that terminates only when $a_s = a_s*$; that is, he had in mind a *finite* policy change, the magnitude of which is determined by a_s* and the initial value of a_s.

In summary, Pareto would have the Ministry of Production choice $a_s = a_s*$, to compensate those, who would otherwise be harmed by the choice and later consider how the residual might best be distributed. After the compensatory transfers, the society as a whole "will have made a gain;" after the distribution of the residual, a gain might be enjoyed by each member of the society.

3 Analysis: Pareto, Interpreted by Chipman

Chipman (2006) offers the following comment on Kemp and Pezanis–Christou (1999):

> '... I do not quite agree with the statement of these authors that Pareto's words, "we can take as much of commodity *A* from the individuals for whom the λs are positive ... as is needed to bring the negative λs back to zero," imply that "in the formulation of economic policy compensation should be a consideration only if it is to be carried out." As I read the statement, it simply points to the possibility of universal improvement starting from a particular situation if transfers are made. Pareto's statement does not seem to imply an ethical obligation on the part of the Ministry of Production of the collectivist state to carry out the distribution.'
>
> [Chipman (2006, p. 466, footnote omitted)]

However, in the quoted passage, Chipman makes it appear that the conclusion of Kemp and Pezanis–Christou (that, in Pareto's view, "in the formulation of economic policy compensation should be a consideration, only if it is to be carried out") had been derived solely from the simple arithmetic that Chipman quotes from the *second* of the two Paretian paragraphs. In fact, as the reader may easily verify by consulting Sect. 2, our conclusion relied heavily on the *first* of the two paragraphs, where Pareto made it clear that, if some λs were positive and others negative, he would not be prepared to say that social utility had increased or decreased. Taken together, the two paragraphs call for complete compensation by the losers. Thus, unintentionally, Chipman has seriously misrepresented the reasoning of Kemp and Pezanis–Christou. His case against their interpretation of Pareto's Principle of Compensation is without secure foundation.

That is, I think, all that need to be said in defense of the Kemp–Pezanis–Christou interpretation of Pareto. However, in this final paragraph, and without emphasis, attention is drawn to a pair of contradictory and therefore puzzling statements in Chipman's essay. The first of these (on p. 465) is an emphatic re-affirmation of his views (1976):

> 'Certainly, it cannot be questioned that Pareto was the analytic originator of the compensation principle, on which the New Welfare Economics was based ... '

However, hard on the heels of that statement comes his profession (on p. 466) that, in 1976,

> '... I did not intend to imply that Pareto would have approved of the extreme Kaldorian view [Kaldor (1939)], largely embraced by Hicks (1939), that distributional problems could be ignored by economists, since that was the job of other disciplines.'

4 Final Remarks

Much has been made of the so-called "Scitovsky paradox;" see Scitovsky (1941). Accepting the reasoning of Kaldor and Hicks, economists might approve a new policy and later approve the dismantling in the policy. However, the paradox is not a problem, if governments make the political decisions expected by Kaldor and Hicks.

In Sects. 1–3, I have followed Pareto himself, and all who have taken part in the debate about his Principle of Compensation, in focusing on a finite competitive economy, with price-taking households and firms, and on lump sum compensation. However it must be borne in mind that, given the assumption of price-taking behavior, a finite economy is internally consistent only if all agents are irrational or ill-informed about the economy in which they are part; see Kemp and Koji Shimomura (2005). If irrationality and imperfect information are unacceptable ingredients of the economy, the assumption of price-taking behavior must be abandoned. It must then be accepted that, in some non-competitive contexts, governments are able to achieve complete compensation only by resorting to non-lump sum means of compensation; see Kemp and Shimomura (2001, especially Sects. 3 and 4).[11] The neglect of this fact can lead to serious error; see, for example, the comments of Kemp and Shimomura (2001, page 297) on the work of Tito Cordella (1998). Moreover, it must be keep in mind that, in imperfectly competitive contexts of the kind described by Kemp and Shimomura (2001), a change in government policy unaccompanied by any scheme of compensation might induce a Pareto-deterioration of well being; see Kenji Fujiwara (2005).[12] Such a change in policy might be difficult to "sell", to an electorate.

[11] Kemp and Shimomura focused on the problem of achieving complete compensation after autarky has been abandoned in favor of free trade. However, their message is valid in the context of any politically-devised reform.

[12] It is well known that if the economy is finite and competitive and if there are missing markets after a change in policy then, even though there exists a lump sum scheme of complete compensation, the uncompensated change in policy might be Pareto-harmful; see Kemp and Wong (1995). The finding of Fujiwara (2005) is noteworthy, for in the model of Kemp and Shimomura (2001), there are no missing markets. However, in Fujiwara's chapter, homogeneous labor is assumed to behave competitively, as though ignorant of the fact that it is homogeneous and might behave cooperatively. Fujiwara's example would be even more convincing, if it allowed for cooperative behavior by labor as an alternative possibility.

Clearly the agenda of academic debate about compensation has changed radically since 2001: If the perceptions of the preceding paragraph had been available to Pareto in 1894, he would have understood that it is no longer a question of lump sum versus non-lump sum compensation but of the optimal mixture of lump sum and non-lump sum compensation and he would not have focused exclusively on lump sum compensation. And if the perceptions of the preceding paragraph had been available to Kaldor and Hicks in 1939, they might have been more qualified in their advocacy of hypothetical compensation.

References

Barone E (1908) Il ministerio della produzione nella stato colletivista. Giornale degli Economisti 37:267–293, 391–414. Translated in: Hayek FA (ed) Collectivist economic planning, Routledge & Kegan Paul, London, 1935

Chipman JS (1976) The Paretian heritage. Revue Européenne des Sciences Sociales et Cahiers Vilfredo Pareto 14:65–171

Chipman JS (2006) Pareto and contemporary economic theory. Rivista Internazionale di Scienze Economiche e Commerciali 53:451–475

Cordella T (1998) Patterns of trade and oligopoly equilbria: an example. Rev Int Econs 6:554–563

Fujiwara K (2005) Unilateral and multilateral gains from trade in international oligopoly, Econ Rec 81:404–413

Hicks JR (1939) The foundations of welfare economics. Econ J 49: 696–712

Hicks JR (1981) Wealth and welfare, vol 1. Harvard University Press, Cambridge MA

Jaffé W (1965) Correspondence of Léon Walras and related papers. North-Holland, Amsterdam

Kaldor N (1939) Welfare propositions in economics and interpersonal comparisons of utility. Econ J 49:549–552

Kemp MC (2008) Trade theory: a critical review. Routledge, London

Kemp MC, Pezanis–Christou, P (1999) Pareto's compensation principle. Social Choice Welfare 16:441–444

Kemp MC, Shimomura K (2001) Gains from trade in a Cournot–Nash general equilibrium. Jpn Econ Rev 52:284–302

Kemp MC, Shimomura K (2005) Price taking in general equilibrium. Am J Appl Sci (Special Issue):78–80. Reprinted in: Kemp MC (2008: Chap. 24)

Kemp MC, Wan HY Jr (1993) The welfare economics of international trade. Harwood Academic, Chur, Switzerland

Kemp MC, Wan HY Jr (1995) On lump sum compensation. In: Moore JC, Riezman R, Melvin JR (eds) Trade, theory and econometrics: essays in honour of John S. Chipman. Routledge, London

Kemp MC, Wong K–W (1995) The gains from trade when markets are possibly incomplete. In: Kemp MC, The gains from trade and the gains from aid, Routledge, London

Pareto V (1894) Il massimo di utilità dato dalla libera concorrenza. Giornale degli Economisti 9: 48–66. Translated in: Chipman JS (ed) Collected papers of Vilfredo Pareto in mathematical and quantitative economics, vol II, Academic Press, San Diego (forthcoming)

Pareto V (1895) Theoria matematica del commercio internazionale. Giornale degli Economisti 10: 476–498. Translated in: Chipman JS (ed) Collected papers of Vilfredo Pareto in mathematical and quantitative economics, vol II, Academic Press, San Diego (forthcoming)

Pareto V (1897) Cours d'economie politique, vol II. Rouge, Lausanne

Pareto V (1909) Manuel d'economie politique, Giard and Brière, Paris

Pareto V (1913) Il massimo di utilità per una collecttività in sociologia. Giornale degli Economisti & Rivista de Statistica 46:337–341. Translated in: Pasinetti LL (ed) Italian economic papers, vol I, Società editrice il Mulino and Oxford University Press, Bologna

Pareto V (1916) Trattato di sociologia generale, 2nd edn. Barbera, Firenze. Edited in English translation by Livingston, A (1935) under the title The mind and society, Jonathan Cape, London

Schumpeter JA (1949) Vilfredo Pareto (1848–1923). Quar J Econs 63:147–173

Scitovsky T (1941) A note on welfare propositions in economics. Rev Econ Stud 9:77–88

Wan HY Jr (1997) A note on compensation schemes. Jpn Econ Rev 48:147–155

FSC
www.fsc.org
MIX
Papier | Fördert gute Waldnutzung
FSC® C083411

Kolibri 360 GmbH
Ferdinand-Jühlke-Straße 7
99095 Erfurt, Deutschland
produktsicherheit@kolibri360.de